'An excellent encyclopedic explanation of the root cau[se of] environmental issues, this book provides an impressive [array of] models and tools to address them, while welcoming deba[te ...] decades of academic research and practice, the book is [...] tion tool and a practical guide.'

  Dr. Stephen Knight-Lenihan, School of Architecture and Planning, University of Auckland, has a particular research interest in local government urban biodiversity and climate change adaptation decision-making

'This is the essential textbook for every design practitioner. Janis uniquely synthesizes the vast ground of interdisciplinary practices required to transform the world of both physical and institutional design and assessment – and thoroughly details the what, why and how of it.'

  Peter A. H. James, engineer and director of Gatchi Pty Ltd, has had sustainability leadership roles in multinational firms including Arup, SKM, Davis Langdon and E.C. Harris

'Birkeland's visionary proposals for environmental planning leave no stone unturned. She carries the reader through a critical outline of models for sustainability to her own path-breaking conception of the "net-positive" approach. A comprehensive textbook on design and governance for architects and town planners alike.'

  Dr. Ariel Salleh is a sociologist with the University of Sydney who writes extensively on environmental ethics and ecopolitics. She is co-editor of *Pluriverse: A Post-Development Dictionary* (2019)

'From the author who developed Positive Development theory comes another tour de force – a delightful guide for those of us disappointed with the direction of conventional approaches to wicked problems. By integrating the technical and creative dimensions of sustainable development (free online app included!), Birkeland's new odyssey is a must-read primer for anyone considering deeds more important than words.'

  Mirek Dymitrow, PhD in Human Geography and Researcher at Chalmers University of Technology, Lund University and University of Gothenburg, Sweden

'Birkeland is a true pioneer in the field of sustainability theory. This book sets out her key arguments and proposes a design tool to enable collaborative creation for "positive development". Like Birkeland's advocacy, it is comprehensive and challenging and offers real options for going beyond sustainability.'

  Dr. Paul Downton, architect, writer, urban evolutionary, proprietor Ecopolis, founder Urban Ecology Australia, co-founder Ecocity Design Institute

'In the wake of the catastrophic impacts of climate change and global warming, Birkeland's new book brings hope. By re-engineering our approach to urban development, she reveals how CITIES could become our most powerful resource in reversing the trends associated with climate change. Advocating "positive development", her evidence-based methodology centres on design and ethics, rather than policy and planning, to apply measurable principles, tools and strategies. Essential reading for all decision makers.'

Dr Kathi Holt, Vice-President UDAL, Urban Design Alliance, Director TANDEM, is an architect and strategic urban designer, specializing in cities research and design

Net-Positive Design and Sustainable Urban Development

'Sustainable' urban planning, policy and design professes to solve sustainability problems, but often depletes and degrades ever more resources and ecosystems and concentrates wealth and concretize social disparities. Positive Development theory holds that development could create more net ecological and social gains than no construction at all. It explains how existing conceptual, physical and institutional structures are inherently biased against the preservation and expansion of social and natural life-support systems, and proposes explicit reforms to planning, design and decision making that would enable development to increase future options and social and natural life-support systems – in absolute terms.

Net-Positive Design and Sustainable Development is aimed at students, academics, professionals and sustainability advocates who wonder why existing approaches have been ineffective. It explains how to reform the anti-ecological biases in our current frameworks of environmental governance, planning, decision making and design – and suggests how to make these changes. Cities can increase both the 'public estate' (reduce social stratification, inequity and other causes of conflict, increase environmental quality, wellbeing and access to basic needs, etc.); and the 'ecological base' (sequester more carbon and produce more energy than used during construction and operation, increase ecological space to support ecological carrying capacity, ecosystem functions and services, restore the bioregions and wilderness, etc.). No small task, this book provides academic theory and professional tools for saving the planet, including a free computer app for net-positive design.

Dr. Janis Birkeland is Honorary Professorial Fellow, Faculty of Architecture, Building and Planning, University of Melbourne. She was Professor of Sustainable Design at the University of Auckland, New Zealand and Professor of Architecture at Queensland University of Technology in Brisbane, Australia. Before that, she was a lawyer, architect and planner in San Francisco. She originated the theory of net-positive design, design for eco-services and other increasingly popular concepts, and taught and published various aspects of sustainable development for over two decades. Her PhD was Planning for Sustainability (1993) and her books include *Positive Development, Mapping Regional Metabolism* and *Design for Sustainability*.

Net-Positive Design and Sustainable Urban Development

Janis Birkeland

Routledge
Taylor & Francis Group
NEW YORK AND LONDON

First published 2020
by Routledge
52 Vanderbilt Avenue, New York, NY 10017

and by Routledge
2 Park Square, Milton Park, Abingdon, Oxon, OX14 4RN

Routledge is an imprint of the Taylor & Francis Group, an informa business

© 2020 Taylor & Francis

The right of Janis Birkeland to be identified as author of this work has been asserted by her in accordance with sections 77 and 78 of the Copyright, Designs and Patents Act 1988.

All rights reserved. No part of this book may be reprinted or reproduced or utilised in any form or by any electronic, mechanical, or other means, now known or hereafter invented, including photocopying and recording, or in any information storage or retrieval system, without permission in writing from the publishers.

Trademark notice: Product or corporate names may be trademarks or registered trademarks, and are used only for identification and explanation without intent to infringe.

Library of Congress Cataloging-in-Publication Data
Names: Birkeland, Janis, 1945- author.
Title: Net-positive design and sustainable urban development / Janis Birkeland.
Description: 1 Edition. | New York : Routledge, 2019. | Includes bibliographical references and index.
Identifiers: LCCN 2019036212 (print) | LCCN 2019036213 (ebook) | ISBN 9780367258559 (hardback) | ISBN 9780367258566 (paperback) | ISBN 9780429290213 (ebook)
Subjects: LCSH: City planning–Environmental aspects. | Cities and towns–Growth. | Sustainable buildings–Design and construction.
Classification: LCC HT166 .B5197 2019 (print) | LCC HT166 (ebook) | DDC 711/.4–dc23
LC record available at https://lccn.loc.gov/2019036212
LC ebook record available at https://lccn.loc.gov/2019036213

ISBN: 978-0-367-25855-9 (hbk)
ISBN: 978-0-367-25856-6 (pbk)
ISBN: 978-0-429-29021-3 (ebk)

Typeset in Sabon
by Swales & Willis, Exeter, Devon, UK

Contents

List of Figures ix
List of Boxes xi
Preface xii
Overview xiii

PART I
Design and Analysis: Synopsis of Part I 1

SECTION A
Introduction to Positive Development

1 Overview of Net-Positive Development 5
2 Centrality of the Built Environment in Sustainability 37

SECTION B
Sustainability Revisited

3 Sustainability Paradigms in Historical Context 61
4 Sustainability and Positive Development Theory 87

SECTION C
Built Environment Solutions

5 Eco-Positive Retrofitting 111
6 Design for Nature Exemplified 136

SECTION D
Systems Mapping Themes (SMT) Analyses

7 SMT Analyses for Physical Design 155
8 SMT Analyses for Institutional Design 181

PART II
Decision Making and Assessment: Synopsis of Part II   **201**

SECTION E
Development Governance

9   Governance and Futures Planning   205

10   Development Control and Assessment   228

SECTION F
Rating Tools Critiqued

11   Rating Tools and Procedures   253

12   Rating Tools and Substance   268

SECTION G
Eco-Positive Design Review (A Qualitative Tool)

13   Eco-positive Design Review (Social Issues)   287

14   The Eco-Positive Design Review (Ecological issues)   309

SECTION H
STARfish (A Quantitative Tool)

15   The STARfish Tool Described   335

16   The STARfish Tool Benchmarks   353

Index   371

Figures

1.1	Code to diagrams	8
1.2	Distinguishing design and decision making	12
1.3	From reducing harm to increasing benefits	13
1.4	From efficiency/recycling to life-giving systems	14
1.5	From differing views of nature protection in design	16
1.6	From nature adapting to humans evolving?	16
1.7	From eco-restoration to increasing ecological carrying capacity	18
1.8	Increasing ecosystems/biodiversity in the bioregions	19
1.9	Social and/or systems change	20
1.10	From consumer preferences to analyses	21
1.11	From trade-offs to net-positive frameworks	22
1.12	From efficiency to the net public good	23
1.13	From value adding to maximizing benefits	26
2.1	Supply and demand	38
2.2	Affirmative action for the environment	39
3.1	The black box approach	67
3.2	The simple circular approach	68
3.3	Differing closed-system views in sustainable design	69
3.4	Closed and open systems	73
3.5	Beyond closing loops to virtuous cycles	78
4.1	NEPA: Balancing resources and growth	90
4.2	WCS (balancing land for people and nature)	92
4.3	WCED: Balancing benefits and burdens of growth	93
4.4	Mainstream donut model	98
4.5	Part-earth model	98
4.6	Whole-earth model	99
4.7	Positive Development theory	99
5.1	Space for nature in competing models	115
5.2	Urban form and material and energy consumption	116
5.3	Reducing cars or reducing driving	118
7.1	Code to SMT (System Mapping Themes) diagrams	163
7.2	Designed Waste (DW) Analysis	164
7.3	Ecological Waste (EW) analysis	165
7.4	Development/Design Functions (DF) aAnalysis	166
7.5	Hierarchy of Innovation (HI) analysis	167
7.6	Passive Maximization (PM) Analysis	168

x *Figures*

7.7	Multifunctional Space (MS) analysis	169
7.8	Resource Security (RS) Analysis	170
7.9	Risk Avoidance (RA) analysis	171
7.10	Negative Space (NS) analysis	172
7.11	Highest Ecological Use (HU) analysis	173
7.12	Ecological Transformation (ET) analysis	174
7.13	Ecological Space (ES) analysis	175
8.1	Reverse sunk cost (SC) analysis	181
8.2	Source of Energy (SE) analysis	182
8.3	Costs of change (CC) analysis	183
8.4	Benefits of action (BA) analysis	184
8.5	Institutional Design (ID) Analysis	185
8.6	Cumulative Decision (CD) analysis	186
8.7	Democratic Impact (DI) analysis	187
8.8	Economic Impact (EI) analysis	188
8.9	Resource Transfer (RT) analysis	189
8.10	Green Optimum (GO) analysis	190
9.1	From changing people to designing relationships	206
9.2	From adversarial politics to conflict resolution by design	207
9.3	From decision-based to design-based tools	208
9.4	Beyond bureaucracy to reasoning	210
9.5	Balancing competing demands versus expanding options	212
9.6	Settling disputes versus resolving systems problems	214
9.7	Pareto Optimum versus Green Optimum	215
9.8	Precautionary versus proactive principle	216
9.9	Minimizing change versus maximizing gains	217
9.10	Zoning for economic, social and ecological land uses	218
9.11	Comprehensive/master planning	219
9.12	Incremental Decision Making	220
9.13	Scenario Planning (Source: Birkeland 2008)	221
9.14	Back-casting and least-cost planning (Source: Birkeland 2008)	222
9.15	Scenario and back-casting versus PD	223
9.16	Planning to diversify environments and options (Source: Birkeland 2008)	224
10.1	Development control versus judicious consent processes	230
10.2	From performance thresholds to adaptable design	231
10.3	Participation in advance/future planning	232
10.4	Participation in development control (consent processes)	234
15.1	The constituent diagrams	339
15.2	Reverse impact wheel (Source: Birkeland 2008)	340
15.3	The STARfish diagram	341
15.4	The circles on the STARfish diagram	342
15.5	A typical leg (radius) on the radar diagram	342

Boxes

1 Sustainable design paradigms — 27
2 The technocratic orientation in sustainability — 79
3 Reframing sustainability principles as positive design challenges — 102
4 Impediments to retrofitting — 131
5 Hierarchy of innovation — 196
6 Sample biases to be reversed — 322
7 The STARfish net-positive design app — 347

Preface

Net-Positive Design and Sustainable Development poses a challenge to academics and professionals who still believe in the capacity of current decision-making processes to solve sustainability issues. 'Sustainable' urban planning, decision making and design continues to underwrite most sustainability problems. About half of global biodiversity and coral reefs have been destroyed in under fifty years. Development has perpetuated the degradation of resources and ecosystems while concentrating wealth and concretizing social disparities. Roughly eight people on the planet now have the combined wealth of half its population. This is entirely unnecessary. Urban environments can be designed to increase nature and advance society.

Positive Development posits that development could create more net socio-ecological gains than no construction at all. The urban environment could become generators of eco-positive sustainability. This book attempts to explain how current conceptual, physical and institutional structures are inherently biased against the protection and expansion of social and natural life-support systems. It then suggests how development can improve universal life quality and increase nature and public options beyond any damage caused during building manufacturing, construction and operation. Debate is always welcome. Any reader may contact the author via email to dispute or discuss any of the propositions in the book.

Overview

PART I DESIGN AND ANALYSIS

Section A Introduction to Positive Development

1. Overview of Positive Development

Provides a brief book overview, highlights some Positive Development (PD) concepts, defines the key terms, introduces PD theory and differentiates sustainable design paradigms.

Today, sustainable development strategies seem to rely more on changing people's values and behavior than on systems redesign. Without the transformation of physical and institutional systems, however, social change will be futile. The built environment could be the fulcrum for creating a sustainable, just and healthy society. However, with the arrival of green building and urban certification schemes and point-scoring systems, the goal became incremental improvements upon the norm. In contrast, net-positive design/development would increase future sustainable options by increasing the natural environment (ecological base), and the general welfare (public estate), well beyond the rates of global consumption and degradation.

Positive Development (PD) rethinks standard approaches to environmental governance, planning and design. It shifts urban design models, mindsets, methods and metrics: (1) from closed-system models of reality that only internalize negative impacts, to open-systems design that can externalize positive impacts/benefits; (2) from negative mindsets (doing no harm), to doing good by improving society-wide conditions and sustainable options; (3) from reductionist decision-based methods that simplify and compare choices or divide costs to design-based approaches that multiply public choices and benefits; and (4) from quantifying inputs-outputs using metrics that exclude cumulative and remote impacts, to baselines and benchmarks that consider whole systems.

2. Centrality of the Built Environment

Explains the potential of urban design to address most sustainability issues and explores why design is under-valued as a driver of systems change.

Built environment design is seldom creatively applied to many basic public health/safety issues, such as carbon sequestration, fire and flood prevention, air and water quality, emergency preparedness, sea level rise and so on. This chapter examines why the transformative potential of urban design is greatly underappreciated, even by many design academics and practitioners. Design has traditionally been regarded as a subset of decision making: merely a means of implementing decisions, plans or policies in physical form. The sequential decision-based approach to policy and implementation is usually derailed by changing market and political forces. Thus, sustainable systems need to be 'designed'.

Positive Development (PD) theory investigates the conceptual barriers and institutional inertia caused by the Dominant Paradigm (DP). Among these is the belief that society must await political, statutory or policy change before designing biophysical solutions. Yet, since energy and health savings can pay for retrofitting cities, direct design actions that benefit everyone could be implemented immediately. Although urban/building design cannot stop corporate greed, sociopathic leaders and/or warfare, it can counteract many contributing factors in inequity and poverty around the world that empower them, including the 'created need' for status, wealth and power, and the resentment caused by destitute living conditions.

Section B Sustainability Revisited

3. Sustainability Paradigms in Historical Context

Traces and describes the restrictive influence of pervasive closed-system sustainability models on the evolution of thought past design solutions (referencing landmark sustainability books).

Before the 1960s, ecosystems were sometimes described as 'open systems', where organisms were immersed in their environments, such that the earth was one interconnected ecosystem. The closed-system paradigm took hold in the 1960s with the popularity of the 'spaceship earth' metaphor. This vision of technocratic efficiency inspired a fledgling sustainable design movement, and even influenced descriptions of nature among ecological designers. Ecosystems soon came to be described as bounded systems within larger systems or nested hierarchies (perhaps to facilitate computational research or input-output analyses). Human and urban systems were conceived as independent organisms in a metabolic balance with their environment.

Self-sufficiency found early expression in the built environment as the 'resource autonomous' house. This was believed to be possible through efficiency, recycling and closing resource loops. The idea of sustainability as 'balance' reinforced the deeply embedded dualistic worldview (e.g. inside-outside, soft-hard, nature-society, inputs-outputs, costs-benefits). This bounded paradigm is seen today in zero-energy or zero-waste buildings. This aligns with the limited ethic of 'do no harm' by internalizing negative impacts – not externalizing positive impacts. Closed-system analyses, with their system boundaries and reductionist units (e.g. money, energy or carbon), conveniently excluded indirect but important, ubiquitous issues that are hard to quantify.

4. Sustainability Policy in Historical Context

Describes key elements of the closed-systems frameworks (limits, boundaries and balance) embedded in government policy that create institutional barriers to physical systems change.

The preamble to the first US environmental impact statement legislation (NEPA 1969) centered on intra/inter-generation equity and the 'limits to resources'. It sought to balance current and future resource use (not expand future options). An international declaration (WCS 1980) redefined the problem as ecological carrying capacity and the 'limits to nature'. The solution was to balance land for people and nature (not increase nature). The subsequent Brundtland Report (1987), although a political landmark, was a conceptual setback. While it aimed to balance the economic demands and environmental impacts of third and first worlds, it emphasized the economy (GDP) over ecology.

The Brundtland Report unintentionally sidelined the nascent environmental/sustainability movement. Although concerned with distributive justice, it saw equity as an economic, not a biophysical, problem. It presumed sustainability could be achieved through current institutions, simply by adding new goals. However, the underlying economics-based structures and decision rules are geared for dividing the pie among competing interests, not expanding the life-support system. The report mainstreamed sustainability and brought it back into the fold of the dominant closed-system, transactional paradigm, where it lost its transformative value. This chapter explains PD theory, upon which the book's proposed conceptual, physical and institutional reforms are based.

Section C Built Environment Solutions

5. Eco-positive Retrofitting

Compares mainstream urban design positions (e.g. consolidation, eco-cities, dispersal) and argues that they omit many fundamental sustainability issues, which eco-positive retrofitting could address.

There is a spectrum of planning approaches that advocate 'green growth'. Most advocate high-density development that restricts urban boundaries and consolidates urban areas through infill development and taller buildings. Others support decentralized, low-density development, semi-rural permaculture settlements or entirely new eco-cities. A compromise position is posed by the UN's New Urban Agenda (2016) which calls for growth through both 'sensitive' consolidation and expansion. These strategies rely primarily on urban morphology (urban form, massing, transport and land use patterns). These can only mitigate the impacts of growth. Urban form, in itself, cannot achieve socio-ecological sustainability. Sustainability is a biophysical design problem.

Urban design and development control has not prevented the decrease in ecological and public space. It has abdicated many sustainability design elements to architects/planners, such as adaptability, multifunctional space and design *for* nature. While cities are largely a product of industrialism, many areas were subsequently modified to suit local needs/conditions (if only to be destroyed by new development). Retrofitting could instead retain these positive features while

xvi *Overview*

reducing net impacts and saving resources and money. However, efficiency-centred retrofitting must be supplanted by 'eco-positive' retrofitting. Some new design concepts that illustrate the potentialities of eco-positive retrofitting and practical implementation strategies are presented.

6. Design for Nature Exemplified

Describes one flexible, adaptable, reversible eco-positive retrofitting concept that serves multiple functions and provides eco-services, to illustrate how change could be rapidly implemented.

The variations on eco-positive retrofitting of buildings and cities are limitless, so this chapter describes one concept in detail. PD Green Scaffolding (building-integrated space-frame structures) create spaces for diverse opportunities to integrate natural systems and eco-services into urban areas for net public gain. This is not a universal solution to be pasted onto buildings, but a structural concept adaptable to different contexts, which can be easily modified to meet changing social, climatic and technological needs/demands. It can support myriad sustainability functions (e.g. urban agriculture, renewable energy, fresh air and water, fire prevention/evacuation, or even ecosystem incubators for restoring the bioregions).

Green Scaffolding illustrates one means to create ecological spaces that can collectively compensate for the cumulative ecological losses that occur upstream-downstream from construction. A self-funding, physical approach to sustainability can by-pass indirect planning and development approval/consent systems, bonuses, offsetting mechanisms and rating tools that only steer conventional development toward less negative impacts. The chapter concludes with a discussion of many ways to incentivize Green Scaffolding or net-positive design more generally. It shows that design incentives could be incorporated into existing tools without legislative or administrative restructuring. Ultimately, however, institutional change is necessary to achieve net-positive sustainability (discussed in Part II).

Section D Systems Mapping Themes (SMT) Analyses

7. SMT Analyses for Physical Design

Outlines SMT analyses which support spatial planning and urban design strategies for increasing the ecological base, the public estate and future public choice.

Design can create healthy, diverse environments that provide more life quality, security and equity while generating compound savings. However, current analytical tools seldom use: a cross-disciplinary perspective that can capture the interconnections between urban design and complex issues like poverty, equity and ecosystems; measures of ecological carrying capacity and biodiversity that show losses in relation to growing rates of human consumption; material flows analyses that identify opportunities for increasing public benefits through multifunctional design; or indicators that show trends relative to diminishing resource stocks. New analyses are proposed that identify opportunities to intervene in systems to generate positive ripple effects.

Overview xvii

SMT analyses reverse the typical approaches. They identify socio-ecological deficits that can be addressed by design. The SMT analyses are arranged here as four (overlapping) levels of investigation: (1) design standards – development or building design issues of concern to project design teams; (2) planning standards – municipal planning, development control and project review considerations; (3) assessment standards – decision making and performance evaluation; and (4) ethical standards – frameworks of governance for protecting basic needs/rights. These forensic flows analyses are part of SMARTmode (system mapping and redesign thinking), a community planning process that was outlined in *Positive Development* (2008).

8. SMT Analyses for Institutional Design

Outlines SMT analyses to guide institutional design changes that enable comprehensive urban/regional planning and set priorities for transforming cities as drivers of sustainability.

Most analytical frameworks are geared toward measuring, mitigating and monitoring the repercussions of economic growth or predicting future trends. They do not guide or measure net-positive public gains. Material flows and metabolic analyses at urban, regional or global scales can help to reduce waste streams throughout supply chains using efficiencies, recycling and/or upcycling measures. While this can reduce the adverse impacts of additional development, reductions in total (global/regional) impacts require the redesign of development itself. Rather than enumerating negative impacts, SMT analyses identify socio-ecological deficits to guide urban and building design interventions supported by PD development control and assessment concepts.

The previous SMT chapter outlines analyses that are relevant to local development/design issues, and provides a framework for developing project 'briefs' or design criteria and community action plans. This chapter pertains to institutional design, decision making and governance. By exposing omissions left by conventional frameworks/processes in environmental governance, planning, decision making and design, SMT analyses contribute to the PD design and assessment processes set out in Part II: the eDR process (design review) and STARfish tool (quantitative assessment). It concludes by providing sample exercises for each SMT analysis which can be undertaken as discussion topics, mind-mapping exercises or postgraduate theses.

PART II DECISION MAKING AND ASSESSMENT

Section E Development Governance

9. Eco-positive Governance

Explains how (despite growing public acceptance of sustainability) frameworks of governance are inherently biased against ecological sustainability and suggests principles for basic reforms.

xviii *Overview*

Part I suggested that built environment design can leverage biophysical sustainability without waiting for social change or institutional reform. Eventually, however, social and institutional change will be necessary. This is because anti-ecological concepts are embedded in the decision-making processes of government and the professions, and political, administrative, religious and business levers for social change rely on people and are easily subverted. The structures and principles underlying governance and management can and must be reconstructed upon ecological foundations, called 'eco-governance'. PD proposes decision frameworks that can increase whole-system and socio-ecological sustainability, rather than just add new policies onto old decision frameworks.

This chapter briefly recaps a PD proposal for constitutional restructuring, which essentially involves the addition of a new ethics-based, decision-making arena for sustainability/planning issues. Although constitutional change is unlikely under present geopolitical trends, decision systems could be altered in minor ways to emphasize positive over zero-sum approaches. Hence, positive principles for modifying land use and environmental planning systems are outlined, regarding comprehensive, incremental and policy planning; statutory consent/control processes; and futures planning (e.g. back-casting and scenario planning). Converting the objectives and decision rules from negative to positive, while simultaneously raising standards, could begin to shift the socio-cultural barriers to sustainability.

10. Development Control and Assessment

Compares eco-positive planning to traditional means of development control and design assessment used by councils to increase built environment safety, quality and sustainability.

Having explained the need to redesign systems of environmental governance on PD principles, this chapter examines strengths and weaknesses of current development control and assessment methods. Green building rating/marketing tools (RTs) have come to dominate this area. RTs are voluntary, private-sector certification schemes for top-end developers that want to market their buildings as green. They have made sustainability fashionable in mainstream development – a huge achievement. However, ordinary buildings do not seek certification, and their impacts nullify any reductions made by RTs. Further, since the clients of RT companies (building councils) are primarily industry, industry brokers the pace of reform.

To see what RTs have contributed, they are compared to traditional quality control mechanisms. These include codes, regulations, design review processes, genuine progress indicators, trading schemes, lifecycle analysis, community participation, ecosystem service and environmental impact assessment (EIA) schemes. In addition, design firms are increasingly relying on building information modelling and management (BIM) tools. These are powerful and promising technologies, but they have conflated sustainability with efficiency. The emphasis on efficiency marginalizes the social and ecological dimensions. Adding more green buildings increases the pressure on life-support systems. To develop criteria for PD assessment, the next section compares EIAs and RTs in depth.

Overview   xix

Section F Rating Tools (RTs) Critiqued

11. Rating Tools compared to EIAs in Procedures

Examines whether 'procedural' pros and cons of EIAs were addressed or exacerbated by RTs, in order to develop assessment criteria for PD tools.

In many developed nations, the building industry was coming under pressure to regulate itself or be further regulated. RTs were in part a response to the threat of regulations and the intrusion of environmental impact assessment (EIA) into the building domain. EIAs required upstream-downstream impacts to be traced back to the natural environment, which spurred the development of material flows and life-cycle analyses. However, this was seen as a growing burden on development proponents. RTs, a checklist of efficiency measures, simplified the assessment. Although EIAs were still required for some large-scale developments, RTs arguably forestalled a paradigm shift in design.

To develop criteria, this chapter compares EIAs and RTs. It asks, do RTs: (1) apply to all or only certain kinds of projects? (2) introduce a science culture or just set rules? (3) examine basic alternatives or simply score points? (4) promote capacity building or outsourcing? (5) increase community involvement or create an expertariat? (6) prevent harmful projects or legitimize them? (7) require transparent findings or simply make judgements? (8) allow as-of-right approvals or foster improvements? (9) require adaptability or rely on durability? (10) consider lost eco-productivity or increase opportunity costs? or (11) devalue the future or consider resource scarcity?

12. Rating Tools Compared to EIAs in Substance

Examines whether 'substantive' pros and cons of EIAs were addressed by RTs, or if RTs added problems, to form criteria for PD tools.

This chapter compares RTs to EIA processes regarding substantive issues. Apart from major development projects, EIAs and/or other review processes are sometimes by-passed when a high RT score is achieved. Among other basic issues: RTs do not really consider on-ground ecological or social impacts (the fact that RTs only measure 'less harmful' impacts went largely unnoticed because they label reductions in negatives as 'positive'); they often list criteria concerning social and economic matters in the environmental column, so many assume that the ecological requirements are extensive; and they often mention biodiversity but this is deemed a matter of external landscaping.

Substantive questions are, do RTs: (1) require public or just client benefits? (2) treat buildings as parts of open or closed systems? (3) allow automatic or judicious decisions? (4) use conflict resolution or choose winners? (5) include elements of time/space or just efficiency? (6) consider regional or just onsite impacts? (7) consider public or just stakeholder interests? (8) consider ethical/ecological or just financial issues? (9) consider whole systems or use system boundaries? (10) address resource scarcity and extinctions or just relative losses? or (11) prioritize highest sustainable land use over economics? Afterwards, the suitability of RTs to disadvantaged regions/nations is discussed.

Section G Eco-positive Design Review (A Qualitative Tool)

13. The Eco-positive Design Report (social issues)

Proposes a low-cost process for guiding community-led design briefs or collaborative design processes concerning socio-ecological issues, with particular applicability to socio-economically disadvantaged regions.

The eDR is a process for developing specific planning/design criteria for particular places. It is not unlike design guidelines, but asks questions and covers sustainability issues that are rarely included in guidelines or assessment tools. Design teams, community groups or city councils can use it in developing design briefs, guiding self-assessment or establishing criteria for an official local review process. It aims to replace rules with reason, compliance activity with creativity and methods for choosing among designs with designing eco-positive environments. The particular example given is meant to be adaptable to disadvantaged regions, for which RTs have been poorly suited.

Social issues are arranged under these categories: (1) increase security and access to the means of survival; (2) foster healthy living, sustainability education and social change; (3) address basic community needs (values, justice, fairness, etc); (4) provide space for changing family needs; (5) increase economic equity, opportunity and affordability; and (6) stimulate safer, healthier jobs. Economic issues are subsumed under the social category as economics should be a means, not the end, to sustainability. Both eDR chapters reference SMT analyses (above) to link the design process to needs analyses. Ideally, the information for these analyses would be collected by governments.

14. The Eco-positive Design Report (Ecological Issues)

Outlines the ecological questions that should be resolved and provides a template for developing site-specific eDR processes (although based on a particular location).

Although social and ecological issues intertwine, the previous chapter focused on social issues while this emphasizes ecology. Ecological design is always contextual, and the sample eDR was developed with a particular city/region in mind. Meanwhile, local political issues changed dramatically, so the eDR was converted to a generic example. Any template should, of course, be grounded in participatory processes that allow for early community engagement and final approval of the eDR. Whether circumstances or resources allow for adequate community-based planning, this example may serve to remind planners, designers and developers of some urban sustainability issues that should not be forgotten.

Ecological objectives should have primacy, as the planet is the foundation of social and economic existence. Development can and should contribute to sustainability by expanding the ecological base as well as stimulating social and economic regeneration. Some criteria concerning ecological issues that should be considered in the eDR are organized under the following categories: (1) restore and increase natural systems and eco-services; (2) create eco-positive onsite and offsite impacts; (3) reduce waste and total material flows; (4) eliminate fossil fuels and sequester carbon; (5) increase ecological and human health; and (6) recognize socio-ecological complexity and interdependency through open systems methods.

Section H STARfish (A Quantitative Tool)

15. The STARfish Tool Description

Proposes a quantitative design tool that facilitates an interactive, collaborative design process in a computer app where a design team competes with itself.

The STARfish tool is the quantitative counterpart to the eDR. This tool uses a blend of radar, spider and impact wheel diagrams. It creates an interactive collaborative 'game' in which a design team competes with itself to create the most sustainable design possible among alternatives. Among the aims of the tool are to foster a whole-systems view; emphasize creativity and fun; reframe design as opportunity creation (versus problem mitigation); emphasize the preliminary design stage; avoid the transaction costs and low transparency of RTs; draw upon common sense but make assumptions/values explicit; and prioritize multifunctional adaptive design to maximize eco-positive structures/spaces.

The chapter explains the STARfish tool, which is a (free) computer app on a website. The digital tool provides call-outs that inform the designers of benchmarks/criteria. Various eco-solutions that might be applicable to a particular problem/context can be posted over time. In contrast, the current tools discourage designers from continuing when a score is achieved or a threshold is passed, such as 'use of 20% less water than a typical building'. There is no upper limit on positive impacts, so all should count. Similarly, negative impacts do not disappear simply because they are offset, so they should not be hidden.

16. The STARfish Tool Benchmarks

Explains the fixed, biophysical (versus relative) criteria and benchmarks that set eco-positive standards for the design/assessment of positive development for each impact category.

This chapter defines the baselines and benchmarks for each of the impact categories that represent net-positive design actions. For comparisons or transferability of information with other tools, categories common to many RTs were used, namely: materials/waste, efficiency/energy, planning/spatial relationships, ecology/biodiversity, health/life quality and greenhouse/carbon. Most other major sustainability criteria can fit under at least one of these headings. The net-positive criteria are based on stationary biophysical baselines, unlike restorative/regenerative criteria which are relative to existing conditions. Because conventional tools compare onsite improvements to pre-construction conditions (not pre-urban/pre-industrial), reductions in 'additional' impacts are seen as positive. This ignores escalating global problems.

The assessment layers of the STARfish allow negative, restorative and net-positive impacts to be estimated using available knowledge. As the design is refined or more information on impacts becomes available, it is easily expanded. The tool is geared for identifying opportunities for positive actions and synergies, to develop the best design among many concepts. Since it calculates scores automatically and transparently, it could be used for project assessment by city councils. If the tool is used for development approvals or third-party certification, the decisions of the design team would be detailed in writing. The app's appearance can be modified visually.

Part I
Design and Analysis
Synopsis of Part I

Essential design and decision-making principles and standards are still missing from all dimensions of sustainability theory and practice in urban design and architecture.

Many proponents of sustainability have argued that efficiency is not enough and that systems change is needed at all levels of society. However, it has largely been assumed that a change of values and public policy would trickle through the interstices of governance and urban planning would automatically transform the built environment. Yet urban theory and practice has not addressed the basic sustainability dilemmas. Omissions are found at all levels of urban planning: planning analyses, development controls, decision methods, design processes and building rating tools. This book explores each dimension and suggests means to make the transition to eco-positive cities.

To have socio-ecological gains without adverse economic impacts, urban planning, decision making and design need to be reconceptualized and restructured for net-positive outcomes.

The sustainability crisis is a whole-system problem, requiring the redesign of development, yet circuitous arguments over policy plans persist. This is partly because design has been marginalized in the culture. It is portrayed as a subset of decision making, concerned mainly with communication, but it is a different way of thinking. Both decision making (choosing solutions) and design (opportunity-creating) are necessary and, ideally, complementary. However, neither processes nor practices evolved with sustainability in mind. They need to be reconceived upon ethics-based and positive principles. This book therefore proposes a reconceptualization of both biophysical design (built structures) and institutional design (decision-making structures).

Part I concerns biophysical design concepts and processes, and proposes paradigm shifts:

- From negative/fatalistic mindsets that assume development must be ecologically terminal – to reconceiving development as a means to increase socio-ecological sustainability [Chapters 1–2].
- From closed/bounded system models – to open-system paradigms that enable design that externalizes public impacts and expands positive future options [Chapters 3–4].

2 Design and Analysis

- From efficient innovations that create more products and material flows – to structural and spatial design solutions that reduce inequities and increase public gains [Chapters 5–6].
- From analyses that share the same conceptual roots as neo-classical economics – to whole-system analyses that prioritize the correction of socio-ecological deficits [Chapters 7–8].

Part II concerns institutional or decision-making structures, and proposes paradigm shifts:

- From reductionist decision-making – to design-based 'methods' that can create synergies and multiply public benefits [Chapters 9–10].
- From numerical standards for green building assessment tools that only reduce the project's damage – to design tools based on whole-system sustainability [Chapters 11–12].
- From either top-down or bottom-up but ineffective consultation processes – to new community-based collaborative processes for developing design criteria [Chapters 13–14].
- From 'metrics' that assess design outcomes relative to typical projects – to measurements that allow for net-positive impacts by using stationary benchmarks standards [Chapters 15–16].

The specific outcomes from a critical examination of sustainable planning and design methods are a community planning process, a design review process and a design tool (with a computer app).

Section A
Introduction to Positive Development

1 Overview of Net-Positive Development

1.1 Introduction

Given the massive environmental material and energy flows throughout the construction lifecycle, the re-design of urban environments is a prerequisite to genuine sustainability.

Cities could become catalysts for social, ecological and economic sustainability. However, to do so, they must increase the natural and social life-support systems and expand future options.[1] So-called 'sustainable' development is not yet sustainable. It transfers and concentrates wealth, reduces cultural/biological diversity, does irreversible ecological damage and impedes adaptability. In addition to curtailing the means of human survival and wellbeing, contemporary cities and buildings lock in negative pathways that eliminate future sustainable public choices.[2] Further, they have huge opportunity costs,[3] because they divert land, money, effort, time and resources away from creating environments that proactively increase sustainability and public benefits.

Most urban development outcomes were shaped by concepts and methods that evolved within an anthropocentric and exploitative ethic called the Dominant Paradigm (DP).

The planning and design of the built environment mirrors post-enlightenment worldviews that saw nature as a threat – if not antithetical to genuine human progress. It was assumed that development must have adverse environmental impacts, so sustainable design only aimed to mitigate negatives and increase positives relative to the norm. Sustainability is therefore still often described as a 'balance' between conservation and development.[4] Hence, environmental management/planning tools have evolved largely for deciding how/where to balance trade-offs.[5] The fallacy of the middle, the sweet spot between good and bad, still predominates urban design and architecture practice. This means doing less harm.

Frameworks of sustainable governance, planning and design should aim to improve urban/regional social conditions and increase the natural environment relative to pre-industrial/pre-urban conditions.

Sustainable design was always 'positive' in intentions, though not in outcomes. It has aimed to 'restore the environment, regenerate the community and revitalize the economy'.[6] Designers have long realized that sustainable design can pay for itself, be profitable, and stimulate socio-economic development.[7] However, the aim has only

6 *Design and Analysis*

been to leave the environment 'better than before construction' or to regenerate remnant natural landscapes.[8] Even if the earth's original environment were restored, however, nature could not support the current needs/demands of 'modern' society. To counteract the depletion/degradation of ecosystems, communities and resources, therefore, our institutional and physical infrastructure must be entirely reconceived.

Despite the massive cumulative and irreversible impacts involved in construction, development could increase positive social and ecological conditions in absolute terms (i.e. globally).

Over recent decades, there have been steady improvements and innovations in resource efficiency, upcycling and innovation.[9] Nevertheless, land use patterns, building design and construction practices still embed ecologically harmful lifestyles and land uses in urban development. Even if population, consumption, pollution and fossil fuels declined rapidly, current development standards and practices would not halt climate change and regenerate nature. For example, 'zero-energy' buildings sound optimal,[10] but these seldom count the 'embodied' resources lost during resource extraction/manufacturing, let alone cumulative losses of biodiversity. Even ecological compensation or offsetting schemes cause net ecosystem/biodiversity losses. Nevertheless, as argued herein, net-positive development is now possible.

Positive Development *(PD) posits that built structures and spaces, despite many unavoidable impacts during their construction, can become net contributors to biophysical sustainability.*

Simply adding more green design criteria and indicators to urban design, planning and architecture conventions has little effect. While these are important components of sustainable development, they do not contribute public and ecological gains in excess of their negative impacts – let alone increase the positive ecological footprint of nature.[11] This is because sustainable development, despite claims, still largely ignores basic sustainability issues, such as ecology, equity, poverty or resource security. In order to shift the trajectory of development from negative to net positive, PD proposes different physical, intellectual and institutional structures.[12] These are derived from ethics-based principles and net-positive standards.

PD refers to basic prerequisites of sustainability – physical/institutional structures that expand positive future options by increasing the ecological base and public estate.

As sustainable urban design gradually became professionalized, the design professions did not really change their underlying philosophies, frameworks or methods. Although sustainability initially meant making everything better, it came to mean reducing harm through efficiency, recycling and closing resource loops. These cannot protect biological and cultural diversity, reverse the pyramidal transfer of resources/wealth, increase adaptability to unpredictable change or convert cities from sterile machines to fertile gardens. Design cannot change economic systems, but it can reduce the impacts of disparities, by providing universal, direct access to basic needs, life quality and security,[13] and increasing public social spaces, or 'the commons'.[14]

A positive, open-system lens reveals alternatives to the negative DP intellectual and institutional constructs that underlie the planning and design of urban environments.

The general approach in sustainability fields has been to improve the same (failed) frameworks and processes. In contrast, PD aims to reconstruct them from ethical, ecological foundations. Increasing nature and positive future prospects requires a shift from reductionist decision-based frameworks to synergistic design-based ones, and from closed and fatalistic mindsets to open and positive ones. This text aims to show how open-systems mindsets, models, methods and metrics are better matched to the multi-dimensional environmental challenges facing society. PD methods reverse the pervasive closed-system approaches to environmental governance, planning and design and reconstructs their conceptual and procedural frameworks on eco-positive principles.

1.1.1 Implementing Change

Most presume that society must change before sustainable built environments can be implemented yet, conversely, built environments also influence social values and behaviors.

Initially, sustainability was about ethics: fairness to future and present generations, or 'inter/intra-generational equity'. Equity was understood to require preserving nature, not just resources, for survival and wellbeing. After the seminal *Brundtland Report* in 1987,[15] however, sustainability became transactional. While new 'sustainable' branches emerged in almost every field, they essentially kept their old paradigm frameworks and methods. Physical and institutional change was expected to follow automatically, once people embraced more enlightened sustainability values. Pushing people to change so they will adopt better policies, targets, strategies or designs, without changing the conditions that cause insecurity, inequalities and resentment, has not worked.[16]

Social and institutional reform through socio-political channels often causes adverse reactions, while physical environments can have direct, positive impacts on behavior and culture.

Positive socio-ecological policies and programs are often reversed by election cycles or powerful interests. However, there is nothing to stop physical environments from transcending current codes and standards to 'give back more than they take'.[17] Design can act independently to meet many competing goals at once. 'Conflict resolution by design' is a proven, though much neglected, process. This means that incompatible interests/positions of adversaries are resolved by alternative designs that make both sides better off while reducing negative public impacts. This is a role of planners/designers: to identify means to correct deficits and add benefits through whole-system analyses [Chapters 7–8].

While biophysical sustainability need not wait for social, economic or political change, the institutional systems that shape the built environment still need reform.

Design can over-compensate for past losses in cultural/biodiversity, environmental justice, social equity and future options, partly because this can be done in ways that save money for investors, occupants and/or the general public. There are no confirmed examples of a net-positive development, however, since they are not yet measured. Current assessment tools do not contemplate, let alone assess or verify, net-positive outcomes. They support efficiency and environmental amenity measures, but not increases in the ecological base and public estate. The institutional frameworks and planning methods to achieve this are discussed in Part II. Part I focuses on built environment design.

8 *Design and Analysis*

1.1.2 Guide to 'Balance' Diagrams

Diagrams are included to illustrate how PD approaches differ from the limited choices that dominate the discourse in urban planning, policy and design.

When couched in a reductionist decision framework, sustainability is often represented as 'a balance between environmental quality, social equity, and economic efficiency'.[18] In practice, and often in theory, 'balance' translates into trade-offs between the 'three pillars of sustainability' or triple bottom line (TBL): economic, environmental, social – and sometimes a fourth one such as governance. This deeply rooted notion of balancing pluralist interests still pervades the literature.[19] The TBL is often misapplied to legitimize trading off nature for short-term socio-economic demands, but it also keeps systems change off the agenda. Restricting debate to conventional choices reinforces dualistic thinking and excludes new perspectives.

The diagrams aim to suggest how traditional binary decision frameworks obscure new and diverse options and opportunities that can be constructed by design.

The concept of balance can limit debate to the two sides of the same coin (e.g. left versus right). The left-hand side of each diagram shows the prevalent 'either-or' dualisms that pertain to the issue at hand [Figure 1.1]. Over time, policies swing from one side of the status quo to the other, like a pendulum, but little actually changes. 'Less negative' choices are generally ecologically terminal or inequitable. The right-hand side of the diagrams shows positive alternatives that flow from a design-based approach. These positive options are overlooked, partly because design is seen as a subset of decision making.

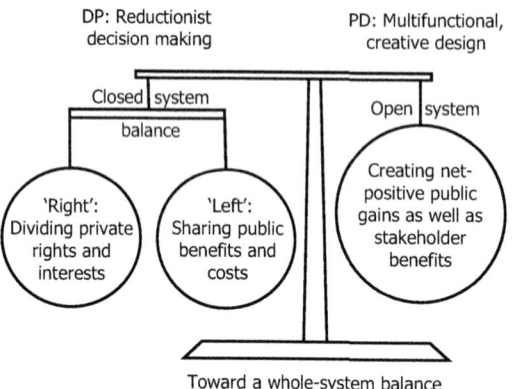

The current choices tend to be between false dualisms (ecology v. economy, planning v. market systems, right v. left politics, etc.). Seen as opposites, a binary tug-of-war is created between what are often public and private interests. Calls for balance usually mean making compromises and trade-offs, not meeting both needs. 'Third' design alternatives are not taken seriously, because they are out-of-the-box.

*PD = Positive Development
*DP = dominant paradigm

Decision-based approaches aid making chooses
Design-based approaches aid creating more choices

Figure 1.1 Code to diagrams

1.2 Definitions and Basic Concepts in Positive Development (PD)

1.2.1 PD Standards and Baselines

***The PD Test** is whether a design, policy, rule or action can increase positive future public options, the ecological base and public estate.*

PD provides baselines for ecological and social design standards in built environment design, along with specific benchmarks in the digital design tool. These baselines mean a design/action would increase sustainable public choices, so that present and future generations gain greater opportunities for a higher quality of life, as well as freedom from risks and threats. These two primary standards (the ecological base and public estate), discussed in many different contexts in this book, are reiterated here for the reader's convenience. These are followed by basic definitions and distinctions commonly used in PD, followed by some examples of net-positive design strategies.

***The ecological base** is an umbrella term encompassing nature (biodiversity, ecosystem functions and services, ecological carrying capacity, wilderness, species, the food chain, etc.).*

Sustainable design fields often advocate emulating, incorporating, restoring or regenerating nature. However, they have not recognized the need for absolute/global increases in ecological carrying capacity and ecosystem services relative to expanding human populations and consumption. It is feasible for vertical urban structures to achieve this. For example, buildings can sequester more carbon than is emitted over their lifecycles,[20] and support integrated natural systems that provide building and environmental functions (eco-services).[21] In PD, 'eco-services' include both intrinsic/inherent value of nature as well as instrumental values.[22] Eco-positive cities would provide urban eco-services, and also regenerate their bioregions, in combination with 'net-positive offsetting' (below).[23]

***The PD ecological standard:** To be ecologically sustainable, construction must increase nature's 'positive ecological footprint' beyond humanity's negative footprint (on a floor area, not ground over, basis).*

To be ecologically net positive, development must increase natural life-support systems beyond the global rate of environmental devastation, as well as preserve/enhance ecological diversity. Closing loops in domestic and industrial processes does not compensate for the embodied and cumulative ecological damage/waste during resource extraction.[24] Given current rates of environmental destruction, therefore cities must over-compensate for more than their own negative impacts. This entails increasing 'ecological space' beyond pre-historic/pre-urban conditions,[25] and maximizing the benefits/services of nature, not just replacing natural resources used in construction. For example, vertical peri-urban structures can support small representative ecosystems that could one day reseed damaged bioregions.

***Design for eco-services,** which includes the practical, cultural and social benefits of natural environments, can combine to help meet the PD ecological standard.*

In theory, a simple green roof or wall can provide up to two-dozen eco-services in itself, such as air filtration, water cleansing, stormwater reduction, oxygen production, endangered bird or bee habitats, building insulation, urban heat mitigation and so on.[26] However, good design is always contextual – ecologically and socially, not just aesthetically. Thus, design for eco-services is based on an analysis of region-wide ecological needs and deficiencies. Whether new or retrofitted/remodeled, good development would address local and regional sustainability issues while meeting the unique constraints of the site and brief [Chapters 7–8]. Urban design should aim for symbiotic development-environment relationships.

The public estate requires direct, universal access to public spaces that provide the prerequisite of sustainability (e.g. health/wellbeing, environmental equity/quality and community engagement/participation).

Development should reduce regional social deficits and disparities of wealth, equity and opportunity, and increase public spaces and direct access to basic needs (e.g. shelter, food, energy, water). Engineering and economic efficiencies have not improved the distribution of social costs and benefits.[27] 'Design efficiency' means maximizing public benefits relative to resources used. 'Direct access' means uninterrupted by markets or delivery systems that make people vulnerable to the threat of deprivation. PD advocates 'direct physical design action', not just indirect policy levers.[28] Unlike economic indicators, such as money or gross domestic product (GDP),[29] improvements in physical conditions and relationships are verifiable.

The PD social standard: To be socially sustainable, construction must increase direct access to basic needs and environmental justice and correct social deficits/ equities (on a regional basis).

Development has generally transferred wealth from poor to rich and future to present generations.[30] Yet sustainable design generally aims to benefit stakeholders (i.e. investors, neighbors and occupants) not to increase the public domain.[31] Sustainable building tools mainly identify efficiency measures (which usually improve profitability anyway) and mitigate the public costs of the project. Basic ethical concerns like environmental justice or equity are forgotten. In fact, many celebrated sustainable buildings do little for the surrounding area, except raise property values. PD aims to increase universal life quality/equity and improve human-environmental health on a regional basis – not just for project stakeholders.[32]

Public space can increase direct, universal access to basic needs and environmental security, which are essential components of democracy: physical and political security.

Studies show that open green spaces contribute to a sense of place, social cohesion, community building improved health and reduction of stresses.[33] 'Urban acupuncture',[34] the term for targeted improvements in disadvantaged areas (e.g. new community centers, parks, libraries, playgrounds) have stimulated positive community interaction and helped to revitalize communities. However, there has been little attention to making disadvantaged areas more independent of economic forces/interests beyond local control, a prerequisite of sustainable democracy. Unlike socio-economic policies which are subject to myriad exogenous factors, design can ensure everyone has direct access to basic needs and safe havens in civil or environmental emergencies.

1.2.2 Types of Design Distinguished in PD

***Mainstream green design** paradigms have been implicitly or explicitly based on closed-system models, which lead to improved efficiency (cleaner production) and reduction (recycling).*

To reduce environmental damage and increase social welfare and amenities, mainstream sustainable design downsizes resource inputs and pollution/waste outputs. In building, this is often done by reducing space for people as well as reducing materials and energy. This generally saves money but does not allow space for nature. Nature is squeezed into a preconceived (sterile) architectural aesthetic. However, reductions relative to typical building design and construction practices or prior site conditions cannot be net positive. Even where zero waste or closed-loop energy and water systems are achieved, this does not increase the social or natural life-support system in whole-system terms.

***Technocratic design** has various meanings but implies industrialism and is more about decision making than design (choosing among alternatives rather than creating choices).*

The term design in business and organization management fields usually refers to improving the organizational processes/practices – from the perspective of the firm. The term 'positive design' has also been taken up in business fields but with a focus on value adding.[35] Since the business culture is transactional by nature, positive usually means benefitting shareholders and stakeholders, but not the environment. 'Adding value' in built environment design has meant marginal change, not changing the nature of urban environments.[36] In contrast, design in PD aims to create built environments that improve distributional and environmental justice and increase social and ecological space.

***Sustainable design** paradigms challenge the belief systems underlying industrial development, but largely only concern the human environment, not social justice and environmental protection.*

The recognition of the centrality of urban design in sustainability issues is growing rapidly.[37] This has led to new sustainable design paradigms that built on different insights from the sustainability movement, as summarized in Box 1. Each paradigm centers on somewhat different though compatible overlapping sets of concerns and priorities. They emphasize different orientations (psychological, cultural, biological, etc.), different dimensions (innovation, recycling, transportation, urban greening, etc.), or different target audiences (manufacturers, business, homeowners, designers, etc.). Over time, mainstream green building organizations are integrating these insights/concepts into their criteria and assessment tools.[38] However, continuous improvement does not shift frameworks and baselines.

***Design** in PD refers to thinking in open systems or flows to create environments that generate reciprocal benefits for both nature and society.*

Design in PD means creating synergistic, symbiotic systems. This requires open-systems thinking.[39] Early on, models of sustainability were based on closed-system metaphors, such as 'spaceship earth' [Chapter 3]. Such metaphors focused the designer's mind on 'limits': containing impacts within boundaries (e.g. property lines, duty of care, resource constraints or urban borders). Closed system frameworks have tended to seek a balance between inputs-outputs or costs-benefits. This has led to solutions that are efficient or even self-sufficient, but not net-positive. 'Internalizing externalities' is not net positive. Although recycling and closing loops are essential, design could increase resources, nature, future options and adaptability.

***Net-positive design** uses borderless, open-systems thinking to benefit the public, whereas conventional sustainable design paradigms can reinforce closed mindsets, models, methods and metrics.*

Designers have always aimed to leave things better than they found them. Design 'with' nature (e.g. permaculture, regenerative design) and design 'like' nature (e.g. biomimicry, biophilic design), in themselves, cannot preserve wilderness. If society were already sustainable, sustainable design approaches might be enough. However, greening cities without increasing nature globally to keep pace with development is shortsighted. Net-positive sustainability requires that design for development aims to 'increase nature's carrying capacity relative to human consumption'.[40] In PD, structures are reconceived as landscapes designed to increase nature's instrumental and intrinsic values. Net-positive development is that which gives back 'more than it takes'.[41]

1.2.3 Decision Making as Defined in PD

Decision making, by its very nature, is about reducing problems to alternatives and comparing them using select criteria in order to facilitate choices.

Generally, environmental decisions allocate resources or distribute costs-benefits among various objectives or stakeholders. Decision tools simplify alternatives to enable comparisons or distribution. They usually weight alternatives according to various priorities. For example, lifecycle assessment may prioritize carbon emissions over biodiversity. Although usually called 'design tools', green building rating/marketing tools (RTs) exemplify a decision-based approach [Chapters 10–12]. Design, in contrast, is 'an interactive, imaginative process for creating something that has never existed before, such as sustainability'.[42] New sustainable systems must be designed, they cannot be chosen. Decision making divides costs, while design can potentially multiply benefits and synergistic relationships [Figure 1.2].

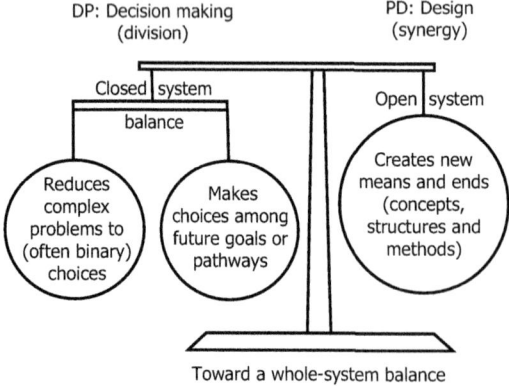

Figure 1.2 Distinguishing design and decision making

Decision making can aim for conflict resolution, but this usually requires creating new 'out-of-the-box' alternatives by design – which requires different mental processes.

Decision making involves reduction and design involves synthesis. It is apparent that design and decision making use different mental processes. Recent research supports this observation: designs and decisions use distinct cognitive functions and neural networks.[43] This does *not* suggest a simplistic distinction between right and left hemispheres of the brain.[44] In fact, design is ideally both an intuitive and intellectual process, requiring the active engagement of both the left and right hemispheres.[45] Design has been marginalized by reductionist decision-making frameworks. Chapters 7–8 propose a number of planning/design analyses that are essential to sustainable design, yet are not undertaken.

1.2.4 Negative and Positive as Defined in PD

Negative *in PD refers to constructs/concepts that have terminal results, because they contribute to anti-ecological or inequitable outcomes that eventually close off options.*

Many advocate the protection, but not expansion, of remnant ecosystems for human benefit (e.g. pharmaceuticals, recreation, amenity). This position tacitly accepts the idea that technology will eventually replace nature,[46] making the demise of nature inevitable. Even efforts at preservation are often dismissed as naïve or sentimental. After all, pollution, poachers and feral species will eventually invade any reserve on earth. Conversely, losing 50% of global biodiversity in fifty years, while spending billions of dollars searching for life on other planets is patently irrational. When humans reach another living planet, they may destroy it instantly with their 'invasive' bodily microbes.

Positive *(without the prefix 'net') refers to actions/outcomes that reduce negative impacts relative to existing conditions or on a project-specific (not planetary) basis.*

PD was first expressed as 'reversing negative impacts': meaning beyond zero (a net gain).[47] This was misinterpreted to mean 'positive': cleaning up industry and resuscitating the environment. While remediation/regeneration activities are essential, however, they seldom offset a project's lifecycle impacts, let alone its share of the adverse cumulative impacts of development in total [Figure 1.3]. Similarly, a building that treats all its organic waste in a building-integrated composting system is positive vis-à-vis soil

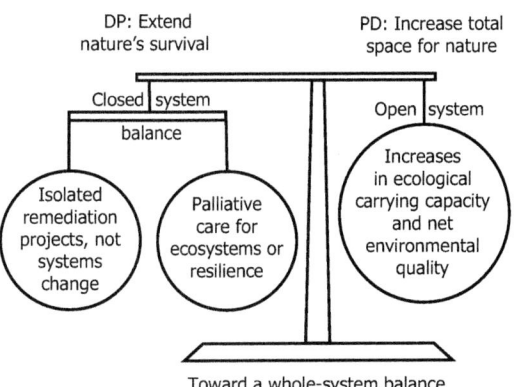

Figure 1.3 From reducing harm to increasing benefits

14 Design and Analysis

but not overall. To be *net* positive, it would need to support more soil ecosystems than those damaged during resource extraction and/or displaced by the building.

1.2.5 Net as Defined in PD

Net positive *means socio-ecological gains in society's and nature's positive ecological footprint created by a development, after deducting the negative human-made ecological footprint.*

Activity that slows the rate of socio-ecological degradation is 'good', but *not* net positive.[48] Net benefits for society and nature should ideally over-compensate for global *rates* of environmental depletion/contamination and growing disparities in wealth, power and life quality. PD phrases such as net positive are still misused by some to mean leaving the site better than 'before construction'.[49] Likewise, 'more nature than in pre-development conditions' was misconstrued to mean more than existed at the time of the particular development proposal, not pre-urban times. 'Pre-industrial' is relevant to European locations and 'pre-European occupation' is more relevant to Australia or North America.

Net *is commonly misappropriated to mean just shifting benefits across borders (e.g. property lines) or between developments, rather than increasing benefits in total.*

The term 'net positive' has been misused to describe energy or water that is collected and sent across borders or property lines.[50] Where onsite *operating* energy usage is reduced to zero by combining renewable and passive systems, and energy is transferred between buildings, this is not necessarily net positive. Since energy cannot be increased due to the laws of physics, 'energy-positive' or 'net-positive energy' are somewhat oxymoronic. Similarly, water is largely a closed global system. When water or energy is moved around to benefit others, it counts as regenerative in PD tools, as they are not net gains [Figure 1.4].

Examples *may help illustrate how net-positive design and development requires an open and whole-system framework, as opposed to reducing damage caused by development.*

Producing resources, air, water, energy, food and so on usually has associated impacts and is not net positive in itself, yet some tools count them as such by

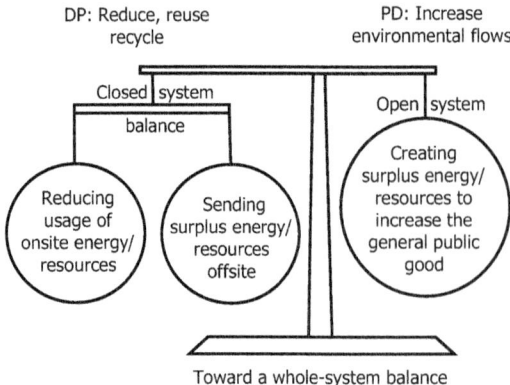

Figure 1.4 From efficiency/recycling to life-giving systems

ignoring some of their associated impacts. Conversely, restorative and eco-positive actions, in combination, can produce net positive outcomes in some cases. The PD design tool [Chapters 15–16] enables these to be quantified and summed. Some examples may help to distinguish positive/restorative from net positive:

- Waste reused in recycling systems, or even upcycled to a higher value, does not usually contribute to the environment, and the recycling/upcycling process itself involves waste, toxins and/or energy. Some organic products, once used, can contribute to habitat creation (as opposed to just circulating organic materials and money): called 'eco-cycling' in PD.
- Contaminated water circulated through natural or artificial wetlands can cause toxins to build up in reeds and even birds. The amount of clean water for humans and the environment is not actually increased. Technically, water can be produced in fuel cells, but this requires energy and materials, and has no ecological benefits.
- Buildings usually have mechanical air treatment equipment that emits contaminated air to the outdoors. Planting walls involves maintenance, but these costs are seldom compared to the maintenance and upgrade costs of mechanical equipment. Apart from plants, there are some substances such as titanium that can purify air, but are harmful in production.
- Land reserved in perpetuity in exchange for using greenfield land for a development is not a net gain since the reserved land was already there. However, if a new building also provides substantial building-integrated ecosystems and eco-services, such that it compensates for its ecological footprint, the combined actions could be net positive.
- Energy produced by a building with substantial wall or roof solar cells and window-integrated solar cells or solar window shades could provide 'surplus' energy, once these features pay back their 'embodied' energy (i.e. used in construction). However, in a whole-system perspective, surplus energy used for negative purposes would need to be deducted.

1.2.6 Nature as Defined in PD

PD planning and design begins from the ecological base, recognizing that social and economic sustainability ultimately depends on protecting and increasing natural environments.

Anthropocentric perspectives, if internally consistent, would support nature as it is the basis of human life. Nevertheless, anthropocentric philosophies have legitimized social and environmental exploitation. For centuries, slaves, women and animals were deemed 'closer to nature' and 'lesser beings' that were put on earth to serve Man [Chapter 4].[51] However, even if everyone became eco-centric, ethical, physical and institutional structures would still need redesign. While ecological design paradigms are relatively less anthropocentric, they do not yet advocate for design *for* nature [Figure 1.5]. If ecological space and carrying capacity is not created in urban-rural environments, nature will not survive.

Sustainable design calls for conserving, restoring or regenerating nature, but has not accepted the possibility of increasing nature to offset past human consumption.

Historically, Man's destiny was to outgrow or transcend nature. Cities largely excluded nature,[52] which was meant to be converted to products, with some wilderness areas set aside for spiritual renewal. Even sustainable design paradigms appear to

16 *Design and Analysis*

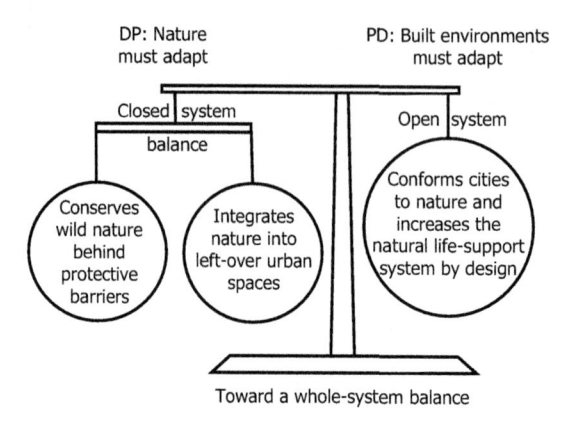

Figure 1.5 From differing views of nature protection in design

assume that nature need only be made more 'resilient', and that urban nature can survive in leftover spaces around the edges of buildings and roads. Concepts like resilience and regeneration challenge the view that nature can be replaced by technology.[53] However, preserving wilderness areas legislatively will not last long, due to politics, genetically modified organisms, toxic dust, poaching, disease, warfare, climate change and so on.

Although well intentioned, concepts like 'co-evolving in partnership with nature' are euphemisms that conceal or excuse the destructive dominance of humans over nature.

A number of theorists like to describe nature and humans as 'co-evolving' in a partnership. This is reflected in the traditional green design expression: working with nature.[54] However, nature cannot evolve fast enough to cope with climate and land use change, as shown by losses in ecosystems/biodiversity.[55] Co-evolving is also eerily reminiscent of past aboriginal 'assimilation' policies [Figure 1.6]. The notion that aboriginals were meant to be integrated into Eurocentric societies made their annihilation sound somewhat benign or, at worst, paternalistic. Today's reality is that humans must evolve, not nature. It is only human society that can evolve fast enough.

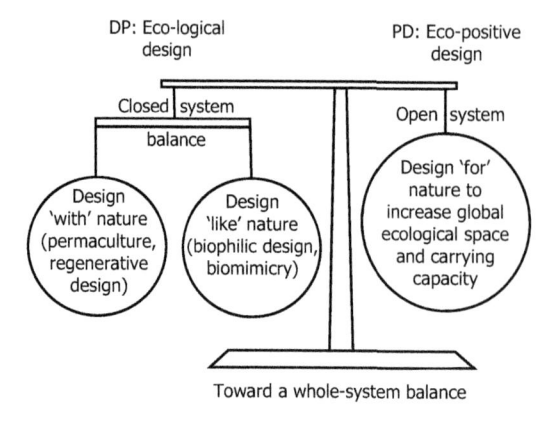

Figure 1.6 From nature adapting to humans evolving?

Some believe that nature has no meaning other than what people assign to it: that nature is a 'reification' (abstraction confused with reality).

Several academics have argued that nature is just a 'social construction'.[56] This implies that environmentalists are projecting a romantic ideal onto material reality, and that the intrinsic value of nature is 'all in the mind' – a uniquely negative social construction. This view has internalized the precepts of neo-classical economics: an ideological construct that reduces nature to raw materials. The idea that a living planet, taking over 3.8 billion years to create, has no inherent value, is not a sound mental outlook. Clinging to physical and institutional structures that have negative outcomes for humans and nature is not rational.

1.3 The Critique of the Triple Bottom Line (TBL) in PD

1.3.1 The Environmental Dimension in PD

To be eco-positive, development must collectively increase the ecological base, not just increase nature's ability to rebound or recover to a recent condition.

Rating tools (RTs), by comparing projects to current environmental conditions or typical construction, can be misleading. For example, '20% less energy' than the norm can mean '80% more than necessary'. A reduction in the damage that might have been caused by a hypothetical code-compliant project, or relative to 'other buildings of the same type', does not increase sustainability. Further, buildings may provide biodiversity habitats in their landscaping, but this does not compensate for the lifecycle ecological impacts or increase net carrying capacity. PD therefore uses fixed, whole-system biophysical baselines and benchmarks, as discussed in Part II [Chapters 15–16]. For example:

- The 'ecological' baseline is more ecological space than in pre-industrial/pre-urban times on a lifecycle and floor area basis.[57]
- The 'social' baseline is a measurable increase in regional environmental justice and equitable access to needs (see below).

Note: 'Eco-positive' and 'net-positive' are generally interchangeable except when measuring net impacts; that is, in the PD design tool [Chapters 15–16]. A project can have remedial/restorative/regenerative design elements which, in combination with eco-positive elements, may constitute net-positive impacts. If the negative impacts are extensive, however, eco-positive actions may fail to exceed net-zero impacts.

Sustainable design uses nature for greater efficiency, health benefits and amenities, but cities must also be converted into structures providing ecosystems and eco-services.

Rainforests and cities each occupy roughly 2–3% of the earth's surface. If cities worked more like landscapes, instead of 'black holes',[58] they could conceivably contribute equivalent positive impacts [Figure 1.7]. Given a finite planet surface, increases in ecological carrying capacity require vertical structures. For example, Green Scaffolding can contribute biodiversity incubators with little land, energy or materials [Chapter 6]. These diverse space-frame structures, constructed around/between/inside existing buildings, can support various eco-

18 *Design and Analysis*

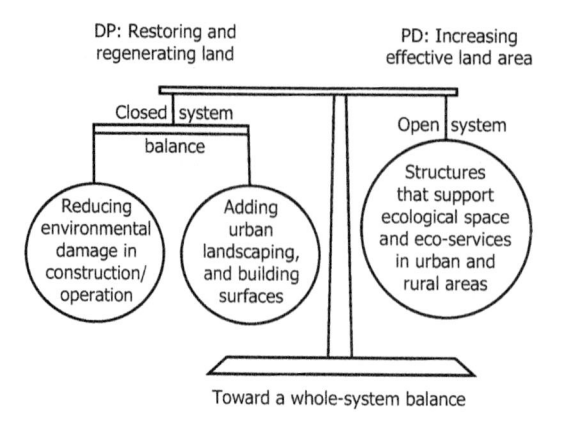

Figure 1.7 From eco-restoration to increasing ecological carrying capacity

services, micro-habitats or ecosystem enclaves/incubators to regenerate the bioregions and provide a hedge against ecological uncertainty. They can be supported financially by building in additional social and/or economic functions. For example:

- Central city restaurants can grow their own food on their rooftops, simultaneously mitigating the urban heat island effect, reducing transportation impacts and ensuring supply chain purity.
- Offsets for surplus ecological gains or land/building area for producing eco-services can be leased to existing developments that cannot physically meet regulations or rising community expectations.

While indigenous ecosystems and pre-human ecological conditions can now be mapped, a return to original ecosystems (if viable) is not always ecologically appropriate.

As demonstrated by the rate of global biodiversity losses and extinction rates, the planet's surface area cannot support the human population and maintain biodiversity. Moreover, a return to prior indigenous ecosystems/species may not be ecologically appropriate anyway, due to past irreversible human interventions.[59] Nonetheless, nature must be increased just to stabilize the rate of deterioration. Buildings may soon be grown with nanotechnology or low-impact materials that consume few natural resources or ecosystems.[60] In any case, they should support urban habitats and micro-ecosystems to reseed the regions. Such ecosystem nurseries will require a new profession that integrates the biological sciences and design.

Rural structures for vegetable/legume production could free up rural land to enable wilderness restoration and compensate for unavoidable past and present environmental destruction.

Although cities can contribute biodiversity banks and ecosystem nurseries, land area in the regions must still be restored/regenerated. A major cause of land degradation is from land-intensive grazing animal and grain production systems.[61] Many have argued for shifting to vegetarian diets which have fewer ecological impacts. However, vertical vegetable food production in scaffolding structures in rural areas will also be necessary to restore productive land and increase overall efficiency.[62] Some of the land currently used for grain and meat production could be regenerated, and remote areas could be restored to relatively natural conditions using Green Scaffolding systems as wilderness buffers [Figure 1.8].

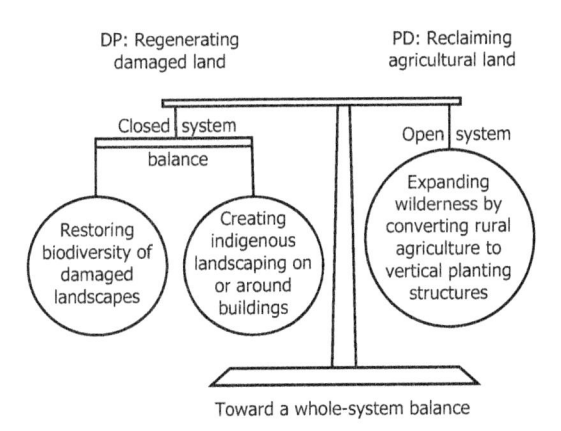

Figure 1.8 Increasing ecosystems/biodiversity in the bioregions

1.3.2 The Social Dimension in PD

Sustainable design literature generally underestimates the potential of built environment design to address social deficits, increase equity and foster social and cultural change.

Well-designed projects enhance the life quality of building occupants, not just property values. While social factors have always been concerns in sustainable design, the focus is typically on either the preferences or psychological, physiological, behavioral and/or experiential effects of buildings on users or stakeholders. This is not the same as equitable living environments.[63] Design can create environments that at least reduce the experience of systematic economic injustices. Ironically, many sustainable designers call upon consumers to adopt better behaviors and/or purchasing choices. This is buck passing, as most can only choose what the building industry and designers put on the market.

Social sustainability requires eco-productive living environments that ensure inbuilt access to basic needs and security but that also reduce social and/or wealth stratification.

While sustainable design emphasizes concepts like 'sense of place' and 'community building',[64] it often leaves basic issues (e.g. environmental security) to the realm of politics or markets. Reliance on remote economic mechanisms for the provision of basic needs can create community vulnerability and dependency.

20 *Design and Analysis*

Democracy requires freedom from coercion through direct, universal access to basic needs. Future government, corporate and/or military powers could withhold supply. In fact, today's voters/consumers are limiting the rights of future generations, just as politicians are limiting the options of future elected officials. Only physical environments can ensure and verify that everyone can access basic needs [Figure 1.9].

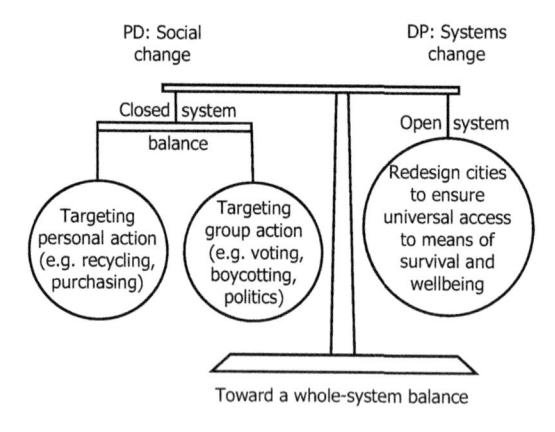

Figure 1.9 Social and/or systems change

Since built environments affect social issues well beyond property lines, social sustainability also requires positive contributions in local/regional social and environmental equity/justice.

The prevailing definition of sustainability, 'meeting present needs without disadvantaging future generations', relies on a trickle-down theory.[65] Policy/political decisions may occasionally divide resources more fairly or extend their usefulness, but this is only a reprieve. Postponing problems does not solve them. Hoping that policies will have positive spill-over effects ignores the scale and speed of accumulating impacts, biodiversity losses and power/wealth differentials. Only physical solutions provide guarantees. While built environment design cannot change socio-political systems or cultures, it can make everyone better off. Public environments can alleviate the impacts of poverty, by increasing environmental amenity, equity and even public shelters.

Leverage points for design interventions can be identified by PD forensic flows analyses that help identify gaps that planning and/or design should address.

Typically, planning and design methods follow political and professional trends. Surveys, community participation and consultation are used to glean user preferences, but often in ways that elicit desired responses. Most consumers/stakeholders can only choose from what they already know or is presented to them. Similarly, indicators are used to reveal general consumer/producer trends, but these usually relate more to wobbly economic variables than issues relevant to physical design. PD diagnostic analyses, arguably not yet undertaken in professions/academia/government, address such gaps.[66] Twenty-two 'missing' planning and design analyses are discussed later [Chapters 7–8]. New digital tools could soon make them more practical [Figure 1.10].[67]

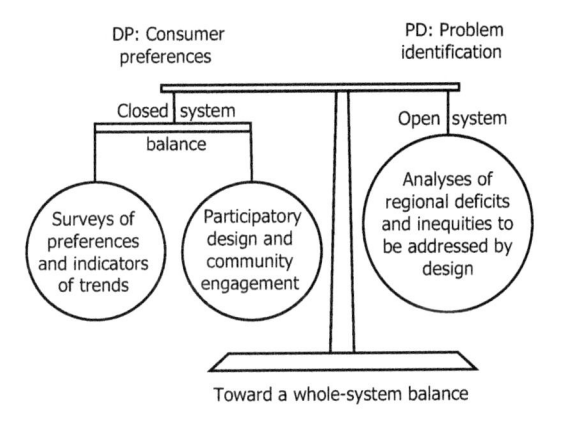

Figure 1.10 From consumer preferences to analyses

1.3.3 The Economic Dimension in PD

While business has embraced efficiency innovations, this has often meant more material components, which can often increase other lifecycle impacts of green buildings.

Design, in business, is used to sell more products, rather than to leverage systems changes that can reduce net material flows. Changing systems always costs extra, but the costs of change can be reimbursed from future savings through simple mechanisms like cross-subsidies. The collective causes of unsustainability, and barriers to sustainability, are interrelated with the global economic system in general and business sector in particular. Nonetheless, economics and business are not barriers to sustainability as such, since ecological design generally saves money through efficiencies, and need not cost extra.[68] The built environment is therefore a strong lever for social/systems transformation.

The triple bottom line (TBL), in business, has meant balancing off long-term social and environmental needs for economic gains, despite the initial intention.

The TBL is a popular translation of sustainable development into a business framework.[69] It was intended to integrate environmental and social concerns into business decisions. However, it has been misused to suggest that the economy, society and environment can be 'balanced' in an imaginary three-column ledger. This has entrenched a cost-benefit framework that legitimizes incremental trade-offs between social/economic/ecological columns, as long as none are destroyed [Figure 1.11]. Incremental development decisions mean that present generations are deciding now how future generations must live, which violates the principle of intergenerational equity [Chapter 9]. PD

2   Design and Analysis

ıstead avoids trade-offs by expanding/multiplying positive diverse pathways and environments [Figure 1.11].

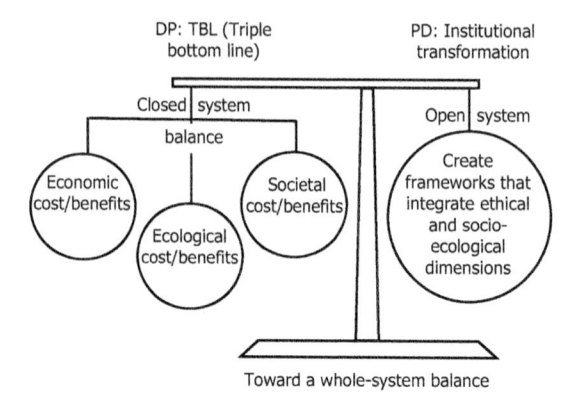

Figure 1.11 From trade-offs to net-positive frameworks

Business and engineering fields have many tools to ensure efficiency or profitability, but none aim for net ethical and ecological gains by design.

RTs are voluntary, industry-led green building assessment/marketing schemes for certifying buildings as 'sustainable'. This classic business-oriented approach to problems is critiqued extensively in Part II [Chapters 9–12]. RTs generally set criteria that are easy to measure, such as 'use 10% recycled material', '20% less water' or 'add twenty bicycle parking spaces'. However, such reductions in negative impacts, which usually save money anyway, are deemed environmental gains. Adjectives like 'ecological', 'ecosystem-based' or 'biodiversity' frequently appear in promotional material, giving the impression that nature is somehow being looked after.[70] Yet RTs do not contemplate or require positive or eco-positive ecological outcomes.[71]

The business approach to urban/building design, green building rating/marketing tools (RTs) emphasize efficiencies (financial benefits) but only slow the pace of ecological destruction.

RTs came about because sustainability was being ignored by most developers.[72] Yet most RT provisions focus on efficiency, which normally corresponds with a financial payback. Ironically, some now claim that RTs emphasize the environment at the expense of finance. They call for more 'balance' between economic and environmental criteria, as if economics was not still the bottom line. If designs are efficient and cost effective, developers make profits and designers gain further employment, and projects that are not cost-effective are usually cancelled anyway.[73] RTs reflect the DP in rewarding businesses that do 'relatively' less harm, but not positive public gains [Figure 1.12].

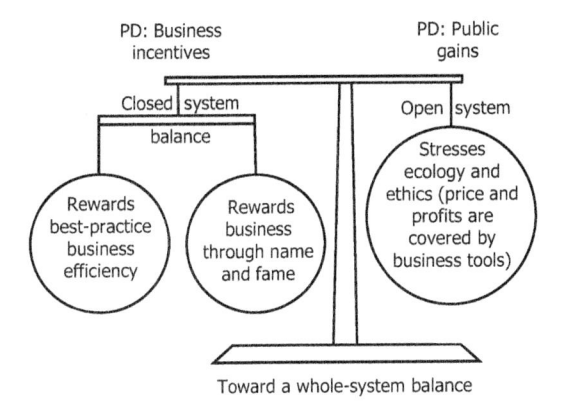

Figure 1.12 From efficiency to the net public good

1.4 Introduction to Some Basic Design Strategies

Design can increase the ecological base, public estate and public choice through, among other things, 'multifunctional design', 'design for eco-services' and 'eco-positive retrofitting'.

Recycling and/or upcycling to a higher economic value are an essential part of sustainable design and are leading to greater efficiencies,[74] through reductions in inputs and/or outputs. In buildings, however, efficiency often means spatial reduction. Reduction makes sense in regard to money, energy and materials, but not in regard to spatial environments.[75] A fixation with (economic) efficiency instead of socio-ecological gain has distracted designers from increasing the functions and values of low-cost, low-impact space. Structures should maximize benefits relative to both resources and space use. Advocates of sustainable design have collected sustainable design ideas that are available on frequently updated websites.[76]

Eco-positive retrofitting: Both ordinary and green buildings will need to be retrofitted, not only for higher performance standards, but for greater adaptability, eco-productivity and biodegradability.

Biophysical sustainability is not technically possible without retrofitting or renovating cities, due to their huge past/ongoing/future impacts [Chapters 5].[77] In contrast, retrofitting for increased worker health and productivity was proven to be profitable decades ago,[78] as costs can be recouped from the energy/resource savings. Any construction, including retrofitting, requires substantial materials,[79] and will require maintenance. However, new construction represents only 1–3% of the building stock.[80] Hence, new cities and buildings cannot reverse overall impacts of development. Replacing cities with new buildings, even zero-energy ones, would cost too much in materials, money, energy and especially time. Retrofitting cities is therefore imperative.

Although retrofitting could support the ecology while improving the human environment and economy, the aim is usually only to make the 'least change'.

Past eco-retrofitting emphasized efficiency measures to reduce costs, energy, water usage and/or occupant health impacts. However, the emphasis was generally on minimizing change to reduce costs – not to increase public benefits or equity in the surrounding area.[81] This is a lost opportunity because adding public benefits by design need not cost more. Retrofitting can 'decouple' financial gains and environmental costs.[82] Costs depend more on design than reduction by 'value management' or cost cutting after by project managers.[83] Where extra costs are entailed, mechanisms like net-positive offsetting can be used to compensate developers for their contributions to society. For example:

- Traditional eco-retrofitting usually concerns single-function measures that improve the thermal performance of the building envelope (e.g. insulating walls, painting the roof white for reflectivity, adding skylights, using double glazed windows). This is a safe and profitable investment.[84] An eco-positive retrofit would aim to send energy to the grid, clean air and water to adjacent properties and provide community benefits such as public garden areas to alleviate stress, produce oxygen and build community [Chapter 5]. Rather than aiming for the least change to reduce the payback time, buildings retrofits should provide the most socio-ecological benefit with the least ecological footprint.

Multifunctional Design: *Multifunctional vertical structures, spaces and surfaces can create garden-like environments that enhance basic physical, physiological and psychological conditions, while contributing to practical functions/services.*

While traditional modes of building design and construction assume that reducing space equals more efficiency and cost savings, PD suggests space should be maximized or optimized. For example, attached solar greenhouse balconies and atriums that collect, store and circulate heat in temperate climates can provide low-impact indoor-outdoor spaces in cold weather. Spaces for vegetation and ecosystems in cities seem small and plants seem high maintenance and of little financial value.[85] Yet plants provide oxygen, and space itself costs nothing – only the structures that define the space use resources.[86] Moreover, new materials are emerging for producing low-cost, less material-intensive structures.

Good design can fit into existing systems of production/construction, while simultaneously transforming them into eco-productive environments that provide multifunctional structures, surfaces and spaces.

Despite the embodied energy and resources caused by production processes, buildings in many climates can be designed to sequester more carbon and toxins, and produce more food, oxygen, energy and water than destroyed during construction. Designed as multi-functional urban landscapes, buildings could also create positive ripple effects throughout the wider region. Although the contribution of each structure may be small, each building or city could contribute economic, natural and social gains. Multifunctional surfaces and spaces that support building-integrated eco-services are easily integrated with buildings (see below).[87] These multifunctional design elements could 'over-compensate' for the ecological footprint of buildings. For example:

- Green walls can add to property values and support mechanical air cleaning functions, but they can be costly to maintain. In tall residential or office buildings, however, whole horizontal floors have been dedicated to open gardens to provide social/meeting spaces. In fact, some double-skin buildings keep some upper floors 'open' with gardens to facilitate air flow up between the two glass walls. These could be maintained by residents that enjoy gardening. Similarly, many building concept drawings over the years have shown how each floor could have roof gardens that are open to the sky and accessible to all residents.

Design for Eco-services: The integration of natural systems with urban structures can provide low-cost building services and environmental amenities, while meeting basic needs and resource security.

Ecosystem services are the basis of the economy, not to mention human existence. Nonetheless, current forms of development have incrementally destroyed them to the point of ecological collapse. 'Ecosystem services' is a problematic term due to its economistic/anthropocentric baggage and association with economics, as it reduces complex interconnected life forms to monetary values.[88] As stated earlier, therefore, the term 'eco-services' is used to include the priceless multiple values of nature.[89] 'Ecological space' in PD, again, is the space dedicated to ecological functions like biodiversity habitats or nature corridors. Even were the human population to suddenly decline, nature must be increased.

'Ecological space' provides an indicator of the ecosystem and biodiversity nurseries created by buildings, and the social/cultural/psychological/physiological benefits they provide to building users.

Recent advances in eco-productive technologies could be integrated with structures. These include mycology,[90] algaetecture,[91] Living Machines,[92] passive solar systems and so on. PD adds practical concepts such as Green Scaffolding,[93] Green Space Walls,[94] Solar Core,[95] Playgardens,[96] Piggyback Roofs and other passive solar retrofit modules [Chapter 5].[97] These are scalable and moveable to other locations. They can fit into existing construction systems while adding 'garden environments', or be used in new construction as well (as was demonstrated by a proposed sustainability center).[98] In combination, they could convert cities into 'ecological arks' while society moves toward ethical and ecological maturity. For example:

- An existing example of design for eco-services is the Living Machine (around since the 1990s) which is like a compact artificial wetland.[99] Contaminated water goes through a series of translucent tanks with different ecosystems, which sequentially process different harmful elements. Usually, the water is simply purified and reused or sent back to the natural environment. These systems could be combined with vertical landscapes and Green Scaffolding that provide biodiversity habitats. These vertical/horizontal landscapes can include ecological spaces designed to support particular threatened birds, frogs or other species, in combination with social spaces, solar cells, food gardens and so on.[100]

26 *Design and Analysis*

1.5 Institutional Reform

Part II describes how environmental governance, planning and design is negative (as it destroys life-support systems) and suggests conceptual, methodological and institutional reforms.

Built environment design can solve most sustainability issues, by: increasing the natural life-support system to reverse ecological losses; bypassing socio-political barriers; improving everyone's health and wellbeing; reducing impacts of disparities of wealth and opportunity; and creating eco-positive environments that increase future options. Using a positive, open-systems lens, PD helps to deconstruct and rethink the negative-fatalistic and reductionist-dualistic thought patterns in contemporary development decision making and design. Paradoxically, exposing the negative biases in design and decision frameworks can be mistaken for 'negativity'. However, reforms cannot happen within old problem descriptions, so Part II provides extensive critiques before the remedies are presented.

1.6 Conclusion

Most green design has been only concerned with benefits for the owners, occupants and neighbors, not global gains for the public and environment.

Sustainable development has relied on recycling and value adding which only improves upon conventional development. Integrating nature into cities increases amenity but does not increase the socio-ecological life-support systems. Relative reductions in energy and material usage bring benefits to building stakeholders, but do not increase the survival options of present and future generations [Figure 1.13]. In a time of unprecedented wealth transfers, consumption and pollution, decision-making systems as well as design tools must consider the public value, functions and eco-services provided relative to the resources and space used. Part II therefore proposes new processes, standards and tools for PD.[101]

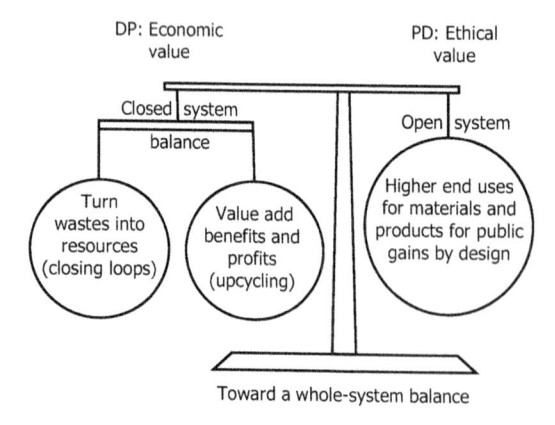

Figure 1.13 From value adding to maximizing benefits

1.7 Exercises

1. Share your current personal definition of sustainable with the group. Develop a group definition by consensus and write it down (revisit the definition at the end of the semester or book). Share negative stereotypes of sustainability you have heard with the group and select the most convincing example. Divide into pairs and debate the pro and con side of the opinion. Arrive at consensus.
2. Locate your position on a spectrum between nature-centered or human-centered (on a scale between 1 and 10). Then trace the origin of your views to early sources of knowledge/influence or personal experiences (e.g. religion, culture, science, family, media, education). Do you lean toward Social Darwinism (survival of the strongest/fittest) or the cooperative model of human relationships. Which is most useful to sustainability and why?

Box 1 Sustainable design paradigms (Source: Birkeland, 2013)

Some prominent schools of design thought are encapsulated here for the reader's convenience. Primary sources should be consulted for further information, as capsule definitions cannot begin to capture their depth and detail. Sustainable design paradigms can be distinguished by their location on various spectrums. For example, some are relatively anthropocentric or ecocentric; focus more on social or ecological aspects; emphasize private or public benefits; concentrate on the building or city scale; or emphasize resources or nature. However, design paradigms that allude to the logic of ecosystems, or at least use nature as a design metaphor, can be considered 'sustainable design'.[102]

Passive solar: Passive design uses building form and natural forces (e.g. convection, conduction, evaporation, radiation) to capture, store and/or circulate solar energy.[103] There have long been passive solar homes and buildings that provide enough operating energy for heating, cooling and ventilating, even in harsh climates, and normally use 'healthy' or organic building materials.[104] Dating back thousands of years,[105] passive design enjoyed a rebirth in the 1970s,[106] and was supported briefly by the US government during the 1970s oil crisis.[107] Today, many new green buildings add on passive solar elements, but many are often under-designed (optimized financially) and thus require costly backup systems.

Permaculture: Permaculture uses ecological principles to design 'with nature' to create living landscapes composed of integrated food production systems. Initially, it focused on the domestic scale and was largely confined to the spaces between building envelopes and property lines.[108] Permaculture more recently includes home renovations and has been incorporated into sustainable building design.[109] It sometimes prioritizes instrumental uses of nature over ecological integrity. For example, some of its advocates emphasize 'co-evolution' and 'succession' or the use of non-native species to restore agricultural productivity.[110] At the farm scale, Natural Sequence Farming is similar, but has been primarily concerned with regenerating drought-affected farmland.[111]

Resource autonomous design: Resource autonomous building was promulgated in the early 1970s.[112] It uses low-impact materials and techniques to collect, treat and store the building's own water and energy on site, along with providing food gardens. This is quite feasible on a domestic scale, by combining passive solar, renewable energy, organic construction materials and permaculture principles. Resource autonomous buildings do not usually offset material flows and other impacts caused during construction or manufacturing processes. Zero energy/resource usage in building operation is a worthy goal, but development could also compensate for the energy and resources embodied in construction, and increase ecosystems, species and biodiversity.

Green buildings: Many green homes, green buildings and green design guidelines had appeared by the turn of this century.[113] Growing awareness that buildings could reduce operating expenses and public costs (compared to ordinary buildings) gradually captured the attention of business. Green building councils were formed which promulgated certification processes. Subsequently, any certified building was considered 'green' by definition. However, many highly-ranked green buildings have prioritized engineering feats and celebrated the ethos of 'machines for living'.[114] Since most 'certified' green buildings do net damage to the environment, they reduce humanity's prospects for survival/wellbeing. Part II explores green building certification tools at length.

Sustainable buildings: Since business interests gradually changed the definition of green buildings to mean 'more efficient than ordinary buildings', many started using the term 'sustainable' building to distinguish them from what they saw as technocratic green design. Sustainable implies buildings that go beyond negative resource, energy and health impacts to include a wider range of sustainability criteria. While sustainable design has always aimed to regenerate the environment, community and economy, it usually only reduces a wider range of adverse impacts within the constraints of existing supply chains and construction processes. Sustainable buildings have not really been catalysts for social and system transformation.

Zero-carbon/energy: Resource autonomy is now experiencing a reincarnation as 'zero-energy buildings'.[115] Zero-energy buildings are quite feasible, assuming not too much electronic equipment is housed in the building.[116] (It should be remembered that net-positive energy is not technically possible due to the second law of thermodynamics.) Zero-energy usually only refers to a building's operating energy. The embodied energy used in construction is currently roughly equivalent to the operating energy. Embodied energy would exceed operating energy usage if passive solar design were maximized. Therefore, zero-energy buildings are really only 'half' zero-energy buildings. They often prioritize economic efficiency over sustainability, and sterility over fertility.

Bioregional planning: This approach, which seems to have dwindled, suggests that planning/design should begin from a regional perspective.[117] It argues that systems of governance, social relationships and economics systems, along with resource extraction, production and manufacturing, should derive from the unique ecological attributes and carrying capacity of each bioregion. This means social, industrial and economic structures should be reorganized to align with the natural resources, flora and fauna of the bioregion.[118] Bioregionalism stresses 'living in place' and 'community building' through environmental education and participatory planning.[119] Some of its contributors were concerned about globalization and sought more regional autonomy and less trade dependency.

Regenerative design: The term regenerative design was introduced in the 1990s.[120] It initially focused on landscapes, but with obvious applications to buildings. The term regenerative is used to mean restoring or enhancing the site's ecology and leaving the community and environment better than before construction. It adds a spiritual dimension to 'design with nature', where nature is a source of inspiration: 'engaging in living processes that regenerate rather than deplete, we become more alive'.[121] Nature appreciation and integration does not guarantee nature's preservation. Thus far, in practice, regenerative design is oriented toward homeowners/clients or architect/designers with less clear relevance to social justice.

Biomimicry: The notion of investigating nature's 'innovations' to develop better technologies has a long history (also called biomimetics or bionics).[122] Nature as a means of stimulating creativity became popular by the turn of the century,[123] and many exemplars of technologies that emulated natural processes began to appear.[124] It was initially geared toward product design: bringing better products to the market through an entrepreneurial business orientation.[125] Although sometimes similar to green capitalism in approach,[126] it has evolved from a focus on inspiring business-led research and innovation into a broader philosophy of design, and has incorporated a broad range of sustainable design principles.

Biophilic urbanism: Substantial research has shown that exposure to nature can measurably benefit people's psychological and physical wellbeing.[127] The concept that humans have an innate need for contact with nature was given more credence when a 'biophilia hypothesis' was proposed by a scientist in 1984.[128] Like regenerative design, biophilic urbanism draws on green design principles to integrate nature into cities. It also encourages design 'references' to nature: elements that are not 'natural', but feel natural, by mimicking natural forms and motifs from nature.[129] It has been less concerned with providing benefits to nature, such as increasing ecological carrying capacity or biodiversity habitats.[130]

Conclusion: Although moving toward whole-system sustainability, sustainable design paradigms initially concerned 'greening the built environment'. They do not generally aim to increase global ecosystem carrying capacity to over-compensate for the net embodied waste/energy/resources used in the construction process. This means they do little to address resource depletion and nature degradation. Likewise, apart from bioregionalism, they do not link social/environmental justice with design. To encourage adoption, sustainable design has been geared toward elites, by making it more fashionable and prestigious. Merely increasing environmental and public amenities through life quality would not reverse the basic development patterns: terminal resource consumption and inequitable wealth distribution.

Notes

1 Inter-generational equity, the original meaning of sustainability, cannot be achieved by closing off future sustainable options.
2 Birkeland, J. (1993) *Planning for Sustainability: Social Transformation and Institutional Reform*, Department of Geography and Environmental Studies, University of Tasmania, Hobart.
3 Opportunity cost is the lost potential to save or make money or acquire other benefits.
4 The 'fallacy of the middle' is the proposition that the truth must be found as a compromise between two opposite positions.
5 This is explored at length in Part II. For example, the idea of trade-offs is embedded in cost-benefit analysis which is the basis of many decision tools.
6 Early books on ecological design include: Papanek, V. (1971) *Design for the Real World: Human Ecology and Social Change*, Pantheon Books, New York; Johnson, R. (1979) *The Green City*, MamMillan, Melbourne; Mackenzie, D. (1991) *Green Design: Design for the Environment*, Lawrence King, London; Lyle, J. T. (1994) *Regenerative Design for Sustainable Development*, John Wiley, New York; Yeang, K. (1995) *Designing with Nature: The Ecological Basis for Architectural Design*, McGraw-Hill, New York; Van der Ryn, S. and Cowan, S. (1996) *Ecological Design*, Island Press, Washington, DC; Wann, D. (1996) *Deep Design: Pathways to a Livable Future*, Island Press, Washington, DC.
7 This is well-established in research: Kats, G. (2003), *The Costs and Financial Benefits of Green Buildings: A Report to California's Sustainable Building Task Force*, CA; RICS (2005) *Green Value-Green Buildings*, Growing Assets, London; Lucuik, M. (2005) *A Business Case for Green Buildings in Canada*, www.usgbc.org/resources/business-case-green-buildings-canada.
8 While the mining industry sometimes tries to regenerate the environment after extracting resources, the built environment professions have not proposed to compensate for resource extraction. See Birkeland, J. and Knight-Lenihan, S. (2016) Biodiversity Offsetting and Net Positive Design, *Journal of Urban Design* 21(1), pp. 50–66.
9 Many books since the 1990s have surveyed efficiency innovations, such as van Weizsacker, E., Lovins, A., and Lovins, H. (1997) *Factor 4: Doubling Wealth – Halving Resource Use*, Earthscan, London; von Weizsacker, E., Hargroves, C., Smith, M. H., Desha, C., and Stasinopoulos, P. (2009) *Factor Five: Transforming the Global Economy through 80% Improvements in Resource Productivity*, Routledge, London.
10 The International Living Future Institute developed the Net Zero Energy Building Certification in 2011. In 2009, future 'zero energy' targets for federal buildings were created by President Obama (October 5, 2009). Executive Order 13,514: Federal Leadership in Environmental, Energy, and Economic Performance, United States Government Printing Office.
11 The ecological footprint refers to human impacts. A 'positive' ecological footprint would logically be where nature is increased globally. The ecological footprint was introduced in Wackernagel, M. and Rees W. E. (1996) *Our Ecological Footprint: Reducing the Human Impact on the Earth*, New Society Publishers, British Columbia.
12 Birkeland, J. (2008) *Positive Development: From Vicious Circles to Virtuous Cycles through Built Environment Design*, Earthscan, London.
13 See Myers, N. (1996) *The Ultimate Security: The Environmental Basis of Political Stability*, Island Press, Washington, DC.
14 The 'commons' is having a rebirth in the literature. See Anastasopoulos, N. (2017) Buen Vivir, sostenibilidad y bienes comunes: el contexto ecuatoriano y mundial, *Estado and Communes* 4(January), pp. 39–55.
15 The *Brundtland Report* and its precedents are discussed in Chapter 4.
16 Discussed further in Birkeland, J. (2014) Systems and Social Change for Sustainable and Resilient Cities, in Pearson, L., Newton, P., and Roberts, P. (eds) *Resilient Sustainable Cities*, Routledge, Abingdon, Oxon, UK, pp. 66–82.
17 Birkeland, J. (2005) Reversing Negative Impacts by Design, in *Sustainability for the ACT: The Future's in Our Hands*, Office of Sustainability, ACT Government, Canberra; Birkeland, J. (2005) Design for Ecosystem Services – A New Paradigm for

Ecodesign, in *SB05 Tokyo: Action for Sustainability, The World Sustainable Building Conference*, September, pp. 27–29.
18 Windhager, S., Steiner, F., Simmons, M.T., and Heymann, D. (2010) Emerging Landscapes: Toward Ecosystem Services as a Basis for Design, *Landscape Journal* 29, pp. 107–13, at p. 108.
19 Birkeland, J. (1988) Redefining the Environmental Problem, *Environmental and Planning Law Journal* 5(2), pp. 109–33.
20 Renger, C., Birkeland, J., and Midmore, D. (2015) Net Positive Building Carbon Sequestration, *Building Research and Information* 43(1), pp. 11–24.
21 Birkeland, J. (2014) Resilient and Sustainable Buildings, in Pearson et al., *Resilient Sustainable Cities*.
22 Design for ecosystem services (eco-services) was proposed in Birkeland, J. (2002) *Design for Sustainability: A Sourcebook of Eco-logical Solutions*, Earthscan, London. See also Birkeland, J. (2004) *Building Assessment Systems: Reversing Environmental Impacts*, Nature and Society Forum, ACT, Australia, www.naf.org.au/naf-forum/birkeland; Birkeland, J. (2007) Design for Eco-Services, Part A – Environmental Services, *Environment Design Guide* 77, Architects Institute of Australia, Canberra, pp. 1–13; and Part B – Building Services, *Environmental Design Guide* 78, Canberra, Architects Institute of Australia, pp. 1–9, in *BEDP (Built Environment Design Professions)* Australia. www.environmentdesignguide.com.au/
23 Birkeland and Knight-Lenihan, Biodiversity Offsetting.
24 Birkeland, J. (2003) Beyond Zero Waste, in *Societies for a Sustainable Future*, Third UKM-UC International Conference, Canberra, ACT, April, pp. 14–15.
25 The terms pre-historic, pre-settlement, pre-urban, pre-development or pre-industrial conditions are used almost interchangeably, as locations differ. They generally refer to ecological carrying capacity since past ecosystems cannot usually be recreated. Each term has issues. For example, 'pre-development' was misunderstood to mean 'the particular development' instead of 'all development'. 'Pre-settlement' was considered to be potentially offensive to aboriginals.
26 Velazquez, L. S. (2008) Box 14: Advantages of Eco-Roofs, in Birkeland, *Positive Development*, p. 292. Hopkins, G and Goodwin, C. (2011) *Living Architecture: Green Roofs and Walls*, CSIRO Publishing, Collingwood, VIC, Australia.
27 One percent of the world population now has 99% of the wealth, and eight men have the equivalent wealth of half the world's population. See Elliott, L. (2017) World's Eight Richest Men have the Same Total Wealth as the Poorest Half of the World Population, *Guardian*, 16 January. www.theguardian.com/global-development/2017/jan/16/
28 See Birkeland, J. (2002) Legislative Environmental Controls, in Birkeland, *Design for Sustainability*, pp. 210–14.
29 See Waring, M. (1998) *Counting for Nothing: What Men Value and What Women are Worth*, Bridget Williams Books, Wellington, New Zealand; Hamilton, C. (1999) The Genuine Progress Indicator: Methodological Developments and Results from Australia, in *Ecological Economics* 30(1), pp.13–28.
30 This is called Resource Transfer Analysis in Birkeland, *Positive Development*, chapter 8, and discussed further in Chapters 7–8.
31 See Daly, H. E. and Cobb. J.B (1989) *For the Common Good: Redirecting the Economy Toward Community, the Environment, and a Sustainable Future*, Beacon Press, Boston, M.A.
32 The term stakeholders can be used to include members of the public, but it is a problematic term as it suggests a transactional paradigm. For example, see Cole, R.J. (2011) Motivating Stakeholders to Deliver Environmental Change, in *Building Research & Information* 39(5), pp.431–435.
33 Wolverton, B.C. (1996) *Eco-friendly Houseplants: 50 Indoor Plants that Purify the Air in Homes and Offices*, Weidenfeld and Nicolson, London. Also see Coutts, C. (2016) *Green Infrastructure and Public Health*, Routledge, NY.
34 Lerner, J. (2005) Keynote talk at *SB05 Tokyo: Action for Sustainability, The World Sustainable Building Conference*, September pp.27–29. www.sb05.com/

homeE.html. See also Lerner, J. (2014) *Urban Acupuncture*, Island Press, Washington D.C.

35 Desmet, P. M. A. and Pohlmeyer, A. E. (2013) Positive Design: An Introduction to Design for Subjective Well-Being, *International Journal of Design* 7(3), pp. 5–19. This is the banner of a design institute at Delft University in the Netherlands. See Birkeland, J. (2009) Eco-Retrofitting with Building-Integrated Living Systems, *SASBE09: Proceedings of the 3rd CIB International Conference on Smart and Sustainable Built Environment*, Delft, Netherlands, June.

36 Positive design has appeared since in the context of green business, but does not include the concept of net positive (where biophysical baselines beyond zero are used): Thatchenkery, T., Cooperrider, D. L., and Avital, M. (eds) *Positive Design and Appreciative Construction: From Sustainable Development to Sustainable Value (Advances in Appreciative Inquiry, 3)*. Emerald Group Publishing, Bingley, UK. I presented a paper on positive design at the conference from which the book's papers were drawn: Global Forum (2009), Business as an Agent of World Benefit, Case Western University, Cleveland, OH.

37 One of the earliest publications to discuss the global impact of the built environment was Roodman, D. M., and Lenssen, N. (1995) *A Building Revolution: How Ecology and Health Concerns are Transforming Construction*, Worldwatch Paper 124, Worldwatch Institute, Washington, DC.

38 A time of writing (April 2019), the Green Building Council in Australia has released a consultation paper proposing basic changes to their green building rating tool which incorporates more green design principles. https://gbca-web.s3.amazonaws.com/media/documents/consultation-paper.pdf

39 The term 'design thinking' is not new but is used in a special sense here. See Buchanan, R. (1992) Wicked Problems in Design Thinking, *Design Issues* 8(2), The MIT Press, MA, pp. 5–21.

40 Birkeland, *Positive Development*, p. 6.

41 Thank you to D. Eisenberg for transferring the concept to The LBC (Living Building Challenge), a green building rating tool (see https://living-future.org/lbc/). However, in the LBC it is used to mean simply 'give back', rather than an actual increase in benefits after negative impacts are deducted.

42 Birkeland, *Positive Development*, p. xx.

43 Alexiou, K., Zamenopoulos, T., Johnson, J. and Gilbert, S. (2009) Exploring the Neurological Basis of Design Cognition Using Brain Imaging: Some Preliminary Results, *Design Studies*, 30, pp. 623–47; Larsen, T. and O'Doherty, J. P. (2014) Uncovering the Spatio-Temporal Dynamics of Value-Based Decision-Making in the Human Brain: A Combined FMRI – EEG Study, *Philosophical Transactions of the Royal Society B: Biological Sciences* 369(1655), pp. 1–12.

44 Abraham, A. et al. (2012) Creativity and the Brain: Uncovering the Neural Signature of Conceptual Expansion, *Neuropsychologia*, 501, pp. 1906–17.

45 Birkeland, *Design for Sustainability*.

46 This was known as the 'technical fix' view in the 1960s. See Drengson, A. R. (1984) The Sacred and the Limits of the Technological Fix, *Zygon* 19, pp. 259–75.

47 The term 'reversing negative impacts' was used from 2002 to refer to net gain, but this was interpreted to mean remediation/restoration. The term net positive was used from 2003, but was misinterpreted to mean just positive.

48 The term also appears as 'net-positive'. Some authors writing on the subject have misinterpreted it. Cole, R. (2015) Net-Zero and Net-Positive Design: A Question of Value, *Building Research and Information* 43(1), pp. 1–6.

49 Green building designers have always aimed to leave things better than an ordinary building would have been.

50 The LBC (https://living-future.org/lbc/), calls for 'net positive' energy, water and waste but this is used to mean only positive or good: using only renewable energy in operation, or recycling all water and waste.

51 The idea of natural hierarchies allows for the idea that there are lower orders of being that can be used as resources (animals, women, slaves, other races and nature

generally). See Merchant, C. (1980) *The Death of Nature*, Harper, San Francisco, CA. Birkeland, J. (1993) Linking Theory and Practice, in Gaard, G. (ed.) *Ecofeminism: Living Interconnections with Animals and Nature*, Temple University Press, PA, pp. 12–59.

52 See Birkeland, J. (2016) Net Positive Biophilic Urbanism, *Smart and Sustainable Built Environments* 5(1), pp. 9–14.
53 Social-ecological resilience, or evolutionary resilience, interprets resilience as the ability of systems to adapt, change, or transform in response to shocks or stressors. See Carpenter S. R., Westley, F., and Turner, M. G. (2005) Surrogates for Resilience of Social-Ecological Systems, *Ecosystems* 8(8), pp. 941–4.
54 The expression 'working with nature' is attributed to Ian McHarg (1969) *Design with Nature*, Museum of Natural History, New York.
55 50% of biodiversity has been lost in fifty years: World Wildlife Fund (2016) *Living Planet Report 2016: Risk and Resilience in a New Era*. WWF, Gland. www.wnf.nl/custom/LPR_2016_fullreport/
56 Reification is where a social construct or belief is treated as if it were a concrete reality. Some have argued that nature is romanticised or reified. However, that idea is a very negative social construct. It is better to have positive concepts that lead to a better world for everyone.
57 Birkeland, *Positive Development*, p. 6.
58 Rees, W. E. (2002) Box 9: Eco-Footprints and Eco-Logical deSign, in Birkeland, *Design for Sustainability*, p. 73.
59 Birkeland, J., Renger, C. and Midmore, D. (2013) Positive Development: Design for Climate Mitigation and Ecological Gains, in *Pushing the Boundaries: Net Positive Buildings*, Sustainable Building conference proceedings SB13, Vancouver, BC, Canada, June 4–6.
60 Buildings are already being printed like products that are laser printed (discussed later), e.g. www.telegraph.co.uk/technology/2017/03/03/incredibly-cheap-house-3d-printed-just-24-hours/ or www.cnet.com/news/worlds-first-3d-printed-apartment-building-constructed-in-china/
61 Foley, J. A., Ramankutty, N., Brauman, K. A., et al. (2011) Solutions for a Cultivated Planet, *Nature* 478 (7369).
62 Some visuals of vertical food production systems are found in Hes and du Plessis, *Designing for Hope*.
63 Equity usually comes into play in green design with regard to inclusiveness among building stakeholders, and just treatment of workers and access to nature, not equality of living environments. See Living Building Challenge, https://living-future.org/lbc/ pp. 51–2.
64 See Cilliers, E. J. and Timmermans, W. (2014) The Importance of Creative Participatory Planning in the Public Place-Making Process, *Environment and Planning B* 41(3), pp. 413–29. See also Kaufman, P. (2002) Place, Community Values and Planning, in Birkeland, *Design for Sustainability*, pp. 105–7.
65 World Commission on Environment and Development (1987) *Our Common Future*, Oxford University Press, Oxford/New York. Also known as *The Brundtland Report*.
66 These SMT analyses are outlined in Chapters 7–8. Birkeland, J. (2014) Positive Development, in Bryne, J., Sipe, N. and Dodson, J. (eds) *Australian Environmental Planning*, Routledge, London.
67 For an introduction on Big Data and digital mapping, see *D_City: Digital Earth/Virtual Nations/Data Cities – Connecting Global Futures for Environmental Planning*, D. Jackson and R. Simpson, http://dcitynetwork.net/manifesto/
68 Again, savings from green building is well established. See Esty, D. C. and Wilston, A. S. (2006) *Green to Gold*, Yale University Press, New Haven. GBCA (2006) *The Dollars and Sense of Green Buildings*, Green Building Council Australia, Australia.
69 Elkington, J. (1997) *Cannibals with Forks: The Triple Bottom Line of Twenty-First Century Business*, Capstone, Oxford, UK.
70 E.g. the UN's New Urban Agenda uses the term 'ecosystem-based' planning but its policies bear little relationship to the concept. See Birkeland, J. (2018) Challenging Policy Barriers in Sustainable Development, in Dymitrow, M. and Halfacree, K. (eds) *Bulletin*

of Geography. Socio-Economic Series, 40(4), Nicolaus Copernicus University, Toruń, pp. 41–56.
71 Several tools use net positive to mean positive, such as The Living Building Challenge, https://living-future.org/lbc/; and EcoSpecifier (Green Tag) www.ecospecifier.com.au/certifications/green-tag-certification/
72 The Australian Prime Minister John Howard warned the building industry that if they did not regulate themselves, the government would. The Australian Green Star rating tool was established in 2003.
73 Sometimes EIAs have been blamed for stopping projects when they were not really financially sound to begin with.
74 McDonough, W. and Braungart, M. (2002) *Cradle to Cradle: Remaking the Way We Make Things*, North Point Press, New York. This seminal book popularized closed loop systems and introduced the idea of upcycling, or recycling to a higher value.
75 There have long been structures that shelter large areas with very little materials and embodied energy, as seen in the work of Shigeru Ban at the turn of this century. At the domestic scale, attached solariums or greenhouse-type structures on roofs or balconies can add low-impact living space.
76 The Treehugger and Inhabitat websites offer many examples on a regular basis. See www.treehugger.com and https://inhabitat.com/
77 There are now many sources on the impacts of cities, so they are not listed here. See UNEP (2013) *Buildings and Climate Change: Summary for Decision Makers*, United Nations Environment Programme (UNEP), Nairobi; UN-HABITAT (2011) *Cities and Climate Change: Global Report on Human Settlements*. www.unhabitat.org/downloads/docs/GRHS2011_Full.pdf/
78 An early study on the greenhouse emissions of buildings and how to reduce them was Romm, J. (1999) *Cool Companies*, Island Press, Washington, DC.
79 See Roodman and Lenssen, *A Building Revolution*.
80 New buildings added to the total building stock each year vary by country and time. See Wilkinson, S., Dixon, T., Miller, N. and Sayce, S. (eds) (2018) *Handbook of Sustainable Real Estate*, Routledge, Abingdon, UK, and New York.
81 Eco-retrofitting has generally been about energy efficiency, not green infrastructure and ecosystem services.
82 Birkeland, *Positive Development*, pp. 23–41.
83 See Kelly, J., Male, S. and Graham, D. (2015) *Value Management of Construction Projects* (2nd ed.), Wiley, Oxford.
84 This has long been established but only recently appreciated. See Heede, R. et al. (1995) *Homemade Money*, Rocky Mountain Institute with Brick House Publishing, Harrisville, NH. For current building retrofitting, see Pacheco-Torgal, F., Granqvist, C.-G., Jelle, B. P. et al. (2017) *Cost-Effective Energy Efficient Building Retrofitting: Materials, Technologies, Optimization and Case Studies*, Woodhead Pub., Elsevier, Cambridge, MA.
85 Plants were associated with the soft, decorative and feminine side of western culture, and not seen as having instrumental value, until NASA published their pollution-absorbing characteristics. See Freundlich, N. J. (1986) Purify Air the Space-Station Way: With Plants, *Popular Science* 229(2), p. 73.
86 Of course, real estate prices do not reflect ecological values.
87 E.g. see Birkeland, Design for Eco-services, Part A – Environmental Services, and Part B – Building Services.
88 Some of the influential works on the subject of ecosystem services include Costanza, R. et al. (1997) The Value of the World's Ecosystem Services and Natural Capital, *Nature*, 387, pp. 253–260; Heal, G. (2000) *Nature and the Marketplace: Capturing the Value of Ecosystem Services*, Island Press, Washington, DC; Folke, C., Jansson, Å., Larsson, J. and Costanza, R. (1997) Ecosystem Appropriation by Cities, *Ambio* 26, pp. 167–17; Daily, G. and Ellison, K. (2002) *The New Economy of Nature*, Island Press, Washington, DC; Beattie, A. and Ehrlich P. (2004) *Wildsolutions* (2nd ed.), Yale University Press, New Haven, CT.

Overview of Net-Positive Development 35

89 Thank you to former professional development student, S. Rooney, transferred the concept of design for ecosystem services to the CSIRO, the leading government research agency in Australia.
90 See Stamets, P. (2005) *Mycelium Running: How Mushrooms Can Help Save the world*, Ten Speed Press, Berkeley, CA; and McCoy, P. (2016) *Radical Mycology: A Treatise on Seeing and Working with Fungi*, Chthaeus Press, Portland, OR. See https://theconversation.com/scientists-create-new-building-material-out-of-fungus-rice-and-glass-98153
91 See *Algae Industry Magazine* (2011) Algaeindustry.com.
92 Todd, N. J. and Todd J. (1994) *From Eco-Cities to Living Machines*, Atlantic Books, Berkeley, CA. For short description see Todd, J. (2002) Living Technologies, in Birkeland, *Design for Sustainability*, pp. 114–17.
93 Birkeland, J. (2014) Resilient and Sustainable Buildings, in Pearson et al., *Resilient Sustainable Cities*, 146–59.
94 Birkeland, J. (2008) Space Frame Walls: Facilitating Positive Development, in *Proceedings of the 2008 World Sustainable Building Conference*, Melbourne, Australia, September 22–25.
95 These SMT Analyses are outlined in Chapters 7–8. Birkeland, J. (2014) Positive Development, in J. Bryne, N. Sipe and J. Dodson (eds) *Australian Environmental Planning*, Routledge, London.
96 Birkeland, J. (2002) Playgardens and Community, in *Design for Sustainability*, pp. 109–12. Birkeland, J. (1994) Ecofeminist Playgardens, *International Play Journal* 2, pp.49–59.
97 A student I paid to draw up my passive solar retrofit modules submitted them for his Masters thesis, representing that the ideas were his own, so I could not publish them.
98 Australian National Sustainability Initiative, see Hes and du Plessis, *Designing for Hope*, p. 98.
99 See www.toddecological.com/. Living machines are summarized in Todd, J. (2002) Living Technologies, in Birkeland, *Design for Sustainability*, pp. 114–17.
100 Birkeland, J. (2009) Eco-Retrofitting with Building Integrated Living Systems, in *Smart and Sustainable Built Environment Conference Proceedings*, Netherlands, Delft, www.sasbe2009.com/
101 PD was earlier defined as 'a net positive living environment that reverses ecological impacts and creates natural as well as social and economic capital'. Birkeland, Reversing Negative Impacts by Design.
102 Two books that survey ecological design paradigms are Hes, D., and du Plessis, C. (2014) *Designing for Hope: Pathways to Regenerative Sustainability*, Taylor and Francis, London, and Birkeland, *Design for Sustainability*.
103 An early text on (technical) green design is Olgyay, V. (1963) *Design with Climate: Bioclimatic Approach to Architectural Regionalism*, Princeton University Press, Princeton, NJ.
104 Passive design can involve embodied energy due to the extensive use of (natural) materials for thermal mass, but it lasts much longer than renewable energy systems.
105 Rudofsky, B. (1964) *Architecture Without Architects*, UNM Press, New York.
106 An entire passive solar suburb was built in Davis California in the 1970s, but the surrounding suburbs followed convention. Bainbridge, D., Corbett, J. and Hofacre, J. (1979) *Village Homes Solar House Designs*, Rodale Press, Emmaus, PA.
107 Many books on passive solar design were available in the 1970s. See e.g. Shurcliff, W. A. (c. 1979) *Solar Heated Buildings of North America: 120 Outstanding Examples*, Brick House Publishing, Harrisville, NH; Anderson, B. (1976) *The Solar Home Book: Heating, Cooling and Designing with the Sun*, Brick House Publishing, Harrisville, NH; AIA Research Corporation. (1976) *Solar Dwelling Design Concepts*, US Department of Housing and Urban Development, Washington, DC.
108 Mollison, B. (1996) *Permaculture: A Designers' Manual*, Tagari Publications, NSW, Australia. Holmgren, D. (2002) *Permaculture: Principles and Pathways beyond Sustainability*, Holmgren Design Services, Hepburn, VIC, Australia.
109 Holmgren, D. (1992) *The Flywire House: A Case Study in Design Against Bushfire*, Nascimanere Pty Ltd, Maleny, Queensland.

110 Ecological succession is the natural process of change in an ecological community over time. In permaculture, this is a human-guided process used to restore natural landscapes and/or increase food productivity.
111 Andrews, P. (2006) *Back from the Brink: How Australia's Landscape Can Be Saved*, ABC Books, Sydney.
112 Vale, B. and Vale, R. (1975) *The Autonomous House: Design and Planning for Self-Sufficiency*, Thames & Hudson, London; Vale, R. and Vale, B. (2002) Autonomous Servicing, in Birkeland, *Design for Sustainability*, pp. 182–5. Mobbs, M. (1998) *Sustainable House*, Choice Books, Sydney.
113 Mackenzie, D. (1997) *Green Design: Design for the Environment*, Nippan Books; Yeang, K. (1995) *Designing with Nature: The Ecological Basis for Architectural Design*, McGraw-Hill, NY; Edwards, B. (ed.) (1998) *Green Buildings Pay*, E&FN Spon, London.
114 The house as a 'machine for living' reflected early twentieth Century mechanistic industrial paradigm. The term is attributed to Le Corbusier. See Corbusier, L. (1931) *Towards a New Architecture*, Courier Corporation.
115 See Kibert, C.J. and Fard, M.M. (2012) Differentiating among Low-Energy, Low-Carbon and Net Zero-Energy Building Strategies for Policy Formulation, in *Building Research and Information* 40(5), pp.625–637.
116 Net-Zero Energy buildings only achieve a net annual energy balance in their operations and exclude energy used in construction.
117 See Dodge, J. (1981) Living by Life: Some Bioregional Theory and Practice, *CoEvolution Quarterly* 32, pp. 6–12; Bailey, R. G. (2002) *Ecoregion-Based Design for Sustainability*, Springer-Verlag Inc., New York.
118 See Brunckhorst, D. J. (2000) *Bioregional Planning*, Harwood Academic Publications, Amsterdam.
119 See Aberley, D. (ed.) (1994) *Futures by Design: The Ecological Practice of Ecological Planning*. New Society Publishers, Gabriola Island, BC.
120 Lyle, J. T. (1994) *Regenerative Design for Sustainable Development*, John Wiley, New York; Van der Ryn, S. and Cowan, S. (1996) *Ecological Design*, Island Press, Washington, DC; Mclennan, J. F. (2004) *The Philosophy of Sustainable Design*, Ecotone Publishing, Kansas City, MO.
121 Van der Ryn and Cowan, *Ecological Design*.
122 Birkeland, J. (2016) Net Positive Biophilic Urbanism, *Smart and Sustainable Built Environments* 5(1), pp. 9–14.
123 Benyus, J. (1998) *Biomimicry: Innovation Inspired by Nature*, Quill, New York.
124 This approach was challenged in Waterhouse, G. (2002) The Bionic Method in Industrial Design, in Birkeland, *Design for Sustainability*, pp. 84–8.
125 For instance, patentable high-tech products could replace more passive and environmentally benign ones, reinforce wealth differentials or increase material flows.
126 Hawken, P. (1993) *Ecology of Commerce: How Business Can Save the Planet*, Weidenfeld & Nicolson, London.
127 See Cooper Marcus, C. and Barnes, M. M. (eds) (1999) *Healing Gardens*, Wiley, New York.
128 Wilson, E. O. (1984) *Biophilia*, Harvard University Press, Cambridge, MA.
129 There is an emphasis on the human experience, such as natural shapes and forms as opposed to 'design for nature'. See discussion in Birkeland, Net Positive Biophilic Urbanism.
130 Kellert, S. (2016) Biophilic Urbanism: The Potential to Transform, *Smart and Sustainable Built Environment* 5(1), pp. 4–8.

2 Centrality of the Built Environment in Sustainability

2.1. Review and Preview

This chapter summarizes the importance of the design of cities and buildings in most sustainability issues, to show why urban transformation is necessary.

The annual amount of natural resources used by cities in 2010 could double by 2050, according to the United Nations Environment Program.[1] However, flows of raw materials do not convey their diverse, cumulative and irreversible impacts on complex ecosystems. For instance, a third of coral reefs have died in the last 30 years, and they may be gone by 2100.[2] Their lost value under climate change scenarios is estimated at only US $4 to $24 billion annually, yet reefs are essential to human survival.[3] As the incubators of ocean biodiversity (as forests are to land biodiversity) they are of infinite value.

As presently designed, the built environment often exacerbates civil and environmental risks, yet it could be a force for social and cultural change.

Conventional urban design, and non-design, can worsen so-called 'natural' disasters, such as fires, landslides, floods, heat inversions, thunderstorms, air pollution or climate change.[4] It can also limit opportunities to escape danger or obtain food and water in crises. Moreover, although physical environments are improving the material living standards for many, they also underwrite the widening gaps in wealth and health.[5] While urban design cannot stop corporate greed, sociopathic leaders and/or warfare, it can counteract many contributing factors/forces. These include the 'created need' for status, wealth and power, and the resentment caused by inequitable living environments that reinforce social hierarchies.

The transformative potential of design is still underrated, not only by government, industry and the lay public, but by the design fields themselves.

As stated above, urban design is far more than a means of implementing decisions and/or policies. It is a different way of thinking. This chapter outlines ways that urban planning and built environment design can not only solve a range of sustainability problems while reducing consumption, but serve as a lever of socio-ecological sustainability. These are sensible, non-controversial actions that can be implemented by planners and designers immediately, without prior political, statutory or policy directives, since they can pay back any extra costs. This chapter looks at how conventional design drives demand before surveying ways that buildings can increase sustainability.

built environment shapes the demand for resources from most primary industries (e.g. forestry, mining, transport, manufacturing) which, in turn, draws down nature.

Before the turn of this century, the contribution of cities to material and energy flows, carbon emissions and biodiversity losses was barely researched or documented.[6] Nonetheless it is now accepted that cities account for roughly 75% of carbon emissions, 60–80% of energy, 40% of solid waste, 40% of pollution, 12% of water and 40% of material resources, including 55% of harvested timber.[7] Cities also shape lifestyles that amplify the demand for goods. For example, suburban land use patterns encourage car ownership and the duplication of appliances, tools and services for each house (e.g. lawn mowers, washing machines, extra bathrooms, driveways).

Nature supplies the essentials, yet traditional depictions of 'supply and demand' show the relationship as closed loops between producers and consumers (excluding nature).

The traditional view of supply and demand assumed that natural resources and land were in endless supply [Figure 2.1]. The supply-demand relationship was supposed to balance resource usage automatically. Theoretically, if particular materials became scarcer, their price would go up and slow consumption.[8] As the jobs and profits that depend directly on nature such as tourism were diminished, demand for wilderness 'preservation' would magically increase. However, today's rich class continues to demand ever more luxuries. Further, developers or producers can always get more public land/resources released for resource exploitation or construction through political persuasion or market pressure, if not corruption.

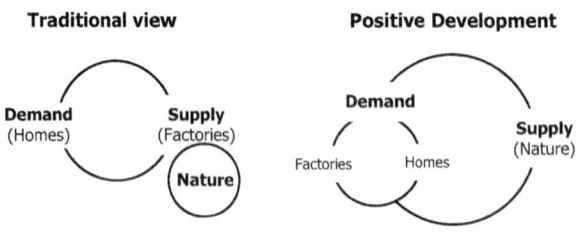

Traditional view

Demand (Homes) — Supply (Factories) — Nature

Positive Development

Demand — Supply (Nature); Factories, Homes

Design can reduce demands upon nature, but net-positive design would also increase the supply of nature.

As resources become scarcer, their price often goes up, so those that control them become more powerful. It can be more lucrative to deplete a resource and move on than to maintain a resource. This is exemplified by the trade in endangered species. Their value goes up as they become scarcer, so poachers and traders benefit. Once gone, other animals can be made scarce.

Figure 2.1 Supply and demand
(Source: Birkeland 2002)

Urban design/architecture could reduce much of the demand for goods but instead has narrowed long-term survival prospects, resilience and adaptability to contextual change.

The design of cities/buildings defines much of the demand for resources, yet most advances have been about efficiency, not design. The green building movement drew upon 'cleaner production' which reduces materials/pollution through technological improvements,[9] and 'industrial ecology/metabolism' wherein industries use wastes from other industries as resources (closing loops).[10] These efficiency strategies reduce harmful/wasteful inputs-outputs through their supply chains, but not the overall demand for materials and products. Even buildings that claim to achieve zero waste often have unnecessary 'ecological waste' (cumulative ecological damage) due to, for example, the use of excessive amounts of materials for reasons of aesthetics or prestige.[11]

Cities can mitigate the underlying causes of unsustainability while increasing resilience, diversity and adaptability, but this requires a radical increase in ecological-social space.

Some advocate alternative low-impact lifestyles as a means to dramatically reduce personal consumption and overall resource flows. It is difficult to get people to relinquish their high-tech toys, ostentatious homes, fashion, travel and other socially engrained expectations. While behavior change may be necessary, however, it is not politically realistic. To achieve 'degrowth' without pain – a necessity in democracies – the requisite sense of progress and optimism requires a continual increase in environmental amenity and equity for everyone [Figure 2.2]. That means more urban space must be dedicated to better living conditions and public spaces, as well as more life-support systems.

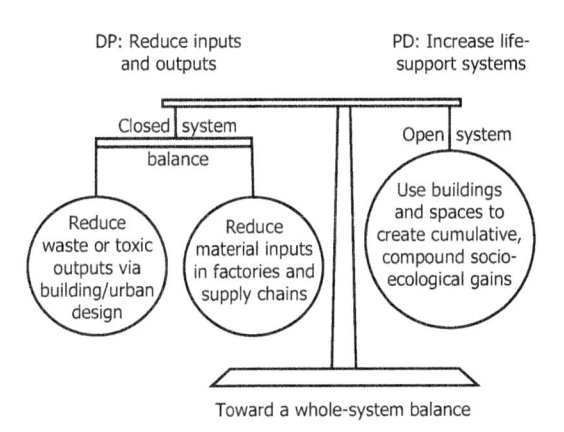

DP: Reduce inputs and outputs   PD: Increase life-support systems

Closed system balance — Open system

Reduce waste or toxic outputs via building/urban design

Reduce material inputs in factories and supply chains

Use buildings and spaces to create cumulative, compound socio-ecological gains

Toward a whole-system balance

The built environment provides means to reduce or reverse many negative, impacts while fostering 'benign' economic growth through public services and infrastructures. Buildings and cities can reduce demands upon nature, while they also increase its supply by creating more ecological carrying capacity. This requires a fundamentally different approach: instead of green growth - positive 'degrowth' via design.

Figure 2.2 Affirmative action for the environment

2.2. Potentially Positive Built-Environment Impacts

The following are examples of how built environment design can reduce or even reverse many familiar sustainability problems without waiting for socio-political change.

Most designers are already aware of the interconnections between built environment design and the following list of social/environmental issues. However, the potential to maximize public gains through design is not attempted as the target is still only 'zero'. This is partly due to the legacy of the dominant paradigm (DP) which creates conceptual barriers, even in the built-environment design fields.

These include the inbuilt bias toward: reductionism over design thinking; closed-systems over flows analyses; and narrow problem-solving over creating positive options. A sustainable, equitable urban environment could do more to shift the imbalances in the culture than divisive debate.

Carbon can be reduced by retrofitting cities and buildings using materials and plants that sequester carbon, while incorporating multiple public functions and eco-services.

Climatic and ecosystem changes are already in train due to excessive atmospheric/oceanic carbon. This will be cataclysmic,[12] unless there is radical change to urban environments. Large-scale industrial solutions are being tested, such as huge industrial machines that suck carbon out of the air.[13] While extreme industrial approaches may be necessary, these would also cause carbon emissions during resource extraction, construction and possibly operation. An arms race between emissions adaptation and mitigation technologies could be avoided if cities reduce sources of carbon emissions throughout the supply chain and use suitable vegetation and construction materials that sequester more carbon that they emit.

Some renewable materials such as timber sequester carbon but, since much of these products are wasted, there is often a net carbon increase.

There are various organic building materials that can sequester carbon emissions.[14] They can be less expensive than ecologically damaging products that involve mining, and can save significant health costs (below). For instance, although biochar emits carbon in production, it sequesters carbon in soil, increases crop yields, and is quite suitable for use in green walls.[15] High-rise buildings can now be made from timber, which sequesters carbon.[16] Although much timber is lost in harvesting and processing, it is recyclable. However, building guidelines usually only target timber waste on construction sites, which is just a fraction of the waste generated during timber production.[17]

Energy usage in buildings as a whole is growing, yet designers under-utilize passive solar design/retrofitting, even though it can offset its embodied energy.

70% of global energy use is traceable to the built environment.[18] Much of this, in turn, is linked to fossil-fuel-based energy. This has huge public costs,[19] affecting economic performance, national security and public health – including atmospheric toxins such as mercury.[20] Building operating energy can be reduced by half, simply by using more efficient equipment.[21] However, passive solar design does not need as much maintenance or periodic replacement, and can usually be modified by homeowners when necessary. It sometimes employs substantial thermal mass (e.g. stone), but design can reduce the embodied energy relative to the overall benefits it produces.[22]

While passive solar systems can require major alterations to existing structures, bolt-on passive retrofit modules can reduce energy costs and add other amenities/benefits.

Building heating, cooling and ventilating systems can be reduced to zero operating energy in smaller buildings by using passive and renewable systems in combination.[23] Windows with built-in electricity-generating elements, or phase change materials incorporated into interior walls, do not occupy floor space.[24] There are many semi-passive retrofit concepts that could reduce energy use in buildings [Chapter 5]. For example, passive 'mini Trombe walls' could be placed over parts of facades, roofs or redundant windows to capture, store and circulate solar heat. The costs of such additions/modifications can be recouped from energy savings and the increased market value of energy-efficient buildings.[25]

Material flows through construction processes have huge upstream-downstream impacts such as compounding waste throughout supply chains and toxin accumulation in people and environments.

Researchers state that cities occupy only 2–3% of the earth's surface but use 75% of its resources.[26] Put differently, the ecological footprints of cities can be many times greater than their geographical footprint.[27] Buildings are composed of many manufactured products, and the material input into manufacturing processes greatly exceed outputs by weight and volume.[28] Post-consumer waste is a tiny fraction of production, construction and demolition waste that ends up in landfill.[29] During the drawing stage, new digital design tools can automatically calculate the materials that a design will use.[30] However, they cannot calculate site-specific cumulative ecological impacts.

Organic and new high-tech materials may reduce impacts, but rarely provide eco-productive and multiple functions to offset their portion of global resource flows.

Vast quantities of low-impact materials will be required to house the earth's 7+ billion people.[31] Materials science is producing stronger, lighter and less wasteful building materials. These also tend to be costly and have high embodied energy.[32] In disadvantaged regions, renewable and organic materials are widely used, but often not in ways that are earthquake, flood or cyclone proof.[33] In such places, existing structures can be reinforced by low-impact/light-weight scaffolding that incorporates space for thermal and eco-productive functions [Chapter 6]. Unanticipated sustainability issues may arise soon if buildings are 'printed' from low-impact materials or nanotechnology is used (discussed later).

Waste caused during resource extraction/manufacturing usually exceeds onsite waste during building construction and operation although it could be substantially reduced by sustainable design.

The percentage of waste per capita is increasing along with population growth.[34] While downstream waste caused by human activities in homes or offices is increasingly recycled, it pales in comparison to waste in mining and extracting materials.[35] Architects can, however, influence the supply chain by specifying renewable materials that reduce upstream-downstream waste. This is because fashion creates much of the demand for wasteful products and processes in the first place. For example, timber harvesting/manufacturing efficiencies can reduce timber waste per unit of production, but only design can reduce the end use and thus the overall environmental destruction these processes cause.

Low-waste processes can still produce wasteful social purposes such as conspicuous consumption, but positive public benefits can at least be added by design.

Project purposes are generally ignored in design tools [Chapters 10–12]. Socially detrimental products, such as weapons, cigarettes, pornographic materials and most disposable products, transfer resources away from more productive uses. Hence efficiency standards do not always meet common sense and ethics.[36]

Ethical design considers the public purposes of proposals. Where harmful purposes are beyond the control of designers, they can ensure the projects perform additional beneficial functions (in addition to being as efficient as possible). Until development control systems consider ethical issues, design could still ensure that any unavoidable waste of materials, spaces, functions or uses are offset by socially constructive functions.

Bio-based building materials (e.g. straw, hemp, mushrooms), being biodegradable, non-toxic, grown from natural ingredients and widely available, make net-positive impacts easier to achieve.

Mycelium (mushroom roots) convert hydrocarbons into carbohydrates and can be grown without external energy sources or light to produce healthy building materials.[37] When injected into agricultural waste, mushrooms grow a fibrous network that becomes as strong as fiberglass. It can be poured inside walls to insulate and strengthen structures. For instance, mushroom-based particle board is purportedly lighter, stronger and cheaper than ordinary particle board which contains formaldehyde (a carcinogen).[38] Mushrooms also have many other uses. For example, they can decompose petrochemicals and heavy metals in contaminated environments.[39] Biodegradable mushroom-based cups/containers can replace expanded-foam cups which, currently, are not usually recycled.

Hemp board and other relatively healthful, biodegradable agri-waste building materials can replace conventional plaster, bricks, particleboard, cladding, plastic and panel or spray-on insulation.

Hemp is a very durable building material. Hemp-based building products are insect and fire resistant, and vapor-permeable, yet impermeable to liquid water. Like most organic products, hemp is non-toxic and biodegradable. For a strong concrete-like material, hemp can be mixed with lime to form 'hempcrete', and then poured as a floor or formed into bricks. Entire homes have been composed of a variety of hemp building components.[40] Other agricultural waste building products (e.g. strawbale, timber, bamboo) are also high-performing 'natural' building materials.[41] However, they require more land area to grow than mushroom-based materials and should be limited to ecologically suitable regions.

Plastic waste is now recognized as a critical global problem, threatening human and environmental health with irreversible consequences, despite there being better alternatives.

More than 9 billion metric tons of plastic have been produced since 1950.[42] It eventually ends up as microplastics which animals mistake for food. Some is eaten by fish and then moves up the food chain until humans eat it. Regulations are being enacted in some places to minimize plastic waste, and some substitutes are being developed. Nonetheless, the plastic that is already in the environment must be removed to avoid ongoing harm. Work is underway to collect plastic waste from the huge ocean garbage patches (oceanic gyres).[43] Fortunately, plastic waste is a suitable filler for road and building materials.

Degraded plastic materials can be recovered as a resource for various kinds of boards and panel products and sequestered in the built environment.

Bacteria exists that can consume plastics but, so far, this is a slow process which is difficult to upscale to match the scope of the problem. Research is progressing on fungal building materials composed of agricultural and manufacturing waste. The fungus binds together waste products like rice husks and glass to form panelling and insulation products, and could potentially bind plastic waste particulates as well. These fungal bricks are termite and fire resistant, and produce less smoke and carbon dioxide than common construction materials.[44] Harmful plastics will not be removed from the environment until there are profitable uses for it.

Sea level rise impacts can be mitigated by modifying coastlines to extend the liveability/safety of coastal cities and time to shift urban populations.

Unless climate change is reversed, major coastal cities will eventually become uninhabitable. At least two physical mitigation strategies are necessary to reduce/postpone the myriad impacts and costs of sea level rise. One approach is to modify the coastline in ways that enhance the coastal ecology while reducing damage from storm surges. For example, giant concrete 'jumping jacks', have been used to mitigate rogue waves. These could be integrated with other socio-economic functions such as walkways for recreational, civic and commercial activities. Some could simultaneously support new reefs to regenerate ocean biodiversity, and/or be combined with tidal or wave energy production.

The underground and ground-level floors of vulnerable buildings could be reinforced to withstand saltwater, with occupied levels being shifted up a few floors.

A second mitigation measure is to modify large urban structures to shift ground-level uses of durable urban buildings to higher levels, to buy time. The concrete structures below maximum water levels could be reinforced and coated with materials impervious to saltwater. A new street level could support light transport systems such as small people movers or monorails.[45] People would leave personal vehicles at the inland periphery of cities to access public transport. Saltwater will contaminate the inland aquifers of most coastal cities.[46] However, in some climates, some saltwater could be pumped into 'solar ponds' for energy production and other functions.[47]

Urban heat build-up, or 'heat island effect', is often treated as an act of nature, when in fact it is caused by design.

Denser cities can be 10°C hotter than their hinterlands[48] due to building/road materials that absorb heat.[49] Heat inversions also cause major pollution/heating events in cities, sometimes killing thousands within days, especially the elderly or disabled who lack access to air-conditioned spaces.[50] The average deaths per month/year from the heat island effect has sometimes exceeded the rates of deaths in wartime.[51] White and green roofs, and street trees reduce urban overheating.[52] Additionally, large residential buildings could be retrofitted with a reinforced central space that can be cooled/heated with fuel cells in brownouts, hot or cold spells, excessive pollution or minor earthquakes.

There are many urban/building design strategies to mitigate extreme urban temperatures and especially their effects on the more vulnerable, while adding public benefits.

Although the heat island effect was known by the 1820s,[53] it was not initially linked to health and safety risks such as cyclones, lightning, wind damage, biodiversity losses or other climate-related threats. Many heat reduction strategies can support additional practical functions, such as shading structures with embedded solar cells, or green walls/roofs that pre-filter the air and water.[54] Retrofitting facades with heat-mitigating, pollution-absorbing materials and even plant containers would also reduce public health costs. Sprinkling systems built into facades, Playgardens or parks could provide heat relief through evaporative cooling since, even in humid climates, water mists can cool paved areas.[55]

Food security *is a human right and must be directly accessible so that people's ability to exercise political freedom is never at risk.*

In many regions, people are still forced to move to cities to seek work, where they often remain impoverished, or become homeless and/or ill due to unhealthy (or too little) food. Growing numbers of urban poor lack direct access to food for maintaining sound levels of nutrition. The only affordable foods in some core urban areas are processed or 'fast foods'.[56] Safety nets like food stamps, charitable soup kitchens or community farm plots, let alone rations, cannot be guaranteed in military, civil or environmental emergencies. Hence, diverse forms of domestic food production should be built into every block and suburb.

Buildings can make food, air and water quality/quantity universally available and provide security to whole districts during periods of crises, neglect or conflict.

A significant portion of nutritional needs can be met by a few square metres of vegetable garden on a roof, yard or wall, which people can also trade for protein.[57] In most central areas, however, all but decorative plants were excised to rid cities of 'pest' birds and bugs. Few urban apartments provide suitable spaces for community or private gardens, let alone space for aquaponic systems or vertical planters. Even informal settlements could increase food security by using window boxes or bamboo scaffolding systems above or around homes to produce vegetables, compost, rain water and other essential goods [Chapters 5–6].

Oxygen *can be created through permanent greenery in buildings, infrastructure and landscape structures for producing and purifying outdoor air using simple design concepts.*

Even if the 80% of lost oxygen-producing forests were somehow replaced,[58] the carbon surplus will last for centuries. Air quality and oxygen levels in cities is often deficient due to inadequate air flow. Additionally, air conditioning equipment from buildings often expels pollution to the exterior. Fortunately, permanent building-integrated vegetation can improve urban air quality and sequester the amount of carbon emitted during building construction and operation.[59] Layered planting structures on top of buildings or multistory Green Scaffolding systems could filter air for the surrounding areas [Chapters 5–6]. Street trees and green walls arguably circulate fresh air down to street level.[60]

Green walls and atriums in offices have been shown to increase worker productivity and mental performance in both actual buildings and test facilities.

It was not until NASA investigated the use of vegetation for oxygen production during space travel that using plants for indoor air quality gained credibility on earth.[61] It is now accepted that indoor air pollution can be absorbed by plants and some other materials. However, most green buildings still use plants largely as decoration, or simply place them in pots.[62] To be effective, buildings must be designed for plants. For example, atriums, balcony greenhouse structures, enclosed courtyards and many similar spatial design strategies can create the conditions for permanent vegetation that filters indoor air while creating healthy, attractive living/ working spaces.

Water consumption by cities was essentially subsidized (like oil), and degraded water infrastructure is expensive to repair because pipes are buried in streets/ buildings.

The built environment has substantial embodied water as it is composed of manufactured products.[63] The amount of embodied water is seldom a big consideration in materials or product selection, let alone the energy involved in delivering water, since these costs are usually passed onto occupants. However, deteriorated water pipes are now a growing health concern. Leaky underground waterpipes and aging sewer systems cause water pollution, soil contamination, erosion and water-borne illnesses, often before the leak is found. It is expensive to replace water pipes in core urban areas because of urban density, and in suburbs where pipes span long distances.

Localized water collection, storage, distribution and recycling systems can be more efficient and contain less embodied energy/resources, while providing water security and safety.

Rainwater storage tanks can be made safe (if petrochemical tanks are avoided) and filters can ensure there is little contamination. Rainwater tanks can double as wall- or floor-integrated thermal insulation and can be connected to firefighting systems to provide onsite sources of water in case of emergencies. Non-potable water can be recycled onsite for landscaping or other purposes. Neighborhood-scale Living Machines can collect, treat and store water safely while adding ecosystem services to public spaces or parks and aesthetic appeal.[64] These distributed systems can become polluted, but this does not compare to past terrorist threats to poison centralized water sources.[65]

Fire risks are exacerbated by the location, shape and detailing of homes, partly because fire-resistant design has been superficial and yet expensive.

In rural residential areas, especially in eucalypt bushlands as in California, Australia and Spain, small mishaps, such as embers escaping fireplaces or electrical faults, periodically destroy forests, homes, human lives, wildlife and livestock. Design recommendations often involve expensive but minor changes to building facades and shapes.[66] Major land-clearing for fire prevention has damaged watersheds and/or contributed to subsequent mud slides, avalanches, floods or famines, especially in underprivileged regions.[67] There are more eco-productive options than permanently clearing woodlands or building extra fire roads.[68] For instance, Australia has fire-resistant native plants that, if strategically planted, could slow fires while supporting native fauna.[69]

Ecological, social and economic benefits should be combined with firefighting and water-storage facilities as determined by an analysis of local needs and conditions.

Eco-sensitive landscaping can channel storm or flood waters into reservoirs, be lifted (using solar/wind power) to uphill reserves, or be stored in water tanks within fire observation structures. Seasonal run off in mountainous areas can be

46 *Design and Analysis*

captured to create small reservoirs with minimal disruption to surrounding habitats. Such strategically located water storage systems could help to contain fires (with fire pumps) before they become unstoppable firestorms. To offset costs, additional functions should be included. For example, earth from constructing public storm/fire cellars (with oxygen tanks) in fire-prone areas could be reused to build above-ground visitor camps, storage dams or biodiversity habitats.

Risks of and vulnerability to terrorist attacks, energy blackouts, extreme weather, water or food shortages are exacerbated by traditional centralized, industrialized urban infrastructure.

Centralized industrial infrastructure with linear service and distribution systems once increased personal freedom and independence (e.g. wires, cables, roads, pipes and railroad tracks). Today in congested cities, however, these systems are vulnerable to many kinds of failure. For example, blackouts and power shortages due to centralized electricity generation/transmission systems have caused deaths from over-heating or freezing, especially among the elderly or disabled.[70] Industrial systems also reduce access to central water, food or energy supplies in emergencies (means of survival) and are vulnerable to terrorist attacks. Generally, resource autonomous and/or distributed energy and water systems would provide more safety and resilience.

Centralized industrial distribution systems sometimes create inflexible and brittle systems, whereas sustainable design works within a given context to transform the larger system.

It is difficult to quantify how centralized urban systems create risks,[71] but many casualties of environmental crises could have been avoided by design (e.g. 2005 storm surge in New Orleans). There are no universal templates because scale is a matter of case-specific design. For example, autonomous water and energy systems are often most efficient at the neighbourhood scale instead of the household or city level, because of the cost and complexity of facilities management and maintenance. In addition to realizing the optimal scale and design, each urban system should be multifunctional and backed by independent energy systems (e.g. solar energy).

Floods are often magnified by urban design or even flood barriers (especially in flood plains) by channelling and speeding up urban water flows.

Throughout history, major natural calamities were caused by the siting of cities near potential flood plains, landslide areas, coastlines and so on, as the terrain shifts over time.[72] For example, after the 1927 Mississippi River flood whole towns had to be moved inland. This added social dislocation to the financial/human costs of flooding. Although zoning has discouraged new construction on flood plains, buildings have been rebuilt after floods anyway due to their prime locations and property values.[73] Engineering barriers built after major floods have increased future flooding impacts.[74] 'Once in a hundred year' floods are increasing due to climate change.

Landscapes can be retrofitted to store overflow from floods for storage, habitats and eco-services and/or public amenities like recreation, hiking, camping, and sightseeing.

Sometimes land previously damaged by water or oil pumping, mining or lands reclaimed from bays or swamps have subsequently caused buildings to collapse.[75] Such terraformed environments cannot be restored, but they can be converted to assist biodiversity or various practical economic functions. For example, where sink holes are suitably located and non-toxic, they might serve as mini-aquifers for water storage. To restore river catchment functions and past ecosystem/biodiversity losses, water diverted into upstream ponds could help maintain biodiversity habitats (e.g. frog refuges). Using these waterscapes for recreational uses could offset their costs but they should be designed for changing water levels.

Mobility is reduced by congestion due to urban densification, causing time, money, energy and health costs, and sometimes closing off emergency escape routes.

When the urban model originated, cities were designed to protect their inhabitants from invaders with physical barriers such as moats and fortress walls. Escape routes in instances of civil and environmental emergencies were seldom available to the masses. Today, dense urban form and hard, brittle structures continue to constrict mobility. Narrow passages like rails, roads or runways in cities, and stairways in tall buildings, can increase casualties in earthquakes, floods, fires, civil disorder, terrorist bombs, sport stadium stampedes, not to mention war. Meanwhile, regular traffic jams and rail breakdowns increase pollution, blood pressure, aggression, road rage, expense and lost time.

Urban greening/regeneration projects that provide nature corridors, green bridges, elevated bikeways and ecological spaces could alleviate congestion, while also providing for emergency evacuation.

The lack of escape routes in dense urban areas can be partially addressed with elevated bike/pedestrian pathways to provide emergency evacuation routes, combined with nature corridors. Instead, freeways have been dismantled at great public expense and waste, such as the elevated San Francisco Embarcadero freeway. Repurposing infrastructure to benefit the public and environment would also attract tourists and businesses, as seen in the conversion of streets to malls and roads to bike and skate parks. A celebrated example is New York's High Line Park, which converted an abandoned elevated railway into a public garden/walkway and revitalized the surrounding urban area.

Environmental education/awareness has suffered from built environments that separate people from nature and reinforce the illusion that humans can/should become independent of nature.

A big architecture fad of the 1960s was to expose/celebrate the mechanical systems of buildings. Today, architecture still conceals the natural systems that sustain life, reflecting/reinforcing the illusion that humans are 'progressing' to escape nature's apron strings. To city residents, it appears that resources materialize from factories, ducts, cans, bottles, pipes, faucets, and wires as if they were 'man-made', and that waste disappears in garbage trucks, smokestacks, drains and sewers, as if evaporating without leaving toxic residues. When system failures occur due to 'minor' malfunctions in complex technical, financial and internet systems, few are able to fix these problems.

Making integrated, eco-productive natural systems in buildings and cities 'visible' can inculcate the possibility of going 'beyond' recycling and regeneration to net-positive sustainability.

There are many environmental education/action programs like Land-care, Water-watch, Habitat for Humanity and Engineers without Borders. In addition to remediation services, these programs combine environmental education with action learning and contribute to a public-minded ethos. The lived experience of healthy environments that have visible, net-positive impacts would also contribute to positive psychology. Tours of green buildings/homes have demonstrated that better living environments (if only for the affluent) can be 'responsible'. While small-scale individual actions are futile in the context of an industrial-corporate-military complex, they help people to imagine a sustainable environment where everyone has some agency over their basic needs/impacts.

The ecological footprint of homes for the rich shows that some individuals use the equivalent resources, water and energy of hundreds of others.

Children in poor regions use a fraction of the material resources used by children in privileged nations.[76] Per capita, underprivileged nations cause fewer impacts than wealthier nations.[77] For example, Australian per capita carbon emissions are 70 times those of Bangladesh.[78] Using 'average' per capita ecological footprints hides the impacts of the rich. Disparities of wealth encourage wasteful consumption (e.g. space tourism).[79] Some high-rise buildings have elevators for trophy cars so they can be admired within the apartment behind glass. An upper limit on individual consumption is a taboo subject, and there is scant research on how urban design transfers wealth.

Economic security is known to reduce population growth, but this could also apply to domestic environments that provide resource security and life quality.

Wealth generally correlates with waste, such as ostentatious homes, yachts and cars.[80] On a finite planet, the definition of waste must include the extravagant and/or inequitable uses of resources. It is also the case that access to means of income for women strongly correlates with a reduction in the birth rate and the shift from expenditure on luxuries to family, child and community welfare. However, wealth is not the operative concept, as life quality depends more on one's living environment than money per se (an abstract construct). Hence, multifunctional community facilities are one way of jumpstarting improved local living conditions.

Environmental refugees, in addition to exiles from political, economic and religious conflicts, would usually prefer to remain in their home communities/cultures if possible.

Abysmal living environments in impoverished regions reinforce social hierarchies, inequities, class segregation and large-scale immigration. Dislocation leads to more conflict or migration. Physical separation no longer guarantees the safety of the privileged.[81] Swanky central districts, often surrounded by miles of decaying peri-urban areas (similar to medieval towns), cannot protect the haves from the have nots forever. One way to prevent the overflow of environmental/political refugees would be to improve their daily living conditions, as opposed to conventional foreign aid.[82] The causes of resentment, conflict and migration would be reduced by green, self-sufficient homes and pleasant public spaces in underprivileged areas.

Homelands have a magnetic quality, so creating low-impact, culturally expressive, resource-autonomous living environments in disadvantaged regions should cost less than over-populating already over-crowded cities.

Urban design cannot prevent colonization, invasions or genocides. It can, however, mitigate some of their causes and reduce the appeal of extremist views.

Foreign aid has been politically unpopular, but direct action to improve the living conditions of the poor and/or disenfranchised is less subject to local government corruption. Retrofitting disadvantaged communities with inexpensive but self-sufficient environments would improve resource security and even create socio-economic opportunities [Chapter 5]. Low-cost loans have usually been for business start-ups instead of funds to eco-retrofit homes (to be repaid from energy savings).[83] Naturally, any interventions should be informed by multi-scalar planning analyses [Chapters 7–8].

Air and water pollution and consequent health issues in both developed and developing regions of the world can be corrected by urban design.

Medical problems are a significant cost to society.[84] Indoor air quality is affected by outdoor air pollution that seeps into buildings but, more crucially, industrial building materials/products that offgas toxins.[85] Sick leave and worker compensation from 'sick building syndrome' has necessitated the demolition of some new buildings that were designed after the problem was well-known.[86] Causes include radon gas, which often enters buildings through concrete basements,[87] mould in buildings in coastal regions, and other common toxins like volatile organic compounds, formaldehyde and asbestos. Even if removed by experts to special disposal sites, toxins eventually re-enter the air, water and/or soil.[88]

Many well-known eco-solutions are ignored because the public health costs of air and water pollution in urban areas are seldom fully accounted for.

Organic building products emit relatively few pollutants as they do not require harmful glues or coatings. However, the least costly means of absorbing indoor pollutants may be design 'for' plants. Worker health and productivity has been measurably improved by low-cost systems like indoor greenery and fresh air.[89] Similarly, water pollution can be pre-filtered by green roofs, wetlands and Living Machines combined with landscaping and parks.[90] A major barrier is that the costs to individuals are prioritized over the costs to the public. If costs and benefits of 'natural' solutions were divided among the whole population, these balance sheets would change.

Stress and sensory overload caused by unnatural levels of noise and light in urban areas are increasingly recognized as exceeding human biophysical tolerances.

Some new eco-cities appear to be modeled on shopping malls. A recent architectural fashion in sustainable building was to light up whole facades with LEDs that 'dance' like giant TV adverts. These mimic the 2D world of flat screens in smart phones, computers and TVs. Some see the potential of 'media facades' for spontaneous international grassroots communication (and public surveillance).[91] If this trend continues, however, cities/buildings may become more electrifying and enervating. This new urban 'reality' could create a modern version of the Gilded Cage Syndrome (referring to a monarch imprisoned in an ornate, luxurious palace who went barking mad).

Many 'sustainable' buildings contribute to urban environments that cause nature deprivation and fail to respect biophilic needs, despite adding potted landscaping and greenery.

There is growing evidence that humans have an innate need for regular contact with nature.[92] Since humans evolved for millennia in relationship with nature, they

50   *Design and Analysis*

may also suffer mental and emotional malaise in sterile, artificial environments.[93] Similarly, research indicates that 'light noise', or constant artificial lighting at night, challenges people's circadian rhythms, and is linked to health problems.[94] At the urban scale, stress levels of residents, office workers and even commuters in dense areas are now understood as manifestations of 'nature deprivation disorder'.[95] Contact with urban nature and/or trips to natural areas ('forest bathing') builds immunity and reduces stress hormones.[96]

Toxins and heavy metals from industrial and urban processes are already concentrated in urban environments and should be isolated and perhaps eventually 'mined'.

Demolition waste is generally very toxic (e.g. lead, asbestos, formaldehyde),[97] and exporting it to landfill is expensive. Urban pollution eventually contaminates local supplies of water, air and food, flowing back to cities in a circle of poison. The expression 'there is no waste in nature' (meaning it recycles everything) is ironic since nature cannot process current levels of toxins, which are biomagnifying in organisms and ecosystems. Fortunately, natural systems can be enlisted to remediate environments. For example, mushrooms can detoxify environments, bacteria can bioremediate the soil, and worms collect heavy metals. Toxins can be mined from waste/worms and reused.[98]

While sustainable design has always included cleaner production and waste reduction, it now increasingly integrates natural systems to decontaminate and restore the environment.

Methane gas is captured from landfill sites, urban forests remediate brownfield urban land, and mining sites are rehabilitated and repurposed. While such actions make the constructed environment better for humans, they do not (in themselves) restore nature. The ecosystems contaminated during resource extraction and construction processes seldom recover to the same level of biodiversity or complexity. This is partly due to uncertainties created by intervening in nature, even to remediate sites or 'enhance' biodiversity. Therefore, a greater investment in urban/regional environmental management will be necessary. This would provide very green jobs for those in fossil-fuel-dependent trades who will become redundant.

2.3 Future Trends

Trends are still toward massive, single-function, brittle industrial approaches to urban infrastructure, instead of using adaptable eco-logical design that provides multiple public benefits.

Eco-logical planning and design that works with or celebrates nature has been around for decades. Many business leaders embrace design, although mainly as a means to produce efficient goods and services. However, current decision frameworks and technologies remain biased toward industrial solutions. This is in part due to the computerization of design. Computers have brought many advantages and are necessary. However, thus far, the programming is usually done by people with a cybernetic rather than a symphonic worldview.[99] Computer-aided design tools and design by genetical algorithms seem more relevant to life in outer space than life on earth [Chapters 3–4].

While computer-aided design can integrate lifecycle analyses with the design process, they have not yet integrated environmental impact assessment to create net-positive impacts.

The data processing ability to deal with LCA and MFA is advancing rapidly, although data is often commercial-in-confidence. However, the full lifecycle impacts of developments are difficult to assess, as industry data seldom include cumulative ecosystem impacts. Computer drafting tools can now quantify the materials, energy, pollutants and water in schematic designs. Some tools can generate and compare many alternatives, but they largely only consider energy/efficiency, and do not trace these flows back to actual sites of materials extraction. They do not link impacts to the total remaining resources and original ecosystems, let alone the health impacts on affected ecosystems.

New green buildings may soon be printed (the way products are laser-printed now) but deeper sustainability issues are still unlikely to be considered.

Buildings can already be 'printed' with automated systems that follow engineering drawings. It is possible that low-impact materials (e.g. hempcrete or mycelium-based materials) could be used in such processes with a fraction of the impacts of traditional materials. Nanotechnology is also promising to bring improvements in the performance of building materials. However, product/material fabrication will probably have little input from ecologists or ecological designers and will ignore the potential for positive socio-ecological impacts. Further, like computer-aided design, the capacity to print buildings may be used to create fancy building shapes, instead of overcoming the impediments to retrofitting cities for sustainability.

2.4. Conclusion

Cities could increase sustainability in excess of their costs and impacts, but this is only possible with a different approach to urban design.

This chapter has surveyed ways that urban design contributes to most sustainability problems, yet could have a positive influence on most dimensions of life. For decades, design has been dominated by methods and concepts that favour fossil-fuel-based industrial approaches that prioritize efficiency and profit over ethical considerations. Sustainability awareness may be expanding, but the potential of urban design and architecture to address sustainability issues is not. Therefore, the next two chapters revisit sustainability, and how it might escape colonization by the DP. This is followed by two chapters on how to retrofit/remodel cities to correct inequity, poverty and past/ongoing environmental impacts.

2.5 Exercises

1. Try to think of any human-made sustainability issue (i.e. leaving aside forces like meteors, volcanos and tsunamis) that is *not* affected by the design of the built environment. Think again. Then think of ways that built-environment design could address these issues.
2. Examine an award-winning sustainable building in relation to the factors listed in the chapter. Identify ways in which these issues are addressed (or not). Then

think of ways that the building could be modified to include these other benefits.
3. Make a table with sustainable materials on one axis and sustainability issues on another (e.g. flood, fire, ultraviolet light and pest resistance, embodied energy, adaptability, lifecycle impacts). Fill in the performance of each material in relation to each issue. Then discuss design solutions to the problems of each material and/or suitable substitutions.

Notes

1 'The annual amount of natural resources used by cities could grow from 40 billion tonnes of raw materials in 2010 to 90 billion tonnes by 2050'. www.resourcepanel.org/reports/weight-cities.
2 *Sydney Morning Herald* citing David Attenborough's *Blue Planet II*. www.smh.com.au/environment/climate-change/great-barrier-reef-will-be-dead-by-2100-says-david-attenboroughs-blue-planet-ii-20171211-h026zv.html.
3 Chen, P. Y., Chen, C. C., Chu, L., and McCarl, B. (2015) Evaluating the Economic Damage of Climate Change on Global Coral Reefs, *Global Environmental Change* 30, pp. 12–20.
4 See www.unenvironment.org/news-and-stories/press-release/resource-experts-call-new-strategy-build-better-cities. This article lists means to slow the deterioration of cities but they would not reverse the trajectory.
5 Thornton, R. L. J., Glover, C. M., et al. (2016) Evaluating Strategies for Reducing Health Disparities by Addressing the Social Determinants of Health, *Health Affairs (Project Hope)* 35(8), pp. 1416–23.
6 An exception was Roodman, D. M. and Lenssen, N. (1995) A Building Revolution: How Ecology and Health Concerns are Transforming Construction, in *Worldwatch Paper 124*, Worldwatch Institute, Washington, DC.
7 Recent figures are provided in the United Nation's Sustainable Development Goals available at www.un.org/sustainabledevelopment/cities/June 2018. In 2010, the building sector alone accounted for 32% of global final energy use and 19% of all GHG emissions, according to Chalmers, P. (2014) Climate Change: Implications for Buildings, in *Key Findings from the Intergovernmental Panel on Climate Change*, Fifth Assessment Report, http://bpie.eu/publication/climate-change-implications-for-buildings/. See also UN-Habitat (2011) *Cities and Climate Change: Global Report on Human Settlements*. www.unhabitat.org/downloads/docs/GRHS2011_Full.pdf
8 For a concise discussion of economics and sustainability, see Hamilton, C. (1994) *The Mystic Economist*, Willow Park Press, Canberra.
9 Most articles in the *Journal of Cleaner Production* reflect a reductionist paradigm that aims to reduce pollution and other impacts. www.sciencedirect.com/journal/journal-of-cleaner-production.
10 Most articles in the *Journal of Industrial Ecology* concern the flows of resources and energy through industrial systems and only aim to close resource loops. https://onlinelibrary.wiley.com/journal/15309290. For a short overview of closed-loop systems, see Tibbs, H. (2002) Industrial Ecology, in Birkeland, J. (ed.) *Design for Sustainability: A Sourcebook of Eco-logical Solutions*, Earthscan, London, pp. 210–14.
11 In an energy efficient building, the embodied energy might be up to 46% of total energy. Sartori, I., and Hestnes, A. G. (2007) Energy Use in the Life Cycle of Conventional and Low-energy Buildings: A Review Article, *Energy and Building* 39(3), pp. 49–57. In an energy efficient home, the embodied energy might be up to 60%. Thormark, C. (2007) Energy and Resources, Material Choice and Recycling Potential in Low Energy Buildings, in SB07, Sustainable Construction Materials and Practices, CIB Conference.
12 HM Treasury (2006) *Stern Review: The Economics of Climate Change*, UK Government, London. webarchive.nationalarchives.gov.uk/+/www.hm-treasury.gov.uk/stern_review_report.htm.

13 For examples of machines developed to suck carbon out of the air to create fuels or support nurseries see www.technologyreview.com/s/601490/go-inside-an-industrial-plant-that-sucks-carbon-dioxide-straight-out-of-the-air/.
14 Carbohydrate or bio-based materials such as hemp, strawboard and cork can sequester carbon (and mycelium can embed materials that sequester carbon). www.circularecology.com/embodied-energy-and-carbon-footprint-database.htm.
15 Biochar, in a sense, sequesters carbon. However, advocates seldom deduct the carbon used in producing it through 'pyrolysis', which involves placing biomass in an oven with little or no oxygen. www.biochar-international.org/biochar/carbon.
16 Timber high-rises are being built in Brisbane, Portland, Norway, London and elsewhere. www.theguardian.com/sustainable-business/2017/jun/21/tall-timber-the-worlds-tallest-wooden-office-building-to-open-in-brisbane.
17 The practices of reusing timber waste are well advanced, but information on upstream timber waste are not readily available. Taylor, J., and Warnken, M. (2008) *Wood Recovery and Recycling: A Source Book for Australia*, Forest and Wood Products Australia. www.fwpa.com.au/images/marketaccess/PNA017-0708_Wood_Recycling_0.pdf. For a summary of the causes of upstream waste, see Santana, M. E. (2002) Timber Waste Minimization by Design, in Birkeland, *Design for Sustainability*, pp. 188–191.
18 See UN Sustainable Development Goals www.un.org/sustainabledevelopment/cities/Other figures were provided in UN-Habitat. (2011) Cities and Climate Change: Global Report on Human Settlements. www.unhabitat.org/downloads/docs/GRHS2011_Full.pdf.
19 6.5% of global GDP still goes to subsidizing dirty fossil fuels. Coady, D., Parry, I. et al. (2017) How Large are Global Fossil Fuel Subsidies? in *World Development* 91, pp.11–27.
20 Scheer, H. (2004) *The Solar Economy*, Earthscan, London.
21 The savings depend on many site-specific conditions. Cost-effectiveness of actions for a typical US home in the USA were itemized by Heed, in Heede, R. et al. (1995) *Homemade Money*, Rocky Mountain Institute with Brick House Publishing, Harrisville, NH. See also Galante, A. and Pasetti, G. (2012) A Methodology for Evaluating the Potential Energy Savings of Retrofitting Residential Building Stocks, in *Sustainable Cities and Society* 4, pp.12–21.
22 For example, rock walls can be designed to provide nooks for small nests for endangered species.
23 Vale, B. and Vale, R. (1975) *The Autonomous House: Design and Planning for Self-sufficiency*, Thames and Hudson, London. Vale, B. and Vale, R. (2000) The New *Autonomous House: Design and Planning for Sustainability*, Thames and Hudson, London.
24 Lee, J. and Park, J. (2018) Phase Change Material (PCM) Application in a Modernized Korean Traditional House (Hanok), in *Sustainability* 10(4), p.948.
25 Bruegge, C., Carrión-Flores, C. and Pope, J.C. (2016) Does the Housing Market Value Energy Efficient Homes? Evidence from the Energy Star Program, in *Regional Science and Urban Economics* 57, pp.63–76.
26 According to UNEP, the world's cities occupy 3% of the Earth's land (other say 2%) but account for 60-80% of energy consumption and 75% of carbon emissions. www.unenvironment.org/explore-topics/sustainable-development-goals/why-do-sustainable-development-goals-matter/goal-11. Cities represent 80% of global GDP. www.resourcepanel.org/sites/default/files/documents/document/media/city-level_decoupling_summary_english_0.pdf.
27 In 2017, Earth Overshoot Day (the day when humans have used the resources that it takes a full year to regenerate) was August 2 according to the Global Footprint Network. www.footprintnetwork.org/our-work/ecological-footprint/
28 Data on material and energy flows is increasingly available, but does not adequately represent toxic flows into the environment from materials processing and construction. www.resourcepanel.org/global-material-flows-database; also, https://resourcewatch.org/data/

54 *Design and Analysis*

29 80% of gold mining, which generates extensive waste and toxins ends up in jewellery. www.theworldcounts.com/counters/environmental_effect_of_mining/environmental_effects_of_gold_mining.
30 BIM or building information modelling tools are not yet relevant to ecological or social sustainability, but they are advanced in terms of energy.
31 Cities use 65% of the earth's resources according to UNEP (others state 75%). UNEP (2013) City-level Decoupling: Urban resource flows and the governance of infrastructure transitions, United Nations Environment Program. www.resourcepanel.org/sites/default/files/documents/document/media/city-level_decoupling_summary_english_0.pdf. See also Riffat, S., Powell, R. and Aydin, D. (2016) Future Cities and Environmental Sustainability, in *Future Cities and Environment* 2, p.1.
32 The use of nanotechnology in building materials is improving the performance of existing materials such as concrete. See Pacheco-Torgal, F. and Jalali, S. (2011) Nanotechnology: Advantages and Drawbacks in the Field of Construction and Building Materials, in *Construction and Building Materials* 25(2), pp.582–590.
33 Buildings have collapsed for other reasons as well, such as failure to meet code requirements. See Figueroa Fernandez, R.H. (2014) *Strategies to Reduce the Risk of Building Collapse in Developing Countries*, Carnegie Mellon University, Pittsburgh, PA.
34 In 2013, the USA generated 254 million tons of trash and recycled about 34% of waste. Individuals disposed of 4.40 pounds of non-hazardous waste per person per day. https://archive.epa.gov/epawaste/nonhaz/municipal/web/html/.
35 For example, the production of 1 tonne of copper generates 110 tonnes of waste ore and 200 tonnes of overburden. However, the amount of waste generated by the mining industry globally has not been quantified. Das, R. and Choudhury, I. (2013) Waste Management in Mining Industry, in *Indian Journal of Scientific Research* 4(2), pp.139–142.
36 An efficient 'green bomb' was touted as a sustainable product at a life-cycle assessment conference by a member of the US Department of Defence in Washington DC. circa 2000. Stegall argues that consumer behavior is as important as systems design, as an axe can be recyclable but be used to fell a forest. Stegall, N. (2006) Designing for Sustainability: A Philosophy for Ecologically Intentional Design, in *Design Issues* 22(2), pp.56–63. However, the separation of design from user behavior is problematic.
37 Jones, M., Bhat, T., Huynh, T. et al. (2018) Waste-derived Low-cost Mycelium Composite Construction Materials with Improved Fire Safety, in *Fire and Materials*, Wiley, pp.1–10.
38 See www.ecovativedesign.com/
39 Stamets, P. (2005) *Mycelium Running: How Mushrooms Can Help Save the World*, Random House Digital, Inc.
40 Danenburg, J. (2002) Hemp Architecture, in Birkeland, *Design for Sustainability*, pp. 205–8. See also www.hempcrete.com.au/
41 Cusack, V., and Yiping, L. (2002) Bamboo as a Building Resource, in Birkeland, *Design for Sustainability*, pp. 201–4; St. Jacques, L. (2002) Strawbale Construction, ibid., pp. 197–9; Burroughs, S. (2002) Earth Building, ibid., pp. 193–6.
42 www.pbs.org/newshour/show/plastic-lasts-more-than-a-lifetime-and-thats-the-problem.
43 Great Pacific Garbage Patch weighs more than 43,000 cars. Lebreton, L., Slat, B. et al. (2018) Evidence that the Great Pacific Garbage Patch is Rapidly Accumulating Plastic, *Scientific Reports* 8(4666). www.nature.com/articles/s41598-018-22939-w.
44 Huynh, T., and Jones, M. (2018) Scientists Create New Building Material Out of Fungus, Rice and Glass, The Conversation (June 20) https://theconversation.com/scientists-create-new-building-material-out-of-fungus-rice-and-glass-98153.
45 Masdar used small people movers or 'podcars' but the scheme ran into problems.
46 https://climate-adapt.eea.europa.eu/metadata/adaptation-options/adaptation-of-ground water-management.
47 Solar ponds trap heat at the bottom of ponds through the use of salt which prevents the hot water rising. The hot brine can then be used for many purposes. For examples see Birkeland, J. (2008) Box 3: Examples of Net Positive Development, in *Positive Development: From Vicious Circles to Virtuous Cycles in Built Environment Design*, Earthscan, London, pp. 279–80.

48 Air temperatures in cities can be as much as 22°F (12°C) warmer than in neighboring, less developed regions. www.epa.gov/heat-islands/heat-island-impacts.
49 Reflecting surfaces lose some energy, some of which is absorbed in nearby structures.
50 IFRC (2004) *World Disasters Report 2004*, International Federation of Red Cross and Red Crescent Societies. www.ifrc.org/publicat/wdr2004/chapter2.asp.
51 Heat deaths in US cities could rise ten-fold due to climate change. In 45 of the largest cities, excess deaths on dangerously hot days could increase from 1,360 each summer (1975–2010) to 13,860 (mid-2040s). Knowlton, K., Chen, L. J., and Kalkstein, L. (2012) Killer Summer Heat: Projected Death Toll from Rising Temperatures in America Due to Climate Change, in *NRDC Issue Brief*. http://publichealth.med.miami.edu/documents/Killer_Summer_Heat.pdf.
52 White roofs reflect heat into the urban environment rather than absorb and use it productively.
53 Howard, L. (1833) *The Climate of London*. Cited in Golden, J. S. (2003/2004) The Built Environment Induced Urban Heat Island Effect in Rapidly Urbanizing Arid Regions: A Sustainable Urban Engineering Complexity, *Environmental Sciences* 1(4), pp. 321–49.
54 Velazquez, L. S. (2008) Box 14: Advantages of Eco-roofs, in Birkeland, *Positive Development*, pp. 292–3.
55 Evaporative cooling works in humid outdoor areas although it is less effective.
56 In wealthy nations, urban design is correlates with obesity and even poor motor coordination in children. www.ajpmonline.org/article/S0749-3797(04)00087-X/fulltext.
57 However, this depends on design, management and maintenance. See Specht, K., Siebert, R., et al. (2014) Urban Agriculture of the Future: An Overview of Sustainability Aspects of Food Production in and on Buildings, *Agriculture and Human Values* 31(1), pp. 33–51.
58 Rainforests produce about 28% of the earth's oxygen but most (70%) of the atmospheric oxygen is produced by marine plants. www.ecology.com/2011/09/12/important-organism/. Deforestation causes about 10% of greenhouse emissions. www.rainforest-alliance.org/articles/relationship-between-deforestation-greenhouse-gas-emissions.
59 Renger, C., Birkeland, J., and Midmore, D. (2015) Net Positive Building Carbon Sequestration: A Case Study in Brisbane, *Building Research and Information* 43(1), pp. 11–24.
60 Air circulation caused by trees and plants can counteract the tendency for heat inversions and pollution to concentrate at street level, according to the Nature Conservancy among others. https://thought-leadership-production.s3.amazonaws.com/2016/10/28/17/17/50/0615788b-8eaf-4b4f-a02a-8819c68278ef/20160825_PHA_Report_FINAL.pdf. Others argue the opposite. See www.theguardian.com/environment/2016/dec/01/trees-may-increase-air-pollution-on-city-streets.
61 Duffy, K. (2004) NASA Studies How to Cool Area as Heat Builds Up, *Atlanta Journal Constitution*, April 18. See also Elton, B. (1989) *Stark*, Sphere books, London.
62 Some green buildings add green plant pots to floor plans but have to send pot plants in petrol-powered trucks back to nurseries for resuscitation.
63 Embodied water in construction is usually estimated at around 12%.
64 Living Machines are self-contained networks of (solar-powered) ecological systems that are designed to support the micro-organisms that eat toxic wastes. Todd, J., Brown, E. J., and Wells, E. (2003) Ecological Design Applied, *Ecological Engineering* 20(5), pp. 421–40. Todd, N. J., and Todd, J. (2002) Living Technologies, in Birkeland (ed.) *Design for Sustainability*, pp. 173–5.
65 In Melbourne nuclear and other waste leaks into the Yarra River which goes through the city, contaminating the whole region. See www.theage.com.au/national/victoria/parks-victoria-washing-toxic-waste-into-yarra-river-20160109-gm2gr1.html. See EPA Victoria (2013) *The Origin, Fate and Dispersion of Toxicants in the Lower Sections of the Yarra River*, Scientific Report no. 1529. www.epa.vic.gov.au/~/media/Publications/1529.pdf

56 Design and Analysis

66 Ramsay, C., and Rudolph, L. (2003) *Landscape and Building Design for Bushfire Areas*, CSIRO publishing, Canberra.
67 https://soe.environment.gov.au/theme/overview/topic/land-use-change-and-habitat-fragmentation-and-degradation-threaten-ecosystems.
68 www.environmentalscience.org/roads.
69 Fire-resistant and retardant plants include saltbush. https://apsvic.org.au/fire-resistant-and-retardant-plants/
70 https://medicalxpress.com/news/2017-06-deaths-cities-fold-climate-isnt.html.
71 Gas explosions, for example, have destroyed whole residential buildings.
72 Some ancient cities were built next to rivers but had to be abandoned when the rivers changed course.
73 This was the case in Brisbane, which had a major flood in 1974 and again in 2011.
74 Both levies and floodways can increase subsequent flooding events. After the 1927 flood on the Mississippi River, the government constructed levies and floodways. These levies changed the flow of the river. The floodways reduced the absorption of seasonal rains by the flood plains, which increased the currents and prevented the deposit of new soils.
75 Many urban buildings are constructed on reclaimed land from bays or marshes which are subject to subsidence or liquefaction in earthquakes.
76 Children in disadvantaged countries consume relatively very little as they have few commercial toys and clothes. www.huffingtonpost.com.au/entry/your-kids-toys-are-killing-the-planet_us_58ffa383e4b0f5463a1a9472
77 Slash and burn of tropical forests for cash crops is an exception. See Tinker, P. B., Ingram, J. S., and Struwe, S. (1996) Effects of Slash-and-burn Agriculture and Deforestation on Climate Change, *Agriculture, Ecosystems and Environment* 58(1), pp. 13–22. See also http://agrihomegh.com/do-not-slash-and-burn/.
78 Bangladesh emits 0.38 CO2 equivalent emissions while Australia emits 26.54 per capita. UN statistic division-environmental indicators. http://unstats.un.org/unsd/environment/air_greenhouse_emissions.htm.
79 Space exploration is important, but children should clean their rooms before they go out to play.
80 Poverty creates waste as well, as exemplified by the destruction of the Amazon basin by individual farmers as well as organized entities.
81 E.g. the Twin Towers, New York.
82 Direct action is practiced by some NGOs that build housing in poor regions, but these are seldom very sustainable.
83 Some developed countries have had loan programs for energy retrofitting.
84 Health care in the USA is over 17% of GDP according to the Center for Disease Control and Prevention. www.cdc.gov/.
85 See www.epa.gov/indoor-air-quality-iaq/introduction-indoor-air-quality.
86 Sick building syndrome has received less attention in recent years. Burge, P. S. (2004) Sick Building Syndrome, *Occupational and Environmental Medicine* 61(2), pp. 185–90.
87 Keller, G., Hoffmann, B., and Feigenspan, T. (2001) Radon Permeability and Radon Exhalation of Building Materials, *Science of the Total Environment* 272(1–3), pp. 85–9.
88 Renou, S., Givaudan, J. G., et al. (2008) Landfill Leachate Treatment: Review and Opportunity, *Journal of Hazardous Materials* 150(3), pp. 468–93.
89 Estimates of net oxygen production of different trees vary, but over seven trees per person may be necessary. Villazon, L. (2015) How Many Trees Does It Take to Produce Oxygen for One Person? *BBC Focus Magazine*, September 6. www.sciencefocus.com/qa/how-many-treesare-needed-provide-enough-oxygen-one-person.
90 Large-scale Living Machines have been built. https://en.wikipedia.org/wiki/Living_machine
91 See e.g.: www.archdaily.com/344971/light-matters-what-media-facades-are-saying. www.archdaily.com/tag/media-facades.
92 Wilson, E. O. (1984) *Biophilia*, Harvard Press, Boston, MA.
93 Haney, C. (2012) Prison Effects in the Age of Mass Incarceration, *The Prison Journal* 20(10), pp. 1–24.

94 For light pollution, see http://darksky.org/light-pollution/wildlife/. For noise pollution, see www.science.org.au/curious/earth-environment/health-effects-environmental-noise-pollution.
95 Nature deprivation disorder is discussed in Louv, R. (2008) *Last Child in the Woods: Saving Our Children from Nature-deficit Disorder*, Algonquin books, Chapel Hill, NC.
96 See Li, Q. (2010) Effect of Forest Bathing Trips on Human Immune Function, *Environmental Health and Preventive Medicine* 15(1), p. 9.
97 www.epa.gov/smm/sustainable-management-construction-and-demolition-materials.
98 Heavy metals in worms can be harvested by putting them in a centrifuge according to G. Gillespie (2006), then President of Zero Waste Australia, pers. comm.
99 Cybernetics is concerned with automatic systems of communication and control. It tends to be a mechanistic approach to systems which analogizes electronic machines and humans.

Section B
Sustainability Revisited

3 Sustainability Paradigms in Historical Context

3.1 Review and Preview

Despite advances in diagnosing the causes of the sustainability crisis and the barriers to geo-political and cultural change, progress toward sustainability has waned.

The values and goals of the sustainability movement(s) have not changed dramatically since the 1970s: environmental and social regeneration, social justice/equity, community building and engagement, more symbiotic human-nature relationships and so forth.[1] Familiar analyses of escalating climatic and socio-ecological problems, and associated strategies for tackling them, are periodically recycled and sometimes even rebadged as epiphanies. Yet the movement's persistent efforts have not slowed extinction rates or environmental devastation,[2] and inequalities of wealth/power continue to mount.[3] Meanwhile, the percentage of people that identify as environmentalists or are otherwise interested in structural and systems change to save the planet is arguably dwindling.[4]

Inspiring sustainability policy manifestos and communication strategies have been put forth over the years, with little examination of reasons for their apparent failures.

There are many explanations for the lack of sustainability, most relating to the DP (dominant paradigm) or cultural marinade of modernity. However, there are few analyses of why sustainability strategies have not worked. This chapter suggests that the circular model that characterizes most schools of sustainable design, while 'revolutionary', has basic limitations. This closed-system model, whether in its more radical or conservative manifestations, cannot really reverse direction. It does not encourage direct action to expand the natural life-support system, challenge the DP (which sees relationships as transactional and solutions as interest balancing), or address mounting cumulative impacts and biodiversity losses.

The circular model shapes problem descriptions, analyses and strategies that are inherently remedial, so direct design action and institutional transformation is also necessary.

As the capsule history below illustrates, sustainable design has aimed to balance environment and development by encouraging behavior modification and technological efficiency to minimize negative impacts. This circular view sees nature as a complex recycling system writ large. In this model, human-made systems should work like organisms that interact with their environment in closed loops that balance consumption and production. Transposed onto the built environment, this means that each building should be in balance with its environment. However, closed-loop systems dissipate energy, resources and nature. They neither correct the underlying problems created by past design nor compensate for accumulated imbalances.

Since buildings benefit from surrounding urban development, major projects should be responsible for their share of the overall ecological damage caused by cities.

Current sustainable design, assessment and measurement practices, although purporting to be comprehensive, do not 'seriously' consider cumulative ecological impacts. The impacts of the built environment cannot be corrected by adding more green buildings that incrementally reduce the ecological base. An open-systems model aligns with the understanding that all things, being interdependent, eventually have system-wide impacts. It helps to expose conceptual barriers that have prevented the design of positive physical and institutional systems. Negative impacts have tipping points, but positive impacts have no limits. Design can create a 'positive butterfly effect',[5] that can give back to nature more than it takes.

Revisiting the development-nature relationship through an open-system lens may help to explain the apparent inability of contemporary society to imagine eco-positive urban environments.

This chapter first attempts to put to rest some widely held misconceptions that impede sustainability. Then it summarizes the DP for those not familiar with the philosophical roots of the negative (anti-ecological) worldview. In doing so, it reminds readers of some influential sustainability books. These offered diverse and profound problem descriptions, although they reflected/reinforced a closed-system view. Next, three streams within closed-systems views are distinguished: hard/technocratic, soft/social and living systems. The question is whether these conceptual frameworks inspire or inhibit net-positive design possibilities. Finally, the chapter describes how closed-system thinking is manifested in the built environment, and has constrained sustainable planning/design.

3.2 Misconceptions about Sustainability

The possibility of sustainability (peace, justice and environmental quality) is still sometimes dismissed as unrealistic, often due to stereotypes, myths and uniformed assumptions.

Many have called sustainability a 'contested subject' that 'no one understands'.[6] To those outside the movement and ethos of sustainability, the premises, values and reasoning sometimes appear confusing. Nevertheless, paradigms have an inbuilt logic of consistency.[7] Therefore, they have relatively correct understandings, regardless of individual interpretations. As in the parable of three blind men who examined different parts of an elephant and formed different conclusions – the elephant did not change. However, any concept that threatens business-as-usual will be misrepresented, and subsequently co-opted, redefined and diluted. This may explain why stereotypes can be inconsistent with the original (pre-Google) sustainability literature.[8]

Initially, grassroots sustainability concerned intra/inter-generational equity (ethics), but some outside observers interpreted it to be about mere 'survival' or making resources 'last longer'.

Although sustainability was about fairness, when filtered through the DP it was sometimes reinterpreted as sustaining material wealth for those who already have it. Similarly, others thought that sustainability meant sustaining society 'as we know it'. In either case, 'sustaining un-sustainability' would not make sense. Some complain that the term sustainability has been co-opted by industry, so it is now too weak and/or tainted. However, alternative terms like resilience and regeneration are weaker.[9] Similarly, the notion of going 'beyond' sustainability presupposes a 'weak' definition of sustainability.[10] There is no real 'beyond' the continual reform of social, institutional and physical constructs.[11]

Taken to its logical conclusion, sustainability would embrace an ecofeminist paradigm (i.e. beyond power): 'caring' for the ecological and social foundations of life.

Sustainability is necessarily grounded in ecology because human existence relies on nature. Just as social and economic sustainability cannot be constructed without solid environmental foundations, physical and institutional structures must be designed to support both community (public estate) and nature (ecological base). While it would help if people felt a part of nature, this is not the same as caring/acting for it.[12] The emphasis on the self has led some to claim (falsely) that sustainability is 'misanthropic' or prioritizing nature humanity.[13] A view that excludes social justice would not be a sustainability paradigm, and would eventually self-destruct, in any case.[14]

3.3 An Overview of the Dominant Paradigm (DP)

With the industrial revolution, 'progress' became intertwined with the domination of nature and, subsequently, the objectification of nature as a 'source and sink'.

Early cultures purportedly had a cyclical view of life, where the seasons of birth, life and death repeated forever. Nature was seen as a nurturing although sometimes harsh mother.[15] This view was gradually replaced by urbanization, and buttressed later with the industrial revolution and enlightenment ideal of 'progress'. It depicted civilization as created in Man's (then) self-image as conqueror, and nature was meant to be conquered. Gradually, a belief in perpetual growth became synonymous with European culture, and dominion over nature became manifest destiny.[16] 'Lesser' peoples and species that were 'closer to nature' were meant to fall by the wayside.

The crisis of modernity has been described, dissected and traced back to its origins by many scholars from different schools of sustainability thought.

Key elements of the DP have been traced back to pivotal historic figures.[17] 'Reductionism' is attributed to Newton (1642): understanding reality by dividing it into parts and particles.[18] The interpretation of nature as a clockwork-like 'mechanism' is associated with Descartes (1596).[19] Bacon (1561) was known for the scientific method which involved the dissection/mastery of nature.[20] Hobbes (1588) saw people as 'autonomous', self-interested individuals, who submit to be governed by representatives in an implied social contract. How these elements combined to create a systemic bias against sustainability and nature was explained by numerous authors from various perspectives in the 1980s (below).[21]

- The Death of Nature (1980) showed how the scientific revolution ushered in a reductionist, mechanistic, power-based worldview that helped to legitimize unlimited industrial growth, colonization, the exploitation of nature and patriarchal relationships.[22] The organic view of a cyclical, regenerative natural world was gradually replaced by a social construction of nature as inert material existing only to serve human needs/desires. While others also linked this Eurocentric view of progress to the devaluation and degradation of nature,[23] this book explained the intrinsically gendered dimension of structures of domination, exploitation and hierarchical social relationships and the subordination of women, nature and slaves.[24]

Many societies, not just those later influenced by European culture and industrial ideology, saw reality in terms of opposing cosmic forces in balance.

The tendency to see reality in terms of fundamental forces in some kind of binary tension is found in many philosophical traditions (e.g. yin-yang, hard-soft, good-evil, mind-spirit, science-art, private-public, rational-emotional, objective-subjective). The ideal state has often been seen as being in balance or harmony. However, the 'hard' side of each dualism usually represented values associated with the social construction of masculinity and which were valued more highly.[25] Hence, traditions many consider unbalanced, such as slavery, were unconsciously accepted as part of the natural order. That also meant challenges to unjust aspects of the status quo were seen as unbalanced or deviant.

Characteristics of the DP, discussed further below, have gradually created in-built mental barriers that are now impeding the design of a sustainable society.

The interrelated elements of the DP (below) have been explored by various authors and activists. They have created a systemic imbalance in the culture toward values once historically associated with masculinity. These imbalances may have served 'progress' well, in the past, but they have now outlived their use-by date. As argued throughout, development still largely prioritizes expediency and efficiency over ecology, linear-reductionist decision making over multifunctional design, and rights-based and exchange relationships over ethics. The list is followed by a capsule history of the sustainability movement. Together, these should shed light on why a circular paradigm was adopted in sustainable development.

- *Linear progress:* Mankind was meant to transcend, control and dominate nature (and lesser beings) over time, still seen today in some industrial infrastructure projects.
- *Autonomy:* Mankind (or at least elite white males) was believed to be, by nature, independent, assertive, dispassionate, competitive, rational, objective and freedom seeking.
- *Public-private dichotomy:* Private ownership of the product of other's labor was accepted and the domestic private sphere became increasingly invisible and thought of as inconsequential.
- *Hierarchical dualism:* The world was understood as sets of gendered opposites, and the masculine side of each dualism was deemed to be more worthy.
- *Essentialism:* Humans have an 'essential nature', and the ideal characteristics/values which correspond to masculinity stood for the higher virtues of humanity in general.

- *Transactional relationships:* Because humans were conceived of as autonomous beings, practical relationships between people and/or groups could be described in terms of exchange networks.
- *Reductionism:* The world can be understood as a composite of separate, elemental physical mechanisms, so problems can be solved by simplification and specialization.
- *Linear causality:* Adverse consequences can be traced back to single sources through linear cause-effect relationships, and therefore outcomes can (eventually) be predicted and controlled.
- *Instrumentalism:* Nature's value lay in how 'useful' it was, so it was wasted when it was not harnessed in the service of humanity.[26]
- *Mechanism:* For many purposes, flora and fauna were considered soulless, mechanistic entities and, therefore, human-made artificial environments could eventually replace disorderly natural processes.
- *Anthropocentrism:* Humans were the center, or top, of a great chain of being, so nature was a backdrop or stage for human activity.[27]

3.4 Historical Strands in the Sustainability Movement

The opposite of linear growth appeared to be circular systems (recycling on many scales and levels) which corresponds with closed-system models of reality.

In the beginning, the sustainability movement drew attention to the problems of unlimited industrial pollution and population growth. The first stage (1960s) was awareness raising about the human health impacts of industrial/agricultural pollution and waste. Industrial systems were analogous to conveyor belts, delivering resources from nature to garbage dumps. Pollution was filtered or dispersed by add-on controls, while post-production recycling programs diverted small amounts of post-consumer waste. Hence, most people saw the solution to be a matter for markets or regulations, so the strategies were political (not a matter of design). Therefore, the movement focused on changing hearts and minds.

Awareness raising: Because the early sustainability writings were about raising awareness, they did not yet have practical physical solutions and, consequently, often presented doomsday scenarios.

The warnings of the 1960s and 1970s concerning the limits to growth and pollution were understated, while other problems, such as plastic pollution, were not yet recognized.[28] Nonetheless, any suggestion of resource or population limits was poorly received. In fact, limits on consumption were hard to grasp for people who were cradled in visions of perpetual growth and unbridled materialism. Some influential books that raised the potential of tipping points were met with personal attacks on their authors. Soon, an industry backlash painted environmentalism as slowing progress and threatening to impose hardships, if not to overthrow democracy (meaning consumer sovereignty).

- The Silent Spring (1962) explained how pesticides were harmful to the entire food chain. The author was harshly condemned and ridiculed by the chemical industry. She was called a communist and 'a fanatic defender of the cult of the balance of nature'.[29] Ironically, anti-environment elements of industry later appropriated the term 'balance' to mean incrementally dividing up remaining natural environment between conservation and development.[30] The book generated public debate about whether or not unforeseen technological fixes would come in time. This only diverted attention from more constructive discussions on how to make everyone better off while repairing the planet.

- The Population Bomb (1968) warned of the limited capacity of the world to feed the growing human population.[31] It suggested that intensive agricultural technologies might not increase food production fast enough to meet the demands of a growing population.[32] It advocated population control – and even suggested sterilization.[33] The ensuing population debate was a lightning rod for hostility from many directions. Population control and family planning remains a taboo subject in many places today. These disputes also sidelined other emerging environmental issues such as biodiversity, urbanization, chemical pollution, climate change and the depletion of raw materials, fish, wildlife, etc.
- The Limits to Growth (1972) charted some alarming trends that had largely been ignored, such as 'accelerating industrialization, rapid population growth, widespread malnutrition, depletion of non-renewable resources, and a deteriorating environment'.[34] Attempts to prove the obvious, that there are material and spatial limits to land and space on a finite planet, were again met by vitriolic attacks on the authors.[35] The concerted industry pushback served to block collective efforts to address problems in constructive ways by design. Sustainability was coupled with extremism. The counterarguments were revisited decades later in a sequel called *The Limits to Growth: The 30-Year Update*.[36]

Appropriate technology: Attention shifted from the limits to industrial growth, pollution and population to socio-economic change: smaller-scale development, appropriate technology, community building and ecological restoration.

Prior to the 1970s, sustainability usually just meant the sustainable 'yield' of resources.[37] By the 1970s, however, more writers began to express an appreciation for the multiple values/benefits of the natural environment, not to mention nature being the foundation of human life and the economy. There were calls to balance the environment and development (consumption and reproduction), and to build community by humanizing economic policy. Collectively, this literature proposed a restructuring of all dimensions of society: political, social, technological, economic and spiritual.[38] However, it also reflected the faith that people would act rationally to improve society through traditional political processes.

- Blueprint for Survival (1972) argued that fundamental policy change was necessary to address the problems of human population, consumption and pollution.[39] First published in *The Ecologist*, it was endorsed by many leading scientists at the time. Like many policy plans since, it underestimated the resistance from powerful industrial lobbies. Presenting a policy plan was positive and proactive but, in the end, possibly no more effective than the awareness raising of the 1960s. While the book recognized that development needed to support the environment and community (not just the economy), it did not recognize the centrality of built environment design.
- Small is Beautiful (1973) argued that health, happiness and life quality was being replaced by commercialism and materialism.[40] It challenged the premises

of neo-classical economics and globalization, and warned of international super-corporations that denied responsibility for their systemic global impacts. In arguing for 'bottom up' democratic decision-making at the lowest practical level (known as the 'subsidiary principle'), it appealed to those with a desire for simpler, decentralized living, de-industrialization, appropriate technology and 'living in place'.[41] This aligned with a subsequent bioregional movement that advocated for industrial and governmental systems that are structured to fit the bioregion's natural environment.[42]

Ecological modernization: Meanwhile, the mainstream technological approach gradually moved from end-of-pipe pollution control and waste management to improving the engineering of factories, processes and products.

By the 1990s, industrial systems used for materials extraction and manufacturing were being re-engineered for efficiency and materials substitution.[43] 'Cleaner production' and 'pollution prevention pays' programs emphasized the public and private savings of waste/toxin reduction. Since the public health savings could offset the private or public investment in new technologies, industries were given loans and other incentives to invest in efficiency upgrades.[44] However, the design of the industries themselves was still treated as a 'black box' [Figure 3.1]. While they reduced waste and pollution, they seldom aimed to reduce overall production and consumption, and their public purposes were never questioned.

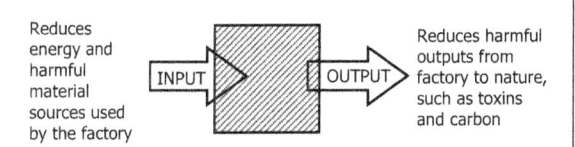

Figure 3.1 The black box approach

Circular/metabolic systems: Having articulated the problems of centralized, linear systems of production, distribution and consumption, the sustainability movement proposed the 'opposite' development model: circular systems.

The next stage was circular systems, where nature was no longer a mere source and sink, but a model for human systems of production. The idea of closed-loop systems, using wastes as resources on all levels and scales, had been percolating for some time, as suggested by the examples below.[45] However, it did not become mainstream sustainable development/design until this century.[46] Circular systems were validated by claiming to be analogous to nature, organisms and/or metabolic systems – an 'appeal to nature' argument.[47] However, the goal has often remained more commercial output and/or less waste/pollution per unit (the definition of efficiency).[48]

68 *Design and Analysis*

- The Closing Circle (1971) warned that the cycles of soil, air and water were being broken by a swathe of post-war industrial technologies.[49] It focused on how industrial chemicals were harming nature and people, and causing more cumulative toxic waste than the earth could absorb. The book presaged the idea of designing human systems to mimic the interconnected cyclical systems of nature, as in biomimicry.[50] Although it was about circular production systems, not construction, the concepts were easily transferable to the built environment. However, mimicking nature's cycles is not the same as designing environments to increase net biophysical sustainability.

The circular model stimulated metabolic studies and material flows analyses that track material and energy throughout production processes to identify where waste occurs.

The Metabolism of Cities (1965) was perhaps the earliest study to quantify material flows in and out of cities.[51] Materials balance and industrial metabolism/ecology fields soon appeared,[52] followed by construction ecology.[53] These map consumption and waste, not just pollution. Closed-system analyses have now been applied to nations, regions, cities, industries, buildings, farms and products.[54] This was put into practice when an industrial park in Denmark (1970s) began to create an exchange network of wastes and resources, gradually mounting to 30 connections.[55] This was for financial reasons, reputedly uninformed by theory. However, it demonstrated that industry was compatible with resource 'conservation'.

While the circular model is essential to reducing waste, it does not, in itself, reduce cumulative negative impacts, let alone create positive impacts.

Metabolic studies trace/measure energy and materials flows in and out of industries, cities, regions or buildings. Recycling of waste materials can occur at every stage of manufacturing: from resource extraction to eventual demolition; between different sectors from farming to forestry; and on different scales from products to buildings/cities. However, the overarching aim is usually a resource balance [Figure 3.2].[56] Closing loops creates financial savings/gains, but seldom socio-ecological gains. 'Upcycling' refers to converting low-grade waste to higher-value products.[57] However, even a product/project that uses waste profitably and productively can be anti-social. In PD, therefore, 'eco-cycling' is used to mean upcycling that is eco-positive.[58]

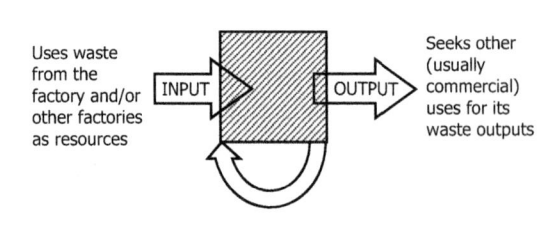

| Uses waste from the factory and/or other factories as resources | INPUT → ▓ → OUTPUT | Seeks other (usually commercial) uses for its waste outputs | Circular systems usually link processes together, including other industries, so that waste or even pollution becomes a saleable or tradeable product and is not simply dumped in the environment. However, the socio-ecological value of the industries or products themselves are not considered. That is, the resource uses, even if recycled, can be a waste in terms of their overall sustainability value |

Figure 3.2 The simple circular approach

Circular systems may be all that can be expected from manufacturing at present, but it is not an adequate model for sustainable building.

Product manufacturing cannot easily be eco-positive because it generally converts natural materials into consumer items. However, there are rapid advances in technology that could substitute many manufactured components in the built environment. For example, insulating bricks can be made of recycled plastic, filled with materials that produce and store electricity from the interior-exterior heat differential.[59] Energy can also be produced from converting saltwater into hydrogen peroxide using sunlight, which is then used to generate electricity in fuel cells in buildings.[60] However, the built environment adds a whole other dimension: space. Spaces can create synergistic relationships and diverse public benefits.

3.5 Three Streams within Circular Approaches

Soon, a divergence in circular approaches appeared in the literature, which can be categorized in three broad orientations: hard/technocratic, soft/social and living/organic systems.

Systems theories simply describe and improve systems. There are myriad system approaches but, in sustainable systems, most can be placed on a spectrum between extremes: hard (reductionist, mechanistic, top-down), to soft (complex, interactive, bottom-up). Both concern linkages or communication. Generally, soft systems concern the multiple perspectives involved in networks,[61] while hard systems focus on controlling networks (e.g. cybernetics).[62] In built environment design fields, a more recent soft-system approach, 'living systems', centers more on social revitalization and environmental regeneration than networks. (Paradoxically, buildings that claim to be living systems are sometimes quite barren and sterile.) These positions are briefly distinguished below [Figure 3.3].

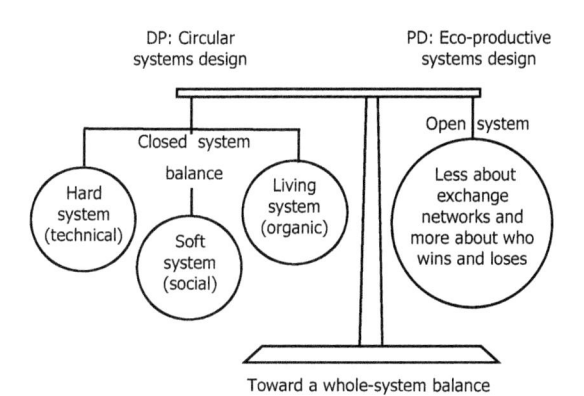

Figure 3.3 Differing closed-system views in sustainable design

The hard (technocratic) orientation: In the 1960s, the metaphor of 'spaceship earth' (representing engineering efficiency, environmental conservation, spatial minimization and closed-loop recycling systems) captivated many designers' imaginations.

Inspired by the US space program,[63] some sustainability advocates proposed that the planet itself should be thought of as a spaceship where everything must be recycled. 'Spaceship earth' was an early closed-system metaphor that greatly influenced sustainable design.[64] This model can be 'innovation forcing': if a factory's water and air supply came from its smokestacks and waste-water outlets, the equipment would soon be re-engineered to be clean and efficient.[65] Looked at differently, spaceships could also be said to symbolize real-world design today: there is so much space junk that one rogue item could set off a chain reaction among them.[66]

The spaceship metaphor corresponded with the 'technological fix' position, which did not address issues such as environmental quality, social justice, biodiversity or equity.

The idea that the earth could be designed and managed like a spaceship expressed a tacit faith in technocracy-led progress. Being an inherently earth-denying image, it was ironic that the mechanistic spaceship metaphor became a banner for 1960s environmentalism. Yet today, the impulse to conquer nature has expanded its horizons to outer space: escaping the planet has priority over protecting the environment. Billions are being invested in space exploration before life on earth is understood, or this limited knowledge can be redirected toward preventing the earth's destruction. (Ironically, the sustainability movement has often been accused of being 'merely about survival'.)

- Environment, Power and Society (1971) ushered in a hard, technocratic stream of research.[67] To enable a whole-system analysis, it reduced natural and human systems to energy flows. It suggested that ecosystems could be represented as electrical circuit diagrams. The analogy of ecosystems with networks facilitated a numerical, diagrammatic approach to environmental analysis. This hard-systems orientation, combined with the 'oil crisis', of the early 1970s (and other factors), contributed to the association of sustainable buildings with energy efficiency alone. This technocratic stream led to the development of green building rating/marketing tools, which marginalized the 'softer' orientation in design [Chapters 11–12].
- The Soft Energy Path (1976) was a phrase used to argue for efficient and renewable energy such as wind and solar, instead of fossil fuel or nuclear sources.[68] The paper argued that there was a choice: a centralized, toxic path or a more safe, equitable path. The US was heading in a dangerous direction. The alternative soft path was less high-tech and more focused on innovation. The argument was couched in benefits to business and industry. However, it spelled out the connection between energy efficiency and 'natural security' and world peace, as well as environmental protection and public health/wellbeing.

Soft (social) systems orientation: Because the technocratic 'hard' orientation sidelined the human dimension, soft-systems approaches emerged to describe human interactions and activities, and to improve their effectiveness.

While the hard-system approach concerned interconnections among inanimate entities and forces, the soft-system approach emphasized the social and psychological dimension.[69] Soft-systems thinking generally involves examining the linkages between people in organizations in order to determine where to intervene to improve connectivity/communication. Since it originated in the field of operations research, however, it was concerned with effective business management.[70] It was later applied to sustainability, as it is well suited for analyzing problems that involve competing values, perspectives and interests. However, the role of the physical environment in improving the quality of interaction is often forgotten in social change strategies.

Soft-systems views have generally been more about fostering/managing change through organizational processes and social evolution, and less about improving physical and institutional systems.

There are many different perspectives on social transformation. Hard systems analyses and strategies are often left to an expertariat who select legislative or economic mechanisms and/or technological fixes. At the soft end, responses to the sustainability challenge are often about changing people and assume that political change will flow from democratic processes.[71] Many sustainable design texts call for changing values, cultures and behaviors,[72] so that people will make better consumer and lifestyle choices [Chapter 9]. In other words, soft systems seldom look at the physical and spatial dimension or the inherent potential of environmental design to shape positive human-society-nature relationships.[73]

- Wicked Problems (1967) are those that are interdependent with other problems and usually involve both natural and human components.[74] Sustainability issues are by definition 'wicked' or multifaceted since people do not share problem descriptions, let alone the same values, goals or criteria for success. This influential article recognized that understanding complex policy issues depends on the problem definition,[75] and argued for ensuring wide stakeholder involvement in problem-defining and problem-solving activities.[76] In planning, solutions often center around communication structures that accommodate different values and interests. However, perhaps because business/management is about manipulating people, the soft-systems approach can sometimes be top-down.[77]

The living systems orientation: The early grassroots sustainability movement was largely a bottom-up approach which called for transforming and/or healing relationships on individual-society, people-people and human-nature levels.

The grassroots movement of the 1980s, like the peace movement of the 1960s and feminist movement of the 1970s,[78] had many levels – from a reconceptualization of self[79] to resistance to the industrial-military-corporate state.[80] This movement spawned new philosophies from a range of perspectives, that explored means to create ethics-based relationships.[81] It was often validated by new descriptions of the evolution of nature and society as being a product of cooperation. Although, for about 150 years, relationships among flora and fauna have been understood to be symbiotic (even if sometimes parasitic or competitive),[82] injustices have been excused as being 'natural'.

Eco-philosophies were constructed upon views about nature being inherently priceless, human nature being essentially good, and hence a belief that reform is possible.

Sustainability advocates plainly believe that humans can evolve to create a more civilized society. They share core ideas such as that nature has inherent value beyond its usefulness to people, and that personal, social and institutional transformation is possible.

72 Design and Analysis

Pessimists and reactionaries tend to favor more authoritarian solutions, in the conviction that the world is a dangerous place.[83] They assume it is up to future generations to adapt to artificial environments that are devoid of nature. Interestingly, some researchers claim to have linked people's socio-political orientation to brain structure, although which comes first is unknown, as brains change with experience.[84]

- Gaia (1979) suggested that the earth's biosphere, including organisms and their inanimate environments, act as a single living being that regulates its own environment.[85] The idea that the earth is a complex, interactive, self-managing ecosystem had earlier precedents.[86] Biological, physical and chemical systems operate as feedback mechanisms to automatically balance changes in the external environment in order to maintain stable conditions. Thus, the earth has a tendency, like an organism, to maintain constant internal conditions despite shocks and changes in the environment. In this view, merely regenerating natural systems may appear adequate, as this would emulate the earth's restorative function.
- The Sacred Balance (1997) and similar books placed emphasis on changing individual values, behaviors and worldviews.[87] It encouraged people to live 'in balance' with nature, and prioritize basic needs (clean air, water, soil, energy and biodiversity, etc.). It called for re-igniting a spiritual kinship with nature and practicing lifestyles that emulate the 'circularity of natural cycles'. Bottom-up community-based action was the lever for change, rather than changes in design and decision systems. However, power relationships do not melt away, and circular systems require changes in design on all levels. Design must be not only recyclable or biodegradable but fool-proof.[88]

Living buildings: The idea of buildings functioning as living entities interconnected with larger ecosystems became an inspiration, although this is arguably yet to be achieved.

'Living buildings' are meant to function like a flowering plant, although buildings do not grow, pollinate, wilt, decay, become food or contribute nutrients back to the environment. Some are nearly resource autonomous, or produce their own energy, water and sewage treatment.[89] Others operate almost as Living Machines, treating the district's water or sewage,[90] although this has not yet been properly measured. However, due to the scale of human activity in general, development can no longer rely on nature to keep producing resources and absorbing wastes. Therefore, a building needs to make a net contribution to the bioregion's ecosystems and biodiversity.

3.6 Open- and Closed-Systems Distinction

Circular models/metaphors assume environments can regain their functional structure, if development impacts are neutralized, such that systems and their environment are in balance.

If hard (technical), soft (social) and living (biological) systems thinking were different, one might suppose that they only need to be integrated to create a comprehensive system. First, these fields would have to communicate with each other. However, circles only internalize the impacts they create, not the collective

Sustainability Revisited 73

and cumulative impacts of development. The circular model and metaphors do not suggest increasing nature or space for ecological growth, even to offset ongoing losses of ecological carrying capacity. Hence, the past distinction between linear and circular systems may not be as heuristic as that between positive open-system and neutral closed-systems design.

The dominance of closed-system paradigms may be due more to legal, economic and measurement convenience/conventions than the appeal of aligning with natural systems.

Before the 1960s, ecosystems were sometimes described as 'open', where ecosystems, organisms and environments were one.[91] However, this model did not meet the need to fit reality into existing intellectual constructs, exchange relationships and measurement conventions. This may explain why species and ecosystems began to be described as bounded systems, linked to their environment in circuits, networks and feedback loops. This also aligned with descriptions of the environmental crisis which saw the solution to pollution or resource exploitation to be establishing boundaries. As discussed in the next chapter, early sustainability declarations emphasized the creation of borders to assign management responsibilities.

- The Commons (1968) associated environmental protection with property lines.[92] This influential paper suggested that shared resources would always be overexploited. It used an analogy to herding sheep to argue for private management. If shepherds have to keep sheep within their own property lines, they will maintain their pastures. However, if they have access to shared, public land they will all overgraze it.[93] This parable was sometimes used to support the privatization of public land.[94] In the real world, however, the richer shepherds would keep buying bigger, greener pastures and continue to externalize the effluent into shared rivers and streams.[95]

The old industrial paradigm was called an 'open' system, because wastes/pollution were 'externalized' beyond property lines, and positive impacts were as yet inconceivable.

Generally, the environmental impacts of development were only considered negative if they were externalized [Figure 3.4]. What happened on a given property was largely up to the owner. Negative impacts were accepted as natural or unavoidable, so the problem was defined as reducing impacts by filtering or dispersing them –

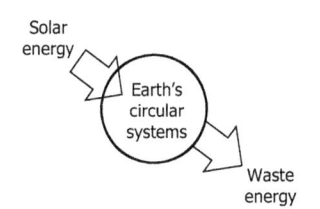

Closed: The closed-system view is that, apart from solar energy which enters from outside the planet and then dissipates, everything is cyclical. Thus, only efficiency and recycling systems can reduce the rate of waste and energy losses. The idea of wilderness being increased is off the table.

Open: Entropy (gradual decay of energy) may nullify all human activity eventually, but the time scale of entropy is millions of years. Meanwhile, on the human time scale, nature tends to grow in complexity and diversity, in between catastrophic events like volcanoes, meteors or rapid climate change. Development and nature need not be in a zero-sum relationship, as buildings, if reconceived, could support ecological growth.

Figure 3.4 Closed and open systems

end of pipe mechanisms. Therefore, factories and later buildings only needed to 'internalize' impacts within project borders to, ideally, achieve zero 'onsite waste' (a fraction of production waste) or zero 'operating energy' (about half of lifecycle energy). The logical solution therefore seemed to be closing loops, but this ignored biomagnifying environmental impacts.

3.7 Hard and Soft Streams in Sustainable Design

Just as environmental and social problems can be linked to the DP, built environments can be understood as a projection of the DP.

In recent decades, architecture has had a diversity of styles. At the hard end is architecture as a 'technical enterprise' (buildings as machines), and at the soft end is architecture as 'cultural expression' (buildings as stage sets). This dualism is also seen in green/sustainable architecture. They have been called the 'nuts and bolts' and 'nuts and berries' traditions/styles respectively. The technocratic lineage celebrates efficiency, and some shiny new green buildings seem to be inspired by science fiction. Despite some potted plants, they seem to spurn nature. More recently, however, some of them are touted as 'inspired by' nature or biomimicry.[96]

Neither the 'hard' technical and 'soft' organic traditions in urban design and architecture accept full responsibility for escalating upstream and downstream socio-ecological impacts.

Many technically oriented theorists/practitioners see the aesthetic stream as too superficial,[97] and many aesthetically oriented theorists/practitioners see the technocratic wing as too mechanistic. However, neither the hard nor soft wings appreciated the complicity of design in social or environmental injustices. Probably every negative impact stemming from the built environment can be linked to decisions or non-decisions that reflect the absence of positive design thinking. Yet until 25 years ago, the socio-ecological impacts of buildings were scarcely examined.[98] Buildings owners/developers/designers were not expected to contribute to the public good – beyond stimulating economic growth. Responsibility stopped at the building envelope or property line.

Nuts and bolts architecture: *Mainstream green architecture generally tends to replicate the hard-edged 'international style' and therefore often fails to accommodate changing socio-ecological needs and climatic conditions.*

The legacy of the DP is still seen in architecture.[99] Modernism culminated in the International Style (or Bauhaus movement) in architecture, often known by the mantra 'form follows function'.[100] This philosophy called for designing from first principles, rather than following cultural traditions. But in this case, the 'first principle' was reductionism/rationalism. It therefore advocated mass production and one-size-fits all design, regardless of context/climate. This style explains the sterile, minimalist buildings around the world that make central cities indistinguishable, with skylines resembling tombstones. Oddly, these buildings often had excessive embodied energy, and were therefore inefficient from an energy and ecological standpoint.

Even 'green' mega-structures and industrial infrastructure tend to conflict with local climates, cultures, natural forces and flows of earth and water over time.

The ethos of controlling/constraining nature inspired massive infrastructure and rigid buildings. However, displays of corporate power and grandeur do little for the life-support system. Although durable, skyscrapers are difficult/expensive to maintain, upgrade or adapt to changing needs, uses and conditions. They are designed for what can be predicted, including earthquakes, bombs, hurricanes or airplane strikes. However, mile-high skyscrapers may well end up in a war zone where they make attractive targets. Similarly, when massive flood barriers along urban rivers are eventually breached, buildings magnify the impacts of floods, and large storm-water tunnels spread erosion, contamination and other ecological damage downstream.

Because industrial construction systems are often brittle and hard to modify, social and ecological costs are shifted onto future generations and the environment.

The industrial approach to controlling water is illustrative of how nature is repressed. Water was originally underpriced, as was the energy used to transport it, and these costs were paid for primarily by the public. Water was piped into cities from great distances and delivered to buildings as if fuel in machines. The pipes were hidden below paving or inside buildings. Future costs, such as leaks/repairs, were not considered, let alone the fact that pipes eventually degrade and allow cross-contamination of water and soil. Pipes also break or lose electricity during emergencies such as fires, heat waves, blackouts or earthquakes.

Industrial-era architecture shaped subsequent investment in development, and the sunk cost (i.e. past investments) created a force of inertia against more sustainable alternatives.

In rigid urban environments, problems are usually fixed by repairing existing conditions, or demolishing and rebuilding, rather than taking the opportunity to create socio-ecological gains. For example, although roads, garages and car parks create vast amounts of spatial and ecological waste, the public costs of removing the resulting concrete megaliths appear prohibitive. Therefore, the response to congestion has been to add more lanes and parking areas, which encourage ever more car production and congestion.[101] Similarly, today, because of the investment in mass-produced cars (and the ability to sell more cars than buses), robotic cars will displace buses or light-rail transport.

Nuts and berries architecture: *Until recently, not even the 'soft' wing of sustainable design regarded urban environments as leverage points for achieving greater social and ecological sustainability.*

The design fields were slow to adopt any form of sustainability. The Garden Cities movement (turn of the twentieth century) had sought healthy human environments simply by separating housing from industry and creating moats of gardens and green belts. There were a few visionary books such as *Design with Nature* (1969),[102] and *Architecture without Architects* (1964),[103] and a passive solar design movement in the 1960s. However, ecological design was largely deprecated as effeminate, and ignored by mainstream (corporate) management, planning and architecture. There was virtually no concern for how the cities/building might affect, let alone support, nature and social justice.

Gradually, schools of sustainable design evolved which built on the ideas of working with nature and resource autonomy, though not design 'for' nature.

In general, the core principles and design concepts of the competing schools of thought at the soft end of sustainable design are similar, but priorities differ.

76 *Design and Analysis*

Therefore, they appeal to different audiences and are sometimes competitive. Nonetheless, the human relationship with nature is a central theme in most of them [Box 2]. The main themes are:

- Working with nature (e.g. permaculture) emphasizes the utilitarian or instrumental use of nature, or co-evolution guided by humans for humans.
- Emulating nature (e.g. biomimicry) focuses on innovation that is eco-efficient (like nature), and therefore minimizes impacts while providing material benefits.
- Experiencing nature (e.g. biophilia) concerns how people feel and even artificial representations of nature are believed to provide psychological/physiological benefits.
- Restoring nature (e.g. regenerative design) prioritizes the integration of natural and human environments to improve environmental/human health and social wellbeing.

The emphasis on balancing inputs and outputs reflects a closed-system view that does not recognize overall past/present losses of biodiversity and nature generally.

The various schools of sustainable design have aimed to restore a notional balance between development and nature by incorporating nature in cities, working with nature and/or reducing the impacts of development on the natural environment. In general, they still evince a closed-system paradigm (internalizing and balancing inputs) which aims for zero impact, not whole-system sustainability. The closed-system model does not allow for rising to the real challenge: increasing nature relative to current rates of consumption. The closed-system model can be described by how it appears at various scales of development: industries, cities, regions, landscapes, buildings homes, and products (summarized below).

3.8 Sustainable Design at Different Scales

Industrial scale: The potential for a balanced relationship between industrial growth/consumption and environmental conservation that could provide 'abundance' with life quality dates back 50 years.

The idea of a 'biotechnic' society, which aimed for a balanced relationship between natural resources and development, appeared by 1970.[104] It was argued that technological growth could support both nature and 'plenitude', now usually called abundance.[105] The biotechnic society would seek satisfaction (not hoarding) and technologies would be designed on the model of organisms. Methods to examine pollution flows from development to the environmental as a whole appeared by the 1970s,[106] and methods to analyze material flows through development appeared by the 1990s.[107] However, it was not appreciated that outcomes depend on more design and resource use (purposes) than technology.

City scale: The idea that cities should be in balance with their regions also dates back 50 years, although the region-urban relationship remains largely unilateral.

The idea of cities having a circular or metabolic relationship with their regions is not new,[108] but the initial concern was for a balance of food-in and nutrients-out to maintain agriculture.[109] Ecological restoration and urban ecology emerged in the 1970s as subsets of the ecology field, and focused more on the 'study' of ecosystems in developed areas than how to protect and enhance urban ecosystems. Urban ecology as a branch of sustainable design (from 1990) advocates revitalizing urban communities and reconnecting them with nature.[110] However, modelling cities on metabolisms or ecosystems does not inspire designing cities as generators of ecosystems.

District/landscape scale: The idea of working with nature (also dating back 50 years) has emphasized the instrumental uses of nature and prevention of environmental risks.

Design with Nature (1969) described how a site could accommodate different land uses in ways that are compatible with the natural environment by analyzing natural systems: topography, soil, hydrology, prevailing winds, climate and so on.[111] This seminal book was written at a time when biodiversity itself was not widely believed to be under immediate threat. What it called 'working with nature' generally referred to optimizing nature's contributions to development. The idea of 'balancing nature and development' has meant maintaining the relationship between development and environment that existed prior to a given development project, not increasing nature's scale, capacity and resilience.[112]

Site-development scale: Permaculture initially focused on increasing domestic food production and self-sufficiency through efficient onsite spatial relationships, but it could reduce land consumption by agriculture.

Permaculture (1978) was defined as an 'integrated, evolving system of perennial or self-perpetuating plants and animal species useful to man'.[113] Permaculture suggests ways to zone gardens for integrated domestic food production and to close loops between different elements.[114] It proposes a closer relationship between people and their means of sustenance. Permaculture has applications to both low-density settlements in disadvantaged regions and middle-class suburbs. New greenfield development providing land area sufficient for private food gardens is questionable.[115] However, integrating food gardens into existing suburban areas (in lieu of lawns) could enable the restoration of some degraded rural land for sustainable functions.

Building scale: In the built-environment fields, ecological design usually refers to incorporating nature in living environments for human benefit rather than for supporting nature.

The Ecological Basis for Architectural Design (1972/1995) focused on tall buildings in anticipation of dense urban development in Asian cities.[116] It took the position that urban densification was necessary to protect the environment. Accepting that all buildings have negative impacts, it suggested that environmental mitigation could be performed by the building itself. For example, climatically and culturally appropriate urban buildings can use natural systems (e.g. passive solar design, vertical gardens, natural ventilation, shading, etc.) that are functionally integrated with the building shapes and facades. Many buildings now incorporate green facades, but are not yet designed to contribute to the natural environment.

Domestic scale: There has long been the occasional passive solar suburb and/or co-housing developments, but they seldom aim for resource autonomy at the neighborhood/regional scale.

After the incorporation of plumbing and electricity in housing, autonomous architecture was possibly not proposed until the 1960s,[117] or built and tested until the 1970s.[118] The Autonomous House (1972/1975) applies closed-loop design to

78 *Design and Analysis*

homes, where most energy, waste, food and water is collected and recycled within property lines.[119] Subsequently, the Passive Haus movement (1990s) emphasized superinsulation.[120] Co-housing projects, in which many domestic functions are shared, such as cooking/dining, laundry and garden equipment, are more efficient. However, most eco-village and co-housing projects do not really challenge the suburban model – separate homes surrounded by gardens or lawns available to the privileged.[121]

Product scale: *Some products are designed for recyclability or biodegradability, but they seldom reduce material flows except when replacing other products, which consequently become waste.*

Cradle to Cradle (2002) concerned the waste and toxins caused by consumer products including the many manufactured products of which buildings are primarily composed.[122] Products, and buildings conceived as products, it said, should be designed to be recycled as either organic materials that re-enter the environment as biological nutrients, or mined materials that are contained within closed-loop industrial cycles (technical nutrients). This extended the more linear 'cradle to grave' concept to a circular, closed-loop model. This was highly influential, but did not overcome the issues related to industrial or urban metabolism (discussed earlier) or aim for net-positive impacts [Figure 3.5].

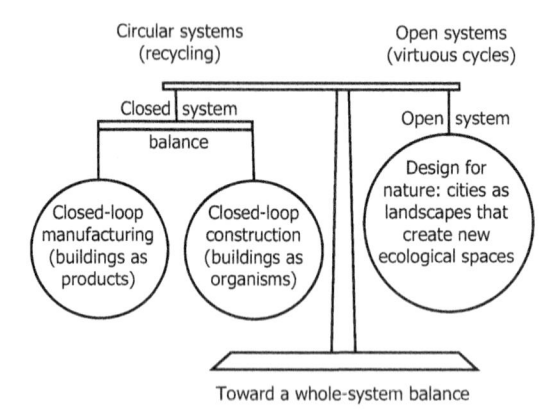

Figure 3.5 Beyond closing loops to virtuous cycles

3.9 Conclusion

Sustainable design avoided harmful practices but did not champion 'direct action by design' to redress past/continuing imbalances in the natural and social environment.

When projected upon reality, a model shapes one's understanding but, more importantly, what one does *not* see.[123] This chapter has discussed how the three major closed-system orientations in sustainable urban design – hard (technical), soft (social) and living (organic) – vary in minor ways but share the idea of balance via closing loops. Circular models and metaphors reflect and reinforce closed-system thinking in these sustainable design paradigms. This is seen at all scales of building. The emphasis on efficiency, recycling and closing loops has meant that the sustainability fields can only achieve neutral impacts, despite the recent adoption of new terminology.

3.10 Exercises

1. Read 'The Tragedy of the Commons' posed by G. Hardin,[124] where shared land gets exploited because producers use more than their share – and the converse, where negative impacts on private land are externalized. How are these twin problems reconciled?
2. Read *The Closing Circle* by B. Commoner (1971),[125] and compare to a more recent seminal book (e.g. *Cradle to Cradle* by McDonough and Braungart).[126] Then outline the conceptual and practical shifts that have been made.

Box 2 The Technocratic Orientation in Sustainability

Metabolic analyses are powerful tools, but they have been conducted in closed-system frameworks They generally limit analyses to measurable units like resource and energy. Nonetheless, metabolic analyses could be converted into a net-positive framework [Chapters 7–8]. While circular, closed systems throughout the supply-chain could slow the impacts of industrial growth and consumption, the framework does not overturn the many premises that were embedded in the linear-reductionist industrial worldview that still block efforts to increase sustainability. For example:

- *Reduction*: because the environmental impacts of development supply chains were pervasive, cumulative and often unavoidable, it was assumed that negative impacts could only be reduced and that even zero impacts were unrealistic.
- *Negativity*: because the problems were seen as unlimited growth in population, consumption and/or pollution, the solutions were to dampen their speed/impacts through efficiencies, recycling and, later, trading mechanisms (not increasing nature).
- *Proxies*: because environmental impacts were expressed as their energy equivalence for analysis/accounting purposes, and since energy cannot be increased (by definition) it was deemed impossible to increase nature on a global basis.
- *Measurement*: because of the notion that there are negative reactions to every positive action, net-positive actions seemed impossible and were therefore not measured, so positive impacts were assumed not to be measurable.
- *Separation*: because environmental management and urban planning evolved from different disciplines (although both originally aimed to control nature) and both regarded nature as belonging outside cities, positive city-nature symbioses were not considered.

- *Individualism*: because of the association of rights and responsibility with property ownership, and the equation of rationality with self-interest, acting to benefit the general public was regarded as charitable but not 'rational'.
- *Property*: because human legal responsibilities for environmental impacts were defined by project boundaries or property lines (if at all), sustainable development was only expected to balance or offset negative inputs and outputs.
- *Boundaries*: because negative cross-boundary impacts were the issue, sustainable urban development was assumed to be answered by constricting city borders, even if that increased other kinds of sustainability impacts (which were forgotten).
- *Offsets*: because public investments that benefit private development such as green infrastructure are paid for by the general public, and private developers expect compensation for providing public benefits, they cost more overall.
- *Trade-offs*: because the value of natural resources on environmentally sensitive land increases over time, especially during economic downturns, every tract of land will eventually be exploited regardless of their importance to life-support systems.

Notes

1 The human need for wild nature has often been expressed in poetry and books such as: Leopold, A. (1949) *A Sand County Almanac*, Ballantine, New York; Thoreau, H. D. (1854, 1995) *Walden, or Life in the Woods*, Minneola, Dover, NY; Carson, R. (1962) *Silent Spring*, Houghton Mifflin, Boston, MA.
2 On extinctions, see www.un.org/sustainabledevelopment/blog/2016/05/rate-of-environmental-damage-increasing-across-planet-but-still-time-to-reverse-worst-impacts/
3 Inequality within countries has grown faster than between countries yet, since 1980, the richest 1% in the world have captured twice as much growth as the bottom 50% individuals. Alvaredo, F., Chancel, L., and Piketty, T. (2018) *World Inequality Report*. https://wir2018.wid.world/
4 E.g. in 1991, 78% of Americans identified as environmentalists, but only 42% did in 2016. Millennials are reputedly less environmentally oriented. www.statista.com/statistics/319145/percentage-of-environmentalist-americans-by-generation/. In 2014, the proportion of Americans between the ages of 18–33 that identified as environmentalist was only 32%, whereas 44% between the ages of 69–86 did so. Jones, J. M. (2016) Americans' Identification as 'Environmentalists' Down to 42%, *Social and Policy Issues* https://news.gallup.com/poll/190916/americans-identification-environmentalists-down.aspx
5 The butterfly effect refers to a wing flap that causes complex and unpredictable chains of reactions that result in a tornado on the other side of the planet.
6 I have been told this several times by academic colleagues, even in recent years.
7 Kuhn, T. S. (1970) *The Structure of Scientific Revolutions*, 2nd ed., University of Chicago Press, Chicago, IL.
8 See Porritt, J. (1985) *Seeing Green: The Politics of Ecology Explained*, Blackwell Publishers, Oxford; Dobson, A. (1990) *Green Political Thought*, Unwin Hyman, London; Dobson, A. (1991) *The Green Reader: Essays Toward a Sustainable Society*, Mercury House, San Francisco. For a discussion on definitions of sustainability, see Hopwood, B., Mellor, M., and O'Brien, G. (2005) Sustainable Development: Mapping Different Approaches, *Sustainable Development* 13, pp.38–52.

9 The regeneration and resilience literature, like sustainability literature, has not called for increasing nature in absolute or whole-system terms.
10 Some define 'weak sustainability' as meaning nature can be substituted for by technology, but this is not sustainable. See Turner, R. Kerry (ed.) (1993) *Sustainable Environmental Economics and Management: Principles and Practice*, Belhaven Press, London. See also Neumayer, E. (2013) *Weak versus Strong Sustainability: Exploring the Limits of Two Opposing Paradigms* (4th ed. 2003), Edward Elgar Publishing, Cheltenham, UK.
11 Birkeland, J. (2003) Beyond Zero Waste, in Societies for a Sustainable Future, 3rd UKM-UC International Conference, UKM-UC, University of Canberra, Australia.
12 Some green philosophies, such as deep ecology, start from the self, but some authors have adopted more eco-socialist and ecofeminist orientations.
13 There are still many false stereotypes of sustainability being published, to the effect that environmentalists are misanthropic or that humans do not need nature, let alone air and water. See e.g. www.aaronmoritz.net/2014/01/20/in-defense-of-humanity/(January, 2014); www.firstthings.com/web-exclusives/2013/01/environmentalisms-deep-misanthropy.
14 Salleh, A. (ed.) (2009) *Eco-Sufficiency and Global Justice: Women Write Political Ecology*, Pluto Press, New York.
15 Merchant, C. (1980) *The Death of Nature: Women, Ecology, and the Scientific Revolution*, Harper & Row, San Francisco, CA.
16 Manifest Destiny was the nineteenth-century USA doctrine that they were meant to expand to the West Coast.
17 Fritjof, C. (1982) *The Turning Point: Science, Society, and the Rising Culture*, Simon & Schuster, New York.
18 Isaac Newton (born 1642) was a founder of the scientific revolution and is known for the laws of motion, gravity and calculus, but contributed to a mechanistic understanding of the natural world.
19 René Descartes (born 1596) was a philosopher-mathematician, known for the use of reason as the means to understand the world, but also for mind–body dualism.
20 Francis Bacon (born 1561) was known for the scientific method or inductive reasoning based on careful observations of nature, but likened the exploration of nature to rape.
21 Ehrenfeld, D. (1978) *The Arrogance of Humanism*, Oxford University Press, New York. He challenged the idea that nature was created for humans to manipulate for their own ends.
22 Merchant, *Death of Nature*, traced the urge to control nature to the 'enlightenment' and further back to patriarchy.
23 Horkheimer, M., and Adorno, T. W. (1944) *Dialectic of Enlightenment*, translated by Cumming, J., Continuum, New York.
24 Ecofeminist theory explains the inter-relationships between these categories as it focuses on the rejection of 'softer' values and abuse of power at personal and political levels. Gaard, G. (ed') (1993) *Ecofeminism: Women, Animals, Nature*, Temple University Press, Philadelphia, PA. Salleh, A. (1997) *Ecofeminism as Politics: Nature, Marx and the Postmodern*. Zed Books, London. Warren, K., Warren, K. J., and Erkal, N. (eds) (1997) *Ecofeminism: Women, Culture, Nature*, Indiana University Press, Indianapolis. Mies, M., and Shiva, V. (1993) *Ecofeminism*, Zed Books, London.
25 Hierarchical dualism refers to the traditional understanding of the world as sets of opposites, where one side (reason, power, control) was seen as 'higher' than empathy, nurturing, collaboration and empowerment, which were seen as weak, feminine traits.
26 For example, water going to the ocean.
27 For instance, nature is often trivialized as something that people 'value', whereas the housing transport and/or food are called basic 'needs'.
28 About 6.3 billion tonnes of plastics have been produced since the 1950s and only about 9% recycled and 12% incinerated. The full effects of endocrine disruptors in plastics are uncertain. See *The Economist* (March 3, 2018) www.economist.com/international/2018/03/03/the-known-unknowns-of-plastic-pollution.

82 Design and Analysis

29 Quoting chemist R. White-Stevens in Lear, L. (1997) *Rachel Carson: Witness for Nature*, Henry Holt & Co., New York, p. 434.
30 Developers adopted and reversed the term 'balance between conservation and development' in the 1980s to suggest too much of the natural environment was being locked up.
31 Ehrlich, Paul R. (1968) *The Population Bomb*, Sierra Club/Ballantine books, New York. Brown, L.R. (1963) *Man, Land and Food: Looking ahead at World Food Needs* (No. 143,860). US Dept. of Agriculture, Economic Research Service, Washington, DC.
32 Parts of Cuba were untouched by chemical agriculture and thrived with organic farming methods. The literature disputes whether organic agriculture has proven to be more productive. Block, B. (2018) Traditional Farmer Knowledge Leads Cuba to Organic Revolution, Worldwatch Institute, www.worldwatch.org/node/6435.
33 Sterilization was associated with fascism and racism.
34 Meadows, D. H., Meadows, D. L, et al. (1972) *The Limits to Growth: A Report for the Club of Rome's Project on the Predicament of Mankind*, Universe Books, New York. This presented the results of computer simulation of population and economic growth with a finite supply of resources.
35 Attacks on limits to growth included Cole, H. S. D. (1973) *Models of Doom: A Critique of The Limits to Growth*, Universe Books.
36 Meadows, D., and Randers, J. (2012) *The Limits to Growth: The 30-Year Update*, Routledge, New York. A counter-argument was that everything is substitutable (including nature), e.g. Worstall, T. (2012) *The Club of Rome's Limits to Growth Updated: Entirely Bizarre*, Forbes, New York.
37 See Wall, D. (ed.) (1994) *Green History: A Reader in Environmental Literature, Philosophy and Politics*, Routledge, London.
38 Brown, L. (1982) *Building a Sustainable Society*, W. W. Norton & Co. Inc., New York; Porritt, *Seeing Green*; Spretnak, C. (1991) *States of Grace: Recovery of Meaning in the Postmodern Age*, HarperCollins, New York.
39 Goldsmith, E. (1972) *Blueprint for Survival*, special issue in *The Ecologist*, and reproduced in paperback form in 1974. See also Abel, B., Anderson, J. M. et al. (1972) Blueprint for Survival, *Nature*, 235.
40 Schumacher, E. F. (1973) *Small is Beautiful: Economics as if People Mattered*, Blond & Briggs, London. See also McKibben, B. (2007) *Deep Economy: The Wealth of Communities and the Durable Future*, Macmillan, Basingstoke.
41 Forsey, H. (ed.) (1993) *Circles of Strength: Community Alternatives to Alienation*, New Society Publishers, Gabriola Island, BC; Meyer, C., and Moosang, F. (eds) (1992) *Living with the Land: Communities Restoring the Earth*, New Society Publishers, Bowen Island, BC.
42 Aberley, D. (ed.) (1994) *Futures by Design: The Practice of Ecological Planning*, New Society Publishers, Philadelphia, PA; McGinnis, M. (ed.) (1999) *Bioregionalism*, Routledge, London; Brunckhorst, D. J. (2000) *Bioregional Planning: Resource Management Beyond the New Millennium*, Harwood Academic Publishers, Amsterdam.
43 Frosch, R. A.,, and Gallopoulos, N. E. (1989) Strategies for Manufacturing, *Scientific American* 261(3), pp.144–52. The *Journal of Cleaner Production* dates from 1993. www.journals.elsevier.com/journal-of-cleaner-production
44 Birkeland (2002) Pollution Prevention by Design, in *Design for Sustainability: A Sourcebook of Integrated Eco-logical Solutions*, Earthscan, London, pp. 69–72.
45 Wolman, A. (1965) The Metabolism of Cities, *Scientific American* 213(3), pp. 179–90; Tibbs, H. (1992) Industrial Ecology: An Agenda for Environmental Management, in *Pollution Prevention Review*, Global Business Network, Emeryville, CA, pp. 167–80; Baccini, P. (1996) Understanding Regional Metabolism for a Sustainable Development of Urban Systems, *Environmental Science and Pollution Research* 3(2), pp. 108–11; Ayres, R. U., Simonis, U. E. (eds) (1994) *Industrial Metabolism: Restructuring for Sustainable Development*, UN University Press, Tokyo and New York.
46 For a short summary, see Tibbs, H. B. C. (2002) Industrial Ecology, in Birkeland, *Design for Sustainability*, pp. 52–5.
47 This logical fallacy is where something is good because it is like (the way we describe) nature.

48 Efficiency is generally the ratio of useful output to total input or the avoidance of waste.
49 Commoner, B. (1971) *The Closing Circle: Nature, Man and Technology*, Knopf, New York.
50 The term biomimetics is attributed to Otto Schmitt; bionics is attributed to Jack Steele but the more recent term, biomimicry, is attributed to Benyus, J. (1997) *Biomimicry: Innovation Inspired by Nature*, William Morrow & Co., New York.
51 Wolman, Metabolism of Cities. Boyden, S., Millar, S., et al. (1981) *The Ecology of a City and its People: The Case of Hong Kong*, Australian National University Press, Canberra, ACT.
52 For a history of the metabolism concept in industry, see Fischer-Kowalski, M. (2003) Exploring the History of Industrial Metabolism, in Ayres, R. U., and Ayres, L. W. (eds) *A Handbook of Industrial Ecology*, Edward Elgar, Cheltenham, pp. 16–26.
53 Kibert, C. J., Sendzimir, J., and Guy, G. B. (eds) (2003) *Construction Ecology: Nature as a Basis for Green Buildings*, Routledge, New York; Birkeland (2002) Construction Ecology, in *Design for Sustainability*, pp. 64–8.
54 For brief articles on Industrial Ecology, Urban Ecology and Construction Ecology see Birkeland, *Design for Sustainability*, pp. 52–68.
55 Kalunborg Park is discussed in Tibbs, Industrial Ecology, in *Design for Sustainability*, pp. 52–5.
56 Kneese, A. V., Ayres, R. U., and d'Arge, R. C. (1970) *Economics and the Environment: A Materials Balance Approach*, Resources for the Future, Washington, DC.
57 McDonough, W., and Braungart, M. (2002) *Cradle to Cradle: Remaking the Way we Make Things*, North Point Press, New York.
58 Eco-cycling is defined as 'up-cycling that contributes to human and ecological health and does not increase total resource flows', in Birkeland, J. (2008) *Positive Development: From Vicious Circles to Virtuous Cycles through Built Environment Design*, Earthscan, London, p. 271.
59 www.linkedin.com/pulse/energy-generating-bricks-offer-affordable-housing-tom-breunig/.
60 https://futurism.com/theres-a-new-way-to-generate-power-using-seawater.
61 An early example is Katz, D., and Kahn, R. L. (1966) *The Social Psychology of Organizations*, Wiley, New York, pp. 14–29.
62 An early example is Weiner, N. (1948) *Cybernetics*, MIT Press, New York. This theory purports to unite the control and communication in machines and animals alike.
63 The first manned space flight was Apr. 12, 1961. President John F. Kennedy announced the USA moon flight plan in Sept. 1962.
64 Fuller, B. (1963) *Operating Manual for Spaceship Earth*, E. P. Dutton & Co., New York. This was taken up by Ward, B. (1966) Spaceship Earth, George B. Pegram lectures, no. 6, and Boulding, K.E. (1966) The Economics of the Coming Spaceship Earth, in H. Jarrett (ed.), *Environmental Quality in a Growing Economy*, Resources for the Future/Johns Hopkins University Press, Baltimore, MD, pp. 3–14. http://arachnid.biosci.utexas.edu/courses/THOC/Readings/Boulding_SpaceshipEarth.pdf.
65 Amory Lovins may have been the first to use this example of the closed loop strategy.
66 www.nature.com/articles/d41586-018-06170-1, Sept. 2018.
67 Odum, H. T. (1971) *Environment, Power and Society*, Wiley-Interscience, New York.
68 Lovins, A. B. (1976) Energy Strategy: The Road Not Taken, *Foreign Affairs* 55. This was followed by a book (1979) *Soft Energy Paths: Towards a Durable Peace*, Harper & Row, New York.
69 Checkland, P. (1972) Towards a Systems-based Methodology for Real-world Problem Solving, *Journal of Systems Engineering* 3(2), pp. 87–116. Checkland is credited for developing the field of soft-systems methodology.
70 Checkland, P. (1985) From Optimizing to Learning: A Development of Systems Thinking for the 1990s, *Journal of the Operational Research Society* 36, p. 757.
71 Birkeland, J. (2014) Systems and Social Change for Sustainable and Resilient Cities, in Pearson, L., Newton, P., and Roberts, P. (eds), *Resilient Sustainable Cities*, Routledge, Abingdon, UK, pp. 66–82.

84 *Design and Analysis*

72 E.g. Pullen, S., Chiveralls, K., Zillante, G., et al. (2012) Minimizing the Impact of Resource Consumption in the Design and Construction of Buildings, Australian and New Zealand Architectural Science Association Conference, Brisbane.
73 See Birkeland, J. (2016) Net Positive Biophilic Urbanism, *Smart and Sustainable Built Environments* 5(1), pp. 9–14.
74 Churchman, C. W. (1967) Wicked Problems, *Management Science* 14(4), p. 141, attributed the term 'wicked problems' to Horst Rittel. Churchman proposed that ethical issues be included in systems thinking.
75 Rittel, H. W. J. and Webber, M. M. (1973) Dilemmas in a General Theory of Planning, *Policy Sciences* 4(2), pp. 155–69.
76 Davidoff, P. (1965) Advocacy and Pluralism in Planning, *Journal of the American Institute of Planners* 31(4), pp. 331–8.
77 Checkland, Systems-based Methodology.
78 Representatives of ecofeminism are: Mies, M., and Shiva, V. (1993) *Ecofeminism*, Zed Books, London; Gaard, G. (ed.) (1993) *Ecofeminism: Women, Animals, Nature*, Temple University Press, Philadelphia, PA; Salleh, A. (1997) *Ecofeminism as Politics: Nature, Marx and the Postmodern*, Zed Books, New York; Warren, K. J. (1997) *Ecofeminism: Women, Culture, Nature*, Indian University Press, Bloomington, IN.
79 Representatives of the mystic end of eco-philosophy are: Næss, A. (1973) The Shallow and the Deep Long-Range Ecology Movement: A Summary, *Inquiry* 16, 95–100; Sessions, G., and Devall, B. (1985) *Deep Ecology: Living as if Nature Mattered*, Gibbs M. Smith, Salt Lake City; Nollman, J. (1990) *Spiritual Ecology: A Guide to Reconnecting with Nature*, Bantam Books, London.
80 Representatives of the socialistic end of eco-philosophy are: Bookchin, M. (1982) *The Ecology of Freedom: The Emergence and Dissolution of Hierarchy*, Cheshire Books, Palo Alto, CA. Pepper, D. (1993) *Eco-Socialism: From Deep Ecology to Social Justice*, Routledge, New York; See also *Capitalism Nature Socialism: A Journal of Socialist Ecology* at www.cnsjournal.org/.
81 For a brief overview of different green philosophies, see Birkeland (2002) Green Philosophy, in Birkeland, *Design for Sustainability*, pp. 20–4.
82 According to Wikipedia, Albert Bernhard Frank used the term 'symbiosis' in 1877 regarding mutualistic relationships among lichens. The mycologist Heinrich Anton de Bary also used the concept in 1879.
83 Psychological differences can purportedly determine whether one is liberal or conservative. See Business Insider Australia www.businessinsider.com.au/psychological-differences-between-conservatives-and-liberals-2018-2?r=US&IR=TFeb.
84 Research suggests that progressives have more grey matter in the anterior cingulate cortex, and conservatives have more grey matter volume in the amygdala. Schreiber, D., Fonzo, G., et al. (2013) Red Brain, Blue Brain: Evaluative Processes Differ in Democrats and Republicans, *PLoS ONE* 8(2), e5297.
85 Lovelock, J. (1988) *The Ages of Gaia: A Biography of our Living Earth*, Norton, New York. Lovelock, J. (1979) *GAIA – A New Look at Life on Earth*, Oxford University Press, Oxford. The Gaia hypothesis was developed in the early 1970s with microbiologist Lynn Margulis.
86 James Hutton, in 1785, anticipated the Gaia hypothesis. Alexander von Humboldt, in 1883, described the idea that the cosmos (heavens and earth) is one entity.
87 McConnell, A., and Suzuki, D. (1997) *The Sacred Balance: Rediscovering our Place in Nature*, Douglas & McIntyre, Vancouver. See also: Spretnak, C. (1991) *Stat es of Grace: The Recovery of Meaning in the Postmodern Age*, Harper, San Francisco, CA; Capra, F. (1996) *The Web of Life: A New Scientific Understanding of Living Systems*, Anchor Books, Garden City, NY.
88 Corruption has been rife in the waste management industry. www.abc.net.au/news/2017-08-07/four-corners-australias-organised-waste-trade/8782866.
89 Vale, B., and Vale, R. (1975) *The Autonomous House: Design and Planning for Self-Sufficiency*, Thames & Hudson, London.

90 Todd, N. J. and Todd, J. (1994) *From Eco-Cities to Living Machines*, North Atlantic Books, Berkeley, CA.
91 Von Bertalanffy, L. (1950) The Theory of Open Systems in Physics and Biology, *Science* 11, pp. 23–9.
92 Hardin, G. (1968) The Tragedy of the Commons, *Science* 162(3859), pp. 1243–8 (Dec. 13).
93 Factories have been known to close and move when the costs of modernization are too high, leaving clean-up costs to the local community.
94 See Obeng-Odoom, F. (2018) Enclosing the Urban Commons: Crises for the Commons and Commoners, *Sustainable Cities and Society* 40, pp. 648–56.
95 E.g. a major environmental problem in New Zealand is cattle poo runoff into waterways.
96 Presentations in professional journals sometimes appear to claim projects have used biomimicry – after the fact.
97 E.g. an engineering department would not let their students take my cross-faculty sustainability units on the grounds that architect-led units could only be about aesthetics (despite the unit outlines).
98 Among the first books on this subject was Roodman, D. M., Lenssen, N. K., and Peterson, J. A. (1995) *A Building Revolution: How Ecology and Health Concerns are Transforming Construction*, Worldwatch Institute, Washington, DC.
99 From Birkeland (2002) Urban Forms and the Dominant Paradigm, in *Design for Sustainability*, pp. 114–17.
100 The Bauhaus school was founded by Walter Gropius in 1919 and later headed by Mies van der Rohe before closing under pressure from the Nazis in 1933. It emphasized sterile, minimalist design that ignored the natural or cultural heritage of the region.
101 It was well known, when I worked as a planner in the early 1970s, that more lanes and parking spaces increases driving. Influence of compact cities on car trips is debated. See Stevens, M. R. (2017) Does Compact Development Make People Drive Less? *Journal of the American Planning Association* 83(1), pp. 7–18 – in contrast with Ewing, R., and Cervero, R. (2017) Does Compact Development Make People Drive Less? The Answer Is Yes, *Journal of the American Planning Association* 83(1), pp. 19–25.
102 McHarg, I. L. (1969) *Design with Nature*, Natural History Press, Philadelphia, PA.
103 Rudofsky, B. (1964) *Architecture without Architects: A Short Introduction to Non-Pedigreed Architecture*, UNM Press, Albuquerque, NM.
104 Mumford, L. (1970) *The Pentagon of Power*, Harcourt Brace, New York.
105 McDonough, W., and Braungart, M. (2013) *The Upcycle: Beyond Sustainability – Designing for Abundance*. Macmillan, Basingstoke. Schaller, D. (2004) Beyond Sustainability: From Scarcity to Abundance, *BioInspire Newsletter*. https://biomimicry.typepad.com/newsletter/.
106 This is discussed in subsequent chapters. See Kneese, A.V., Ayres, R. U., and d'Arge, R. C. (1970/2015) *Economics and the Environment: A Materials Balance Approach*, Routledge, London.
107 Hawken, P. (1993) *Ecology of Commerce: How Business Can Save the Planet*, Weidenfeld & Nicolson, London; Allenby, B., and Deanna R. (eds) (1994) *The Greening of Industrial Ecosystems*, National Academy Press, Washington, DC.
108 Wolman, Metabolism of Cities.
109 Matthews, E., et al (2000) *The Weight of Nations: Material Outflows from Industrial Economies*, World Resources Institute, Washington, DC; Girardet, H. (1992) *The Gaia Atlas of Cities: New Directions for Sustainable Urban Living*, Gaia (revised and republished in 1996 for UN-Habitat, New York).
110 www.urbanecology.org.au/.
111 McHarg, *Design with Nature*.
112 Design for nature is a distinguishing feature of net-positive design. Birkeland, *Positive Development*, p. xxii.
113 Mollison, B., and Holmgren, D. (1978) *Permaculture 1: A Perennial Agricultural System for Human Settlements*, Transworld Publishers, Melbourne.

86 *Design and Analysis*

114 E.g. see Mollison, B. (2002) Functional Analysis of the Chicken, in Birkeland, *Design for Sustainability*, p. 172.
115 Only vertical farming seems justifiable.
116 Yeang, K. (1995) *Designing with Nature: The Ecological Basis for Architectural Design*, McGraw-Hill, New York. This book was written as a thesis in the early 1970s.
117 See Chermayeff, S., and Alexander, C. (1963) *Community and Privacy*, Doubleday, New York.
118 The Vales were perhaps the first to build and quantify an autonomous house although they were proposed before then and energy autonomy was common in pioneer homes. Vale, B. (1972) *The Autonomous House*. University of Cambridge, Department of Architecture, Technical Research Division, Cambridge. Vale and Vale (1975) *The Autonomous House.*
119 At the neighborhood scale, Village Homes, in Davis California, was built on passive solar design principles. Conceived in the 1960s, construction began in 1975. www.villagehomesdavis.org/.
120 The Passivhaus movement, which began in Germany, has stringent energy efficiency standards. Many passive homes were built in the 1970s in the USA, perhaps mainly in response to the energy crisis.
121 The Regen Village project in Holland, Crystal Waters and Currumbin Eco-villages in Australia are examples of passive solar settlements that are essentially suburban. www.regenvillages.com/;. https://crystalwaters.org.au/; https://crystalwaters.org.au/.
122 Closed-loop design was popularized by McDonough and Braungart, *Cradle to Cradle*. For a synopsis, see Tibbs, Industrial Ecology, in *Design for Sustainability*, pp. 52–5.
123 Birkeland, J. (2012) Design Blindness in Sustainable Development: From Closed to Open Systems Design Thinking, *Journal of Urban Design* 17(2), pp. 163–87.
124 See n. 92 for details.
125 See n. 49 for details.
126 See n. 57 for details.

4 Sustainability and Positive Development Theory

4.1 Review and Preview

This chapter puts the old closed-system paradigm (still found in environmental problem descriptions and solutions), in historic context and proposes an alternative framework.

The previous chapter suggested how circular models in both technical (hard) and social (soft) orientations tend to limit goals to recycling and restoration. Closed-system concepts perpetuate incremental balancing processes in design and decision making that ultimately compromise the long-term public interest. This chapter looks at key components of closed-system frameworks (limits, boundaries and balance) in historical context, as revealed in government-level policy declarations. The environment still appears as a constraint on human development. This suggests that there have been few conceptual advances in sustainability thinking, at least at the public level. Therefore, a more open eco-logical and positive theory is introduced.

The ideal of 'balance' sounds positive but, in the context of socio-ecological imbalances, balancing processes are used to legitimize incremental losses and trade-offs.

Since the traditional linear growth model ignored the limits to growth (resources, energy and nature), circular models and methods seemed a logical way to curb unlimited growth. Closed-systems strategies can eliminate waste and increase efficiency. Recycling, exchange networks and efficiencies create jobs and profits. However, while reducing externalities and costs they conceal incremental losses of the life-support system. Recycling is not the same as creating eco-productive environments with socio-ecological benefits. Although circular systems are an essential part of the solution, a new designed-based approach is needed to guide investments in eco-productive systems solutions that benefit nature as well as society.

The basic components of closed-system thinking (limits, boundaries and balance) are seen throughout sustainability theories/literature – and work to reinforce the status quo.

This chapter looks at some representative sustainability policy declarations, from 1972 to the present, which under-represent ethics, ecology and built environment design. Government statements are naturally written to offend no one. However, they also avoid dealing with basic physical prerequisites of ecological sustainability and socio-economic justice. This chapter suggests that the closed-systems paradigm, although necessary in reducing negative impacts, cannot increase future options because of its focus on limits, boundaries and balance. It then summarizes PD theory.

88 *Design and Analysis*

Theory is important because, to the extent theory is ignored, practice will continue to be shaped by outdated, subliminal theories that contradict sustainability.

4.2 Limits to Growth and the 1972 UN Stockholm Conference

The 1972 UN Stockholm Environment Conference declared that development precedes environmental protection, and that countries had the right to exploit their environment.

The first major international environment conference led to the establishment of United Nations Environment Program (UNEP). It presumably represented the global position. Many of its pronouncements are still common today, the need to: maintain the earth's capacity to produce renewable resources and absorb pollution, assist developing nations in protecting their environment, and conduct rational, integrated planning to balance environment and development. It also declared that environmental policies should not limit development, as economic growth was supposedly necessary to improve the environment. States could over-exploit their own resources to the extent that this did not endanger the wellbeing of other states.[1]

Descriptions of the environmental crisis centered on the earth's finite surface area and its limited capacity to absorb pollution and provide natural resources.

Early environmental policy was largely concerned with 'sustainable yield'. Sustainable yield meant balancing the needs of future generations with the right of current generations to exploit resources. The solution was development that could meet competing demands through the 'wise use' of resources. Many conflated 'wise use' with allocating resources to their highest economic use. Even so, sustainable yield fueled debates between evidence-based and faith-based adversaries over whether limits were 'real', or if divine forces (i.e. markets, technologies or gods) would provide for future needs. Counter-balancing environmental degradation/depletion by expanding the natural environment to keep pace with consumption was not considered.[2]

The 'limits to growth' position was generally heard as threatening (demanding constraint), yet it did not call for changing the nature of growth.

The concern in early sustainability thought was the human health consequences of pollution and resource depletion, not ecological sustainability.[3] The emphasis on limits to growth or pollution/resources concentrates the mind on dead ends and makes many not want to think about the future. By analogy, if a beginning snowboarder stares at the cliff looming on the horizon, the board will head straight for it. Although the consequences that await beyond the cliff's edge are unknown, the force of inertia makes reversing direction not seem feasible. To novice snowboarders, the only alternatives appear to be stopping in their tracks or crashing.

4.3 Limits to Resources and the 1969 NEPA Legislation

The preamble to NEPA, 'the USA National Environmental Protection Act', introduced environmental impact assessment (EIA), which was meant to improve development decision making.

NEPA (1969) was an early national legislative response to excessive pollution, resource depletion, environmental degradation and biodiversity losses.[4] The preamble emphasized health and resources for future generations. It aimed to 'promote efforts which will prevent or eliminate damage to the environment and biosphere and stimulate the health and welfare of man'.[5] Its practical solution was to 'inform' decisions regarding environmental damage that results from development.[6] The EIA process required decision makers to consider the environmental impacts of major development approvals involving the federal government. It was hoped that this would improve the management culture in government bureaucracies.

NEPA relied on evidence-based, cross-disciplinary and participatory decision making, rather than changing the principles, regulations or institutional structures that shape the physical environment.

NEPA required development approval authorities to explain their reasoning and consider project alternatives. It did not, in itself, require design changes in response to the EIA process. Some thought the process might act as a Trojan Horse to shift the ubiquitous industrial-age ethos in government and industry. However, it accepted that decision makers would balance (trade-off) short-term socio-economic factors affecting individuals/stakeholders with long-term environmental issues affecting society as a whole. While the legislation forced the consideration of environmental impacts, it did not recognize that development could benefit the wider public and nature, except as a putative side-effect of economic growth.

NEPA stated principles that reappeared in most subsequent sustainability declarations, which generally express the aim of mitigating the bad and enhancing the good.

The following decision principles are common to most early definitions of sustainability. However, this was probably the first time they were endorsed at a national level and implemented by specific mandatory processes. This was followed rapidly by EIA legislation in several other countries. The US Congress, in adopting NEPA, acknowledged:

- The self-evident limits to resources
- Inter-generational equity (i.e. present-future)
- Intra-generational equity (local-foreign, rural-urban, rich-poor, etc.)
- Conservation of biological diversity and ecological integrity
- Recognition that environmental problems lack boundaries
- Multidisciplinary and participatory decision making

The legislation was 'process-forcing' (not outcome forcing), in that it established certain administrative procedures in development approval decisions, especially the scope of considerations.

Although some have described EIAs as 'action-forcing',[7] they did not really force physical actions or outcomes. Instead, EIAs manifested the common belief at the time that if the process is right the outcome will be right, because decision makers are rational and act for the common good.[8] (Box 3 reframes these same principles in a more action-oriented, design-based framework to illustrate the difference between following procedural norms and aiming for tangible outcomes.) In contrast, PD shifts the focus to substantive, not just procedural, standards. Actions are then compared to intentions and outcomes, not just adherence to rule-based processes [Chapters 7–8].

90 Design and Analysis

Although there was a backlash against the costs of compliance, EIAs spawned many advances in the ability to trace and quantify environmental flows/impacts.

EIAs were not intended to interfere in the discretion of government officials or developers – only to improve decision making. However, there was resistance by industry due to the time, costs and intellectual challenge that EIAs entailed, and a perceived imposition on business freedom/profits. Although EIAs were meant to be accessible, the growing weight of the documents was seen as disempowering to lay citizens, if not obfuscating. Ironically, they did not deal with limits, cumulative and regional impacts or consider positive impacts [Figure 4.1]. However, because EIAs required tracing the impacts of development, they fostered new analytical methods and tools.

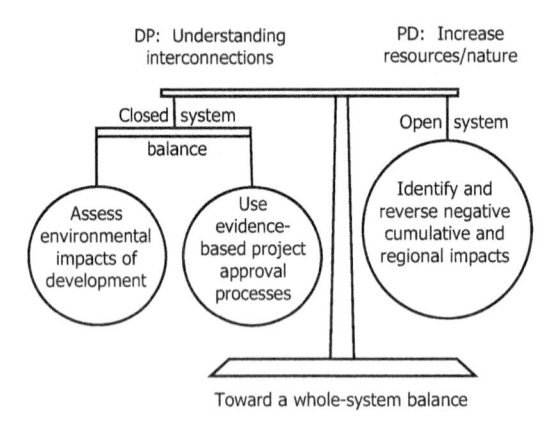

Figure 4.1 NEPA: Balancing resources and growth

4.4 Boundaries and the 1980 World Conservation Strategy

Early on, a common problem description was the borderless nature of environmental media and pollution, which suggested the need for establishing management boundaries.

In the 1970s, a central concern was that environmental protection laws and procedures were national in scope, whereas the oceans, Arctic and atmosphere were transnational and affected by the cross-border impacts of others. Similarly, shared resources within countries such as river basins, coastal areas and oceans needed to be managed through integrated, cross-sectoral management systems. Since only international laws and treaties could conserve certain threatened regions from exploitation or pollution, such as the Antarctic, conservation required the cooperation among world governments. It was not foreseen that international cooperation and environmental leadership might one day not be supported by 'advanced' nations.

In 1980, the 'World Conservation Strategy: Living resource conservation for sustainable development' (WCS), emphasized transboundary issues such as ecology, pollution and shared resources.

The WCS took a global view.[9] It emphasized improving life quality within the earth's regenerative capacity: 'the maintenance of essential ecological processes and life-support systems, the preservation of genetic diversity, and the sustainable utilization of species and ecosystems'. It attributed some of the growing environmental pressures to poverty in third-world nations and proposed policies to support their economic advancement. It also proposed procedural remedies to ensure 'compensation for damage to shared natural resources, and to persons in other countries that are harmed'.[10] Nonetheless, it implied that growth could protect the environment and wealth could compensate developing nations for resource exploitation.

By calling for living within the earth's carrying capacity, the WCS was a shift from the limits of growth/resources to 'limits of nature'.

Unlike some previous and subsequent academic/professional definitions of sustainability, the WCS regarded nature as living, not inert. In valuing other species and ecosystems, it recognized that human wellbeing depends on the ecological base, and presented a relatively eco-centric viewpoint. It did not inspire the kind of following from as many in the sustainable design fields that the technocratic spaceship earth metaphor had done [Chapter 3]. Nonetheless, the WCS greatly influenced the more well-known Brundtland Report or WCED in 1987. Despite these roots, the WCED shifted the emphasis from nature back to resources, and even implied that technology could ultimately replace nature.

The limits to nature position was positive, but implied that protecting and/or regenerating nature within areas left over by development would be sufficient.

The limits to nature were obvious long before extinction rates and ecosystem losses were formally quantified in 2005.[11] The WCS indicated that biodiversity could be preserved if humans reduced negative impacts, remediated the damage, and balanced the remaining undeveloped land for humans and nature. Since the 1980s, however, biodiversity has been lost at an explosive rate, due to transboundary pollutants, habitat losses, and so on.[12] Simply confining ecosystems to spaces left over by development is no longer adequate. Living 'within' the earth's ecological carrying capacity means little in a depleted, degraded environment, where each new development contributes additional environmental damage.

The emphasis of the WCS on ecological carrying capacity gained currency in some circles, but made little headway in public discourse and policy.

While the WCS emphasized boundaries, it did not address the problem of transboundary impacts that it noted. It simply called for more rational planning which, apparently, did not really happen. As in NEPA, a missing element was the potential of urban design to replace consumerism with a higher life quality and lower material flows.[13] Cities can provide for the spatial expansion of nature by, for example, reducing agricultural land through vertical farms. To preserve the natural environment, new ecological space must be created to support gene banks for gradually restoring the bioregions, not just sustaining remnants of the natural world.

The idea of protecting nature within geographic boundaries and compensating for environmental damage elsewhere was a good plan that passed its used-by date.

The WCS called for humans to recognize/respect natural boundaries [Figure 4.2]. However, the ability of society to manage nature was tested in an artificial enclosed microcosm called Biosphere II. This recreated natural ecosystems/eco-services to serve the needs of human settlements under geodesic domes. The project ended in 1991 in failure. There were many reasons for this, including personal issues that

92 Design and Analysis

develop between people confined in crowded spaces. In trying to mimic life on earth, however, it may have presaged the current situation of trying to survive on what some believe is the figurative knife edge of an irreversible tipping point.

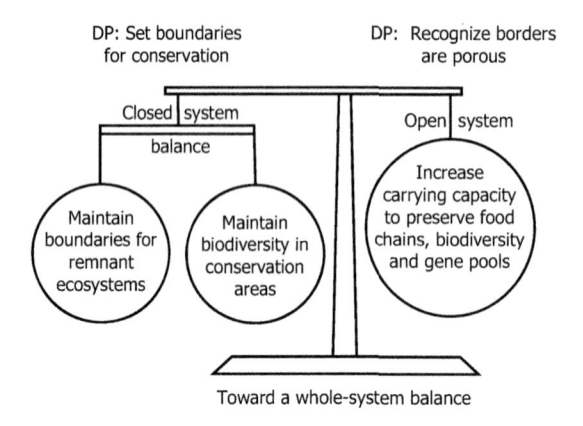

Figure 4.2 WCS (balancing land for people and nature)

4.5 Balance and the 1987 World Council for Environment and Development

The 'World Commission on Environment and Development' (WCED), known as the 'Brundtland Report' (1987), essentially redefined sustainability to fit into the mainstream worldview.

Few in the professions, academia or government had been across the earlier sustainability literature when the WCED arrived in 1987.[14] It put sustainability on the global agenda for a while. 'Sustainability' was soon attached as a prefix to established fields and agencies. However, their operative paradigms changed little.[15] The inclusion of wiggle words like 'mitigate', 'enhance' and 'balance' watered down any transformative conception of sustainability or of human responsibility.[16] This may partly explain why some academics saw sustainability as a passing fad.[17] The WCED has often been proclaimed as heralding the grassroots sustainability movement but, in reality, it sidelined ecology.

The WCED was an attempt to make sustainability acceptable to leaders of rich and poor nations, but focused on resource distribution, not the environment.

Nature preservation and pollution reduction had been seen by some leaders in disadvantaged nations as only benefitting privileged nations. Many even saw it as a threat to their country's right to catch up materially. While the WCED made sustainability a household word, it lost the earlier concern for ecological carrying capacity. It imposed a definition of sustainability used by most professionals and academics today: 'development that meets the needs of the present

Sustainability and Positive Development Theory 93

without compromising the needs of future generations to meet their own needs'. This not only marginalized ecology but assumed existing institutional structures and processes could make sustainability happen.

Despite being an impressive political achievement, the WCED narrowed sustainability to mean resource distribution, and largely omitted environmental ethics, ecology and environmental design.

The WCED was essentially a return to sustainable yield and interest balancing.[18] Like NEPA, it offered no viable plan for the preservation of wilderness or even resources, and even suggested that it sufficed if humans merely 'understand' their impact. Further, it implicitly endorsed the economic concept of the 'substitutability' of nature.[19] Substitutability means that future generations can be left with the 'means of production' (farms, forests, factories, fisheries and fossil fuels) in lieu of the 'means of survival' – nature.[20] Equitable distribution of resources, were it to happen, would not ensure the sustainability of the ecology or economy in itself.

The WCED suggested that environmental quality and fair distribution of resources could be achieved by increasing GDP and efficiency while reducing relative impacts.

Earlier UN environmental conferences/reports had presumed that environmental protection must be preceded by economic advancement (meaning resource consumption).[21] Likewise, the WCED called for more economic growth – as measured by GDP.[22] This ignored how economic accounting systems were implicated in most sustainability problems and failed markedly in achieving economic fairness, social equity or environmental conservation.[23] Further, the WCED saw equity as more an economic issue than a biophysical design problem. Instead of redesigning human systems to fit ecological realities then, it redefined 'sustainability' as democracy in consumption and relied on traditional management and government levers and pulleys (called 'weak sustainability').[24]

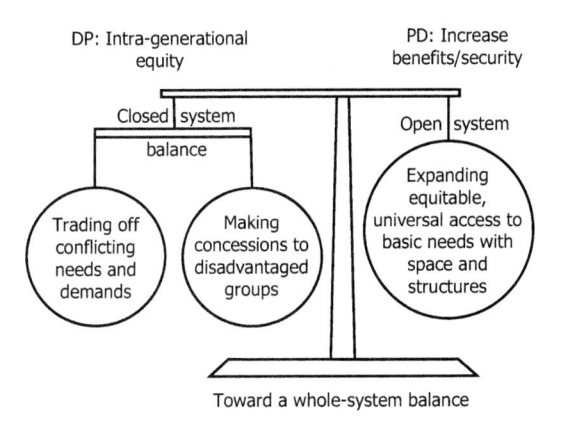

Figure 4.3 WCED: Balancing benefits and burdens of growth

94 Design and Analysis

The WCED supplanted the more optimistic WCS conception of sustainability with the idea of adopting better policies and decisions through existing socio-economic conventions.

With the WCED, sustainability became equated with meeting competing human material needs, primarily through economics-based structures and tools [Figure 4.3]. These are good at dividing the pie among competing interests, but not expanding and diversifying the pie. If the wise use of resources and accommodating a broader range of values/interests in economic development was a 'new' goal, then governments had never honored their 'social contract'.[25] Moreover, the WCED gave many the impression that the government/corporate sector now had sustainability issues under control. Thus, while sustainability became mainstreamed, it lost its transformative edge. Currently, ecological sustainability seems barely on the agenda.

4.6 Government Declarations and Policies Concerning Urban Development

The WCED led to 'Agenda 21' which enlisted the participation of community groups in conservation activity, but also diverted effort/attention from global issues.

Major UN declarations on sustainability followed the WCED approach that added specificity, targets and indicators, but did not advance upon the idea of sustainability itself. As a follow on from the WCED, the Rio Declaration and 'Agenda 21', was announced at a UN Earth Summit in 1992 and endorsed by 178 governments.[26] It called for the engagement of local governments and community volunteers in sustainable development. Community-based cooperation and action in conjunction with government gave hope to many. Some, however, saw this action agenda as offloading responsibility from authorities. Conversely, others saw it as part of an international anti-human conspiracy.[27]

After another major UN conference, the Millennium Summit in 2000, sustainable development targets were adopted which were intended to be achieved by 2015.

'Millennium development goals' were adopted that concerned the usual sustainability issues (sanitation, water, child mortality, environmental quality, gender equality, poverty, education, etc.), but were somewhat lacking in ecological sustainability and community participation.[28] In 2010, another major UN conference led to a global action plan to accelerate progress towards those goals. While calling for environmental quality, however, there was little on sustainable cities and buildings, apart from affordable housing. In 2015, Agenda 2030 reaffirmed the principles of the Rio Declaration and promulgated new Sustainable Development Goals (SDGs).[29] These 17 goals fell under the themes of 'people, planet, prosperity, peace, and partnership'.

Like the sustainable development goals, most national and state government sustainability policies have tended to marginalize urban design and ecology (the biophysical dimension).

Sustainability policies at the urban scale generally rely on economic levers and pulleys, not physical design solutions. This can be illustrated by a representative document, an Australian 'Smart Cities Plan' (2016).[30] 'Smart' is now often used in lieu of sustainability and often mainly concerns 'business sustainability'. This 'plan' was, typically, a position paper, with the usual references to 'striking a balance' between the public interest in health, environment and resource security, versus individual/corporate entitlements to exploitation. Moreover, it framed regulation as a problem or an impediment to 'compromising the needs of future generations to meet the current demands of business'.

A 'Smart Cities Plan' exemplifies many government and corporate vision statements which omit design and are almost the opposite of the PD Test.

- *'Reduce development assessment processing time and inconsistencies so that we strike the right balance between appropriate quality, sustainability and safety standards and responsiveness to housing supply and affordability.'* Decoded, the above provision translates to: 'the supply, quality and affordability of housing is increased by transferring more land and resources to development interests who may, in turn, lower costs by increasing sales'. It proposes watering down design and assessment processes, not redesigning development approval systems to make them more relevant to implementing sustainability, while being more efficient and effective. Where design is left out, sustainability/safety and supply/affordability are often put in a zero-sum relationship that can only be balanced. In a return to the era of the 1972 Stockholm Convention, it paints sustainability as something to be traded off.
- *'Subject planning and zoning rules to a public interest test to ensure the benefits of restrictions to the community outweigh the costs.'* This language treats planning and zoning as being bureaucratic restrictions that impose upon the 'community' (business). It also has a 'public interest test' that deftly equates business (private profits) with the public interest. This is convergent with a trickle-down theory, and is couched in terms of balancing costs and benefits. Unlike the Stockholm Convention, however, it does not state that those aggrieved should be compensated. Basically, it equates freedom to do harm with freedom from being harmed. The provision can be read as: 'urban planning is against the public interest when it restricts or imposes obligations on the business community'.

The New Urban Agenda, or 'UN Habitat III' (2016) is an international statement calling for improvements in urban policy, governance, planning and financing.

The New Urban Agenda (NUA) states a four-pronged approach:[31] (a) development of policies for sustainable integrated urban development; (b) stronger urban governance that empowers and includes urban stakeholders and promotes predictability, social inclusion, economic growth and environmental protection; (c) more long-term, integrated urban and territorial planning and spatial design; and (d) effective financing frameworks 'to create, sustain and share the value generated by sustainable urban development in an inclusive manner'. This is inspirational, but similar policy planning, management and financing mechanisms have failed to improve the environment and social equity. Some representative statements illustrate how balancing is regarded as strategy.

> 'We will implement integrated planning that aims to balance short-term needs with long-term desired outcomes of a competitive economy, high quality of life, and sustainable environment. We will also strive to build in flexibility in

our plans in order to adjust to changing social and economic conditions over time.'

This section suggests a balance between profit, people and planet can be achieved through 'integrated planning'. However, this is not defined, or distinguished from earlier uses of the term that have not proven operational.[32] The document emphasizes 'flexible planning' to accommodate the social and economic change that has resulted from market determinism, not structures that can adapt to change. It does not mention how cities might be redesigned to reverse growing social inequities and/or biodiversity losses. That is, it recommends that plans be responsive to socio-economic pressures, rather than that built environments be adaptable to climatic, ecological and social change.

> 'We will promote planned urban extensions, infill, prioritizing renewal, regeneration, and retrofitting of urban areas, as appropriate, including upgrading of slums and informal settlements, providing high-quality buildings and public spaces, promoting integrated and participatory approaches involving all relevant stakeholders and inhabitants, avoiding spatial and socio-economic segregation and gentrification, while preserving cultural heritage and preventing and containing urban sprawl.'

This section calls for opposite forms of growth simultaneously, such as urban infill/densification along with urban expansion or 'planned urban extensions'.[33] Apparently the hope is that 'sensitive' growth in all directions will lead to more balanced growth. Like most urban sustainability declarations which balance competing policies, it does not suggest how urban planning might work to resolve these basic contradictions. Balancing competing growth strategies to expand inward and outward does not question how different planning strategies/methods might enable better decisions and designs, or refer to studies that do. Further, it considers neither degrowth nor an increase in the ecological base.[34]

While a clarion call, such policy plans and declarations do not discuss why these policies should work now when they did not previously.

NUA appears to favor exchange and incentive-based approaches over regulation. Regulations traditionally define and enforce behavior, while incentives reward business initiatives.[35] However, incentives are hit and miss, and rely on (volatile) markets, which is akin to gambling. While markets are efficient in reducing prices (not reducing net resource consumption), the costs of market failures in the socio-ecological spheres have been incalculable. On the other hand, there are many valid arguments for also seeking non-legislative means to protect the environment. For example, legislatures are subject to powerful interest groups and (sometimes corrupting) campaign financing. Moreover, environmental protections can simply be reversed.

Both regulations and incentives need to be redesigned to over-compensate for the indirect and cumulative impacts of waste, environmental damage and social inequities.

Environmental damage prevention saves lives or increases people's life expectancy. Therefore, it cannot fairly be portrayed as an infringement on rights, especially where the savings are used to compensate those that are disadvantaged by regulations. Nonetheless, conventional regulations or market-based tools cannot keep pace with socio-ecological problems, since they only offset negative impacts, instead of creating net-positive ones. Sustainability therefore requires the redesign of physical and institutional structures on positive principles. Existing regulations, policies and tools could be assessed according to whether they reflect the legacy of negative concepts and assumptions or question existing practices. Some clues are, do they:

- Portray sustainability as 'sustainable supply' of resources, presupposing that the wise use of natural resources is enough to preserve the life-support system?
- See nature as a source of materials and sink for wastes that only becomes a problem when waste exceeds nature's assimilative capacity?
- Assume that nature, within its current reserves or reservations, can be made resilient enough to withstand external pressures, interventions, depletion and pollution?
- Presume that better policies can lead to sustainable development without a paradigm shift to guide the redesign of institutional and biophysical structures?
- Rely on strategies implicitly aligned with an economic ideology that caused the sustainability crisis – without a vision for actual biophysical sustainability?
- Trust that a change in societal values and better information through electoral politics and social movements will lead automatically to behavior change?
- Accept the idea that incentives for businesses and firms will spontaneously lead to systems that achieve more than efficiency, recycling and trade-offs?
- Suggest that inter-generational equity is met where future generations are left with merely the 'means of production' in lieu of nature (substitution)?
- Subscribe to the traditional idea that a strong economy will trickle down and lead people to choose sustainability over survivalism and hoarding?
- Assume better management within given institutions will lead to better decisions, without recalibrating technical methods and tools to align with sustainability goals?
- Convey the idea that sustainability and nature preservation only require more effort by government agencies and volunteer community organizations (i.e. palliative care)?

The next section outlines PD theory, after first distinguishing two current (closed-system) approaches to sustainability, represented by simplified diagrams that emphasize their differences.

4.7 Three Differing Models of Sustainability

The mainstream donut model (wise use of resources, waste reduction, fair resource distribution) relies on private and public sector goodwill, generosity and rationality.

The traditional view of sustainability, as represented by government declarations (above) portrayed society as bounded by limits to growth and resources (tipping points). It assumed that the environment could be sustained if a balance of inputs and outputs was achieved through efficiencies, recycling and closing resource loops. This remains the general view in sustainability today – redirecting investment toward the common good rather than growth at any costs [Figure 4.4].[36] As

98 *Design and Analysis*

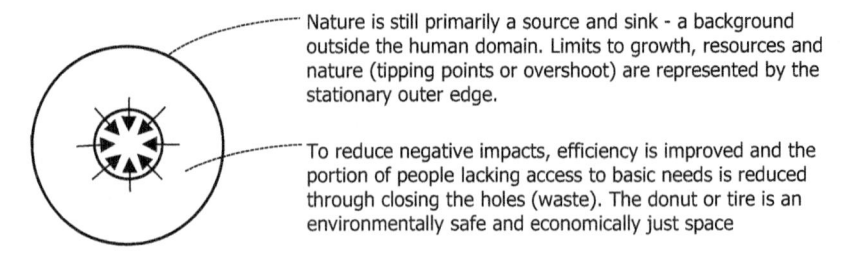

- Nature is still primarily a source and sink - a background outside the human domain. Limits to growth, resources and nature (tipping points or overshoot) are represented by the stationary outer edge.
- To reduce negative impacts, efficiency is improved and the portion of people lacking access to basic needs is reduced through closing the holes (waste). The donut or tire is an environmentally safe and economically just space

Figure 4.4 Mainstream donut model

expressed in the recently christened donut model,[37] no one need be in the hole (deprivation) if society lives within the donut (within planetary limits).[38] This is still basically efficiency.

***The part-earth** model (reserving half the earth's land and water surface for wilderness) provides a target and helps people to grasp the challenge.*

Current proposals for either dispersed or concentrated cities fail to offer means to preserve or increase the ecological base or public estate in real terms, because of their reliance upon incremental either/or decision making. Therefore, some advocate developing only half the earth's surface,[39] or limiting cities to current boundaries.[40] Even if half the earth's surface was reserved for the remaining 50% biodiversity by fencing off development, investment in different kinds of urban design might not occur. Just as the 'limits to growth' argument licensed environmental depletion/degradation up to a limit, urban boundaries would license more destruction within a spatial limit.

*A **whole-earth** model would improve social and environmental justice but also redesign cities to conform with their bioregions and return land/water to wilderness.*

A half-earth image suggests specific limits to growth and resources [Figure 4.5].[41] In arguing for a bigger nature reserve and living within the human carrying capacity of half the planet, however, it is similar to the WCS (above). It assumes that sustainability can be achieved through technological innovation, driven by regulations, technology and markets. It is unclear why these approaches would begin to work now. Further, geographical borders can be reversed by politicians, just as environmental protections were reversed recently in the USA.[42] Instead, a whole-earth approach, as represented by Figure 4.6, could be more politically realistic than setting limits.

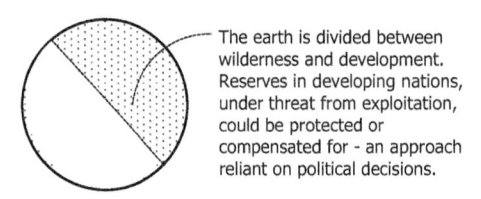

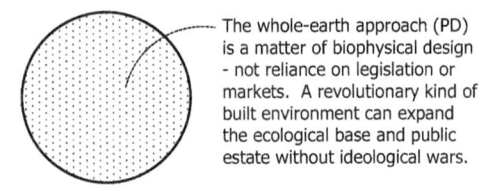

- The earth is divided between wilderness and development. Reserves in developing nations, under threat from exploitation, could be protected or compensated for - an approach reliant on political decisions.
- The whole-earth approach (PD) is a matter of biophysical design - not reliance on legislation or markets. A revolutionary kind of built environment can expand the ecological base and public estate without ideological wars.

Figure 4.5 Part-earth model

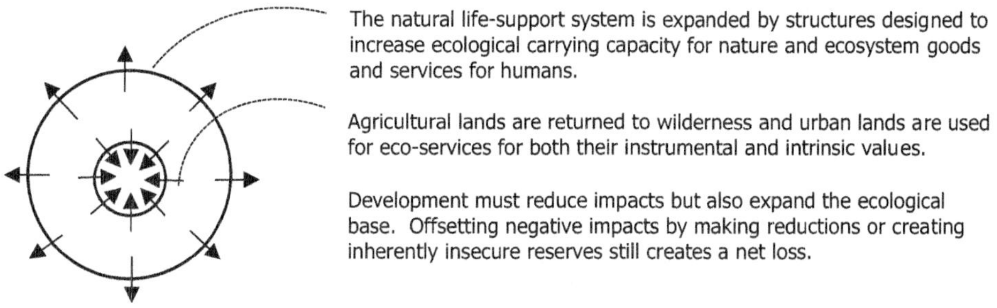

Sustainability and Positive Development Theory 99

The natural life-support system is expanded by structures designed to increase ecological carrying capacity for nature and ecosystem goods and services for humans.

Agricultural lands are returned to wilderness and urban lands are used for eco-services for both their instrumental and intrinsic values.

Development must reduce impacts but also expand the ecological base. Offsetting negative impacts by making reductions or creating inherently insecure reserves still creates a net loss.

Figure 4.6 Whole-earth model

4.8 Positive Development Theory in Shorthand

PD examines why environmental governance, planning, decision making and design are currently 'negative', and suggests conceptual, methodological and institutional reforms, not just policies.

Using an open-systems lens, PD provides a prism for deconstructing the negative-fatalistic, reductionist-dualistic thought patterns in mainstream development planning and decision making [Figure 4.7]. Critiques of system biases are often paradoxically seen as signs of negativity, while so-called positive viewpoints often avoid critique. However, identifying new pathologies and diagnoses requires different frameworks. Being profitable, built environment design can bypass socio-political barriers to create environments that solve most/many sustainability issues. Urban design can increase the

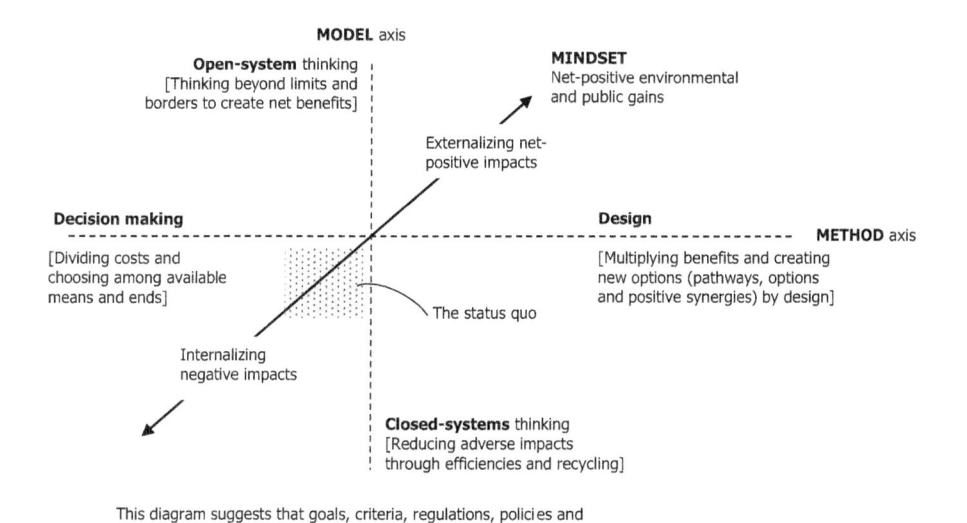

MODEL axis

Open-system thinking
[Thinking beyond limits and borders to create net benefits]

MINDSET
Net-positive environmental and public gains

Externalizing net-positive impacts

Decision making
[Dividing costs and choosing among available means and ends]

Design
[Multiplying benefits and creating new options (pathways, options and positive synergies) by design]

METHOD axis

The status quo

Internalizing negative impacts

Closed-systems thinking
[Reducing adverse impacts through efficiencies and recycling]

This diagram suggests that goals, criteria, regulations, policies and design solutions can be located along a continuum from current negative or zero-sum choices to positive means and ends.

Figure 4.7 Positive Development theory

100 *Design and Analysis*

natural life-support system, create eco-positive environments that reverse ecological losses, improve everyone's health, wellbeing and life opportunities, reduce apparent disparities of wealth and increase future options.

4.8.1 Models of Reality: From Closed- to Open-systems Thinking

A shift from closed-system models that reduce negative impacts using efficiency and recycling strategies – to open-systems design that externalize positive public benefits.

Key features of closed systems are reductionism (a telescopic/microscopic view) and use of system boundaries. In the closed-system view, systems are analyzed as interconnected networks or nested hierarchies. These express linkages between systems or components, but focus on exchange at system borders. Closed-system models lead logically to methods geared to exchange/transactional relationships, and aim for balance or net zero impacts. Hence, this view aligns with input-output and cost-benefit analyses. Circular solutions in urban systems are limited to reducing/internalizing negative impacts (through efficiencies, recycling and, closing loops) with added urban amenities/greenery. Though important, these insular approaches are only half the solution.

4.8.2 Mindsets: From Negative (Do No Harm) to Positive (Doing Net Good)

A shift from a limited rights-based ethic, or 'do no harm' – to improving society-wide conditions by creating eco-positive social and ecological environments.

The dominant rights-based ethic, where negative actions are constrained by other's rights/territory, only limits harmful actions to one's property. Defensive mindsets lead to a focus on limits and threats which foster selfish responses/reactions. This does not inspire development that gives back more than it takes. 'Positive' systems (versus net-positive ones) have relatively good outcomes – better than the past. However, they do not pass the PD Test (expanding the public estate and ecological base to increase adaptability, resilience and future public choice). Ecologically net positive means an increase in ecological carrying capacity beyond pre-historic/pre-urban conditions to over-compensate for cumulative impacts.

4.8.3 Methods: from Decision- to Design-Based Strategies and Processes

A shift from decision-based methods and tools that simplify and compare choices or divide costs – to design-based approaches that multiply public choices/benefits.

The dominance of linear-reductionist binary decision making (choosing) over design (synthesis, symbiosis and synergy) has created a cultural lobotomy. Decision making requires closed-system frameworks to simplify choices, divide burdens-benefits and/or compare alternative plans, policies or actions, often through a process of elimination. While decision frameworks help in assessing existing or foreseeable choices and find the best available practice or product, design envisions environments/products that do not yet exist. Design aims for multiplier/spillover effects that increase symbiotic relationships, often at a saving. Hence, PD aims to counterbalance reductionist, dualistic methods and exchange processes with design-based ones that create net public benefits.

4.8.4 Metrics: From Counting the Costs to Assessing Net Benefits

A shift from quantifying flows at borders which exclude complex cumulative or remote impacts – to transboundary methods that look at whole-systems flows.

The built environment could be designed to increase space for nature and the public in lifecycle and global terms. This requires assessing design against fixed biophysical standards. PD uses metrics that aim to assess the net benefits of multifunctional design. While typical multicriteria analyses only assess reductions in negative impacts, PD tools help to expose negative impacts and net gains that are not currently counted. These include tools: for community planning via SMARTmode (*Positive Development*, 2008);[43] for development of briefs and design criteria/review via the eDR [Chapters 13–14] and; for collaborative design and quantitative assessment via the STARfish [Chapters 15–16].

4.9 Conclusion

Mainstream sustainable development has aimed to set limits and then aspire toward more equal resource consumption, but this cannot happen without systems redesign.

Both the destruction of the natural environment and disparities of wealth are much greater today than imagined 50 years ago when sustainability legislation and government programs began. Nonetheless, in general, sustainable development relies on policies that set limits on damage, reduce consumption and/or work toward equalizing consumption. The element of design, or spatial and structural dimension, is largely missing (or confused with efficiency, recycling and closing loops). Restoration/regeneration is seen as optimal. Hence, we see (futile) efforts to implement:

- Regulatory processes that require offsets of some of the damage through ecological restoration at the sources of extraction, but do not give back to nature.
- Manufacturing processes that fabricate building components more efficiently or effectively, but do not replace mechanical equipment (requiring more regular maintenance/replacement) with passive or natural systems.
- Recycling processes that use waste as a resource, but still increase overall embodied waste each time they are remanufactured and often do not even upcycle.
- Construction methods that use less energy and resources relative to typical buildings, accepted practices or prior site conditions, but do not provide additional public benefits.
- Urban form that occupies less land by constricting urban boundaries, but does not reduce ecological impacts outside those urban areas during the resource extraction processes.

Such strategies are a part of the mix, but they only aim for less bad or zero. The other side of the coin is eco-positive design that creates positive trickle-up effects. There are no limits to positive impacts and synergies that can be created by design.

Circular, bounded models can enable material and energy savings within (largely unenforceable) limits, but only design can create net benefits, diversity and choice.

The circular model might once have sufficed, had the limits, boundaries and balance of nature not been outstripped. Depicting humans-nature relationships in circular diagrams and mandalas is heuristic, charting flows of energy, carbon or materials through production systems to find waste and close loops is strategic. However, if the goal is still just to divide up and use more resources expeditiously and equitably, and to define and limit the responsibilities of those given access to those resources, nothing has changed. The constitution of physical and institutional systems themselves must change, if development is to generate net ecological and social benefits.

4.10 Exercises

1. Using a case study from a green building council, critique a highly ranked sustainable building in terms of its social and ecological as well as environmental impacts. To what extent has it compensated or offset its share of the total impacts of buildings in the region? This depends on currently available data, so assumptions must be clearly stated. What data are available and what are not?
2. Most green buildings greatly reduce carbon emissions and energy usage. Thus far, however, most design has been aimed at post-construction impacts such as the use of energy and water during building operation. Survey developers and designers to ask what they do to avoid pre-construction impacts at the sites of resource extraction, or if their suppliers provide information about impacts throughout the chain of custody?
3. Examine one or more of the declarations or action proposals discussed in the chapter from NEPA (1969), WCS (1980), WCED (1987), UNCED (1992), NUA (2016) (or other comparable policy statements) against the list provided above of commonly held assumptions that characterize the DP.
4. Challenge PD theory and send class critique to janis.birkeland@unimelb.edu.au for a considered response.

Box 3 Reframing sustainability principles as positive design challenges

Sustainability principles that form the basis of built environment decision and design tools can be converted from value statements to action-oriented design objectives that, if operationalized, would have positive biophysical outcomes. Basic sustainability 'headlines' are drawn from the preamble to the USA National Environmental Protection Act (1969): an early governmental statement on sustainability (which suggests that there have been few conceptual advances since). However, these principles are applied to design and reframed here in the positive tense. They aim for planning and design that increase the ecological base, public estate and future options. General performance standards are also suggested.

Inter-generational equity: Urban environments should provide future generations safe, healthy and eco-productive environments, not just leave enough capital and/or industry to meet future economic needs.

Sustainability has often been represented as preserving basic necessities for future generations, rather than leaving them more life quality opportunities and environmental benefits than people have today. Popular interpretations of sustainability often fail to recognize that the planet itself is a basic need (including its ecosystems, biodiversity and wilderness). These basic survival needs are not created by economic growth and, clearly, natural environments are not protected when economies are booming. Inter-generational equity thus requires affirmative design to reduce environmental crises/risks from natural or man-made disasters. Design should create the most public benefits with least public resources. To achieve inter-generational equity:

- *Security*: Design should proactively increase public security, improve health, sequester carbon, produce renewable resources and energy, and create positive ecological impacts. The worse-case scenario should determine the investment in preventing future environmental crises/risks (such as costs of inaction).
- *Adaptability*: Design should use adaptable, demountable, interchangeable or biodegradable building components that can be easily modified in response to unexpected change. The future costs of upgrading designs to a sustainability standard should be considered in development assessment processes.
- *Future choice*: Design should ensure that the means of production (industry) does not replace nature – means of survival ('substitutability'). Future generations should have the same or greater range of responsible life opportunities, including experiencing ecological and cultural heritage.

Intra-generational equity: Developments should alleviate inequities between privileged and disadvantaged groups/regions, since injustices resulting from political-economic and physical development systems are 'social constructions' (not natural/inevitable).

Built environments are a form of inherited wealth that shapes class identity and individual destiny. Rich-poor and north-south relationships are shaped by global political/market structures that have entrenched systemic economic power imbalances. However, low-cost built environments in disadvantaged regions could provide residents with direct universal access to basic needs, along with public social spaces/facilities for self-help socio-economic development. Aid in the form of sustainable, low-cost built environments can pay for themselves eventually (whereas charity may not literally pay back). Developments should improve the whole community, respect cultural heritage/identity and sense of place, and foster responsible lifestyles. To achieve intra-generational equity:

- *Distribution*: Design should offset unavoidable impacts by creating sustainable built environments in socio-economically deprived regions. Government investment in trading schemes and incentives that benefit disadvantaged communities should consider the future costs of environmental refugees and problems of migration.
- *Equity*: Design should reduce the impacts of disparities of wealth and consumption within/between urban areas, and slavery in the supply

chain, distribute urban amenities and provide each neighborhood its share of social space in proportion to population density.
- *Opportunity*: Design should improve social conditions in the surrounding area. Where projects promise jobs, the value and quality of jobs should be considered in relation to resources used and the relative value of alternative land and/or resource uses.

Recognition of resource limits: *Built environments should create the space, conditions and biological systems to regenerate natural environments and regrow the (equivalent) materials that the developments use.*

For decades, the limits to resources argument was met by volitional statements that the 'technological fix would come'. For example, a safe means for storing nuclear waste has been 'just around the corner' for over 50 years. Even renewable energy involves mined materials, but self-perpetuating 'biological' resources could potentially provide net-positive benefits. For example: fungi can remove environmental toxins and grow building materials; algae can produce fuels; bacteria can operate solar cells; worms can convert waste to fertile soil, and so on. Bio-based building products could replace industrial materials, but these are under-examined. To recognize the limits to natural resources:

- *Fertility*: Design should support appropriate eco-productive systems that grow back the equivalent resources used in construction, including soil (e.g. vertical composting systems) and urban areas should provide the amount of vegetables that are needed by the urban population.
- *Reversibility*: Design should ensure that development does not exceed global rates of consumption (let alone cause permanent destruction) and should be evaluated in terms of reversibility, given that development closes off future land use options and public choices.
- *Resource share*: Design should not remove natural resources from socio-economically deprived regions if their resources cannot satisfy future needs, or if the recipient development far exceeds its 'environmental space' (the total available world resources divided by the global population).

Conservation of ecological diversity and integrity: *Urban and rural development should support vertical agriculture and ecosystem/biodiversity reserves, as well as take actions to return degraded rural land to wilderness.*

Development that irreversibly damages the environment causes public costs even if the impacts are not yet visible (thus representing 'unjust enrichment'). Conservation is impossible if shrinking reserves are subject to exogenous forces such as pollution, feral species and indirect interference. Although humans lack the knowledge to recreate wilderness or biodiversity, multifunctional ecological spaces in buildings/landscapes can contribute public/private functions, socio-economic benefits and ecological restoration. Vertical (vegetable) farming in rural and/or urban areas could free up land for regenerative or protection purposes, while urban biodiversity incubators can produce (small) ecosystems to reseed the bioregions. To preserve biological diversity and ecological integrity:

- *Eco-services*: Design should produce built-in eco-services and urban biodiversity habitats. As a rule of thumb, the volume of ecological space in new urban development in cubic meters should aim to exceed the gross floor area in square meters.
- *Cumulative impacts*: Design should over-compensate for the past and ongoing development that has caused ecological degradation, by supporting ecological gains that are proportionately greater than the rate of ecological losses in the region/planet (i.e. create a net-positive ecological footprint).
- *Offsetting*: Design should contribute to the ecological restoration of the regions by using net-positive offsetting systems, where direct onsite ecological gains are not feasible. Net-positive biodiversity offsetting should return degraded land to wilderness, rather than simply remediate damage.

Recognition that environmental problems lack boundaries: Built environments affect virtually all sustainability issues (which are borderless), so they should have positive onsite/offsite impacts that anticipate environmental change and uncertainty.

It was once cliché to say that environmental problems and development impacts have no boundaries. However, most urban analyses continue to balance inputs and outputs at project or property boundaries – creating artificial divisions to enable arithmetic. Therefore, solutions still largely focus on internalizing negative impacts or closing loops. While essential, reduction and efficiency constitute only a partial solution. In addition to reducing total resource/energy flows over the project lifecycle to near zero waste, urban developments will need to support their cities and bioregions by contributing positive socio-ecological impacts beyond their geographical borders. To understand the environment as lacking boundaries:

- *Positive externalities*: Design should aim to use adaptable and multifunctional design so developments can adjust to changing circumstances and generate net-positive public benefits. Buildings should be designed for retrofitting. Flexible design is not the same as flexible (negotiable) rules.
- *Time and energy*: Design should aim to reduce total resource/energy flows over a development's lifecycle and lifespan. Energy and resource usage should be assessed relative to public need, recognizing that some uses/functions are inherently wasteful or anti-social, even if efficient.
- *Full costs*: Design should prioritize renewable and passive energy systems (e.g. microbial fuel cells, algae-based fuels) before considering industrial equipment. When comparing costs of natural and mechanical systems, future maintenance, repair and replacement of equipment needs to be considered.

Interdisciplinary and participatory decision making: Urban planning/design should incorporate interdisciplinary, collaborative and participatory processes that begin from agreed ethical principles to ensure developments meet societal needs and values.

The involvement of immediate building users/stakeholders in development is often a given as they are the clients. Interdisciplinary and participatory processes that include community groups have been best practice in urban planning for decades. Urban design is a conflict resolution mechanism that can meet competing public and private needs/interests, not just provide means of dividing goods/benefits among stakeholders. Community engagement activity has often focused on dampening the objections to win-lose decisions, or making trade-offs (interest balancing) – rather than ethics. In such cases, the outcomes of consultation and compromise can mirror power imbalances. To foster trans-disciplinary and participatory decision making:

- *Ethics-based*: Design should fully integrate the ethical dimension into decision and design processes as the built environment shapes relationships. As suggested by the PD SMARTmode process, a constitutional framework can help to ensure substantive and procedural due process.
- *Optimization*: Design should accommodate all interests (present-future, public-private, nature-people) by exploring design alternatives that not only meet client needs and preferences but meet the PD Test (i.e. not just use economics-based tools that compare, choose or trade-off positions).
- *Assessment*: Designs should be assessed by community-expert panels. However, juries should be impaneled where there are irresolvable disputes, or major projects, and include a consideration of both ecological space (ecological compensation) and environmental space (per capital resource/space consumption).

Notes

1 What stays within property lines is still generally considered to 'do no harm'.
2 If there is evidence to the contrary, contact Janis.lynn.birkeland@gmail.com.
3 Norton, B. G. (2005) *Sustainability: A Philosophy of Adaptive Ecosystem Management*, University of Chicago Press, Chicago, IL.
4 NEPA, National Environmental Policy Act of 1969, 91st United States Congress. It concerned the quality of the 'human' environment.
5 Back then, 'Man' presumed to represent different generations, classes, regions, genders and races, at least to the extent they accepted the white male European culture.
6 Earlier legislation established reserves or parks and the like, but did not affect development decision making. Many countries have enacted impact assessment processes.
7 Although certain processes must be followed, this requires administrative processes, not physical action.
8 Simon, H. A. (1957) *Models of Man Social and Rational: Mathematical Essays on Rational Human Behavior in a Social Setting*, J. Wiley & Sons, New York.
9 IUCN/UNEP/WWF (1980) *World Conservation Strategy*, republished 1991 as *Caring for the Earth: A Strategy for Sustainable Living*, IUCN (The World Conservation Union), UNEP (United Nations Environment Program) and WWF (World Wide Fund for Nature), Earthscan, London.
10 *World Conservation Strategy*, p. 6. See also COAG (1992) *The National Strategy for Ecologically Sustainable Development* (NSESD), Council of Australian Governments, Canberra.
11 Millennium Ecosystem Assessment Program (2005) *Ecosystems and Human Well-being: Our Human Planet – Summary for Decision-makers*, Island Press, Washington, DC. Species extinctions are now estimated to be about 1,000 times greater than normal.

12 Over 50% of global biodiversity has been lost in under 50 years according to the World Wildlife Foundation. See www.theguardian.com/environment/2014/sep/29/earth-lost-50-wildlife-in-40-years-wwf.
13 Resort-like environments can obviate the need for material luxuries.
14 Brundtland, G. H. (1987) *Report of the World Commission on Environment and Development: Our Common Future*, United Nations General Assembly, Oslo. The World Council on Environment and Development was formed in 1983.
15 Ecological economics sees economics as being about the environment, whereas environmental economics usually fits environment within an economic framework.
16 In the 1970s I wrote urban design and planning policies and was asked to add 'mitigate' or 'enhance' before statements to avoid committing anyone to action.
17 I was told by several colleagues in the mid-1990s that sustainability was out of date and that 'we are now into post-modernism'.
18 Until the 1960s, there were very few if any writings on sustainability that were not really about sustainable 'yield' (the instrumental value to humans). See Wall, D. (1994) *Green History: A Reader in Environmental Literature, Philosophy and Politics*, Routledge, London.
19 Substitutability implies that natural resources can be sacrificed as long as human capital or welfare is increased.
20 Brundtland, *Report*, p. 45.
21 At the first major international conference on the environment, United Nations Conference on the Human Environment, in Stockholm (June 1972) the general view was that growth was necessary in order to fund improvements to the environment. In this century, the UN Millennium Goals still include GDP as an indicator.
22 The WCED called for growth in GDP, but see Perrings, C., and Ansuategi, A. (2000) Sustainability, Growth and Development, *Journal of Economic Studies* 27(½), pp. 19–54.
23 Saunders, C., and Dalziel, P. (2017) Twenty-Five Years of Counting for Nothing: Waring's Critique of National Accounts, *Feminist Economics* 23(2), pp. 200–18.
24 Weak sustainability has been defined as accepting that nature can be substituted for by technology (leaving out ecological sustainability). See Turner, R. K. (ed.) (1993) *Sustainable Environmental Economics and Management: Principles and Practice*, Belhaven Press, London.
25 The 'social contract' suggests that governments have power only because citizens have agreed to devolve power to them.
26 UNCED (1992) *Earth Summit 1992: United Nations Conference on Environment and Development, Rio de Janeiro*, Regency Press, London.
27 Harman, G. (2015) Agenda 21: A Conspiracy Theory Puts Sustainability in the Crosshairs, *Guardian*. www.theguardian.com/sustainable-business/2015/jun/24/agenda-21-conspiracy-theory-sustainability.
28 www.un.org/millenniumgoals/.
29 www.un.org/sustainabledevelopment/sustainable-development-goals/.
30 Smart Cities Plan www.dpmc.gov.au/cities.
31 Habitat III (2016) *The New Urban Agenda* (Quito declaration on sustainable cities and human settlements for all). http://habitat3.org/the-new-urban-agenda/.
32 Section 94 of Habitat III (2016).
33 Section 97 of Habitat III (2016).
34 Birkeland, J. (2018) Challenging Policy Barriers in Sustainable Development, in Dymitrow, M., and Halfacree, K. (eds), *Bulletin of Geography, Socio-economic series* 40(4), Nicolaus Copernicus University, Toruń, pp. 41–56.
35 Birkeland, J. (2002) Legislative Environmental Controls, in *Design for Sustainability: A Sourcebook of Ecological Solutions*, Earthscan/Routledge, London. Incentives are usually given to businesses that created the problem.
36 E.g. Daly, H. E., Cobb Jr, J. B., and Cobb, J. B. (1994) *For the Common Good: Redirecting the Economy toward Community, the Environment, and a Sustainable Future*, Beacon Press, Boston, MA.
37 Raworth, K. (2017) *Doughnut Economics: Seven Ways to Think like a 21st-Century Economist*, Chelsea Green Publishing.

38 The 'donut model' was stated in *Positive Development* but in reference to embodied waste net-positive design: 'One can reduce the size of the hole, or turn the donut holes into positives. In other words, we can have our doughnut and eat it too.' Birkeland (2008) *Positive Development: From Vicious Circles to Virtuous Cycles through Built Environment Design*, Earthscan, London, p. 75.
39 Wilson, E. O. (2016) *Half-Earth: Our Planet's Fight for Life*, W. W. Norton & Co., New York.
40 Shellenberger, M., and Nordhaus, T. (2007) *Break Through: From the Death of Environmentalism to the Politics of Possibility*, Houghton Mifflin, New York.
41 Wilson, *Half-Earth*.
42 www.vox.com/energy-and-environment/2018/1/26/16936104/epa-trump-toxic-air-pollution.
43 SMARTmode process is described in Birkeland, *Positive Development*, pp. 251–73.

Section C
Built Environment Solutions

5 Eco-Positive Retrofitting

5.1 Introduction

Debates regarding sustainable urban design have concentrated more on the form of urban development (consolidated, dispersed or new eco-cities) and less on retrofitting.

A central debate is whether to concentrate people and structures to minimize urban sprawl, to disperse low-impact settlements into nature, or to build new eco-efficient cities. In these growth models, nature is peripheral: polycentric urban nodes separated by green landscapes; self-sufficient semi-rural villages each with food gardens; or new eco-cities surrounded by greenfield land. There is no universal template, but any model must include retrofitting existing settlements to increase public space for greater equity, access and security, to integrate nature into buildings, and to increase ecological space in cities in ways that can enable the eventual regeneration of their bioregions.

Mainstream retrofitting approaches conserve materials, energy, ecosystems and money, but have not addressed the need to be eco-productive or increase nature's positive footprint.

The high-density model of urban development would restrict urban boundaries and consolidate urban areas through infill development and/or taller buildings.[1] Essentially, this means eliminating urban open space or squeezing people into taller vertical spaces. Cities would theoretically occupy less land, so more landscapes would be conserved, except resources would be still drawn from their hinterland. The opposing low-density model would disperse people spatially in low-impact, permaculture-like settlements. These dwellings would help to ground people in nature, but ecosystems would be altered by direct physical disturbances. Both strategies hope to protect ecosystems but relegate them to land left over by development.

Retrofitting existing urban environments can increase residential density, amenity and eco-services with less ecological destruction during extraction of construction materials from natural environments.

Although energy conservation is just one aspect of sustainability, there are many ways that this can be financed. To meet current targets of reducing energy usage to 50% of 2005 levels by 2050, over half of existing buildings would need comprehensive energy-efficiency retrofits. Several countries are aiming to renovate 2% of their

112 *Design and Analysis*

buildings each year.[2] Since this is roughly the amount receiving ordinary renovations each year anyway, this pace is feasible. With upskilling in sustainable design, energy retrofitting programs could be converted to eco-positive retrofitting to create net public and ecological gains. However, there are still systemic barriers [Box 4].

Many of the gaps and omissions concerning socio-ecological sustainability shared by the competing models of urban form could be addressed by eco-positive retrofitting.

Retrofitting is quicker, cheaper and less disruptive than new development, and it can provide more diversified (specialized and/or generalist) local employment. The green-growth agenda will take too much time, is subject to political distractions, and is not easily reversed if contexts/circumstance change. In contrast, energy savings can pay for retrofitting (below), so construction can pay for itself. Retrofitting can be cheaper than doing nothing, especially if the full public costs are considered, not just the costs to owners. However, retrofitting has been focused on monetary aspects (health costs, worker productivity, energy savings, etc.) instead of ways to contribute socio-ecological gains.

Eco-positive retrofitting could happen incrementally yet simultaneously in every city and pay for itself while increasing direct access to the means of survival.

Eco-positive retrofitting can go beyond energy/carbon reductions to produce eco-positive cities.[3] Green-growth proposals have diverted attention from the need for retrofitting. The public resource savings from retrofitting, if accounted for, could be rolled over into further urban retrofitting initiatives. This chapter discusses some of the problems of three basic proposals for urban sustainability: densification or dispersed urban nodes, integration or isolation of people and nature, and new eco-cities. The usual approach to eco-retrofitting, which only aims for efficiency, is then critiqued. Finally, some examples of bespoke or commercial retrofitting modules are provided for cases where whole-of-building design approaches are difficult.

5.2 Alternative to Green Growth

Current urban policies call for 'sensitive' growth in all directions: new urban centers/ eco-cities, urban extensions, infill and densification, but without tangible ecologically based criteria.

Green-growth policies tend to call for 'sensitive' incremental growth anywhere [Chapter 4].[4] There are no agreed principles for prioritizing competing values (e.g. densification and expansion), for filling existing policy gaps (e.g. ecology, equity), for ways to implement these policies, or for assessing results.[5] Determining whether standards are met is left to local governments, as long as local developers and councils subscribe to *any* sustainability values and virtues.[6] While retrofitting is sometimes thrown into the mix, it is not usually differentiated from upgrading mechanical equipment, or adding insulation and solar panels.[7] Ecology is always mentioned, but without regard for ecosystem destruction.

The three green-growth strategies (eco-cities, densification or dispersal) each have rationales, but under any development scenario, virtually all existing structures must be retrofitted.

Current policies, represented by the extensive list in the *New Urban Agenda* [Chapter 4], support all three green-growth models and presume existing physical and institutional frameworks are adequate. However, despite the use of (undefined) phrases such as 'ecosystem-based' planning, there are no plans or policies that would reduce net environmental destruction or increase the total space dedicated to nature. All three urban growth proposals support the use of greenery and amenity, but not increasing nature beyond that depleted/degraded in the past and present. Nature is still objectified as a means to satisfy human material, economic and physiological or psychological needs.

The alternative to 'greener' growth is retrofitting existing cities for eco-positive gains by identifying and correcting problems caused by past/present planning and design.

Despite 50 years of sustainable development, cities still reflect the twentieth-century industrial ethos which assumed that everyone had the same psychological, spiritual, biological, aesthetic and emotional needs [Chapter 3].[8] Cities are zoned like factories, with virtual pipelines of freeways connecting different economic sectors (commercial, residential, recreational, etc.). Over time, however, economic and social forces have had uneven influences on urban environments. Cities have divided further into strip malls, parking lots, slums or even decaying central commercial areas (abandoned for new regional shopping centers). Simply building more cities or replacing parts of them will not address the causes of degeneration.

Design templates based on urban form tend to miss lessons that could be learned from the ongoing degeneration/regeneration of urban and natural environments.

New development, whether infill, expansion at the periphery, urban renewal or new towns, is initially shiny and sterile and counteracts human needs for meaning, identity and sense of place. Since most new developments not designed for adaptability, new, permanent eco-cities that replace diverse urban areas may not suit future generations. Moreover, within decades 'modern' development seems to become old, smelly and grungy. Although many love the buzz of city life, as central urban areas become decadent, they are also stressful and unhealthy. Noise, traffic jams, public transport delays, dirt, crime, exposure to disease and toxic chemicals can destroy their charm.

Retrofitting can target negative features and convert them into positives by being responsive to local conditions, heritage, local culture and sense of community.

Because retrofitting does not need to disrupt existing communities, how the changes will affect people can be tested. Also, existing urban conditions evolved incrementally over time. For instance, residential areas have been gradually diversified, as outdoor spaces, landscapes and facades are gradually individualized. Thus, local needs and preferences can be gleaned from bottom-up changes. Further, deficits unique to each area can be detected and targeted, such as public health threats (e.g. asbestos, formaldehyde). Most importantly, eco-positive retrofitting can be a lever for sustainability by identifying local gaps and potential gains, for which a set of analyses is provided [Chapters 7–8].

5.3 Shared Problems of Competing Growth Models

The three countervailing green-growth models would be better than laissez-faire and opportunistic development, but they fail to address many fundamental sustainability issues.

Broadly speaking, form-led approaches specify an ideal shape or massing of cities. Although they offer diametrically opposed forms of development to accommodate growth, they implicitly accept the inevitability of increasing population and material consumption. It is not clear how each model will deal with the problems of existing cities, environmental depletion/degradation and the changing climate, or how they will mitigate current destructive technological directions (robotic cars, personal air transport, etc.). They sometimes support particular lifestyle preferences, such as rural or urban and low- or high-density living, but do not spell out how they will resolve the unintended consequences of these alternatives.

5.3.1 Shared Growth Issues

Green-growth strategies (dispersed, compact and new eco-cities) center on universal geographic templates for urban forms without built-in direct physical access to basic needs/security.

Most strategies in sustainable urban design belong in the category of green growth or efficient buildings, technologies and land use arrangements.[9] Green growth is an oxymoron because development usually increases net material flows or consumption and reduces the natural environment in some respect. Advocates of the three geographical strategies acknowledge the need for accessible and protected natural environments. However, they do not explain how they would prevent cumulative impacts on the natural or social environment. They reduce 'relative' impacts but do not increase the proportion of nature to development. That is, they confuse design (opportunity creating) with engineering (problem solving).

The extent to which consolidation/infill development, the expansion of low-density settlements and new cities affects sustainability depends more on design than urban form.

Dense cities have benefits.[10] They may reduce car travel,[11] or increase social interaction, but crowding also contributes to social conflict, pollution, stress, congestion, anomy and/or a sense of isolation.[12] Low-impact rural residential development also has benefits and many have a romantic view of rural living. However, its independence from manufacturing and from vulnerability to global economic and climatic forces is generally overestimated. Since planners do not have means of controlling the human population, cities must increase sustainability relative to current rates of consumption. Fortunately, cities create edges and spaces, so they can contribute to increased biodiversity and environmental amenity simultaneously.

The three positions disregard many sustainability issues and instead emphasize common measurable factors, such as transportation fuels, yet technology is changing these factors.

Those who like high-density living tend to select reductionist measurements such as 'people per unit of land area' or 'floor area per person' as indicators of sustainable planning. If density were an adequate measure, the poorest, most over-crowded shantytown in India would be the paragon of sustainability. Conversely, 'average per capita consumption' conceals inequities and favors those with elite lifestyles. Per capita impacts are lower, but individual land use and transport impacts can be excessive. Indicators like liveability or conviviality tend to replace regional social justice with local consumer satisfaction. For example, rural residential development is very liveable but exclusionary.

5.3.2 Shared Resource Issues

The high-density approach focuses primarily on reducing the horizontal land area occupied by cities, but taller buildings often have a greater ecological footprint.

The three green-growth models would not substantially reduce resource extraction in regional areas.[13] While most city planners favor greater urban density (more residents per unit of land/floor area),[14] some would restrict all development to strict urban boundaries [Figure 5.1].[15] Theoretically, this could give natural environments time to recover.[16] Growth could occur through decontaminating and redeveloping urban brownfield sites, replacing suburbs with higher-density residential developments, converting open spaces (golf courses, parklands, etc.) to infill development, and building taller office/residential structures. However, the necessary resources to do so could not be obtained from within urban boundaries, unless and until radical new technologies are created.[17]

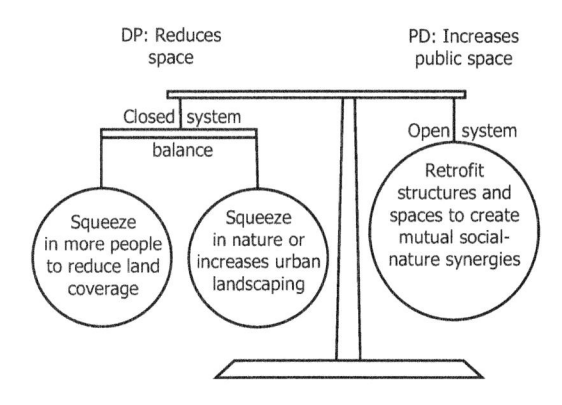

Figure 5.1 Space for nature in competing models

Extremely compact cities may require nuclear energy yet not reduce consumerism, travel, use of high-tech entertainment or need for the experience of nature.

Since densification demands centralized energy, some advocates support nuclear-powered cities,[18] despite the specter of terrorism. There is, of course, enough solar/wind energy to support a 'sustainable' society (assuming world peace) and the rural land they occupy can be used for multiple purposes. Energy from renewable energy production outside urban boundaries can be generated with relatively few impacts, despite transmission losses. However, the

116 *Design and Analysis*

technology-dependent urban culture currently tends to correspond with consumerist lifestyles, ever-changing demands for new fashion, personal robots or fancy cars. Moreover, the idea of confining people to vertical zoos ignores substantial research on the psychological/physiological need for nature.[19]

Dispersed settlements can encourage low-impact lifestyles, solar design and permaculture, but occupy extensive land area (e.g. roads and parking) and interfere in ecosystems.

Proponents of the dispersed model contend that low-density living can increase sustainability and reduce waste and energy by facilitating passive solar energy, low-impact lifestyles and community-building activity.[20] However, transport systems for access to (and construction of) dispersed settlements would occupy ever more (relatively) natural areas and contaminate remnant ecosystems. Roads involve substantial material flows, pollution, terraforming and ecological damage due to seed dispersal on tires and travel by feral animals.[21] New forms of air/water transport (blimps, hover craft, drones) might reduce some impacts but increase others. Generally, 'co-evolution by integration' could cause greater extinction rates, biomagnified toxins and simplified ecosystems.

Formulaic approaches to urban form create some efficiencies (e.g. transport) at the expense of others (e.g. open space and adaptability to changing conditions).

The current debates about whether compact or dispersed cities can best contribute to sustainability tend to reduce complex design challenges to a matter of efficient massing of buildings based on patterns, solids and voids [Figure 5.2].[22] Any urban form can be optimized for energy efficiency by retrofitting, but new forms designed for energy efficiency often reduce the space necessary for other dimensions of sustainability. Further, changing urban form is less efficient than retrofitting, which is necessary regardless of form. Any new or retrofitted development, whether in dense, dispersed or satellite cities, should be designed for future retrofitting along with other sustainability criteria.

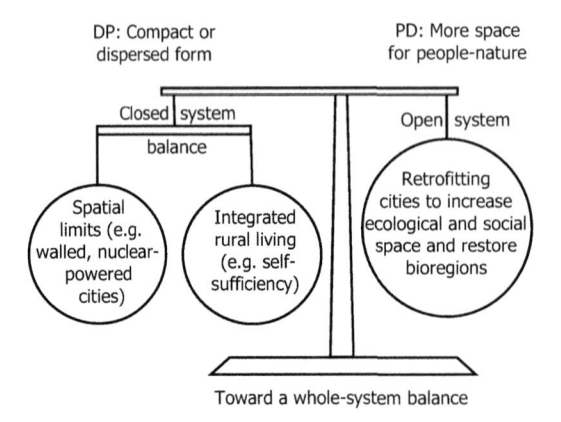

Figure 5.2 Urban form and material and energy consumption

5.3.3 Shared Regional Issues

Few debates about the most efficient land-use patterns and urban forms have real solutions for protecting the bioregion's ecology and improving social equity.

Proponents often compare well-designed dense cities to poorly designed low-density developments – or vice versa. However, the results of any comprehensive analyses that attempt to compare these basic models would depend upon many assumptions and, especially, what is not counted. For example, the ongoing omissions of old buildings or their demolition impacts (e.g. toxic waste, radon, asbestos) affect the urban poor more than others, but environmental justice is seldom counted. Similarly, comparisons often claim that a particular model would preserve more of the remaining species/ecosystems without evidence. They do not consider how their preferred model would compensate for past/ongoing ecological losses.

Although most green-growth strategies could improve urban life quality and amenity, they should also address material flows in the regions and urban-regional relationships.

Each green-growth model would drain the materials, water, soils, non-renewable resources and essential ecosystems from the regions. Some urban and regional developments claim to be zero carbon or zero energy, but do not count the external sources of manufactured products or impacts on the region.[23] Even when development notionally achieves zero carbon, it seldom reduces pressure on the bioregion.[24] Further, the deficits in regional areas that are causing the migration to cities globally are not considered. New central or regional developments for the privileged do not necessarily trickle down to environmental, economic or political refugees that are migrating into cities.

Rural settlements and new regional eco-cities do not mitigate the ongoing depletion and pollution, poverty and stress in the cities that they abandon.

Most eco-cities and eco-industrial parks do not accommodate a cross-section of humanity, and in some cases have displaced local populations.[25] Generally, they do not address regional problems, correct the ongoing impacts of urban decay/waste in old cities, or compensate for the land clearing and other ecological impacts. Eco-cities typically aim for energy self-sufficiency, but use more than their fair share of environmental space: total available resources divided by the global (or regional) population.[26] Masdar, an eco-city close to Dubai, claims socially sustainable design, but only addresses onsite social matters such as integrating immigrants or treating workers humanely, not environmental justice issues.

5.3.4 Shared Transport Issues

Densification and dispersal have not reduced driving, congestion, parking garages and intra-city car travel, let alone the ecological damage caused by car production.

The 'built environment' includes transportation systems (although not a focus of this book). Urban space dedicated to parking, roads, trains and filling stations have been estimated to take up a third of the total land area.[27] Cars have greater life-cycle impacts than some homes,[28] and many people have less dedicated living space

118 *Design and Analysis*

than cars. They have killed literally millions of people with little denunciation, while deaths from sharks, snakes and spiders spark calls for revenge. The investments in annual car fashion changes are huge, yet bumpers are still not designed to protect pedestrians or cyclists, presumably due to aesthetic judgments.[29]

Driverless cars are being prioritized over public transport in cities, with little consideration of the long-term planning issues, public costs and ecological impacts.

A leading densification strategy in planning is transport-oriented development (TOD): increasing residential development near public transport hubs so people need not drive, and families may get rid of one of their cars. This model of urban form is sensible, except that transport modes are rapidly changing. Driverless, robotic vehicles will ensure that vast paved urban wastelands dedicated to roads and parking remain. They may reduce costly accidents, barring electrical hiccups or hacking. However, they will not likely reduce the impacts of car production and urban congestion, or encourage public transport, unless perhaps only taxis are allowed, not private robotic cars [Figure 5.3].

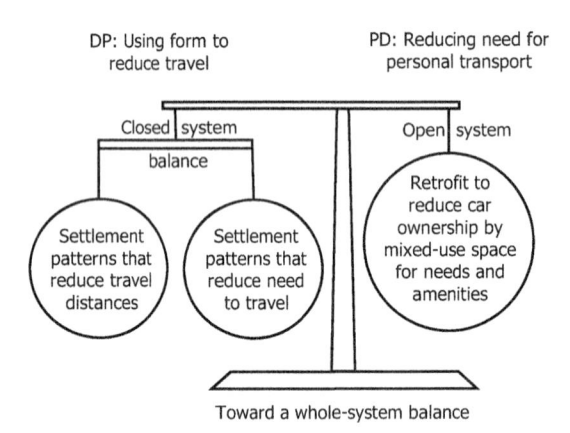

Figure 5.3 Reducing cars or reducing driving

Robotic cars may be inevitable in profit-driven societies, but their impacts can be reduced by converting roads, bridges and garages into eco-productive systems.

While urban designers advocate public transport systems to reduce environmental impacts, save money and improve mobility, little work has been done to reduce the onslaught of robotic cars or car infrastructure.[30] The only remaining option may be to add some positive functions to this infrastructure. For example, Green Scaffolding systems above or beside parking lots and roads could absorb pollutants and noise and create biodiversity corridors [Chapter 6]. Regional roads provide the scale to support elevated linear 'algaetecture' systems for producing fuel, oxygen, fertilizer, shade and carbon sequestration. Alternatively, roads can be used to collect heat, or produce kinetic energy.[31]

Personal air transport will have different impacts in rural and urban areas, but may cause ecological damage in both compact and low-density scenarios.

Personal air transport such as jet packs is inherently dangerous but might allow for paved urban space to be converted to cycling lanes, sports hardtops, elevated gardening boxes for the elderly/disabled, pedestrian paths, seating and other social spaces. However, personal air transport will also mean freedom for city dwellers to invade relatively pristine areas at will. Hence, even walls around cities and rural road removal would not protect the region's ecosystems. The increase in personal road and air transport could lead to unsustainable increases in material and energy flows and, like all digital networks, be subject to hacking and mischief.

5.3.5 Shared Ecological Issues

In compact, dispersed and eco-city approaches, the regeneration of onsite or offsite landscapes can seldom compensate for the lifecycle (embodied) impacts of construction.

Researchers have found that one square kilometer of urban development uses about 1,000 square kilometers equivalence of varied ecosystems: a ratio of 1,000 to 1.[32] Hence nature regeneration/restoration cannot really compensate for the ecological footprint (EF) of development. While the EF or equivalent land area is a useful concept, however, it can also be misleading. First, it implies one ecosystem can substitute for another. Second, a high-rise development may leave more ground area for landscaping yet have a larger EF than low-rise buildings. Third, reductions in a project's embodied materials, ecosystems, waste and/or energy cannot compensate for its additional EF.

Biodiversity offsetting can compensate for some environmental damage, but the building footprint (i.e. ground coverage) is often offset rather than the ecological footprint.

Preserving land that already exists cannot compensate for land that is irreversibly lost through development. For example, a shopping center reportedly set aside a 'permanent' nature reserve to compensate for the greenfield land. This reserve was larger than the land occupied by the building site, but was a small fraction of the tributary area affected by resource extraction, transport and construction or the EF. The reserved land was already in existence, so it could not result in an increase of nature. Similarly, a so-called zero-energy or zero-waste building does not increase global ecosystems or compensate for the upstream ecological damage.

Generally, to offset the ecological impacts of development, it is necessary that vertical structures increase ecological carrying capacity and eco-services beyond pre-urban conditions.

If a greenfield development clears 20 acres for resource extraction or construction and regenerates 20 other degraded acres in compensation, there is still a net loss of 20 acres. That is, only half of the total 40 acres that have been damaged are remediated. If a brownfield development (i.e. contaminated land) redevelops 20 acres of degraded land within urban boundaries, only the portion of the 20 acres not covered by buildings can be regenerated. This does not compensate for the many lifecycle impacts of construction that affect distant ecosystems. New ecological space can be 'net positive', but regeneration cannot be.

Increasing species richness and ecosystem resilience in existing natural landscapes does not ensure the maintenance of ecosystems and biodiversity or address ecological uncertainty.

Returning landscapes to earlier ecological conditions in the bioregion may often be impossible, as past and present interventions in nature have unpredictable outcomes. Moreover, urban environments cannot accommodate larger species, as some individual bird/animal species require huge tracts of land or territories to maintain adequate numbers and genetic diversity.[33] Nonetheless, since buildings provide vertical structures, they can increase the total 'effective' land area allocated to the smaller 'building blocks' of biodiversity, along with the food chains and microorganisms that support them. This is parallel to more progressive zoos that use habitats instead of cages to preserve species and gene pools.[34]

5.3.6 Shared Social Issues

The market-based political system cannot permanently prevent sprawl or greenfield development, although urban/rural residential living could theoretically instill low-impact lifestyles and environmental values.

Advocates of semi-rural settlements presume inhabitants would adopt more self-sufficient lifestyles and cultivate more ecological sensitivity/awareness. Even if future generations embraced the 'settler' model over virtual reality, however, rural living has not always ignited people's biophilic needs. Further, permaculture-type housing also requires active citizens, and many disabled or elderly people need centralized, specialist services. Future generations may soon be locked out of rural home/land ownership due to cost, as many are in cities. Since there is a limit to land, the wealthy might acquire ever more land for personal resource security.[35] They are not likely to be restrained by politicians.

New cities and buildings cannot alleviate the negative, cumulative disparities of health and wealth, unless existing cities/buildings are also retrofitted for net-positive sustainability.

New eco-positive cities could, hypothetically, provide substantial ecological space and conceivably offset many of their own impacts over their lifespans. However, if built on greenfield land, they would add greatly to the ecological impacts of existing cities. If they replace old cities, they would cause substantial demolition waste/pollution. New construction only accounts for 2–4% of the total building stock, depending on the region, economy, etc.[36] The money, energy, time, displacement and resources involved in building new cities would destroy the environment long before they could replace old toxic cities. The priority in PD has therefore been to retrofit cities.[37]

Eco-retrofitting has significant social benefits (e.g. creating skilled employment and public health improvements) and additional costs to employers/developers can be recouped from savings.

Costs related to the health impacts of conventional buildings include absenteeism, worker compensation, low morale, medical costs or shortened work lifespans.[38] Common retrofitting strategies for improving health and productivity include replacing degraded or toxic materials with bio-based building products, substituting fossil fuels with passive solar heating/cooling/ventilating, and improving air quality and ambience with plants and natural lighting systems. The investment in eco-retrofitting buildings for health and productivity has greater returns than the operational energy savings.[39] Jobs in retrofitting can be created everywhere, unlike in urban renewal or greenfield eco-city construction which often involve the displacement of either workers or residents.

5.4 Retrofitting

The benefits of retrofitting are well-known but it is not as glamorous as new building and remains justified/judged only by its potential profitability.

If the population explosion continues, urban expansion as well as densification may be inescapable. However, building new eco-cities will take substantial time, money and resources, no matter how efficient design and construction processes may become. Meanwhile, old cities will continue to cause greenhouse emissions and pollution, whether they thrive or decay economically. Although retrofitting saves money, reduces pollution and greenhouse emissions, increases public health and life quality and so on, uptake has been slow. One reason is that new buildings double as corporate billboards. Retrofitting can change a building's exterior, but taller structures do more to project power and virility.

Retrofitting cities can create more varied, interesting environments than uniform modern buildings that generally lack human scale and diversity, despite postmodern stylistic variations.

Since eco-retrofitting decouples environmental impacts and economic growth, retrofitting buildings in developing nations would be a better investment than foreign aid. It would reduce the breeding ground for political violence, create jobs, revitalize local areas, stimulate economic activity, reduce emissions and improve public and environmental health. Many poor live in older buildings that preceded building codes and earthquake provisions and that have not been upgraded for decades. Retrofitting could also respect the local cultures and heritage. However, there has been little interest in retrofitting deteriorated living conditions in disadvantaged regions of the world, although the costs of prevention are cheaper.

Retrofitting almost always has fewer adverse impacts than replacing a building and, in any case, all buildings need regular maintenance, renovations and upgrades.

The benefits of ordinary eco-retrofitting for energy/water savings, in place of new construction, have long been documented.[40] By re-using structures and materials, retrofitting can generally save a third of the cost of new buildings.[41] Instant increases in property values, due to better energy ratings, can cover the construction costs.[42] There is a growing recognition of the benefits of retrofitting beyond resource and financial savings.[43] Sometimes, the value to the general public is evaluated using hedonic pricing schemes,[44] but these seldom include all public

122 *Design and Analysis*

benefits. The retention of local character, sense of place and irreplaceable heritage features also increase market/rental value.

Eco-retrofitting is more complicated than demolition and construction of a new building, and its long-term performance relies more heavily on competent sustainable design.

Eco-retrofitting has typically aimed for energy savings and appearance. However, positive design actions are also necessary to create net public gains.[45] One cannot achieve positive socio-ecological gains by only reducing impacts. Design represents about 5% of the total costs of a building but can reduce up to 80% of its lifecycle impacts.[46] Therefore, investing more effort in the design stages or 'frontloading' pays off for investors and the general public. Nonetheless, design is often the first thing sacrificed because it is still seen by many as decoration or cosmetics to conceal unsightly mechanical functions or bare surfaces.

The easiest place to kick-start net-positive sustainability from a practical/financial standpoint is to retrofit cities and infrastructure for socio-ecological gains, or eco-positive retrofitting.

While reducing material, water and energy impacts reduces public and private expenditure, sustainable buildings and retrofits are seldom designed with social justice or equity issues in mind. Although design cannot correct disparities of wealth or change trickle-up economics, again, it can mitigate the deprivations caused by urban poverty and wealth disparities. Better physical environments can reduce some reasons for excessive hoarding and defensive expenditure by the 'haves' and avoid consigning the 'haves nots' to living environments that feel like detention centers. However, eco-retrofitting has been efficient but not eco-positive. Existing built environments could be redesigned to create happy, healthy places.

5.5 Eco-Positive Retrofitting

Eco-positive retrofitting goes beyond energy or eco-retrofitting to create opportunities to meet the PD Test, while making the economy more sustainable and resilient.

The economic, social and cultural benefits that urban ecosystem services provide are now being appreciated, as is the economic value of nature to human wellbeing/survival.[47] However, the benefits of nature to the economy as a whole are still under-valued. Most research has focused on the economic costs of environmental damage and/or benefits of remediation, not the potential to use natural forces and features to increase economic sustainability.[48] Eco-positive retrofitting can build on existing structures to create multifunctional landscapes that support ecosystem services through simple modifications to walls, atriums, decks, spaces and surfaces or simply adding Green Scaffolding (GS) [Chapter 6].

Integrated eco-services can be combined and incorporated over, in and around structures to increase ecological, economic and socio-cultural benefits for owners, occupants and the general public.

The benefits of ecosystem services are well known. For example, they treat organic wastes, help regulate the local (and global) climate, alleviate floods, droughts and storm-water runoff, sequester carbon, produce food, fibers and pharmaceuticals, develop fertile soils, prevent erosion, control pests, purify air and store, treat and recycle water.[49] The term 'ecosystems services' usually refers to instrumental benefits that can be expressed in monetary values. Reducing them to financial values diminishes their infinite value: existence itself depends on them. This is, again, why PD uses the term 'eco-services' to include ecological functions and intrinsic values, not just goods and services.[50]

Building-integrated eco-services only provide minimal ecological carrying capacity and/or biodiversity habitats but, collectively, they create significant urban functions (e.g. nature corridors, clean air).

The mere addition of green roofs and/or walls can provide at least two dozen eco-services,[51] along with other direct or incidental biodiversity benefits. Increasing ecological space involves identifying the needs of 'at risk' species, their co-dependent species and food chains, spatial requirements for their territories and nesting sites, and other needs. Therefore, the aim should be biodiversity gains far greater than global depletion rates, not improvements over existing conditions. For example, if endangered butterflies coincidentally lay eggs in green walls, this is a reprieve, not a net benefit. An eco-positive design for butterflies would involve providing building-integrated greenhouses for breeding them.

To reduce the costs of public benefits (e.g. health, amenity), Green Scaffolding can be integrated with other functions, such as renewable/passive energy systems.

No expense is spared in the quest for the 'world's tallest buildings' by proponents who have sometimes claimed that sustainability is too expensive. Design for eco-services in building/retrofitting can be justified on financial grounds alone, as it can increase market values, reduce energy and health costs, and improve marketability. Although the provision of ecosystems and eco-services also costs money, this will not be adequately funded unless it makes profits as well as saves money. While full-cost accounting is not yet practiced in reality, due to the legacy of narrow accounting methods, the data and methods for measuring eco-services are evolving.

Vertical agriculture in both cities and regions may be necessary to support sustainable urban living and enable the ecological restoration of rural/regional land.

Using either land for free-range grazing animals or compact factory farming raises a number of serious ethical and ecological issues. The land area that is being depleted by food production to support the growing human population/consumption is outpacing any land that is being regenerated.[52] A shift to vegetarian diets alone is not sufficient to restore the ecological base or enable the regeneration of wilderness or relatively natural areas. To ensure adequate land for ecosystems and settlements, vertical (vegetable) agriculture will be necessary. However, to have ecological restoration/regeneration, rural land will need to be converted back to wilderness in due course.

Provisos are that eco-positive retrofitting must not only have public benefits but be designed to enable future upgrades to meet increasing sustainability standards.

Retrofitting is almost always better than doing nothing. However, it usually only improves buildings and does little to undo past ecological damage or ameliorate

124 *Design and Analysis*

local social problems. That is, it seldom addresses problems elsewhere in the urban system. An increase in sustainability requires not only impact reduction and the creation of additional positive impacts, but the ability to improve environmental conditions and building performance continually. Buildings that claim to increase 'resilience' are often designed for durability/permanence rather than for easy upgrading. If buildings are not adaptable to ongoing environmental change, they cannot meet higher standards if these become politically feasible.

5.6 Implementing Retrofitting

Although the retrofitting of cities is essential to sustainability, little as yet has been done to overcome the needless systemic barriers to retrofitting.

There are many forces of inertia operating against retrofitting, despite it being a good business opportunity and the existence of some national programs that encourage it. Barriers include a disaggregated construction industry with practices that are passed down through trades, the lack of concern for waste when it does not register as a financial cost/savings, and a lack of political support for sustainable development generally [Box 4]. Also, retrofitting is site-specific, unique and one-off, so it is difficult to capture economies of scale or make much use of prefabrication. Therefore, government needs to speed up eco-positive retrofitting with tangible incentives.

Means of funding retrofitting projects have long been available and many disincentives have been identified, yet little has been done to support eco-retrofitting.

An eco-positive version of the performance contracting model could be used to facilitate net-positive outcomes. Credits are often awarded to developments that use green design principles that are already well established. Sometimes these efficiency measures only offset a small portion of the added environmental and/or social costs of the development. Currently, there is a proposal to add a zero-operating energy target for a voluntary rating tool, following prolonged consultation. However, industry does not need time to prepare for 'voluntary' standards. A sliding scale to reward net gains (versus specific targets) could be implemented immediately while developers choose their own pace.

Performance contracting, where an energy contractor recovers the costs of retrofitting from future energy savings, can be applied to eco-positive retrofitting as well.

Performance contracting begins with setting an energy reduction target. In one version, the building owner pays the amount of the last energy bill to an energy retrofit contractor, who pays the bill but pockets the savings from the reduced amount. When the contractor has been remunerated, the owner resumes paying the energy supplier, but it is a greatly reduced energy bill. Since business loans are always available for non-sustainable ventures, there is no reason that loans should not be available for eco-positive retrofitting projects. Government incentives and/or regulations could speed up the adoption of this well-established but long-delayed implementation strategy.[53]

A portion of tax savings from building depreciation could go towards funding ecologically/socially positive building improvements, if building owners and contractors are reimbursed.

Passive and renewable eco-retrofitting could eliminate most heating, cooling and ventilating bills. However, energy contractors have tended to upgrade lighting systems rather than design for public benefits. The owners' annual savings from energy retrofits or tax breaks for depreciation could be rolled over into a building improvement fund. This approach has longstanding precedents (e.g. the US EPA Green Lights program began around 1992). Retrofitting is often most efficient when the whole building or block is considered as a whole. For example, properties on an urban block could invest in a collective solar dish as well as solarize their own buildings.

Performance contracting incentives might include government programs that reward or bank and exchange any net public benefits that are achieved by retrofit projects.

Eco-retrofitting can be achieved at no net financial cost to anyone, including developers and building owners, so it is potentially self-funding, if not profitable. For decades, energy contractors have retrofitted buildings for energy efficiency at no net cost to owners.[54] However, expertise and experience are generally lacking. Therefore, specialist retrofit companies with the capacity to manage retrofitting projects and guarantee the specified performance level could be funded by 'retrofit banks'. These banks could collect fees from projects involving greenfield development. Alternatively, developers could acquire (strictly controlled) development credits or transferable development rights if they fund retrofit projects via specialist companies.

A green building rating tool encourages new construction to be offset by retrofitting other properties, although it does not yet require eco-positive outcomes.

Although a new building may offset its impacts by protecting a larger area of natural environment in perpetuity or by retrofitting the same amount (or more) of floor area in another building, such actions may not necessarily be net positive. If the impacts of new buildings are offset by an energy retrofit of an old building, for example, the total reduction of the life-support system could be greater (or lesser) than if the new building was not constructed. Clear rules of benchmarking and measuring credits for building, infrastructure or neighborhood retrofits for resource/energy savings and urban eco-services are therefore essential.

Until eco-productivity can be easily assessed/measured, ecological gains could be appraised by the volume of ecological space to floor area (not ground coverage).

It is not difficult to introduce natural and passive systems into existing buildings to improve performance and add amenities. Some ways of doing so are suggested in the examples below. Ecological space (which supports eco-services that benefit the public/nature) could serve as an interim measure of eco-productivity. In short, net-positive gains would be where the volume of ecological space exceeds the gross floor area. Public and work spaces can be combined with ecological space, as sometimes provided by some atriums, aviaries, large terrariums or aquariums. These could be reinvented as building-integrated systems that create eco-services and reduce mechanical building equipment.

5.7 Sample Eco-positive Retrofitting Design Concepts

Eco-positive retrofitting is a self-funding (comprehensive-incremental) strategy that can occur everywhere at once with diverse design solutions to fit any building or block.

The following lists some sample design concepts for possible eco-positive retrofitting, while the next chapter discusses one example in detail. They are generic concepts that can be adapted to different sites and conditions, although all sustainable design requires site/project specific detailing. Retrofitting could create unlimited employment for 'non-robots'. Job creation and skills training is not a political priority at present, but the cost-benefit ratio is such that jobs would be higher paid than in many fields (e.g. military work is very expensive, although soldiers earn relatively little). Moreover, clients can be created, since they get a benefit for no net cost.

Solar Core: The PD Solar Core can collect, store and distribute passive solar heating/cooling in insulated heat banks in attics or other unused internal spaces.

The Solar Core is a means of storing heat/coolness from passive solar collectors on roofs. Solar heat is collected on a roof or attic of the house,[55] and sent using solar fans to an internal area such as an unused central fireplace or insulated hall closet. A frame of galvanized fencing can hold a vertical tower of pebbles, pumice or clean brick rubble in a central closet. This provides thermal mass, without causing construction dust in an existing home, and allows for adjusting and removing the system later. The concept can be adapted for use in two-story buildings as well.[56]

The Solar Core uses natural forces (radiation, convection and conduction) to distribute heating and cooling when or where needed, during night or day.

The Solar Core combines the attributes of a 'solar chimney', which pulls hot air out of a building, a 'wind tower' which draws cool air into a building, and a 'Trombe wall' which stores and circulates heat/coolness using thermal mass. The rock container stabilizes the building temperature by radiation, and heat is distributed through natural convection and/or solar-powered fans and vents. The rocks can be cooled in summer through ducts from underneath above-ground homes.[57] The Solar Core can be used to retrofit any house, apartment building or a set of units to reduce heating and cooling costs in 'non-tropical' regions.

Piggyback Roof: The PD Piggyback Roof adds a transparent skin on roofs for collecting, storing and distributing winter heat and blocking and expelling summer heat.

At least 50% of roofs in typical suburbs face enough sun to support solar cells or hot water collectors. The Piggyback Roof is a means to retrofit a roof surface so it can collect, store and/or distribute (or expel) heat around the house, assuming adequate insulation. A batten frame on the existing roof supports a polycarbonate or other transparent cover but allows for upward heat flow. Small vents at the bottom of the roof unit enable air movement and prevent mold. As heat rises, a solar fan at the roof peak sends heat into the rooms or central storage area.

Passive Solar Piggyback Roof units can be home-made with simple carpentry skills, or be commercially mass-produced units to be added onto new/existing roofs.

In summer, Piggyback Roofs works like 'double roofs' that are sometimes used in hot climates. However, conventional double roofs are more expensive. In summer, it can be covered with a canvas tarp, or more high-tech equivalent, with the hot air passively vented out the top or aided by a solar fan. Where a roof does not face the sun, the roof shape can be modified with a functional roof addition that adds extra interior space such as a loft. Such additional space involves expense, but in some cases might also enable a growing family to avoid the need to relocate.

Passive Solar Modules: *PD Passive Solar Retrofit Modules can increase energy collection/storage without the structural change or construction waste that passive solar design retrofits can entail.*

Different versions of eco-positive retrofitting modules can be used in retrofitting homes and apartments to direct light, heat or coolness passively throughout the home.[58] These should be designed for both energy performance and aesthetics. Homes must be appropriately insulated and draft-proofed first, but these necessary actions quickly pay back their costs. The spaces these modules add can provide practical, aesthetic or environmental benefits in addition to passive thermal functions, as is the case with greenhouse windows. Such modules can be designed to blend in with the unique features of existing buildings and would mitigate the monotony of shoebox homes.

Additions such as solar dormers, bays, gables or loft units can be adaptable to different roof shapes and either commercialized or custom made.

Retrofit modules can double as functional roof elements like gables. They should be adaptable to different site conditions and microclimates, or to being taken by owners if they move. They could be prefabricated commercially or home-made. Thus far, corporations (the market) have largely ignored passive retrofitting opportunities, largely because they do not fit easily into the conveyor belt of industrial systems and its supply chains. Passive systems are not proprietary as 'no one owns the sun'. While mass-produced systems can cost less than site-specific custom design, any number of concepts suiting any number of structures can be built by homeowners.

Reverse Curtain Wall Units: *PD Reverse Curtain Wall Units can mitigate many of the adverse impacts of over-glazed walls that are so common in large urban buildings.*

Curtain glass walls are found on many large modern buildings. Reflective glass and other materials can marginally reduce the heat gain in buildings, but some reflected heat is absorbed by nearby structures.[59] There are now a variety of technological innovations in glass that can reduce some impacts of curtain glass walls, such as internal heat loss/gain, urban noise, and reflected glare and heat. Windows can now even generate electricity. Older curtain glass walls could be retrofitted with various modules using new transparent films that resist heat gain/loss, filters that treat pollution, or glass with embedded photovoltaic cells for electricity production.

Tall buildings have modular facades which allow components to be added over parts of facades to contribute public benefits (e.g. urban air cleaning).

Parts of existing windows could be covered by modular pollution, and/or sound-absorbing materials, or even planting modules where accessible for maintenance. There are limits to the use of retrofitting modules that protrude beyond the facade, due to wind, maintenance, site boundaries and other issues. At lower levels (below 10 floors), however, modifications can add interest to barren walls, such as shade structures combined with solar panels. Additions such as greenhouse windows, built-in bird or bat nests and Green Scaffolding [Chapter 6] could increase the eco-services of facades. The designs should also address urban environmental or ecological problems such as pollution.

Reverse Trombe Walls: *PD Reverse Trombe Walls differ from the usual Trombe walls (e.g. do not obstruct existing views) and are better suited for retrofitting buildings.*

Trombe walls typically have a small air space between a masonry wall and an exterior sun-facing window.[60] The hot air is stored in the thermal mass wall and warms the room by radiation when the temperature cools, or by vents using convection. On cold sunny days, hot air enters the room through vents at the top of the space in the Trombe wall and cool air re-enters the same space through vents at the bottom. In summer, the glass is shaded, and the hot air is vented to the outside. Ordinary Trombe walls often block what could otherwise be views.

Reverse Trombe walls can be modified or moved, as they essentially add a special kind of window frame over a new/existing masonry wall.

Reverse Trombe wall systems are placed outside an existing blank wall which avoids blocking views. Alternatively, where there is no suitable masonry wall, a rock stack in a wire frame/gabion can be added.[61] Such added rock walls can serve as a design 'feature' as well. The inside-facing wall of the rock gabion is made air-tight with an inexpensive, insulative material while the outside-facing surface is glazed. This system is 'reversible', as rocks can be moved. For example, a building occupant might choose to add on a new room, window or doorway where the demountable thermal mass wall was located.

Playgardens: *PD Playgardens are botanical 'exploratoriums' that go beyond the ordinary child development functions (socialization, motor skill development, etc.) and immerse children in nature.*

Playgardens aim to counteract the increasing separation of children from nature in bleak urban/suburban environments by functionally integrating nature and play experiences, which allow urban children to experience nature up close and personal.[62] Playgardens are completely integrated with native gardens. That is, they are not just gardens with play equipment. While they provide the developmental benefits of other kinds of playgrounds, they encourage children to move, rather than passively riding on equipment. Being combined with native gardens, they can complement rather than clash with the surrounding urban landscape. Contrary to the expectations of some, the vegetation in Playgardens has thrived.[63]

Playgardens can support ecosystems, eco-services and urban biodiversity, as well as meet diverse educational and social needs of children and encourage family interaction.

Playgardens bring nature into cities, provide eco-services, create urban biodiversity habitats and develop children's creative, imaginative, social and motor skills. They encourage interaction among different age groups/families, as parents can play in them along with their children. By integrating support structures with low-scale, landscape-integrated equipment, the 'play value' (inventive, developmental, interactive and exploratory activities) is increased at far less cost. Plants serve practical functions, like soft landings, or slowing children down where they might otherwise fall or collide with others. Vegetative groundcover is renewable, less subject to dispersal than sand or bark chips, and generally softer than expensive rubbery paving.[64]

Suburban Bootstrapping: PD Suburban Bootstrapping can double suburban occupancy while avoiding the social displacement and demolition waste involved in replacing homes with new apartment blocks.

Multistory apartment buildings are replacing homes in many cities today. However, preserving a diversity of housing choices is a hedge against unexpected future change. Adding units above single-story suburban homes, supported on structural 'tables' as necessary, could solarize both units while maintaining desirable neighborhood characteristics. This bootstrap approach would accommodate more families quickly without displacing existing residents. It would also enable the elderly to stay in their communities. Since construction could be funded from the prospective rent or sale of the additional unit(s), government funding might not be necessary. Countless owners could act simultaneously and independently to increase housing availability.

Suburban houses need upgrading, but remodeling homes is usually done in ways that enlarge them or add substantial impacts rather than solarizing them.

Even modest suburbs are becoming exclusionary now, due to escalating populations and property values. When suburban homes are upgraded, it is often to increase the space per occupant and, often, more ground area is covered. Moreover, renovations usually involve demolition which releases toxic waste (e.g. polyvinylchloride, radon, formaldehyde, asbestos). 'Proper' disposal processes only slow the dispersal of toxins in the environment,[65] so until solutions are found, encasing toxic parts of buildings may be safer. The structural table concept allows the original unit to be encased in an ecological envelope for passive solar heating and eco-services and avoids toxic demolition waste.

5.8 Conclusion

This chapter has suggested a basic modification to green-growth models which have focused on where new buildings should occur, not on retrofitting existing cities.

Sustainable buildings are often designed for permanence/durability rather than future maintenance, adaptability or upgrading, let alone public sustainability gains. Durability assumes that buildings will not need to meet higher standards or changing functions. For example, the embodied energy and maintenance costs of mechanical equipment, and the cost of cleaning tall building windows is seldom counted, let alone their many negative impacts. All equipment requires repair/replacement, but up-front costs are prioritized over the ease of periodic changes or upgrades. In contrast, passive systems can last as long as the building, support eco-services, pay back their public costs and provide public benefits.

130 *Design and Analysis*

The social and ecological gains created by eco-positive retrofitting might individually be small, but collectively could improve sustainability and resilience in real terms.

To some, retrofitting seems like individual recycling, which would have no overall impact unless everyone does it. It is true that unless and until retrofitting addresses sustainability issues and the basic design of buildings, it will be tokenistic. While government programs in many countries have encouraged retrofitting, these have mostly relied on exemplars, exhortations, incentives and volunteerism. Problem-driven approaches that center on one variable like energy often have unintended consequences on other sustainability issues. In contrast, eco-positive retrofitting could stimulate changes upstream-downstream on all scales of development, but only if undertaken seriously, with ecological base and public estate in mind.

The next chapter expands on one design concept to illustrate how eco-positive retrofitting can provide multiple sustainability benefits for both owners and society.

Adding ecological space to buildings for social, environmental and ecological gains can have measurable benefits. Some buildings now dedicate entire floors to vegetation to reduce the amount and costs of mechanical air conditioning and purification equipment. More visionary building proposals have overlapping floors, exposing many 'green roofs' to the sky, or 'sky gardens'.[66] These alone probably cannot provide enough ecological space, unless in combination with other strategies, such as vertical urban/regional agriculture and building-integrated eco-services. The following chapter provides an example of how retrofitting can provide solutions for many sustainability issues and support ecological space and eco-services through Green Scaffolding.

5.9 Exercises

1. This chapter highlights only a few arguments for and against new eco-cities, consolidated/compact and decentralized/dispersed settlement patterns. List arguments above for each of the three different green-growth scenarios and then think of others. Then think of planning/design alternatives that address these issues.
2. Assign different houses in the same older, homogenous suburb to individual or small groups of students. Develop and share a variety of retrofit solutions for each house with the class. Then, as a group, develop design solutions at the suburban scale or a block of homes, such as multifunctional public spaces or facilities that address local socio-ecological deficits.
3. Distinguish durable parts/products from durable structures. For instance, a durable building product such as a window may be designed to last as long as a building, but if it is locked into a wall, it cannot easily be deconstructed when the building is modified or demolished.

Box 4 Impediments to retrofitting (Source: Birkeland, *Positive Development*, 2008)

Despite many efforts to promote eco-retrofitting, and its established financial benefits, there has been relatively little uptake so far. Some of the many reasons for this are:

- Incentives to counter the lingering misconception that 'sustainable design and retrofitting costs extra' are rare. Loans could be given for retrofitting buildings that can be paid back from the energy savings. Credits or transferable development rights should be awarded for providing demonstrable benefits to the public (versus saving money).
- Eco-positive retrofitting demonstration projects are needed to show people how sustainable design can provide more quality of life or healthy work environments. Many demonstrations have emphasized energy savings through reductionist measures like air-tightness and lower ventilation rates. Sterile cubicles for workers without access to nature are not inspirational.
- Using indirect market-based or regulatory incentives to influence building has tended to focus attention on reductionist approaches instead of stimulating investment in urban design. Direct design solutions do not need carrots and sticks, but do require a new planning/design paradigm, since most incentive schemes still reinforce the old paradigm.
- There are many sectors that influence the built environment: clients, builders, government, designers, investors, tenants and so on. The lack of sustainable design knowledge among any of the diverse participants in a development project can lead to decisions that undercut the logic of the design, causing more long-term costs.
- Codes, regulations and incentives sometimes require the best available technology, which supports the purchase of eco-efficient products and services rather than passive solar design. This mechanistic approach focuses on thermal comfort and misses many opportunities to create semi-outdoor spaces (e.g. atriums, greenhouse balconies) that create interesting yet functional forms.
- The fragmentation, segregation and adversarial processes that characterize the building industry make retrofitting projects (lacking economies of scale) more difficult. The oppositional structural relationships among designers, builders and owners has also delayed the adoption of integrated design, procurement, construction, commissioning and management processes (such as partnering and quality-based selection).
- There is relatively little monitoring of the performance of existing buildings. Some green building rating/marketing tools (RTs) assess energy retrofitting, but these do not penalize existing buildings that use or leak excessive energy. RTs do not apply to ordinary buildings, old or new, so poor performers are not identified.
- There is little attention paid to ensuring building products, materials and equipment are not only 'green' but adaptable. A building is only as durable as

its weakest link (e.g. errors that permit mold to grow can destroy a new building), so even retrofits must be capable of being easily retrofitted.
- The standard of 'best practice' means marginal improvements over standard buildings will obtain a high 'star rating'. For example, RT points can be obtained for using conventional materials or equipment exceeding a specified level of efficiency, but often not for using passive design that replaces these materials or equipment.
- Building owners and homeowners will often invest in upgrading before selling a property but are seldom aware of the investment potential of energy retrofitting (as TV property shows demonstrate). That is, extensive retrofitting occurs, but real estate agents seldom advise homeowners of the opportunities to simultaneously reduce environmental impacts.
- In many jurisdictions, there are free or subsidized thermal audits of existing buildings, but most will select the lowest-cost renovation option, rather than a more efficient whole-of-building retrofit. Systems for tradable credits for public benefits from major buildings are possible but not likely to be instituted for private homes.
- In the case of rental properties, planned unit developments or strata title properties, the landlord generally pays for retrofits while the tenant saves money (a split incentive). This problem has been recognized and is gradually being addressed. Nevertheless, there are high transaction costs involved in organizing rental building retrofits.
- Passive solar retrofitting often requires some design talent, so it can be simpler to purchase an energy-efficient thermal product which has a definite warranty and cost. The design fields have not been proactive in this area. Some building organizations provide energy advisory services, but also favor product sales.
- Estimates on the return of investment or payback from retrofitting buildings are uneven as existing buildings differ substantially. Also, buildings may change hands before the investment is recouped from energy savings. However, some jurisdictions require energy ratings when homes are sold, which provides a market advantage for green homes.
- There is a tendency for builders and designers to want to continue their customary ways/practices (modus vivendi), even when they know capacity-building in retrofitting could lead to increased profits. Green building councils depend on industry support so they must moderate the pace of change to suit their clients.
- Most consumers favor new buildings, and the belief that bespoke design is a luxury prevails, although it can be a modest portion of the total life-cycle cost of the building. Design is generally devalued. Even environmental management has emphasized measuring, monitoring and mitigating impacts over design to avoid impacts.
- Risk aversion and the perceived lack of 'customer demand' has caused developers to prefer light green projects. These are deemed more marketable although this has not been substantiated. In rewarding light green projects, RTs have postponed regulations that might prevent buildings from failing to correct unnecessary adverse environmental impacts.

> - Generally, complex, reductionist and prescriptive building codes and RTs still favor new construction over retrofitting, and urban planning policies and strategies fail to consider the ongoing public costs of existing development. Policies still encourage inefficient new buildings to be built and old buildings to continue to operate without improvements.

Notes

1 See Bay, J. H. P. and Lehmann, S. (eds) (2017) *Growing Compact: Urban Form, Density and Sustainability*, Taylor & Francis, Abingdon, UK.
2 Sebi, C., Nadel, S., Schlomann, B., and Steinbach, J. (2019) Policy Strategies for Achieving Large Long-term Savings from Retrofitting Existing Buildings, *Energy Efficiency* 12(1), pp. 1–17.
3 Birkeland, J. (2018) Eco-positive Cities, in Kothari, A., Salleh, A., Escobar, A., et al. (eds) *Pluriverse: A Post-Development Dictionary*, Authors Up Front and Tulika, Delhi.
4 UN Habitat III (2016) *The New Urban Agenda* (Quito declaration on sustainable cities and human settlements for all). http://habitat3.org/the-new-urbanagenda/.
5 UN millennium goals www.un.org/millenniumgoals/2015_MDG_Report/pdf/.
6 Birkeland, J. (2018) Challenging Policy Barriers in Sustainable Development, in Dymitrow, M. and Halfacree, K. (eds), *Bulletin of Geography, Socio-economic Series* 40, Nicolaus Copernicus University, Toruń, pp. 41–56.
7 E.g. there are few programs for recycling solar cells, which have a limited lifespan and toxic residues.
8 See Birkeland, J. (2002) Urban Form and the Dominant Paradigm, in *Design for Sustainability: A Sourcebook of Integrated Eco-logical Solutions*, Earthscan, London, pp. 114–17.
9 For a discussion of 'degrowth', see Demaria, F., and Kothari, A. (2017) The Postdevelopment Dictionary Agenda: Paths to the Pluriverse, *Third World Quarterly* 38(12), pp. 2588–99.
10 The assumption that people interact more positively in dense cities is questioned in Bramley, G., and Power, S. (2009) Urban Form and Social Sustainability: The Role of Density and Housing Type, *Environment and Planning B: Planning and Design* 36(1), pp. 30–48. Dempsey, N., Brown, C., and Bramley, G. (2012) The Key to Sustainable Urban Development in UK Cities? The Influence of Density on Social Sustainability, *Progress in Planning* 77(3), pp. 89–141.
11 Newman, P., and Kenworthy, J. (1999) *Sustainability and Cities: Overcoming Automobile Dependence*, Island Press, Washington, DC.
12 The experience of over-crowding is influenced by cultural backgrounds/upbringing as people's sense of personal space varies. For a literature review, see Gray, A. (2001) *Definitions of Crowding and the Effect of Crowding on Health*, Ministry of Social Development, New Zealand, Wellington. www.msd.govt.nz/documents/about-msd-and-our-work/publications-resources/archive/2001-definitionsofcrowding.pdf.
13 The emphasis has been on energy efficiency, technical systems and/or material flows, not ecology. See Bergesen, J. D., Suh, S., Baynes, T. M., and Musango, J. K. (2017) Environmental and Natural Resource Implications of Sustainable Urban Infrastructure Systems, *Environmental Research Letters* 12(12). http://iopscience.iop.org/article/10.1088/1748-9326/aa98ca.
14 A discussion on definitions of density is found in Dovey, K., and Pafka, E. (2016) Urban Density Matters – But What does it Mean? The Conversation, May 2016. https://theconversation.com/urban-density-matters-but-what-does-it-mean-58977.
15 Blomqvist, L., Brook, B. W., Ellis, E. C., et al. (2013) Does the Shoe Fit? Real versus Imagined Ecological Footprints, *PLoS Biol* 11(11), p. 1700.
16 This is parallel to a 'half-earth' proposal, discussed in Chapter 4, except it does not set a global target.
17 For discussion on differing views, see Birkeland, J. (2015) Prospects for Nature in Proposals for Urban Growth, *Smart and Sustainable Built Environment* 4(3), pp. 310–14.

18 Shellenberger, M., and Nordhaus, T. (2007) *Break Through: From the Death of Environmentalism to the Politics of Possibility*, Houghton Mifflin, New York.
19 Following Wilson, E. O. (1984) *Biophilia*, Harvard University Press, Cambridge, MA, there has been substantial research on the human need for contact with nature.
20 Pearce, F. (2015) The Big Green Divide, *New Scientist* 226(3026), pp. 26–7. (Note that this is the author of *The New Wild: Why Invasive Species will be Nature's Salvation*).
21 Daigle, P. (2010) A Summary of the Environmental Impacts of Roads, Management Responses, and Research Gaps: A Literature Review, *BC Journal of Ecosystems and Management* 10(3), pp. 65–89.
22 See Oliveira, V. (2016) *Urban Morphology: An Introduction to the Study of the Physical Form of Cities*, Springer, New York.
23 Studies of Masdar have claimed zero waste but do not count lifecycle impacts such as procurement of products and materials from outside the region.
24 Beillo, D. (2012) Gigalopolises: Urban Land Area may Triple by 2030, *Scientific American*. www.scientificamerican.com/article/cities-may-triple-in-size-by-2030/.
25 Shenzhen, near Hong Kong, for example, was a small fishing village in the 1970s, which became encircled by a mega city.
26 Environmental space is a measure of equitable per capita consumption, introduced in the 1990s by an environmental NGO, Friends of the Earth.
27 In peri-urban areas and within city height limits, there is a lot of open space that could be used for human and environmental benefits.
28 The embodied carbon of making a car is as great as driving it. Berners-Lee, M., and Clark, D. (2010) What's the Carbon Footprint of … a New Car?, *Guardian*, Sept. 23. www.theguardian.com/environment/green-living-blog/2010/sep/23/carbon-footprint-new-car.
29 Bumpers were aesthetically unpleasing, so design for safety was left to technology, such as electronics and airbags.
30 Until about 1950 public transport was the dominant form of mobility for the overwhelming majority of the urban population.
31 Some advocate replacing roads with thick solar panels, see www.climatecouncil.org.au/these-solar-roads-could-power-an-entire-country/, 2014 Aug. Others advocate using the mechanical energy of roads, see https://iecetech.org/Technology-Focus/2018-02/Harvesting-energy-from-roads. These would have more embodied energy than freeways with solar cell 'roofs' that have added functions (e.g. noise control and animal crossings).
32 Wackernagel, M., and Rees, W. E. (1998) *Our Ecological Footprint: Reducing the Human Impact on the Earth*, New Society Publishers, Bowen Island, BC. See also Folke, C., Jansson, Å., Larsson, J., and Costanza, R. (1997) Ecosystem Appropriation by Cities, *Ambio* 26, pp. 167–72.
33 The home range of territorial animals limits their number, although it varies with food supplies.
34 This does not suggest that sentient animals or people should be kept in zoos.
35 A notable exception is the owners of the North Face chain of stores that purchased extensive land in Chile and put it in reserves.
36 Estimates vary between 1 and 4%, depending on the region and researchers. See Wilkinson, S. (2012) Analyzing Sustainable Retrofit Potential in Premium Office Buildings, *Structural Survey* 30(5), pp. 398–410.
37 See Birkeland, J. (2008) The Case for Retrofitting, in *Positive Development: From Vicios Circles to Virtuous Cycles through Built Environment Design*, Earthscan, London, pp. 23–42.
38 Romm, J. (1999) *Cool Companies: How the Best Businesses Boost Profits and Productivity by Cutting Greenhouse-Gas Emissions*, Island Press, Washington, DC.
39 Examples are found in Von Weizsacker, E., Lovins, A. B., and Lovins, L. H. (1998) *Factor 4: Doubling Wealth – Halving Resource Use*, Earthscan, London. Von Weizsacker, E. U., Hargroves, C., Smith, M. H., Desha, C., and Stasinopoulos, P. (2009) *Factor Five: Transforming the Global Economy through 80% Improvements in Resource Productivity*, Routledge/Earthscan, London.
40 Heede, R., et al. (1995) *Homemade Money: How to Save Energy and Dollars in Your Home*, Rocky Mountain Institute with Brick House Publishing, Harrisville, NH.

41 It is generally accepted that retrofitting is a third the cost of new construction and can save over a third of energy usage. E.g. see El-Darwish, I., and Gomaa, M. (2017) Retrofitting Strategy for Building Envelopes to Achieve Energy Efficiency, *Alexandria Engineering Journal* 56(4), pp. 579–89.
42 EPA (1998) *Market Values for Home Energy Efficiency* (a study by Nevin and Watson), Environmental Protection Agency, Washington, DC.
43 See Wilkinson, S., Dixon, T., Miller, N., and Sayce, S. (eds) (2018) *Handbook of Sustainable Real Estate*, Routledge, Abingdon, UK.
44 Hyland, M., Lyons, R. C. L., and Lyons, S. (2013) The Value of Domestic Building Energy Efficiency: Evidence from Ireland, *Energy Economics* 40, pp. 943–52.
45 Birkeland, J. (2009) Eco-retrofitting with Building-integrated Living Systems, Proceedings of the 3rd CIB International Conference on Smart and Sustainable Built Environment (SASBE09) 15–19 June, Delft, Netherlands.
46 This is an oft-cited figure. https://ec.europa.eu/jrc/en/research-topic/sustainable-product-policy. It is disputed in Barton, J. A., Love, D. M., and Taylor, G. D. (2001) Design Determines 70% of Cost? A Review of Implications for Design Evaluation, *Journal of Engineering Design* 12(1), pp. 47–58.
47 Costanza, R., d'Arge, R., de Groot, S., et al. (1997) The Value of the World's Ecosystem Services and Natural Capital, *Nature* 387, pp. 253–60.
48 Birkeland, J. (2014) Resilient and Sustainable Buildings, in Pearson, L., Newton, P., and Roberts, P. (eds) *Resilient Sustainable Cities*, Routledge, Abingdon, UK, pp. 146–59.
49 See Heal, G. (2000) *Nature and the Marketplace: Capturing the Value of Ecosystem Services*, Island Press, Washington, DC; Daily, G., and Ellison, K. (2002) *The New Economy of Nature*, Island Press, Washington, DC; Beattie, A., and Ehrlich, P. (2004) *Wildsolutions* (2nd edition), Yale University Press, New Haven, CT.
50 See Birkeland, *Positive Development*.
51 Valezquez, L. (2008) Advantages of Eco-roofs, in Birkeland, *Positive Development*, box 14, pp. 292–3.
52 See www.theguardian.com/environment/2017/sep/12/third-of-earths-soil-acutely-degraded-due-to-agriculture-study
53 Birkeland, J. (1995) Rethinking Pollution, Turning Growth into ESD – Economically, 1995 EIA National Conference, Brisbane, Oct. 26–27.
54 Performance contracting has been around for decades, and was used in the Empire State Building which reportedly saved millions of dollars in the first year (2012). www.prnewswire.com/news-releases/empire-state-building-saves-millions-of-dollars-in-first-year-of-energy-efficiency-plan-155892635.html.
55 If an attic is used if would have a translucent skylight in the roof with an insulated storage space in the attic.
56 See Birkeland, J. (2005) Solar Core, in Hargroves, K., and Smith, M. H. (eds) *The Natural Advantage of Nations*, Earthscan, London, pp. 367–8.
57 Alternatively, ducts can go underground or through ponds to cool the external air.
58 Drawings are available from the author.
59 Reflected heat does not lose all its energy so this can contribute to the urban heat island effect.
60 Usually the space between the thermal mass and glass is about 50 mm.
61 This kind of Trombe wall can create rock features that also support small wildlife like lizards, assuming ducts or other features isolate the ecosystems from the indoor environment and air.
62 Playgardens were probably first conceived and built in Australia in the 1980s. See Birkeland, J. (1994) Ecofeminist Playgardens, *International Play Journal* 2, pp. 49–59.
63 Playground codes were later imposed that would have required Playgardens to be built in less safe ways.
64 Plant selection is important to avoid inviting the wrong kinds of bugs or birds.
65 Disposal sites are lined but they eventually all leak.
66 See Yeang, K., and Richards, I. (2007) *Eco Skyscrapers*, Images Publishing, Melbourne; Yeang, K. (2008) *Ecodesign: A Manual for Ecological Design*, Wiley, New York.

6 Design for Nature Exemplified

6.1 Introduction

This chapter canvasses ways of retrofitting cities with one sample design concept to illustrate how they could quickly increase eco-services and biophilic benefits.

Excluding warfare, the impacts related to the built environment cause the biggest threat to sustainability. Although 50% of biodiversity has been lost in the last 40 years,[1] ecosystem and species extinctions are not a real concern in government, business or industry. It certainly does not rate as high as sports stories in the media. A Martian would think humans are only debating the color of the Koolaid: carbon, food, air or water poisoning. There is a positive alternative: to convert urban environments into health spas and gardens that also increase the ecological base and public estate and future public options.

Possibilities for eco-positive retrofitting are limitless, so one design strategy is examined in detail to illustrate how retrofitting can deliver 'design for eco-services'.

Green Scaffolding (GS) was introduced before as a retrofitting concept. Here it provides an example of ways to integrate natural systems with urban living for symbiotic human-nature benefits.[2] When design for eco-services is illustrated to provide a visual design example, some assume such elements are intended to be a 'single design solution' that is pasted onto any building in any context. It is important to understand that sustainable design is always contextual.[3] GS can be very diverse to integrate with different contexts and functions, or modified later to meet changing social, climatic or technological needs and hopefully higher future standards.

Retrofitted structures that increase sustainability need not wait for socio-political or technical change, since they can generate immediate public benefits and private savings.

Solutions like GS can pay for themselves in savings (with full costs/savings accounting). However, incentives have been necessary to redirect the business culture and actions toward positive public objectives. Ultimately, institutional change will be required to ensure sustainable outcomes. As currently devised, traditional means (e.g. approval/consent systems, development credits, assessment tools and/or offsetting schemes) only mitigate damage.[4] They do not expect full compensation for (otherwise unavoidable) ecological losses. Hence, this chapter suggests ways to incentivize GS and net-positive design generally. Happily, net-positive standards can also be included in regulatory systems without major legislative/administrative restructuring, simply by changing their design standards.[5]

6.2 Green Scaffolding (GS) Functions

Creating space: PD Green Scaffolding capitalizes on 'empty' spaces around-above-between buildings to support natural and/or passive systems and other positive building, social, and environmental services.

GS is one among many eco-positive retrofitting concepts that can increase structural performance, eco-services and the other economic or socio-ecological values of buildings.[6] Essentially, it adds exterior or interior layers to an existing building envelope to create a triple-skin building. It can utilize 'empty' spaces between or above buildings, parks or pathways.[7] As a spaceframe structure, it can use efficient low-cost materials with little additional embodied energy, materials or waste, and supports passive solar or renewable energy systems to amortize the construction costs. GS can add to many functions and spaces, while also providing multiple eco-services and offsite environmental benefits.

Security: GS can create private or public spaces that provide food, safety and other basic human needs in case of social or natural emergencies.

Modern urban and building forms have exacerbated many emergencies. The GS concept can provide temporary shelter and structural reinforcement in case of floods, fires, storms, heatwaves or earthquakes. The evacuation of urban areas in crises has proven difficult due to the lack of escape routes from buildings (e.g. Twin Towers) or cities (e.g. New Orleans). Although no structure can withstand every large-scale earthquake, terrorist attack, tsunami, volcano, asteroid or nuclear accident, GS could reinforce building clusters and connect them at different lower levels,[8] to enable people to evacuate from several buildings at once or seek refuge above.

Adaptability: Where a basic building is difficult to update, the adaptable skeletal frame can give it flexibility to meet changing needs/functions, micro-climates and conditions.

GS forms a kind of 'ecological envelope' around buildings, or parts thereof, to support eco-services and/or ecosystems. However, it also reinforces older buildings structurally, adds functional spaces and incorporates private or public benefits into the building. For example, social or work spaces can be integrated into GS that extends over sidewalks or rear yards, assuming they solarize the dwelling. Planning permission or incentives would be granted on the basis that the dwelling or small building substantially reduces energy consumption through the new integrated renewable/passive energy system. The added floor area can offset the construction cost by raising the property value.

Disadvantaged regions: The GS concept is suited to impoverished communities where people lack secure structures and spaces to provide for community safety and resource security.

GS can be used by communities as low-cost multifunctional structures in their village center to support neighborhood scale renewable (wind, biogas, solar, etc.) energy systems. Risks from floods can be provided by a cross-braced tower that supports elevated platforms.[9] GS can also be structurally attached to mud brick or structurally weak buildings, connected with wires through walls to reduce earthquake damage. These ultra-fortified structures could serve as community refuges during or after hurricanes or earthquakes. While the structure is like a spaceframe, it can be designed to provide any functional priority and blend into any aesthetic or local cultural heritage.

Employment*: GS, being minimalist in materials and adjustable to different locations, could provide geographically distributed and productive jobs that provide training in transferable skills.*

Many kinds of jobs simply redistribute wealth and circulate money, or are actually 'wasteful' of resources because they provide no public benefit (e.g. trading in weapons, sex, endangered animals and slaves, pornography and related entertainment). Retrofitting the built environment can create productive, and even self-funding jobs for the under-employed, as well as designers, while greening and diversifying cities visually. GS will require significant maintenance but so do mechanical/electrical building systems, which would be reduced. Arguably, much of the employment created to maintain these passive and natural systems in GS structures would be akin to gardening or other relatively healthy work.

Eco-efficiency*: GS, as low-cost skeletal structures, can increase the eco-efficiency of buildings by allowing suitably located passive solar and natural systems (e.g. ventilation, air-cleaning, daylighting).*

GS provides the physical framework to support more environmental benefits in new or old buildings or, ideally, a whole city block. It can combine additional building functions with passive and/or natural systems that supplement heating, cooling and ventilating costs or possibly replace them in the case of homes or small buildings. For example, GS can combine, in strategic locations, photovoltaic panels, passive solar design (e.g. gabion wall sections for thermal mass, attached greenhouses), light-weight vertical wind generators, light tubes, light shelves and/or mirrors for daylighting, solar stacks for natural ventilation, and vertical composters, wetlands or even algae fuel production systems.

Environmental education*: In addition to supporting passive systems that provide building services, GS can support educational displays of biodiversity incubators or local micro-ecosystems and habitats.*

Some modules created by GS can support various kinds of habitats to house small endangered species for the eventual ecological restoration of the bioregions, such as bird or small animal nests, pollinators and so on. From inside the buildings, such mini-habitats serve as 'living wallpaper'. Integrated GS or internal GS could display the activity/growth of underground plant roots, insect colonies or lesser-known invertebrates for educational purposes by demonstrating how natural systems can support building services/functions and vice versa. Public buildings could also provide for nature interpretation displays through wall-mounted microscopes/telescopes or videos, such as are now found in many museums and zoos.

6.3 GS Applications in Cities

Diverse forms of GS can be developed for different sizes, types and scales of development suited for either congested or dispersed settlement patterns.

GS would enable cities to blend into the landscape. The extensive use of GS in one precinct might sound somewhat monotonous. However, GS can have a vast variety of appearances or work to harmonize a typically cacophonous urban environment. GS can be prefabricated in portable components and can easily be modified for changing needs.[10] It can cover part or all of facades or roofs, be used in large buildings or small homes, be attached to the interior or exterior of walls or compose the facade structure itself, be a free-standing structure or be combined with fences, plazas or landscape features.

Large building scaffolding: *The adverse impacts of curtain glass walls could be reduced with GS, which can operate like triple-skin walls, yet build in more benefits.*

The facades of older buildings are sometimes given new curtain glass walls to increase their rental/market value. Curtain glass walls usually increase glare, noise, energy use and urban heat. They even occasionally drop glass on sidewalks due to the contraction/expansion of their window frames.[11] GS can incorporate materials or multifunctional modules that absorb noise, glare and air pollution, while improving their aesthetic value.[12] Unlike single- or double-skin facades,[13] they can enable safer maintenance, repair and window cleaning, as well as add earthquake and wind load bracing, integrate protected fire escapes, and even incorporate water storage for central city fire sprinklers.

GS need not increase the cost of new buildings and it can prolong the life of older buildings to delay their replacement/demolition impacts.

Due to its versatility, GS allows for myriad variations to suit the unique conditions and changing functional needs of new or old buildings.[14] Retrofitting costs less than constructing new buildings, and it could be subsidized at no net public cost where it adds socio-ecological gains. For example, planning exemptions could allow GS that supports eco-services such as urban air cleaning, or permit integrated decks, greenhouses or balconies (which also increase the market/rental value). Similarly, planners could allow GS above height limits, sidewalks or integrated with skybridges in business districts, or in legislated setbacks, as appropriate, to provide additional financial incentives.[15]

Wall integrated scaffolding: *The PD Green Space Wall is GS that forms the exterior structure itself, as opposed to scaffolding outside or inside the building envelope.*

The Green Space Wall is a GS for new buildings that combines extra functions within the building wall structure itself.[16] The wall supports modules with glass or other surfaces as appropriate to the location, orientation, function and/or needs of each wall segment. The modules can: provide storage or social spaces; insulate, store and circulate heat/coolness; produce clean energy, air, water and soil; and/or support ecosystem functions or habitats for small endangered species. The GS wall structure would generally be modular, so it can be contracted or expanded in size to accommodate changing uses, or even (potentially) be deconstructed and moved.

The Green Space Wall provides practical spaces as well as eco-services and accommodates biophilic functions, and can house ecosystem habitats and biodiversity incubators.

As above, GS can include educational displays on the inside wall of public spaces for environmental education and awareness-raising, but it can also provide biodiversity incubators.[17] The double-skin wall structure can support a range of

140 *Design and Analysis*

micro-habitats to house mini-gardens, butterfly breeding spaces, ant or termite farms, frog or reptile sanctuaries and small endangered species.[18] If the microclimate proves not to be ideal, exhibits can be moved to other modules. Modules with terrariums or aquariums can be maintained by student or naturalist groups such as horticulture, herpetology or entomology societies. They should allow for maintenance/access from the GS interior or exterior.[19]

Historic building scaffolding: *The PD 'interior GS' can reinforce historic structures without altering the facade, while increasing amenities for occupants/visitors such as attractive, interesting work spaces.*

Many historic buildings are not permitted to modify their facades, yet need earthquake proofing or other structural upgrades in order to continue to be used. Sometimes, only the facade is preserved, either to stand alone or to attach a new building behind it. Where retained, the historic buildings usually need major interior renovations as their floor plans are not amenable to modern activities and expectations. Since floors have often settled, they are sometimes gutted so new floors can support square walls. Interior GS could reinforce heritage structures from the inside and create internal atriums for public exhibits and social functions.

GS can allow for flexible open-plan interior spaces to accommodate changing office needs, tourist activities, public social spaces, and/or daylighting and fresh air.

The new interior spaces in historic buildings are usually better than the 'rabbit warrens' that often preceded them. However, they still often have little daylight or views across their open spaces. Interior GS can create interior open spaces for arcades, exhibition spaces or reception areas with, for example, 'vertical landscapes'. Light and air can be brought in from the roof level using skylights, mirrors and/or light shelves that are not visible from the street. In one design, for example, the light from skylights strike a PD 'green chandelier' that reflects light onto plants and sitting spaces in the interior GS.[20]

Domestic structure scaffolding: *PD 'domestic GS modules' can support domestic needs and cost-saving functions like passive solar or renewable energy systems, insulation or vertical vegetable gardens.*

Domestic GS can be combined with homes, carports, roofs or garden structures (e.g. gazebos, sheds, fences), or other landscape features. The modules could provide food production pots, water cleaning, rain collectors/storage, daylighting using integrated light shelves, sleeping areas for pets, thermal and sound insulation, air ventilation, passive and/or renewable energy systems, clothes drying areas accessible from inside, earthquake and cyclone protection using cables, etc.[21] Since many older suburban homes lack adequate insulation, scaffolding with integrated insulation can offset some costs of renovations. External appearances can blend into individual house styles, and modules can support greenery where visual screening is appropriate.

GS can increase the security/functionality of homes in developing nations, where some people lack the funds to make home improvements with conventional construction.

GS is suited to rural 'third world' villages that often lack affordable construction materials or personal space. Using timber or bamboo versions of GS (preferably with cables), these scaffolds could provide planting walls for food production, water collection, treatment and storage, and/or storage space with roof decks. If the GS is partly internal, the inside layer can provide practical functions like shelves and bunks. If the GS is partly external, it can support inexpensive walls of recycled plastic bottles and/or earth brick.[22] They can fit into spaces in crowded villages because the ground level can be left open for pedestrians.

6.4 GS Applications at Urban/Regional Scales

Urban farming: GS can support urban farming, a significant movement to increase urban food security and health while reducing truck transport to and from cities.

Demand for more varieties of food is increasing in urban areas, which can best be accommodated by specialist food production in vertical urban farms. Urban farming can reduce truck transport between farms and cities, and within cities as well. Vertical farming captures economies of scale and takes up less land area. In some cases, urban farming structures are greenhouse structures that use rotating trays to facilitate watering and harvesting and to control the amount of light they receive from skylights.[23] In other cases, abandoned urban warehouses have been repurposed with internal scaffolding structures that support vertical vegetable and/or flower production.

Rural farming: GS in rural areas can convert land used for monocultural food production back into biodiversity habitats and buffers to (partially) protect natural areas.

Significant amounts of rural land are currently used for grain and meat production, which can be damaging to nearby ecosystems, waterways, land productivity and even soil biology. Land currently used for meat production could be gradually reclaimed for vegetable and legume production using rural GS structures. Such vertical structures could also free up land for biodiversity habitats and wilderness restoration. Their cost could be offset by savings from substituting more costly processes. For example, they could reduce the use of enormous agricultural machines that dwarf the embodied energy in the solar- or wind-powered equipment needed to construct/operate the vertical farming.

Desert cities: GS for food production in desert cities could ameliorate the housing problem in a relatively benign way while also respecting fragile desert ecosystems.

A third of the planet's land area is now desert,[24] and many bioregions are being destroyed. Some argue that the physical footprint of solar-powered desert cities would do relatively less harm. Although many species have adapted to deserts, they have fewer ecosystems and species. Water is an issue in deserts, but passive technologies can now capture mists or evaporation of ocean breezes sufficient to support large GS greenhouses.[25] The water harvested from the air is pumped through roofs to cool the buildings during the day and water the plants. These structures can be elevated to reduce damage to desert ecologies.

Other regional applications: GS can provide demountable and/or adaptable means of increasing/protecting urban biodiversity and creating a hedge against invasive species, while serving diverse local functions.

There are schools and small communities in rural areas on flood plains or hurricane alleys, or near woodlands that are especially prone to bushfires. GS 'functional

142   *Design and Analysis*

fences' with water storage and sprinkling systems located between fire-prone areas and settlements could hinder the spread of fire while providing local benefits.[26] Horizontal or vertical gardens in GS structures above or around schools could support outdoor classrooms, social areas, and/or places for children to grow and prepare food while learning about health and nutrition. These structures could serve as backup refuges and relief facilities for communities in case of a natural disaster.

6.5 Green Scaffolding (GS) and Eco-Services

The following suggests how GS systems can provide specific benefits for humans and nature in ways that also directly or indirectly support biodiversity.

It should be emphasized that the following examples of GS concern design 'concepts', not specific systems or technologies. Since every site and context is different, every application or design of GS might differ in structure, shape and appearance. Design thinking is required to apply them to site-specific environments and constraints. By definition, sustainable design must be responsive to climatic, cultural and biophysical circumstances, while meeting many functional parameters and unique priorities. It would be easy to conjure up situations in which an abstract design concept might not work, but it would be equally easy to resolve these problems by design.

6.5.1 *Eco-Services that Support Energy, Materials and Transport*

Electricity/fuel production: Distributed energy systems are not considered as efficient as large-scale facilities such as regional solar thermal plants.[27] However, they provide for energy security when electricity distribution networks fail or in a crisis. GS combined with signage and billboards could support solar cells which can provide electricity to adjacent buildings. 'Algaetecture' (where transparent tubes of algae are supported by and integrated with facades) can produce biofuels/biogas.[28] Algae tubes have doubled as shading devices and other architectural features. A form of GS was proposed for producing biofuels using fast-growing algae in the empty spaces above existing filling stations for feeding non-electric vehicles.

Integrated wind power: Regional or peri-urban wind power systems can be combined with GS functions for additional productive purposes. Some micro-wind generators work on the sides or roof edges of buildings. The use of building-integrated wind generators is problematic due to variable wind velocities, turbulence and intermittence. However, the cavity created by the GS can stabilize the air flow and reduce wind turbulence. The air flow becomes uniform as it moves through the cavity (regardless of wind direction). Therefore, the area between GS exterior panels could harvest wind energy.[29] Potentially, then, GS could be combined with small-scale wind turbines for building energy autonomy.

Materials substitution: Although all buildings need occasional upgrades, longevity generally reduces the rate of environmental degradation and resource depletion caused by extracting materials for new construction. GS can increase the longevity of buildings in several ways. They can enable buildings to meet changing circumstances, as in the case of renovating the interior of historic buildings (above). They can prolong the life of older buildings that are vulnerable to earthquakes or gradual earth movement, by providing (multifunctional) structural reinforcement. When used as walls, GS could reduce the materials used in building facades to achieve better structural/environmental outcomes, and could enable major future modifications.

Land reclamation: Freestanding GS can make use of land that is degraded and being remediated. Since GS is generally on piers/posts and can be energy and water autonomous, it can be installed over brownfield sites (land contaminated by past industrial uses), and/or integrated with urban forests, while the soil is gradually rehabilitated for human use. While decontaminating land, urban forests can also provide timber or bamboo (where appropriate) for construction materials. During the years that bioremediation processes and urban forests are remediating the damaged land, elevated GS walkways, greenhouses and public venues in the landscape will ensure the land is well used.

Transport reduction: Regional transport impacts include human fatalities and road kill, isolation of species into 'islands', the climatic and biodiversity impacts of excavating construction materials, and the spread of seeds by vehicle tires. Urban transport impacts include pollution, congestion and the heat island effect from roads and parking garages. Transport to and from the country can be reduced not only by urban agriculture, but by vertical urban composters combined with other functions, such as GS structures that support solar cells. Rural freeways/railways could have Green Scaffolding roofs that support linear algae biofuel production systems along with biodiversity bridges and other locally appropriate functions.

6.5.2 Eco-Services Providing Comfort and Health (Heating, Noise, Pollution, Oxygen)

Thermal comfort: GS can integrate passive solar heating systems into existing buildings and avoid the use of high-cost building facade materials. Passive systems have been underutilized, in part because purchasing new energy-efficient products is preferred to site-specific design. However, passive solar design is widely considered more comfortable, as it generally heats or cools the whole wall, as opposed to space heaters that do not warm the whole space and create vertical temperature differentials.[30] GS retrofits can create space for additional passive solar heating, cooling, insulation, thermal storage, or incorporate ventilation systems (e.g. wind scoops, thermal chimneys or solar core features) [Chapter 5].

Urban acoustics: Noise pollution is now recognized as contributing to unwelcome stress in humans and animals. Over-glazed and/or metallic facades transfer noise in and out of buildings and reflect street noise. Portions of GS facades could have panels of materials that absorb urban traffic noise, and portions could filter street dust and pollution (being three-dimensional). Noise can also be tempered by GS structures that are designed and shaped to break up sound waves. For example, soil containers in GS can be designed to refract sound while supporting soil which absorbs some noise, in addition to growing plants to treat air and water.

UV radiation and daylighting: Interior lighting uses significant energy, and even energy-efficient light bulbs have negative impacts. Daylight is more beneficial for people and ecosystems than artificial lighting.[31] Methods used in double- or even triple-glazed facades for optimizing daylighting automatically during the day can be adapted for GS.[32] Automated light shelves and mirrors built into the GS structure can bounce light further into the building. Similarly, shade cloth, vines, EFTE products,[33] and so on, supported by the GS, can control the light levels to create the proper habitat conditions for ecosystem nurseries within the GS and/or shield micro-habitats from excessive light and UV radiation.

Particulates, pests and pathogens: Plants are known for their ability to reduce particulates and toxins that affect ecological as well as human health. GS can support exterior filters to remove toxic urban dust or plants that absorb particular toxins found in building interiors.[34] Since some eco-toxins bioconcentrate in plants, they may eventually require composting in special processes.[35] Mosquito-borne illnesses are reportedly moving into urban areas due to climate change,[36] so flytraps that attract but kill pests could be included in the GS. Where such multifunctional GS systems are used, the GS would need to be designed for access from inside the building or scaffolding.

Urban heat island: Extreme temperatures and pollution in urban areas can be mitigated by GS over streets or parks. Free-standing GS structures can provide public functions which would offset their costs. The plants in elevated GS garden structures can clean the air, and also cause stagnant air near ground level to rise which mitigates heat inversions. Street trees are also beneficial in this regard, but not always suitable (e.g. narrow roads) and can even expose pedestrians to falling limbs or drop bears.[37] Unlike trees, GS does not require regular pruning for powerlines. Where trees are removed, GS can provide some of their amenities.

6.5.3 Eco-Services that Provide Essential Needs like Food, Soil and Clean Air

Soil production: Global losses of topsoil and desertification is a serious issue that has been largely ignored for decades.[38] However, soil can be produced in vertical composting systems without competing with other land uses. There are now many large-scale, stand-alone urban composting systems. Biogas digesters have even been housed in buildings for energy and heating.[39] GS systems can be used to create small-scale vertical composters braced by urban structures to produce soil for urban farms. Most regenerated soil is used for decorative landscaping or food gardens in cities, but if scaled up it could be used in repairing depleted, eroded agricultural land.

Food diversity: GS can support various forms of greenhouses in garden seating areas or above roof gardens for production of specialized organic foods to supply local shops. For example, boutique restaurants could use GS to produce herbs, honey, mushrooms or more novel foods. Micro-gardens in urban areas, being relatively sheltered from genetically modified organisms that circulate over the hinterland, can help protect indigenous and medicinal plants, which are rapidly being lost.[40] They can also provide a hedge against diseases that threaten monocultural crops upon which society is now dependent, and provide additional repositories for diverse plant gene stocks to supplement seed banks.

Omega 3 production: Omega 3 is essential for health, but fish stocks are rapidly diminishing.[41] Fish production in suitable rural areas could eventually reduce the pressure on ocean fisheries. Urban aquaculture can grow fish and fertilizers for plants in closed-loop arrangements supported structurally by GS systems. Many sizes and scales of aquaponic systems are now available. These can be combined with structures for processing the fish to save land cover and help support the weight. GS could also provide mini-aquarium windows substitutes on lower floors (which avoid blocking views). There are examples of aquarium structures in interior work spaces where views are unavailable.

Oxygen generation: Urban office workers can experience fatigue from oxygen deficits. This is increasingly recognized as a financial cost to businesses. A few square meters of vertical planting walls can meet the oxygen requirements of an individual,[42] so GS could theoretically make buildings self-sufficient in oxygen. Nonetheless, few buildings are designed to support interior plants, let alone to treat indoor air pollution. Since plants produce almost as much oxygen as they absorb carbon, it is difficult to have too many plants. Similarly, 'algaetecture' systems (above) can consume carbon while producing oxygen.[43] Both could provide 'fresh air' and amenity to oxygen-deprived inner-city areas.

Protected or invasive species: Nature corridors enable select species to escape areas invaded by predators or find food and genetically diverse mates. GS can support vertical, multi-layered nature corridors for small animals, insects, birds and especially endangered species, to reduce impacts of habitat fragmentation caused by cities.[44] Some green roofs have been designed to grow plants that attract particular species. GS on roofs or walls can support food chains or custom-designed habitats for endangered species, although their designs must also deter invasive species. Conversely, some native species can control invasive urban pests. For example, peregrine falcons have reduced the pigeon problem in many cities.

6.5.4 Eco-Services Treating or Storing Water for Humans and Ecosystems

Treating water pollutants: Living Machines are a well-established technology with many demonstration centers around the world.[45] Living Machines are similar to a series of filtration basins in the natural environment or constructed landscapes, but use less acreage.[46] Typically, these treat water through a series of translucent water containers with different bacterial communities that evolve micro-ecosystems around the particular pollutants which, to the bacteria, are food. They can be integrated into built environments at any scale from nature strips to regional wastewater treatment facilities. The concept can work vertically or horizontally in a large-scale GS if it is accessible for ongoing testing and maintenance.[47]

Reducing storm water runoff: Vertical landscapes can reduce storm-water runoff and thus soil erosion, sediment loss and water pollution. This protects biodiversity by preventing contaminated water from reaching the local creeks/rivers and oceans downstream. Water collected on the roof can be gravity filtered through soil, pebbles and other media in a GS wall. Where a roof structure cannot support gardens and water, a vertical GS attached to a building can do the job. Interior vertical wetlands in atriums can also treat water, provide fresh air and (paradoxically named) negative ions. These could be designed to be more easily maintained in an accessible GS atrium space.[48]

Water collection: In humid climates, water can be harvested from the air. For example, evaporative 'water cones' can collect and clean water by evaporation.[49] Dew harvesting and evaporative systems, or commercial water filter systems, can be integrated into GS structures. Water can also be harvested in dry climates, or even in some deserts. GS can support vertical screens for extracting water from mist or

146 *Design and Analysis*

fog, which were used in a Peruvian desert in the 1950s.[50] Rainwater treated by gravity filters can be stored in GS containers below these drip screens for use in food production or even potable water for local residents.

Water for thermal mass: Water tanks, used as walls, can double as a heat storage medium that absorbs excess heat or insulation (thermal mass). Another existing concept that is suited to climates that have hot days and cold nights (typical in many deserts) is the 'camel roof'. Translucent water containers on a flat metal roof collect and store solar heat through a translucent cover. At night, an insulating cover slides over the top, and heat radiates into the building. The water containers cool off overnight, ready to cool the building the next day. Then the sun heats up the water containers again by evening.

Emergency water: The loss of food and water supplies in natural or civil emergencies (e.g. the Irma, Harvey, Maria and Jose hurricanes of 2007) sometimes kill more people than the event. Survivors cannot always escape to safety, or even be reached by emergency brigades within a reasonable time. Elevated flood and earthquake-resistant GS structures could provide district evacuation centers (and water supplies) as well as store interim water and food supplies. Their cost can be offset by supporting solar thermal power structures.[51] Alternatively, in fire-prone areas, elevated GS neighborhood emergency centers (over fire bunkers) can support water storage and fire sprinkler systems.

6.6 Incentivizing GS and Design for Eco-Services

This section looks at incentives for net-positive offsetting or design for eco-services which can compensate for (not be used to permit) biodiversity losses.

Existing legislative and regulatory processes do not yet set net-positive standards.[52] PD terms are increasingly being used by those who omit to call for compensation adequate to offset ecological uncertainty and/or biomagnification. Sometimes, urban planning and building codes, point systems, discretionary development conditions or performance assessment schemes encourage partial offsets, but not full (lifecycle) ecological compensation. Many planning and design incentives schemes, such as biodiversity offsetting, have the 'potential' to encourage positive compensatory actions. Thus far, however, agency decisions and case law has tended to interpret 'net benefit' as allowing the destruction of ecosystems if other degraded parcels are regenerated.

Barriers to PD are created by current codes, development control mechanisms and building rating tools, largely because they set low (voluntary) socio-ecological standards.

Planning and building codes and development control schemes treat development as a right to do a certain amount of damage to the environment, and simply place upper limits on that right. Green building rating/marketing tools (RTs) now reward reductions in environmental damage relative to the damage allowed by such regulations [Chapters 11–12]. There are also various means to encourage developers to do good rather than just less harm (e.g. developer contributions/exactions) discussed below. However, these contributions usually only compensate for some of the extra public costs, such as public infrastructure used by the development.[53] They never demand net positive results.

Developer offsetting schemes sometimes allow 'extra' (beyond code) negative onsite/offsite ecological impacts because they do not require compensation for the full public costs.

Offsetting schemes do not aim to compensate for the ecological damage allowed by code.[54] They only aim to compensate for some of the extra (beyond code) damage. At best, offsetting is ecologically remedial. If a project clears 20 greenfield acres and regenerates 20 other degraded acres in compensation, there is a net loss of over 20 acres. It is not net positive because only half of the 40 acres that have been or will be damaged are regenerated. If a construction redevelops 20 acres of degraded brownfield land within urban boundaries, only a part of these 20 acres is regenerated.

One reason that credits for biodiversity 'gains' often mean a net ecological loss is that post-construction landscapes are assessed relative to pre-construction landscapes.

A recent proposal for biodiversity offsetting will give credits for more biodiverse landscaping.[55] This proposed credit scheme emphasizes two things: discouraging buildings on previously undeveloped or greenfield sites and conducting scientific studies that assess the biodiversity before and after construction. First, this means 'uncertified' buildings will be located on sensitive sites. Second, it also means a building could get biodiversity credits even if, in constructing the building, there were excessive impacts on vegetation, water, ecosystems and soil during offsite materials extraction. That is, developments that do net ecological damage can get biodiversity credits for regenerating the landscape around the new buildings.[56]

Vertical GS structures that support biodiversity nurseries/incubators at urban boundaries can provide protection from invasive species, along with environmental services/security for urban residents.

Seed banks may preserve plant species, but they cannot preserve unique and complex ecosystems. Land ecosystems require the maintenance of soil biota, insects, plant diversity and everything else that was there to begin with. Efforts to increase urban biodiversity usually only concern individual species and landscapes are vulnerable to invasive species. Since measuring ecosystem viability is underdeveloped and complicated, the PD rule of thumb is: 'the cubic meters of ecological space in a building or site should exceed the gross floor area'. GS is one way to meet this standard, but incentives would need to be provided for ecosystem enclaves.

6.7 Sample Incentives

The following reviews several types of planning instruments that can be modified to incentivize full compensation for (unavoidable) losses of ecosystems and biodiversity.

Planning tools could easily limit land uses that are harmful to the community, and require net-positive impacts, were it not for customs. These include a philosophical/legal heritage that prioritizes private property rights over the public good and, of course, vested interests. There are many possible ways to create incentives that might gradually alter these biases. However, none of these schemes, summarized below, have yet aimed for a net-positive contribution to the public estate and ecological base. This would only require minor modifications to existing systems. (Part II discusses reforms to institutional principles/practices that would involve modifications to constitutions or charters.)

- *Street/yard easements*: In dense cities, most urban buildings exploit the 'allowable' building envelope, as defined by planning set-back and height limit regulations. As an incentive, GS could be allowed, in appropriate circumstances, to effectively extend the floor area or building envelope.[57] Partial extensions over alleyways, streets, yard requirements or height limits, for eco-services like noise and pollution reduction or biodiversity habitats, would need to meet variance requirements.[58] The additional floor area provided by the GS, such as bay windows and balconies, create a financial incentive to owners, but can be designed to benefit the public, neighbors and nature as well as occupants.
- *Developer contributions/exactions*: When a large greenfield development or housing estate entails significant public infrastructure costs (e.g. roads, sewers, water, electricity), contributions/exactions are sometimes negotiated from the developers. For example, some of the land may be dedicated to public uses such as parks or sports-fields. However, some public uses convert grasslands to lawns or otherwise adversely impact native bushlands/woodlands. Where unavoidable, these impacts could be offset by GS that provides eco-services. For example, GS over park paths, lawns or Playgardens to support native ecosystems, or integrated with Living Machines between the natural and urban landscape, could create buffers and provide biodiversity habitats.
- *Reversing green tape*: Costly prescriptive regulations and assessment tools can add 'green tape' that delays projects or increases transaction costs. For example, to conduct the paperwork for green building certification, it is often necessary to hire a dedicated staff person for many months. Some councils will expedite development applications, or 'streamline' approval processes, for buildings that receive high scores on RTs. However, since few certified green buildings provide significant public or environmental gains, expediting conventional 'sustainable' buildings simply increases the speed of environmental depletion/degradation. It would make more sense to impose fees on buildings that do not score well on RTs [Chapters 11–12].
- *Planning code variances*: Planning code variations/variances allow minor exemptions from rules where they cause undue hardship or undesirable outcomes in the particular context. They are more likely to be approved if no neighbors object, and they benefit the wider public. An extension into a rear yard for an attached GS on a sun-facing back wall of a building can support balconies or sun porches. If it also supports a passive solar greenhouse, significant vegetation, nesting boxes, vegetable trays and/or solar cells on shading devices, it could become net positive. The variance criteria could require a significant gain in eco-services or urban biodiversity habitats.
- *Transferable development rights*: Transferable development rights (TDRs), reportedly used since 1916,[59] move development entitlements or property rights around for equitable purposes. TDRs have enabled new planning provisions that increase development controls, such as new height limits, by transferring the property rights elsewhere. The reduction in the 'allowable' floor area can also be transferred or sold to another property owner. A PD approach would enable 'surplus' eco-services or biodiversity gains on one site to be transferred to another, to incentivize net-positive gains.[60] This way, the best locations for particular biodiversity enclaves/habitats could be created in suitable urban areas without burdening any property owners.

- *Offsetting on other sites*: Biodiversity offsetting is now a well-established concept in regional areas for ecological compensation when relatively unspoiled land will be damaged by resource extraction. For example, some urban buildings have been allowed more floor area where developers contribute financially to a rural eco-restoration project. The additional harm from the extra development is, theoretically, offset by rural remediation. Although the biodiversity impacts due to the extra floor area may be offset, the impacts of the basic building seldom are – even where the legislation calls for 'net benefit'. That is, offset schemes do not compensate for the development, only the extra development.
- *Credit and banking schemes*: Development credit systems occur in many forms. For example, farmers might set aside and restore existing land for biodiversity conservation in order to deposit the credits in a biodiversity bank, which developers can purchase.[61] Private exchanges are also sometimes arranged. For example, grocery stores and restaurants have leased large roof spaces on nearby properties to grow fresh produce. GS on these roofs could add vertical space for more produce along with auxiliary functions like bee hives and bird refuges. Trading and banking eco-services could be facilitated by establishing credits for ecological space, assuming the values of ecosystem services are formalized.

6.8 Conclusion

Energy retrofit schemes have been attempted with little ecological design input, and eco-positive retrofitting for social and ecological gains has not been tried.

The general approach to environmental problems has been to seek large-scale industrial solutions without institutional reform. Although the scale of the problem is huge, most problems were caused by industrial development. For example, large-scale energy supply and carbon sequestrating technologies use resources, emit carbon and, in the case of nuclear power, have many other unresolved issues. Meanwhile, they do not address the problems caused by millions of new buildings. Regardless of whether a soft or hard energy path is followed, each precinct, building complex or individual building could begin to contribute to sustainability by retrofitting to create positive socio-ecological impacts.

Unless exchange systems require net-positive biodiversity gains, they will continue to legitimize negative trade-offs, even where they could be avoided by better design.

Buildings that leave the environment worse off than no development are not sustainable. The above schemes tend to use (weak) building and planning code requirements as the baseline. When these were developed, biodiversity or ecology was not considered, only health and safety. Hence, codes create a de facto license to deplete the environment. Fortunately, standards in codes, regulations and design review processes could be improved by simply adding term 'net positive' – as long as this is defined in accordance with PD theory and not merely relative to current conditions or practice (i.e. relative to pre-urban, pre-settlement or pre-industrial conditions).[62]

6.9 Exercises

1. Divide into groups and design a bamboo GS system that would contribute to the sustainability of impoverished 'third world' villages or refugee camps. Each group should select a different culture and climate, and explain their priorities and solutions.
2. Examine an urban planning code's incentive provisions which may appear as variances, point systems, developer contributions or offsets, and so on. Analyze why and how they fail to encourage net-positive gains and modify their provisions to change this, while minimizing compliance and transaction costs.
3. Acquire the plans for an old building that needs structural reinforcement or modernization for earthquake resistance. Retrofit the building with an internal and/or external GS system to improve its earthquake resistance. Ensure that the cubic meters of ecological space exceed the gross floor area.
4. Take a whole city block for which plans are obtainable (for convenience) and retrofit the block with GS in the empty spaces, for appropriate eco-positive functions and accessibility for maintenance and so on (avoid access by, or dangerous conditions for, building climbers, and other misuses).

Notes

1 World Wildlife Fund (2016) *Living Planet Report 2016: Risk and Resilience in a New Era*, WWF, Gland, Switzerland. www.wnf.nl/custom/LPR_2016_fullreport/.
2 Birkeland, J. (2009) GEN 77: Design for Eco-Services: Environmental Services, pp. 1–12, and GEN 78: Design for Eco-Services: Building Services, pp. 1–8, in *BEDP Environmental Design Guide of the Australian Institute of Architects* (online and hard copy journal) ACT, Canberra, www.environmentdesignguide.com.au/.
3 See Birkeland, J. (2002) Responsible Design, in Birkeland, J. (ed.) *Design for Sustainability: A Sourcebook of Integrated, Eco-Logical Design*, Earthscan, London, pp. 26–30.
4 Birkeland, J., and Knight-Lenihan, S. (2016) Biodiversity Offsetting and Net Positive Design, *Journal of Urban Design* 21(1), pp. 1–17.
5 Birkeland, J. (2014) Positive Development, in Bryne, J., Sipe, N., and Dodson, J. (eds) *Australian Environmental Planning*, Routledge, London.
6 Birkeland, GEN 77 and GEN 78.
7 See Birkeland, J. (2008) *Positive Development: From Vicious Circles to Virtuous Cycles through Built Environment Design*, Earthscan, London.
8 Flexible joints in GS can reinforce structures without increasing brittleness.
9 Some people have survived tsunamis by climbing on stable structures.
10 An example of Green Scaffolding that is integrated into the building wall is in Birkeland, *Positive Development*, pp. 281–2, and Hes, D., and du Plessis, C. (2015) *Designing for Hope: Pathways to Regenerative Sustainability*, Routledge, London, pp. 93–111.
11 This happens fairly often. www.washingtonpost.com/local/trafficandcommuting/for-the-third-time-glass-falls-from-a-bethesda-office-building-onto-sidewalk-below/2019/02/19/.
12 It is generally considered that levels above roughly eight stories have strong wind loads and would not be suitable for appendages.
13 Safamanesh, B., and Byrd, H. (2012) The Two Sides of a Double-Skin Facade: Built Intelligent Skin or Brand Image Scam, *Proceedings of the 46th Architectural Science Association Conference*, Griffith University, NSW, Australia.
14 For example, GS could blend into historic wrought iron terrace houses. See figure 1 and 3 in Birkeland, *Positive Development*, pp. 9 and 31 respectively.
15 Mirrors could bounce light into unshaded areas at street level.
16 Birkeland, J. (2008) Space Frame Walls: Facilitating Positive Development, in Proceedings of the 2008 World Sustainable Building Conference, Melbournea.
17 Two-way mirrors can be used so that animals are not frightened.

18 Birkeland, J. (2012) Integrating Building Design and Solar Industries, *Solar Progress*, Journal of the Australian Solar Energy Society, summer issue. http://issuu.com/commstrat/docs/sp_2012.
19 This design was designed by the author for a National Sustainability Center in Canberra but it was not funded.
20 Green chandelier was proposed in Birkeland, *Positive Development*, figure 4, p. 33.
21 Birkeland, J., Renger, C., and Midmore, D. (2013) Positive Development: Design for Climate Mitigation and Ecological Gains, Sustainable Building Conference SB13, Vancouver, June 4–6.
22 Many self-help homes use recycled glass bottles and other reject materials artistically. E.g. https://insteading.com/blog/glass-bottle-walls/and www.pinterest.com.au/luttepetut/glass-bottle-walls-earthship-/.
23 See Hes and du Plessis, *Designing for Hope*, pp. 93–111.
24 Over 75% of the planet's land area is degraded, and over 90% could become degraded by 2050. By 2050, up to 700 million people may be displaced due to scarce land resources and this figure could reach up to 10 billion by 2100. https://ec.europa.eu/jrc/en/news/new-world-atlas-desertification-shows-unprecedented-pressure-planets-natural-resources.
25 In Morocco, fog water collectors reportedly can capture 22 litres per square meter which will serve 1,300 people. See Dodson, L. L., and Bargach, J. (2015) Harvesting Fresh Water from Fog in Rural Morocco, *Procedia Engineering* 107, pp. 186–93. There is a new solar-powered technology for removing salt from brackish water. See https://reneweconomy.com.au/unsw-looks-to-solar-powered-desalination-to-help-bust-droughts-josh-39604/.
26 Rural fires are subject to differing conditions such as wind and heat, and pumps can soon fail in a fire, but mechanical drips over a fly screen are more reliable. Effectiveness of fly screens is discussed in Holmgren, D. (1992) *The Flywire House: A Case Study in Design Against Bushfire*, Nascimanere Pty Ltd, Queensland.
27 The GS structures that support the parabolic concentrators in large-scale solar thermal plants could be combined with vertical food production systems.
28 An algae power building, the BIQ building, in Hamburg, Germany, has been operating since about 2013. www.fastcompany.com/3033019/this-algae-powered-building-actually-works.
29 Hassanli, S., Hu, G., Kwok, K. C., and Fletcher, D. F. (2017) Utilizing Cavity Flow within Double Skin Façade for Wind Energy Harvesting in Buildings, *Journal of Wind Engineering and Industrial Aerodynamics* 167, pp. 114–27.
30 People experience discomfort when the room temperature is stratified.
31 Daylighting has several health benefits. See https://sustainability.ncsu.edu/blog/changeyourstate/benefits-of-natural-light/.
32 Triple-glazed windows are sometimes used where street noise is a problem and is used in very cold climates. The frame must be well insulated. www.homebuilding.co.uk/does-triple-glazing-make-sense/.
33 EFTE, a synthetic fluoropolymer, considered a relatively sustainable material, uses less raw material costs, weighs little, has good light-transmittance, thermal insulation compared glass. However, it is easily damaged and emits chemicals in fire. www.builtjournal.org/built_issue_7/01_Touchaphong.pdf.
34 E.g. internal air can be circulated through filters and plants in the GS.
35 It is theoretically possible to extract chemicals from 'hyperaccumulator' plants and earthworms that are cleaned from the air and water. Reeves, R. D., van der Ent, A., and Baker, A. J. (2018) Global Distribution and Ecology of Hyperaccumulator Plants, in *Agromining: Farming for Metals*. Springer, Cham, pp. 75–92.
36 Mosquito-borne diseases are spreading due to global warming. www.scientificamerican.com/article/mosquito-borne-diseases-on-the-uptick-thanks-to-global-warming/.
37 This is a test to see if anyone is reading this.
38 About 1% of topsoil is lost each year, and half the earth's topsoil has been lost in the last 100 years. www.worldwildlife.org/threats/soil-erosion-and-degradation.
39 Cotanaa, F., Petrozzia, A., Piselloa, A. L., et al. (2014) An Innovative Small Sized Anaerobic Digester Integrated in Historic Building, in *Energy Procedia 45, 68th Conference of the Italian Thermal Machines Engineering Association 2013*, Cham, pp. 333–41.

40 Roughly 15,000 medicinal plant species may be threatened with extinction. www.biological diversity.org/publications/papers/Medicinal_Plants_042008_lores.pdf.
41 Around 85% of global fish stocks are depleted. www.bbc.com/future/story/20120920-are-we-running-out-of-fish. There are other sources of Omega 3 such as flax seed.
42 There is little consensus on how much greenery is needed and there are myriad variables to consider.
43 Algaetecture is being explored for its aesthetic potential. See https://carloratti.com/project/algaetecture/and www.iaacblog.com/projects/algaetecture/.
44 Multi-story bird refuges have been proposed for roofs of buildings that are designed for protection from predators. Register, R. (2006) *Ecocities: Rebuilding Cities in Balance with Nature*, New Society Publishers, Bowen Island, BC, p. 123.
45 Todd, N. J., and Todd J. (1994) *From Eco-Cities to Living Machines*, Atlantic Books, Berkeley, CA.
46 For short description see Todd, J. (2002) Living Technologies, in Birkeland, *Design for Sustainability*, pp. 114–17.
47 Some wetlands and Living Machines have failed in droughts.
48 There are sometimes maintenance issues, partly because facilities managers lack the relevant background/interest to maintain them.
49 www.watercone.com/mage.html.
50 Water can be extracted from mist or fog, as done in Peruvian and Chilean deserts. https://newatlas.com/how-the-fogcatchers-of-the-atacama-are-bringing-water-to-the-driest-desert-on-earth/39040/.
51 www.eia.gov/energyexplained/?page=solar_thermal_power_plants.
52 Birkeland and Knight-Lenihan, Biodiversity Offsetting.
53 E.g. the public may pay for sewerage or electricity to be delivered to the new development, and the exaction may cover part of that cost.
54 Birkeland and Knight-Lenihan, Biodiversity Offsetting.
55 GBCA (2017) Land Use and Ecology Category Review, Green Building Council of Australia, Sydney https://gbca.org.au/contact/.
56 The author provided a critique of this biodiversity credit scheme but the outcome is unknown at time of writing.
57 The author proposed this in the early 1970s and the San Francisco Planning Department approved something similar.
58 Variances often require consent by adjacent landowners to a finding that they do not affect their property values and environmental amenity.
59 Nelson, A. C. (2012) *The TDR Handbook: Designing and Implementing Successful Transfer of Development Rights Program*, Island Press, Washington, DC.
60 Birkeland, *Positive Development*.
61 Bayon, R. (2008) Banking on Biodiversity, in *State of the World 2008*, Worldwatch Institute, Washington, DC, pp. 123–239. www.worldwatch.org/files/pdf/SOW08_chapter_9.pdf.
62 Again, the ecological baseline varies with the location. Pre-industrial is relevant to Europe which was greatly changed by various human civilizations for thousands of years, whereas pre-European settlement might be more appropriate for Australia.

Section D
Systems Mapping Themes (SMT) Analyses

7 SMT Analyses for Physical Design

7.1 Review and Preview

Mapping invisible systems that shape and are shaped by built environments can uncover sustainability gaps left by current planning methods and design tools.

Two young fish swam by an older one who greeted them with: 'how are you finding the water today?' After swimming on, one young fish asked the other: 'what the heck is water?' The fish did not 'see' the water because it had always been there. Some take the earth for granted and see social constructs as natural. In this way, mainstream environmental management frameworks reflect/reinforce the illusion that humans can become independent of the land, water and sky, and that ecosystems are expendable. The SMT, or systems mapping themes, are flows analyses that aim to expose these invisible currents.

SMT analyses aim to assist in developing physical solutions that reverse the losses of the ecological base, public estate and future public choice.

Conventional planning and design tools aim to accommodate economic growth with fewer impacts and/or more stakeholder benefits within regulations. To go beyond measuring, mitigating and monitoring environmental damage, new analytical frameworks are needed that can reverse the negative precepts (below) that are embedded in the dominant paradigm (DP). SMARTmode (system mapping and redesign thinking) is a community planning process discussed in *Positive Development* (2008) and summarized below.[1] This process includes forensic flows analyses that have since been expanded and are called SMT (systems mapping themes).[2] Governments and professional planning/building organizations would ideally map these undercurrents and make the information publicly available.

Since planning analyses and tools used in sustainable development fields only measure what has traditionally been studied, they do not identify net-positive potentials.

As discussed earlier, management considers what is easily unitized and measured, and closed-system methods are suited to predicting and controlling a complex reality by reducing phenomena to separate, measurable factors. For example, data on depletion or contamination of land, air and water are usually expressed as units,

156 *Design and Analysis*

not extra deaths/extinctions.[3] Numerical analyses and tools cannot yet capture the interrelatedness of multidimensional issues like poverty, equity or ecosystems. Although the understanding of the socio-ecological effects of urban development are improving, assessments do not examine losses of the local ecological or social domain in the context of global rates of human-driven consumption.[4]

The complex reciprocal relationship between the built environment sector and resource extraction/manufacturing industries, and their cumulative impacts, are seldom captured by linear-sequential analyses.

The built-environment fields can draw upon various material flows analyses at urban, regional or global scales, although they were developed for other purposes.[5] However, these studies generally trace flows downstream to/from 'primary industries', not from nature. Moreover, they do not trace the potential positive, multiple effects of good design back upstream. For example, replacing highly processed building materials with non-toxic substitutes and low-impact designs can generate compound savings throughout resource extraction, construction and manufacturing processes.[6] Yet most analyses only concern reducing waste streams (costs) in supply chains through recycling and upcycling measures, not reducing total flows by changing urban design.

In these two chapters, SMT analyses are contrasted with environmental analyses that trace energy/material conversions through time (upstream-downstream), but largely omit non-material impacts.

Impact assessment (EIA) traces negative impacts, such as pollution and waste, from the building components in proposed developments back through industries to their sources in nature. Material flows analyses trace reductions in material resources from places of extraction in nature through industries to their final location. Lifecycle assessment looks at a number of impacts, from carbon emissions to biodiversity impacts, at each processing stage of the development cycle. All three generic approaches can identify areas of waste and pollution that can be reduced. In contrast, SMT analyses concern the spatial and non-material dimension, and support multifunctional design to address opportunities.[7]

Many SMT Analyses concern spatial relationships that are overlooked in planning, urban design and architecture, even though these are generally considered 'spatial arts'.

Some SMT analyses concern space, as this has been overlooked. These include:

- NS (Negative Space) Analysis: maps underdeveloped or available space in urban areas, and tracks trends in the loss of public space, basic needs and amenities and eco-services over time. This can establish priorities for planning interventions that will increase net sustainability, and assist in identifying opportunities for increasing urban socio-ecological functions.
- MS (Multifunctional Space) Analysis: matches available public and private spaces with PD criteria (and other general sustainable design principles), and assesses the value of benefits and eco-services per unit of space (rather than the floor area per capita) while ensuring that spaces remain flexible enough to enable adaptability to unforeseen needs/problems.
- ET (Ecological Transformation) Analysis: determines ecosystems and species that are most likely to succeed in particular urban areas to support the eventual

regeneration of the bioregions. This can help to guide the design of habitats for representative ecosystems and endangered species, including their 'biological supply chains' and control of invasive species.
- ES (Ecological Space) Analysis: sets the amount of space for ecosystems and eco-services that a development should support in its structures and/or landscapes to offset the ecological damage caused during the resource extraction and manufacturing process. The aim is for every development to contribute directly or indirectly to the ecological base.
- PM (Passive Maximization) Analysis: looks at building form and site planning to ensure both solar access and substantial vegetation, while importing minimal energy and water. While not new, this has been de-emphasized due to rating tools (RTs) that set rules based on impact reduction and assume that zero-sum trade-offs are necessary.

SMT analyses would contribute background research to support other PD methods including the SMARTmode planning process, the eDR method and the STARfish tool.

SMT analyses are meant to be used in PD planning/design processes, by filling gaps left by conventional frameworks and processes in environmental governance, planning, decision making and design.

- SMARTmode provides a framework for developing community action plans, policy guidelines or project briefs (architectural criteria). It intends to create a more inclusive, positive lens for collaborative planning/development issues, as proposed in *Positive Development* (2008).
- The eDR process helps to develop a community consensus for urban or regional plans and provides a qualitative project and self-assessment method that includes basic sustainability issues that are often forgotten in RTs [Chapters 13–14].
- The STARfish tool provides a quantitative net-positive design assessment tool for use during the design process in the form of a free computer app, which can be downloaded from a website – sustainability.org.au [Chapters 15–16].

Outline: A review of the PD SMARTmode process is provided below. The SMT analyses listed and described in these two chapters are also referenced in the chapters on the eDR and STARfish tools to underscore how and when they should be consulted or applied. The descriptions of the SMT analyses may be further clarified by the discussion topics and research exercises provided at the end of Chapter 8 which apply them to actual sustainability problems. The SMT analyses are sorted into different although overlapping levels of investigation from local to national scales of decision making and grouped into four general categories:

- Development or building design issues of concern to project design teams – design standards.
- Municipal planning and development control or project review considerations – planning standards.
- Decision making and assessment system design – assessment standards.
- Governance frameworks that concern basic needs or rights – ethical standards.

158 *Design and Analysis*

By exposing and filling in gaps in urban planning and design, these analyses are intended to better align urban governance with sustainable design.

These analyses may not address every issue that has been omitted from urban planning and decision making. However, they indicate how the built environment plays a pivotal role in sustainability issues that currently are barely considered. These omissions exist because the philosophical basis of planning and design tools evolved before there was any awareness of ecology, let alone resource limits. Institutional reform could help to shift some of the anti-ecological biases that have culminated in a perverse economic system. Built environment design cannot change an economic system, but it could alleviate many of that system's harsher social and environmental impacts.

The potential functions of SMT analyses include:

- Support for SMARTmode, and the eDR and STARfish tools (described later).
- A research framework for sustainable planning and urban design.
- Additional considerations to fill in gaps in building assessment tools.
- Information to supplement that which was collected only for economic growth.
- Means to identify priority sites where design interventions could be most effective.
- Topics for mind-mapping exercises or design charrettes in community planning.
- Means to draw attention to the ethical dimensions of urban environments.
- Support for large-scale flows analyses at bioregional scales.
- Ways to apply big data analytics in support of the public good.
- Information to inform design briefs for the planning and design of particular projects.
- Means to make who wins or loses in development decisions more transparent.

7.2 Review of the SMARTmode Planning Process

SMT analyses contribute to the SMARTmode process for participatory planning, and that process, summarized here, also provides a capsule review of PD principles.

Because problem definitions and analytical frameworks evolved in the pre-ecological era, the anti-ecological biases in development decision processes are baked in. Since resources seemed infinite, progress became associated with exploiting natural resources as rapidly as possible. Resource exploitation became a race, and governments often subsidized resource exploitation.[8] Resource allocation processes picked winners and sometimes compensated losers, but did not distribute benefits well. Conflict resolution by design provides an antidote. Design-based processes can make everyone better off, because competing public needs and interests can usually be met simultaneously through out-of-the-box and/or multifunctional solutions. The SMARTmode process aims to aid collaborative design:

- *Establish common ground on sustainability concepts*: The SMARTmode process skips to the conclusion of typical workshop processes. Most sustainability workshops have revolved around defining sustainability and never seem to get beyond the views that people come to share. PD bypasses this stage, however worthwhile, because it is circuitous. Instead, participants are expected to arrive with a commitment to inter/intra-generational equity and nature preservation (i.e. sustainability). It is not about converting those who apparently need to consume luxuries that are not available to most others. The starting point is the PD sustainability standard which, again, means expanding future options by increasing the ecological base and public estate.

- *Adopt a constitution for decision-making*: A basic principle of PD is that sustainability is the fundamental right and responsibility of current and future generations. It is more than just a set of values or beliefs (contrary to the position of some post-modern writers). Since most construction harms the earth and thus reduces long-term options, everyone has stakes in how the earth is modified by development. The organizational structure/constitution of a major project, community plan or project partnership should ensure substantive due process (fair outcomes) and procedural due process (fair rules of engagement). An informal constitution to that effect should be agreed to by the participants.
- *Articulate project objectives and criteria*: A set of general PD social and ecological criteria was stated in *Positive Development* (2008).[9] These can assist in guiding project-specific, bioregionally appropriate planning and design criteria. The question is: what would be sustainable in a perfect world? Whereas sustainable building guidelines and tools aim for incremental improvements on current practices, and label that 'sustainable', the eco-positive design review (eDR) process asks questions to stimulate design and self-assessment before and during the design activity. It can also be used by third-party development consent/control processes. A sample eDR, which is oriented toward developing regions is provided as a general reference [Chapters 13–14].
- *Conduct forensic audits for new information*: PD forensic flows analyses (SMT) are a means to identify areas of waste, hazards, social inequities (slavery in the supply chain) where urban design interventions can speed up the transformation to sustainability. Soon, digital technology or big data will enable the targeting of design opportunities on multiple scales.[10] Currently, digital tools are being applied to complex urban systems but generally leave out impacts on ecosystems and bioregions. SMT creates a framework to broaden the application of these highly reductionist tools and synchronize them with design. Where digital mapping is impractical, the SMT analyses can serve as workshop/discussion topics to stimulate ideas.
- *Consider 'how and what' to trace and measure*: An over-emphasis on numbers leads to reductionism instead of finding means to increase life-quality opportunities. Numbers generally require system boundaries or artificial limits in time and space to enable arithmetic. By ignoring crucial 'remote' impacts, boundaries conceal cumulative, bio-magnified impacts.[11] Likewise, buildings and urban systems are usually seen as bounded systems and are examined using reductionist factors (e.g. energy, materials or water) which sideline ecological impacts. Again, comparing developments to typical buildings, pre-construction site conditions, conventional practices, and so on, means that irreversible impacts on the global life-support system are treated as gains, as if they somehow increased ecological sustainability.
- *Select appropriate methods and tools*: Tools are often selected for ease of use or to enable the use of pre-existing information. That is, they define problems and set targets that match the tools, and then select data that match

the tools, rather than the reverse. For example, most built-environment assessment methods (often mis-labelled 'design tools') have conceptual roots in cost-benefit balance sheets. These encourage trade-offs. Where only the impacts within system boundaries are counted, closing loops are seen as solutions. In essence, closed-loop systems recycle, downcycle or upcycle materials/products.[12] Hence they are mitigation measures. Instead of 'internalizing negative impacts', PD aims to externalize positive impacts.[13]

- *Develop planning information, concepts and strategies*: SMT analyses aim to determine priority planning and design issues for particular sites, cities and/or regions. There are many sets of generic criteria and indicators.[14] However, they are often forgotten when local councils compete to attract development to increase tax revenue. Councils should provide relevant sustainability data and criteria to ensure that economic development contributes to social and ecological gains. Governments or planners have the unique capacity to access this kind of information in the public interest, but they do not yet provide many data relevant to SMT analyses. Hence, university students and researchers may need to fill these gaps.

- *Develop design strategies/solutions*: The SMT analyses are a kind of social and ecological 'needs analysis' of the site and surrounding areas. Sustainable planning should correct local deficiencies. It is not just a matter of efficient, compact, mixed land uses.[15] Whereas architectural design traditionally ends at the building envelop or property line, PD sees design as thinking in flows,[16] and 'cities as landscapes' that support regional ecosystems.[17] PD therefore starts with the highest ecological use of land/water site. This re-prioritization leads to different kinds of design solutions that focus on multifunctional, adaptable design: multiplying benefits, rather than reduction, or subtracting impacts from unsustainable designs.

- *Apply self-assessment*: Since the conventional baseline is typical developments, buildings advertise reductions beyond the harm an ordinary (hypothetical) building might have caused. The basic criteria for self-assessment before, during and/or after the planning and design process is the PD Test. To review, the PD *ecological* baseline is increases in ecological carrying capacity beyond pre-development or pre-settlement (not pre-construction) conditions.[18] The PD *social* baseline requires increases in social equity at the local or regional scale. To increase future *options*, the Hierarchy of Eco-innovation (HI) provides a scale based on the public benefits of projects, including increases in future options and opportunities [Box 5].[19]

- *Obtain external assessment*: Green building rating/marketing tools (RTs) set efficiency standards ranging from 'better than the norm' to 'do no harm'. These are not genuine gains.[20] Efficiency is essential but has remote benefits to nature. For example, a factory using child or slave labor, producing toys with toxic materials, or otherwise creating unjust enrichment for investors or developers,[21] could score very highly on most RTs. In contrast, PD assessment considers the social 'purposes' of projects. The qualitative eDR process and quantitative STARfish tool, although geared for use in self-assessment by design teams, can also be used by commercial assessors or government approval officers.

- *Select and apply relevant measurements*: Tools do not always measure relevant things in relevant ways. For example, using land for conventional buildings reduces or delays prospects for the transformation to a sustainable society.

Since land use can be zero sum, the opportunity cost of green buildings keeps growing.[22] Yet impact assessments do not consider reductions in the earth's remaining land area. Government environmental reporting looks at depleting/degrading resource stocks, but not how it is caused by buildings.[23] Moreover, land uses are still determined less by planning than by property and/or construction prices, even though prices fluctuate, are speculative and are not grounded in biophysical reality.

- *Assess accountability and performance*: Post-occupancy evaluation (POE) is well established. POE compares the completed project to goals defined in the project brief, the predicted technical performance and/or occupant satisfaction. However, POE does not compare outcomes to a sustainability standard. Few if any POEs adequately investigate reasons for design shortcomings, let alone explain why projects intended to be exemplars of sustainability were later converted into ordinary developments. How industry structures, organizational cultures, modus operandi or tools have undermined the brief is not systematically investigated. PD requires deficiencies to be corrected after construction, which is possible if adaptable design is used to facilitate future sustainability upgrades.

7.3 Overview of SMT Analyses

SMT analyses aim to reverse negative assumptions and omissions in planning processes while stimulating design that generates positive social and environmental ripple effects.

The following outlines the SMT analyses before describing them in detail (as suggested by a reviewer). Government agencies should provide this information, as they are responsible for managing environment-development conflicts. New digital technologies could make it possible to collect and map information relevant to sustainability. The following analyses overlap and ideally would be combined as one overarching urban-bioregional analysis. They are 'divided' to accommodate specialization and suggest that design could be compatible and even symbiotic with reductionist research. They are arranged below from smaller-scale (building design, development consent, local planning) to larger-scale decision-making frameworks and institutional arrangements for environmental governance.

7.3.1 Design Issues at Building or Project Scale

- *Avoiding upstream and downstream waste*: Planning and design methods should go beyond impact reduction to avoid both: post-production waste during project/product usage, such as wasteful functions, luxuries, status symbols or contributions to wealth differentials; and pre-production waste, taking into account the ecological restoration time at resource extraction and building sites (i.e. embodied and ecological waste).
- *Increasing positive public purposes*: In the context of escalating sustainability issues, projects and products should be assessed according to their net public benefit and contribution to systems change (not just efficiency/effectiveness). This includes social purposes and functions. Where anti-social projects cannot be modified, positive public benefits can usually be included at no net cost.

162   *Design and Analysis*

- *Maximizing natural systems and ecological spaces*: Project planning should first address basic ecological and social deficits/needs in the surrounding area, and building design should first maximize passive solar, multifunctional and adaptable design principles. Since economic uses are becoming less site-dependent (partly because of the internet), they should cease to be the primary determinant of land use.

7.3.2 Urban Planning Issues at Municipal or Regional Scale

- *Prioritizing preventative actions*: Each development should ensure that the surrounding community has direct access to basic needs to provide physical security in environmental and civil emergencies (e.g. escape routes, safe refuges) and political independence. The worst-case scenario should determine the investment, rather than balancing the likelihood of problems against the cost of prevention.
- *Setting eco-positive site planning principles*: Design review and assessment processes as well as building, site and zoning regulations, should begin from an ecological analysis of the site or region, in part by examining the site and bioregion's natural history. Cities should support appropriate ecosystem nurseries, biodiversity incubators and nature corridors for eventually reseeding the bioregions.
- *Mapping opportunities for public benefits*: Planners and/or researchers should proactively and systematically identify 'negative space' (i.e. lacking social or ecological benefits). These are a resource in urban core areas, as they provide opportunities for multiple public uses/benefits. Ecological space should not be limited to ground-level landscapes, and includes space around, above or within building envelopes.

7.3.3 Decision Making at Development Assessment Scale

- *Moving from transactional to transformational tools*: Proposed design-based tools with different standards, baselines, frameworks and measurement concepts are discussed in Part II. However, a couple of basic concepts in development control and assessment that need change are introduced here: the lack of whole-system baselines and benchmarks, and reliance on decision processes where design is more suitable.
- *Setting whole-system baselines (time and space)*: Projects should be assessed against fixed sustainability standards, as opposed to moving targets (i.e. typical buildings, or current conditions and practices). Alternatives should be compared against fixed baselines as if neither project/system yet existed. This would account for the cost of projects that perpetuate harmful energy sources (e.g. nuclear, coal).
- *Instituting whole-system accounting*: Planners should consider the costs of low standards for long-life building projects, including the opportunity costs and added expense of upgrading buildings later. Both costs can be avoided by design for diversity and adaptability. Instead of discounting the future, the 'compound benefits' of immediate, direct action would also be considered.

7.3.4 Governance at Regional or National Scale

- *Charting impacts of governance systems*: Government reporting systems seldom examine whether institutional systems, agency decisions, and/or their on-ground outcomes are consistent with their specific enabling legislation and/or stated policies (e.g. an environmental protection agency that authorizes unnecessary environmental damage).[24] Development decisions should be transparent/public and show judicious reasoning that links decisions logically to sustainability principles.[25]

- *Increasing socio-economic independence*: The ways that centralized infrastructure and electronic/financial systems affect democratic needs/rights and distributive justice should be examined. Indicators of engagement like voting and/or purchasing only reflects aggregate activity, not substantive choice. Similarly, how economic policy affects resource scarcity and, in turn, the economy itself is seldom assessed (i.e. a whole-system view).
- *Maximizing equitable outcomes*: Cities concretize social inequities, concentrate wealth and reduce social mobility. Nonetheless, there is scant research on how built environment transfers wealth between regions, classes or other social divisions (e.g. public and private sectors), or facilitates unjust enrichment. Physical conditions, not monetary transactions, are what most directly reflect genuine life quality.

7.4 Code to the SMT Diagrams

The diagrams that accompany the SMT analyses below aim to accentuate differences while suggesting how conventional approaches tend to reinforce the status quo 0].

There is a tendency to adopt plans, policies or actions that involve the *least* change, because they are assumed to have the least financial and/or political cost [Chapter 9]. Consequently, efficiencies are made incrementally, at the margins. Conventional design likewise aims to fit into the status quo. However, a design that works within an unsustainable context often tends to perpetuate the outdated parent systems. For example, gentrification stimulates revitalization, but often exacerbates disparities of wealth. SMT analyses are meant to guide design that stimulates positive change in the wider urban context while addressing specific local issues, as in 'urban acupuncture' [Figure 7.1].

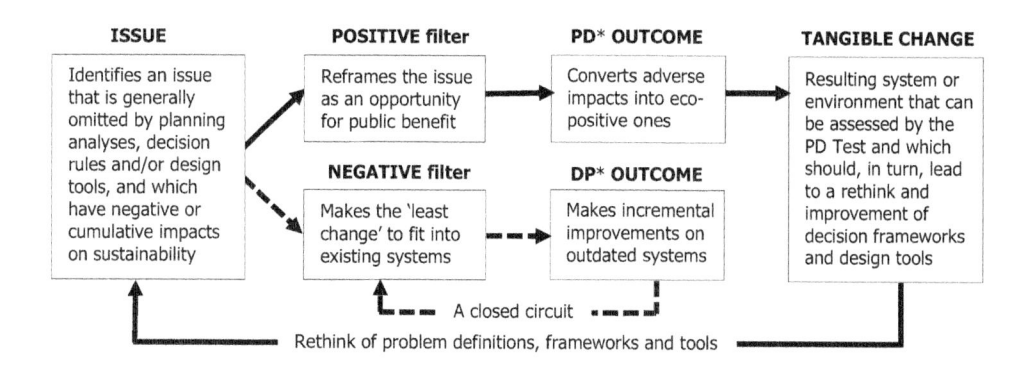

ISSUE	POSITIVE filter	PD* OUTCOME	TANGIBLE CHANGE
Identifies an issue that is generally omitted by planning analyses, decision rules and/or design tools, and which have negative or cumulative impacts on sustainability	Reframes the issue as an opportunity for public benefit	Converts adverse impacts into eco-positive ones	Resulting system or environment that can be assessed by the PD Test and which should, in turn, lead to a rethink and improvement of decision frameworks and design tools
	NEGATIVE filter	**DP* OUTCOME**	
	Makes the 'least change' to fit into existing systems	Makes incremental improvements on outdated systems	

⊢ ─ ─ A closed circuit ─ ─ ⊣
Rethink of problem definitions, frameworks and tools

***PD** = Positive Development
***DP** = dominant paradigm
━ ━ ▶ Closed circuit = leads to vicious circles

Figure 7.1 Code to SMT (System Mapping Themes) diagrams

7.5 Design Issues at Building or Project Scale

7.5.1 Avoiding Upstream and Downstream Waste

Designed Waste (DW) Analysis *anticipates and traces likely upstream-downstream waste resulting from design itself to reduce impacts during product usage (e.g. planned obsolescence, redundancy, deferred maintenance, extravagant materials or harmful disposal impacts).*

Much waste is caused by poor design: lack of adaptability, longevity and/or biodegradability, or high maintenance and operating costs. DW analysis anticipates the likely waste resulting from a design over its lifecycle, including disposal. Unlike manufacturers, designers seldom benefit financially from product duplication, disposability, breakage or the 'rebound effect'.[26] Therefore, in the absence of more demanding regulations and building code provisions, the responsibility for waste reduction falls upon designers by default. Low-impact, multifunctional products and resort-like living environments can replace the emotional 'needs' for excess consumption, pressures from changing fashions, retail therapy or the 'keeping up with the Jones' effect.[27]

Despite superficial differences, there are few substantive choices among most 'modern' urban environments. Buildings are standardized for the convenience of the construction industry, not the planet. Yet the investment in trivial 'stylistic' product variations in buildings (not just cars or disposable items) is huge.[28] Even if 'efficiently' produced, these expensive environments do not benefit nature or humanity. Job creation is sometimes used to justify the production of luxury homes, jewelry, expensive electronic equipment (with toxic e-waste) or building facelifts.[29] In contrast, eco-positive retrofitting would create interesting, diverse skilled jobs that pay for themselves and reduce long-term public costs [Chapter 5].

The lifecycle impacts of commercial construction products are increasingly being calculated and reported. However, specification tools have focused more on efficiencies in manufacturing processes than on avoiding wasteful design, extravagant uses or excessive maintenance costs.[30] For example, by rewarding the use of certified timber products, building certification tools have encouraged excess timber usage for unnecessary purposes [Chapters 11–12]. Green 'mansions' have received top energy ratings despite extra rooms with expensive, imported (high-embodied energy) furnishings that are only used on special occasions. If ostentation is necessary, low-impact substitutes can look just as expensive as luxuries like marble walls or gold faucets [Figure 7.2]

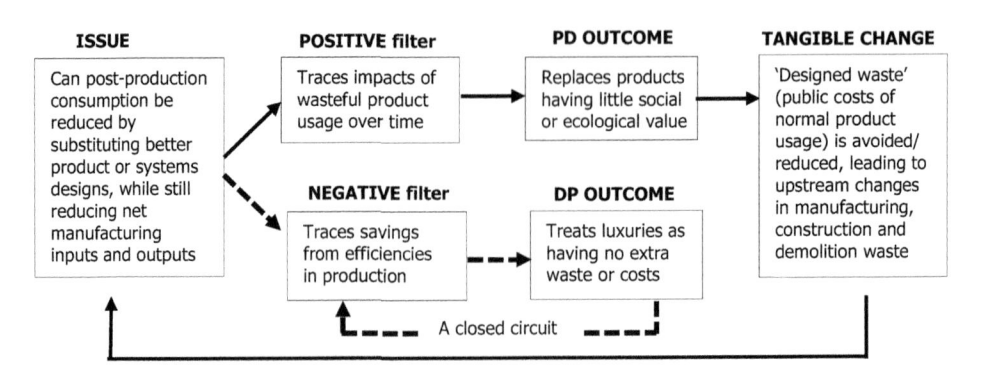

Figure 7.2 Designed Waste (DW) Analysis

Systems Mapping Themes (SMT) Analyses 165

Ecological Waste (EW) Analysis *considers the restoration time and space that specific ecosystems need to recover, in addition to the costs of regeneration and quantities of materials used or embodied in production.*

Normally, the consumption of natural resources is measured simply by quantities of materials used or wasted. This often omits 'embodied waste': the cumulative loss of materials during forestry, mining and construction.[31] Although environmental impact assessments trace the damage between resource extraction sites and buildings, they tend to ignore the time and space needed for ecological functions to repair themselves. Similarly, when assessments use the (hypothetical) financial costs of replacing lost ecosystem services,[32] they assume that land and water ecosystems can recover their original condition. PD adds 'ecological waste' to account for the time and space that ecosystems require to regenerate.[33]

Even if the full costs of restoring land and water ecosystems were included in assessments, long-term human health impacts are generally underestimated. For example, the eco-restoration of mining sites is often undertaken, but there is no meaningful compensation for the human and environmental health impacts. This includes exposure of miners in developing nations to cyanide, and toxic waste and mercury in coal dust that circulates in the atmosphere and settles almost everywhere.[34] Wage increases, improved working conditions or social offsets for mining (e.g. Aboriginal cultural centers) seldom compensate for the individual health costs, let alone public human and environmental costs.

When losses of biodiversity habitats are factored in, they are often regarded as a one-off, not ongoing, cost. Hence, regrowing a forest sometimes counts as full compensation, as if seeds could replace an ecosystem. While the viability of replacement ecosystems is often presumed, there is no guarantee that the new forest will end up as healthy or biodiverse.[35] Trees can be felled again in, perhaps, a half century,[36] but many ecosystem values take longer to recover.[37] Even 'successfully' regenerated forests may be less disease resistant than the original forest, and altered ecosystems may harbor invasive species that invade nearby areas [Figure 7.3].

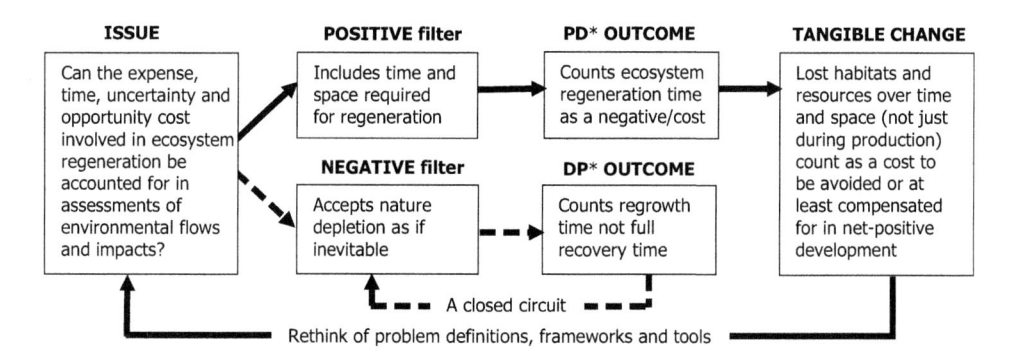

Figure 7.3 Ecological Waste (EW) analysis

7.5.2 Increasing Positive Public Purposes

Development Functions (DF) Analysis *assesses the 'social waste' inherent in a development or product that has negative public purposes/functions, to encourage the incorporation of public benefits where harmful outcomes cannot be prevented.*

Developments that have unnecessary negative impacts, lack humanitarian value and/or do not otherwise contribute to sustainability take space/resources away from other uses. Since approval processes are first-come-first-served, they do not consider the opportunity costs. Inherently wasteful if not anti-social functions (e.g. cigarette factory, tavern, race track, casino or shooting range) or its location (e.g. near a school, stream or beach) divert land and resources from development that could provide public benefits. Currently, socially unproductive land uses are not required to incorporate public benefits. Hence, DF analysis considers the waste and lost opportunities caused by an undesirable land use or building function.

Developments are seldom subjected to competing land uses, because building proposals are usually approved if they comply with planning codes – especially if certified as 'green'. Some design review processes allow for suggestions, but few RTs processes do [Chapters 11–12]. When EIAs are required, 'alternative' projects or land uses are sometimes examined, but there is no obligation for approval authorities to require revisions to projects or designs. Although the economic value of some developments is considered to override environmental concerns, designs could nevertheless include positive impacts. Design can at least 'value add' positive functions and economic benefits for the community.

Land uses with negative social impacts can have 'measurable' costs to local economies which are not recouped. Socially harmful businesses tend to degrade neighborhoods, as those neighbors that can move are likely to. Such businesses may be profitable, but other property owners lose out when the local economy declines. The location of land uses can also have public costs. For example, new regional shopping centers that wipe out central business districts can result in vacant buildings. Councils could accommodate critical public needs in such areas (subsidized by offsets), such as affordable housing, recreational uses, meeting halls, training centers and/or business incubators [Figure 7.4].

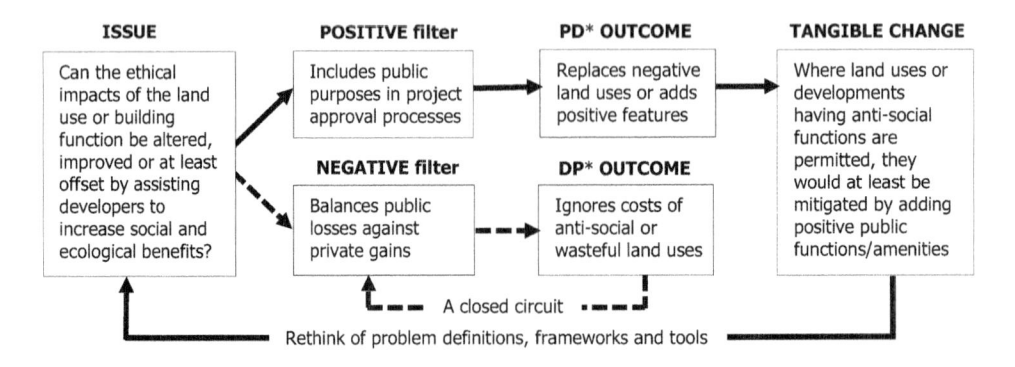

Figure 7.4 Development/Design Functions (DF) aAnalysis

Hierarchy of Innovation (HI) Analysis *assesses the public and environmental values of innovations/designs against a seven-step scale, similar to ethical technology assessment but more applicable to the spatial dimension or urban environment.*

Most assessment tools compare quantities of variables in design alternatives (e.g. energy, water, materials, pollution) relative to conventional development, without regard for their long-term outcomes. They do not consider potential system-wide public and environmental contributions that developments could make. While DF analysis (above) focuses on project or product purposes, and DW analysis (above) looks at likely waste during occupancy/usage, HI analysis is an ethics-based assessment.[38] It assesses increases in the ecological base, public estate and future public options (PD Test). It creates a hierarchy of planning and design intentions and outcomes on a scale from efficiency to recycling [Box 5].

The term 'innovation' is usually favored in business fields, perhaps because it sounds more 'hard' (technical) than design, which is subconsciously seen by some as decorative, trivial or feminine.[39] However, today eco-innovations prioritize commercialization, and often simply achieve 'efficient' increases in the use of fossil fuels, water or materials.[40] Similarly, some RTs use expert design panels to award extra points for innovation *per se* (i.e. originality), with little regard to the net effects on global material/energy flows. Sometimes, the new application of an existing technology to a building has counted as an innovation, regardless of any measurable contribution to sustainability.

HI analysis can be used to assess innovations, guide product/project design teams, set criteria for development project review boards, or be integrated into existing RTs to assess innovations. To incentivize design, the ability to privatize knowledge creates incentives for business to 'implement' ideas. However, when businesses commercialize ideas that were long advocated in environmental or indigenous circles, this disincentivizes the originators. In business, the ends justify the means, but it does not cost extra to recognize the origin of ideas. In PD, the proponents would acknowledge the origins of an innovation and show how the commercialization advances the concept [Figure 7.5].

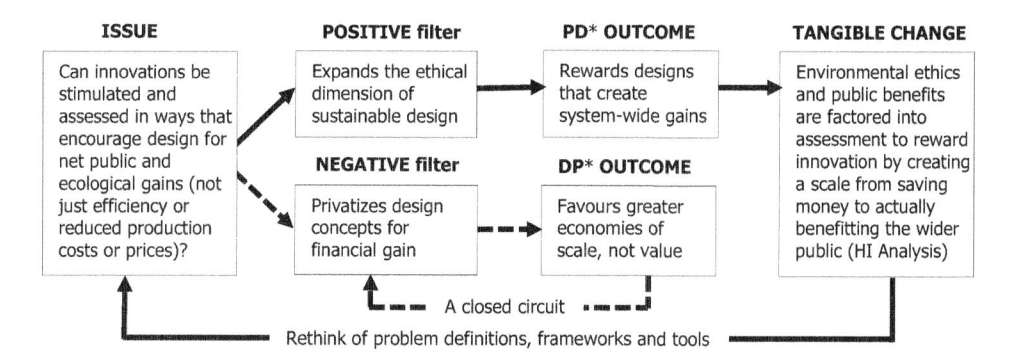

Figure 7.5 Hierarchy of Innovation (HI) analysis

7.5.3 Maximizing Natural Systems and Ecological Spaces

Passive Maximization (PM) Analysis *ensures that passive/natural systems are maximized before renewable and/or efficient mechanical energy systems are added on, since energy-efficient equipment reduces heating/cooling costs, but not necessarily total energy usage.*

Many case studies over the decades have demonstrated that passive solar design can achieve huge operational energy savings. Although passive solar design enjoyed USA government support during the 1970s oil crisis, this was short-lived, perhaps due to the influence of powerful petrochemical industries or geopolitical means of accessing oil. Biases against passive solar design then circulated, such as the idea that design added costs, or that solar access required the elimination of trees.[41] Also, a limited range of unattractive passive design prototypes were presented.[42] Meanwhile, the demand for cooling buildings/cities was growing, although the heat island effect was already recognized.[43]

Energy efficiency reduces costs per unit but can require more energy overall.[44] Hence, despite renewable energy technologies, passive design is essential.[45] Maximizing passive and renewable systems before specifying mechanical systems can reduce the size of backup heating-cooling-ventilating systems.[46] The impacts of energy 'sources' (not just quantity of energy) are examined in Source of Energy (SE) analysis, below. PM analysis maximizes passive energy collection-storage-circulation at building and/or precinct scale. It involves consideration of area-wide design factors and forces, such as the urban wind tunnel, heat island effect, latitude, topography and so on. This was customary green design practice before RTs emerged.[47]

Some developers/designers prefer off-the-shelf, energy-efficient equipment over passive solar design. However, RTs do not prioritize passive design either. Thus, many certified buildings rank higher in energy performance than 'typical buildings of the same type' due to efficient equipment, yet use excessive amounts of energy overall.[48] Other certified buildings are less efficient than ordinary buildings because they have acquired extra points in non-energy categories.[49] While passive solar design may use substantial thermal mass involving embodied energy,[50] renewable energy involves fossil-fuel-based fabrication processes.[51] Moreover, mechanical equipment has limited lifespans, and replacement costs are usually not included when comparing passive and renewable options [Figure 7.6].

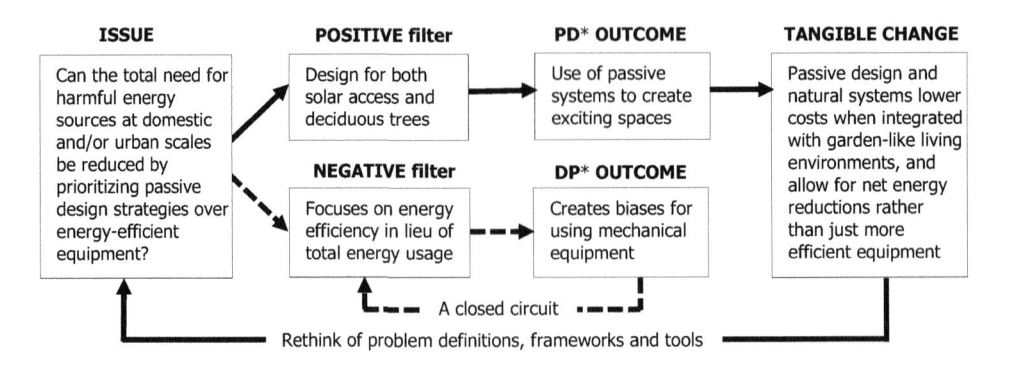

Figure 7.6 Passive Maximization (PM) Analysis

Multifunctional Space (MS) Analysis *assesses the potential for additional public benefits in the urban environment to counteract the single-function design strategies of modernism, to provide ecological space and allow for future adaptability.*

A PD strategy is using mixed-use multifunctional design to maximize public benefits in private and public development.[52] Since the 1960s at least, multifunctional design and mixed-use development planning have been considered good practice.[53] While mixed-use and transport-oriented development generally reduce car travel, this is often counteracted by people owning cars or periodically escaping congested cities in cars/planes to have some semi-wilderness experiences. Most people that can afford to will travel, so hindering car usage by making driving inconvenient is not very effective.[54] Instead, substantial, accessible urban 'natural' environments and multifunctional public green spaces can reduce the desire/need to escape cities.

Design can increase the multifunctional uses of community facilities and open spaces for people and nature. Currently, open spaces in central cities are mostly paved and used for moving people/objects around. Less open space does not mean less loitering or homelessness: it simply concentrates it. Negative Space analysis (below) identifies spatial opportunities, and MS analysis maximizes the benefits of that space and ensures future adaptability. It identifies missing social, psychological and ecological functions, and optimizes the way these are integrated with spaces, surfaces or structures. For example, design for eco-services can exploit otherwise underutilized spaces while greening the built environment.

Many site-specific social needs can be met while increasing the public estate (e.g. social places that strengthen community bonds), and ecological base (e.g. food gardens and natural water collection/storage/treatment). For example, instead of closing schools in response to demographic changes (a widespread trend to capitalize from one-off land sales), community functions/benefits are sometimes included, such as after-hour uses that provide some rent. School gyms are commonly rented for evening sport activities or public meetings. Other uses that preserve green public areas might include elderly facilities, urban farms, local craft shops, botanical gardens and/or public refuges in case of environmental disasters [Figure 7.7].

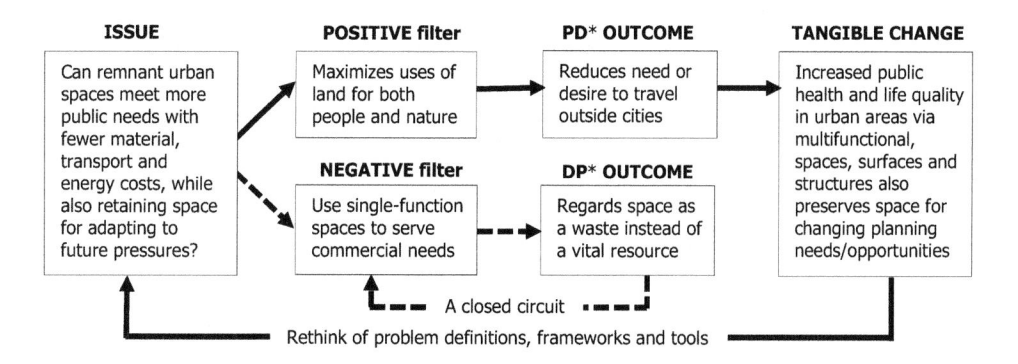

Figure 7.7 Multifunctional Space (MS) analysis

7.6 Urban Planning Issues at Municipal or Regional Scale

7.6.1 Prioritizing Preventative Actions

Resource Security (RS) Analysis *determines where environmental amenities and services are best located to provide for universal safety/security on a bioregional scale consistent with 'environmental space', while ensuring facilities/provisions for any emergency.*

In PD, direct and universal access to healthy food, clean water and air, shelter and safety in natural and civil emergencies is taken to be a basic human right. To ensure that the means of survival, health and wellbeing are universally available, local industries and cities must align with the bioregion.[55] Bioregional planning calls for living within the constraints of local natural resources and using systems of production and construction that conform to local/regional resources.[56] RS analysis identifies specific sites for facilities or services that increase local resource security, meet basic needs and ensure emergency facilities are within everyone's reach.

Whereas bioregionalism usually begins with inventories of local resources, RS analysis begins by calculating the 'environmental space'. This equals the available renewable resources divided by the relevant population to ensure sustainable consumption and fair distribution.[57] The amount can vary with changing populations, environmental conditions and efficiencies in production. RS analysis then determines the amount and location of provisions for civil/natural emergencies to ensure access from wherever people live, work or play. This is parallel to 'equity mapping',[58] which measures the proximity of people to environmental goods like parks. However, RS Analysis focuses on guiding design interventions that increase 'natural security'.

The funding for safety and/or security is often treated as a political issue: a process that depends on relative power or money, rather than design for geographical and environmental conditions (see RA analysis below). Thus, investments in urban safety have generally been limited to mitigating risks.[59] In contrast, Curitiba, Brazil, resettled squatter villages from flood plains to safe areas before the next flood occurred.[60] Existing 'escape routes' from large buildings have been modeled for efficient evacuation plans. Instead, urban high-rise buildings should be retrofitted with built-in escape routes for emergencies via elevated green corridors/bridges on lower floors, helicopter pads, etc. [Figure 7.8]

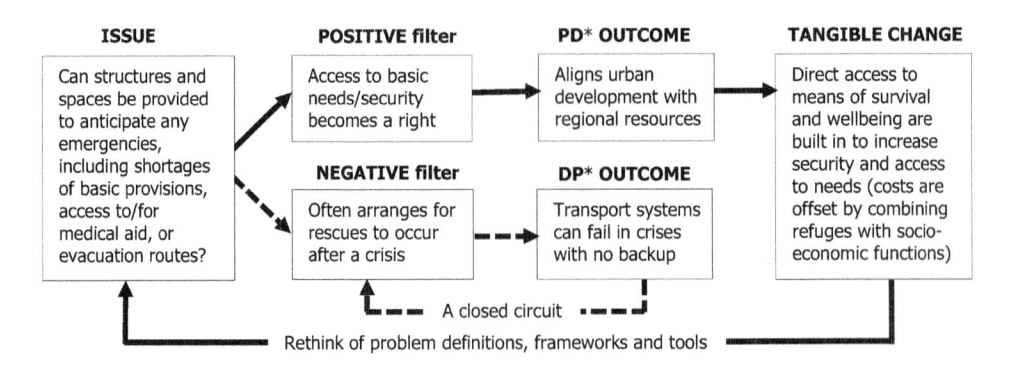

Figure 7.8 Resource Security (RS) Analysis

Risk Avoidance (RA) Analysis *determines the likely (economic, social, environmental) costs of a worst-case scenario in order to establish the 'minimum' amount that should be invested in preventative or corrective safety measures.*

Risk-benefit analyses inform decisions concerning future actions. However, decisions are often based on the odds that something 'will not happen'. The risks caused by the status quo are not cost-neutral. Discounting the future costs and impacts of unexpected ecological consequences is gambling. Cost predictions seldom adequately account for emotional and post-traumatic stress from environmental catastrophes. Meanwhile, in the belief design adds to total costs, opportunities for creating greater physical security are often ignored. Therefore, while RS analysis (above) distributes emergency facilities and provisions, RA analysis sets the amount of money/resources to be invested in preventative actions based on worst-case scenarios.

Volcanos, meteorites, and gamma rays have no design solutions. However, most environmental risks do have physical design solutions. Nonetheless, environmental risks are generally treated as an economic or insurance matter. Investments in prevention will not be made if their occurrence is unlikely. For instance, floods on flood plains are almost inevitable, and 'hundred-year floods' are happening ever more often. Yet preventative measures are often delayed. When storm surges or hurricanes strike, the costs of recovery usually exceed what prevention would have cost, especially since preventative measures can be offset by including income generators, such as recreational, social or commercial activity.

The risk and costs of forest or bush fires in near residential areas have been increasing.[61] However, housing design 'solutions' are often superficial and expensive. Changing the roof shapes and rain gutters are often recommended,[62] without modifying building surfaces or creating reliable sources of stored water with fire pumps.[63] Well-distributed public facilities with inbuilt water storage could be strategically positioned in bushlands/woodlands to fight fires before they become unstoppable fire storms.[64] Likewise, rural Green Scaffolding biodiversity habitats could create (eco-productive) fire barriers with built-in water tanks, fire pumps, sprays and fly-wire screens to reduce radiant heat, flames, embers [Chapter 6] [Figure 7.9].[65]

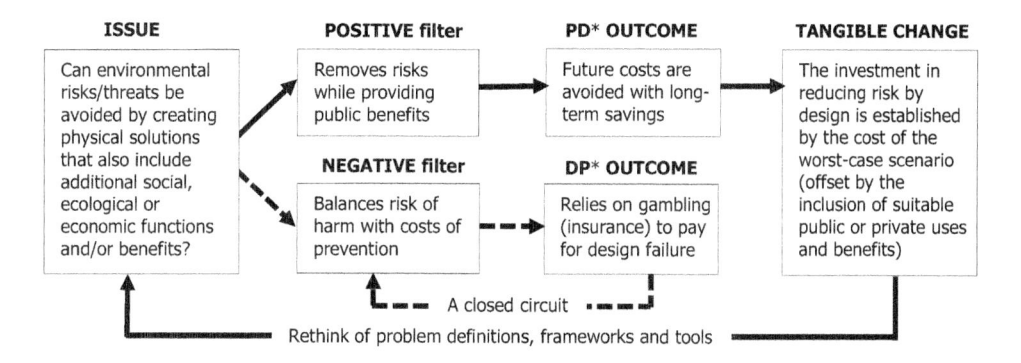

ISSUE	POSITIVE filter	PD* OUTCOME	TANGIBLE CHANGE
Can environmental risks/threats be avoided by creating physical solutions that also include additional social, ecological or economic functions and/or benefits?	Removes risks while providing public benefits	Future costs are avoided with long-term savings	The investment in reducing risk by design is established by the cost of the worst-case scenario (offset by the inclusion of suitable public or private uses and benefits)
	NEGATIVE filter	**DP* OUTCOME**	
	Balances risk of harm with costs of prevention	Relies on gambling (insurance) to pay for design failure	

A closed circuit
Rethink of problem definitions, frameworks and tools

Figure 7.9 Risk Avoidance (RA) analysis

7.6.2 Mapping Opportunities for Public Benefits

Negative Space (NS) Analysis *maps empty urban space in three dimensions to identify appropriate places to support added public benefits and track the conversion of space to private control, or vice versa.*

Urban 'density', often measured by the number of people/households per hectare, is a questionable indicator of sustainability. For instance, in developed nations, less space per person is often seen as a sustainability indicator, while more space per person is usually seen as more sustainable in disadvantaged regions.[66] Densification goals imply space is waste, but a lack of outdoor space for unanticipated future needs can cause more waste in the future. Also, spaces and surfaces that fail to absorb noise, treat pollution, reduce urban overheating, improve air quality or provide eco-services are lost opportunities to improve urban sustainability and public benefits.

Not only does high-density development lack sufficient space to adapt to social, technological and climatic change or unexpected problems, it seldom has lower material flows than medium-density alternatives.[67] Further, public needs are not being met, being increasingly left to market forces alone. Therefore, new spatial strategies are necessary. NS analysis maps urban space (using drones) in 3D (as opposed to ground-level mapping) to identify and prioritize opportunities for positive economic, social and/or ecological interventions.[68] Urban land densification should also be tracked in 3D over time, so its positive/negative effects on social cohesion, resilience, health and other values can be examined.[69]

Developers sometimes gain offsets/credits for providing public benefits on private property, such as public mini-parks or plazas.[70] Similarly, spaces that are made available for public health and amenity (e.g. multi-layered Green Scaffolding) could be granted 'transferable development rights' [Chapter 6].[71] That is, ecological space could be transferred/sold to other properties as floor area bonuses.[72] However, such development bonuses should be restricted to areas designated for urban revitalization. Developers could also be given other kinds of development bonuses for application in socially sustainable developments.[73] Planners could map areas of the city where revitalization is a priority and determine an appropriate 'credit rate' [Figure 7.10].

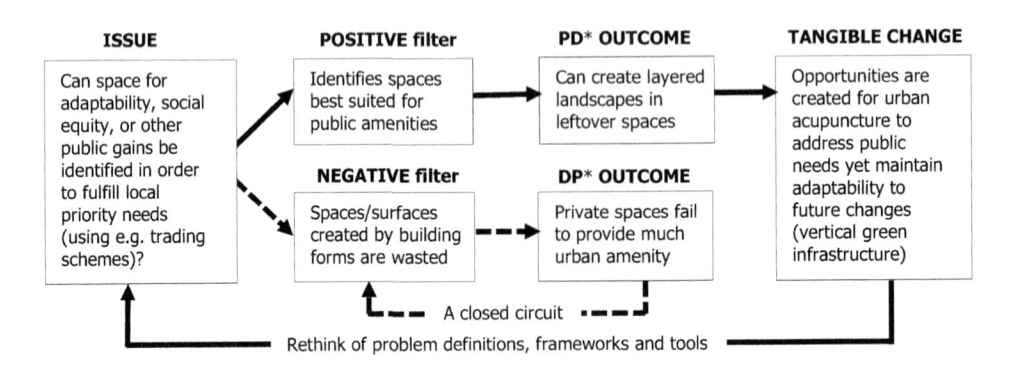

Figure 7.10 Negative Space (NS) analysis

Highest Ecological Use (HU) Analysis *considers the ecological deficiencies of the area in order to increase the ecological health of the site, before selecting preferred economic uses (which are temporary and transitory).*

Historically, ecological values were considered irrelevant to urban development, and zoning prioritized the 'highest economic use' of land. Specific land uses were determined by developers who would usually select the best site permitted by zoning, based on financial prospects. However, economic conditions are often transitory, and property values fluctuate. When economic circumstances change, buildings often change their functions. City planners could set criteria that optimize the ecological functions of a site, and then create incentives to attract developments or land uses that are compatible with them. HU analysis determines its 'highest ecological use' with the assistance of ET analysis (below).

Zoning positioned the natural environment as an urban land use primarily for recreational use. Despite the growing appreciation of the natural environment and open space, nature has not yet been well integrated with cities. Many urban areas remain sterile and gray, like mausoleums. Some jurisdictions promulgate code requirements and/or design guidelines to protect the environment, that may discourage development that conflicts with ecologically sensitive sites and heritage areas or even protect biodiversity. However, urban ecology is largely left to remnant ground-level open spaces, and urban biodiversity guidelines usually encourage tokenistic actions, such as water-efficient landscaping or pervious paving in left-over spaces.

The highest ecological use of a site might require keeping significant parts of the ground level open, dedicating some higher-level floors for biodiversity reserves, or it could recommend not developing the site at all. In one such instance, a new library building would have replaced an historic agricultural research plot on a crowded university campus. This was resolved by building the library under it (which also provided substantial thermal insulation).[74] However, when only waste and efficiency in production and operation is measured, and the benefits of open space are not really counted, designs that preserve land would seldom be considered [Figure 7.11].

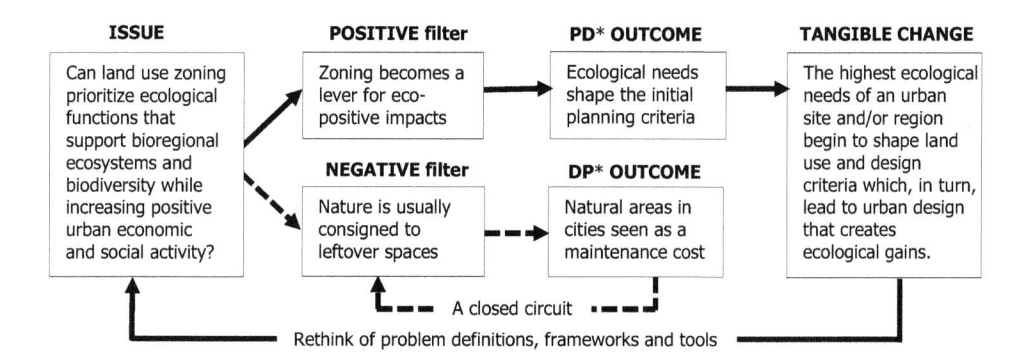

Figure 7.11 Highest Ecological Use (HU) analysis

7.6.3 Site Planning for Ecological Gains

Ecological Transformation (ET) Analysis *traces the ecological evolution of the area from pre-historic times to identify appropriate ecosystems/species, guide actions for offsetting unavoidable ecological losses, and increase ecological carrying capacity and/or eco-services.*

What has been called ecological design has often largely concerned resource/energy conservation, at the expense of nature. When design does not increase nature in proportion to past/ongoing ecological losses, it usually amounts to a net ecological loss. Although ecologically sensitive ground area landscaping around buildings could help weave the bioregion back together, it cannot increase net ecological carrying capacity. However, if cities and buildings dedicated substantial floor area or surface area to ecosystem enclaves and biodiversity incubators, they could aid the future restoration of their bioregions. Cities could become living landscapes that constitute a unique yet integral part of the bioregion.

Urban 'empty' spaces can be mapped using NS analysis (above) and socio-ecological needs/deficits can be matched to spaces using MS analysis (above). Then ET analysis can help establish appropriate eco-productive ecosystems.[75] While current knowledge may be insufficient, ET analysis can guide the biological mix for addressing ecological deficits and increasing the ecological base.[76] Among other things, this would involve overlaying hydrological, geological, botanical maps at a bioregional scale. Of course, attempts to regenerate past ecosystems may be unsuccessful in future contextual/ecological conditions.[77] Nonetheless, tracing changes in indigenous landscapes over time can shed light on what may now be most appropriate.

Many indigenous buildings were optimized for their unique micro-climates, passive solar requirements and local materials.[78] Some even had (relatively) symbiotic relations with their local ecology. Modern examples of ecologically appropriate buildings are hard to find, since eco-positive design is not yet assessed. Lanzarote, one of the Canary Islands off the west coast of Africa, built tourist facilities decades ago, designed for local materials and in forms that reflected the unique landscape of each island. This created a sense of place and fostered a local identity. However, perhaps because these islands were not threatened by over-development, these projects did not support ecosystems [Figure 7.12].

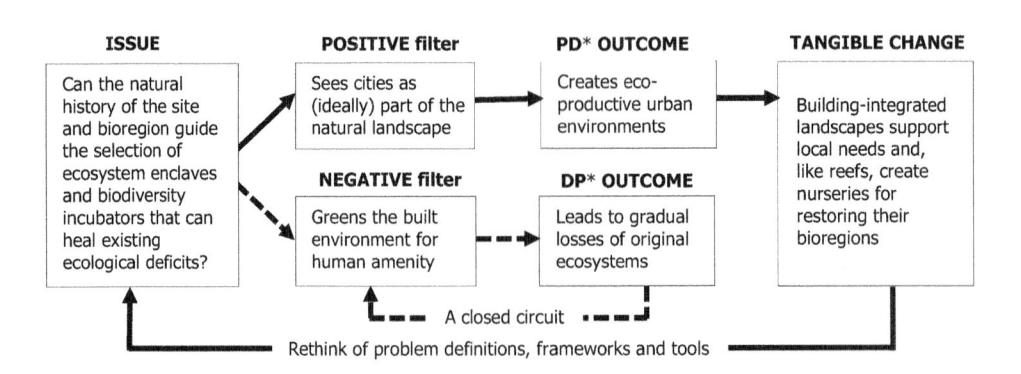

Figure 7.12 Ecological Transformation (ET) analysis

Ecological Space (ES) Analysis *determines the amount of space for ecosystems needed by an urban development to meet the ecological sustainability standard: more eco-services and ecological carrying capacity than in pre-industrial/pre-urban times.*

Since increases in ecological carrying capacity are necessary, in the absence of a catastrophic decline in the human population, cities should support 'ecological space' (ES). This is again the effective area allocated to building-integrated, eco-productive systems (e.g. biodiversity incubators, ecosystem enclaves and/or nature corridors).[79] These can be integrated with buildings or constructed above buildings, parking areas, walkways, train tracks and so forth. While NS analysis (above) identifies spatial opportunities in a city, ES analysis determines the amount of space that a building needs to qualify as 'eco-positive' (i.e. by creating more ecological space, biodiversity and eco-services than in pre-historic times).[80]

Some tools assume that 'preserving' land elsewhere, avoiding sensitive sites or installing ecological-sensitive landscapes constitutes ecological 'gains'.[81] Such actions do not offset the ecological footprint of construction.[82] Likewise, buildings with green roofs cannot offset the floor area, let alone ground area, that they occupy. Roof landscaping seldom provides adequate environmental media (e.g. healthy soil and water) to ensure ecosystem self-maintenance. In some cases, however, vertical layered roof or wall structures could create net ES, after construction impacts are deducted. Assessing the ecological value of introduced ecosystems is arguably not yet really possible, but many methods are evolving toward this goal.[83]

Where measuring ES is impracticable, as in small projects, a PD rule of thumb could be used: a cubic meter of ES for every square meter of gross floor area. That is, a ten-story building would need almost ten times the ES as a single-story building. This is possible by combining atriums, building-integrated greenhouses, living roofs, walls, plazas, nature corridors and garden levels. Some tall buildings have dedicated whole floors to gardens merely to improve the performance of their double-skin walls.[84] Where necessary, easements, credits or trading schemes could allow any ES deficiencies to be transferred to other sites [Figure 7.13].

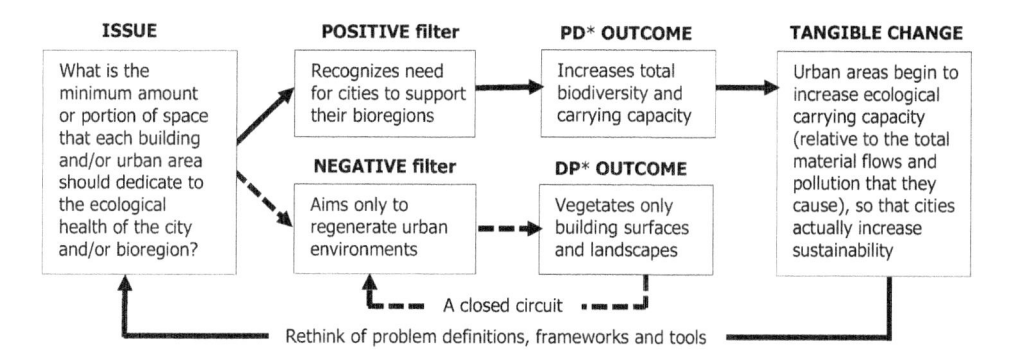

Figure 7.13 Ecological Space (ES) analysis

7.7 Exercises

1. Take one of the analyses in Chapters 7 to 8 and critique it in depth (citing pros and cons) as a term paper, using case studies and examples. Send paper to author for an appraisal or response. See end of Chapter 8 for exercises pertaining to each analysis.

Notes

1 SMARTmode can be undertaken as a community planning process or means to develop a design brief. See Birkeland, J. (2008) *Positive Development: From Vicious Circles to Virtuous Cycles through Built Environment Design*, Earthscan, London, pp. 251–73.
2 A version of SMT appears in Birkeland, J. (2015) Planning for Positive Development, in Byrne, J., Dodson, J., and Sipe, N. (eds) *Australian Environmental Planning: Challenges and Future Prospects*, Routledge, New York, pp. 246–57.
3 Lifecycle assessment depersonalizes impacts, such as the fact that 60% of primate species are threatened with extinction. Estrada, A., et al. (2017) Impending Extinction Crisis of the World's Primates: Why Primates Matter, *Science Advances* 3(1), e1600946.
4 See e.g. Australian Green Building Council (2017) *Land Use and Ecology Category Review*, Discussion Paper, AGBC, Oct. See also critique in Birkeland, J. (2018) Challenging Policy Barriers in Sustainable Development, in Dymitrow, M., and Szymańska, D. (eds) *Bulletin of Geography Socio-Economic Series* 40(40), Nicolaus Copernicus University, Toruń, pp. 41–56.
5 E.g. see Hendriks, C., Obernosterer, R., Muller, D., et al. (2000) Material Flow Analysis: A Tool to Support Environmental Policy Decision Making, *Local Environment* 5, 311–28; and Baccini, P., and Brunner, P. H. (1991) *Metabolism of the Anthroposphere*, Springer Verlag, Berlin and New York.
6 Compounding is a concept discussed in von Weizsacker, E., Lovins, A., and Lovins, H. (1997) *Factor 4: Doubling Wealth – Halving Resource Use*, Earthscan, London. Many materials and mining processes are toxic, which is not always adequately considered in material flows analyses.
7 Thank you to S. Knight-Lenihan for comments on the first draft.
8 Sometimes public resources are sold off at below cost. Repetto, R. C., and Gillis, M. (1988) *Public Policies and the Misuse of Forest Resources*, Cambridge University Press, Cambridge; Ridgeway, J. (2004) *It's All for Sale: The Control of Global Resources*, Duke University Press, London.
9 See Birkeland, *Positive Development*, pp. 256–57.
10 Jackson, D. (2018) *Data Cities: How Satellites are Transforming Architecture and Design*, Lund Humphries, London.
11 See Birkeland, *Positive Development*, pp. 262–3.
12 Tibbs, H. B. C. (1992) Industrial Ecology: An Agenda for Environmental Management, *Pollution Prevention Review*, Spring, pp. 167–80; McDonough, W., and Braungart, M. (2002) *Cradle to Cradle: Remaking the Way we Make Things*, North Point Press, New York; Tibbs, H. B. C. (2002) Industrial Ecology, in Birkeland, J. (ed.) *Design for Sustainability: A Sourcebook of Integrated Eco-Logical Solutions*, Earthscan, London, pp. 52–5.
13 See Birkeland, J. (2008) Box 30: Evolution Towards Positive Development, in *Positive Development, Ibid*, p.315.
14 For example, see Environment Australia (1998) *Indicators for the Nation State of the Environment Reporting*, Environment Australia, Department of Environment, Canberra. Some themes include human settlements, biodiversity, the atmosphere, the land, inland waters, estuaries and the sea, natural and cultural heritage.
15 The *New Urban Agenda* does not suggest criteria or indicators for infill or retrofitting. Habitat III (2016) *The New Urban Agenda* (Quito declaration on sustainable cities and human settlements for all). http://habitat3.org/the-new-urban-agenda/.

16 See Birkeland, *Positive Development*, pp. 97–114. The PD phrase, design as thinking in flows (rather than input-output and cost-benefit analyses) has been adopted, but only as a metaphor.
17 See Birkeland, J. (2017) Net-Positive Design and Development, *Landscape Review* 17(2) (special issue on integrated urban gray and green infrastructure), pp. 83–7.
18 Birkeland, *Positive Development*, p. 269.
19 See also Birkeland, *Positive Development*, pp. 235–50.
20 When people use the terms net-positive energy and water, it generally indicates a closed-system view, as energy and water cannot really be increased, only shipped across borders.
21 For discussion on unjust enrichment and planning, see Birkeland, *Positive Development*, pp. 131–46.
22 'Opportunity cost' is the lost opportunity to save or make money/resources.
23 When I worked for the federal government in 2000, management decided to downplay the State of Environment Report because it was not good news. Many thought environmental reporting was no longer conducted. https://soe.environment.gov.au/.
24 Corporate sustainability reporting has mushroomed as it enables organizations to claim improvements in performance over time, but many are selective in presentation.
25 While many decisions systems are prescribed by legislation, agencies usually have wide discretion regarding decision rules and processes.
26 See Harrison, D., Chalkley, A. M., and Billet, E. (2002) The Rebound Effect, in Birkeland, *Design for Sustainability*, p. 129.
27 See Hill, G. (2002) Designing Waste, in Birkeland, *Design for Sustainability*, pp. 43–5, which explores how new designs often prematurely replace the old, resulting in more total products. Also, Davidson, S. (2002) Market-Led Design, in Birkeland, *Design for Sustainability*, pp. 125–8.
28 See Pryor, F. (2008) Box 54: Reversing the Role of Fashion, in Birkeland, *Positive Development*, p. 342.
29 See Tennant-Wood, R. (2008) Box 19: E-Waste, in Birkeland, *Positive Development*, p. 300.
30 See www.globalgreentag.com/ and www.geca.eco/. These focus on lifecycle impacts of products.
31 See Santana, M. E. (2002) Timber Waste Minimization by Design, in Birkeland, *Design for Sustainability*, pp. 188–91.
32 An early analysis of the economic value of nature was in Costanza, R., et al. (1997) The Value of the World's Ecosystem Services and Natural Capital, *Nature* 387, pp. 253–60.
33 See Birkeland, J. (2007) GEN 6: Ecological Waste: Rethinking the Nature of Waste, in *Environmental Design Guide of the Australian Institute of Architects*, ACT, Canberra. www.environmentdesignguide.com.au/.
34 Coal ash and dust includes toxins that gets into the air, water and soil, such as arsenic, lead, mercury, cadmium, chromium and selenium. See Physicians for Social Responsibility, www.psr.org/assets/pdfs/coal-ash-toxics-damaging-to-human-health.pdf.
35 E.g. in another realm, cod were wiped out in the Great Lakes at great cost to the economy and ecology.
36 Rate of growth depends on timber species and myriad other factors.
37 After a major flood, the ecology of a region reportedly takes decades to recover fully, although the GDP usually increases because it is based on economic activity, not whole-system benefit.
38 Ethical technology assessment does not generally concern buildings. Palm, E., and Hansson, S. O. (2006) The Case for Ethical Technology Assessment (ETA), *Technological Forecasting and Social Change*, 73(5), pp. 543–58.
39 Birkeland, J. (2002) Urban Forms and the Built Environment, in Birkeland, *Design for Sustainability*, pp. 114–17.
40 E.g. Katerva promotes eco-innovation with an emphasis on likely commercial success https://katerva.net.

41 More recently, wind power was widely discredited as killing birds, although more birds die flying into building windows, and the damage of fossil-fuel systems to habitats causes greater damage.

42 Books in the 1970s presented passive solar design as if it were mechanical equipment. See Shurcliff, W. A. (c. 1979) *Solar Heated Buildings of North America: 120 Outstanding Examples*, Brick House Publishing, Harrisville, NH; AIA Research Corporation (1976) *Solar Dwelling Design Concepts*, US Department of Housing and Urban Development, Washington, DC; Anderson, B. (1976) *The Solar Home Book: Heating, Cooling and Designing with the Sun*, Brick House Publishing, Harrisville, NH.

43 The building cooling load in urban areas is increasing rapidly. White roofs reflect some heat into the urban area, whereas Green Scaffolding (of bamboo or galvanized pipe) could support garden roofs above the homes to cool the roof and supply food.

44 Efficiency does not mean that less harmful sources of energy or less overall energy are used. For example, energy usage for air conditioning systems. See David, L. W., and Gertler, P. J. (2015) Contribution of Air Conditioning Adoption to Future Energy Use under Global Warming, *Proceedings of the National Academy of Science* 112(19), pp. 5962–7.

45 2016 was the hottest year yet recorded and the last five years have been the hottest ever. Carbon dioxide levels have not been as high and the climate has not been as hot in 4 million years. www.nasa.gov/sites/default/files/atoms/files/noaa-nasa_global_analysis-2016.pdf.

46 Mechanical building equipment, again, has a short life span and needs repair more often than passive solar design elements.

47 Even the progressive LBC rating tool mentions passive design in a footnote, in effect, favoring renewable energy.

48 Newsham, G. R., Mancini, S., and Birt, B. J. (2009) Do LEED-certified Buildings Save Energy? Yes, But ..., *Energy and Buildings* 41(8), pp. 897–905. Scofield, J. H. (2009) Do LEED-certified Buildings Save Energy? Not Really ..., *Energy and Buildings* 41(12), pp. 1386–90.

49 Curwell, S. (1996) Specifying for Greener Buildings, *The Architects' Journal*, Jan., pp. 38–40.

50 Passive solar design has always recognized that stone, earth, timber and other materials used in passive systems should be sourced locally.

51 The embodied energy in solar cells takes about two years to pay back, and this is improving, so it is a good investment.

52 Public open spaces have tended to promote commercial goals alone.

53 Mixed-use development became a planning goal in the 1960s. Marina City, two skyscrapers in Chicago, was an example of mixed-use residential and commercial development. Completed in 1968, they looked like corn cobs, biomimicking a dominant agricultural crop in Illinois.

54 There was a marked tendency to design for the 'inconvenience' of cars rather than the convenience of pedestrians and bicycles, but it was still car-oriented design. Birkeland, *Positive Development*.

55 Bioregionalism is sometimes associated with an anti-trade or even nationalist stance, but that does not necessarily follow. See Breckwoldt, R. (1996) *Approaches to Bioregional Planning, Part I: Proceedings of the Conference*, Department of Environment, Sports, and Territories, Canberra.

56 Brunckhorst, D. J. (2000) *Bioregional Planning: Resource Management Beyond the New Millennium*, Harwood Academic Publications, Amsterdam; Dodge, J. (1981) Living by Life: Some Bioregional Theory and Practice, *CoEvolution Quarterly* 32, pp. 6–12; Aberley, D. (ed.) (1994) *Futures by Design: The Practice of Ecological Planning*, Envirobook Publications, Sydney.

57 Again, 'environmental space', a Friends of the Earth concept, suggests everyone has the right to a fair share of resources within the carrying capacity of the earth. 'Ecological space' is a PD term meaning the effective area allocated to building-integrated, eco-productive systems. These are discussed further in subsequent chapters.

58 For a description of equity mapping, see Byrne, J. (2008) Box 48: Equity Mapping, in Birkeland, *Positive Development*, p. 336.

59 The inadequate flood barriers in New Orleans were an example. Reportedly, the same inadequate levels of protection are being replaced, not reconceived.
60 See Lerner, J. (2014) *Urban Acupuncture*, Island Press, Washington, DC. For a short description of Curitiba, see Birkeland, *Positive Development*, pp. 12–13.
61 A Climate Council report predicts that the economic cost of fires, including insured losses and broader social costs, will double in Victoria. Boyd, S. (2017) Bushfire Costs to Reach $378 Million by 2050. www.stawelltimes.com.au/story/4412432/behind-the-flames-the-cost-of-more-severe-bushfire-seasons-graphs-photos/?mc_cid=3221a083d0&mc_eid=f4b936a136.
62 See Ramsay, C., and Rudolph, L. (2003) *Landscape and Building Design for Bushfire Areas*, CSIRO Publishing, Victoria, Australia. The detailing of buildings can avoid collecting dry leaves or flying embers but provides no protection in a major fire.
63 Fire pumps can be turned on by remote control or use sensors.
64 Storage areas could support biodiversity habitats for endangered species such as frogs (not to mention as yet unknown invertebrates).
65 For the use of flyscreens or flywire, see Holmgren, D. (1992) *The Flywire House: A Case Study in Design Against Bushfire*, Nascimanere Pty Ltd, Maleny, Queensland.
66 Third-world barrios are not necessarily more sustainable because they use more space or less space. Most references advocating high-density development do not seem to make a distinction between indoor and outdoor space per person.
67 The material flows caused by a development depend on product and materials selection. Space can be framed far more inexpensively than is the case with typical buildings. See Ban, S., and Bell, E. (2001) *Shigeru Ban*, Princeton Architectural Press, Princeton, NJ.
68 While equity mapping evaluates access to needs and amenities, negative space analysis maps spatial opportunities. Urban consolidation/urbanization has been regarded as a virtue largely because it reduces transportation fuel, but electric vehicles could change this. Adaptable urban open spaces are essential for basic resources like clean air, and enable things like clean public transportation or urban agriculture.
69 The technology to do so has progressed dramatically in the last decade. See Jackson, D., and Simpson, R. (eds) (2012) *D_City: Digital Earth, Virtual Nations, Data Cities*, Sydney. Also, Jackson, *Data Cities*.
70 For a further discussion on positive and negative offsetting, see Birkeland, *Positive Development*, and Birkeland, J., and Knight Lenihan, S. (2016) Biodiversity Offsetting and Net Positive Design, *Journal of Urban Design* 21(1), pp. 50–66,
71 Nelson, A. C. (2012) *The TDR Handbook: Designing and Implementing Successful Transfer of Development Rights Program*, Island Press, Washington, DC.
72 The combined spaces should meet the sustainability standard.
73 This is in keeping with the current skills set and practices of planners. Common incentives are waivers of development application fees, expedited assessment processes and transferable development rights.
74 Library at the University of Illinois, Urbana. Underground corridors that link the buildings surrounding the plot was a bonus to pedestrians in harsh weather.
75 See Renger, C., Birkeland, J., and Midmore, D (2015) Net Positive Building Carbon Sequestration: A Case Study in Brisbane, *Building Research and Information* 43(1), pp. 11–24.
76 Designers would need to work with ecologists and others to create spaces with the right conditions for the right species and species mix.
77 To reemphasize, a return to pre-human or indigenous conditions would not suffice to offset or balance current human consumption (ecological footprint) and is only a preliminary guide to the kinds of ecosystems and species that might be appropriate.
78 See Rudovsky, P. (1964) *Architecture without Architects: A Short Introduction to Non-Pedigreed Architecture*, Museum of Modern Art, Doubleday, New York.
79 For examples, see Todd, N. J., and Todd, J. (1994) *From Eco-Cities to Living Machines*, Atlantic Books, Berkeley, CA.
80 The ecosystems and species themselves should always be determined by people in the ecological sciences.
81 Birkeland, Challenging Policy Barriers, pp. 41–56.
82 The ecological footprint is the total land/water area equivalence used by the building, not the 'building footprint'. See Wackernagel, M., and Rees, W. E. (1996) *Our*

Ecological Footprint: Reducing the Human Impact on the Earth, New Society Publishers, Bowen Island, BC.

83 Martínez-Harms, M. J., and Balvanera, P. (2012) Methods for Mapping Ecosystem Service Supply: A Review, *International Journal of Biodiversity Science, Ecosystem Services and Management* 8(1–2), pp. 17–25. Compare to UNEP (2005) *Millennium Ecosystem Assessment: Strengthening Capacity to Manage Ecosystems Sustainably for Human Wellbeing*, United Nations Environment Program, New York. http://ma.caudillweb.com/en/about.overview.aspx.

84 There are a number of books showing double-skin wall buildings. See Shameri, M. A., Alghoul, M. A., Sopian, K., et al. (2011) Perspectives of Double Skin Façade Systems in Buildings and Energy Saving, *Renewable and Sustainable Energy Reviews* 15(3), pp. 1468–75. See also Safamanesh, B., and Byrd, H. (2012) The Two Sides of a Double-Skin Facade: Built Intelligent Skin or Brand Image Scam? *in Building on Knowledge: Theory and Practice*, 46th Annual Conference of ANZAScA, Griffith University, Australia, Nov. 14–16.

8 SMT Analyses for Institutional Design

Reverse Sunk Cost (SC) Analysis *sets stationary baselines for project assessment and compares all alternatives as if no development yet existed, so that each alternative carries its full share of lifecycle costs-benefits-risks.*

The sunk cost is the proverbial 'spilt milk'. The past investment in a failed system does not ordinarily matter much in business, as firms are expected to cut their losses.[1] In resource industries, however, there is resistance to even upgrading a system unless the payback is very rapid as they are using resources below cost.[2] Some industries have milked resources until costs exceeded profits. For example, some firms have continued to pollute while opposing regulations in court, and then abandoned substandard factories.[3] As evidenced by thousands of superfund sites,[4] the public is left to clean things up after the fact.

Ironically, the sunk cost in existing harmful systems counts as positive. The sunk cost has made systems change appear more expensive. Not using industrial systems seems wasteful because they are already there. However, the past expense of constructing, maintaining and later decommissioning nuclear or coal-powered electricity plants is seldom counted when considering new nuclear plants. Similarly, fossil-fuel-based plants and building equipment are not expected to pay back their costs – yet renewable energy systems must show a fast payback.[5] Commercial 'energy-saving' building equipment is also favored over passive solar design because the impacts of producing fossil-fuel-based equipment are seldom counted.[6]

When development uses fossil-fuel-based energy, pollution is locked in for decades. Lifecycle assessment (LCA) looks at the portion of impacts from resource extraction, energy production, transportation systems and so on that feed into the particular project. It may, for example, count the portion of energy required to produce/operate the trucks used during construction. While the impacts of trucks may be divided into each project, the project's contribution to perpetuating fossil-fuel-based systems is not. Tracing impacts too far back becomes too complex since impacts merge with industrial development as a whole. Therefore, SC analysis compares alternative systems as if neither system existed [Figure 8.1].

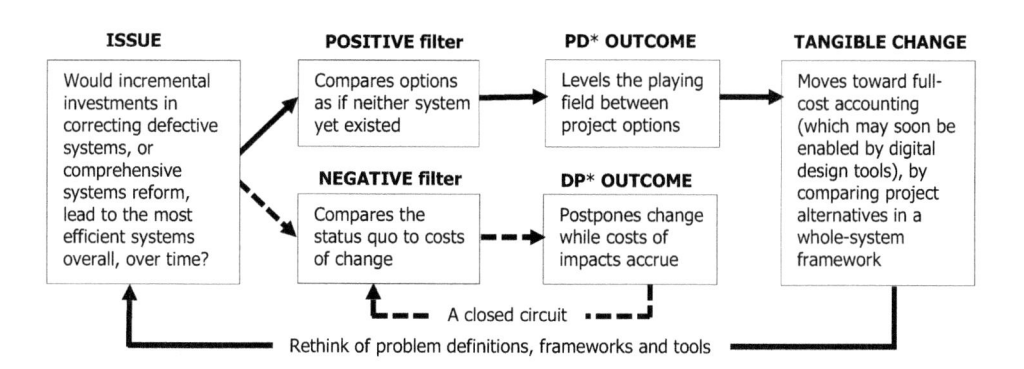

Figure 8.1 Reverse sunk cost (SC) analysis

182 *Design and Analysis*

Source of Energy (SE) Analysis *assesses the impacts caused by the source and type of energy, in addition to the amount of energy used by development or the efficiency of its use.*

There is enough solar energy to power the needs of 'sustainable' systems and societies.[7] Passive and renewable energy can provide most of the heating, cooling and ventilating needs of smaller buildings in many climates.[8] The source of energy determines most of the harmful environmental and human health impacts of powering buildings.[9] For instance, fossil and nuclear fuel systems are damaging throughout their production and distribution, and well beyond their useful life.[10] Nonetheless, most assessment tools emphasize the efficiency, not the source of energy. SE analysis emphasizes the source of energy (e.g. coal, gas, solar, wind) including transmission and distribution impacts.[11]

When only the efficiency of energy use counts, losses of energy through transmission/distribution systems generally only register as less efficient (i.e. more expensive). The toxins such as mercury, distributed by fossil-fuel-based energy, are often left out. Efficiency figures can be misleading in other ways. For example, 'black coal' is frequently advertised as '40% more efficient', but this is relative to brown coal – not renewable energy. Further, public health costs are decoupled from the profits of companies that gain by damaging public health. Although renewable energy is now financially competitive, a 'multiplier' could help to account for harmful energy sources.

The optimal energy mix depends on the context. Energy flows through urban areas can be mapped to determine the best location and scale for energy production-storage-distribution systems. Passive solar design may often be the most cost-effective because it collects, stores and circulates air 'for free' and needs less maintenance.[12] In some cases, windows that generate and distribute surplus energy to adjacent buildings or batteries may be better than adding single-function solar cells.[13] Neighborhood solar thermal disks are often more efficient than solar cells or distant wind farms.[14] In dense cities, fuel cells can provide backup systems when renewable energy fails [Figure 8.2].[15]

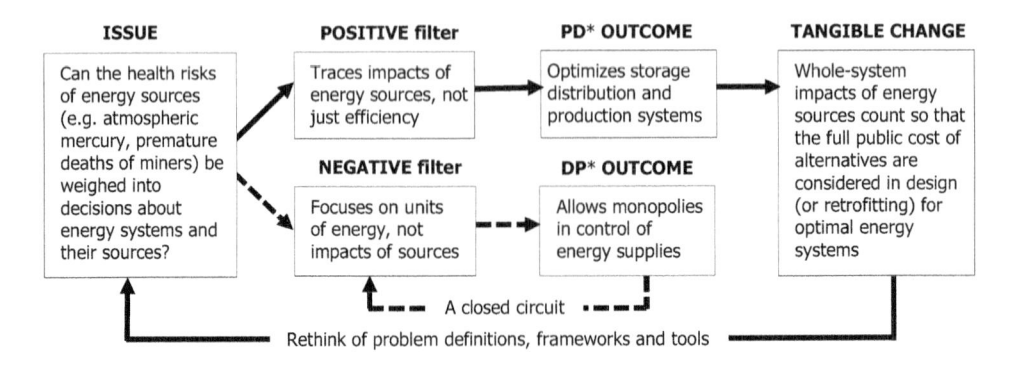

ISSUE	POSITIVE filter	PD* OUTCOME	TANGIBLE CHANGE
Can the health risks of energy sources (e.g. atmospheric mercury, premature deaths of miners) be weighed into decisions about energy systems and their sources?	Traces impacts of energy sources, not just efficiency	Optimizes storage distribution and production systems	Whole-system impacts of energy sources count so that the full public cost of alternatives are considered in design (or retrofitting) for optimal energy systems
	NEGATIVE filter	**DP* OUTCOME**	
	Focuses on units of energy, not impacts of sources	Allows monopolies in control of energy supplies	

--- A closed circuit ---
Rethink of problem definitions, frameworks and tools

Figure 8.2 Source of Energy (SE) analysis

Costs of Change (CC) Analysis *estimates the costs of converting conventional development projects into net-positive structures in the future, including the extra costs of renovating buildings that were not designed/retrofitted for adaptability.*

Planning approvals do not compare alternative land uses or development options in relation to a sustainability standard. Moreover, industries are often 'grandfathered' when planning or building codes change.[16] In addition to implicitly counting sunk costs as positive (above), the 'least change option' is generally assumed to be cheaper or less complicated. Because impact assessment is based on current conditions, the future cost of retrofitting to meet higher standards is not considered. However, the public costs of pollution and clean-up continue to increase. Hence, PD suggests 'design for adaptability' so that higher standards can be met less expensively in the future.[17]

The least change option often costs more over time. Since road transport systems are established, more roads and parking garages are approved in cities, although it is widely understood that they increase driving and congestion.[18] The least change also favors electric and robotic cars over shifting to public transport, because they use existing roads. However, investments in electric cars and ongoing road improvements take resources away from public transport systems. Environmental standards are likely to rise, assuming humanity survives. Therefore, unless changes begin now, today's cities will involve expensive future upgrades and maintenance costs, as well as incalculable opportunity costs.

Sustainable systems save money, but the act of changing existing systems is, in itself, usually quite expensive. However, the transformation to sustainability is not really optional.[19] To correct the biases toward least change, CC analysis estimates the future costs of upgrading developments to the PD sustainability standard. Where private costs are incurred in retrofitting buildings, government loans could be provided and reimbursed from the resultant savings.[20] If building structures and facades are 'printed' rather than constructed, their designs could be modular, demountable and biodegradable in order to enable the conversion of printed buildings to higher sustainability standards in the future [Figure 8.3].

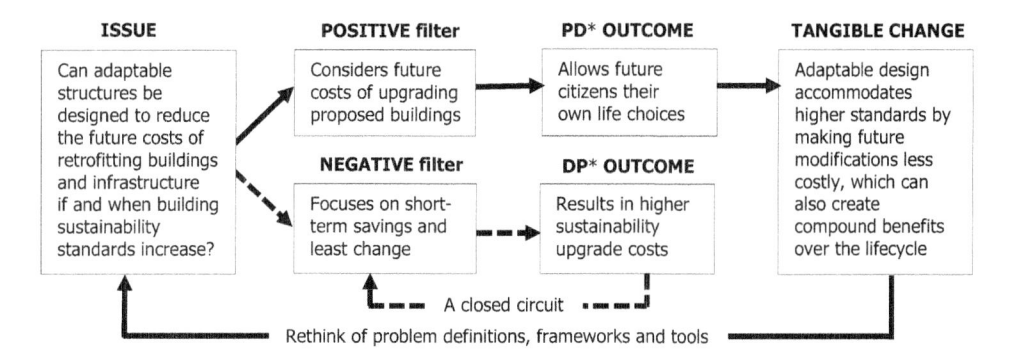

ISSUE	POSITIVE filter	PD* OUTCOME	TANGIBLE CHANGE
Can adaptable structures be designed to reduce the future costs of retrofitting buildings and infrastructure if and when building sustainability standards increase?	Considers future costs of upgrading proposed buildings	Allows future citizens their own life choices	Adaptable design accommodates higher standards by making future modifications less costly, which can also create compound benefits over the lifecycle
	NEGATIVE filter	**DP* OUTCOME**	
	Focuses on short-term savings and least change	Results in higher sustainability upgrade costs	

A closed circuit
Rethink of problem definitions, frameworks and tools

Figure 8.3 Costs of change (CC) analysis

184 *Design and Analysis*

Benefits of Action (BA) Analysis *supplements 'cost of inaction' analysis by identifying opportunities for positive and/or pre-emptive actions that capture compound savings from the future social and ecological benefits of natural areas.*

Environmentalists have consistently argued that the costs of *not* correcting social and environmental problems almost always escalate over time. The phrase 'costs of inaction' was mainstreamed by the influential *Stern Review*.[21] However, in practice, the use of this concept has largely centered on the relative future financial costs of alternative policies.[22] This discourse tends to compare financial costs of mitigation/prevention to doing nothing, rather than to the benefits of increasing positive options, or natural and social capital. The need to change development systems and increase nature in global terms has been derailed by the emphasis on reducing future environmental impacts.

Assessing the cost of inaction will usually show that sustainable systems cost more in the short term but save more money in the long term.[23] Environmentalists argue that ecological and human health should be seen as an investment, not a cost. For example, renewable energy immediately begins to reduce and/or pay back total costs, as well as reducing health costs.[24] In contrast, fossil-fuel-based energy perpetuates and accumulates health impacts, while depleting and degrading the life-support system permanently. However, long-term costs are not persuasive to politicians who often represent corporate interests. Therefore, BA analysis emphasizes the 'opportunity gains' of sustainable design.

Financial contrivances such as the economic concept of 'discounting' (i.e. devaluing the future as people prefer to have things now) exacerbates many environmental issues, yet still goes largely unchallenged. The consequence of devaluing future options, ironically, raises the exploitation value of resources and wilderness. As forests become scarcer, their value goes up, so companies with timber rights, and their governments, gain advantage from their rapid exploitation and growing scarcity. Forests with higher heritage or ecological values have been deliberately felled before citizen can be organized to protect them.[25] BA analysis helps to reverse the tendency to discount the future [Figure 8.4].

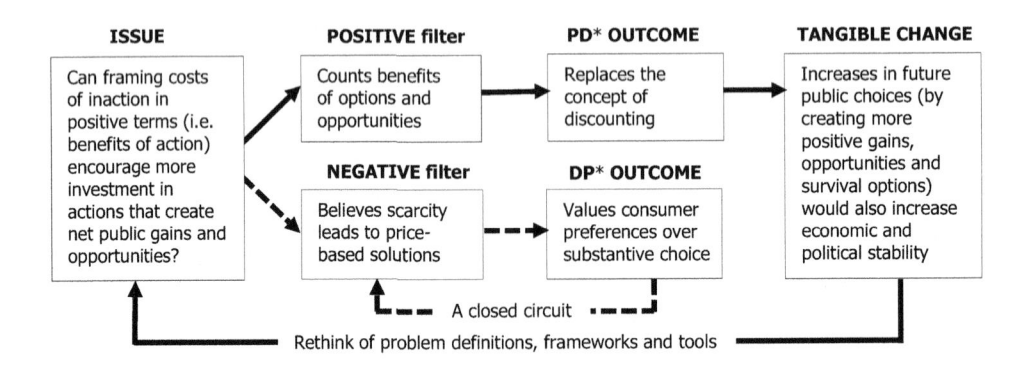

Figure 8.4 Benefits of action (BA) analysis

Institutional Design (ID) Analysis *supplements conventional criteria and indicators that reflect trends, with performance measures based on 'total' stocks and flows to diagnose problems that stem from the design of the institution.*

Governance theoretically concerns ethics and due process while, in business, the ends justify the means. Due to the 'revolving door' between the regulated and regulators, agency 'capture' has been normalized.[26] Thus gradually there has been a growing fusion of private and public organizational cultures and management mindsets. Judgments about whether public or private sectors work best depends on the perspective of the observer, but analyses in both sectors look at growth figures and money in an annual budget, not an environmental budget. Many radical analyses focus on who gains or loses, but not the effects on remaining social/natural resource stocks.

Neither side of mainstream politics appears to look at the depletion of resource stocks relative to growing demand. This is partly because progress indicators are usually snapshots in time and focus on trends, instead of remaining reserves. Government and corporate environment reports alike read like promotional documents.[27] Like weathervanes, they lack grounded, stationary baselines. For instance, the amount of land remediated and/or reserved is seldom juxtaposed with land clearing rates.[28] Similarly, the number of individuals reportedly better off is seldom compared with those either unaffected or worse off, let alone the effects of increasing or shifting populations on these numbers.

Public and private sector perspectives have blended as governments increasingly subscribe to a transactional and processed-based ethos, instead of a public interest in social and environmental outcomes.[29] The abdication to market-based approaches has meant, among other things, that nature is treated as just another stakeholder/customer.[30] The environment becomes a player at the poker table where it is entitled to bargain for its 'fair share' of water. Meanwhile fresh water supplies continue to decline.[31] ID analysis, in contrast, proposes that resource agency performance should be assessed by the increases/decreases in relevant public goods or resource stocks, or other fixed biophysical baselines [Figure 8.5].

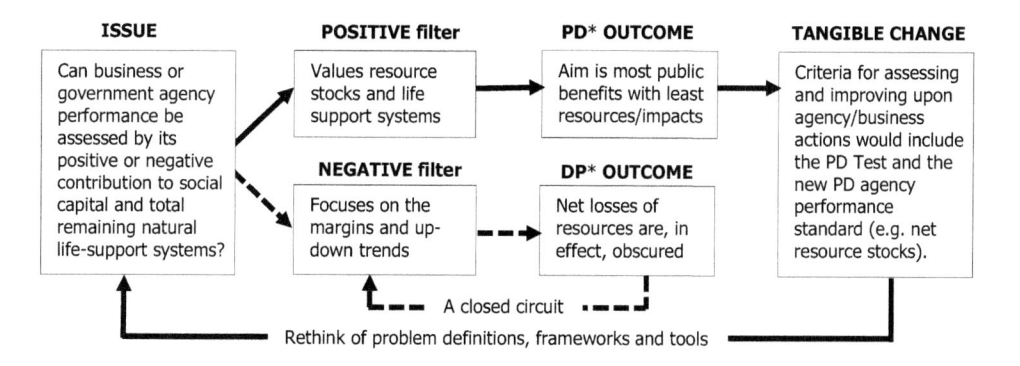

Figure 8.5 Institutional Design (ID) Analysis

Cumulative Decision (CD) Analysis *compares the original charter and legislative intent to agency policies with specific decision rationales and on-ground outcomes, to ascertain how well decisions and overall outcomes match official objectives.*

Development consent/approval frameworks and environmental legislation/regulations evolved back when negative impacts in construction were assumed to be unavoidable and nature lacked any financial value. Nonetheless, there was a countervailing belief in a public interest and a high value placed on cultural/natural heritage.[32] The enabling legislation of land and resource management authorities often refers to a public interest, but decisions did not always explain how this objective was fulfilled. Ideologies and politics are often the determining factor. Advocates of regulatory schemes shift burdens onto business to increase public welfare, while advocates of market-based schemes shift externalities onto taxpayers in order to shrink government.

Tracking changes between intention and outcomes can expose factors that have undermined judicious decision making. Since decisions that adversely affect the natural environment are largely irreversible, such statements should be able to make a logical connection to the organizational or legislative purposes. Decision rationales of development approval authorities should link to sustainability goals. This could save money, since actions that threaten critical environmental, social assets often result in public-interest law suits.[33] To increase accountability, therefore, CD analysis maps and compares the agency's enabling legislation and/or preambles, not only to their long-term outcomes, but to specific decisions and their rationales.[34]

An agency charter may call for the 'wise use of resources'. However, perhaps due to a belief in the trickle-down effect,[35] some agencies have effectively 'given away' public resources at below cost.[36] For instance, some authorities have spent more auctioning off forests than it would cost to conserve them: a perverse subsidy.[37] If an environment agency does more harm than no agency, it violates its reason for being and would certainly fail the PD Test. Instead, the net amount of wilderness area preserved should be increased in proportion to the growing human population (e.g. number of visitors using the wilderness area).

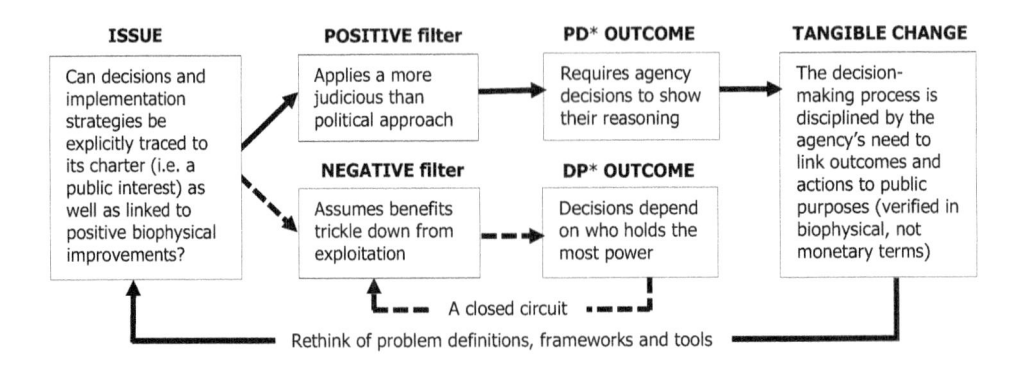

Figure 8.6 Cumulative Decision (CD) analysis

Democratic Impact (DI) Analysis *examines how built environments affect distributive justice and thus future political fairness, since equitable physical conditions and accessibility are necessary to ensure the long-term preservation of democratic rights.*

Meaningful civic engagement requires opportunity and security. If democracy is a right, direct physical access to basic needs must be a right (RS analysis). Concentrated/centralized urban forms do not always increase social interaction, civic engagement or access to the means of survival and wellbeing. In the name of economies of scale, centralized cities can create dependency on unreliable economic and electronic systems. In centralized, privatized systems, civic engagement requires monetary, mechanical and electronic systems as well as access to transport, which can easily be withdrawn by future rogue governments or corporations, or fail in cases of environmental crises or terrorism.

The socio-economically deprived in urban areas do not always enjoy full citizenship benefits in the best of times. The lower classes are sometimes consigned to the outskirts of cities where accessibility is limited by fewer transport and other services.[38] Although sustainable design emphasizes health benefits and access to amenities, it sometimes leaves basic needs to centralized and often privatized mechanisms over which local residents have little control (e.g. pipes, cables, rails and wires). While social impact assessment examines the likely distributional impacts of projects, it does not require action by governments to ensure or enhance personal political freedom and democracy.

Whereas RS analysis (above) concerns proximity and accessibility so that basic needs and resource security are available to everyone, DI analysis concerns another aspect of urban governance: political freedom and democracy. This requires electronic, financial and transport systems that have adequate backup systems and/or cannot be disrupted. Distributed energy is one example where flexibility and redundancy can be built in to avoid the kinds of large-scale energy blackouts that occur in extreme weather or power outages with associated transport and communication breakdowns. Physical environments provide a means to verify, as well as provide, the prerequisites of individual freedom, security and democracy.

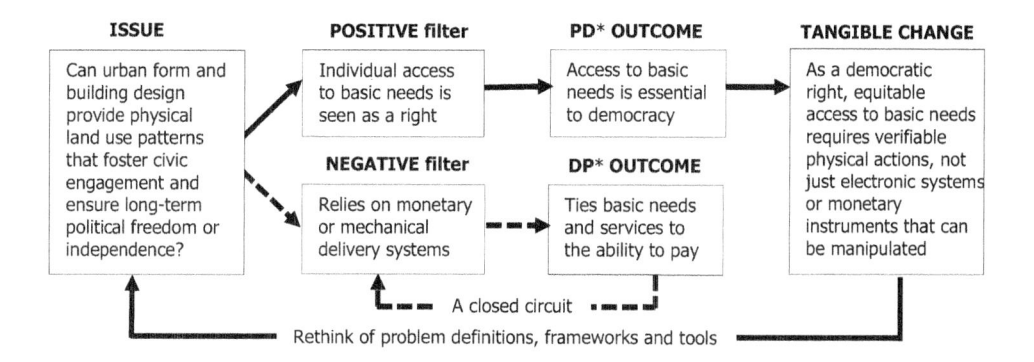

Figure 8.7 Democratic Impact (DI) analysis

188 Design and Analysis

Economic Impact (EI) Analysis *links economic outcomes with environmental policies to assess the long-term costs of ecological and resource depletion on the economy itself, rather than just the costs of environmental damage.*

Until recently, environmental and human health impacts were considered externalities. Regulatory impact assessments were introduced during the Reagan era (1980s), primarily to estimate the economic costs of environmental regulations. These include the costs of compliance and other burdens on industry. The financial value of lives saved[39] and the benefits of regenerating damaged ecosystems, and protecting endangered species, were gradually expanded in assessments. However, while some economic benefits of pollution prevention and environmental protection were quantified, the long-term impacts on the economy itself were not, such as the escalating costs of scarce resources and the repair of the natural life-support system.

In the 1990s, the financial costs of replacing ecosystem services began to be considered, and 'useful' flora and fauna (e.g. pollinators, iconic and keystone species) were increasingly monitored.[40] However, habitat and biodiversity losses, and the growing environmental debt are still arguably under-reported.[41] Ironically, the costs of environmental protection are widely attributed to government 'bureaucracy', while protecting endangered species often relies on under-funded researchers and community volunteers to remediate habitats through schemes such as Waterwatch, Earthwatch and Landcare. EI analysis is not about the long-term public costs of economic policies on the environment, but rather the costs to the economy itself.

The long-term impacts of environmental destruction on the economy are illustrated by the saga of nuclear power.[42] Nuclear accidents affect the economy/environment immeasurably, yet the costs and risks to the economy (e.g. the permanent contamination of land) seldom register in comparisons of energy systems.[43] In the USA, a cap was placed on nuclear accident liability, so no one was responsible for the full costs of accidents. There was no incentive for industry to use its innovation skills to solve the problems of nuclear waste, because the risks and long-term costs of decommissioning, and accountability were put under the table.[44]

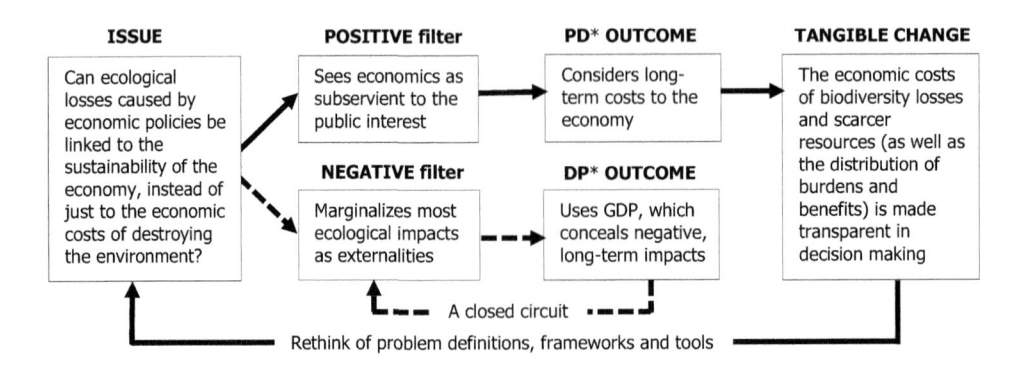

Figure 8.8 Economic Impact (EI) analysis

Resource Transfer (RT) Analysis *links physical development with the transfer of wealth and resources that are embodied in physical structures, and examines how materials embodied in built environments correlate with socio-economic disadvantages.*

Historically, raw materials and cheap/free labor from economically challenged nations meant a transfer of materials, and thus wealth, from poorer to richer regions.[45] This cumulative wealth transfer increased the bargaining power of governments/corporations to exact more resources from poorer regions at lower cost. Disadvantaged countries were left with diminished resource stocks and less resilient environments. Today, large construction projects, even in developing nations, are often built by offshore corporations using imported labor. Many such buildings serve international firms with little direct benefit to local residents beyond consumerism. Thus, urban centers in both developed and developing nations now reflect/reinforce disparities of wealth.

Most Hollywood stars and dictators alike live in ostentatious mansions that hog vast amounts of environmental space (again, the individual share of total resources). The money spent on conspicuous consumption corresponds roughly with the amount of embodied energy and materials. However, using money as a measure obscures the physical dimension and its impacts on equity and opportunity. The embodied energy/materials in physical structures could therefore be a better measure of wealth transfers from poor to rich, or rural to urban, and so on. RT analysis proposes tracing the value of physical materials through construction processes to their final property value.

There are many development assessments that inform the social justice impacts of built environments: EIAs evaluate the impacts of development on nature; material flows analyses trace resource consumption/pollution through production systems; and social impact assessments assess the effects of development among different demographic groups. Currently, these sources of information are largely privatized and fragmented. With advances in digital tools, past assessment data could be mined to correlate environmental with social impacts. For example, since the price of raw materials from disadvantages regions does not reflect the end value (minus processing-manufacturing-construction costs), their inhabitants seldom benefit from the resources they relinquish.

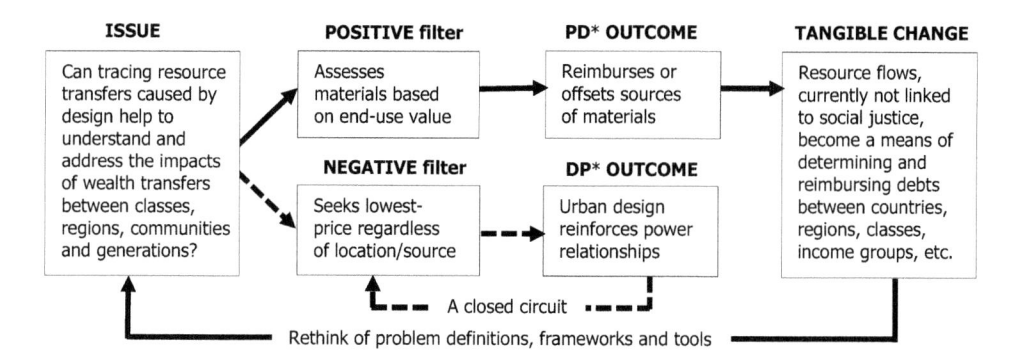

Figure 8.9 Resource Transfer (RT) analysis

190 Design and Analysis

Green Optimum (GO) Analysis *reverses a basic decision rule of capitalism, the Pareto Optimum, to encourage developments that maximize public benefits, compensated for as necessary by reciprocal benefits for investors and developers.*

The Green Optimum (GO) is the flip side of the Pareto Optimum (PO).[46] The PO means that an action or development is optimal if it makes individuals or corporations better off without unduly burdening others [Chapter 9]. The GO reverses this: a development is optimal if it benefits the general public without unduly burdening others.[47] Developments are generally only profitable due to prior/ongoing public investments in transport, power grids, infrastructure and so on. Conversely, the public may benefit from economic development, but not necessarily enough to compensate for the long-term pollution/depletion costs. This is especially the case in speculative projects.

Developers, again, are sometimes asked to make 'contributions' to offset some of the public financial and environmental costs, but these amounts seldom cover the ecological impacts.[48] The lack of compensation for a project's externalities is a relic of the view that any growth is good. Information about the distribution of environmental costs between public and private sectors, or who pays what costs, is seldom transparent. Project approval processes should come early enough to make positive suggestions for designing in environmental/public gains. Developers that provide net gains could be compensated after the public is reimbursed for any contributions made toward the project.

Any public contributions to a project should be considered if public benefits from private development count toward project approvals. For example, lifecycle analysis generally only records the percentage of environmental impacts caused by a resource extraction and construction process that can be assigned to the specific project. They do not consider the public value that is extracted from the resources, or even who benefits. EIAs record the adverse environmental costs that are directly attributable to a project, however, they seldom count the benefits to developers and owners that accrue from access to public resources.[49] Excessive public costs indicate unjust enrichment.[50]

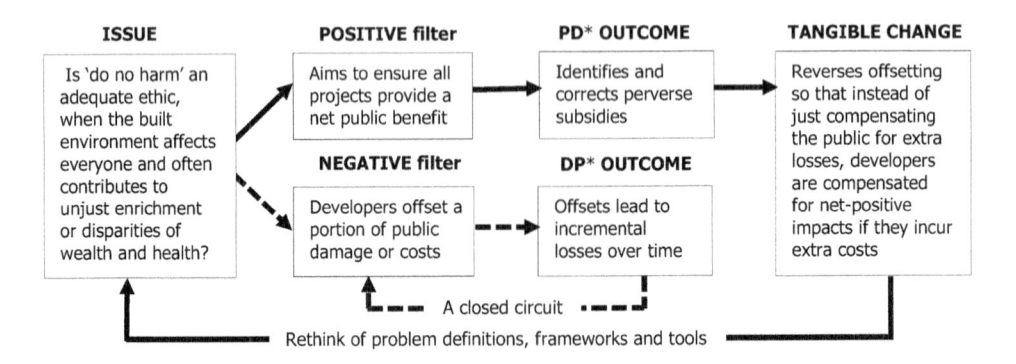

ISSUE	POSITIVE filter	PD* OUTCOME	TANGIBLE CHANGE
Is 'do no harm' an adequate ethic, when the built environment affects everyone and often contributes to unjust enrichment or disparities of wealth and health?	Aims to ensure all projects provide a net public benefit	Identifies and corrects perverse subsidies	Reverses offsetting so that instead of just compensating the public for extra losses, developers are compensated for net-positive impacts if they incur extra costs
	NEGATIVE filter	**DP* OUTCOME**	
	Developers offset a portion of public damage or costs	Offsets lead to incremental losses over time	

A closed circuit
Rethink of problem definitions, frameworks and tools

Figure 8.10 Green Optimum (GO) analysis

8.3 Exercises

The following lists some exercises that could be undertaken as discussion topics, group mind-mapping exercises or postgraduate theses. Like the SMT analyses themselves, they overlap and can be considered part of one comprehensive urban/regional analysis. If all were undertaken, they could guide plans and priorities for the eco-positive retrofitting of a city. Many of these research or workshop topics would benefit by starting with plans of an existing building, or of a project assessment, such as a lifecycle assessment, green building rating tool, material flows analysis or regulatory impact assessment. They should be re-examined in the context of net-positive sustainability.

8.3.1 Design Issues at the Building or Project Scale

8.3.1.1 Avoiding Upstream and Downstream Waste

Designed Waste (DW) Analysis: Obtain lifecycle analyses (LCAs) for two different products with similar functions. To what extent do LCAs consider waste caused by the product design itself? Think through the secondary/downstream wastes that products would likely entail during their operational life, the hours/days/weeks they would normally be used and recycling costs/impacts. How can this waste be reduced/avoided by substituting alternative products or redesigning them? Everyday examples include high-fashion gowns versus work clothes, hand shavers versus electric shavers, or a lawn (needing mowing, fertilizer, weed pulling, watering) versus a native landscape (e.g. providing ecological functions, eco-services, etc.). *Alternative topic*: Critique the LCA tool itself.[51]

Ecological Waste (EW) Analysis: At the end of the twentieth century (in Australia anyway), embodied timber waste was estimated at 90%.[52] How much have operations improved to ensure more timber waste is recycled or upcycled? Compare timber preserved in end-use building products to the volume of timber felled. Trace losses through each stage of timber production (e.g. losses from logging, warping, milling, surfacing, transport, onsite cut-offs). Then trace the losses of biodiversity and eco-services that were incurred during the regeneration period, called 'ecological waste'.[53] How might this study modify the debates regarding timber sourced respectively from clear-felled native forests, selective logging or plantations?[54]

8.3.1.2 Increasing Positive Public Purposes

Development Functions (DF) Analysis: To what extent are public purposes/benefits taken into account in planning/building codes and project approval processes? Find some proposed or existing developments that are of questionable social value and have had a social impact assessment, EIA or similar assessment. Do these consider opportunity costs, or take up land, resources and space where the site/land could serve more vital socio-ecological or economic functions? Do they limit options for adapting to changing conditions or for increasing their public value over time? Was any effort made to design in additional community gains? What can be done to improve the development's overall positive public functions?

192 *Design and Analysis*

Hierarchy of Innovation (HI) Analysis: Have some eco-innovations had adverse ethical consequences? Should disruptive innovations only be subject to market competition, not social impact assessments? Examine some eco-innovations that have been assessed in sustainable design competitions (e.g. green building awards run by national architecture institutes, the Cradle-to-Cradle program, the Katerva organization, the Ellen MacArthur Foundation).[55] To what extent do competitions count market success factors (e.g. potential sales) relative to public benefits/risks? Rank the designs using the criteria of HI analysis [Box 5] which highlights ethics and public benefits, instead of marketability, potential uptake, profitability or inventiveness. Propose means to integrate these ethical criteria into the award scheme.

8.3.1.3 Maximizing Natural Systems and Ecological Spaces

Passive Maximization (PM) Analysis: Some green buildings with poor energy performance have been certified because they were able to gain enough points through other actions that were easier. Obtain a green building certification that was highly ranked for energy even if it is below contemporary expectations. Using passive solar principles, do a desktop retrofit with the aim of substantially reducing the energy needed for heating, ventilating and air conditioning. Conduct an energy modeling of both building plans and estimate their embodied-operating energy usage. Project these energy savings to the number of similar buildings city wide to calculate the relative savings over the lifespan or 50 years.

Multifunctional Space (MS) Analysis: Assess a whole urban block or building cluster against the list of PD social and ecological criteria.[56] How many of these general criteria are met? Assess the number and portion of building users that benefit directly from the positive features and functions of the project over time (e.g. oxygen produced by vegetation, work spaces in interior/exterior garden areas). What portion of visitors and occupants benefit from the environmental/spatial amenities (e.g. windowless work cubicles versus open pleasant foyers)? What is the ratio of resources/space used to public benefits? Retrofit the block to match spaces and PD criteria and maximize public benefits.

8.3.2 Urban Planning Issues at Municipal or Regional Scale

8.3.2.1 Prioritizing Preventative Actions

Resource Security (RS) Analysis. Identify locations for safe havens from various plausible disasters in a specific region (earthquakes, fires, hurricanes, floods, etc.). Design a public facility which provides security in case of a crisis while meeting other social needs and ecological functions. *Alternative topic*: Identify the main materials for local construction used by a particular town. Map the physical supply chain back to their sources. Identify locally available organic materials that could substitute for industrial materials transported from long distances. In some bioregions, this might include strawboard, bamboo, hemp or clay. Map the alternative supply chain. Discuss the relative costs, risks, impacts and benefits.

Risk Avoidance (RA) Analysis. Chart the potential impacts of a potential disaster in a region or town due to environmental risks and secondary costs (the worst-case scenario) to set the design budget. Explore several solutions. For example, in a bush/forest area fires, a solution might be multifunctional observation towers with bunkers and oxygen supplies that incorporate socio-ecological and economic functions (e.g. recreational uses). To delay/mitigate the impacts of sea level rise, a solution might involve moving ground level uses up one floor and treating the surfaces of lower levels with saltwater-proof coatings.[57] Calculate the costs of these measures and compare to the worst-case costs.

8.3.2.2 Mapping Opportunities for Public Benefits

Negative Space (NS) Analysis. Identify local environmental, social and public needs in an urban block or district (e.g. vegetation for air quality, social space, urban heat island mitigation, escape routes in case of and environmental or civil emergency). Map the available open space around, between or above buildings. Find the best means to optimize these elevated open spaces without reducing natural daylighting and desirable views. For example, multi-story scaffolding systems above and/or between buildings could support skybridges, seating areas, specialty food production or multi-layered planting structures for passive air filtering.[58] Then develop planning and design incentives and code changes that would encourage such improvements.[59]

Highest Ecological Use (HU) Analysis. Select a site in a core urban area that is experiencing rapid growth, such as a vacant, dilapidated or underdeveloped site. Identify the major ecological deficits/issues in the surrounding vicinity. What is the highest ecological use, as informed by the ET analysis(below). Develop a set of site planning and design guidelines for the site.[60] For example, these might require nature corridors at various levels linking nearby developments to natural areas, or provisions for limiting the ground coverage of the structure and exposing (daylighting) a stream that was previously covered.[61] What economic uses are compatible with the highest ecological uses?

8.3.2.3 Site Planning for Ecological Gains

Ecological Transformation (ET) Analysis. Map the pre-industrial or pre-historic conditions of a site (whichever is most applicable to local issues) that may be or has been developed.[62] Compare these to current conditions and ecosystems to identify deficits/potentials. Then determine which species and ecosystems can and should be protected, restored or discouraged, to the extent possible. How does this differ from selecting whatever provides more 'species richness' (numbers) for purposes of gaining development credits, or whatever plants grows best? Design biodiversity habitats and/or ecosystem nurseries in conjunction with appropriate natural systems (e.g. water and air cleansing). Remember to design means of impeding invasive predatory species.

Ecological Space (ES) Analysis. Model an existing building using available digital design tools to assess the amount of ES required so that the cubic meters of ES exceed the floor area. Determine where and how to incorporate some or all eco-

194 *Design and Analysis*

services listed in Chapter 6. Estimate how many ecosystem functions can be effectively and synergistically integrated in these spaces. For example, where there is excessive heat gain from curtain glass walls, consider covering half of each window with a pollution-noise absorbing panel that supports micro-habitats and/or includes accessible plant containers. Compare the previous eco-productivity of the site to that created by the new design.

8.3.3 Decision Making at Development Assessment Scale

8.3.3.1 Setting Whole-System Baselines (Time and Space)

Reverse Sunk Cost (SC) Analysis. Obtain or perform a lifecycle analysis (LCA) of a building, that includes the resource extraction/manufacturing processes involved. Examine the stated and unstated baselines used in LCAs. For example, does the LCA count the impacts of a harmful manufacturing process as pre-existing and thus neutral? Does the LCA capture just the industrial impacts that are connected to the project, or does it also consider the contribution of the project to the perpetuation the status quo? That is, does the LCA include the contribution of the project to the perpetuation of a harmful industry itself (e.g. toxic emissions, oil spills, landslides, deforestation)?

Source of Energy (SE) Analysis. Trace the energy flows through an existing area, such as a suburb, back to a coal-fired or nuclear power plant, or find a study that does. Estimate the environmental impacts of the construction and operation of this power source, including such things as the atmospheric toxins emitted in mining the coal/uranium. Count the portion of the energy sent to a particular neighborhood/suburb and the energy lost in production and transmission. Count associated impacts related to habitat destruction, pollution and human health impacts. Compare this to whole-system costs of a solar thermal disk or similar system that just serves the suburb.

8.3.3.2 Ensuring Whole-System Accounting

Costs of Change (CC) Analysis. Obtain plans for a building that is being replaced or retrofitted, perhaps from a city council, and the new/proposed project from the architect or owner. Compare both the old building and new building against PD sustainability standards. How easily will the replacement building be retrofitted in the future to meet these sustainability standards or at least achieve zero operating energy? Design desktop retrofits for both the old and new building. Estimate the costs/impacts of all options. The new building should include the cost of a future retrofit as well, if necessary to achieve the PD sustainability standard in the future.

Benefits of Action (BA) Analysis. Consider the health costs of sick building syndrome (SBS), or a particular cause of SBS in a region, such as mold problems in a coastal town. What will be the medical costs over the next 50 years? Estimate the construction costs of fixing the problem now. Estimate the time required to pay back the costs of retrofitting through medical (and energy) savings. *Alternative topic*: Examine a large building in a polluted city like Bangkok or Beijing. Design solutions that would improve the health of building occupants but also clean the outdoor air in the surrounding area. Estimate the medical savings.

8.3.4 Governance Issues at Regional or National Scale

8.3.4.1 Charting Impacts of Governance Systems

Institutional Design (ID) Analysis. Examine the criteria and indicators in an environmental reporting system of a government agency. Do they meet the PD Test (i.e. increase future options, ecological base and public estate)? In what respects do they conflict with it? For example, does the report consider environmental losses or gains in relation to the previous reporting period or to overall losses of environmental stocks and flows over time? Do the criteria and indicators consider environmental improvements or losses relative to what originally existed, what currently exists, trends, expected losses, likely future costs, increasing rates of population, consumption and pollution, or to no action?

Cumulative Decision (CD) Analysis. Examine a government policy or regulation and implementation measures intended to improve the sustainability and resilience of the natural and built environment. Then trace subsequent agency actions based on that policy or regulation to the on-ground impacts. Compare the outcomes to the stated legislative intent. For example, a Murray Darling River Basin Plan, in Australia, was enacted to increase water flows and allocations to the environment. Did these flows increase or decline after the trading scheme was initiated?[63] Examine the various reasons for the environmental or sustainability conditions becoming better or worse than expected (e.g. political, economic, technological, planning methods).

8.3.4.2 Assessing Socio-Economic Independence

Democratic Impact (DI) Analysis: Review some SIAs (social impact assessments) for large-scale development projects with regard to the PD Test. Does the SIA discuss the provision/absence of physical facilities for social and civic engagement, public forums? Are there adequate physical backup systems to ensure direct access to basic needs? To what extent do delivery systems for food, water and energy in the event of a natural, economic or military crisis depend on monetary and/or electronic systems? For example, are there means to ensure that communication systems remain operative, that building-integrated water and food supplies cannot be contaminated, and that power sources cannot be disabled?

Economic Impact (EI) Analysis: Examine a representative regulatory impact assessment of a recent (USA or other) regulation and examine what 'counted' (e.g. jobs, shortened lifespans, medical costs, transaction costs) and what did not count. Does it consider the costs of ecological waste and restoration, the future costs to the economy of land and resource scarcity, and lost ecosystems/biodiversity? Is the substitutability of nature a viable option? *Alternative topic*: Many economists have argued that higher prices due to resource scarcity lead to behavior change or adjustments that prevent resource scarcity. Are there cases where scarcity has led to resources being increased to a sustainable level?

196 *Design and Analysis*

8.3.4.3 Ensuring Equitable Outcomes

Resource transfer (RT) Analysis. Trace a mined building material to its place of origin in a disadvantaged region/country (e.g. Amazon, Papua New Guinea). Did this involve toxic mining processes (cyanide, coal dust, etc.), unsafe working conditions with low-cost labor, or clear-felled native forests that indigenous people relied on? How much monetary value did these resources gain when embodied in a building, after the costs of production and construction are deducted? Should reparations be made in some way? What portion of the embodied wealth might be used as an amount to reimburse the environmental or human health costs in regions from which the resources came?

Green Optimum Analysis. Examine cases where biodiversity offsets were used to gain approval for a project.[64] Establish the extent to which total negative impacts were increased or reduced from a whole-system perspective (nature restored and/or increased minus the ecological damage or destruction, etc.).[65] What concessions or incentives were given to developers in exchange for the biodiversity offsets, such as extra floor area beyond code allowance? Were the impacts of the extra floor area assessed? *Alternative topic*: Examine a court decision regarding biodiversity offsets granted by a government agency. Were biodiversity 'gains' awarded according to the land area restored or to the ecological footprint?

Box 5 Hierarchy of innovation (Source: Birkeland, 2008)

There are myriad innovation tools that are accessible on the internet. However, most of these processes are oriented towards creating – sometimes unnecessary – products and then finding or creating a market. If they are not designed for sustainability, they could have the effect of increasing consumption. Given that there is an infinite amount of work that needs to be done, and an infinite number of design opportunities, design tools should prioritize net-positive sustainability. Designs, tools and implementation strategies should therefore be reviewed to see whether improvements are possible, according to a hierarchy of solutions from lowest priority to highest.

Level 1: New products or production systems that reduce 'relative' negative impacts per unit (compared to ordinary ones) often increase net resource flows and are, therefore, the lowest order on the hierarchy. New designs, products or production systems that increase resource flows, but at less negative impact per unit than the norm, still can increase future impacts. In general, these should be the last in this list to be publicly supported.

Level 2: The next level is innovations that reduce the waste from ongoing processes or activities by closing resource/energy loops. Closing loops means either downcycling where the outcome has less economic value, or upcycling where the outcome has more value.[66] Innovations that reduce the impacts of waste from ongoing processes or activities through reuse, recycling or reassembly, often have some negative impacts and a reduction in use value or 'downcycling'.

Level 3: The third level is actions that reduce the impacts of past as well as ongoing development (e.g. Living Machines that remove toxins already in the environment). Innovations that reduce the impacts of toxins or waste already in the environment)add economic value, but upcycling can involve an increase in conspicuous consumption and resource flows.

Level 4: Zero waste innovations/outcomes are 'no loop systems'.[67] 'No-loop' refers to innovations where waste is 'designed out' of an existing, ongoing or future system entirely. These actions could still create unnecessary products, which are inherently wasteful, or have a rebound effect, where the resource savings are spent on harmful activities. These design waste out of a system entirely (notwithstanding entropy). The term zero waste usually excludes embodied waste.[68]

Level 5: PD adds 'eco-cycling' which would contribute net gains, without increasing conspicuous consumption or net resource flows.[69] Whereas upcycling can include unnecessary luxury items because these add economic value, eco-cycling would need to increase nature, equity and/or justice. Eco-cycling is upcycling that contributes to human and ecological health (i.e. is net positive) and does not increase total resource consumption. However, this may still not increase access to the means of survival and resource security (the public estate).

Level 6: Net positive, the highest level, refers to either non-physical systems or physical environments that improve whole-system health, or create positive externalities (beyond the project scale), and increase positive future options, the ecological base and public estate (the PD Test). Innovations can be at the building or system level:

- Net-positive development reverses existing impacts and increases the ecological base and public estate beyond pre-development or pre-urban conditions.
- Net-positive systems innovations create levers for biophysical improvements and social transformation at the global-local scale (e.g. converting cities from fossil to solar energy).

Notes

1 A point made by Amory Lovins.
2 Ridgeway, J. (2004) *It's All for Sale: The Control of Global Resources*, Duke University Press, Durham, NC, and London; Myers, N., and Kent, J. (2001) *Perverse Subsidies: How Tax Dollars can Undercut the Environment and the Economy*, Island Press, Washington, DC.
3 This is parallel to burning down buildings for insurance to avoid upgrading them.
4 Superfund sites are places contaminated by hazardous waste in the USA, determined by the EPA to risk human and environmental health.
5 Investments in green buildings have long been known to be sound business investments. Edwards, B. (ed.) (1998) *Green Buildings Pay*, E&FN Spon, London. However, the public costs of buildings, such as the mining impacts, should also be counted.
6 Most energy ratings of homes often do not give credit for passive design elements such as external shade structures and other effective passive features.

198 *Design and Analysis*

7 The amount of solar energy that hits the earth in one hour would power civilization for a year.
8 The energy needed in operating buildings can be highly variable due to differing needs for electronic equipment.
9 Global mercury levels caused by fossil fuels is left out of public debates on solar versus fossil energy.
10 For summary, see Scheer, H. (2004) *The Solar Economy*, Earthscan, London.
11 Energy sources can be mapped in a way that makes the costs of energy sources more apparent or transparent such as in Sankey Diagrams.
12 Most architecture students are taught about thermal mass, insulation, passive air flows and shaping building to collect, store and distribute energy, but are not expected to use this knowledge when employed in firms.
13 Solar windows could power all buildings but would not address ecological or social sustainability. See Latimer, C. (2017) New Tech Could Turn Windows into Solar Panels, *Sydney Morning Herald*, Oct. 30. www.smh.com.au/business/energy/new-tech-could-turn-windows-into-solar-panels-20171027-gz9goq.html.
14 See Lovegrove, K. (2008) Box 18: Solar Powering the Future, in Birkeland, J. (ed.) *Positive Development: From Vicious Circles to Virtuous Cycles through Built Environment Design*, Earthscan, p. 299.
15 Fuel cells can ensure energy provision in large buildings. See CHP Group of the Chartered Institution of Building Services Engineers (CIBSE) www.cibse.org/chp. www.cibse.org/getmedia/59beaaf3-0669-4a33-9248-c68fd588851f/Fuel-Cells-for-buildings_data sheet-4_May-2017.pdf.aspx.
16 Grandfathering is where old rules apply to some existing situations while new rules apply to all future cases.
17 Permanence is an asset to landmark buildings, and their heritage value may ensure that they are maintained.
18 Simply discouraging cars by reducing car lanes without adequate public transport is no more effective than creating more parking spaces to reduce congestion.
19 Smith, Michael H., Hargroves, K., and Desha, C. (2010) *Cents and Sustainability: Securing our Common Future by Decoupling Economic Growth from Environmental Pressures*, Earthscan/Routledge, London.
20 As discussed in Chapter 5, some businesses provide energy efficiency services at little or no cost to clients and recover their costs and make profits from the reduced energy, water or sewage bills.
21 HM Treasury (2006) *Stern Review: The Economics of Climate Change*, UK Government, London.
22 The term 'costs of inaction' emphasizes remediation and prevention or defensive actions, rather than exploring the benefits of positive action.
23 Whether or not climate change is real or not, the actions that should be undertaken are still the same, so transition costs should not be the issue.
24 Many costly power plants and dams have been postponed due to community energy efficiency initiatives.
25 Lake Pedder in Tasmania was flooded quickly because of a campaign to save it, losing valuable timber in the process. www.greenleft.org.au/content/lake-pedder-beginning-movement.
26 Many executives of government agencies have been drawn from the ranks of those the agency regulates and vice versa.
27 Milne, M. J., and Gray, R. J. (2013) W(h)ither Ecology? The Triple Bottom Line, the Global Reporting Initiative, and Corporate Sustainability Reporting, *Business Ethics* 118(1), pp. 13–29.
28 E.g. Australia has given carbon credits for reducing the rate of land clearing while clearing rates increase.
29 Daly, H. E., Cobb Jr, J. B., and Cobb, J. B. (1994) *For the Common Good: Redirecting the Economy Toward Community, the Environment, and a Sustainable Future*, Beacon Press, Boston, MA.

30 See Cole, R. J. (2011) Motivating Stakeholders to Deliver Environmental Change, *Building Research and Information* 39(5), pp. 431–5.
31 $13AU billion was spent on water reform yet millions in liters and dollars have been taken by irrigators, at the expense of the many communities that live along the Murray Darling River in Australia. See Thompson, R. M. (2017) Is the Murray-Darling Basin Plan Broken? The Conversation, https://theconversation.com/is-the-murray-darling-basin-plan-broken-81613 (July 26). Grafton, Q., et al. (2018) The Murray Darling Basin Plan is Not Delivering – There's No More Time to Waste, The Conversation, https://theconversation.com/the-murray-darling-basin-plan-is-not-delivering-theres-no-more-time-to-waste-91076 (Feb. 5).
32 E.g. a sense of public interest was expressed in the establishment of the national park system in the USA.
33 See Save Beeliar Wetlands (Inc.) v Commissioner of Main Roads (2017) FCA 4 www.findlaw.com.au/articles/6151/save-beeliar-wetlands-inc-v-commissioner-of-main-r.aspx; Bulga Milbrodale Progress Association Inc v. Minister for Planning and Infrastructure (2013) NSWLEC 48 www.westlaw.com.au.ezp.lib.unimelb.edu.au/maf/wlau/app/document?docguid=I93463be1cdf611e4a5c3e0c0015e82d4&tocDs=AUNZ_CASE_TOC&isTocNav=true&startChunk=1&endChunk=1.
34 For an example, see Swain, I. (2008) Box 40: Linking Policies to Outcomes, in Birkeland, *Positive Development*, pp. 325–6.
35 The trickle-down theory is that subsidies to businesses, or the wealthy more generally, will magically flow to the poor because the economy will grow.
36 Myers and Kent, *Perverse Subsidies*.
37 Repetto, R. C., and Gillis, M. (1988) *Public Policies and the Misuse of Forest Resources*, Cambridge University Press, Cambridge.
38 Some rating tools mention social equity but only concern reducing the impacts of well-healed suburbs by encouraging less consumptive lifestyles, not helping socio-economically deprived regions.
39 Regulatory impact assessment does not really focus on the ecological impacts of economic policies/legislation, or the long-term impacts on the economy of degraded and depleted resource stocks. It focuses on costs and benefits.
40 See Regan, E. C., Santini, L., Ingwall-King, L., et al. (2015) Global Trends in the Status of Bird and Mammal Pollinators, *Conservation Letters* 8, pp. 397–403.
41 The contribution of the rich to the ecological footprint is largely hidden by using averages.
42 www.taxpayer.net/energy-natural-resources/nuclear-power-subsidies/.
43 Nuclear energy was promoted in the post-war USA by labelling defence expenditures as domestic.
44 There is a proposal to improve nuclear waste storage. See www.bloomberg.com/news/articles/2018-03-20/this-father-daughter-team-says-it-has-a-cheaper-safer-way-to-bury-nuclear-waste.
45 The resource drain can be compared to the 'brain drain'.
46 The Pareto optimum, more formally, is where resources are distributed such that one party's situation cannot be improved without making another party's situation worse.
47 Corporations are regarded as persons in US law and have similar rights. See Winkler, A. (2018) 'Corporations Are People' is Built on an Incredible 19th-Century Lie, *The Atlantic*, Mar. 5. www.theatlantic.com/business/archive/2018/03/corporations-people-adam-winkler/554852/.
48 E.g. many politicians oppose subsidies to solar energy but conceal/ignore subsidies to fossil fuels. Analyses by the International Energy Agency showed that fossil fuels received four times more subsidies than renewable energy. See Kavanagh, M. (2016) A World Map of Subsidies for Renewable Energy and Fossil Fuels: Government Support for 'Dirty' Fuels across the World Still Exceeds that for Renewables, *Financial Times*, July 26.
49 Royalties have not covered the public costs. Myers and Kent, *Perverse Subsidies*.
50 For discussion on unjust enrichment, see Birkeland, *Positive Development*, pp. 142–4.
51 The procedures of lifecycle assessment (LCA) are found in ISO 14,000 environmental management standards: ISO 14040:2006 and 14044:2006.

200 *Design and Analysis*

52 Santana, M. (2002) Timber Waste Minimization by Design, in Birkeland, *Design for Sustainability*, pp. 188–91.
53 Birkeland, J. (2007) GEN 6: Ecological Waste: Rethinking the Nature of Waste, in *Environmental Design Guide of the Australian Institute of Architects*, BEDP, Canberra. www.environmentdesignguide.com.au/
54 This comparison has been done, but factors are 'weighted' in varying ways.
55 See www.katerva.net/; www.c2ccertified.org/; www.ellenmacarthurfoundation.org/.
56 See Birkeland, *Positive Development*, pp. 256–7.
57 There are coatings for materials in saltwater.
58 Similar examples can be found on the internet. E.g. see www.treehugger.com and https://inhabitat.com/
59 These might include transferable development credits or other incentives discussed in Chapter 6.
60 Birkeland, *Positive Development*, pp. 257–8.
61 Prairie restoration projects began in the USA in the 1930s in part to repair the dust bowl. See www.wildflower.org/learn/recreate-a-prairie.
62 E.g. see https://welikia.org/explore/mannahatta-map/ or www.gizmodo.com.au/2015/09/what-every-block-of-nyc-looked-like-400-years-ago/.
63 See ABC TV 4 Corners (2017) *Pumped: Who's Benefitting from the Billions Spent on the Murray-Darling?* www.abc.net.au/4corners/pumped/8727826, updated Aug. 17, 2017. See also n. 31 above.
64 Offsets have sometimes been used to make uneconomic development feasible. See Lang, J. (1996) Implementing Urban Design in America: Project Types and Methodological Implications, *Journal of Urban Design* 1(1), pp. 7–22.
65 E.g. the 'no net loss' of wetlands proviso led to net losses. Roberts, L. (1993) Wetlands Trading is a Loser's Game, say Ecologists, *Science*, 260(5116), pp. 1890–2; National Research Council Staff (2001) *Compensating for Wetland Losses under the Clean Water Act*, Committee on Mitigating Wetland Losses, National Academies Press, Washington, DC.
66 The term upcycling was introduced in McDonough, W., and Braungart, M. (2002) *Cradle to Cradle: Remaking the Way we Make Things*, North Point Press, New York.
67 McDonough and Braungart, *Cradle to Cradle*.
68 Birkeland, GEN 6: Ecological Waste.
69 Birkeland, *Positive Development*, pp. 240–2.

Part II
Decision Making and Assessment
Synopsis of Part II

Having examined issues pertaining to design and analysis, this part concerns decision-making structures for governance, planning and assessment that can foster eco-positive environments.

Part I examined ways that the design of physical structures and spaces could create the biophysical conditions for economic, social and ecological sustainability. Conventional sustainable design can mitigate the growing impacts of population, pollution and wealth disparities, and slow the rate of environmental destruction overall. However, it does not increase the total ecological and social life-support systems. The remediation and regeneration of the remnants of nature cannot counteract the ongoing losses of the ecological base. Ultimately, ecological restoration cannot compensate for losses of ecosystems, biodiversity and eco-services unless space for nature is, in effect, increased beyond pre-colonial or pre-industrial conditions.

New frameworks of governance, planning and development control are suggested to overcome current biases against ecological sustainability, in order to embed net-positive sustainability.

Built environment design can leverage biophysical sustainability without waiting for social change or institutional reform, because eco-positive retrofitting can occur immediately and continuously, and can pay for itself. However, institutional redesign will eventually be necessary to embed proactive approaches and positive thinking across the governmental, professional and academic disciplines. To promote net-positive outcomes, institutional structures, planning methods and assessment tools must integrate design thinking with the more reductionist, technocratic approaches. Part II proposes positive institutional frameworks for governance, planning, management and assessment that can guide decision making to expand future sustainable options and increase the ecological base and public estate.

A new constitution could catalyze the transition to a sustainable society but, meanwhile, new decision rules would enable development that supports socio-ecological transformation.

Chapters 9–10 discuss eco-governance generally, review sustainable planning approaches and describe development control/consent processes and participation in planning. It then introduces green building rating/marketing tools (RTs). RTs have come to dominate quality control in urban design and architecture but reinforce the mechanistic approach to problem-solving. Chapters 11–12 suggest that RTs did not learn from or build upon earlier development control strategies.

202 *Decision Making and Assessment*

Since managers need evaluation tools and designers like challenges, two alternatives to RTs are presented to address their problems: Chapters 13–14 present a qualitative approach to support planning, and Chapters 15–16 present a quantitative design tool, the STARfish.

The STARfish design tool assists sustainable design and assessment by establishing eco-positive benchmarks and stimulating processes that can achieve maximum positive public benefits.

The STARfish is an app (computer application) to support net-positive design and assessment. It creates an interactive collaborative 'game' in which a design team competes with itself to create the most sustainable design possible by revealing opportunities for positive design synergies. It draws upon a combination of radar, spider and impact wheel diagrams to assist visualization and communication. The STARfish is geared for identifying opportunities to provide net public gains and increase social and ecological life-support systems in a global sense. It is called the STARfish because it can have any number of legs or discard and grow new ones.

Section E
Development Governance

9 Governance and Futures Planning

9.1 Review and Preview

Although biophysical sustainability is largely a design problem, institutional structures that shape built environments should be reoriented to enable eco-positive problem solving and opportunity creating.

Part I argued that biophysical design can bypass many of the systemic barriers to environmental, economic and social sustainability. Changing the built environment from negative to eco-positive can begin immediately. It need not wait for changes in the operation of politics, profits or power – only a paradigm shift in design. Nevertheless, political and institutional structures and rules of engagement also matter because they shape the debates, decisions and designs. Institutional structures must therefore be consciously redesigned. The chapter suggests a constitutional structure for eco-governance that can take into account environmental ethics and presents principles for urban governance and planning.

This chapter first reviews how institutional and physical redesign can stimulate social change and why socio-political levers and pulleys have not been effective.

It cannot be over-emphasized why design-based strategies to increase biophysical sustainability are urgently needed. Sustainability advocates keep trying to change values and opinions via social movements, persuasion, conversion, politics, or behaviors via markets or regulations – hoping to get different results. The illusion that good values will rise to the top if everyone simply gets a voice in a virtual town hall or marketplace has been contradicted by the realities that the internet and social media have exposed. All levers are important (political, administrative, ideological, spiritual financial, etc.) but indirect approaches are easily derailed by levers that can be easily manipulated.

9.2 Design as a Driver of Systems Change

9.2.1 Beyond Social (Values-Centered) Levers of Change

Though values must change, a more direct approach to social transformation is to create environments that reduce the causes of discontent and inequity.

One negligent person can undo the actions of hundreds of conscientious people. Even if everyone managed to change their beliefs, values and prejudices, individuals can do little beyond 'reduce, reuse and recycle' (3Rs). Any collective reductions in consumption would be outweighed by large-scale global forces well beyond the influence of consumers and voters. The 3Rs alone cannot change the waste and toxins inherent in current development systems from upstream damage during resource extraction/manufacturing to downstream damage during building operation/demolition. However, eco-positive urban structures and environments can address the 'causes' of consumption, such as disparities of wealth and cravings for hoarding/consumerism.

Efforts to change people have delayed the redesign of structural systems which could shape positive socio-ecological outcomes, regardless of conflicting ideologies and values.

Without planning for biophysical sustainability, progress toward more sustainable values will swing left and right, but not forward. A promo for a TV program *Ecosolutions* encapsulated the orthodox approach: 'we talk to people who are taking steps to help balance our environmental challenges and who show us how to make better choices every day'.[1] Institutional and structural change does not happen by holding voters or consumers accountable [Figure 9.1]. Improvements in product choices cannot outpace the mounting impacts of the DP. Conversely, however, built environments could be building community, influencing behavior, values and hope, while creating more mutually beneficial human-nature and human-human relationships.[2]

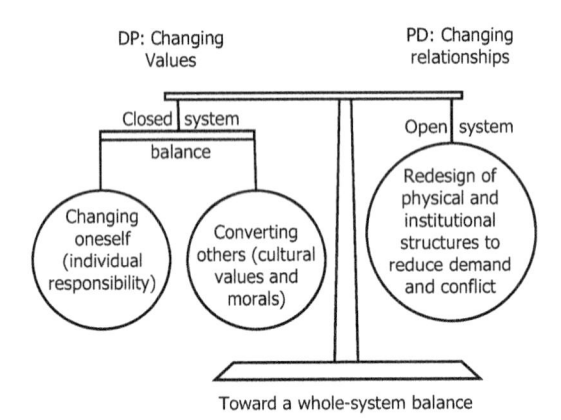

Figure 9.1 From changing people to designing relationships

9.2.2 Beyond Political (Rights-Centered) Levers of Change

Neither reactionary nor progressive politics on their own can change the systemic biases against nature hidden in decision-making frameworks of government and industry.

Right- and left-wing political positions have not really challenged the anti-ecological bias in the DP [Chapter 3]. Information, education and awareness do not seem to alter the ideologies of politicians or bureaucrats, or translate into more ethical/moral political behaviors. The divisive politics surrounding right-left worldviews conceals an uncanny similarity or false dualism between these positions. There are sometimes pyrrhic victories through socio-political channels, but temporary gains do not keep pace with environmental destruction, and can be trumped in any future election. This is especially true where corporate or foreign political donations are allowed, despite the axiom 'one person, one vote'.[3]

The political milieu is ill-suited for collaborative approaches to reform, since political reform relies on representatives who often gain power by fueling division.

Most today would say that politics is a shallow, winner-takes-all process. With the rise of the internet and the cult of personality and celebrity, there are fewer curbs on divisiveness, disruption and distraction. Conflict surrounding personal morals and/or rights (e.g. abortion, gay marriage, marijuana, immigration) diverts attention from long-term sustainability issues that require structural transformation. Politics creates teams but not cooperation in addressing big issues such as disparities of wealth, climate change or disappearing life-support systems. Despite a growing wealth of information, efforts to go beyond sound bites and engage the public or politicians in constructive problem-solving appears futile.

Design can be a conflict resolution mechanism which transcends rigid ideological positions/preconceptions to find physical solutions that address everyone's interests, values and needs.

Basic infrastructure decisions are often made by an expertariat of engineers and/or economists who generally lack design training – before meaningful community input is sought. For example, a dam or pulp mill is often planned and costed before the proposal is subject to public consultation. Community input is therefore limited to making objections to a project or its environmental assessment after it is too late to consider design alternatives that could satisfy both the investors and community [Figure 9.2]. Appeals boards and environmental courts generally limit their review to how procedures were complied with, not on whether win-win design options were available.

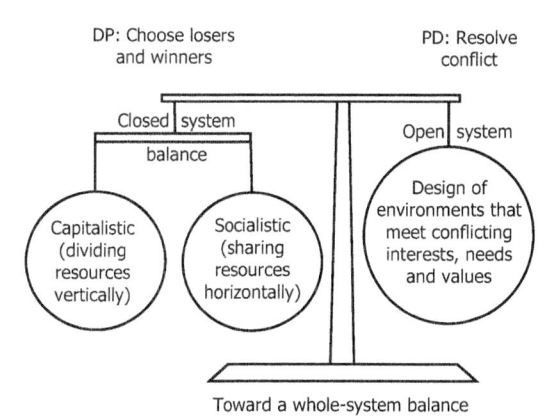

Figure 9.2 From adversarial politics to conflict resolution by design

9.2.3 Beyond Business (Market-Centered) Change

Decision methods in economic and business fields are designed to increase an individual's or firm's relative position, not to improve the whole system.

Business administration tools evolved in parallel with military strategies and aim to optimize a firm's relative position.[4] Competition does not always lead to unethical practices, but it is seldom shown to make systems that work for everyone.[5] Nonetheless, business can change quickly to gain a competitive advantage. In the 1990s, many businesses made impressive strides toward cleaning up industry in response to public and political pressure.[6] In most cases, however, neither regulations nor innovations have increased whole-system sustainability. Reducing toxins or wastes per unit of output has little net-positive effect, and not enough to offset the adverse impacts of development.

Community engagement (marketing research) is considered good business practice, but the choices presented to consumers seldom include alternatives that provide direct public benefit.

In property development, which is business, community participation is geared toward gleaning or shaping consumer preferences, and not toward reducing global consumption. Public involvement in development approval processes often just means variations on surveys or voting, consultation or sales pitches, or opportunities to object – with little opportunity to express views on substance. Consumer demand is largely created by supply-side advertising. The market provides 'consumer choice', but these choices are usually only in regard to styles or products (not systems): diversity within sameness. While there is participation in planning and design itself, it is often directed toward certain pre-conceived ends.

Although business and industry have developed and use many whole-system analyses, the aim is price/resource reduction, not working toward reversing global environmental depletion/degradation.

There are many business tools to stimulate innovation and take a system's view of business issues. However, they tend to focus on marketability and cost efficiency. Alternatives are compared to existing conditions, pathways or goals and generally only consider changes that the firm can capitalize on. There are also analytical tools that trace negative impacts through time and space in order to reduce negative flows and reduce costs, such as industrial metabolism.[7] These analyses use systems boundaries and cost-benefit ledgers that limit their application to the business or industry concern, whereas governments could develop analyses aimed at increasing the general welfare [Figure 9.3].[8]

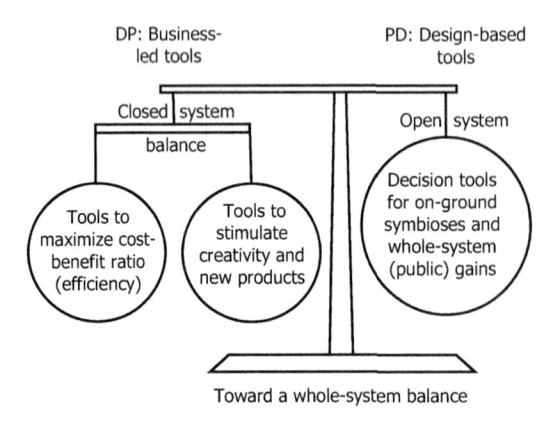

Figure 9.3 From decision-based to design-based tools

9.2.4 Beyond Government (Regulation-Centered) Change

Some governmental (executive branch) agencies have substantial discretion to protect/destroy natural environments, but often cater to short-term demands from industry, consumers and politicians.

Resource management agencies have substantial decision-making powers regarding resource conservation/exploitation (in English-speaking democracies). They were partly set up to take the political heat off of politicians regarding controversial resource decisions. Pressure comes from two directions: bottom-up demands from the public for cheaper goods or relief from recessions, and top-down demands from business and industry for more access to cheaper resources.[9] Demands for more land for suburban housing will come from both directions as long as population growth/immigration continues. The influence of economic-based frameworks on government agencies means that basic issues like human/ecological carrying capacity are scarcely considered in these debates.

Governments are meant to correct the failure of markets to meet demand/needs, but seldom recognize that nature is the ultimate source of supply.

Consumer supply and demand is often balanced at the expense of the life-support system (the basis of supply). With each boom and bust of the market cycle, governments dip into reserves of natural resources to assuage consumer or political unrest. Governments may create more nature reserves, but these can be reversed later by executive order. Once gone, they are often gone forever,[10] so temporary reprieves for ecosystems mean little. Each time environmental protection is reversed by governments there may be accidents, oil spills, toxic leaks or nuclear incidents,[11] where links in the food chain and biodiversity matrix are irreversibly broken.

Agencies use surveys, hearings, public consultation or participatory processes, but these are designed around preconceptions and reflect the interests of politicians and management.

Planners often use similar tools to those of business and military fields. Theories and tools for improving outcomes for a firm or agency can be very different from designing systems that create win-win solutions.[12] Mainstream tools, designed to make trade-offs between alternative pathways or policies, have been modified to include sustainability, but are generally oriented around cost-benefit or risk-benefit frameworks. These rearrange the bumps on a pinball machine – they do not reverse the slope of the playing field itself. The decision principles and participatory processes can modify pre-conceived positions, but do not change the context that creates binary positions [Figure 9.4].

210 *Decision Making and Assessment*

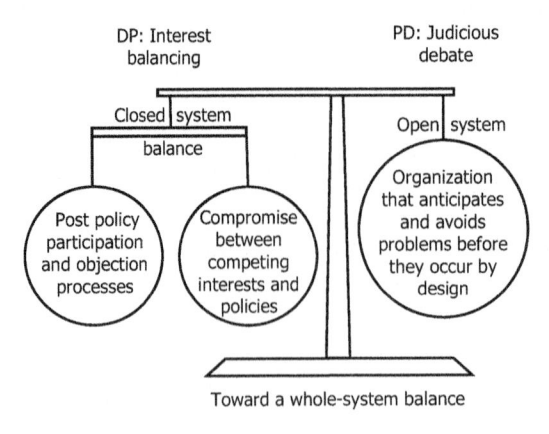

Figure 9.4 Beyond bureaucracy to reasoning

9.2.5 Design-Based Change

Whereas the above strategies for social change can be circuitous, design can provide a direct, non-partisan, more lasting approach to positive systems transformation.

People have finally stopped hoping that, once a 'really big' environmental and social crises occurred, citizens and governments would mobilize to effect change. Greater crises kept occurring, yet little has been done. Direct design action to convert urban deficits into public benefits offers a more constructive approach than continually trying to change people. Design-based approaches can create physical solutions that provide more equitable living conditions without extra cost. However, built environments are still not expected to address socio-ecological sustainability issues. Many think it is enough to build energy-efficient developments that encourage occupants to reduce consumerism, drive less and recycle more.

Physical and institutional structures can provide healing environments that at least reduce the impacts of wealth disparities and other causes of welfare/warfare expenditures.

Governmental or business-led approaches are limited by the legacy of physical and institutional structures that have perpetuated unequal relationships. Solutions are usually directed at producing more buildings and building products efficiently, rather than on creating environments that shape more positive and equitable relationships between individuals, society and nature. Even innovations that are 'inspired by nature' or evoke the subjective feeling of natural environments,[13] often rely on special interests (private initiatives/investments, government subsidies and/or wasteful corporate competition).[14] Environments that increase the ecological base and public estate need not cost extra, so nothing actually prevents designers from designing 'for' nature and society.

The marginalization of design has not only perpetuated low-quality built environments but has limited people's ability to envisage life in eco-positive urban environments.

Since any design that is better than the norm is generally labelled sustainable, basic models and standards of conventional sustainable development have gone unchallenged. Green buildings almost never maximize the possible public benefits or the ecological potential of a site. Since few administrators/politicians/technocrats understand design, they seek to improve performance by increasing the 'numbers' by which problems are measured. It is incumbent upon designers to help people visualize a diverse range of sustainable environments. Until social and ecological standards evolve, however, buildings could be required to be 'reversible' (e.g. de-constructable, adaptable, biodegradable) to allow for future expansion, contraction and upgrading.

In summary, shifts from negative to positive paradigms in all dimensions of life can be fostered by design-based approaches to planning and design.

Some years ago, it became unfashionable in the built-environment field to suggest that the built and natural environment influences people and their values or behaviors (derided as physical determinism). However, in a complex system, everything shapes everything else, and the physical dimension is implicated in virtually all sustainability issues. Thus, the environment can be a solution as well as a problem. Design-based approaches to social, political, financial, regulatory and legal spheres provide a counterbalance to limited, binary reductionist, decision-based approaches:

- From trying to change people by imposing one's own set of values, ideologies or worldviews on others – to constructing physical environments that reduce the underlying causes of conflict or discontent by providing for basic needs and environmental quality.
- From obtaining funds or supporters to protest injustices or get representatives elected (musical chairs) which temporarily move the political pendulum – to creating non-binary decision-making systems that can increase whole-system sustainability in ways that multiply benefits and divide burdens.
- From using market-based tools that aim to maximize profits, exploit opportunities and allow people to manipulate the system for personal gains – to incentivizing development that solves problems, increases opportunities and makes sustainable living both irresistible and foolproof.
- From imposing regulations that are negotiated by powerful financial stakeholders in business/industry or simply encouraging the use of best available technologies – to adopting ethics-based design principles that provide physical solutions to different issues, developments, environments and socio-cultural contexts.
- From relying on adversarial legal systems for settling disputes over access to resources among private and public interests – to implementing collaborative, participatory, creative community design processes that address the underlying environmental causes of negative impacts in urban environments.

9.3 Eco-governance

Without changes in underlying structures of planning and urban design, built environments will continue to lock in unsustainable pathways, regardless of any incremental advances.

The decision-making processes of government virtually exclude any ecological considerations since the underlying structures of governance were conceived before there was an appreciation that the ecological base is the foundation of democracy.[15] Ironically, the term eco-governance has often been used to mean adding new principles and policies to old decision frameworks. While built environment design can benefit everyone, a new system of governance is ultimately also needed. In PD, eco-governance refers to decision frameworks that can increase whole-system sustainability. The first section recaps a PD proposal for constitutional restructuring and some positive institutional design principles before discussing governance in planning.

9.3.1 Government Structures

Three branches of government create checks and balances that can help prevent the abuse of governmental power, yet have not prevented environmental exploitation.

The models of governance in many democracies distinguish three forms of decision-making: legislative, executive and judicial. Congress or Parliament (legislative branch) establishes rights, to avoid future conflicts. However, resource industries and multinational corporations influence these representatives.[16] To the extent that political representatives mirror society, they disproportionately represent the powerful, and a few individuals now have the combined wealth of half the world's population.[17] The executive branch, including resource management agencies, implements/enforces policies, and can make decisions with irreversible ecological consequences.[18] The judicial branch (environmental courts) resolves conflicts after issues materialize, when it is often too late for win-win design solutions.

To address the ethical issues underlying sustainability, a fourth sphere of governance for environmental planning and design must be integrated into decision-making frameworks/constitutions.

Resource decisions, whether influenced/decided through legislative, judicial or executive processes, have been rights-based. They determine whose rights will prevail or, in effect, divide resources among rival interests. These decisions often create precedents that will shape future choices and opportunities. While negotiation/mediation occurs in various forms, the outcome often splits the difference, compromises or mitigates impacts. Sustainability is more about ethics than just rights/claims to resources. Therefore, PD suggests an ethics-based decision arena integrated into constitutions and agency charters.[19] This 'fourth' branch of governance would be designed to deal with the multifaceted ethical and ecological dilemmas underlying development and environment decisions [Figure 9.5].[20]

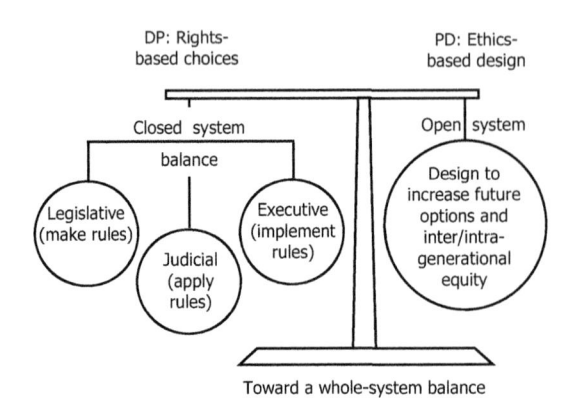

Figure 9.5 Balancing competing demands versus expanding options

The fourth tier of government, at national, regional and/or local levels, would deal with biophysical sustainability issues and guide proactive eco-positive design interventions.

Many land development proposals are initiated through economic prospecting by private investors, and constrained by various planning laws and building regulations. These building codes and regulations were usually enacted due to past mischief, or losses from health and safety defects, resulting from corrupt business practices and/or corporate lobbying. Accumulating layers of incremental, reactive regulations has made compliance ever-more complex and ideocratic/bureaucratic. This complexity means efforts at reform are superficial and seldom challenge underlying problematic premises (e.g. that nature is expendable). Genuine eco-governance will require the reform of constitutions, charters, decision rules and organizational structures ideally to meet the PD Test.

The Constitution of Ecuador recognizes the rights of nature, and every person has standing to demand that public authorities protect the natural environment.

In 2008, Ecuador changed the nation's constitution by referendum. It not only included a declaration of the rights of nature, but allowed anyone to call upon the government to enforce those rights on behalf of species, ecosystems and natural cycles. Nature also has the right to be restored, so the State is obliged to create mechanisms to eliminate or mitigate negative environmental impacts and restore damaged ecosystems. Everyone has the right to benefit from the environment and environmental services, as they belong to the public and cannot be appropriated. Further, organic/inorganic material that would cause irreversible genetic change is forbidden.

Where constitutional change at national levels is not politically feasible, government decision rules could be modified to align better with net-positive sustainability standards.

A widely accepted principle is that government has an implicit social contract with its citizens to protect their rights, interests and basic needs.[21] The idea that individual rights meant freedom from government interference morphed into freedom to exploit resources. Governments have traditionally allocated natural resources to speed up economic growth and development. For example, land grants and resource concessions were allocated to encourage mining and the exploitation of forests in exchange for the 'service' of advancing industrial progress. Given the now diminishing public land and resources, however, it would be reasonable to update archaic principles to meet new rights and realities.[22]

Until legislative reforms that foster ethics-based land use and development decisions are enacted, positive principles could be integrated into lower-level government decision-making processes.

The reorientation and reorganization of charters, constitutions and conventions sounds difficult, but it is not unprecedented (as in France and Ecuador).[23] Moreover, the charters of many government resource agencies, in democracies at least, were created to uphold the public interest. That public interest gradually became equated with corporate interests without direct or deliberative debate, ballots or referenda.[24] The shift to private control of the means of survival was a quiet revolution [Figure 9.6]. Although constitutional reform may currently be politically unrealistic, decision principles, conventions and rules that apply to sustainability issues can be restated in positive terms [as proposed in Box 3].

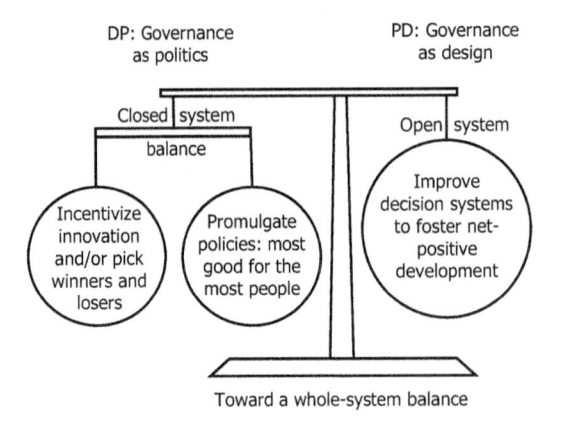

Figure 9.6 Settling disputes versus resolving systems problems

9.3.2 Decision Principles for Eco-Governance

The new sphere of decision making in resource or environment agencies at local, national or international levels would be constructed upon ecological/ethical principles.

There are well-established ethical concepts of governance, such as procedural and substantive due process, which are engrained in the USA constitution. Other governments purport to guarantee a basic human right to a healthy environment.[25] When government and planning institutions began to protect the natural environment, however, many saw this as restraining freedom of exploitation. This contributed to a 'small government' (i.e. deregulation) movement. Whether government is large or small, there is no rational argument against applying planning and design principles that are based on a positive ethic, or proactively doing good, since positive actions cost less in the long term.

9.3.3 Beyond 'Do No Harm'

The Pareto Optimum implies that development is optimal if it does not harm others, and development need not contribute to the public good.

In a closed-system ethic, one only needs to look after one's own property and not violate other's rights. Stimulating economic growth has been deemed an adequate contribution to society, so developers/designers have only been responsible for not (unduly) harming others. This view corresponds with the Pareto Optimum, a basic capitalist decision rule. In the context of physical development, this is fictitious, because virtually all construction does ecological damage. In reality, then, the Pareto Optimum means not causing negative impacts beyond acceptable levels. This places environmental groups in the position of (non-profit) 'objectors' who must prove there will be unreasonable harm.

The PD Green Optimum states that development should increase the public estate, ecological base and future options (while compensating or offsetting) owner/investors where necessary.

The PD Green Optimum is practically the reverse of the Pareto Optimum [Figure 9.7]. It stems from the realization that sustainable design can 'decouple' negative environmental impacts from economic growth.[26] This is because it can make/save substantial amounts of money, energy or social/environmental resources. However, design can also maximize benefits to the general public and nature, to the extent talents and abilities permit.[27] Where it will cost more to achieve this, developers, owners or investors can be compensated for any undue financial burdens they incur. There are many ways to offset any burdens or expenses that do not require direct public subsidies.[28]

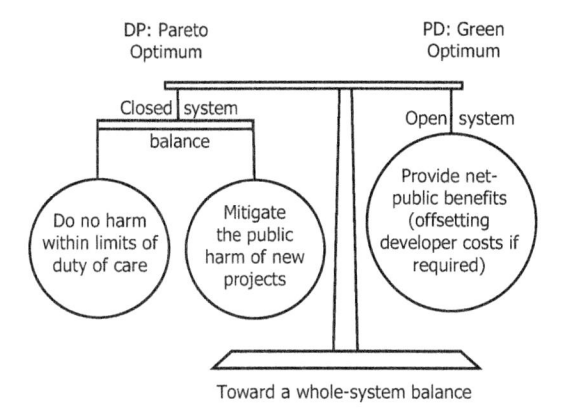

Figure 9.7 Pareto Optimum versus Green Optimum

The free rider *concept, a corollary to the Pareto Optimum, suggests that benefitting society is a problem if any beneficiaries fail to pay.*

The free rider or stowaway concept reflects the neoliberal world view. Since relationships are seen as transactional, one is not expected to do good without receiving benefits in exchange. This concept makes no sense in the built environment context, as developers receive many direct/indirect 'free' benefits from the general public. A commercial building profits from public investments in transportation systems, police and emergency services, sanitation and water supplies, a supply of clients, customers and workers, and gains in prestige that provide market advantages. Developments should therefore give back to society – beyond merely contributing to civic pride and economic growth.

9.3.4 Beyond the Precautionary Principle

The precautionary principle *(not using excuses for not fixing problems) is seldom implemented, but should be reconceived to mean proactively reducing existing/potential risks.*

The principle is often stated as a triple negative and in a reactive form, such as: a 'lack of scientific evidence should not be used as an excuse for inaction in preventing environmental problems'.[29] It is usually raised in objection to a proposed new action, such as adopting a risky technology or using a harmful chemical. It is seldom applied to problems that already exist, such as nuclear and coal power.[30] Since the precautionary principle is weak, a proactive principle is needed to prevent continuing down a path that most scientists believe is harmful to both people and planet.

216 *Decision Making and Assessment*

Recognizing that the failure to prevent planetary destruction is 'reckless disregard for life' (knowing the risks and possible consequences) would shift the burden.

The precautionary principle is meant to shift the burden of proof from the public to the profiteers, but it is not stated directly (and hardly ever occurs). Many politicians choose to believe that evidence of climate change is false and conspiratorial, but the only rebuttal they offer is that eco-efficiency and environmental quality cost more. There is no evidence that climate change does not exist or that measures to improve human health and wellbeing are not worth the trouble. Managers who risk the lives of others for financial gain may one day be liable for recklessness, since positive alternatives are available.

The PD proactive principle *means taking direct design action to correct risks, such as mitigating climate change, even were climate change not evident.*

Those wanting to undertake activities that might unnecessarily expose others to risks, or those blocking positive actions that would benefit everyone, would need to show their position would at least 'do good'. Therefore, since coal mining shortens lifespans, causes extinctions and destroys the natural environment, whereas renewable energy saves money, health and lives, the proactive principle would dictate abandoning coal. Fossil fuel interests would need to prove climate change did not exist, even if it were somehow 'reversible'. To provide work or pensions for redundant miners, renewable energy facilities could be built in most locations where coal mines were closed [Figure 9.8].

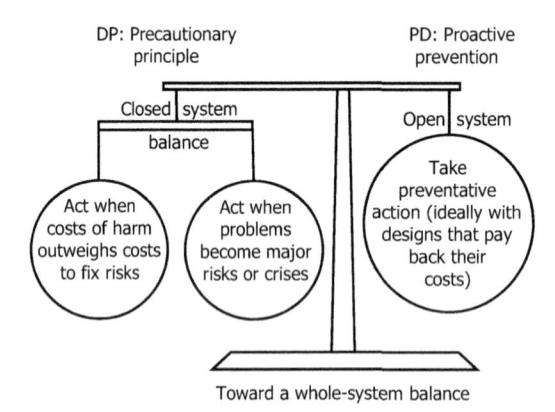

Figure 9.8 Precautionary versus proactive principle

The PD direct action principle *reverses the convention of indirect business incentives, and targets community-wide ecological and social deficits through physical design interventions.*

Design improvements are 'direct' because, unlike regulations and incentives, they are less vulnerable to intervening forces.[31] While good design research can pay for itself and avoid the accumulation of future environmental remediation and medical costs, the public should be reimbursed from the savings brought by government investments.[32] Instead, the recipients of research grants have often set up private companies that essentially privatize knowledge for individual profit. When companies, in effect, exclude others from building upon these innovations, it slows the pace of positive change. Governments could instead proactively fund net-positive solutions and roll over the savings into more such projects.

The least change approach to retrofitting the built environment is the norm, since eco-efficiency is generally confused with monetary savings (price, not value).

Direct action to fix environmental problems – before the costs of inaction exceed the costs of action – begins saving immediately. It is the opposite of the 'least change', price-based approach. Systemic procrastination owes partly to the management credo: 'only manage what can be measured'. Since only 'measurables' are managed, environmental problems usually accrue long before they are visible or quantifiable.[33] For example, since facilities managers are mainly responsible for reducing costs, not reducing externalities caused by aging buildings,[34] the environmental costs of deferred maintenance in buildings increase. Hence, many urban properties degrade until land becomes profitable to redevelop entirely.

Opportunity gain (versus opportunity cost) refers to increasing options/opportunities, as well as building social and natural 'capital', to increase resilience, adaptability and choice.

The opportunity cost means foregoing an opportunity to make money by doing nothing or not value adding. The opportunity costs of wasteful design are seldom, if ever, analyzed [Chapter 7]. The aim of ordinary design and engineering is the 'least change' to the status quo that reduces costs or postpones crises through efficiency [Figure 9.9]. Ordinarily, the 'opportunity gains' from retrofitting the built environment that increase public benefits, future options and adaptability are not really counted. Thus, most industries wait for waste disposal costs, laws or public pressure to increase before investing in environmental systems, even though they start paying back immediately.[35]

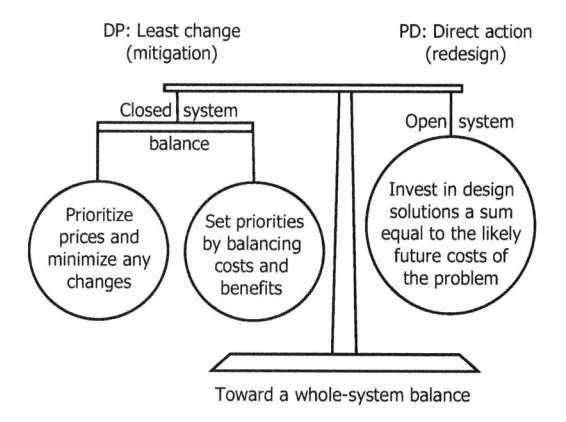

Figure 9.9 Minimizing change versus maximizing gains

9.4 Planning as Governance

Some traditional development control, planning and assessment processes are briefly summarized below, followed by a discussion about ways they can be improved upon.

Having suggested the need to redesign systems of environmental governance on PD principles, the following reviews some planning traditions that license but limit the right to do harm. These are distinguished briefly from potentially more positive counterparts. Traditional planning approaches include: zoning; comprehensive, incremental and policy planning; statutory development consent/control processes; and futures planning (eg. back-casting and scenario planning). This chapter reviews futures planning, and the following chapter reviews development control and community participation processes in the context of PD. The PD community planning process (SMARTmode) was reviewed in Part I because planning analyses must precede site-specific design [Chapters 7–8].

Zoning regulates land use to improve urban efficiency and health but has segregated people by culture and classes and often removed natural amenities.

Zoning has been traced back to early cities where it served to separate royalty and other economic groups, as well as facilitate movement within and between urban areas. From the turn of the twentieth century, zoning was concerned with public health and reducing squalor. However, it did little to reduce the causes of hazards, noise or pollution: it mainly segregated these from housing. Planning initially focused on land use and transportation patterns, and 'gray infrastructure' (e.g. curbs, gutters, bridges, railways, pipes, sewage plants). It generally treated transport, housing, commerce and industry as separate functional components in a larger urban machine.

Zoning became dominated by a mantra – the highest economic use of land – and land use planning evolved largely on economics-based precepts.

Ecological issues were considered relevant in zoning only where nature was a 'threat' due to potential landslides, flooding, storm surges, sinkholes or the like [Figure 9.10]. Nature in cities was sometimes valued for its human benefits, such as recreation, respite or spiritual solace, but not for its three to four billion years of evolution. It was groomed and isolated in parks but generally regarded as an expense:

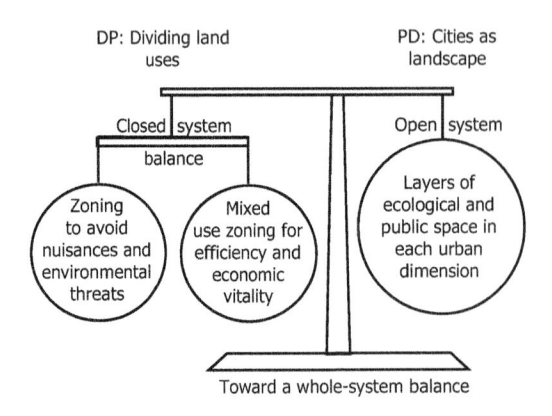

Figure 9.10 Zoning for economic, social and ecological land uses

a maintenance problem or a luxury. PD instead first determines the highest *ecological* use of land, and then seeks appropriate economic uses, and ensures building forms and functions support local/bioregional ecosystems as well as local social needs.

***Comprehensive/master planning** was built upon zoning and assumed that an ideal future form and pattern of urban growth could be determined in advance.*

Post-World War II master/comprehensive planning aimed to create a future stable, sanitary and modern environment. Comprehensive plans resembled zoning maps (colored mosaics), but with overlays. 'Comprehensive' implies a whole-system perspective but, in practice, it meant the enforcement of one particular set of values (a Jetson-like vision) [Figure 9.11]. This technocratic paradigm treated cities as factories, and buildings as 'machines for living'.[36] Permanent plans and structures deny future generations their self-determination regarding (responsible) choices about their own lives. Urban renewal based on comprehensive plans decimated once stable, cohesive low- and middle-income communities.[37] Planning acquired a negative association with slum clearance and top-down control.

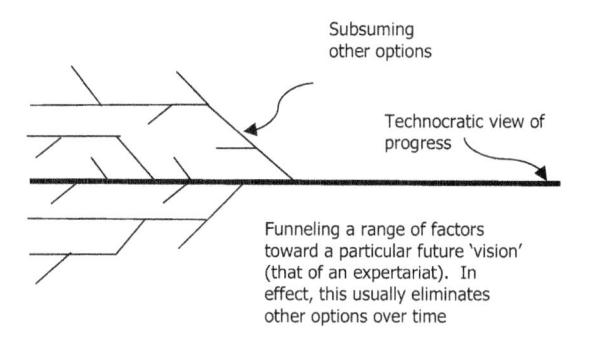

Figure 9.11 Comprehensive/master planning

***Incremental planning** was proposed as an antidote to comprehensive planning and conformed to the realities of planning, but it only mitigates market impacts.*

The 1960s saw the emergence of incremental-adaptive planning theory.[38] To reduce the risks of big planning failures, it advocated small decisions with minor consequences and a continual reassessment of direction.[39] It was also a rationalization for the tendency toward ad hoc, reactive and politicized planning, once described as 'muddling through'.[40] This could be seen as one of the precedents of adaptive management.[41] Incrementalism assumes that short-term plans and policies can be changed when things do not work out. However, in reality, systems inertia works to prevent changes in direction. Planning necessarily involves a strategic mix of comprehensive and incremental actions [Figure 9.12].[42]

220 Decision Making and Assessment

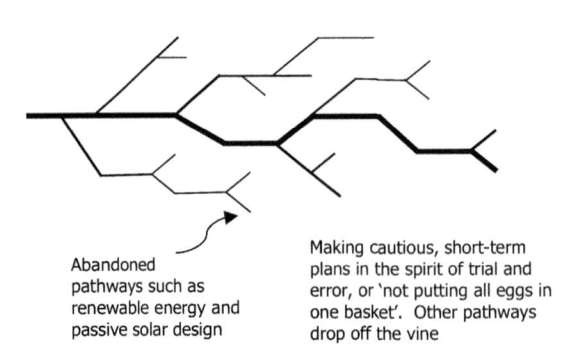

Abandoned pathways such as renewable energy and passive solar design

Making cautious, short-term plans in the spirit of trial and error, or 'not putting all eggs in one basket'. Other pathways drop off the vine

Incremental planning allows for trial and error. However, it does not necessarily lead to sustainability, as 'one cannot cross a great chasm in small steps'. In the urban context, construction is largely irreversible, so changing directions creates waste. Since development decisions are driven by investors, incrementalism is really a market planning model that aspires to mitigate the impacts of business-led activity.

Figure 9.12 Incremental Decision Making

Policy planning*, where aspirational values guide planning decisions, has eclipsed rules-based planning approaches, yet there is little implementation, oversight or evaluation of outcomes.*

A common cliché in the 1980s was: 'planning is politics ... it is all about trade-offs'.[43] This validated negotiation and transactional processes. As discussed in Chapter 4, policy planning sets priorities and their rationales but these are usually platitudinous (e.g. 'accommodate growth with less impact' or 'balance economic and environmental quality').[44] Policies also change in shifting political winds.[45] For example, optimistic policies like 'zero waste by 2000' were later altered when politicians were not likely to meet the targets.[46] Policies are essential but they seldom evaluate or implement new planning strategies and methods that might enable the goals to be realized.

9.5 Sustainable (Futures) Planning

Sustainable planning *appeared in the 1990s to address the shortcomings of comprehensive and incremental planning that had no real effect on sustainability issues.*

Many types of urban planning have been distinguished, but they generally fall under comprehensive approaches that shape the future or processes that manage change through incremental, experimental and adaptive management. Sustainable planning came at a time when regulation was under attack, and when the ability to predict the future was coming to be seen as futile. There was a growing appreciation that planners dealt with – not just systems but – 'complex systems'. Ironically, better forms of prediction were seen as the solution. New predictive methods emerged to negotiate complexity by either choosing the best route or the best destination.

Scenario planning *predicts the consequences of different pathways and their likely outcomes to select the best end state that can 'currently' be envisaged.*

Scenario planning charts the probable outcomes of alternative actions or pathways and compares their likely consequences. In the process, it identifies many kinds of variables that could affect the success of these different directions in order to anticipate constraints and avoid problems (e.g. likely events, changing conditions, institutional barriers, organizational weaknesses). However, selecting the best route tends to predetermine the end state or goal, by eliminating pathways that are not as desirable.[47] That is, scenario planning is about choosing pathways, or deciding futures, not redesigning the context itself or creating diverse pathways that reduce future risks and keep options open [Figure 9.13].

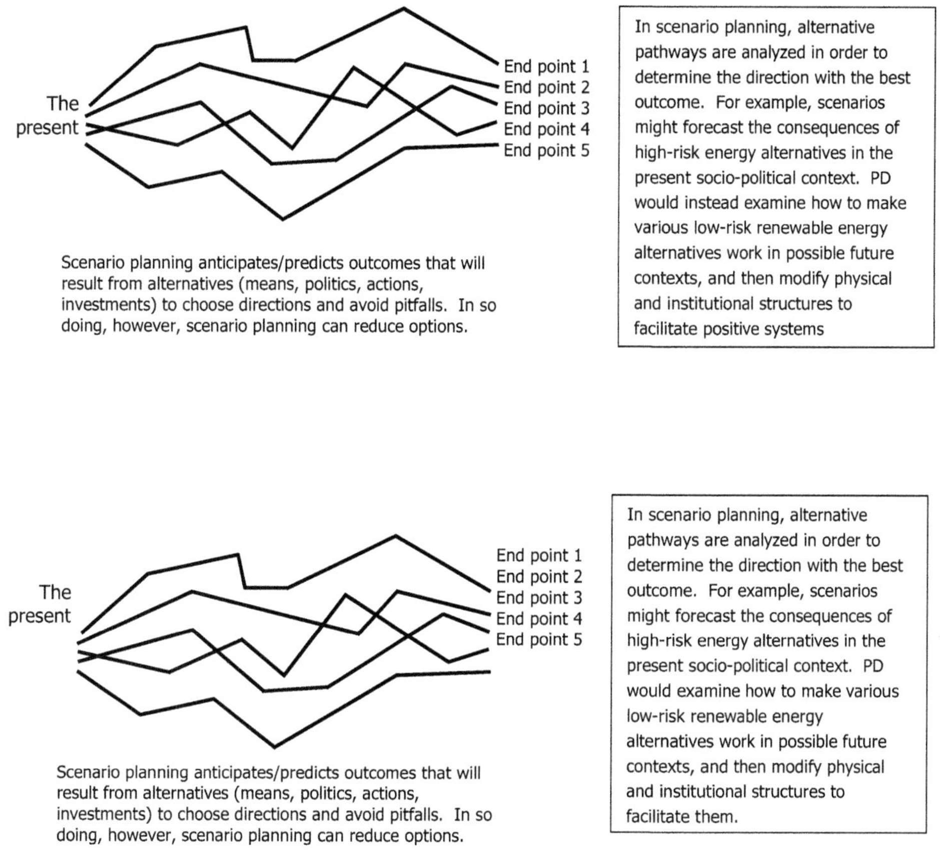

Scenario planning anticipates/predicts outcomes that will result from alternatives (means, politics, actions, investments) to choose directions and avoid pitfalls. In so doing, however, scenario planning can reduce options.

In scenario planning, alternative pathways are analyzed in order to determine the direction with the best outcome. For example, scenarios might forecast the consequences of high-risk energy alternatives in the present socio-political context. PD would instead examine how to make various low-risk renewable energy alternatives work in possible future contexts, and then modify physical and institutional structures to facilitate positive systems

Scenario planning anticipates/predicts outcomes that will result from alternatives (means, politics, actions, investments) to choose directions and avoid pitfalls. In so doing, however, scenario planning can reduce options.

In scenario planning, alternative pathways are analyzed in order to determine the direction with the best outcome. For example, scenarios might forecast the consequences of high-risk energy alternatives in the present socio-political context. PD would examine how to make various low-risk renewable energy alternatives work in possible future contexts, and then modify physical and institutional structures to facilitate them.

Figure 9.13 Scenario Planning (Source: Birkeland 2008)

***Back-casting** is thinking backward from a desired end state to compare ways to get there, then selecting the best strategies, actions and investments.*

Back-casting is almost the reverse of scenario planning. While the latter compares pathways to see where they lead in order to choose the best end state, back-casting chooses a destination and then 'reverse engineers' to find the least risky and costly route. For example, the goal might be a low-carbon future: the best path is then determined by tracing logical steps back. However, selecting the best future that is available or appears attainable at the present time will not diversify opportunities, adaptability or future options. Like scenario planning, back-casting can cut off other potentially more positive futures in the process [Figure 9.14].

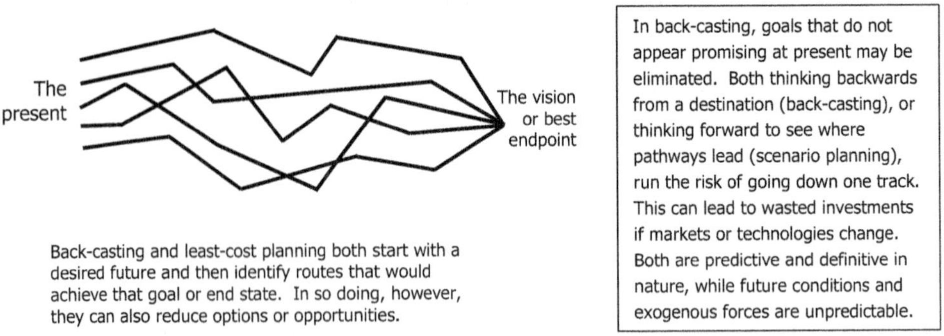

222 Decision Making and Assessment

Back-casting and least-cost planning both start with a desired future and then identify routes that would achieve that goal or end state. In so doing, however, they can also reduce options or opportunities.

> In back-casting, goals that do not appear promising at present may be eliminated. Both thinking backwards from a destination (back-casting), or thinking forward to see where pathways lead (scenario planning), run the risk of going down one track. This can lead to wasted investments if markets or technologies change. Both are predictive and definitive in nature, while future conditions and exogenous forces are unpredictable.

Figure 9.14 Back-casting and least-cost planning (Source: Birkeland 2008)

Scenario and back-casting are crucial tools, but neither are designed to diversify future destinations and/or pathways and both assume optimal conditions are known/knowable.

Exploring directions in order to choose the best destination (scenario planning), or selecting the best destination to find the best route (back-casting), can both miss options that have not been imagined or are not yet conceivable. These methods for making decisions involve processes of elimination and simplification. This is different from creating diverse, new eco-positive environments. This is parallel to 'synaptic pruning' in the growing brain, where unused connections are lost that may later have unexpected survival value. Preconceived pathways or targets cannot expand future sustainable options unless there is a conscious effort to design in redundancy, diversity and/or reversibility.

The above futures planning approaches explore alternatives, but do not build in more life opportunities through a diversity and redundancy of life-support systems.

Current futures planning methods are still basically means of prediction and control. Being methods for making decisions (versus design), they simplify options in order to make choices (versus increasing choices). The selection of initial variables predetermines the outcome. Where construction is not adaptable and space is limited, the ability to adapt cities to new challenges in an increasingly uncertain and complex world is diminished. For example, dense urban areas that are simultaneously too durable and flimsy will be abandoned or bulldozed when needs or conditions change. It will be impractical to modify them due to a lack of retrofit options.

Futures planning and analyses in PD identify public or private investments that expand public options and increase environmental quality, security and life-support systems.

Planning for PD builds on previous planning models but reverses their shared tendency to narrow cultural and biological diversity by, sometimes unwittingly or half-wittingly, eliminating potential pathways, targets or end states. Rather than controlling the future or massaging market forces, PD focuses on maximizing nature, options and opportunities by creating diverse and adaptable physical environments [Figure 9.15]. This means more diversity of form and function in cities to counter the narrowing of meaningful public choices by market forces. To find opportunities for eco-productive urban systems and public benefits, PD analyses identify social/ecological deficits, using the SMT analyses [Chapters 7–8].

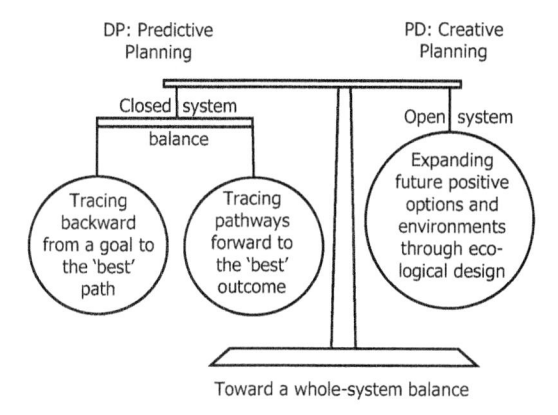

Figure 9.15 Scenario and back-casting versus PD

9.6 Digital Cities

New urban sciences (e.g. informatics) have emerged to apply advances in data-driven research in most conceivable areas of investigation on most urban scales.

Data is being collected and mapped for economic purposes, such as identifying potential economic investments, or facilitating collaborative research between governments, industry and academia; for social advocacy purposes, such as proving toxic industries are located where the urban poor live, or developing platforms that enable citizen participation in planning; for urban management, such as multifunctional sensors that collect most measurable forms of urban phenomena (for anticipating traffic and pollution warnings, or running automatic urban watering systems); for experiential design, such as mapping brain waves to discover how people experience the urban environment. There is, however, remarkably little on urban ecology.

A new smart-city technocracy is headed toward sidelining the advances that have been made in various branches of urban ecology and ecological design.

Digital technologies may change urban planning for the better,[48] if they do not ignore the socio-ecological dimension. This is partly because decisions about what data to collect, how to analyze them and how to present the results can create a self-fulfilling prophecy. Data-driven tools are suited for prediction which, in turn, shapes the future. Current architectural applications of digital technologies are astonishing and tickle the senses with moving lights and impossible building forms. As in planning paradigms that pre-date sustainability, however, these models largely assume that the ecology belongs outside cities, and that cities are largely independent from their bioregions.

9.7 Conclusion

Given uncertainty due to unpredictable socio-political and biophysical forces, cities must be retrofitted to ensure diversity, adaptability and increase the socio-ecological support systems.

Having developed in an industrial era and ethos, planning is gradually morphing with social changes. Over time, planning branched out from zoning (preventing

224 Decision Making and Assessment

nuisances), to comprehensive planning (shaping the future), to incremental planning (minimizing mistakes), to policy planning (steering market forces), to futures planning (navigating a maze). The current stage is future proofing and resilience, a defensive stance which continues to mitigate the adverse impacts of market activity at public expense. Planning that does not embrace big data will be superseded, but digital technology can be redirected toward solving the causes of the sustainability crises, not just creating more sensationalism.

While planning has converged with business management in many respects, business looks for investment opportunities that include means to reduce risks and responsibilities.

Despite an ongoing evolution, the conceptual frameworks of planning still do not differ greatly from business and military planning. Perhaps because of the influence of economic models, and the need to be seen as a science, much of the development of planning theories and methods focused on prediction and strategy. However, this has been defensive: predicting and/or mitigating the impacts/risks of development – not providing for urban social/natural life-support systems. Spatial planning and decision-making systems should propose actions that ensure the preservation and equitable distribution of the means of survival, not just the place of planning in a consumerist system [Figure 9.16].

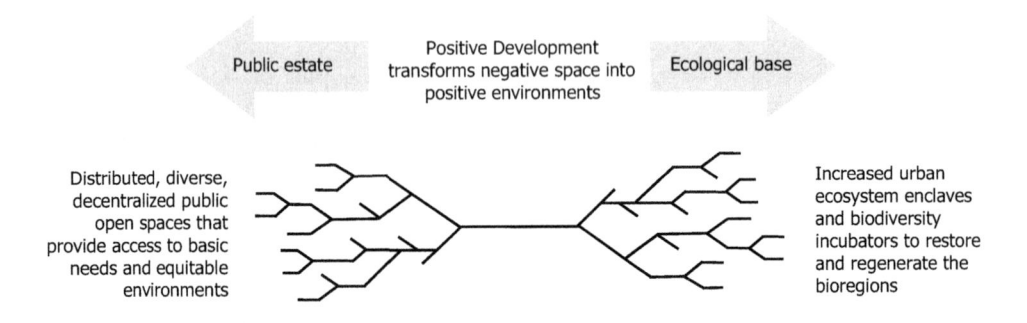

PD Decision tree. Designing wider options for natural security and social choice through a 'rhizomatic approach'. The diagram is intended to indicate how planning in PD reverses both scenario planning and back-casting. Both futures planning concepts are useful if not essential methods but, in application, tend to close off options. They need to be undertaken in ways that avoid 'pruning the synapses' of the decision tree.

Figure 9.16 Planning to diversify environments and options (Source: Birkeland 2008)

This chapter has summarized the PD proposal for constitutional restructuring, which would involve the addition of an ethics-based, decision-making branch for biophysical sustainability issues.

Efforts at positive social change through political, administrative, religious and business strategies cannot keep pace with ecological problems, when compounded by dysfunction and tribalism. Urban design could begin to create biophysical and social sustainability immediately while gradually paying back the investments. Ultimately, however, institutional reform will be necessary, because the decision-making processes of government and professions were developed without any thought of ecological sustainability. The structures and principles underlying governance and management must be reconceived and reconstructed upon ecological foundations. Although constitutional change is unlikely in the current political climate, planning systems can be altered to employ more positive methods.

9.8 Exercises

1. Examine and compare the Equador Constitution,[49] and the French Constitutional Charter for the Environment. Do they meet the PD Test? Examine papers that discuss the Charter and analyze their frame of reference as well.[50]
2. Examine the Earth Charter and consider whether its principles can be achieved in the absence of a change in built-environment design.[51]
3. How can digital technologies and mapping be used by planners to convert cities into sustainable ones, rather than just more resilient ones?
4. How does traditional science, which is often based on prediction, and traditional planning, based on choosing directions for growth, differ from systems redesign based on the PD Test?

Notes

1. The standard advert for the show *Eco-solutions* on CNN in 2018.
2. Birkeland, J. (2002) *Design for Sustainability: A Sourcebook of Integrated Eco-Logical Solutions*, Earthscan, London.
3. Currently in the USA, there is no practical limit on corporate contributions and, in Australia, donations from foreign countries are still allowed.
4. See Keller, G. F. (2009) The Influence of Military Strategies on Business Planning, *International Journal of Business and Management* 3(5), pp. 129–34.
5. The disparities of wealth are growing in many countries and in total. Again, in 2018, three men in the USA had the equivalent wealth of the poorer half the rest of the US population while many can barely survive on the minimum wage.
6. The World Business Council for Sustainable Development (WBCSD) was founded in 1995 by Stephan Schmidheiny. An influential book in this era was Hawken, P. (1993) *The Ecology of Commerce: A Declaration of Sustainability*, HarperCollins, New York.
7. For a discussion on industrial ecology, see Baccini, P., and Brunner, P. H. (1991) *Metabolism of the Anthroposphere*, Springer Verlag, Berlin; Tibbs, H. (2002) Industrial Ecology, in Birkeland, *Design for Sustainability*, pp. 51–3. Few flows analyses consider the built environment. See Boyden, S., Millar, S., Newcombe, K., and O'Neill, B. (1981) *The Ecology of a City and its People: The Case of Hong Kong*, Australian National University Press, Canberra.
8. Girardet, H. (1996) *The Gaia Atlas of Cities: New Directions for Sustainable Urban Living* (2nd ed.), Gaia Books, London. See also Birkeland, J., and Schooneveldt, J. (2003) *Mapping Regional Metabolism: A Decision-Support Tool for Natural Resource Management*, Land and Water Australia, Canberra.
9. See box 49 diagram on supply and demand in Birkeland, J. (2008) *Positive Development: From Vicious Circles to Virtuous Cycles through Built Environment Design*, Earthscan, London.
10. This was brought home when the Trump administration reversed a number of environmental protections and public land reserves.
11. In addition to radioactive waste sites leaking, terrorists can make 'dirty bombs' from the waste.
12. Decision theories and tools tend to assume rational decision makers with perfect information, while some theories suggest decision making is seldom like that. Simon,

H. A. (1957) *Models of Man Social and Rational: Mathematical Essays on Rational Human Behavior in a Social Setting*, J. Wiley & Sons, New York.
13 See Birkeland, J. (2016) Net Positive Biophilic Urbanism, *Smart and Sustainable Built Environments* 5(1), pp. 9–14.
14 While most designers are 'ultimately' funded by corporations, some are doing altruistic work through NGOs like Designers Without Borders, as argued by Stairs, D. (2005) Altruism as Design Methodology, *Design Issues* 21(2), pp. 3–12.
15 Birkeland, J. (2018) Challenging Policy Barriers in Sustainable Development, in Dymitrow, M., and Szymańska, D. (eds) *Bulletin of Geography: Socio-Economic Series* 40, Nicolaus Copernicus University, Toruń, pp. 41–56.
16 Political donations by foreign nationals are not permitted in Australia, but foreign contributions can come in indirectly. www.theguardian.com/australia-news/2017/nov/30/sam-dastyari-told-to-resign-from-senate-positions-after-china-revelation.
17 Elliott, L. (2017) World's Eight Richest Men have the Same Total Wealth as the Poorest Half of the World Population, *Guardian*, Jan. 16. www.theguardian.com/global-development/2017/jan/16/worlds-eight-richest-people-have-same-wealth-as-poorest-50.
18 In the USA, some federal land use and environment agencies effectively combine legislative, executive and judicial functions.
19 Constitutional change is possible, as the need is as great as at the time of the American revolution. Birkeland, J. (1993) *Planning for a Sustainable Society: Institutional Reform and Social Transformation*, Environmental Studies, Department of Geography, University of Tasmania, Hobart.
20 This fourth sphere could be implemented on the agency level if constitutional change is politically implausible at the national level.
21 The social contract theory (from the Enlightenment era) holds that individuals have, in effect, accepted government authority in return for the protection of their rights.
22 Some US government agency charters mention the 'wise use of resources' (meaning sustainable harvesting), which is attributed to Gifford Pinchot, an early advocate of scientific management. The term has been co-opted by a movement in the US that advocates increased use of public lands and reduced environmental regulation.
23 See Turner, S. J., and Marrani, D. (2019) The French Charter of the Environment and Environmental Protection, in *Environmental Rights: The Development of Standards*, Cambridge University Press, Cambridge. See also Bourg, D. (2006) The French Constitutional Charter for the Environment: An Effective Instrument? in Tremmel, J. C. (ed.) *Handbook of Intergenerational Justice*, Edward Elgar Publishing, Cheltenham.
24 E.g. 'standing' in law requires a plaintiff to show they will be directly harmed, which usually means a financial harm. Arguably, all citizens should have standing to protect democracy and sustainability whether it affects their pocketbook or not.
25 Environmental rights are included in more than 90 national constitutions, according to Boyd, D. R. (2013) The Effectiveness of Constitutional Environmental Rights, Yale UNITAR Workshop, Apr. 26–27.
26 Birkeland, *Positive Development*.
27 It is important to reiterate that everyone has some design ability, although it may be repressed by education.
28 E.g. transferable development rights (TDRs) compensate for the lost 'expectation value' of property rights by allowing them to be shifted to another property, as discussed in Chapter 5.
29 As defined in the Rio Declaration on Environment and Development of the United Nations (1992): 'Where there are threats of serious or irreversible damage, lack of full scientific certainty shall not be used as a reason for postponing cost-effective measures to prevent environmental degradation'. See Read, R., and O'Riordan, T. (2017) The Precautionary Principle under Fire, in *Environment: Science and Policy for Sustainable Development*, Taylor & Francis, Philadelphia, PA.
30 Nuclear power is not subject to the precautionary principle, as the genie is out of the bottle.
31 See Birkeland, *Design for Sustainability* p. 210.

32 Ironically, the term 'direct action' was misapplied in Australia by then Prime Minister Tony Abbott to mean that the public should pay; he left out the idea that the public should be reimbursed.
33 Floods and mudslides from deforestation and fires on hills sitting over settlements are predictable but often occur.
34 See Nielsen, S. B., Sarasoja, A.-L., Galamba, K. G. (2016) Sustainability in Facilities Management: An Overview of Current Research, *Facilities* 34(9/10), pp. 535–63.
35 For discussion on insurance, see Greyson, J. (2008) Box 51: Precycling Insurance, in Birkeland, *Positive Development*, p. 339.
36 This was a famous expression by Mies van der Rohe that articulated the view that buildings were machines.
37 Jacobs, J. (1961) *The Death and Life of Great American Cities*, Random House, New York.
38 There are other ways of categorizing types of planning. See e.g. Hudson, B. M., Galloway, T. D., and Kaufman, J. L. (1979) Comparison of Current Planning Theories: Counterparts and Contradictions, *Journal of the American Planning Association* 45(4), pp. 387–98.
39 Davidoff, P. (1965) 'Advocacy and Pluralism in Planning', *American Institute of Planning Journal* 31, pp. 331–8.
40 Lindblom, C. E. (1969) *The Science of Muddling through*, Pengui, Harmondsworth, pp. 41–60.
41 Norton, B. G. (2002) A Pragmatist Epistemology for Adaptive Management, in Keulartz, J., Korthals, M., Schermer, M., and Swierstra, T. (eds) *Pragmatist Ethics for a Technological Culture*, Kluwer, Dordrecht, pp. 171–90. Aldo Leopold is also credited with inspiring adaptive management. Leopold, A. (1949) *A Sand County Almanac*, Ballantine, New York.
42 The distinction between incremental and comprehensive planning is arguably a false dualism, as post-war comprehensive planning was not comprehensive, and incrementalism was arguably a rationale for business-as-usual.
43 For a description of this view, see Broyd, D. (2011) *Where to Planning?* City Futures Research Centre Occasional Paper, UNSW, Sydney. www.be.unsw.edu.au/sites/default/files/upload/wheretoplanning.pdf.
44 In the 1970s, governments seemed to have more power to negotiate design improvements than in many places today.
45 When I was writing what were later called 'sustainability' policies for a planning department, I was told not to imply anyone had to take action, but to simply state 'enhance the good' or 'mitigate the bad'.
46 As was quite literally the case with an ACT greenhouse gas plan.
47 See future planning tools in Birkeland, *Positive Development*, pp. 165–79.
48 Jackson, D. (2018) *Data Cities: How Satellites are Transforming Architecture and Design*, Lund Humphries, London. http://data-cities.net/.
49 www.futurepolicy.org/healthy-ecosystems/ecuador/. Tanasescu, M. (2016) *Environment, Political Representation and the Challenge of Rights: Speaking for Nature*, Springer, Amsterdam.
50 Marrani, D. (2015) Reinforcing Environmental Rights: The French Charter for the Environment, *European Journal of Fundamental Rights* 25, pp. 383–400.
51 http://earthcharter.org/discover/download-the-charter/.

10 Development Control and Assessment

10.1 Review and Preview

Whereas the previous chapter discussed eco-governance and futures/advance planning in general, this focuses more on development control/consent regulations and processes, or statutory planning.

Many planning authorities have subdivided into two main units: futures or advance planning, which deals with where to go, and strategic planning, which deals with how to get there. This chapter centers on statutory planning, or regulation, implementation and enforcement. This includes code compliance, design guidelines, approval processes and quality controls. Regulations set minimum benefits or maximum impacts. They tell developers what they 'should not do' by setting limits on the amount of harm that will be permitted. Design guidelines indicate what developers 'should do' by setting objectives and standards, which can be subjective and open to interpretation and negotiation.

It could be said that there are three approaches to quality control in development approval processes: prescriptive and performance-based controls and community participation.

There are many levers for improving specific development proposals, such as planning and building codes, design review processes, genuine progress indicators, trading schemes, rating tools and so on. In many areas, there has been a progression from more prescriptive regulations toward more flexible performance-based strategies to allow for innovation, modernization and unique conditions. Thus far, however, these processes fail to encourage net-positive design, or address the irreversibility of ecological impacts and the potential reversibility of the urban environment. Community participation, in both adopting planning policies and in consent/control processes (below), is time-honored but often does not significantly alter the outcomes.

Ideally, development approval decisions, like plans, should address the PD Test (again, increase the public estate, ecological base and future options or opportunities).

While eco-governance concerns developing principles and processes for generic planning policies and land use plans, development approvals are site-specific judgments. Development decisions shape future development options in the area and may, in effect, be precedent setting. Politicians have stepped in to approve developments based on ideological orientations or short-term issues like protecting poorly paid jobs, instead of attracting proposals that create more and healthier jobs. The PD Test would force decision makers to consider sustainability issues. Written findings that link decisions to basic sustainability issues (PD Test) would enable meaningful public oversight, discipline decision makers and reduce political interference [Chapters 12–13].

After distinguishing various forms of development controls, guidelines and participatory processes in urban planning, basic quality control mechanisms, particularly assessment tools, are introduced.

RTs have for some decades dominated the scene regarding development assessment and quality control. After summarizing development control methods, some RTs are introduced and their basic advantages and limitations are reviewed. Several authors have stated that RTs are not the answer but, among those, most only mention a couple of shortcomings. Whether pro or con, they seldom examine their effectiveness in relation to sustainability. The question here is whether RTs corrected the shortcomings of existing quality control schemes. Issues arising from this comparison of RTs to assessment tools and in particular, EIAs [Chapters 11–12], provide extensive criteria for PD tools.

10.2 Development Control

10.2.1 Prescriptive and Performance

Prescriptive controls *and consent processes apply generic rules that require minimum standards at the building scale, but these seldom include positive sustainability gains.*

It is necessary to set minimum acceptable health and safety standards. However, building codes and building planning regulations are blunt instruments. Some see these as protecting the public interest, and others see them as government interference in private property rights. Many means to make standardized rules more flexible have been devised to ameliorate any hardships on developers or make compliance easier. These include variances, bonuses, exemptions, transferable development rights, and objection and appeals processes. All have transaction costs, and none guarantee sustainable outcomes. Often these instruments result in conditional approvals that add mitigation measures, but do not design in public benefits.

Prescriptive regulations rely on numerical rules whereas ethics-based questions can challenge design teams to meet PD standards and thus engage with sustainability issues.

Built environments are often described by how they pay homage to certain values. For example: a building with a Braille pattern around the upper facade 'showed respect for the blind' who could not see or touch it; a park segregated trees by species into square blocks was demonstrating 'stewardship of nature'; and buildings have celebrated nature by mimicking naturalistic forms in building environments devoid of living things or composed of mined substances and relicts of dead forests. To answer questions about ethical and biophysical outcomes, designers and approval authorities would have to engage with the meaning of sustainability beyond clichés.

230 Decision Making and Assessment

Regardless of whether codes or guidelines are involved, where a controversial proposal divides the community and/or experts, citizen juries should make the determination.

Variances can be granted or denied where prescriptive codes, rules or score sheets cause unproductive hardships. In each case, administrators should publish reasoned findings concerning major project approvals to ensure quality control in decision making as well as in project design. Although this often occurs, the criteria usually balance the relative rights of neighbors to life quality and of developers to make profits [Figure 10.1]. Sustainability principles, let alone the PD Test, are very seldom involved. Nonetheless, written decisions should not be treated as precedents, because all environmental situations can be unique, and urban environments should be evolving to higher sustainability standards.

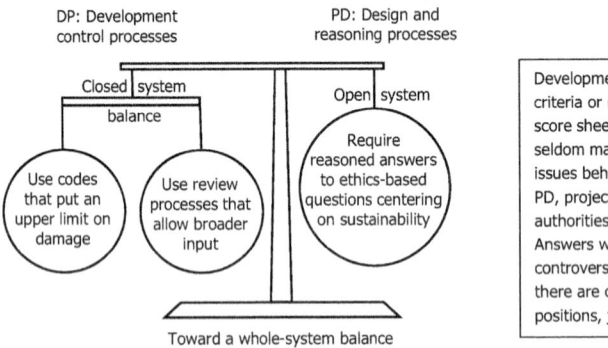

Figure 10.1 Development control versus judicious consent processes

Performance-based standards increase flexibility in meeting regulations, but they have often led to 'flexible' criteria and point-scoring mechanisms instead of encouraging adaptable design.

Performance-based rules were meant to alleviate the problems of inflexible building codes and overly elastic planning policies and design guidelines. Today, various forms of score sheets are often used which require a minimum number of optional green design/planning points for a certain score.[1] These make rules more adaptable to developer needs but have not, thus far, led to the design of buildings that are adaptable to future owners, technological change or sustainability imperatives such as climate change and biodiversity losses. In PD, performance-based rules would encourage development to support public values and amenities or design in adaptability to changing contexts.

Although performance-based rules can be met in creative ways, the outcome will not be sustainable if flexibility allows for a lower sustainability standard.

Chapter 9 suggested that flexible planning is good but thus far has not led to adaptable built environments. Flexible planning may encourage better development, but it has usually allowed irreversible development [Figure 10.2]. Buildings themselves must be adaptable. Proponents of major developments must demonstrate energy and resource conservation, but they are seldom asked to show how the design can be modified in case of rapid changes in sea level rise or global warming, or what the contingency plans for emergency evacuation from the area are (e.g. flood, fire, terrorist threat, earthquake). If such sustainability strategies were in writing, ideas would disseminate faster.[2]

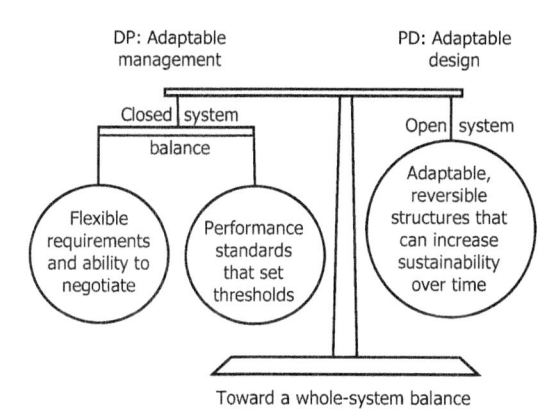

Figure 10.2 From performance thresholds to adaptable design

10.2.2 Development Design Guidelines

Design policies/guidelines attempt to encourage innovation and flexibility by avoiding restrictive rules, but often rely on broad volitional statements and/or discretionary review panels.

Design guidelines provide a checklist of considerations that remind design teams of basic design principles. They can be used in negotiations to suggest ways for developers to increase public benefits in developments, but they are not easily enforced unless they are adopted legislatively. Like policy plans [Chapter 9] and incentive schemes (as presently conceived and structured), they seldom address the basic physical preconditions for intra/inter-generational equity or socio-economic opportunity. The criteria usually aim for 'less bad' design and do not require multifunctional design, or even adaptability so that they can be upgraded in the future to a net-positive sustainability standard.

Design guidelines recognize that good urban/building design depends on site-specific conditions and relationships, but these are more difficult to administer than numerical rules.

Since each site has myriad contextual challenges and each project has diverse functional parameters, overly standardized rules can limit good design. Hence, development control has tended to shift from allowing anything that does not violate codes to generic urban design guidelines that state general virtues. RTs, in a sense, combine both. They apply numbers to green design principles and are quite prescriptive and detailed. Many buildings that score well on RTs are sterile and metallic as if designed

232 *Decision Making and Assessment*

by computers. Several other kinds of development assessment tools are therefore compared to RTs (below), after a discussion on participation in design.

10.3 Community Participation

Participation in advance planning: Community participation in futures planning issues has generally been limited to workshopping vision statements within given parameters, and seldom changes actual future directions.

Public hearings were sometimes seen as a right to object, but not necessarily a right to be heard. Participation in planning is often distinguished from top-down consultation. It is intended to raise awareness, immerse people in problem-solving or unite the community around shared community goals. However, it can be carried out in perfunctory ways. Whether organized by government planners or developers, participation processes are often (unconsciously) structured to lead to preconceived outcomes, shape preferences, endorse plans or simply assuage community concerns.[3] In any case, the outcomes are often descriptive wish-lists that do not resolve difficult issues or conflicting policies.

Participation in planning is an essential process, but should create opportunities to question the planning processes themselves and what is considered 'best practice'.

Participation will usually raise awareness of the community's stake in spatial planning and is therefore inherently worthwhile. Too often, however, contributions gleaned from local workshops, charrettes, surveys or town hall meetings do not actually materialize in urban plans. Moreover, participation in vision statements often occurs after the 'gray infrastructure' is decided, which predetermines future growth.[4] Those orchestrating participatory processes can have political and professional agendas. They often do not believe they can learn from the community. If involvement does not lead to changed perspectives (mutual learning) on the part of both authorities and participants, a rethink is probably called for [Figure 10.3].[5]

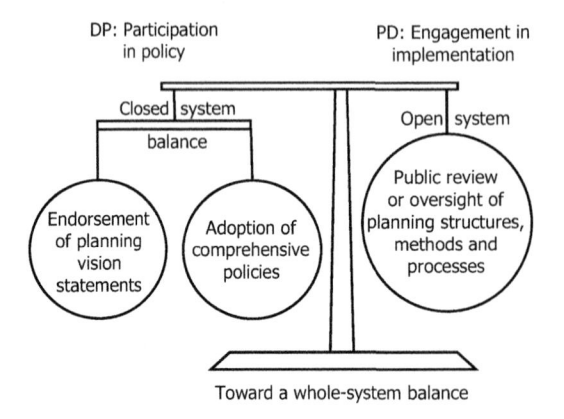

Figure 10.3 Participation in advance/future planning

Participation in development control: Community participation in development consent/control processes has a long history, but many have suggested that participatory programs lack any real depth of engagement.

Community participation in planning and development approvals has been around for many decades.[6] Traditionally, it involved objecting to major project approvals, often in a post-design hearing process. However, advocacy planning, emerging from the 1960s poverty programs in the USA, saw planners and architects engaging with low-income communities, often, in effect, to fight city hall.[7] This sometimes resulted in 'counterplans' to stop urban renewal projects that were then seen as causing community disruption and dislocation. In parallel, the Sydney 'green bans' in the 1970s opposed the destruction of historic areas which, somewhat ironically, were subsequently 'gentrified' due to their heritage value.

Participation in major project approval processes have not altered the tendency of urban development toward segregation of people by class, race and wealth.

Participation in approval/consent processes are a check on development that meets codes but nonetheless threatens neighborhood life quality and sense of place. It does not tend to reduce the social disparities and ecological degradation that contributes to and results from social divisions. If planning can only mitigate the impacts of a global economic machine that transfers resources from poor to rich and from public to private control, participation cannot achieve sustainability either. Hence, regardless of whether commercial decisions are made with popular consent or by an expertariat, only decisions informed by ethical and ecological principles (above) can reverse these trends.

Participation in PD: In the PD planning process, participants first agree to basic ethical principles (to avoid reinventing wheels) and then apply them to planning/design issues.

There are PD tools for community planning, design review and project assessment. As explained earlier, the SMARTmode community planning process is intended for guiding plans or developing criteria for major projects [Chapter 7]. It aims to bring government planners, experts and community groups together to critically re-examine principles underlying sustainable planning and design. It begins by developing or agreeing to a constitution of ethical/ecological principles to ensure substantive and procedural due process.[8] It takes a critical and conscious approach to developing/selecting analyses and methods. When there are disputes regarding major plans or projects, these principles guide the deliberations of juries.

Digital platforms could broaden input/engagement, but need to be more transparent and avoid the way that electronic feedback and survey mechanisms predefine feedback.

In design, face-to-face engagement is important, even amongst people who know each other. Although many people are now more transdisciplinary, design skills and ecological knowledge are limited, and values and perspectives differ. Therefore, collaboration is necessary when making decisions about the shared built environment [Figure 10.4]. Participation in design will inevitably be augmented with digital tools in various ways to increase information, input and interaction among participants. However, all forms of communication are subject to manipulation, especially social media platforms. In addition, digital tools involve binary mechanisms, so their programmers eliminate many basic choices. Therefore, digital tools need to be scrutinized.

234 *Decision Making and Assessment*

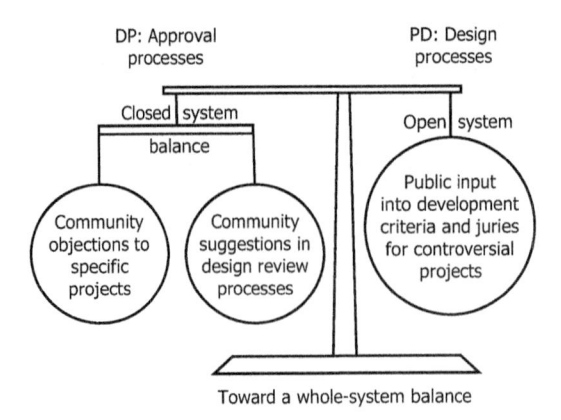

Figure 10.4 Participation in development control (consent processes)

10.4 Introduction to Green Building Rating/Marketing Tools (RTs)

Since RTs have become the dominant means of quality control, it is necessary to dissect RTs in detail to set criteria for improvements.

Industry-led green building councils (GBCs) and their voluntary certification schemes (RTs) began to appear in the 1990s when the concern was primarily energy efficiency. The UK BREEAM tool (1990) was reputedly the first green building RT,[9] but GBCs soon emerged in other countries and promulgated their own tools. RTs served an important educational function, as most developers did not see the relevance of sustainability, let alone eco-efficiency,[10] to building design. Few developers even appreciated that sustainable design criteria would benefit them financially.[11] The uptake of RTs has been impressive,[12] but their effectiveness in achieving a sustainable environment must be questioned.

RTs are means of scoring, acknowledging and certifying good environmental performance by green buildings and the companies, designers and clients who build/operate them.

RTs establish what is considered good practice regarding different building features, such as energy, water and construction waste. They list measurable aspects of buildings and award points for avoiding harmful features (e.g. volatile organic compounds, radon), or adding green features such as daylighting, indoor plants, insulation and certified timber. These features may reduce the amount of materials, energy and water, increase worker productivity or add environmental amenity such as indoor air quality (compared to ordinary buildings). These standards are often set with the advice/consent of advisory groups drawn from industry to ensure that targets are feasible, affordable and broadly acceptable.

RTs use point systems to facilitate comparisons between products and buildings and enable developers/designers to avoid undertaking complex environmental impact or lifecycle assessments.

Points are given for designs that exceed specific threshold levels of performance, and more points are given for attaining higher levels. The sum of the points determines the number of 'stars', or other symbols (e.g. Pearls) that the building earns. Having a standard framework for comparing buildings allows for both competition (sticks) and a marketing advantage (carrots). Most building designers/developers would naturally aspire to outscore other projects. Since the points are relative to standard practice, they are positive. If the points were relative to sustainability, the points gained might be negative, but they would still show which buildings outperform others.

The eagerness for industry self-regulation was partly in response to increasing layers of government-led development quality control and design assessment processes (green tape).

There was a boutique green building movement before the 1990s, but green students would graduate into firms that were oblivious to sustainability. Designers would encounter skepticism from clients, and green clients would be dispirited by mainstream designers, who thought sustainability meant solar cells and were too expensive. However, development consent/control processes were beginning to address sustainability or at least energy efficiency. It became clear that sustainability regulations would eventually impinge upon the development industry. Self-regulation seemed a better alternative.[13] Although RTs curtailed the application of impact assessment to buildings, they offered an opportunity to foster sustainable design awareness and skills.

As the dominant means of promoting sustainable building design today, RTs should not impose standardized templates which work to impede sustainable design solutions.

Today, RTs virtually define green buildings. Being voluntary, GBCs need to attract clients by setting the bar low.[14] Gradually, RTs have been upgrading, by raising efficiency standards (cost savings) and increasing the number of stars that are obtainable.[15] While essential, however, efficient buildings are insufficient to save the planet. RTs share many characteristics with planning/building codes. Codes only set minimum health/safety standards and have been slow to adopt sustainable design principles.[16] Nevertheless, codes apply to all – not just high-end – buildings. If RTs are a sustainability solution, they should be adopted as codes and apply to all buildings.

Because it is assumed that RTs are the least bad option, RTs are rarely questioned regarding their effectiveness in achieving sustainable urban environments.

RTs have been critiqued by some for their transaction costs and fees, although they usually pay for themselves. Others have critiqued RTs on grounds of substance. For example, some complain that they address efficiency, but not socio-ecological sustainability, and others complain that they only concern environmental impacts and not economic performance. RTs have also been critiqued on technical grounds. Some researchers have argued that RT scores often differ greatly from actual energy performance of buildings (below). Therefore, some pros and cons of RTs are listed. Then they are compared to traditional development controls to see whether RTs brought tangible improvements.

10.4.1 Benefits of RTs

RTs vary in the following respects, but generalizations can nonetheless be made as they have many basic conceptual and procedural things in common.

There are a wide range of RTs that focus on different types or scales of development, but most share the basic approach of dividing conventional developments into components that are easily measured or impacts that are easily reduced.

Measurement is important, as long as the things measured improve the sustainability of the environment, the welfare of the wider community and the life quality of building users – relative to other processes. First, some distinctions among RTs should be noted:

- RTs are generally voluntary although many require certain mandatory levels of performance to qualify for any level of certification.[17] Most are operated by private companies, but some councils have adopted RTs as a mandatory layer of quality control, beyond minimal code requirements.
- RTs usually apply to different building types functions or scales, such as office buildings, homes, commercial or infrastructure projects, or whole neighborhoods. Different tools are necessary for each type because the performance standards are based on typical buildings of the same kind.
- RTs sometimes apply to particular stages of a building lifecycle, such as retrofitting, demolition, design, construction and operation. They seldom require reasons for demolishing existing buildings in order to construct new ones, instead of retrofitting. This is considered a separate economic matter.
- RTs often involve third-party assessors, although they could be used by practitioners to guide self-assessment. Since most tools are complex and prescriptive, a large project will generally hire a qualified assessor whose primary function is to do all the paperwork.[18]
- RTs may concern a building's projected performance or its post-construction performance. Some ratings for energy performance have sometimes differed from the results of lifecycle assessments and/or the building's actual performance. However, linking predictions to on-ground results may not help change past practices.[19]

Despite their large number, diversity and range, published comparisons of RTs indicate more similarities than differences, and emphasize the benefits to development stakeholders.

There are common patterns among most RTs. Many comparisons have been conducted which make generalizations about them, and there are few significant exceptions.[20] Before comparing RTs to other development control mechanisms and to EIAs in particular, some positive attributes of RTs are listed below to ensure they are retained. A summary of problems with RTs is then provided [Chapters 11–12]. These form criteria for the PD design review process (eDR) [Chapters 13–14] and the PD design tool (STARfish) [Chapters 15–16]. First, favorable characteristics of RTs, noted by various tool developers, academics and professionals, are reviewed.

- They provide a single overall score against which to compare similar buildings, which gives a basis for rewarding good building performance and construction management.[21]
- They often draw on both expert and developer input and builder experiences in the process of developing criteria and indicators, using extensive stakeholder processes.[22]
- They benefit the public by reducing energy and pollution relative to what otherwise would have occurred, which slows the rate of growing ecological destruction.
- They help to convince developers and contractors that sustainable building practices can generate more profits, while reducing negative impacts: 'do well by doing good'.[23]

Development Control and Assessment 237

- They increase the commercial demand for 'green buildings' by raising the expectations of businesses and their clients and thus building quality standards over time.[24]
- They inculcate a whole-building and lifecycle perspective among design teams, and building professionals/academics generally,[25] to which social and ecological sustainability issues could be added.
- They communicate complex information about system-wide impacts in simple but comprehensive ways,[26] and allow different stakeholders to use them for any number of purposes.
- They provide for comparative case studies, since different buildings use similar criteria and exemplars, which could support continuous learning and ongoing improvements over time.
- They encourage owners, tenants and designers to seek a competitive advantage through sustainability branding, free advertising and improved public relations which rewards high achievers.
- They provide a means of raising goals, standards and de facto guidelines among members of the building industry that are not committed to sustainability.

Being widely used, RTs have clearly demonstrated that reductions in environmental impacts, compared to typical buildings, generally correspond with financial benefits to owners/developers.

A rapidly growing percentage of new buildings use RTs.[27] According to the World GBC global network, of which many GBCs are members, 1.04 billion square meters of green building space, 'an area 10 times the size of Paris', had been certified globally.[28] This gives the impression that GBCs have greened the equivalent land area of ten large cities. Similarly, Green Star (Australia) announcing its 2,000th building certification in 2018, stated that its certified buildings:

- Produce 62% fewer greenhouse gas emissions than average Australian buildings
- Use 66% less electricity than average Australian buildings
- Use 51% less potable water than average buildings, and
- Reduce waste: 'as built' projects (certified after construction) recycled 96% of their construction and demolition waste. However, the more waste, the higher the recycling rate.

Such statistics could explain why so many have concluded that RTs have solved the problem of building impacts, although the cumulative impacts of buildings keep increasing.[29]

10.5 Overview of Issues and Omissions in RTs

Using voluntary schemes to make buildings more sustainable, while impacts from certified and uncertified buildings continue to mount, may delay necessary regulatory reforms.

New buildings certified since 2003 under the Australian Green Star rating system 'saved' 3.8 billion kilograms of carbon or '840 million kilograms of carbon cut from our atmosphere each year', 'the equivalent of 261,000 cars from our roads or the equivalent of 46,700 households' emissions'.[30] Such impressive accomplishments suggest that the GBCs should be in a position to encourage governments to raise the minimum standards of building codes, since most buildings are not affected by RT schemes. Nonetheless, emissions from cars and homes are still increasing, and green buildings continue to increase total energy consumption, water depletion and carbon emissions.

Even the more progressive RTs only envisage positive contributions as defined by project boundaries, which does not necessarily translate into positive whole-system gains.

The current premier rating tool, the Living Building Challenge (LBC), sets broad sustainability criteria and requires certain criteria to be met or there is simply no certification. This relies on the influence of exemplars, a trickle-down approach. Although using the term 'net-positive',[31] the criteria for net-positive water, waste and energy are defined by project boundaries and/or the additional impacts caused by the given development. Nonetheless, it requires the project's embodied energy to be notionally offset and prohibits many harmful materials/chemicals entirely. In other words, the LBC standard is zero 'additional' impact – not quite the same as an eco-positive ecological footprint.

The de facto delegation of responsibility for sustainable buildings from governments to private-sector organizations leaves a significant gap: the majority of buildings.

There is a danger of governments abdicating responsibility for sustainable buildings to private GBCs, whose clients are consultants and developers, not the general public.[32] Being private-sector organizations, they do not censure poor performers who do not bother to seek certification. Inexplicably, several RTs give credits for complying with existing (minimal) laws or set criteria already required by planning or building codes.[33] While perhaps no more protectionist than other professional bodies or lobby groups,[34] they nonetheless set the balance between business interests and sustainability goals. That is, they broker the rate of change and ensure developers do not feel beleaguered.

The value of design/assessment tools depends on whole-system outcomes, including their effect on the capacity of future generations to meet changing environmental conditions.

The voluntary and 'name and fame' strategy of RTs stimulate competition. By focusing on rewards, marketing and recognition, GBCs have been successful in making green/sustainable design almost fashionable among leading developers and design firms (but not yet among average builders). RTs have also created many employment/career opportunities in sustainable development as assessors.[35] Websites with case studies by GBCs display success stories, and subscriptions increase annually.[36] Nevertheless, the built environment is the largest consumer of natural resources and energy (excluding the military).[37] By ignoring ordinary buildings (and not mentioning the net impacts of certified buildings) capacity for real change is diminished.

Being reductionist, RTs arguably divert the attention of building academics and theorists away from larger sustainability problems that are caused/perpetuated by built environments.

Since the existence of RT companies gives many the impression that sustainable building is well in hand, governments and citizens can be distracted from attending to the material flows, pollution and biodiversity losses that even certified buildings are causing. RTs periodically add more comprehensive design principles when the building industry and advisory groups feel ready to raise standards. However, these do not address the more fundamental sustainability issues such as intra/inter-generational equity. RTs may award points for things that reduce waste, energy and water, increase worker productivity/morale or lower health costs, but these usually include reductions in the life-support system.

Despite gradual progress in community participation, the right to damage one's own property still trumps the right of communities to a healthy environment.

The pervasive impacts of development have become better understood. However, development control/consent systems, in most democracies at least, share the basic position that development is a right, subject only to explicit and narrow legal constraints. In line with this, few RTs create opportunities for community participation.[38] If basic code provisions are met, and a project receives a high rating on an RT, community objectors still have the burden of proving that the development will harm their rights/interests. RTs could broaden the range of remedies for malfeasance. For example, a portion of certification fees could be earmarked for a performance bond.

Training programs provided by GBCs are largely about operating particular RTs, and many assessors often lack adequate qualifications in 'sustainable' architecture and planning.

Training programs for prospective tool operators do not really educate design practitioners about deeper sustainability issues or recent advances in sustainable design. For example, one GBC course includes only a couple of hours on sustainable design.[39] This contributes to the undervaluing of design and equates sustainable design with improvements upon ordinary buildings.[40] Some RT provisions promote public education and green consumerism, by rewarding buildings for being displayed as exemplars of green design. As discussed in Chapter 9, however, relying on educating consumers to change purchasing patterns, rather than increasing the knowledge of designers and assessors, shifts responsibility away from GBCs.

Although leading to greater efficiencies, RTs do not deal with the long-term effects of certified buildings on the ecological base and public estate.

RTs are widely assumed to be concerned with the natural as well as human environment that results from new development. However, upon closer inspection, most put economic and social criteria in environmental categories, which implies they contribute ecological gains. For example, green walls contribute to the health of building occupants and are good for the bottom line of the building owners or businesses in the building. However, few green walls create appropriate ecosystems or habitats anywhere sufficient to offset the building's construction impacts. Further, few green buildings increase the public domain or improve the social conditions of the wider community.

By emphasizing numerical criteria, RTs reinforce cost-benefit thinking (choosing the best available plans and products) instead of encouraging a whole-system approach to design.

RTs generally define 'less bad' as 'more good'. RTs count reductions in negative impacts relative to unsustainable buildings as positive, even though they usually do net harm. Merely sending building-generated energy or treated rainwater to other property, or sending no construction waste to landfill, is an improvement. However, it does not pay back the ecological impacts, let alone contribute to net ecological sustainability. Moreover, RTs exclude many negative impacts as well as potentially positive ones, such as those suggested by SMT analyses [Chapters 7–8]. This raises the next question: to what extent did RTs improve upon other forms of assessment?

10.6 Comparison of RTs to Other Quality Controls

The costs/benefits of RTs should be considered relative to other quality control mechanisms or the costs of delay versus direct investment in change.

Most development assessment processes are widely considered to be expensive and bureaucratic, with burdensome transaction costs. The primary concern should not be cost, but cost-effectiveness in achieving sustainability. However, investing effort in making tools less burdensome for users may be pointless if they miss the mark on procedural or conceptual levels. If RTs do not improve upon other tools in addressing basic sustainability issues such as ecology and intra/inter-generational equity, further refinement could waste time and money and have huge opportunity costs. Thus, a comparison of RTs and other tools is necessary for developing criteria for alternative formal/informal approaches.

Building codes *were prescriptive and tended to favor established products/businesses, but have gradually been modified to allow for flexibility in meeting numerical rules.*

Codes largely ignore sustainability issues beyond health, safety and amenity. They set minimum requirements and seldom encourage much flexibility in solving problems in innovative ways. Codes were accused of creating monopolies for manufacturers of traditional products or materials, and their executives sometimes served on code development advisory boards/panels. Since codes favored existing technologies, they were also accused of stifling creativity. From the 1960s, however, codes have become increasingly performance based, meaning that numerical standards can be met in any way a design team chooses.[41] RTs should have addressed the shortcomings of codes, as they were bemoaned long before RTs appeared.

RTs, as voluntary codes, added efficiency to safety and health concerns, but are only recently adding the social and ecological dimensions of sustainability.

Like most codes, RTs set minimum performance thresholds. They also usually do not allow extra points once projects meet certain levels of performance, so thresholds become a de facto maximum. The expected performance is based on best practice or best available technology for buildings with similar functions (offices, homes, apartments, retail, etc.).[42] In order to meet either code or green building certification provisions, it is easier to begin with a building design that conforms to basic conventions and then look for ways to reduce their impacts. Thus, RTs sustain the industrial model of construction but add another layer of activity.

Zoning *segregated land uses for purposes of nuisance avoidance and transport efficiency, but separated people from nature while doing little to support nature.*

Zoning was used for centuries to promote social order and mitigate health problems and nuisances caused by the proximity of domestic areas to industries, factories, brothels, tip sites, etc.[43] Zoning also protected development from the forces of nature – flooding, landslides and other hazards. Apart from reserving public land for parks, recreation and amenities, however, it removed nature from cities. Streams were piped, shorelines were filled in, hills were levelled and parks were fenced off. Once the importance of vegetation to human health was appreciated, there was little public space left for anything other than installing a few street trees.

RTs now encourage using landscaping and/or plants in buildings for human benefit (oxygen, environmental amenity and health, etc.) but not for ecological sustainability.

While zoning aims at land use rationality at the city scale, RTs focus on resource and energy efficiency and environmental amenity at the building scale or within property lines. RTs were slow to encourage design that functionally integrated plants in/around buildings – even after the positive relationship of building-integrated greenery to occupant health was accepted.[44] Many RTs still treat building elements as separate, though nested, systems where decorative plants are one building element: 'add-ons' that provide biophilic benefits for humans.[45] While neighborhood-scale certification schemes may encourage landscaping and some even encourage habitat restoration,[46] they do not include design *for* nature.[47]

Environmental regulations *have encouraged the use of best available technologies, but seldom call for replacing energy-efficient technologies with passive solar and natural systems.*

From the 1970s, environmental regulations that prescribed the 'best available technology' pollution controls were advocated.[48] This was an improvement over mandating more specific technologies that might soon become outdated. However, the technologies back then were mostly 'end-of-pipe' scrubbers and filters (mitigation) or 'cleaner production' (efficiency). In the built environment context, the most efficient technology can mean more efficient fossil-fuel-based heating, cooling and ventilating equipment added onto the traditional building. This can bypass architectural strategies that could avoid fossil-fuel-based systems altogether [Chapters 5–6]. 'Alternative' passive solar design was generally left to owner-builders, most of whom had no formal training in design/architecture.

RTs, while potentially more educational, use rules and measurements derived from traditional building and construction norms, which reinforce conventional design and construction methods.

RTs were meant to deter government interventions into the building sector. However, RTs changed the regulators, not the regulations. While voluntary, they tend to be prescriptive, expensive and end-of-pipe. Even though typical buildings are clearly unsustainable,[49] RT development often begins with extensive measurements of existing buildings to compare the characteristics of existing materials/equipment against various criteria and indicators.[50] In response to criticism, some RTs began to give points for innovation. Often, however, this was without regard to the sustainability value of the innovation.[51] Once the small number of maximum points for innovation are achieved, there is no incentive for research.[52]

Design review *processes aim to improve the design quality of urban development proposals, and allow for flexible solutions through staff-developer collaboration or negotiation.*

Many municipalities have design review processes, conducted informally by staff or formally by design review boards.[53] Developers are usually encouraged to consult planning staff before investing in a particular project or design proposal to ensure there are no surprises. Staff sometimes provide guidelines for sites that are ripe for development, outlining relevant code standards and design guidelines to ensure buildings meet local planning and building design policies.[54] Review boards or staff may suggest design improvements. If an impasse occurs among the parties, a public hearing can usually be requested. (A PD version of design review is provided in Chapters 13–14.)

RTs reflect the latent values, aesthetics and/or cultures of those making the rules, which can conflict with principles of contextual and regional design.

In design review processes, board/panel members with varying expertise sometimes pass judgment on aesthetic and technical matters, which recipients can find too subjective. RTs and design review processes sometimes include aesthetic criteria, such as 'beauty'.[55] All designers theoretically strive for beauty, but opinions by design panels or RT assessors about beauty can be influenced by personal taste. Some municipalities use RTs as design quality controls, since numerical tools are less subject to challenge than design panels. However, RTs seldom show regard for 'regionalism': design principles based on local cultural heritage.[56] These can be defined to provide relatively objective aesthetic criteria.[57]

Environmental reporting *traces the environmental and/or social impacts of decisions or actions made by government agencies or corporations, often throughout their supply chains.*

Many organizations now prepare sustainability reports, covering environment, social, economic and/or management performance. The Global Reporting Initiative (from 1997) provides guidelines for a management-oriented approach to establishing organizational goals, indicators, policies, training programs, monitoring, corrective or preventative actions, and certification. Criteria may include human rights, product responsibility and supply chain performance, or even the impacts businesses have on the communities they operate in, such as health/safety impacts, social displacement, cultural heritage or even slavery and corruption.[58] However, reporting on environmental performance regarding 'inputs (material, energy, water) and outputs (emissions, effluents, waste)' seldom traces project-specific impacts back to the natural environment.[59]

RTs and corporate reporting schemes both encourage continuous improvement, but do not encourage new ventures expressly designed to increase social or ecological sustainability.

Industries that were subject to public suspicion and widespread criticism, such as tobacco and chemical companies, were among the first to produce reports. Corporate reports mainly document and reduce impacts that are already being created. RTs seldom require tangible efforts to improve construction supply chains, other than indirectly by favoring more sustainable procurement processes.[60] To increase sustainability, processes are needed that incentivize businesses, government agencies or private-public-community partnerships to create new projects/businesses that address priority socio-ecological deficits. Government agencies could facilitate this by mapping resource and environmental flows to set priorities for initiatives that can increase sustainability while creating employment.

Genuine progress indicators (GPI), from the 1990s, were intended to correct problems of GDP, which have virtually ignored or worked against sustainability issues.

GDP measures economic transactions as indicators of progress. It ignores negative impacts, since more economic growth was assumed to always be better than less growth. Many people, including Robert F. Kennedy (1968), outlined the anomalies caused by treating GDP as synonymous with wellbeing.[61] For example, oil spills increase GDP because medical and environmental clean-up costs generate more economic activity.[62] Also, so-called 'woman's work' (nursing, housekeeping, child-raising) counts for nothing when performed in the home.[63] Therefore, environmental economists developed GPI to better reflect overall societal wellbeing. Some international NGOs and governments have developed their own indicator sets to assess social/environmental progress.[64]

RTs did not draw upon GPI indicators, although they were available, despite the shared economic orientation among GBCs and their development industry clients.

GPI were intended to broaden the narrow economistic worldview expressed by GDP. GPI went beyond financial transactions to include a range of social and environmental sustainability factors that had been omitted in GDP.[65] Despite the crucial role of buildings in the economy, however, most GPI ignore built-environment issues and many ecological ones, as does economics in general. Further, GPI are generally expressed as the costs of environmental impacts or savings from reducing them, which sideline the potential benefits possible by design. Nevertheless, although indicators primarily chart large-scale trends, GPI provide measurable social criteria which could be used in RTs.

Trading/offsetting schemes assist in improving development outcomes 'efficiently' by allowing developers to reduce negative impacts wherever it is least expensive to do so.

Market-based emission trading schemes are considered more efficient and flexible than regulations. Trading schemes were discussed in Chapter 6. They allow adopters of pollution controls to sell their unused pollution/emission 'rights', so polluters can continue their emissions if they buy the emission rights. They were used in the US Clean Air Act (1977) and an Acid Rain Program (implemented in 1995). In the built environment, 'transferable development rights' (from 1916) are sometimes used to compensate for new planning regulations that restrict property rights.[66] The equivalent of the lost development right (e.g. allowable floor area) can be transferred to another site.

RTs, by using total scores, allow flexibility in meeting criteria but do not encourage trading/exchange among different projects to reduce overall regional impacts.

Single scores mean that difficult standards can be avoided by scoring enough points in 'easy' categories.[67] Token actions (e.g. adding bike racks and showers) can numerically offset more significant impacts, such as energy/water performance. Traditionally, trade-offs are positive impacts that only partially offset major negative ones. Likewise, RTs do not expect total reductions. One RT requires land to be reserved to (partially) offset greenfield development, but this does not guarantee a net reduction in total impacts. There should be insurance that 'extra' development is not allowed in exchange for land preservation/regeneration elsewhere by considering the combined impacts of both developments.

Lifecycle analysis (LCA) assesses product impacts from cradle to grave, but 'normalizes' and 'unitizes' impacts, and generally treats nature as a raw material.

Lifecycle analyses (LCA) trace the materials that go into a building product throughout the supply chain, and add up the impacts using normalization and unitization techniques. 'Normalization' means different impact factors are converted into the same units, such as energy or carbon equivalents. This allows single scores for purposes of comparing built or proposed projects on the same scale. 'Unitization' means that ecosystems and biodiversity are converted (for practical purposes) into sets of resources, as if they were inert materials.[68] This has tended to legitimize trade-offs between the life-support system (e.g. species extinctions), and incommensurate, short-term considerations such as profit.

RTs sometimes encourage the use of building information modeling tools (BIM) which can link LCA data on quantities/impacts of products to digital drawings.

BIM tools enable complex information on materials to be integrated with digital drawings. This gives designers feedback on the lifecycle impacts of building components before they commit to final designs. BIM tools can help decide which products, materials and building shapes to use, such as which roof shape harvests the most sun and/or water.[69] Despite their potential, BIM tools are based on conventional buildings and were not designed by people with adequate training in sustainability. (Thus, students assigned to assess their preliminary building designs with BIM tools had to change their designs to conventional buildings before they could use the tools.)

Ecosystem services assessments, if applied to buildings and not just surrounding landscapes, can provide indicators of a project's contribution to the ecological base.

The public and private savings from retaining the services of natural systems can be cheaper than replacing them with industrial technology.[70] For example, preserving the watersheds around cities has been shown to be more economical than selling the land and using chemical-mechanical water treatment.[71] The evaluation of ecosystem services has generally used monetary equivalents. Monetization links eco-services and economic frameworks. This is important as economics underpins most urban and regional policy making and the financial value of nature is still not fully appreciated.[72] However, monetary values are inherently rubbery and temporal, and subject to fluctuation, speculation and exogenous political/economic forces.

RTs sometimes encourage landscaping for ecosystem services, but only for their instrumental values, not for building functions or the intrinsic values of nature.

The building industry has been slow to learn from the natural sciences, such as biology, mycology or ecology. Some RTs promote urban biodiversity in the surrounding landscape, but ignore the opportunities created by the vertical structures, surfaces and spaces of urban buildings. Design for eco-services is essential for ecological sustainability, yet RTs do not consider the idea that buildings could provide ecosystem services to support building functions.[73] Proposals to include nature in buildings are still often discussed on grounds of maintenance costs. However, these costs are not compared to the frequent maintenance, repair and replacement costs of industrial building equipment.

Environmental impact assessment (EIA) aimed to make decision makers 'take into account' the environmental implications of development, without constricting their discretionary decision-making authority.

EIA was introduced in 1969 by the US National Environmental Protection Act and was quickly taken up around the world. (It is compared to RTs in Chapters 11–12.) EIAs aimed to address several problems in previous development approval systems, such as failing to fully consider alternatives or the effects of environmental pollution on human health, and an over-emphasis on short-term economic factors. Since most of those trained in business, industry and government development agencies had little background in social/ecological sciences, and vice versa, it was assumed that including more information from the natural sciences would lead to better development decisions.[74]

RTs helped to restrict the intrusion of EIA into the building industry, but arguably did not improve upon EIAs in process or substance.

When EIAs emerged, the negative impacts of development upon the natural environment were still underestimated, nature's resilience was overestimated and the potential of design in solving sustainability problems was not appreciated. Nonetheless, by the time RTs appeared, the impacts of construction processes on the life-support system were widely known. While RTs were much simpler to apply than EIAs, they largely excluded ecological issues, focusing instead on matters that can be measured off drawings, and that affect costs (energy, resources, etc.). Rather than tracing the ecological impacts of development back to nature, they set criteria/thresholds that have been achieved in practice.[75]

10.7 Conclusion

While building assessment is continually improving, it has not addressed whole-system sustainability issues (e.g. universal wellbeing, ecological health, environmental quality and intra/inter-generational equity).

The comparison of RTS to other quality control/assessment mechanisms suggests that RTs did not consider the pros and cons of existing building quality control processes. The growth of RTs has been impressive and they are gradually adding more green planning and design principles, but these seldom address the fundamental challenge of sustainability (again, development that expands future options and increases nature to compensate for unavoidable biological/industrial resource depletion and pollution). Hence, they may create a negative force of inertia by supplanting other kinds of built environment quality controls. The following two chapters compare EIAs and RTs to develop specific criteria.

10.8 Exercises

1. Examine the development quality control mechanism(s) of a local municipality in terms of the PD Test.
2. Examine the forthcoming upgraded Greenstar Rating tool under development in Australia against the PD Test. (The discussion paper was published online (April 2019) just after this book was completed. https://new.gbca.org.au/news/gbca-media-releases/ultimate-challenge-sustainable-building/.)

Notes

1 The LBC (Living Building Council) takes a different approach and uses only about 20 indicators.
2 There are many case studies but they emphasize savings, not sustainability.
3 Sarkissian, W. (2002) Pros and Cons of Design Charrettes, in Birkeland, J. (ed.) *Design for Sustainability: A Sourcebook of Integrated Eco-Logical Solutions*, Earthscan, UK, p. 113.
4 As recently as 2006, a major university precinct project stated that they wanted input from sustainable design experts, but not until the basic infrastructure was in place.
5 Post-workshop assessment forms could ask both those running the sessions and the community participants how their views were altered.
6 Kramer, R. M. (1969) *Participation of the Poor*, Prentice-Hall, Englewood Cliffs, NJ. I was once turned down for a planning position in Sydney expressly on the grounds that I had 'too much experience in community participation' (in context meaning pro-community).
7 Birkeland, J. (1972) *The Value and Limitations of Advocacy Planning*, College of Environmental Design, University of California, Berkeley, CA. The San Francisco Community Design Center was founded in 1967.
8 Birkeland, J. (2008) *Positive Development: From Vicious Circles to Virtuous Cycles through Built Environment Design*, Earthscan/Routledge, London, pp. 251–73.
9 BREEAM (Building Research Establishment Environmental Assessment Method) is the main UK tool and LEED (Leadership in Energy and Environmental Design) is the main US tool. See Crawley, D., and Aho, I. (1999) Building Environmental Assessment Methods: Applications and Development Trends, *Building Research Information* 27, pp. 300–8.
10 Birkeland, J. (2002) Box 22: Implementing Design for Environment, in Birkeland, *Design for Sustainability*.
11 In the 1990s, some books were influential in showing that business and environment need not be zero sum. Van Weizsacker, E., Lovins, A., and Lovins, H. (1977) *Factor 4: Doubling Wealth – Halving Resource Use*, Earthscan, London; Hawken, P., Lovins, A., and Lovins, H. (1999) *Natural Capitalism: Creating the Next Industrial Revolution*, Earthscan, London.
12 E.g. LEED projects reportedly 'saved' 2.9 million tons of CO₂ and 1.2 trillion gallons of water in 2009.
13 E.g. the then Australian Prime Minister Howard told the building industries that they would be regulated if they did not regulate themselves.
14 I was told this by several of those involved in RT development in the early years. A winner of a green building design award stated: 'All I did was add pelmets to the windows. I don't know anything about green design.
15 E.g. NABERS (the National Australian Building Environment Rating System) added a sixth star to raise the bar.
16 Passive design principles that were commonplace in the 1960s were adopted by some building codes decades later. See Peterkin, N. (2009) Rewards for Passive Solar Design in the Building Code of Australia, *Renewable Energy* 34(2), pp. 440–3.
17 E.g. a building that is near an ecologically sensitive site, does not meet local codes or fails to achieve a certain level of energy performance may be barred automatically, even if it otherwise would get enough points.
18 Achieving BREEAM Excellent ratings is typically less than 1% of the construction cost of a new office building, according to Prior, J., Ward, C., et al. (2017) *Briefing Paper Delivering Sustainable Buildings for BREEAM UK New Construction 2014*, BRE Global, Watford, UK. However, an in-house assessor told me that the savings exceeded the cost of the certification (which can amount to thousands of dollars) but admitted he was not counting his two-year salary ($150,000 a year in 2008 dollars).
19 It was noted early on that a building that rates poorly in energy consumption can still achieve a high score by meeting other less important criteria. E.g. Curwell, S. (1996) Specifying for Greener Buildings, *The Architects' Journal* (Jan.), pp. 38–40.

20 See e.g.: Reijnders, L., and van Roekel, A. (1999) Comprehensiveness and Adequacy of Tools for the Environmental Improvement of Buildings, *Journal of Cleaner Production* 7(3), pp. 221–5; Ding, G. K. (2008) Sustainable Construction: The Role of Environmental Assessment Tools, *Journal of Environmental Management* 86(3), pp. 451–64; Say, C., and Wood, A. (2008) Sustainable Rating Systems around the World, *Council on Tall Buildings and Urban Habitat Journal* 2, pp. 18–29.
21 Fowler, K. M., and Rauch, E. M. (2006) *Sustainable Building Rating Systems – Summary*, Pacific Northwest National Laboratory, Richland, WA.
22 Gu, Z., Wennersten, R., and Assefa, G. (2006) Analysis of the Most Widely Used Building Environmental Assessment Methods, *Environmental Sciences* 3(3), pp. 175–92.
23 Du Plessis, C. (2012) Towards a Regenerative Paradigm for the Built Environment, *Building Research and Information* 40(1), pp. 7–22.
24 Liew, H. L. (2000) *Environmental Performance Assessment Method for Residential Buildings in New Zealand: A Conceptual Framework*, March, University of Auckland, Auckland.
25 Ali, H. H., and Al Nsairat, S. F. (2009) Developing a Green Building Assessment Tool for Developing Countries – Case of Jordan, *Building and Environment* 44(5), pp. 1053–64.
26 Sev, A. (2011) A Comparative Analysis of Building Environmental Assessment Tools and Suggestions for Regional Adaptations, *Civil Engineering and Environmental Systems* 28(3), pp. 231–45.
27 *Green Building Voice* (2018), a monthly email newsletter of the Green Building Council Australia announced in October 2018 that 2,000 Green Star projects have been assessed across Australia, amounting to 32 million square meters of building space or more than the entire Sydney CBD. https://new.gbca.org.au/news/gbca-news/story-two-thousand-green-star-ratings/?utm_source=gbv&utm_medium=email&utm_campaign=reg.
28 See World Green Building Council website www.worldgbc.org/rating-tools.
29 When I was on a sustainability expert reference group around 2005, the building-related policies I had suggested were deleted because someone said there were now green building rating tools, so buildings were no longer an issue.
30 *Green Building Voice*.
31 Thank you to D. Eisenberg for proposing the net-positive concept to the LBC, based on my 2008 book.
32 E.g. a Green Building Council representative tried to get me fired from the university because I was quoted in a newspaper as saying 'green buildings are not sustainable'.
33 When advising on a building rating tool for tourist facilities, I pointed out that they were giving points for merely 'being legal' but they kept the provisions.
34 E.g. the Victorian Architect's Registration Board has little evidence of pursuing complaints against architects. Lucas, C. (2019) Are Complaints Against Architects Falling on Deaf Ears? *The Age*, Feb. 10. www.theage.com.au/politics/victoria/are-complaints-against-architects-falling-on-deaf-ears-20190209-p50wqw.html.
35 A LEED rating tool prerequisite aimed to ensure that systems perform to specifications reputedly helped create a new industry of commissioning agents. Regulation might have been more effective. See Todd, J. A., Pyke, C., and Tufts, R. (2013) Implications of Trends in LEED Usage: Rating System Design and Market Transformation, *Building Research and Information* 41(4), pp. 384–400.
36 By 2016, LEED claimed to have nearly 80,000 projects across 162 countries. Tufts, R (2016) *LEED by the Numbers: 16 Years of Steady Growth*. www.usgbc.org/articles/leed-numbers-16-years-steady-growth.
37 Huovila, P., Ala-Juusela, M., Melchert, L., and Pouffary S. (2007) *Buildings and Climate Change: Status, Challenges and Opportunities*, Sustainable Buildings and Construction Initiative (SBCI), United Nations Environment Programme (UNEP), Paris. www.unep.fr/shared/publications/pdf/DTIx0916xPA-BuildingsClimate.pdf. See also IEA (2012) *World Energy Outlook*, International Energy Agency, Paris, www.oecd-ilibrary.org/energy/world-energy-outlook-2012_weo-2012-en.
38 Some tools give credit for obtaining community 'endorsement' but this may be an investment in public relation, not design input.

39 I attended one of these courses which covered passive solar design very briefly and then they presented their RT which ignored passive design.
40 Passive design was taught in the 1960s, but the texts and resources were very mechanical and may have put off design students.
41 The need for performance-based codes was a discussion in my architecture school in the 1960s, for example. See Australian Building Codes Board www.abcb.gov.au/Initiatives/All/Performance.
42 E.g. NABERS, an Australian building energy RT, rates a building's energy efficiency, carbon emissions, water and waste over a year, compared to others that have similar size, occupancy, hours of use, local climate, etc.
43 Zoning has both problems and prospects as a tool for sustainability. See Lehavi, A. (2018) *One Hundred Years of Zoning and the Future of Cities*, Springer, Amsterdam; Levine, J. (2010) *Zoned Out: Regulation, Markets, and Choices in Transportation and Metropolitan Land Use*, Resources for the Future Press, Washington, DC.
44 Lee, A. C., Jordan, H. C., and Horsley, J. (2015) Value of Urban Green Spaces in Promoting Healthy Living and Wellbeing: Prospects for Planning, *Risk Management and Healthcare Policy* 8, pp. 131–7; van den Berg, M., Wendel-Vos, W., van Poppel, M., et al. (2015) Health Benefits of Green Spaces in the Living Environment: A Systematic Review of Epidemiological Studies, *Urban Forestry and Urban Greening* 14(4), pp. 806–16.
45 Green roofs were becoming fashionable before RTs appeared. By the 1970s, San Francisco City Planning design review section encouraged buildings that could at least support green roofs.
46 At time of writing, the Australian GBC is developing a biodiversity tool. See GBCA (2017) *Land Use and Ecology Category Review*, Green Building Council of Australia, Sydney. https://gbca.org.au/contact. This is critiqued in Birkeland, J. (2018) Challenging Policy Barriers in Sustainable Development, in Dymitrow, M., and Halfacree, K. (eds), *Bulletin of Geography: Socio-Economic Series* 40, Nicolaus Copernicus University, Toruń, pp. 41–56.
47 Birkeland, *Design for Sustainability*.
48 E.g. the best available technology was specified in the USA Federal Water Pollution Control Act Amendments of 1972.
49 E.g. a 2003 Report by the OECD, *Environmentally Sustainable Buildings: Challenges and Policies*, stated that the built environment consumes 32% of the world's resources – including 12% of global fresh water, 40% of the world's energy, 40% of waste to landfill and 40% of air emissions.
50 König, H., and De Cristofaro, M. L. (2012) Benchmarks for Life Cycle Costs and Life Cycle Assessment of Residential Buildings, *Building Research and Information* 40(5), pp. 558–80.
51 PEARL and LEED only award 2% and 5% of total points respectively to innovation-related criteria.
52 BREEAM gives an additional 10% for exemplary performance, which can encourage innovation, but this requires a special application and evaluation fee.
53 In the US, design review processes are often a formal, mandatory part of local governance. Scheer, B. C. (1994) Introduction: The Debate on Design Review, in *Design Review, Challenging Urban Aesthetic Control*, Springer, Boston, MA, pp. 1–10. For a discussion on design review in the UK, see Carmona, M. (2018) Marketizing the Governance of Design: Design Review in England, *Journal of Urban Design* 24(4), pp. 523–55.
54 As done in the San Francisco Planning Department in the 1970s. See also http://default.sfplanning.org/publications_reports/ResidentialDesignGuidelines_GeneralHandout.pdf.
55 Beauty is one of seven categories or 'petals' in the Living Building Challenge RT. See https://living-future.org/wp-content/.../12/Living-Building-Challenge-3.0-Standard.pdf.
56 Amourgis, S. (ed.) (1999) *Architecture and the Environment*, Pomona State Polytechnic University, Pomona, CA.
57 Contextual design indicators have been used in planning codes, such as the San Francisco Residential Planning Code.

58 Global Reporting Initiative, Society, www.globalreporting.org:80/NR/rdonlyres/D2BC0DF8-FF2C-4BAB-B2B4-27DA868C2A5F/2802/G3_IP_SO_ENG_and_cov.pdfG3_IP_SO08.indd.
59 Global Reporting Initiative, Sustainability Reporting Guidelines G3_GuidelinesENU.pdf http://globalreporting.org:80/NR/rdonlyres/ED9E9B36-AB54-4DE1-BFF2-5F735235CA44/0/G3_GuidelinesENU.pdf.
60 One can sometimes get points for the use of sustainably harvested timber or recycled materials that are surplus to need.
61 Robert F. Kennedy speaking at the University of Kansas, Lawrence, KS, in 1968. https://en.wikisource.org/wiki/Remarks_at_the_University_of_Kansas.
62 See Eckersley, R. (2005) *Well and Good: Morality, Meaning and Happiness*, Text Publishing, Melbourne.
63 Waring, M. (1999) *Counting for Nothing: What Men Value and What Women are Worth*, University of Toronto Press, Toronto.
64 Comparing environmental indicators over time may be more instructive than the changes in measurements. See Commonwealth of Australia (1998) *Environmental Indicators for National State of the Environment Reporting*, Environment Australia, pursuant to the First Commonwealth State of Environment Report in 1996.
65 See Hamilton, C. (2002) Genuine Progress Indicators (Box 6), in Birkeland, *Design for Sustainability*, pp. 38–41. The World Bank, in 2000, questioned why governments rely on GDP when it is a poor indicator of wellbeing. World Bank (2000) *Quality of Growth*, World Bank, Washington, DC. www.worldbank.org/wbi/qualityofgrowth/overview.pdf.
66 See Nelson, A. C. (2012) *The TDR Handbook: Designing and Implementing Successful Transfer of Development Rights Program*, Island Press, Washington, DC.
67 Scofield, J.,H. (2009) Do LEED-Certified Buildings Save Energy? Not Really …, *Energy Build* 41(12), pp. 1386–90. Newsham G. R., Mancini S., Birt B. J. (2009) Do LEED-Certified Buildings Save Energy? Yes, But …, *Energy Build* 41(8), pp. 897–905.
68 The numbers of species is often used as an indicator of biodiversity, but when post-construction numbers of species are compared to pre-construction conditions, it can be too late.
69 Krygiel, E., and Nies, B. (2008) *Green BIM: Successful Sustainable Design with Building Information Modeling*, John Wiley & Sons, New York.
70 Beattie, A., and Ehrlich, P. (2004) (2nd ed.) *Wildsolutions*, Yale University Press, New Haven, CT.
71 Daily, G. C., and Ellison, K. (2002) *The New Economy of Nature*, Island Press, Washington, DC.
72 See Frumkin, H., Bratman, G. N., Breslow, S. J., et al. (2017) Nature Contact and Human Health: A Research Agenda, *Environmental Health Perspectives* 125(7), 075001.
73 Ecosystem services gained world attention in the 1990s. Costanza, R., d'Arge, R., De Groot et al. (1997) The Value of the World's Ecosystem Services and Natural Capital, *Nature* 387(6630), p. 253. Design for (building integrated) ecosystem services was first suggested in Birkeland, *Design for Sustainability*.
74 This was according to the stereotypical 'homo economicus'. Simon, H. (1976) *Administrative Behaviour* (3rd ed.), Free Press, New York.
75 The problem with this is that RTs are directed at leaders in the construction industry, but ordinary developers simply apply the rules to accrue points.

Section F
Rating Tools Critiqued

11 Rating Tools and Procedures

11.1 Review and Preview

The previous chapter suggested that RTs redefined sustainable as 'best practice' and did not improve upon the capacity of existing quality control processes.

In 1990, when RTs were introduced, green building design was widely considered 'alternative' if not hippy. Thanks to RTs, green buildings became accepted as good practice, if not prestigious. However, they also marginalized design by focusing on building-centered efficiency measures and accounting activity. Since natural and passive systems were harder to score, they were often replaced by cost-effective commercial building products. These two chapters critique RTs to develop assessment criteria that can increase the public interest and natural environment. Based on this discussion, alternative assessment processes that can be used from the earliest design stages are then proposed [Chapters 13–16].

EIAs (environmental impact assessments) were meant to protect environmental/ human health, by encouraging decision makers to consider the long-term environmental consequences of industrial development.

When EIAs began around 1970, many in the building industry did not yet see the relationship between buildings and biology. EIAs helped to make the connections between the natural and built environments, and bridge the traditional divide between ecology and urban development. Nonetheless, there were many well-known criticisms of EIAs by the time that RTs emerged in the 1990s, from the perspectives of both developers and environmentalists. RTs could have adopted their good points and/or avoided their shortcomings. The following suggests that RTs did not do so. Further, RTs arguably relieved developers/designers of having to think more deeply about their sustainability obligations.

A reductionist, point-scoring, insular, retrospective approach can distract designers from increasing environmental-public gains, if not measure the wrong things in the wrong ways.

RTs were in part aimed at avoiding harsher codes, standards and especially EIAs through building industry self-regulation. Otherwise, they might have improved upon assessment tools that were available at the time, such as EIAs. (EIAs are still evolving, but this discussion concerns the time when RTs were being developed.) EIAs aimed to apply a whole-system view. In contrast, RTs assess things that are traditionally or easily measured on typical buildings, so they exclude many whole-system issues.

Further, RTs replace the biological dimension with surrogates: rules based on typical buildings, but which are presumed to reduce environmental impacts in most situations.

RTs are being transported to many developing countries, which means that these countries may be side-tracked from leapfrogging industrial development to net-positive sustainability.

Since RTs were based on typical Western (industrial) development, they have redefined sustainable buildings along similar lines. In effect, they endorse materialistic, even elitist, living standards that do not necessarily provide the highest life quality for the least environmental costs. They are being used in developing nations, either directly or as modified to suit local climates and conditions. It may be better to bypass this stage and move towards eco-positive design. Their suitability for these nations is discussed in Chapter 12. An alternative quality control approach for developing nations that emphasizes environmental and social justice is suggested in Chapters 13–14.

11.2 Applies to Total Construction Impacts or Just Certain Types of Projects?

EIAs were limited to certain kinds of projects, and preliminary EIAs could allow 'relatively' harmless projects to escape scrutiny, despite potential for improvements.

Most EIA legislation was limited to listed development types that generally have serious impacts, such as factories or mines. Unlisted types were generally excluded.[1] In the US federal legislation, States regulate land use and construction, so federal action had to be involved, such as funding or permit approvals. Major building projects that were likely to have significant negative impacts were also subject to EIAs. Since EIAs involve expense and delays, a preliminary EIA statement (a mini EIA) was often conducted to determine if a full EIA would be necessary. Thus, many small projects were exempted, regardless of their cumulative damage.

RTs only cover projects that voluntarily seek certification, and the collective impacts of non-certified buildings easily cancel out 'reductions' achieved by certified buildings.

Regulations apply to all buildings but only set minimal standards. Although the use of RTs is growing, they apply to a small portion of buildings.[2] Being optional/voluntary, certification is not usually sought where projects will have significant negative impacts. RTs could raise standards very quickly but would lose subscribers in the process.[3] The cumulative impacts of buildings not subject to RTs are huge. Further, the growing number of green buildings adds to the total negative impacts of cities, buildings and other infrastructure. A process that awards high achievers does not reverse the total environmental impacts of demolition, construction or renovation.

PD tools can be applied to any building, as the baselines/benchmarks relate to stationary and on-ground ecological conditions, rather than contemporary building standards/practices.

Some councils incorporate RTs as regulations to raise design standards. Since RTs are based on typical building templates, however, many green buildings are ordinary boxes with added efficiency measures.[4] Few RTs include sustainable design principles, such as adaptability to changing conditions, climates and cultures, so they tend to lock in current standards.[5] PD requires built environments to be analyzed in relation to their context and, where possible, to ameliorate problems in the surrounding area. Since PD tools are grounded in the biophysical environment (instead of conventional building norms), they are applicable to different project types, sizes, locations or environmental significance.

Does the process: (1) Consider the project's share of the collective impacts of all buildings, given that the impacts of ordinary buildings outweigh those of certified buildings? (2) Ensure projects offset a portion of existing problems in the area (eg. Negative material, energy and environmental flows), rather than just meet performance targets for individual buildings or components? (3) Encourage design that will enable future building modifications, since even green buildings constrain future public choices regarding infrastructure, urban form and lifestyle? (4) Examine how the building will interact with the surrounding areas, to identify opportunities to increase environmental and social benefits in the region?

11.3 Introduces a Culture of Science or Sets Rules?

EIAs added a scientific dimension to development control/consent practices, but did little to cross-fertilize the natural sciences with urban design, planning and architecture.

The EIA process was meant to raise awareness and improve the evidence base of government decisions through the pollination of science and urban development – without any direct interference in decision makers' discretion.[6] Since planning and public works departments had little contact with the environmental fields, agencies often hired environmental scientists to manage the new EIA process. EIA specialists, consultants and assessors, whether inhouse or outsourced, usually remained separate from designers, however. Designers were seldom involved in EIA preparation and learned little from EIAs. Even today, designers are often relatively isolated from those in more technocratic departments in academia or government.

RTs were technocratic and accountancy-oriented, and tended to sideline biological, social and cultural issues, so more efficient equipment was favored over design-based approaches.

Transdisciplinary, integrative and collaborative methods have always been considered integral to sustainable design. Yet RT developers did not consider the biological sciences very relevant to green buildings.[7] The generic rules relate to separate building components and set standards that may conflict with on-ground contextual conditions, such as congestion.[8] Some RTs encourage the use of Building Information Modeling tools which quantify some environmental factors,[9] but mainly only concern efficiency, not ecology. Some RTs have gradually added criteria regarding biological factors, such as 'species richness' or 'permeable surfaces'.[10] However, these concern landscaping outside of developments, not the creation of new ecological spaces.[11]

PD tools emphasize natural systems (e.g. biodiversity, passive solar design), since LCA-based tools are available for the selection of particular equipment or products.

RTs often award points for pragmatic and economic choices, such as the best available technology for a particular building function. Meeting performance targets with equipment is a procurement problem, for which product specification tools now exist.[12] Rewarding best practice benefits owners.[13] It does less to regenerate the economy, environment and community, let alone inspire whole-system transformation at the urban/regional scales. To increase the biodiversity, eco-productivity, resilience and/or ecological carrying capacity of a particular living environment, the integration of natural-ecological sciences into government decision making is necessary. PD attempts to integrate ecologists and designers in the early stages of the design.

Does the process: (1) Educate specialist fields in biological sciences (along with designers and building users) about the potential of built environments to support ecological sustainability? (2) Ensure transdisciplinary teamwork occurs at early, conceptual stages of project design, to enable mutual learning among ecological scientists, building technology/engineering experts, and urban planners and designers? (3) Recognize biophilic features as essential elements in creating culturally transformative and net-positive environments, as opposed to efficient but sterile structures? (4) Trace the ecological impacts of design to on-ground ecosystems rather than just meeting generic numerical thresholds that may have ill-advised or unintended outcomes in different urban and ecological contexts?

11.4 Examines Basic Alternatives or Simply Compares Design Elements?

EIAs came late in the design process, but they required a consideration of project alternatives, even if these were not always seriously examined.

EIAs were post-design predictions of past-future impacts, so project designs were already too highly resolved to enable major changes. They seldom led to significant design improvements or a rejection of the project. Most regarded EIAs as a compliance activity and the investment in time, money and effort required was hardly welcomed as an opportunity to improve the design. Nevertheless, EIAs required a discussion of 'alternative' sites, plans or projects,[14] and/or alternative ways to mitigate adverse impacts.[15] The analyses of alternatives were often tokenistic, however, because few developers wanted to investigate the impacts of alternatives that they would not undertake anyway.[16]

RTs do not require an examination of positive alternatives, sites and/or designs and do not prevent projects that conflict with the surrounding development.

Unlike EIAs, RTs compare proposals to the norm and do not explore basic site/design alternatives. Since most RT criteria involve numerical standards or thresholds, they require a detailed design to measure, or at least a building that is similar to conventional buildings. While post-design assessment is useful for awarding certificates/prizes, it does not encourage investing more thought in alternative projects/sites. RT success stories provide examples and inspiration, but largely only illustrate design concepts or technologies that are already used.[17] Instead of exploring multifunctional design that contributes to the wider community and environment, RTs make it easy to select off-the-shelf technology.[18]

PD tools start from first principles to guide preliminary design and construction, rather than emphasizing accountancy activity after a design has already gelled.

PD criteria aim to link planning and design back to sustainability/ethical principles and to facilitate the investigation of alternatives throughout the design process. This reverses the process of starting with a typical building, or one based on current styles/aesthetics, and then mitigating their likely impacts. The emphasis on reason and design thinking is directed at encouraging design that creates more positive public and environmental functions. The STARfish tool, for instance, would continuously add examples of new eco-solutions for various situations (e.g. air, soil, water treatment) to stimulate ideas [Chapters 15–16]. (These would need to be modified to suit differing situations.)

Does the process: (1) Encourage a serious consideration of alternative sites, projects, functions and designs, especially where the proposed project cannot be modified to produce net-positive outcomes? (2) Apply an iterative process that seeks improvements throughout the planning and design process and avoids making irreversible decisions? (3) Integrate design with assessment activities in ways that inspire a collaborative, creative team exploration of alternative designs concepts and go beyond fine-tuning conventions (which are often impeded by retrospective accounting requirements)? (4) Provide sample eco-innovations that are relevant to particular sustainability issues or which can be used to amplify the positive impacts of the basic plan/design?

11.5 Promotes Capacity Building or Outsources to Private Consultants?

EIAs helped to integrate the natural sciences into government departments, but agencies and developers began to outsource assessment processes, which slowed institutional learning.

Many government agencies recruited personnel for EIA verification/oversight, which increased agency cross-disciplinarity.[19] However, since project proposals needed to be assessed scientifically, specialist EIA firms soon arose to prepare EIAs for project developers. These consultants were usually paid by proponents, so they had a financial and/or ego investment in the projects proceeding, and sometimes took on an advocacy role. Designers were not typically included in the assessment process, where they could learn about the environmental consequences of their designs. Likewise, most consultants lacked design or sustainability backgrounds. Specialists were trained in measuring/predicting impacts, not improving environmental and social conditions by design.

RTs generated many private consultancies, but the process did not integrate design with assessment activity sufficient to ensure a design paradigm shift resulted.

As in the case of EIAs, RTs created openings for external consultancies. RTs are usually conducted by individuals trained by and for the organization.[20] This means that the oversight of decisions is left in the hands of non-government officers whose job is to achieve a numerical score. Many RT operators do not always understand the reasons behind the rules/thresholds, and many lack discretion or flexibility in scoring anyway.[21] Hence, there are often reports of anomalies. For instance, highly efficient timber-aluminum composite windows were specified for a timber building, but were classified as aluminum (poor insulator) and thus received a low rating.[22]

PD tools integrate cross-disciplinary experts and communities with designers to reduce outsourcing and emphasize overall development outcomes over maximizing points in score sheets.

Analyses and assessment processes should be a knowledge transfer process among designers, building scientists and urban ecologists. Therefore, PD planning analyses and processes are designed to encourage design thinking, self-education, and engagement among communities, designers, planning/building approval staff, occupants and professional bodies. Both the more quantitative (STARfish) and more qualitative (eDR) tools do not have clients other than the users themselves. There is no reason to withhold information or massage scores. For instance, the tool is designed as a kind of game (a computer app) wherein the team competes with itself rather than others, to maximize net public benefits [Chapters 15–16].

Does the process: (1) Discourage privatizing information as intellectual property, or otherwise speed up knowledge transfer among/between designers, specialists, assessors and the community? (2) Publish accessible, transparent and reasoned assessments in writing, where the basis of tools are private, to enable learning by the general public as well as design and/or development firms? (3) Ensure verification processes cannot be influenced by the needs/desire of developers or designers to receive positive assessments for marketing purposes and/or impressing clients? (4) Allow people to challenge the evidence behind judgments, and ensure assessors have flexibility to avoid rules that prevent better design solutions or contradict on-ground conditions?

11.6 Increases Community Engagement or Creates an Expertariat?

EIAs provided opportunities for public objections or hearings, based on a public interest in improving environmental/human health, not based on property rights alone.

Development control is a regulatory responsibility of government and is necessary to protect health and safety. Initially, however, councils were more concerned with concrete matters such as curbs and gutters. Nature was seen as messy and unclean, so plants and rainwater were removed from cities.[23] Even though the eradication of public land, space and urban nature affects everyone's rights/interests, public input was generally limited to objecting to particular developments.[24] EIAs instituted community involvement or feedback in major development issues and often involved public hearings. In many cases, public funding would be necessary so that community groups could obtain scientific advice.[25]

RTs, centering on numerical and prescriptive rules, thresholds and targets, do little to encourage designers to identify unique community needs, preferences and concerns.

Sustainable design has always emphasized collaborative, integrative processes, community involvement and mutual education. RTs, in contrast, were developed within an industry perspective, and were somewhat technical and inaccessible to lay citizens. Some RTs award points for community 'consultation', but this falls well short of participatory design and other collaborative design review processes. Being based on generic rules, local citizens cannot really engage in either rule-making or determining if projects meet rules. Since RTs are voluntary, their minimum thresholds often create maximum targets. Thus, if an ordinary project gains enough numerical points to get certified, citizens cannot usually demand better design.

PD tools emphasize community-expert participation in design (versus post-design community consultation), to meet local needs/values and reduce conflict caused by 'yes/no' approval processes.

Generic rules can impede a design-based approach that is responsive to the local ecology and socio-cultural conditions.[26] While checklists can be useful, they do not substitute for community design charrettes and other participatory processes. When these activities occur, they are often divorced from the final design. Built-in opportunities for design questions/critique can remedy this, while helping to avoid obstructionism. PD methods aim to foster site-specific design in part by flexibility, stretch goals, community engagement, transparency and standards that reference the local ecology and cultural heritage. Where major developments entail irresolvable disputes, citizen juries would hear both sides of conflicting issues.

Does the process: (1) Provide for the use of charrettes or similar participatory planning/design methods to foster community engagement in developing the design brief and schematic plans? (2) Ensure basic ethical issues concerning controversial project proposals or their siting can be raised and resolved early in the design stage or before proposals are approved? (3) Provide access to expert input when there are conflicting scientific views, and a jury system if there are serious impasses regarding a significant development project? (4) Enable community groups to challenge both designs and assessments, if there is evidence that the findings and/or decisions are questionable or unprofessional?

11.7 Enables the Prevention of Harmful Projects or Legitimizes Them?

EIAs allowed for the possibility of stopping excessively harmful projects, even back when any form of economic growth was considered better than nothing.

EIAs often included the no development option among the alternatives that were examined. If full-cost accounting was used, 'no development' would have fewer ecological impacts than any green building built thus far. Yet, despite the way durable or non-reversible development can close off future options, the null alternative was seldom seriously compared to the proposal. Since the ability to measure bioaccumulation and/or biomagnification was not well advanced, cumulative, regional impacts and ecological uncertainty could not be enumerated and were therefore discounted. Moreover, many written decisions based on EIAs tacitly expressed an economic framework that balanced economic gains against ecological losses.[27]

RTs do not compare projects to no development (which has zero additional impacts), and do not assess how green building reduce net sustainability.

As mentioned above, RTs do not prevent harmful developments. Since they do not compare 'green' buildings to the null alternative, let alone to a net-positive standard, buildings with significant ecological impacts still rate highly. Where a proposed project would damage a sensitive site, an EIA could provide the basis for stopping a project.[28] In contrast, most RTs would, at most, withhold certification of developments near 'sensitive' environments.[29] Without regulation, ordinary, uncertified developments will be built there. Further, the existence of an RT scheme provides an excuse for States to 'not get around to' legislating to protect sensitive sites from development.

PD tools do not give harmful projects positive scores, and instead aim to provide assistance in finding ways to contribute positive public benefits/functions.

'Zero impact' buildings that claim no operational energy demand or no onsite construction waste still add to total environmental impacts. Hence, they define zero to be better than the norm. A positive score in PD is reserved for projects that are better than no development. Because some degree of 'net-positive offsetting' is usually feasible, merely offsetting impacts caused by resource extraction, construction and operation should not suffice. PD design tools therefore aim for net public gains relative to growing population demands, resource flows and biodiversity losses. Buildings that fail the PD Test should be redesigned or designed for future retrofitting.

Does the process: (1) Provide a mechanism for stopping projects that have antisocial outcomes or cause substantial harm to the environment and public, or at least require net-positive socio-ecological benefits in compensation? (2) Adopt means to encourage projects to be better than no development at all, and get warranties for performance where appropriate? (3) Ensure 'less positive' buildings pay more for approvals or certifications, preferably an amount that covers the full public/environmental costs that the project would cause if permitted? (4) Ensure that the existence of RTs does not delay the adoption of codes that apply to all development and raise minimum standards?

11.8 Requires Public Transparent Findings or Simply Makes Judgments?

EIAs were published but were often too inaccessible to serve a public education function, and not self-reflective enough to expose the underlying values/assumptions.

Some EIAs uncovered new knowledge, but EIAs are voluminous and required significant time and background knowledge to read. Further, some information can be labelled 'commercial in confidence'. Scientific writing norms are necessary for credibility, but they also reduce accessibility. Style and vocabulary are not the only aspects of communication, however. More important is transparency about assumptions behind the philosophical filters through which facts or figures are filtered. Some EIAs make technical assumptions that are not self-reflective about their philosophical bases/biases. For example, the tacit belief that reductionist frameworks represent higher-order thinking can cause more creative design approaches to be ignored.

RTs sometimes have semi-confidential provisions and do little to explain the scientific reasons or ethical bases for many of their numerical performance standards.

All tools make assumptions to simplify considerations for decision making, but RTs seldom explain the specific reasons.[30] While EIA methods are known and results can be challenged, the internal bases of RT rules are usually private. Although RTs may be developed in close consultation with client industries, they provide little opportunity for outside inspection. The use of numbers tends to suggest a greater scientific basis than often exists. When rules/criteria appear self-evident, they are likely to reflect the dominant paradigm. There is no real right to object to ratings if the basis of the scoring and weighting systems is withheld.

PD tools are not 'commercial' and are transparent so they can be modified and/or used in various ways (but can also be misused).

The PD tool baselines/benchmarks derive directly from PD theory [Chapters 15–16], so their bases can be debated. PD attempts to explain: why current built environment decision and design frameworks are unsustainable; how PD tools counter these inbuilt biases; why various issues and factors are excluded/included; why and how the numbers and standards are derived; why different factors are weighted more than others, etc. Because PD design tools are 'free', there is no reason to hide errors.[31] Critiques, suggestions and debates can lead to improvements. However, this means that they could be altered to serve other uses that defeat the purpose.[32]

Does the process: (1) Make reasons available for the standards, weighting some factors highly and excluding others and other scoring features, without making people pay for access? (2) Ensure the potential for net-positive impacts are explored, and convey the idea that public gains have no upper limits, so they can always be increased? (3) Ensure the bases of specific development approvals are in writing and freely available to the community and stakeholders, rather than making an appeal to authority? (4) Provide an explanation of how the rules/standards will meet the PD Test or not, as opposed to comparing the project to the norm?

11.9 Allows As-of-Right Approvals or Fosters Improvements?

EIAs provided bases for requiring design improvements but also, in effect, sanctioned mediocre projects which precluded more positive uses of land and resources.

EIAs raised awareness but did little to change the first-come-first-served approach to land use approvals. Rather than setting minimal criteria, as in codes, EIAs predicted the likely consequences of proposed projects. Then, approval authorities could set conditions on development approvals or require the mitigation of impacts, even where the land use was permitted by zoning 'as of right'. However, by having an EIA, projects with modest adverse impacts can be sanctioned. EIAs do not compare projects to a sustainability standard or the no development option. Moreover, decision makers, in their discretion, can still ignore the EIA or waive it entirely.

RTs are increasingly used for development approval purposes by councils, so designs may be allowed even where they could easily be improved upon.

Where municipalities adopt RTs as de facto regulations, a project that ranks highly on an RT may be considered sustainable and approved almost automatically and expedited. Yet, as noted earlier, buildings with high scores have sometimes been less sustainable than some ordinary buildings.[33] In one case, a mandatory energy rating scheme only counted insulation, and ignored the energy usage per square meter, total annual energy usage and the energy from PV cells. Consequently, a home got a zero score, because one room lacked ceiling insulation – although the room was closed-off and all the electricity in the home was renewable.[34]

PD tools aim to identify ways that all building structures can contribute to positive public impacts, while avoiding prescriptive rules, targets or thresholds.

In the above scheme, reductions in net energy usage did not matter, but the purchase of particular products counted, regardless of the use of passive solar design, thermal mass and renewable energy. As in some early building codes, certain insulation firms and suppliers were involved in developing the RT requirements.[35] Hence, the incentive was to purchase particular products, rather than apply passive solar design principles. While sustainability should create commercial opportunities, sustainability measures that benefit special interests may delay basic reforms.[36] PD would instead target poor energy performers using eco-positive retrofitting programs (where contractors are reimbursed from the energy savings).[37]

Does the process: (1) Recognize that today's low standards can permit developments that effectively block positive future proposals for those sites that would have better sustainability outcomes? (2) Ensure higher standards are achieved where local governments choose merely to adopt private industry RT schemes as their building design quality control mechanisms? (3) Avoid 'as-of-right' building approvals that do not consider basic sustainability issues, or encourage tools like conditional development approvals that can require specific cases/proposals to be improved? (4) Require consideration of the best uses of the development site to enable every project to include elements that make a positive contribution to sustainability?

11.10 Requires Adaptability to Be Designed in or Relies on Durability?

EIAs could lead to improvements to a development project, but did not examine whether projects were adaptable to future socio-ecological and climatic conditions.

Although EIAs could provide councils with a basis for requiring mitigation measures or even rejecting a project entirely, neither were likely if the project was the best proposal on offer at the time, as development increases the tax base. Because buildings were not required to be adaptable, even good designs limited the prospects for future sustainability. Durable design shapes subsequent development, and can bake-in negative impacts, increase future costs or reduce sustainable public choices. While permanence often saves resources, adaptability is necessary for intergenerational equity. In architecture, unfortunately, adaptability usually just refers to flexible spaces within rigid, inflexible outer structure.

RTs are designed around current environmental conditions, yet buildings last decades, so the capacity to adapt to changing climates and contexts is overlooked.

While many RTs update their criteria based on regular client feedback, they do not require buildings to be adaptable to unexpected contextual or climate change. Ecosystems/species cannot survive long enough to 'adapt' to current or future conditions, so buildings must adapt. In many cases, land uses and projects are certified if enough total points are acquired, although they are not designed for future conditions. Buildings are generally meant to last 100 years, when environmental conditions may be far worse. Some RTs encourage urban temperature mitigation, but do not require the avoidance of other climate risks, such as floods or droughts.

PD tools emphasize design for retrofitting/deconstruction to enable adaptability to future socio-ecological and climatic change, not simply for problems that are already visible.

Sustainable design is more about renewability than permanence. In PD, adaptable design includes reversible, demountable, portable and/or biodegradable structures. Eco-positive retrofitting refers to adapting buildings to changing conditions, such as the heat island effect, and ensuring that buildings can be retrofitted to higher standards and unexpected future environmental challenges. Strategically located space on the property is an important element of adaptability. Reserving spaces in and around buildings, as well as creating rural biodiversity reserves, may enable cities to adapt to changing social pressures, climates, land use needs or even food shortages. Urban residents also benefit from vertical green spaces and landscaping.

Does the process: (1) Enable design for eco-retrofitting, so that projects can be modified over time to meet unexpected social, technical or other contextual changes? (2) Foster design that meets possible climate extremes at the end of the building's lifespan rather than just accommodating the current range of normal climatic conditions? (3) Ensure adequate ecological space on buildings, complexes or city blocks is reserved for changing needs or conditions, and encourage onsite eco-positive landscaping where appropriate? (4) Encourage the local authority to implement plans for periodic building upgrading or retrofitting to extend their useful lifespans, even if they meet current RT performance standards?

11.11 Considers Lost Eco-productivity or Ignores Opportunity Costs?

EIAs sometimes tacitly balanced jobs against the economic costs of ecological impacts, but not the economic costs of a reduced natural life-support system.

Traditionally, human appreciation/valuation was often mistaken for the actual existential value of nature. Local people have often been willing to sacrifice nearby lakes and forests for job creation, thinking they can always experience nature elsewhere. The short-term employment potential of forestry or fisheries seems urgent, but the future of their jobs depend on healthy ecosystems. Hence, in the name of democracy, many environmental decisions emphasize 'preferences', but democracy is predicated on a healthy environment. Thus, EIA statements did not count future eco-productivity and jobs that might be lost from resource depletion,[38] and seldom looked for alternative ways to create/replace jobs.[39]

RTs do not take into account the global context or the impacts of development on the depletion of regional resources, ecosystems and biodiversity.

EIAs positioned buildings and development in a systems framework, even if often just in a linear supply chain analysis. Since RTs focus on building components that are easily measured, they fail to reflect the economic benefits of a healthy environment and the opportunity costs of lost/damaged natural resources. For example, RTs do not deduct points if buildings fail to compensate for reductions in nature's positive ecological footprint, or cause ecological disruption at the sites of materials extraction. The impacts of resource/extraction activity due to 'sustainable' buildings are greater now than ever, relative to the remaining biodiversity, ecosystems and natural habitats.

PD tools consider the opportunity costs of irreversible decisions causing depletion, waste and pollution, including reductions in eco-productive environments (and therefore future jobs).

Impacts outside the boundaries of the product, site, property, building or region are often forgotten.[40] For example, many RTs only consider construction waste that occurs during construction within property lines. This is a small fraction of the total waste due to offsite resource extraction/production activities all along the building's supply chain. When offsite waste is counted, ecological waste is excluded (which is, again, the restoration time/land area of affected habitats and natural resources).[41] PD tools aim to draw attention to the future costs to the economy itself, including wasteful resource usage, lost uses during the regeneration period and ecological uncertainty.

Does the process: (1) Assess development in terms of how it will impact future resource stocks, biodiversity and land productivity, not just suit owner/user priorities such as parking, jobs, financial savings and so on? (2) Create incentives that favor designs and designers that are able to contribute to the ecological base, public estate and future options? (3) Assess likely building performance in a whole-system framework that considers ecological uncertainty and ecological waste, as well as eco-productive gains? (4) Recognize that nature has economic and social benefits that can exceed the commercial value of its natural resources when they are converted into commercial products?

11.12 Effectively Devalues the Future or Considers Resource Scarcity?

EIAs often reflected cost-benefit thinking by, for example, reducing the future value of nature to present worth, ignoring the increasing scarcity of nature.

As mentioned earlier, business management paradigms dominate decision theory which, in turn, shape assessment frameworks. Thus, concepts like 'discounting' were often found in EIA statements (where the future environment is reduced to present values) [Chapters 7–8].[42] One rationale for this is the idea of 'willingness to pay': that most people would take less money now than wait. In reality, since the costs of environmental damage increase over time, nature's real value necessarily escalates. Another rationale for discounting is to anticipate inflation. However, prices fluctuate over time for reasons that are unrelated to nature. In reality, environmental impacts are not speculative.

RTs ignore the mounting, cumulative costs/impacts accruing from built-environment design, and the future costs of retrofitting certified buildings to meet sustainability standards.

By merely reducing impacts of buildings relative to the norm, RTs ignore the future costs of dealing with accumulating ecological problems. Designing for present values, or willingness to pay, devalues the future. Bigger problems and higher costs are being passed on to future generations with the promise they will find the 'fix'. By tinkering at the edges, RTs may be delaying the start to fundamental systems change. For instance, more dense, brittle metallic 'green' cities increase material flows as well as reducing opportunities for eco-positive retrofitting. Reducing options for change, while adding to future costs/impacts, violates basic intergenerational human rights.

PD tools would emphasize verifiable physical solutions over abstract economic concepts to increase ecological space and carrying capacity and ensure future public choice.

Discounting is biased against sustainability, like many other economic concepts, such as determining value by cost-benefit analyses, gross domestic product and willingness to pay, or using measurements based on rubbery, ephemeral prices.[43] Meanwhile, the socio-ecological effects of built environments are barely researched.[44] While RTs have increased awareness and motivation among many development professionals, they set relative standards, reward projects that fall far short of sustainability and allow harmful and irreversible planning decisions. Rather than deciding today how others must live tomorrow, then, PD aims to increase multiple positive functions, including urban adaptability, options for change, ecological carrying capacity and eco-services.

Does the process: (1) Avoid accounting frameworks that reduce the value of the environment (or the impacts of resource exploitation) to present values since, in reality, scarcity of resources increases future costs? (2) Avoid using temporary, fluctuating, random market-price indicators that allow the manipulation of the devaluing of natural resources and nature? (3) Recognize that negative ecological impacts are virtually always cumulative and irreversible, and cost more to fix in both absolute and monetary terms as time passes? (4) Take into account how delaying design reform will pass on costs to future citizens and even reduce their capacity to address them at all?

Notes

1. A list is usually interpreted to mean things not on the list are meant to be exempt.
2. E.g. the UK Building Research Establishment Environmental Assessment Method (BREEAM) claims to have certified over 250,000 buildings in more than 50 countries worldwide. www.breeam.com.
3. The client is industry so consensus is necessary to raise standards.
4. Even progressive tools such as the Living Building Challenge (LBC) emphasize renewable energy systems and barely mention passive systems. https://living-future.org/lbc/.
5. PEARL encourages design for disassembly, adaptability and flexibility, but it is unclear how this is demonstrated or verified. See PEARL M-3 and 4, in Abu Dhabi Urban Planning Council (2010) *The PEARL Building Rating System for Estidama: Design and Construction*. http://estidama.org/PEARL-rating-system-v10/PEARL-building-rating-system.aspx.
6. NEPA, National Environmental Policy Act of 1969, 91st United States Congress.
7. The concern at the time was energy and the term ecological often referred to energy.
8. Mechanistic formulas like minimum or maximum parking spaces per tenant can have results that undermine sustainability.
9. BIM (building information modeling) systems are digital tools that take measurements off drawings and facilitate measurements such as the rainwater collection area.
10. BREEAM uses species richness as an indicator of ecological change. The German Sustainable Building Quality Label emphasizes permeable land area. www.breeam.com/.
11. Token landscaping around buildings has little benefit to ecosystems. BREEAM concerns landscaping to protect soil and water (e.g. erosion), minimizing the ground coverage of buildings, and considers protected or threatened species in site selection, but does not assess site ecology and does not provide incentives for increasing biodiversity habitats. See www.breeam.com/. PEARL gives points for restoring or recreating habitats that are self-sustaining and connected to other similar habitats.
12. E.g. see Good Environmental Choice Australia (www.geca.eco/) and Eco-specifier (www.ecospecifier.com.au/).
13. Many papers from industry and government explain how green buildings pay. Kats, G. (2003) The Costs and Financial Benefits of Green Buildings: A Report to California's Sustainable Building Task Force, USGBC ; Kok N. (2009) Doing Well by Doing Good: Green Office Buildings, Profitable Sustainability, in Property Conference of the Australian Property Institute, Sydney, Nov. 10. www.adpia.com.au/.
14. O'Brien, M. (2000) *Making Better Environmental Decisions: An Alternative to Risk Assessment*, MIT Press, Cambridge, MA.
15. See Gibson, R. B. (2013) Avoiding Sustainability Trade-offs in Environmental assessment, *Impact Assessment and Project Appraisal* 31(1), pp. 2–12, also citing Steinemann, A. (2001) Improving Alternatives for Environmental Impact Assessment, *Environmental Impact Assessment Review* 21(1), pp. 3–21.
16. An EIA might discuss whether to build a dam in two different locations on the same river or on different rivers, or whether to build a dam at all. However, a dam builder is unlikely to consider a wind farm, so alternatives were often hypothetical and not fully costed.
17. Developers and bankers want to know that design concepts have worked elsewhere, which means that innovative projects can be hard to fund.
18. Commercial equipment provides information on performance expectations, whereas more 'natural' materials and passive solar systems are not as standardized and often do not have warranties.
19. EIAs written by consultants can be accepted or authored by the government agency. This means the government office is verifying the information.
20. RTs are usually non-profit organizations, but charge fees to cover their costs and promotion.
21. Where a council has adopted an RT as a de facto regulation, the public servants applying the RT may interpret it very literally because they do not have a design-science background to understand a provision (as I have seen first-hand).
22. Schweber, L. (2013) The effect of BREEAM on Clients and Construction Professionals, *Building Research and Information* 41(2), pp. 129–45, 136.

23 See Birkeland, J. (2016) Net Positive Biophilic Urbanism, *Smart and Sustainable Built Environments*, 5(1), pp. 9–14.
24 The right to object is not the same as being listened to.
25 Most community design centers no longer restrict their services to those who cannot pay. Finn, D., and Brody, J. (2014) The State of Community Design: An Analysis of Community Design Center Services, *Journal of Architectural and Planning Research* 31(3), pp. 181–200.
26 Although RTs are written as performance-based codes, they are usually quite prescriptive.
27 This was certainly the case when I used to review EIAs at work.
28 EIAs seldom led to decisions to stop a project, but many projects were arguably stopped due to the delays caused by EIAs, which suggests that they may have been somewhat financially marginal.
29 The LBC does not certify buildings near sensitive sites. https://living-future.org/lbc/.
30 E.g.: 'Use ready-mix concrete for cast-in-situ construction, 8 points' is clear, but the why, what, where and when are not at all clear. Why not consider more environmentally friendly alternatives?
31 Not all tools cost users. For example, BEES is a freely available tool and can be downloaded from the internet. Also, a Built Environment Sustainability Scorecard or BESS is paid for by councils around Melbourne to assist planning applicants.
32 E.g. the PD tool concept could be misused merely to express negative impacts in more positive terms.
33 Newsham, G. R., Mancini, S., Birt, B. J. (2009) Do LEED-certified Buildings Save Energy? Yes, But … , *Energy Build* 41(8), pp. 897–905; Scofield J. H. (2009) Do LEED-certified Buildings Save Energy? Not Really …, *Energy Build* 41(12), pp. 1386–90.
34 The assessors are trained to operate the tools, not to evaluate passive solar design. For example, in Australia, the Nathers rating system rates the thermal performance of homes with software and only counts the energy needed to heat or cool spaces, not passive design elements.
35 This was also the case of a solarization proposal in the ACT.
36 Commercial gain does not always lead to better environmental outcomes, even though efficiency can save all parties money.
37 This principle has been around for decades, such as in the green lights program in the USA. https://nepis.epa.gov/.
38 Mechanization of resource exploitation in forestry, fisheries, fossil fuels, farming and factories is a major cause of job losses, but lack of resources also necessarily causes job losses and social dislocation over time.
39 There is an infinite amount of work that needs doing, so any destructive job can be replaced by jobs that have net benefits to society.
40 An early precedent for whole-system analysis is Meadows, D. H, Meadows, D. L., Randers, J., et al. (1972) *The Limits to Growth: A Report for the Club of Rome's Project on the Predicament of Mankind*, Universe Books, New York; Poldy, F., and Foran, B. (1999) *Resource Flows: The Material Basis of the Australian Economy Resource*, Futures Program, CSIRO Wildlife and Ecology, Canberra; Birkeland, J., and Schooneveldt, J. (2002) *ACT Sustainability Audit: A Material Flows Analysis of the Residential Sector of Canberra*, ACT Planning and Land Management Authority, Canberra.
41 Birkeland, J. (2007) GEN 6: Ecological Waste: Rethinking the Nature of Waste, in *Environmental Design Guide of the Australian Institute of Architects*, AIA, BEDP (Built Environment Design Professions), Canberra. www.environmentdesignguide.com.au/.
42 One proposed solution was to add an ecological factor to account for future costs. Cocks, K. D. (1992) *Use with Care: Managing Australia's Natural Resources in the Twenty-first Century*, NSW University Press, Sydney.
43 Carbon equivalence is a more reliable measure than monetary equivalents, but any single unit will omit other sustainability issues. Different units can be compared using a radar diagram, as seen in Chapters 15–16.
44 Urban morphology and other urban planning paradigms study how built environments shape society and vice versa, but usually without a political-economic perspective. See Obeng-Odoom, F. (2016) *Reconstructing Urban Economics: Towards a Political Economy of the Built Environment*, Zed Books, London.

12 Rating Tools and Substance

12.1 Requires Public Purposes or Just Client Benefits?

EIAs often implicitly balanced the economic value of proposals against negative impacts, but not overall contributions to social sustainability (i.e. the public estate).

EIAs were meant to discipline project approval processes and include environmental considerations among the usual economic factors. While EIA statements discussed social factors,[1] the social purpose or function of the project itself was seldom deemed relevant.[2] For instance, authorities might approve a cigarette factory if its environmental controls were up to standard, regardless of the medical/personal costs of smoking. Also, EIAs framed the process as an either/or decision, so the economic prospects could outweigh social and environmental impacts.[3] Furthermore, EIAs could compare a project to less socially desirable developments to create the 'decoy effect', making the proposed project look better.

RTs, being voluntary, do not require anti-social or anti-environmental projects to undertake certification processes or even meet design standards (creating a perverse subsidy).

EIAs brought greater awareness to governmental/professional decisions and encouraged consideration of the public interest. Some development projects were abandoned due to the prospect of paying for an EIA where the findings would clearly be negative.[4] RTs allow socially harmful projects to escape the time, money and effort for an EIA application, although an EIA might still be required.[5] Neither EIAs or RTs stop political interference in support of projects that communities oppose.[6] Further, most RTs do not require proponents to present proposals at a public hearing so that citizens can object, make design suggestions or seek mediation to resolve the issues.

PD tools enable both public and expert input and consider the project's public purposes and social values, not just relative efficiencies or impacts.

EIAs and RTs can lead to the approval of socially/environmentally detrimental projects, because they largely ignore ethical issues. They focus on efficiency measures (cost savings) rather than public benefits. PD includes a broader range of sustainability/ethical issues that are affected by built-environment design. EIAs and RTs may result in impact reductions, but PD aims to identify and attract development that addresses local socio-ecological issues. The identification of local needs should guide the search to attract new developments.[7] This would reverse the standard approach (seeking any kind of economic growth) and help planners/designers find leverage points for maximizing public benefits.

Does the process: (1) Frame the review process as primarily an opportunity to multiply public benefits and social functions, or just to pick winners or appease objectors? (2) Avoid dualistic (better/worse, either/or, yes/no) frameworks that favor the 'best available' project, without building in opportunities for site-specific community/expert input, or including no-regrets improvements? (3) Avoid a bargaining/trading process that allows trade-offs between private-public and future-present interests, and instead seek opportunities to add net-positive contributions to the social and natural environment? (4) Avoid the decoy effect where proposals are approved because they look better than the other (ordinary) options that are currently on the table?

270 Decision Making and Assessment

12.2 Treats Buildings as Parts of Open or Nested Urban Systems?

EIAs were limited to project assessment but stimulated the development of systems analyses that could trace negative construction impacts throughout the built-natural environment.

When EIAs emerged, industrial pollution was the focal point of environmental issues. Environmental management in the 1970s was largely concerned with adding filters or scrubbers and taller smokestacks that only dispersed pollution more widely. By mapping adverse negative impacts upstream-downstream from factories, EIAs encouraged cleaner production and products throughout construction industry supply chains. It also fostered the development of systems analyses like lifecycle, material flows and total quality analyses. However, little attention was paid to potential positive impacts. While post-design analyses can pinpoint areas for mitigation, they do not address the causes of ecological problems in the design of structures/systems.

RTs delayed the advance of whole-system analyses of buildings due to their mechanistic approach and emphasis on the resource/energy efficiency of separate components.

While EIAs raised awareness of the links between development and natural environments in distant places, RTs divided up buildings conceptually into measurable parcels. Despite the occasional use of metaphors such as 'living buildings' and buildings as ecosystems, RTs apply a mechanistic, reductionist framework.[8] They treat buildings as systems nested within urban systems, which assumes that if building impacts are minimized, cities will be sustainable. Yet many have observed that optimizing separate systems can lead to suboptimal outcomes.[9] For example, the airtightness of buildings for energy savings conflicts with ventilation needs if mechanical systems are used instead of sustainable design principles.[10]

PD tools conceive of buildings/cities as natural landscapes that are interconnected with and supportive of bioregional systems (rather than designing buildings like cars).

Sustainable design, being fundamentally concerned with environmental and social issues, logically aim for a whole-system framework that integrates all sustainability dimensions. While EIAs initially centered on pollution or cleaner production, RTs initially centered on energy or efficiency. These are essential but distract attention from creating positive offsite environmental/social impacts. For example, some RTs include social factors such as the safety and welfare of construction workers onsite, but not wider issues such as how importing cheap labor affects other regions or communities.[11] By exposing local and bioregional socio-ecological deficits,[12] a project's potential ramifications beyond urban boundaries can be improved [Chapters 7–8].

Does the process: (1) Frame the project and its environment as one complex interdependent system, or see buildings as a set of parts, even if bigger than the whole? (2) Assist in helping project proponents to see how developments interrelate with and affect social dimensions of sustainability, including environmental ethics and socio-economic justice? (3) Foster design that supports positive socio-ecological impacts in the bioregion, as well as reducing waste or pollution throughout the project supply chain? (4) Go beyond linear, input-output frameworks that are more suited to efficiency in manufacturing (cleaner production) than spatial design, and view 'cities as landscapes' instead of mechanisms?

12.3 Allows for Automatic Approvals or Judicious Decisions?

EIAs presumed that development decisions were based solely on objective considerations by rational actors, so that information would automatically result in better decisions.

When EIAs were adopted, the mainstream view was that officials made goal-oriented decisions based on objective expert advice.[13] The EIA process assumed that providing information about long-term environmental consequences of development would dislodge preconceptions.[14] Accordingly, it was assumed that the decision was correct if the proper process was followed.[15] Since the focus was on development decisions, EIAs embedded sustainability in the prevailing binary frameworks of business administration and economics – rather than within a sustainable design paradigm. There were no in-built provisions for tracking how development decisions were influenced by EIAs, or for checking if decisions honored the legislative intent.

RTs are largely quantitative and do not explain their thresholds and rules or explain why project outcomes have sometimes been inconsistent with ratings.

While EIAs traced upstream-downstream environmental damage, RTs set thresholds, weightings and targets, usually without clear scientific rationales.[16] Although RTs claim to be 'evidence based', the assumptions behind the rules are seldom stated. Because points can be obtained where it is easiest to do so, uneven results have often been observed.[17] Being numerical does not mean something is objective and may indicate a technocratic bias. Ease of measurement, not research, often appears to be the main criteria. There are many studies on the economic and resource savings attributable to RTs, but little on their contribution to improving overall urban design outcomes.

PD tools aim for a judicious approach where reasons for standards are open to scrutiny, and benchmarks are directly linked to net-positive sustainability.

Development decisions affect everyone, present and future, and shape ethical issues, such as how people share resources and spaces, and how close they live to the natural environment. Such decisions should be a deliberative, not a bookkeeping, process. Since some decision makers have put economic ideology over long-term outcomes, explicit reasoning in approvals should be provided. In contentious issues, a judicious approach should be used instead of executive 'command and control' or reductionist, automated approaches. PD tools build on ethics-based principles, and use stationary, tangible baselines [Chapters 15–16]. Where there are contentious (non-legal) sustainability issues, a jury-based process is recommended.

Does the process: (1) Require transparent explanations of assessment rules (as well as specific development decisions) and not just rely on there being a direct connection between objective information and decisions? (2) Use stationary, tangible baselines and benchmarks relating to objective on-ground conditions, instead of simply aiming for projects that exceed code-compliance? (3) Recognize that development assessments and approvals involve subjective values so they should be explained, instead of simply rewarding things because they are easily enumerated? (4) Use citizen juries that hear both sides of an issue when it appears that factual disputes or value conflicts cannot be resolved by collaborative design?

12.4 Uses Design as Conflict Resolution or Simply Chooses Winners?

EIAs often, in effect, appeared to endorse buildings with 'less' harmful impacts, even though modifications could have met more community needs and interests.

Since EIAs required a detailed design concept to enable quantitative analyses, designs seldom changed much after the EIA was prepared, although development approvals could prescribe conditions.[18] Many developments were exempt from the EIA process, and projects with average EIA results were likely to be approved, even if citizens raised objections. As illustrated in the environmental conflict resolution literature,[19] design can often resolve conflicting needs/interests between communities and developers. Most buildings did not have to prepare EIAs.[20] Therefore, the EIA process did not create much pressure to modify designs so that projects at least mitigated/offset the damage to those adversely affected.

RTs framed sustainability as a technical matter, which reduced opportunities for using the design process to resolve competing demands, interests, needs and preferences.

When RTs emerged, development approval was less often seen as a primarily apolitical, engineering process. Today, there is an even greater appreciation that design is more than technology. However, the emphasis on numerical targets inhibits the identification of conflicting community and developer interests concerning specific projects. RTs divert time and effort from resolving conflicts by design. Numbers can provide rough indicators of future performance, but it is the design that determines stakeholder satisfaction. Some RTs encourage 'site analyses', but do not call for a clarification of conflicting issues or for finding basic design alternatives through community participatory in design processes.

PD tools highlight the ethical issues underlying sustainability issues to guide design processes toward meeting diverse public interests and preventing future social conflicts.

Conventional development approval processes pick winners and losers. Whereas development conflicts are generally framed as 'either/or' disputes, designers can use both stakeholders and public-interest positions as design criteria. Design can circumvent conflict by meeting diverse needs/values through multifunctional environments. Zero-sum conflicts and/or outcomes are minimized where designs make everyone better off. SMT analyses help to identify existing inequities and other contextual issues, before irreversible planning/infrastructure choices are made (e.g. RT analysis). The Hierarchy of Eco-innovation shifts the emphasis from private-public trade-offs to finding opportunities for net-positive benefits [Box 5]. Being iterative, PD tools can be used throughout development/design processes.

Does the process: (1) Explore ways for developments to avoid future social conflict by meeting competing public needs and interests, reducing disparities of wealth and avoiding future land use conflicts? (2) Ensure contextual and ethical issues are resolved before making significant land-use or planning approvals, to avoid irreversible or zero-sum decisions and otherwise avoid closing off future options? (3) Anticipate and overcome potential conflicts/deficits via proactive community planning processes and SMT analyses, and seek development proposals that address those issues? (4) Create development incentives for sustainable design (e.g. fast-track assessment processes or low application fees) where development proposals demonstrably contribute net community-wide improvements?

12.5 Includes Elements of Time and Space or Just Material Efficiency?

EIAs stimulated the development of lifecycle analysis, but the focus on materials, pollution and energy distracted from an appreciation of the spatial dimension.

Buildings are the embodiment of the materials extraction, manufacturing, transport and construction impacts that their designs dictate. EIAs required examining the upstream-downstream impacts of building supply chains and ushered in the nascent lifecycle assessment tools.[21] Nonetheless, impacts of buildings were not taken very seriously before the turn of this century, perhaps partly because EIAs were limited to major developments. Today, LCA-based specification tools rank industrial products/materials by their impacts from cradle to grave or, theoretically, 'cradle to cradle'.[22] However, product lifecycles are generally analyzed separately from their spatial impacts, and do not consider the potential positive uses/benefits of space itself.

RTs omit the impacts of embodied energy/materials and effects of spatial relationships on sustainability issues, concentrating instead on post-construction operational and material/product impacts.

RTs primarily concern resources, energy, water and pollution in the human environment. They do not really encourage/assess the use of space to multiply practical eco-services and/or non-material benefits. Whereas EIAs may trace building impacts back to specific locations in nature, RTs use generic indicators about construction impacts and post-construction performance. As noted earlier, most resource and energy wastage occur before materials even reach the site,[23] and RTs exclude system-wide impacts by using temporal and spatial system boundaries.[24] Not only can a zero-energy building have more embodied energy/materials than ordinary buildings, it may fail to provide spaces with any socio-ecological benefits.

PD tools conceive of space, structure and surface as key design elements for multiplying public gains, not just reducing the impacts of materials/products.

The cost of a building is usually based on its floor area, and its usable space is defined by its two-dimensional area, rather than by its functional benefits. Since space (volume) is seen as empty, reducing space per person or per function appears to enhance efficiency.[25] However, because efficiency is not the same as sustainability, less space is not always more effective in terms of outcomes. The sustainability value of space depends on its functions/uses. In PD, a development is an opportunity to expand social and ecological functions and benefits – relative to the overall impacts, embodied materials and space used.

Does the process: (1) Avoid treating space as empty, since the use of space as well as the surrounding density greatly affects long-term sustainability outcomes? (2) Appreciate and utilize space as a means of increasing multiple benefits for both human and ecological communities, since synergistic relationships between functions and spaces depend mainly upon design? (3) Hold buildings responsible for their share of both ecological and environmental space that is needed to make urban areas sustainable? (4) Avoid specifying thresholds that can be met by simply selecting products or components, at least where this distracts from maximizing the functional benefits of space and surfaces?

12.6 Considers Cumulative, Regional Impacts or Just Onsite Impacts?

EIAs were considered unsuccessful at analyzing cumulative and regional impacts but, because this was acknowledged, some effort was directed toward improving these defects.

EIA methods look at the site-specific impacts of development proposals. This recognizes that development form and function may be well-suited to one location, yet harmful in another (e.g. near a wetland or ecologically sensitive site). It was understood in theory that toxic emissions bioaccumulate and/or biomagnify in many species and even humans. Nonetheless, EIAs did not adequately consider either a project's contribution to cumulative pollution or the reduction of ecological carrying capacity in the region. For example, when coal mining is concentrated in coal-rich regions, total coal pollution will exceed the assimilative capacity of the region's air, water, soils and humans.

RTs and their promotional literature emphasize the savings achieved by certified buildings, but ignore or understate their incremental, collective, cumulative impacts on regions.

RTs do not consider their share of the collective impacts of buildings. The repercussions of particular buildings may be small, but their collective impacts are huge and still growing. For example, the carbon emissions of a green building may be small relative to the typical building, but they add to the overall carbon contribution of buildings (estimated variously at 30 to 40% of human-emitted carbon).[26] Similarly, RTs do not consider how buildings reduce the remaining ecological base. By concealing how far buildings fall short of actual sustainability, many citizens and professionals alike are lulled into a state of complacency.

PD tools hold buildings notionally responsible for their 'share' of total impacts, to encourage attempts to increase the positive ecological footprint of nature.

In a highly vegetated neighborhood or district, greenery does not appear necessary for cooling, pollution absorption, carbon sequestration or oxygen. Given the total impacts of construction, however, each building should make a contribution. Of course, creating even small reductions in atmospheric carbon or urban overheating through development is challenging.[27] Some RTs simply limit the carbon emissions that buildings that can add yet still be certified.[28] RTs that label carbon emission reductions as if they reduce atmospheric carbon is misleading, since buildings can sequester more carbon than they emit over their lifecycle.[29] PD awards negative points for relative reductions in carbon impacts.

Does the process: (1) Treat all projects as opportunities to increase the overall contribution of cities to the sustainability of the bioregion, if not to global sustainability? (2) Consider the building's contribution to cumulative and regional impacts over time, at least notionally (as opposed to rewarding estimates of reductions in future negative impacts relative to hypothetical developments)? (3) Consider whether a project will displace other future more desirable development alternatives and how this affects cumulative, regional, socio-ecological conditions? (4) Set zero lifecycle carbon targets for buildings, since this is theoretically possible, rather than only aiming for zero carbon in a building's post-construction operation?

12.7 Considers Public Interests or Just Stakeholder Interests?

EIAs only aimed for the understanding, documentation and mitigation of harm, rather than encouraging high standards or expecting projects to provide public benefits.

When EIA processes began, pollution was still accepted as unavoidable, and the 'frontier ethic' meant that nature was considered an infinite sink for pollution and waste. In fact, some actually considered not exploiting resources to be 'wasteful'.[30] Likewise, the prevailing ethics was that developers (wealth producers) should maximize benefits to themselves as long as they did not unduly harm others (a trickle-down theory). Thus, while EIA statements discussed social and economic impacts (often indirectly),[31] they overlooked the potential of built environments to improve social equity and environmental health, let alone to improve the natural environment through urban and/or building design.

RTs mostly aim to benefit project stakeholders, although they increasingly encompass land-use arrangements, site planning, landscaping and amenities at the neighborhood scale.

Buildings are often more socially constructive than the no development option, as they provide for social interaction and amenities, as well as jobs, economic activity and so forth. RTs benefit project stakeholders, but do not use development to address wider social issues. For instance, most RTs do not discourage gated communities or large 'green' homes with excessive embodied energy and materials. Elitist projects in privileged areas usually get the same number of points as projects in disadvantaged areas. Some RTs even prioritize development in central high-cost areas, mainly for fuel efficiency,[32] rather than in areas needing social investment and revitalization.

PD tools reflect the Green Optimum where each development contributes something to the public good, since undue burdens on investors/developers can be offset.

Development cannot achieve a social sustainability standard if it imposes unjust risks or distributional outcomes. When projects are considered in interaction with the urban/natural environment, design elements can be found that reduce disparities of wealth and/or multiply public benefits. The public good should not be outweighed by financial benefits to investors. The Green Optimum [Chap. 8], again states that any building should make society better off, without causing burdens to the developers/investors. This means proponents of major projects should consider how their development proposals can contribute to a reduction in social deficits, such as class, race, wealth segregation or disparities.

Does the process: (1) Assess social outcomes relative to a sustainability standard to increase life quality at the local community and/or regional scale (beyond merely providing economic benefits to owners/occupants)? (2) Deduct negative social impacts in assessments of sustainability, whereas RTs thus far largely only consider positive social impacts? (3) Expand the public estate through carefully designed public spaces that increase social interaction, security, place making and community bonds, while addressing local and/or regional social deficits? (4) Consider ways of offsetting any contributions to the public estate or ecological base that impose extra costs upon developers, where the result is a net social/environmental gain?

12.8 Considers Ethical and Social Issues or Just Economic Gains?

EIAs often tacitly considered economic activity to be positive without accounting for the possible future losses of jobs from environmental degradation and depletion.

EIAs helped to counterbalance the emphasis on GDP, which counted all economic activity/transactions as positive.[33] However, when socio-economic benefits were discussed in EIA statements,[34] negative economic impacts were often omitted. Promises of jobs were sometimes stated without deducting the costs of future job losses from resource depletion (e.g. forestry), the health/safety risks of jobs (e.g. mines), worker relocation or the relative benefits of jobs. Jobs in offshore oil drilling, mining, forestry, dam building often end when the resources are gone and involve social impacts, such as community or family disruptions.[35] Hence, social impact assessment was strengthened to address these and other issues.[36]

RTs downplay socio-ecological and ethical issues while emphasizing the financial benefits for developers/owners, such as energy savings, property values, worker productivity and marketability.

Social impact assessment was established before RTs emerged, but RTs did not utilize this source of knowledge. When RTs emerged, indoor air pollution was a big social issue. The costs of productivity losses, absenteeism and worker compensation due to indoor air were widely publicized.[37] In fact, some new buildings had been demolished due to 'sick building syndrome'.[38] Indoor air quality gradually appeared in some RTs, but these provisions usually only consider the health effects on occupants, not neighbors.[39] For instance, RTs seldom consider the wide dispersal of toxic waste from demolition carried out to allow for a new 'green' building.[40]

PD tools discourage the 'double counting' of private financial gains as if they were public benefits, since savings should be their own reward.

While RTs usually only count reductions in negative environmental impacts, they generally only count positive social impacts. Some neighborhood-scale RTs count social amenities, but overlook the disparities of wealth and opportunity or social inequalities that may result from the new suburb. Similarly, investors, owners and developers benefit financially from high RT scores, while also making gains from savings (again, marketing, energy savings, indoor air quality, happier, healthier workers and lower absenteeism). Rewarding them twice over for financial savings/gains made sense when few builders understood that good design saved money. Today, however, monetary gains should count as private, not public, benefits.

Does the process: (1) Recognize that the value of jobs created both in construction projects and in producing construction materials should take account of their relative long-term costs? (2) Provide a means of learning from, and building upon, the experience, defects and successes of past environmental and social impact assessments? (3) Avoid counting what are really economic benefits to project stakeholders (developers, owners and investors) under assessment categories that purport to be about public socio-ecological gains? (4) Consider drawing upon genuine progress indicators which aim to integrate social and environmental factors with economics (although they seldom include factors directly related to built environments)?

12.9 Considers Whole-System Gains or Relies on System Boundaries?

EIAs examined projects in relation to the environment as a whole, although generally within a closed-system framework using system boundaries to facilitate analysis/computation.

EIAs traced construction impacts upstream (resource extraction, materials transport, manufacturing, etc.), if not downstream (operation, refurbishment, eventual demolition, etc.). As discussed earlier, since toxins can affect different individuals, species and ecosystems in different ways, it is still almost impossible to measure myriad interactive chemicals in complex and changing contexts. Therefore, to accommodate arithmetic, outputs-inputs were assessed at system boundaries, such as building envelope, property lines and farm or factory gates. This meant that impacts beyond an arithmetically convenient point in time, space or distance could effectively be ignored. Unfortunately, this also meant EIAs tended to underestimate the overall cumulative damage.

RTs replaced the emphasis on tracing upstream-downstream impacts back to nature with numerical rules that see buildings as a collection of separate parts.

The nature of borderless interactive, regional and/or cumulative impacts were understood when RTs originated. However, embodied impacts were too complex for certification purposes. Therefore, a checklist of numerical factors that were easily measured from drawings was used.[41] This favored conventional building design. Dividing building systems into separate units conflicts with modern understandings of reality as a dynamic flux of interactive forces/substances. Reductionism without design is Yin without Yang. While many provisions are based on conventional buildings, some RTs encourage lifecycle assessments (LCA). However, LCAs are generally weak on social/ethical issues, as these are difficult to isolate, unitize, enumerate and quantify.

PD tools draw upon flows analyses to help visualize information in a whole-system perspective (as opposed to using whatever data are readily available).

Development affects everything eventually, even if in tangential, distant and/or delayed ways. Hence, systems boundaries are problematic. Disregarding impacts that are not proximate in time or space just to apply arithmetic tends to focus attention on accounting instead of reasoning processes and physical design solutions. Further, it is not necessary to measure net-positive impacts as these do no harm (by definition). Using a lens that considers flows of resources, energy and materials from their origins in nature to eventual demolition helps to identify opportunities for design synergies.[42] Design, a mental flows analysis, can be used where quantitative analyses are impractical.

Does the process: (1) Avoid reliance on reductionist system boundaries when they obscure total cumulative impacts, and concentrate on maximizing positive impacts? (2) Include ethical, social or ecological benefits in assessment, even though they cannot always be expressed numerically, especially since net-positive design need not cost more than ordinary design? (3) Give preference to natural systems and materials in design, even where data on their impacts are difficult to obtain/verify, when they promise to have fewer embodied and ecological impacts? (4) Focus on impacts of products or projects in relation to their actual production systems and actual environments, in lieu of generic rules?

12.10 Addresses Resource Scarcity and Extinctions or Just Relative Consumption?

EIAs examined the ecological impacts of individual projects, but did not consider their contribution to the growing scarcity of nature and natural resources.

By not adequately dealing with cumulative and regional impacts (above), EIAs largely ignored the growing scarcity of nature and resources. Meanwhile, in order to open up more resources for exploitation, economic downturns were often blamed on nature conservation ('locking up' land). Some economists actually argued that scarcity would protect nature: as endangered species or wilderness areas became scarce, their value would go up, because people would 'willingly pay' more to protect them. In reality, when species become endangered, their value increases and poaching becomes more lucrative. When species disappear, the animal trade will make another animal more rare and valuable.[43]

RTs do not consider the global rates of species extinctions, declining ecosystems and biodiversity habitats, let alone offset the ecological footprint of development.

Collectively, buildings are using ever more mineral/natural resources.[44] Incremental project-centered assessments hide the ecosystem depletion and land degradation caused by the upstream-downstream resource extraction and construction for buildings. The traditional response to most problems, the promise of technological 'fixes', cannot reverse species extinctions, climate change and cumulative pollution. The potential contribution of the built environment to correcting these issues has been ignored. This is, again, because of the reliance on finding technologies to sustain architectural fashion, not to close the gap between current and sustainable conditions. Representing reductions in the speed of environmental destruction as 'progress' amounts to professional negligence.

PD tools do not equate mitigation (i.e. resilience, adaptation, eco-restoration) with ecological sustainability because, while important, regeneration cannot increase the net ecological base.

Terms like 'resilience' are increasingly used instead of sustainability (a term considered worn out). Resilience implies that nature's capacity to regenerate only needs to be fortified. Yet only returning land to wilderness and creating diverse ecosystem enclaves can reverse past/ongoing losses.[45] Similarly, the term 'climate adaptation' suggests that buildings only need to be modified to withstand increasing weather events. PD posits that cities should go beyond resilience and climate adaptation to reduce extreme weather, absorb atmospheric carbon and cool urban areas.[46] The ecological base and public estate can be increased in real terms by, for example, creating eco-positive vertical spaces.

Does the process: (1) Compare proposed developments to either 'no development at all' or to net-positive sustainability, rather than merely comparing them to typical development? (2) Avoid the traditional fiction that economic gains can compensate for the escalating costs of nature and resource depletion, since nature ignores economic fictions? (3) Recognize that economic growth is a specious concept and requires a concomitant increase in natural resource stocks and ecological carrying capacity to compensate for their consumption? (4) Consider specific means to protect/increase the habitats, food needs and 'species-area relationships' of rare/endangered species that are being affected by total cumulative development in the region?

12.11 Prioritizes Highest Sustainable Land Use or Highest Economic Use?

EIAs often tacitly accepted the premise of the highest economic use of land, despite the lack of correlation between economic and environmental values.

EIAs sometimes assumed the proposed development was the highest economic use of land and did not examine whether it was the highest ecological use of the site. Development increases property values because it attracts economic activity and increases real estate supply and demand. However, developments that thicken markets are not necessarily the optimal land use. Property values are vulnerable to forces beyond the control of economists or planners, and prices do not correlate with sustainability. For example, the negative impacts of high-value central city developments can be greater than those of low-cost regional developments (due to embodied energy, water, etc.).[47]

RTs sometimes give credits for high-density development per se, even where it does not increase the actual sustainability value of the urban area.

Some RTs give points for site location and landscaping, but do not consider the highest ecological or public use for the site. Locational choices are usually based on private financial considerations. For instance, central locations can be more valuable because of the access to clients and public transport. Yet credits are sometimes awarded for high-density urban infill regardless of possible adverse socio-ecological impacts. That is, a project may get environmental points for locating near a central transport hub to attract more customers or charge higher rents – even though it reduces public spaces and the environmental quality in the area.

PD tools start from the highest ecological use of land, since the life-support system is the basis of the economy, sustainability and survival.

Sustainability outcomes depend more on socio-ecological gains than economics. Further, money accruing from economic growth seldom trickles down to the general public or environment. An environment that provides spaces for environmental and/or public benefits can often support more economic activity than ordinary commercial spaces that create either garish or sterile environments. For example, private patios, balconies or green roofs add economic and aesthetic value but are a poor substitute for public spaces that provide, for example, naturally lit ground level areas, elevated pedestrian networks and/or nature corridors. In PD, the starting point is therefore the 'highest ecological use' of the site.

Does the process: (1) Start from the highest ecological use of a site and then identify suitable economic uses to support the public benefits provided by the development? (2) Maximize both ecological and public space by combining these functions where possible and ensuring adaptability to both changing socio-ecological conditions and advancements in planning knowledge and capacity? (3) Ensure that proposals for urban densification provide evidence that other sustainability goals are not sacrificed in the process, such as environmental quality and adaptability to future change? (4) Ensure commercial/office developments do not receive credits for central locations unless they provide other public and/or ecological benefits?

12.12 Transferability of RTs to Disadvantaged Regions

While RTs provide helpful checklists, few RTs for industrialized nations are applicable to critical social, ecological or economic sustainability challenges in developing nations.

Being geared to wealthier nations, RTs do not always align with local priorities, resources or financial realities in disadvantaged regions. Because they are measurement-driven and have high transaction costs, they can divert resources away from resolving local issues. Many governments have difficulty managing informal settlements, for which RTs are almost irrelevant. Consequently, there has been extensive debate about whether locally grown or imported RTs would save more time and costs. RTs also need to interconnect with different systems of governance. For example, while usually non-profit and industry-led, some are government-owned (e.g. Abu Dhabi).[48] Direct, outcome-oriented planning/design investments might be more useful.

Since responsiveness to unique local characteristics of climates, geography, topography and ecology are central to sustainable design, nation-wide RT rules can be problematic.

Most RTs are designed for the range of climatic conditions that are expected in particular regions (e.g. tropics or deserts). Yet the diurnal temperature range in some areas can exceed the annual temperature variation in others. Even within regions there are unique environmental circumstances. For example: the elevation of settlements greatly affects the weather; fires or hurricanes can be a particular problem; coastal areas need to prepare for sea level rise; and the urban heat island effect in some hot climates can be deadly. RTs allow for little flexibility to address extremes of climate, let alone diverse cultural heritage issues.

Debates about the transferability of RTs to developing nations sometimes overlook whether the development outcomes would adversely affect urban social problems and poverty.

Most generic rules in RTs contemplate high-end offices, elite homes and idyllic suburbs, and do not address critical urban problems in disadvantaged regions. Because buildings last decades, tools built on standard building templates for industrial development could prevent them from leapfrogging to a sustainable model. They may also delay local capacity building in sustainable planning and design. For instance, developers may choose to import assessors with experience in operating the particular tools, rather than training local people. If locals are trained to use imported RTs, they are less likely to use traditional passive design methods that support local traditions.[49]

Even if the weightings of the criteria are customized for developing nations, imported RTs may not address the unique priorities of each country.

Some countries have already created hybrid RTs, usually based on the highly developed UK (BREEAM) or US (LEED) systems.[50] Adapting benchmarks and weightings ostensibly enables developing countries to benefit from 'tested' knowledge and experience.[51] However, few of these concern economic or environmental justice.[52] For example, RTs do not consider how residential project location may affect spatial inequity. Isolated social housing projects at city outskirts cost less to build, but can mean occupants cannot access employment due to the lack of public transport and private car ownership.[53] Conversely, moving the disadvantaged to the inner city could cause separations from friends and relatives.

Since RTs were developed with particular cultures and values in mind, they can stifle regional design traditions that reflect the local cultural heritage.

RTs that are transferred or modified for developing nations may transpose an industrial 'modern' aesthetic that undermines the local culture. Most large residential and office construction norms reflect the International Style, which dishonored many cultural or architectural traditions.[54] RTs that were developed for European, Australian or North American residential neighborhoods would do little to enhance community bonds, regional identity or public spaces in developing nations. In parallel with the 'green agriculture revolution' (1950s), certification schemes may someday be regarded as having contributed to a form of colonization.[55] Alternatively, 'regionalism' in design draws upon local knowledge/customs to respect the region's heritage.[56]

Assuming imported RTs could be modified to suit local environments and cultures, they could nonetheless delay any serious efforts to increase net-positive sustainability.

Technical tools such as RTs, LCA and BIM are being rapidly disseminated. However, in disadvantaged countries, the number of 'certified' projects is still relatively low. Such tools are still generally used for large corporate or government buildings, not residential structures or neighborhoods serving/affecting ordinary people (since lower cost or poorly performing buildings generally ignore RTs). They are not designed to use development to address sustainability issues. Even assuming that imported RTs could be modified to suit local conditions and aspirations, they would still delay the transformation to net-positive sustainability. Hence, the potential of more flexible design review processes should be considered.

Since RTs are oriented toward lifestyles and living standards that characterize wealthier developed nations, a design review process may better serve developing cities/nations.

The LBC (Living Building Council) approach, unlike most RTs, is qualitative and focuses on design.[57] Nonetheless, it is geared more toward elite eco-developments rather than to the socio-economically deprived. An RT for disadvantaged regions would need to be applicable to urban redevelopment schemes and/or eco-retrofitting projects, and create incentives for specific net-positive developments that can directly address regional issues. Although the LBC is closer to a design review process and classic sustainable design values/criteria than more technocratic RTs, custom eco-positive design review processes (eDR) would arguably be better suited for developing nations. This is discussed in the next two chapters.

12.13 Conclusion

This review of RTs has highlighted how they buttress current unsustainable industrial construction practices, materials and technologies, and pay scant attention to socio-ecological issues.

This set of chapters has argued that technocratic reductionist tools can divert the user's attention from sustainability. In comparing EIAs and RTs, it emphasized that RTs fail to consider a building's actual impacts in nature, let alone aim for inter/

intra-generational equity (the original core concepts of sustainability). They only seek improvements upon conventional buildings and do not encourage adaptable, passive, multifunctional or eco-positive design. While gradually broadening their scope to include broader criteria, they do not meet net-positive sustainability standards. This discussion produced a wide set of criteria for developing an eco-positive approach to qualitative and quantitative design and assessment processes.

12.14 Exercises

1. Compare an EIA of a large building conducted a few decades ago with a similar one done recently in the same city. Discuss differences. What conceptual advances have been made?
2. Take one of the 22 questions discussed in this pair of chapters and examine how a representative EIA statement and RT scoresheet deal with the particular issue in detail.
3. Apply an RT to an existing building that has received a rating and assess the building using the same RT yourself – before viewing the documentation. Then compare your score sheet to the official one. Discuss any differences.

Notes

1 Social impact assessment was part of the EIA process, as outlined in Interorganizational Committee on Guidelines and Principles (1994) *Guidelines and Principles for Social Impact Assessment*, US Dept Commerce, Washington, DC, NOAA Tech. Memo. NMFS-F/SPO-16.
2 EIA statements often tended to balance the irreparable harm to the environment against the harm that the developers would feel if the project were rejected. That is, the interests of project stakeholders were often balanced against those of everyone else.
3 Again, this either/or framework in part exists because design was seen as a mere form of decision making (i.e. cost-benefit analysis). See Birkeland, J. (2012) Design Blindness in Sustainable Development: From Closed to Open Systems Design Thinking, *Journal of Urban Design* 17(2), pp. 163–87.
4 When working in design review, I was sometimes asked by developers if the community would oppose the project, in which case they might not bother to propose a development in that location.
5 A project that is rated highly on an RT is sometimes relieved of the usual review/compliance processes.
6 A controversial project can be approved by politicians/authorities regardless of the EIA, but a statement on the decision is necessary.
7 In the 1980s, many planners felt their role was to attract economic growth.
8 See Birkeland, J. (2016) Net Positive Biophilic Urbanism, *Smart and Sustainable Built Environments* 5(1), pp. 9–14.
9 Von Weizsacker, E., Lovins, A. B., and Lovins, L. H. (1997) *Factor 4: Doubling Wealth – Halving Resource Use*, Earthscan, London.
10 E.g. some large green buildings have used multi-story atriums with solar heating/cooling systems to provide fresh air and ventilation combined with insulation and thermal mass.
11 Jobs are lost to imported workers or products are imported from countries where health and safety standards are lower. The PEARL rating tool for Abu Dhabi provides for worker accommodation. Abu Dhabi Urban Planning Council (2010) *The PEARL Building Rating System for Estidama: Design and Construction*. http://estidama.org/PEARL-rating-system-v10/PEARL-building-rating-system.aspx.
12 See Brunckhorst, D. J. (2000) *Bioregional Planning: Resource Management beyond the New Millennium*, Harwood Academic Publishers, Amsterdam; McGinnis, M. (ed.)

(1999) *Bioregionalism*, Routledge, London; Birkeland, J. (2008) *Positive Development*, Earthscan, London, pp. 208–15.
13 Known as the myth of the 'rational decision maker' discussed in Simon, H. A. (1957) *Models of Man Social and Rational: Mathematical Essays on Rational Human Behavior in a Social Setting*, J. Wiley & Sons, New York.
14 Preamble to the National Environmental Policy Act of 1969, 91st United States Congress.
15 This was the prevalent view in planning and planning theory at the time.
16 RTs are developed in consultation with industry so criteria cannot be too challenging.
17 RT points can be ignored if difficult, as points can be gained in other ways. For 'uneven results', again, see Scofield, J. H. (2009) Do LEED-certified Buildings Save Energy? Not Really …, *Energy Build* 41(12), pp. 1386–90.
18 Conditional use approvals can require the mitigation of impacts that an EIA has exposed.
19 The US federal government created the US Institute for Environmental Conflict Resolution in 1998. Environmental conflict resolution often involves finding alternative sites, designs or energy sources.
20 Since EIAs could cause substantial delays, expedited EIA processes were often available for less significant projects (mini-EIAs).
21 Although not the first LCA, a private study by the Coca-Cola Company in 1969 is considered to have set the model for cycle assessment in the United States. www.coca-colacompany.com/stories/reduce.
22 McDonough, W., and Braungart, M. (2002) *Cradle to Cradle: Remaking the Way we Make Things*, North Point Press, New York.
23 Most RTs ignore embodied impacts in buildings because, in the past, operating impacts of buildings were greater, but this is because many pre-completion impacts are excluded by system boundaries and because buildings have been highly inefficient in operation.
24 Most RTs set rules that ignore embodied impacts. The Living Building Council considers embodied impacts, but labels water, energy net-positive if sent across a property line (which does not produce energy or water). Nature, however, can increase in diversity and complexity.
25 Birkeland, *Positive Development*.
26 Buildings are 'the single largest end-user of energy', according to the International Energy Agency: IEA (2012) *World Energy Outlook 2012*, International Energy Agency, Paris. www.oecd-ilibrary.org/energy/world-energy-outlook-2012_weo-2012-en.
27 PEARL awards up to six points for reducing external heat gain with passive measures, because overheating in Abu Dhabi is a major issue.
28 'Zero carbon', 'carbon neutral' and 'carbon positive' buildings usually only refer to operating energy, which is not very difficult if both passive and renewable energy are used. The carbon emitted in construction would usually nullify carbon neutral building operation.
29 Only permanent vegetation supported by a building would contribute. See Renger, C., Birkeland, J., and Midmore, D. (2015) Net Positive Building Carbon Sequestration, *Building Research and Information* 43(1), pp. 11–24.
30 Several politicians have stated that water that reaches the ocean is wasted.
31 Social impacts statements are part of most EIAs, such as the Australian Environmental Protection Act 1994 (EP Act) and the US NEPA of 1969.
32 The assumption is that people will drive less if buildings are closer together, but many RTs tend to assume urban densification equals sustainability.
33 Saunders, C., and Dalziel, P. (2017) Twenty-five Years of Counting for Nothing: Waring's Critique of National Accounts, *Feminist Economics* 23(2), pp. 200–18; Eckersley, R. (1998) *Measuring Progress: Is Life Getting Better?* CSIRO Publishing, Canberra.
34 EIA statements were expected to 'balance' socio-economic benefits against ecological costs, but many put the assessment in an economic context, creating a systemic bias.
35 Social impact assessment has financial costs but these are not taken as seriously as financial impacts which are protected by criminal law.
36 Principles for social impact assessment, part of the initial EIA process, were later defined in more detail (see n. 1 above).
37 Miller, N., Pogue, D., Gough, Q., and Davis, S. (2009) Green Buildings and Productivity, *Journal of Sustainable Real Estate* 1(1), pp. 65–89.

38 Redlich, C. A., Sparer, J., and Cullen, M. R. (1997) Sick-building Syndrome, *The Lancet* 349 (9057), pp. 1013–16.
39 Occupancy is sometimes delayed so the building products could off-gas some of their toxins. See www.greenbuildingsupply.com/Learning-Center/Green-Greenwashing-Chemical-Sensitivities-LC/IAQ-and-Your-Health-A-Deeper-Look-at-VOCs-and-Formaldehyde.
40 Beck, C. M., Geyh, A., and Srinivasan, A., et al. (2003) The Impact of a Building Implosion on Airborne Particulate Matter in an Urban Community, *Journal of the Air and Waste Management Association* 53(10), pp. 1256–64.
41 I have been told this by several different individuals involved in developing different RTs.
42 Birkeland, J., and Schooneveldt, J. (2002) *ACT Sustainability Audit: A Material Flows Analysis of the Residential Sector of Canberra*, Planning and Land Management Authority, Canberra.
43 The market-based solution is for socio-economically deprived villagers to sell coupons or permits to Western hunters to shoot poachers.
44 In some places, fossil fuel use is going down, but the consumption of construction materials is increasing. Kalmykova, Y., Rosado, L., and Patrício, J. (2016) Resource Consumption Drivers and Pathways to Reduction: Economy, Policy and Lifestyle Impact on Material Flows at the National and Urban Scale, *Journal of Cleaner Production* 132, pp. 70–80.
45 Although the contribution of a project to biodiversity seems infinitesimal, it can still be positive. However, the use of a degraded site or the preservation of an undeveloped site does not increase the ecological base beyond pre-settlement or pre-industrial conditions.
46 Renger et al., Net Positive Building Carbon Sequestration.
47 Dispersed development projects can increase transportation impacts, but this depends on the specific project, context and design.
48 PEARL, in Abu Dhabi, is government owned and mandatory for buildings.
49 See Rudofsky, B. (1964) *Architecture Without Architects: A Short Introduction to Non-Pedigreed Architecture*, Museum of Modern Art, New York.
50 E.g. Brazil and Mexico have tools based on LEED, the USA RT (Leadership in Energy and Environmental Design)
51 Shi, Q. (2008) Strategies of Implementing a Green Building Assessment System in Mainland China, *Journal of Sustainable Development* 1(2), pp. 13–16; Todd, J. A., and Geissler, S. (1999) Regional and Cultural Issues in Environmental Performance Assessment for Buildings, *Building Research and Information* 27(4–5), pp. 247–56; Guy, S., and Moore, S. A. (2005) *Sustainable Architectures: Cultures and Natures in Europe and North America*, Spon, New York.
52 Sev, A. (2011) A Comparative Analysis of Building Environmental Assessment Tools and Suggestions for Regional Adaptations, *Civil Engineering and Environmental Systems* 28(3), pp. 231–45.
53 Gibberd, J. (2002) The Sustainable Building Assessment Tool: Assessing How Buildings Can Support Sustainability in Developing Countries, presented at the Built Environment Professions Convention, Johannesburg, South Africa.
54 See Hill, R., Bowen, P., and Opperman, L. (2002) Sustainable Building Assessment Methods in South Africa: An Agenda for Research, presented at the Sustainable Building 2002 Conference (SB'02), Oslo, Norway.
55 See Shiva, V. (1991) *The Violence of the Green Revolution: Third World Agriculture, Ecology, and Politics*, Zed Books, Atlantic Highlands, NJ.
56 Amourgis, S. (ed.) (1999) *Architecture and the Environment*, Pomona State Polytechic University, Pomona, CA.
57 ILFI (International Living Future Institute) (2012) Living Building Challenge 2.1, p. 10. Like other RTs, the LBC lacks transparency about the basis of the criteria. http://living-future.org/lbc/about.

Section G

Eco-Positive Design Review
(A Qualitative Tool)

13 Eco-positive Design Review (Social Issues)

13.1 Review and Preview

Design review processes can go beyond prescriptive RTs that encourage best practice green buildings, to increase sustainable design outcomes consistent with ethics-based standards.

Before RTs were introduced in the 1990s, design review processes were often used, and they still are in many cities and countries. Some lack enforceable criteria,[1] while others have been adopted legislatively by elected officials. The criteria can be subject to differing interpretations. However, they provide a basis for negotiating ways to value add by design. Ideally, design review has transparent, timely, non-arbitrary processes, and can be responsive to differing positions/interests among the community and developer-design teams. If there are disagreements, the design panels or council staff can help to find design alternatives. Failing that, an appeal process is often available.

The eDR (eco-positive design review process) is a collaborative, flexible, design-based approach that considers the PD Test and either supplements or replaces RTs.

Traditional design review focused on aesthetic qualities or nuisances like congestion, and often occurred after a design was complete. The eDR is not retrospective and instead occurs at the preliminary design stage.[2] It emphasizes collaborative design and community engagement, and aims to facilitate feedback and dialogue among experts, assessors and community members. It uses questions based on PD criteria,[3] that ideally will guide design research-reasoning efforts toward accomplishing net-positive gains. Design teams can use it in developing design briefs (objectives), or for self-assessment. The eDR process could also be adopted by councils or others as a formal design review process.

Design review criteria can set higher standards than RTs that are restricted by numbers, and the eDR uses questions to compel deeper thinking.

In developing a project review process or its design criteria, planners often start with a relatively blank slate and conduct local workshops or community consultation. There is usually little feedback/critique after that stage. Any design review process should allow citizens to critique the final process and substance in community workshops. However, the outcomes may be filtered through the perspective of local government planners that is marinated in current planning models/trends. To avoid this problem, the eDR asks questions that often require the design team to engage with the local community.[4] The questions for consideration here are based on PD criteria.

The council staff can use the eDR as a means for leveraging public benefits, rather than just for assessing and approving completed proposals.
In the eDR process, the project design team documents its design strategies. Development review staff then work with developers, and any community opponents, for design improvements or, failing that, set conditional use approval criteria.[5] As seen earlier, RTs avoid ethical issues that have not traditionally been measured (e.g. increasing social equity), or are difficult to measure (e.g. improving human-nature relationships). By the time socio-ecological or ethical issues raised by the development are measurable, it is too late to redesign. Transparent reasoning and evidentiary sources, that are usually omitted from RTs and other assessment processes, should enable wider sustainability gains.

Frontloading design, or investing more time and effort in the preliminary design stage, unlike post-design assessment, can enable more benefits at less cost.
Investments in projects are often based on land-use decisions without consideration of design. Therefore, the pre-design decisions determine site planning and infrastructure, which largely determines the environmental/economic costs of development before serious design work begins. Following the design, development approval officers assess code compliance, while RT assessors verify measurements. The eDR would instead shift the burden of proof from assessors to the project proponents. Whereas RTs treat design as a process to aid decision making, the eDR treats decision making as a design process. The design team must explain or provide evidence for how the design achieves PD standards.

The eDR questions relate to whole-systems issues and set higher standards than familiar green building principles (which are deemed incorporated in PD anyway).
The eDR questions are meant to shift the focus from beyond stating conventional design guidelines and setting numerical thresholds/targets to achieving net improvements. The questions aim to push boundaries. Basic sustainable design principles are well known so they are presumed to be incorporated within net-positive criteria.[6] Given practical and political realities, design teams that cannot meet the standards would be allowed to show that net-positive impacts were currently infeasible, even if alternative designs, functions and/or sites were used (as verified by independent experts if necessary). Offsetting would then over-compensate for unavoidable impacts with offsite public benefits, to the extent necessary.[7]

This sample eDR concerns residential construction in socio-economically deprived regions and could be a first step in developing a localized design review process.
An eDR process can easily be adapted to the unique priorities of developing nations, as it uses questions to target local problem areas in relation to sustainability. The development of an eDR would be based on on-ground biological and social research. It would include public workshops and criteria that are adopted by local governments after community feedback and probably formal hearings. This sample

eDR was based on Bogota, and done in collaboration with an architect raised there, María Alejandra García Patino. Local socio-political conditions changed so rapidly that the idea was not pursued, but it serves as a generic example.

13.2 Basic Criteria for an eDR

Design-based: An eDR should emphasize an investigative orientation yet avoid bean accounting activity that segregates building elements or appears more scientific than it is. Because each site and development is unique, the eDR is intended to shift the design process toward reasoning and relational thinking,[8] and away from tick-box approaches that focus the mind on numerical rules. This is still necessary because many mainstream planners and architects are not yet open to considering the fundamental sustainability issues that lie at the heart of urban design. Sustainable design requires ongoing learning through the integration of research, science and design. Because design teams record the research/strategies undertaken to meet local needs, opportunities and outcomes in the eDR, any baseless claim of expert knowledge should be apparent.

An approach that requires investigation and reasoning can help to uncover opportunities for positive innovations, whereas numerical rules tend to favor conventional design.

Numerical indicators or criteria often extract single factors from complex phenomena to create simple standardized rules or thresholds.[9] Therefore, reductionist measures can often be misleading. For instance, statistics indicating a growth of employment levels can obscure the growing disparities of income.[10] In RTs, measurements like the 'percentage of recycled to total water usage' can overlook a project's wasteful baseline water usage. Similarly, more families or 'housing units per square kilometer' can actually mean a lack of adaptability, life quality and amenity. The eDR changes the focus from scoring to multiplying benefits and expanding opportunities for positive socio-ecological gains by design.

Contextual: Since the built environment has systemic impacts, an eDR should include relevant offsite and regional considerations, such as the effects on urban-rural equity.

All aspects of a development affect sustainability, as environments influence human psychological/physiological health as well as environmental conditions.[11] A building-centered orientation distracts attention from regional and wider social issues, and their mutual relationships with urban development. Building occupants and neighbors are not only affected personally and physically by buildings but also by their surrounding developments/environments. Development patterns in the surrounding vicinity can have more impact on local life quality than a proposed project from, for example, excessive pollution, congestion and noise.[12] The eDR therefore requires design teams to consider the reciprocal relation of buildings to their immediate and regional surroundings.

An eDR can use SMT analyses as mind-mapping exercises to help identify regional-scale issues/deficits, or to expose opportunities that the design can exploit.

Although RTs can affect who wins or loses over time, they side-step most ethical issues (e.g. environmental justice). The eDR intends to stimulate and guide design research to avoid win-lose outcomes or trade-offs between financial and social criteria. SMT analyses [Chapters 7–8] are referenced in the sample eDR below. These analyses are especially relevant to developing regions as some consider wealth transfers from public to private interests, poor to wealthy and future to present generations over time.[13] While SMT analyses aim to stimulate design (problem-solving and opportunity-creating), they can eventually be examined quantitatively using new digital mapping tools.[14]

Offsetting: Net-positive offsetting can be delivered in economic-deprived villages by, for example, using inexpensive natural systems that demonstrably improve local environmental and/or socio-economic conditions.

Usually, RTs target either efficiency or restorative/remedial outcomes that generally save money. Many net-positive offsets do not require extra money, time or effort – just a paradigm shift in design. Passive design and natural systems are applicable to disadvantaged regions because they are generally inexpensive and use nature (e.g. bacteria, fungi, trees) without depleting resources or ecosystems. Net-positive offsets can be constructed at a district level to increase efficiency and to avoid inequalities through, for example, living machines or natural water purification systems [Chapters 5–6].[15] The eDR process should encourage creative solutions that provide for basic needs where most needed.

Offsite ecological restoration projects can sometimes over-compensate for negative impacts, but onsite impacts should be deducted and, added together, should have net-positive impacts.

Where a project that has a sound public purpose and developers/designers cannot find a better site or alternative project to correct for acceptable levels of damage, net-positive offsetting may be justifiable. This does not mean granting dispensations for simply undertaking positive actions elsewhere. Typically, offsetting schemes have failed to compensate for total project impacts, as discussed earlier [Chapter 6]. One RT allows compensation for greenfield development by retrofitting other buildings (which can be subcontracted to specialist companies). However, demolition impacts on brownfield sites are also harmful. Ideally, both the retrofit and new project, in combination, should achieve an eco-positive impact.[16]

Bottom-up: The eDR should respect community views/values through participatory engagement, yet also be adaptable to changing demographics, needs, priorities and local cultures over time.

Although some RTs encourage activities to solicit community involvement/support, this does not ensure that input is taken seriously. Once a basic design is conceived and plans are drawn, they seldom change significantly in response to suggestions, due to the extra time, energy, resources and money required. Therefore, many eDR questions aim to require the participation of local communities from the beginning, and discourage outsourcing to consultants who are less accountable. Adaptable design would theoretically enable developments to be modified later to correct any serious breaches or shortcomings, as well as enabling future changes to meet changing socio-economic and ecological conditions.

Most tools hinder lay citizens in challenging the basis of the numerical prescriptions and specific ratings, let alone in suggesting improvements to designs.

The eDR should be an open process that encourages constructive input and challenges to the criteria themselves – as opposed to just after-the-fact consultation or marketing presentations about the project. By being open to inspection, the eDR process recognizes that everyone (citizens, experts, planning staff, etc.) has standing to challenge processes and decisions concerning sustainability. The preliminary design process should also be open to consideration of basic alternatives, such as different sites or even building functions. The risk of abuse of the system would be no greater. Genuine engagement would reduce costly objection processes that sometimes end up in court.

Verification: *The eDR could require that projects be retrofitted in cases where developments fail to meet agreed post-occupancy evaluation criteria, backed by a warranty.*

Many buildings are fast-tracked because they are certified by an RT scheme, yet do not perform as expected. Some RTs have separate, but optional, post-occupancy evaluation (POE) processes to ensure that projects perform according to their ratings. POEs assess building performance in terms of occupant satisfaction and/or environmental impacts, usually after a year of operation. The consequence for not meeting performance targets, however, is often merely 'not getting another certificate'. The eDR process could include a warranty so, if building performance were unsatisfactory, it would be corrected.[17] Again, adaptable design would facilitate post-construction modifications as necessary to meet performance guarantees.

The eDR is a qualitative tool that ideally would be supplemented, or eventually replaced, by a quantitative net-positive planning/design tool (e.g. PD STARfish).

While the eDR is qualitative, this does not prohibit the selection and use of verification measures by governments for any criteria. However, the eDR could gradually be supplanted by more quantitative versions, such as the PD STARfish tool [Chapters 15–16]. Meanwhile, the eDR can be a rapid means to infuse development control systems with a creative design ethos. The aim is capacity building and education in sustainable design, to leapfrog the traditional industrial building model that locked in many sustainability problems. Ultimately, sustainability will require new frameworks of eco-governance: the redesign of planning, urban design and development control systems [Chapters 9–10].[18]

Social criteria for an eDR: *A draft eDR would give local communities an opportunity to define the positive qualities of the unique conditions and cultures in their bioregion.*

This process aims to identify priority ecological/social problems that can be addressed by design interventions, and attract development based on its particular contribution to community needs, not just the profit of distant investors. The idea is for cities/regions to set criteria and then recruit projects that address the local priorities (instead of economic growth regardless of consequences). In this example, the social and ecological issues are separated only for organizational purposes. Financial performance is considered to the extent that it affects social equity or ecological conditions and is subsumed under social issues. SMT analyses relevant to the question are noted.

13.3 Health, Safety and Security

13.3.1 How Will Security and Means of Survival Be Built In?

Changes to the built environment in disadvantaged nations could remedy many causes of environmental crises, social strife and mass migration at low cost.

Dramatic increases in environmental refugees have been predicted, and there may be around 50 million by 2050.[19] Many regions are losing the ability to support their populations. Most would agree that fixing environmental crises in disadvantaged countries would be less costly and disruptive than mass migrations. However, it is still presumed that this requires substantial foreign aid, instead of building in provisions for basic needs. For example, weak structures can be reinforced with scaffolding for earthquake proofing, vegetable production and rainwater treatment/storage.

Urban/building form needs to include more consideration of resource security and self-sufficiency (e.g. direct access to food, water and air) in congested areas.

High density in socio-economically deprived districts can reduce transport distances, but does not necessarily facilitate public transport, as it increases the costs of new infrastructure and ongoing repairs and renovations.[20] It also limits the potential for more resource autonomy, since there is little room for urban farming. In already dense cities, however, aging exterior materials can gradually be replaced with surfaces composed of healthy, renewable materials that absorb urban pollution and provide thermal and noise insulation and other positive functions.

13.3.2 How Will Adaptability to Disasters/Demographic Change Be Provided?

Building and infrastructure that work with nature to prevent/reduce flood impacts are more reliable than 'engineered barriers' and provide more lasting environmental security/safety.

Flooding incidents are increasing worldwide,[21] and urban growth has gradually increased the risks of urban floods. The old approach, large engineering barriers, is prone to serious damage in earthquakes, and they have often exacerbated the damage of large floods.[22] One RT simply does not certify development on 100-year flood plains, but this affects few projects.[23] Due to both land-use and climate change, 100-year flood plains are no longer safe. Risks of future floods are best predicted by tracking past bioregional changes. (See RA analysis.)

Flexible planning and management to accommodate individual cases does not substitute for flexible development that keeps pace with changing demographic and climatic conditions.

Design for adaptability to changing social conditions is still rare.[24] If infrastructure and buildings are not capable of expansion, contraction or relocation, population increases/declines can lead to wasted space and materials, if not demolition. When the elderly require assisted living or high care, they sometimes need to move far from families/friends due to inflexible and uniform design, causing expense, stress and depression. Converting disused buildings into shelters for the elderly, battered women or even the homeless is one offsetting option.

13.3.3 How Will Resource Autonomy Be Increased to Provide Natural Security?

Resource-autonomous design, at appropriate domestic or neighborhood scales, can provide backup energy, food, clean air and water during economic, social or environmental crises.

To increase resource autonomy, some RTs set percentages for onsite electricity generation or water reuse systems.[25] However, the lack of distributed and multiple sources of provisions make it difficult to survive a crisis or enable people to aid their neighbors. That is, systems that provide water treatment, electricity, sewerage, food and other essentials, may be more effectively/efficiently delivered at the house, block or neighborhood level, depending on local conditions. The eDR should explore the most efficient scale for different services.

Food security is increased by dispersed urban gardens, which can also create distributed enclaves for threatened medicinal plants, native flora and small fauna.

Community food gardens can promote community bonds and cooperation, biophilic benefits and local food security. The percentage of the total area to be allocated to urban food production should be assessed, although feasibility depends on the available space (vertical and horizontal).[26] Building-integrated ecosystems can protect medicinal and/or income-generating plants, while providing diverse living seed banks to safeguard essential resources. To alleviate malnutrition in poorer neighborhoods, appropriate plant species that are suited for wall or window planter boxes should be considered. (See RS analysis.)

13.3.4 How Is 'Crime Prevention by Design' Provided For?

Crime reduction and physical security may best be achieved by design strategies that contribute to community building, rather than costly defensive expenditures alone.

For security, some RTs suggest safe areas, fences or 'compliance with local security provisions'. One RT suggests safe access to school pick-up locations.[27] This alters the behavior of potential victims, but does not tackle the underlying causes that are affected by built-environment design. These are only 'defensive' forms of design. 'Urban acupuncture' is a positive approach that provides strategically located public facilities (e.g. libraries, playgrounds and health centers) in deprived or high-crime areas.[28] This improves social cohesiveness, surveillance and security.

Crime prevention by design need not lead to more sterile environments, and could partially replace the process of chasing criminals after the fact.

Families that feel unsafe sometimes leave neighborhoods when they can. This weakens community bonds and increases crime.[29] One RT focuses on secure access to buildings through well-lit footpaths and cycle lanes.[30] An old approach to design for crime reduction was to remove plants as they were deemed hiding places for criminals. These are defensive design approaches. The eDR should consider 'crime prevention by design'.[31] For example, garden areas could work like the 'bait cars' that police use to catch thieves.[32]

13.4 Sustainability Education and Social Change

13.4.1 How Will People Be Motivated to Make Neighborhood Improvements?

Engaging communities in cooperative neighborhood improvement programs can be a more practical and realistic means of leveraging positive change than targeting individual homes.

Some RTs encourage 'open houses' to inspire property owners and increase consumer demand for greener homes. Obviously, these exemplars are out of the reach of most. In contrast, a community in Manila systematically created jobs from waste recycling programs and constructed community facilities to address local poverty, health and education issues.[33] In many poorer areas, residential buildings have a high percentage of renters.[34] Hence, making residential/neighborhood retrofitting programs more attainable to landlords could prove more useful than large-scale urban renewal.

Pollution, a critical issue in many developing cities, requires comprehensive public measures to clean existing environments, as well as reduce additional pollution sources.

In developing nations, urban pollution is a priority health issue. Solid fuels used in cooking and poor construction materials in homes are major causes of illness. However, individual building design and equipment does little to address external air pollution caused by other buildings. For example, diesel-power buses can cancel out the improvements made in individual buildings. The eDR should consider exterior solutions, such as materials/vegetation that filter pollution,[35] and indoor solutions such as portable living walls that renters can install.[36]

13.4.2 How Will the Community Become More Aware of Urban Design?

Bottom-up participation in design is likely to have more positive outcomes in supporting actions for community education, empowerment and action than top-down consultation.

Analyses regarding social and cultural aspects are sometimes undertaken for social housing projects but, in the end, budgets only allow for minimal code compliance.[37] Some RTs give credits for running a 'charrette' (participatory design),[38] hosting a community meeting, or obtaining community endorsement for a proposal. The latter two can often be perfunctory public relations or disingenuous marketing exercises. The eDR can avoid manipulation of the local community by setting out how the final design reflects input from participatory design processes.[39]

Collaborative, participatory design should be structured to reduce indirect costs associated with miscommunication and conflicting agendas that can sometimes occur in local politics.

Community collaboration and participation have always been central tenants of sustainable building design. Construction projects are socially complex, so the integration of diverse stakeholders throughout the design process can help to avoid/resolve conflicting cultural values or competing objectives before any disputes can occur. Nonetheless, there are ever-present risks of distorted communication and accidental exclusion, even without any hidden agendas.[40] The eDR should therefore apply (at least aspects of) the PD SMARTmode planning process, which aims to avoid common communication problems.[41]

13.4.3 How Will Occupants Be Trained in Building Operation and Performance?

Commissioning processes and operating manuals may improve building management, which greatly affects building performance, but design should make responsible living choices largely automatic.

When and if impact assessment capacity improves and passive solar design is maximized, the embodied energy of buildings will be more crucial than operating energy.[42] Some RTs simply give credits for providing instruction manuals for building managers/occupants about equipment, appliances and recycling methods.[43] Nonetheless, people may still, for example, leave doors open in winter. Design should make buildings relatively 'fool proof'. An eDR should include 'commissioning' processes to check equipment/systems performance after construction, as this also greatly affects operational performance.[44]

Metering is useful for well-off individuals who want to save money, but lack of energy usage in some poorer neighborhoods also indicates problems.

Meters help to show occupants how to save money by pinpointing poorly functioning systems.[45] Some RTs encourage smart meters connected to aggregation centers and give credits for sub-metering and monitoring,[46] but these are seldom available in unauthorized properties or disadvantaged communities. A prior step should be to determine which neighborhoods/homes could use public support for retrofitting programs, since these pay for themselves over time. The eDR should consider usage in relation to need, as some energy uses are inherently wasteful.[47]

13.4.4 How Will Awareness and Adoption of Green Technologies Be Promoted?

The 'legibility' of green technologies and passive design can be educational and inspire pride by celebrating the achievements of each neighborhood or building.

Many renovations of heritage buildings have accentuated elements that reflect their history and evolution over time. Along these lines, buildings that display their environmental features can increase the ecological knowledge and literacy of building users. Visual indicators of sustainable performance in buildings, such as reductions in waste, water or energy usage, can encourage more responsible behavior.[48] At the community level, public displays of local neighborhood performance can encourage improvements and create a challenge along the lines of 'tidy town' competitions.[49]

Public tours of green buildings are inspirational, but the exposure of errors and/or critical analyses might be more informative to designers and owner-builders.

RTs promote building companies with green credentials and provide idealized case studies. However, constructive critiques of projects would also be of educational value to designers. Developers of future projects might learn more by avoiding others' mistakes. If the eDR publishes learnings, they would gain respect, and others could avoid repeating mistakes. Similarly, case studies that explain how the RT worked out what it does/does not assess (not just the score), would enable others to get more benefit from the RT.

13.5 Social Needs (Vvalues, Justice, Fairness, Etc.)

13.5.1 How Will the Project Avoid Exclusionary Practices?

Integrated development, assuming good design, can counteract the effects of past real estate practices and exclusionary zoning that have divided residents by status.

The current economic paradigm created the ethical/environmental problems that now demand physical solutions. Class divisions and social segregation perpetuate the lack of equity, opportunity and life quality among the economically disadvantaged. RTs perpetuate these problems by omission. Physical change therefore requires better sustainable urban planning, design and architecture. Now that developers know that good design is compatible with profitability, urban design can shift the emphasis to creating public benefits and opportunities, such as health, heritage value,[50] social equity and recreation.

The integration of mixed uses and nature into cities could quickly ameliorate some of the physical impacts caused by segregation and wealth disparities.

Mixed-use urban development (e.g. ground-level commerce, offices above and residential complexes on top) can reduce social and functional segregation or its effects.[51] At the larger scale, major residential developments can integrate cultural, commercial and recreational functions to draw in the wider community, reduce need for transport, counteract economic segregation and increase distributive justice. Similarly, with improvements in research capabilities, many community gardens have proven to have community-wide social and health benefits,[52] and mitigate the life-quality deficits of the underprivileged.

13.5.2 How Will Social and Cultural Needs/Values Be Identified and Supported?

Sustainable design can preserve historically and culturally significant landscapes that make a place meaningful to inhabitants without sacrificing any practical or economic imperatives.

Heritage is a key element in shaping or enhancing regional identity and sense of place.[53] Although cultural landscapes and heritage buildings contribute to community building, identity and meaning, however, few RTs really address historic preservation and provide for interpretation.[54] By building on unique local/regional qualities, developments that respect heritage can increase tourist income and employment opportunities in cities, towns and rural areas. The eDR should examine the cultural and ecological heritage of the area as potential levers of social sustainability.

Regionalism or place-sensitive design can be helpful in achieving environmental and cultural aims, but can also meet the particular needs of disadvantaged communities.

Vernacular architecture evolved through knowledge of climatic conditions, local species, natural resources and used passive solar design. It almost invariably reflects the bioregion, both aesthetically and pragmatically.[55] In contrast, modernist architecture celebrated the machine at the expense of unique cultural heritage and identity. Recognizing emblematic design elements and local features that respect and complement this heritage can be assisted by local community participation in design. The eDR process should ensure the design references the cultural heritage that the community values.[56]

13.5.3 How Will Social Deficits and Spatial Inequities Be Addressed?

Sustainable design is always contextual, or responsive to the surrounding conditions, but it has seldom actively addressed social deficits in the surrounding areas.

Some RTs aim to operate beyond the individual building scale.[57] One recommends an urban site assessment to ensure that the development is sensitive to its urban context.[58] However, RTs do not really include environmental/social justice issues. Major residential projects could address local sustainability issues that lie beyond site boundaries, rather than relying on some kind of trickle-down effect. Simply providing social amenities such as mini-parks and public open spaces in disadvantaged areas can reduce some impacts of segregation and poverty.[59]

A project should consider how it compensates or mitigates resource transfers from the rural to urban economy and/or from poor to rich neighborhoods.

The concentration and privatization of land and resources is associated with poor resource distribution and cumulative resource scarcity. This is one of the reasons that sustainability will require an increase in nature to compensate for the impacts of past, irreversible actions. Since virtually all biophysical development, even eco-retrofitting, can limit future land use and development options, net-positive offsetting is essential. Offsetting by design can counteract the impacts of past unilateral resource flows in ways that also do not disadvantage developers.[60] (See RT Analysis.)

13.5.4 How Will Impediments to Social Advancement Be Addressed?

Low car ownership in disadvantaged regions could assist in the development of sustainable transport systems, but some RTs indirectly promote private car ownership.

There are places in third-world cities that have the advantage of not yet being car-dominated.[61] Yet some RTs give points for using low-emitting or electric vehicles.[62] The transfer of such car-oriented provisions can work against public transport initiatives, including cycling, jogging and skating paths. With more public transport, roads in some disadvantaged inner-city areas could be converted to multifunctional social/recreational uses like sports hardtops, pop-up markets or wheel-chair gardens.[63] This could increase social cohesion and even security through public surveillance.

Residential developments, even if relatively car free, are often exclusionary and, in some cases, can reinforce social segregation and reduce overall social sustainability.

Road travel can be difficult for the elderly and/or poor. Some RTs call for 'car-free living' through mixed-use development, reward projects near central transport hubs which increase customers[64] or give credit for projects within walking distance of basic services.[65] These may coincidentally favor residences for the upper class, such as gated communities, where homes are accessed by golf carts. Also, access to public transport and commercial services sometimes receives credits for 'design', even though the location is for financial reasons. (See ID analysis.)

13.6 Space for Changing Needs

13.6.1 How Will Flexible Interior-Exterior Spaces Be Provided?

Residential projects should respond to the needs of extended families, including changing requirements as people age, and the provision of semi-private open space.

In many traditional cultures in disadvantaged regions/districts, the elderly are looked after by extended families, and many elderly wish to remain where they know people and raised families. Few RTs consider adaptable design to meet the changing needs of families over time,[66] or acknowledge the need for space for extended families, semi-private outdoor areas, room for disabled and elderly 'flats' or income-generating rental units. Instead, high-rise cupboards for individuals/couples/students are growing, which are intended to meet 'affordability' goals more profitably.

The ongoing conversion of public space to commercial uses means many social activities are on private business property, which limits future community-building opportunities.

Urban space is often regarded as 'empty' if not an invitation for infill development. The costs of public open space can be mitigated by multifunctional design and commercial uses. However, commercial spaces, including the exterior spaces they enclose, are primarily designed to encourage spending and can limit casual community activity and socialization. Similarly, the large (ostentatious) properties of movie stars, financiers and dictators have huge per capita consumption of spatial and material resources. The eDR should consider accessible open space/person.

13.6.2 How Will Social Interaction and Civic Engagement Be Increased?

Public facilities in disadvantaged areas for children or elderly needing special care can reduce total time, money and burdens on the working poor.

Disadvantaged areas usually lack public facilities for elderly family members or children that make it convenient for their care-givers to find work outside the home. Similarly, social facilities and community meeting spaces can reduce social isolation, and stimulate community, social or recreational activities – at little net cost.[67] Such facilities can also produce electricity, food or collect/treat rainwater for the surrounding community.[68] By operating at different times and evening hours they can create part-time jobs and more safety and security.

Creating an identifiable, safe and active community domain, supported by town council activities, can contribute to building more mutually supportive and resilient communities.

Several RTs encourage an active public realm in residential areas to instill the sense of community or belonging and placemaking. These are considered key qualities of healthy communities.[69] Appropriately designed spaces for social gatherings mean neighbors get to know each other, which improves security and can enable mutual support systems. However, such activities should be built in from the project beginning. The eDR process should explore ways to encourage facilitate local councils or non-government organizations to coordinate activities in collaboration with developers/owners.

13.6.3 How Will Accessibility for the Young, Elderly and/or Disabled Be Provided?

Needs of disabled citizens have not been adequately considered in most RTs, as social sustainability criteria are usually generic or geared toward stereotypes.

'Inclusive design' has generally focused on physical access issues (e.g. ramps).[70] Access for children, disabled and elderly (let alone other species)[71] is seldom designed for in underprivileged regions, in the absence of specific legal requirements.[72] For example, the elderly often lack seating near playgrounds when minding grandchildren. People with special needs are silent development stakeholders that should be included in eDR design workshops. For example, people using wheelchairs have different needs and lifestyles, and experience spaces from a different perspective.

The plan should accommodate varying family sizes, student groups or extended families, so that people can choose to live with whom they please.

More than most, disadvantaged groups must adapt to urban environments that are shaped by economic forces rather than human needs. Student groups frequently squeeze into shared apartments in high-rise buildings that can be far from part-time employment opportunities. The floor plans of residential buildings could be designed to enable modifying the number of bedrooms and/or to create duplexes (and change them back again later). Offsetting could help fund small distributed retirement homes so the elderly can stay in their communities. (See ID analysis.)

13.6.4 How Will the Spatial Arrangements Increase Socialization?

Since physical barriers around private open spaces can impede a more active street life, they should be reconceived for more flexibility and functionality.

Fences and high walls are common in underprivileged areas in developing cities.[73] They may increase seclusion, inaccessibility and lack of interaction with neighbors, but may also provide shading for outdoor living which is increasingly important in urban areas.[74] Some RTs give credits for private outdoor spaces, which may not always be feasible in over-crowded districts.[75] Where barriers are necessary, they could be designed to be openable, convertible and to serve additional functions such as vertical gardens, food production and seating.[76]

The potential multiple functions of public open spaces should be optimized to better serve the general public and occupants of affordable residential developments.

Some cities have been selling off open spaces, parks and golf courses, because they are costly to maintain. However, the value of green space is now becoming appreciated.[77] Multifunctional landscaping using passive design features can reduce operational and maintenance costs. For example, water can be lifted up into water towers by playground equipment that also serves as elevated observation/surveillance points.[78] Improvements to public spaces can be subsidized through small business activities that provide community benefits as well as local jobs. (See NS analysis.)

13.7 Economic Equity, Opportunity or Affordability

13.7.1 How Will Affordable Housing Be Distributed?

Housing programs that require affordable units in new residential developments do not usually include enough units to keep pace with growing housing demand.

Policy debates regarding affordable housing often occur within a budgetary context, rather than a design framework. Sometimes councils negotiate with developers to include a percentage of affordable units. Meanwhile, people may be displaced during construction or subsequent gentrification. Thus, the beneficiaries of the affordable units are not necessarily those that were uprooted by the development. The eDR should therefore examine various means to fund appropriately distributed affordable housing projects or units (e.g. a portion of stamp duty on purchasing expensive homes).[79]

Residential projects are often located in central areas, when housing in geographically segregated poorer areas outside central cities can sometimes be more beneficial.

Some RTs encourage affordable housing (e.g. 'fifteen per cent of housing units must meet an affordable housing standard').[80] Such provisions may not encourage homes in locations where need is greatest. The poor that live at the urban periphery may not necessarily benefit, and not everyone wants to move.[81] Subsidized housing in central areas does not necessarily reduce the isolation or insecurity of residents. Given that location is not a settled issue, diversity and distribution in affordable housing may be the safest option.

13.7.2 How Will Opportunities for Affordable Housing Be Increased?

Multi-residential projects with affordable units are replacing some low-density housing but, without environmental amenities, this growth pattern could continue to incur local opposition.

Urban communities are still often segregated by status and wealth, and affordable multi-residential housing remains scarce in greener neighborhoods. Since most inexpensive housing projects lack adequate public infrastructure and public space, new affordable housing projects located in middle-class areas have sometimes had negative local social and environmental impacts on neighbors. If combined with substantial green space, mixed uses and public amenities, however, lower-cost housing units might meet with less local resistance, because they would contribute environmental quality to the neighborhood.

Affordable housing is often based on the sale price instead of the operating costs that the owners or tenants pay (energy, water, maintenance).

Most models for increasing affordability create financial incentives, but not incentives for sustainability outcomes. Lower operating costs (e.g. through insulation, food production, lower maintenance, passive solar design) are often sacrificed after in-principle approval to reduce construction costs. Also, residential projects often reduce upfront costs by eliminating spaces rather than increasing the uses of those spaces. Simultaneously, interior space-saving concepts are overlooked, such as beds and tables that fold into walls or ceilings, sleeping lofts or food-producing greenhouse balconies.

13.7.3 How Will Offsetting Mechanisms Assist Poorer Communities?

Design that gives back more to the community and nature than it takes can benefit developers beyond providing a 'social license' to build.

As discussed earlier, councils sometimes persuade developers to contribute to public facilities to offset the public costs of developments such as infrastructure or, conversely, development bonuses are sometimes provided for public benefits. Developer contributions seldom cover the full public costs of the project. Offsite social contributions in exchange for exemptions or bonuses in wealthier urban neighborhoods (that do no harm) could fund physical improvements in disadvantaged or priority areas. The eDR allows for full-cost accounting or transparent and consistent assessment.

Development in disadvantaged areas should not receive credits and offsets if public health improvements or other sustainability goals are not guaranteed by contract.

Social costs have accumulated due to the past lack of investment in quality rental properties. Being voluntary and rarely used by landlords, RTs exempt most buildings and especially most absentee landlords from making improvements. Similar problems apply to development where units are owned by occupants but corporate bodies must be persuaded to cooperate. If local needs in underprivileged areas are established by planners, then health or safety actions that benefit rental properties can receive more credits or otherwise be incentivized.

13.7.4 How Will Full-Cost Accounting for the Project Be Undertaken?

Full-cost accounting methods are advancing, but are not yet adequately integrated into processes and strategies of city and regional planners and urban designers.

Full-cost or sustainability accounting emerged in the 1970s, and many such tools have been developed over the years, often sponsored by major international organizations such as the United Nations and the OECD.[82] Although full-cost accounting in development was mandated in the USA for government decisions,[83] views about what constitutes full accounting are still largely defined by economists.[84] Like GPI (genuine progress indicators) the measurables are not very relevant to the built environment as economics has been seen as the key determinant of life quality

302 Decision Making and Assessment

[Chapter 10]. Further, some feel that accountancy tools are designed more for obfuscation than for communication.

BIM tools will make measuring materials and energy in construction on a lifecycle basis easier but, thus far, they include few sustainability issues.

Building Information Modeling (BIM) is a digital representation of a building that allows for information sharing among stakeholders throughout the design/operation of the building. Each object in the drawing has associated information. Thus, for example, material quantities can be calculated automatically. If an object on a drawing is changed, related features also change. A new version of BIM (BIM 6D) purports to be about sustainability, but only concerns energy. LCA data can be taken automatically from 3D drawings for real-time assessment of alternatives.[85] As yet, however, it only addresses material issues (pollution, carbon, health, etc.), not ecological and ethical issues.

13.8 Safer and Healthier Jobs

13.8.1 How Will Productive Jobs Be Created?

Rather than moving people to jobs that technology will soon eliminate, technology could be used to create employment in or near affordable housing.

Mixed-use urban development has tended to presume people could and would move closer to employment opportunities – even though jobs are becoming far less permanent. Moving the poor may not increase their employment prospects in the long term. However, mobile phones and new digital technologies are creating and distributing jobs geographically. For example, India is rapidly advancing in digital capacity.[86] Hence job training programs may be better value. The eDR should therefore emphasize ethical project/product purposes, not just promised jobs.

The built environment can be directed more at creating ongoing employment (not just construction jobs), rather than leaving this to separate government initiatives.

Many argue that RTs should pay more consideration to economics, but do not suggest that developments need to play a larger role in supporting a diversified local economy, let alone solving local economic problems or creating ongoing jobs. However, in Curitiba, urban acupuncture reportedly reduced crime rates, increased social cohesion and, in turn, buoyed local businesses and employment.[87] An economic and social needs analysis should, ideally, be provided by relevant government social services and/or planning departments for each urban area.

13.8.2 How Will Construction Workers and Occupants Benefit?

The rights of migrant workers and the effects of migration on regional inequities/deficits need attention, both from where workers originate and where they arrive.

Some RTs mention the welfare of migrant labor.[88] However, when large construction projects import cheap labor, it causes dislocation in their home and destination regions during and after construction. For example, immigrant workers can disrupt housing demand where they come from, work or resettle. Similarly, while some RTs may address regional differences and priorities, they do not deal with inequities between regions caused by major developments.[89] Therefore, the eDR should consider the social and environmental impacts of migrating construction workers. (See BA analysis.)

Employment opportunities in new/retrofitted residential projects in poorer districts of cities could be aided by income-generating spaces, in combination with strategic training programs.

Affordable residential developments can provide spaces for on-site income-generating activities, such as small business incubators, communal workshop spaces, job-creation activities for those that are otherwise not easily employable, spaces serving different uses at different times, rooms that open to the outside for selling products, neighborhood recycling centers, community orchards and so forth.[90] The property managers could also provide training programs for residents that build sought-after skills that are relevant to local/regional needs through, for example, partnerships with local councils.

13.8.3 How Will Fair and Safe Labor Practices Be Implemented?

Worker health/safety standards, including unique needs of migrant labor (or slavery in the supply chain), should be addressed in relation to particular projects/places.

Many people in the construction industry that migrate from the countryside are not prepared or trained. Health and safety conditions on construction sites are often below standard in developing nations.[91] In some places, construction accidents and the abuse of foreign workers have been unacceptably high.[92] At this scale of problem, regulation is essential, and should not be left to RTs.[93] While codes can set minimum standards, the eDR can go further to ensure safety measures at the specific construction sites. (See EI analysis.)

Labor practices should include capacity building in sustainable practices (not just code compliance), to improve the overall health and wellbeing of construction workers.

Few RTs set standards beyond meeting legislative requirements for health/safety.[94] Some training and capacity-building programs in sustainable construction have developed visual information for workers, which include performance monitoring and achievement rewards.[95] To build morale, they can also show workers how they are contributing to healthier living conditions for the community. However, in some socio-economically deprived regions, alcohol, drugs and gambling among construction workers are serious problems. An eDR should identify problems concerning specific groups of construction workers in specific locations.

13.8.4 How Will Local Sustainable Practices, Products and Services Be Supported?

Although RTs sometimes express a preference for local products and materials, they seldom require a justification for using imported or unnecessarily luxurious products.

Locally manufactured materials or light-weight products can mean reduced transport costs and benefits to the local economy. While some RTs encourage heavy, high-density materials to be sourced locally, however, they do not deduct for the addition of lavish or imported products.[96] The eDR should consider local and bio-based products first since they are generally more environment friendly. In some regions, for example, bamboo has good structural performance, is light-weight, replenishes quickly and has far less embodied energy/toxins than many other products.

Self-help housing should be encouraged or designed for, so that disadvantaged families can make code-compliant additions as necessary, when circumstances and budgets allow.

In many impoverished regions, owners increase their dwelling's size gradually, when they can afford materials or when required by changing family needs.[97] As well as meeting individual family preferences, self-help housing can contribute to the expression of cultural and local identity. RTs do little to anticipate or support owner-builder and/or self-help housing in disadvantaged or 'informal' areas. The eDR should consider design that enables safe self-help processes, where homeowners can add on rooms, atriums, lofts or even floors later on.

Notes

1 Dawson, E., and Higgins, M. (2009) How Planning Authorities Can Improve Quality through the Design Review Process: Lessons from Edinburgh, *Journal of Urban Design* 14(1), pp. 101–14; Scheer, B., and Preiser, W. (1994) *Design Review: Challenging Urban Aesthetic Control*, Chapman & Hall, New York.
2 Proposed in Birkeland, J. (1996) Improving the Design Review Process, *CIB Commission Conference Proceedings*, RMIT, Melbourne, pp. 150–5.
3 Birkeland, J. (2008) *Positive Development: From Vicious Circles to Virtuous Cycles through Built Environment Design*, Earthscan, London, pp. 257–8.
4 The questions posed in the first version of the eDR were simply derived from green design criteria. Birkeland, J. (1996) Towards a New Project Review System, *Bogong* 17(2), pp. 10–13.
5 This is consistent with design review processes in many jurisdictions, although they vary from country to country and city to city.
6 Among many books summarizing 'green' design principles: Wann, D. (1996) *Deep Design: Pathways to a Livable Future*, Island Press, Washington, DC; Zeiher, L. C. (1996) *The Ecology of Architecture*, Whitney Library of Design, New York; Mackenzie, D. (1997) *Green Design: Design for the Environment*, Laurence King Publishing, London. See Chapter 1.
7 Birkeland, J. and Knight Lenihan, S. (2016) Biodiversity Offsetting and Net Positive Design, *Journal of Urban Design* 21(1), pp. 50–66.
8 See Birkeland, J. (2012) Design Blindness in Sustainable Development: From Closed to Open Systems Design Thinking, *Journal of Urban Design* 17(2), pp. 163–87.
9 Birkeland, J. (2002) *Design for Sustainability: A Sourcebook of Integrated, Eco-Logical Design Solutions*, Earthscan, London, p. 230.
10 Similarly, the mean and median wealth are quite different because 26 individuals have as much wealth as 50% of the lower half of the global population in 2019. www.newsweek.com/26-rich-wealth-poorest-50-percent-report-1299345.
11 Todd, J. A., and Geissler, S. (1999) Regional and Cultural Issues in Environmental Performance Assessment for Buildings, *Building Research and Information* 27(4–5), pp. 247–56; Guy, S., and Moore, S. A. (2005) *Sustainable Architectures: Cultures and Natures in Europe and North America*, Spon, New York.
12 E.g. pollution kills 9 million people a year and New Delhi sometimes has pollution levels that are 400 times the safe level. At the very least, buildings in such areas should have pollution abatement systems that reduce indoor and outdoor air pollution.
13 Birkeland, *Positive Development*.

14 Jackson, D. (2018) *Data Cities: How Satellites are Transforming Architecture and Design*, Lund Humphries, London. http://data-cities.net/.
15 Todd, N. J., and Todd, J. (1994) *From Eco-Cities to Living Machines*, North. Atlantic Books, Berkeley, CA; Todd, J. (2002) Living Technologies, in Birkeland, *Design for Sustainability*, pp. 173–6.
16 Determining 'appropriate' numbers of species for biodiversity is arguably beyond current capacity.
17 The eDR, if formally adopted by a government, could be enforced by a performance bond or warranty.
18 Birkeland, J. (1996) Ecological Government: Redesigning Democratic Institutions, *Technology and Society* 15(2), pp. 21–8; chapter 13, A New Constitution for Eco-Governance, in Birkeland, *Positive Development*, pp. 219–33.
19 In 1999, the International Red Cross estimated that 25 million people were displaced by disasters. In 2009, the United Nations High Commissioner on Refugees estimated the number to be 36 million, 20 million of whom were listed as victims of climate change-related issues. The American Association for the Advancement of Science (AAAS) estimates the number will be 50 million by 2020.
20 Density provides large numbers of commuters to support public transport, but urban densification makes the costs of building new infrastructure expensive as land must be acquired and buildings demolished.
21 Urban flooding is on the rise in many cities. See https://newsroom.unsw.edu.au/news/science-tech/urban-floods-intensifying-countryside-drying.
22 Daily, G., and Ellison, K. (2002) *The New Economy of Nature*, Island Press, Washington, DC.
23 Things such as flood plains must be regulated, not deprived of a reward.
24 While PEARL encourages design for disassembly, adaptability and flexibility, it is unclear how developers demonstrate that the design is adaptable. PEARL M-3 and 4, in Abu Dhabi Urban Planning Council (2010) *The PEARL Building Rating System for Estidama: Design and Construction*. http://estidama.org/PEARL-rating-system-v10/.
25 The Living Building Challenge adopted the Net Zero Energy Building Certification in 2011. http://living-future.org/lbc/.
26 It is estimated that this would require one-third of a city in Martellozzo, F., Landry, J. S., Plouffe, D., et al. (2014) Urban Agriculture: A Global Analysis of the Space Constraint to Meet Urban Vegetable Demand, *Environmental Research Letters* 9(6), 064025. See also LBC (2013) Imperative 02: Urban Agriculture, in the Site petal of the Living Building Challenge 2.1. http://living-future.org/lbc/about.
27 PEARL, Abu Dhabi Urban Planning Council (2010).
28 Jaime Lerner, when Mayor of Curitiba, Brazil, was credited with the concept of urban acupuncture in the 1970s. See Birkeland, *Positive Development*, pp. 12–13.
29 Brandon, P. S., and Lombardi, P. L. (2011) *Evaluating Sustainable Development in the Built Environment*, Wiley-Blackwell, Chichester, UK.
30 BREEAM. BRI (2010) *Code for Sustainable Homes: Technical Guide*, Dept for Communities and Local Government, Building Research Establishment, London.
31 Marzbali, M. H., Abdullah, A., Razak, N. A., and Tilaki, M. J. M. (2011) A Review of the Effectiveness of Crime Prevention by Design Approaches towards Sustainable Development, *Journal of Sustainable Development* 4(1), pp. 160–73; Schneider, R. H., and Kitchen, T. (2013) Putting Crime Prevention through Environmental Design into Practice via Planning Systems: A Comparison of Experience in the US and UK, *Built Environment* 39(1), pp. 9–30, 22.
32 CCTV spaces and undercover police decoys can catch criminals initiating a crime, as long as they avoid entrapment.
33 Mendoza, S. S. (2008) Box 16: Making Positive Impacts, in Birkeland, *Positive Development*, p. 295.
34 This does not prevent activities such as beach litter cleaning or tree planting parties.
35 Velazquez, L. S. (2008) Box 14: Advantages of Eco-roofs, in Birkeland, *Positive Development*, pp. 292–3.

36 Trees at about 10 years of age at are estimated to absorb 48 pounds of CO_2 per year. urbanforestrynetwork.org/benefits/air%20quality.htm
37 Thwaites, K., Porta, S., et al. (2007) *Urban Sustainability through Environmental Design: Approaches to Time-People-Place Responsive Urban Spaces*. Routledge, London, p. 82.
38 Sarkissian, W., Cook, A., and Walsh, K. (2002) Box 13: Pros and Cons of Design Charrettes, in Birkeland, *Design for Sustainability*, p. 113.
39 Advocacy planning in the 1960s aimed to empower communities in the design process. See Birkeland, J. (1972) *The Value and Limitations of Advocacy Planning*, College of Environmental Design, University of California, Berkeley, CA.
40 Romice, O., and Frey, H. (2007) The Communities in Action Handbook, in Thwaites et al., *Urban Sustainability*, pp. 123–8.
41 Birkeland, J. (2008) Chapter 15: The Smartmode Process, in *Positive Development*, pp. 251–73.
42 Operating energy is assumed to be greater, for example, Mithraratne, N., Vale, B., and Vale, R. J. D. (2007) *Sustainable Living: The Role of the Whole Life Costs and Values*, Butterworth-Heinemann, London. This would not be the case with passive solar design.
43 BRI, *Code for Sustainable Homes*.
44 Bannister, P. (2008) Box 20: Designing for Successful Failure, in Birkeland, *Positive Development*, p. 301.
45 Graham, P. (2003) *Building Ecology: First Principles for a Sustainable Built Environment*, Blackwell Science, Oxford.
46 E.g. LEED, https://new.usgbc.org/leed; BREEAM, www.breeam.com; and PEARL, http://estidama.org/PEARL-rating-system-v10/ address metering.
47 Car racing in cities, for example.
48 Graham, *Building Ecology*.
49 Cities or communities might compete for the most positive sustainability gains annually.
50 Some RTs have discriminated against earth wall, timber or strawbale construction. Some encourage timber usage on grounds of carbon sequestration, but the percentage of the tree that ends up in a timber product is very small and the rest is largely waste.
51 Mixed-use urban development, in modern industrial cities, has been around since the 1960s. https://theconversation.com/a-place-to-live-work-and-play-why-mixed-use-developments-are-making-a-comeback-73142.
52 A list of social benefits of urban gardens and farms is provided by http://community-gardens.ca/content/benefits-community-gardens.
53 PEARL gives a point for solutions inspired by early precedents that demonstrate a contribution to improving water conservation, energy efficiency or comfort.
54 Sev, A. (2011) A Comparative Analysis of Building Environmental Assessment Tools and Suggestions for Regional Adaptations, *Civil Engineering and Environmental Systems* 28(3), pp. 231–45.
55 See Rudofsky, B. (1964) *Architecture without Architects: A Short Introduction to Non-Pedigreed Architecture*, Museum of Modern Art, New York.
56 Sarkissian, W., Bunjamin-Mau, W., with Cook, A., Walsh, K., and Vajda S. (2009) *Speakout: The Step-by-Step Guide to Speakouts and Community Workshops*, Earthscan, London, pp. 215–35.
57 E.g. BREEAM www.breeam.com; LEED https://new.usgbc.org/leed; Green Star https://new.gbca.org.au/green-star/rating-system/.
58 PEARL. http://estidama.org/PEARL-rating-system-v10/PEARL-building-rating-system.aspx.
59 Byrne, J. (2008) Box 48: Equity Mapping, in Birkeland, *Positive Development*, p. 333.
60 Birkeland and Knight Lenihan, Biodiversity Offsetting.
61 E.g. 92% of Bogota residents do not own cars and many others endure pollution and long commuting distances. Cámara de Comercio de Bogotá (2007) *Observatorio de movilidad de Bogotá y la Región*, Bogotá, Colombia.
62 LEED, https://new.usgbc.org/leed.
63 Trainer, T. (1995) *The Conserver Society: Alternatives for Sustainability*, Zed Books, London.

Eco-Positive Design Review (Social Issues) 307

64 LBC, https://living-future.org/lbc/.
65 Gated communities are meant for security but are usually exclusionary.
66 Moore, R. (2002) Box 14: Adaptable Housing, in Birkeland, *Design for Sustainability*, p. 124.
67 Bichard, E. (2015) Developing an Approach to Sustainable Return on Investment in the UK, Brazil and the USA. www.rics.org/uk/knowledge/research/research-reports/developing-an-approach-to-sustainable-return-on-investment/.
68 The LBC encourages walking and pedestrian accessibility for residents, but this assumes middle-class developments. https://living-future.org/lbc/.
69 Schmitz, A., and Scully, J. (2006) *Creating Walkable Pplaces: Compact Mixed-Use Solutions*, ULI (Urban Land Institute), Washington, DC, p. 47.
70 Mathers, A. (2007) Listening to and Understanding the Voices of People with Learning Disabilities in the Planning and Design Process, in Thwaites et al., *Urban Sustainability*, pp. 146–50.
71 A common design student exercise is to design projects for other species to expand empathy.
72 The LBC requires disabled access but this would not affect many projects in disadvantaged regions. https://living-future.org/lbc/.
73 This was recognized by planning authorities to be a problem in Bogota, for example.
74 PEARL, being for a very hot, dry climate, adds credits for shading and natural cooling devices around buildings. http://estidama.org/PEARL-rating-system-v10/PEARL-building-rating-system.aspx.
75 BREEAM Sustainable Homes and PEARL, for example.
76 LEED provides credits for the quantity and quality of open space but, like other RTs, presumes housing models that are typical of wealthier nations.
77 From 2000, to 2003, Bogota reclaimed 1,648,528m² of park land that had previously been enclosed for security. http://institutodeestudiosurbanos.info/endatos/0200/02-070-espacio/02.07.04.htm.
78 This must be designed for efficient maintenance.
79 E.g. in Victoria, Australia, homes costing over $750,000 (below the average house price in Melbourne) pay the same stamp duty as those costing less.
80 ILFI (International Living Future Institute) (2012) Living Building Challenge (LC) 2.1, http://living-future.org/lbc/about, p. 38. Residential developments can be required to provide the units in other parts of the city.
81 Redacción Bogotá (2013) Detalles de enfrentamiento entre Bogotá y Minvivienda por uso de suelo, *El Tiempo*, Jan. 30.
82 See Lamberton, G. (2005) Sustainability Accounting – A Brief History and Conceptual Framework, *Accounting Forum* 29(1), pp. 7–26.
83 Obama required full cost accounting and also set future zero energy targets for federal buildings in 2009. Obama, B. (Oct. 5, 2009) Executive Order 13,514: Federal Leadership in Environmental, Energy, and Economic Performance, United States Government.
84 See Daly, H. E., and Cobb, J. B. (1989) *For the Common Good: Redirecting the Economy toward Community, the Environment and a Sustainable Future*, Beacon Press, Boston, MA; Hamilton, C. (1994) *The Mystic Economist*, Willow Park Press, Canberra.
85 LCADesign takes information directly off CAD drawings and display the information using a radar diagram. https://sbenrc.com.au/app/uploads/2013/10/22-lcadesignbrochure.pdf. See www.evah.com.au/who-we-are.html.
86 https://economictimes.indiatimes.com/news/economy/policy/how-indias-is-leading-digital-revolution-with-speed-and-scale/articleshow/67906932.cms.
87 Birkeland, *Positive Development*, pp. 12–13.
88 PEARL.
89 LEED (2009) created Regional Priority Credits to address the different needs of different regions, but few points are awarded and it may not address inequities.
90 Evans, G., and Foord, J. (2007) The Generation of Diversity: Mixed Use and Urban Sustainability, in Thwaites et al., *Urban Sustainability*, pp. 95–100.
91 Secretaría Distrital de Ambiente (2010) *Guía de Manejo Ambiental para el Sector de la Construcción*, Alcaldía Mayor de Bogotá, Bogota, Colombia.

92 Human Rights Watch (2006) UAE: Workers Abused in Construction Boom. www.hrw.org/news/2006/11/11/uae-workers-abused-construction-boom.
93 PEARL, adopted officially by the government, addresses abuse of foreign labor.
94 BREEAM Sustainable Homes includes criteria to promote fair labor practices during construction, but only as already set by a British certification scheme. PEARL also has provisions for worker safety.
95 Bell, N. (2002) Box 7: Waste Reduction Checklist, in Birkeland, *Design for Sustainability*, pp. 50–1.
96 The LBC (Imperative 14) has generic provisions to encourage projects to use local materials and services. http://living-future.org/lbc/.
97 This is illustrated in Yoff, Senegal, where concrete blocks were stored in many homes until enough could be bought to expand the home in self-help construction.

14 The Eco-Positive Design Review (Ecological issues)

While the previous chapter concerned the social and economic impacts of development that should be covered in an eDR, this concerns ecological impacts.

The eDR is essentially a set of questions that the design teams should consider from the outset. The discussion following the questions is intended to contextualize or help to interpret them. It is a reminder of some of the wider, sometimes indirect, sustainability issues that should be considered. Many of these issues have been covered explicitly/implicitly in the text. The questions also provide a basis for community workshops or design briefs. The final two chapters then present a tool for more in-depth design. It allows design teams to quantify impacts relative to real-world conditions, as opposed to typical development.

14.1 Restore and Increase Natural Systems and Eco-services

14.1.1 How Will Environmental Degradation/Depletion Be Addressed?

Understanding the regional climate and ecology is essential since intervening in nature, even when aiming to increase biodiversity, can irreversibly alter complex ecosystems.

Most RTs have only concerned 'ecologically sensitive' landscaping. In contrast, ecological design traditionally began with a site analysis that considers climate (temperature range, timing and duration of rainy or hot seasons, humidity), latitude/longitude, predominant wind directions, topography, fire danger, wetlands, endangered species and so forth. Nonetheless, sites were usually designed for current rather than potential future conditions due to increasing consumption and climate change. Determining the highest ecological use of the site requires an analysis of the bioregional needs and deficits.

Since the global environment is being degraded, the future needs of people and ecosystems in a changing climatic/ecological context require a safety net.

Again, an increase in nature's positive ecological footprint is necessary to reduce or reverse the rate of environmental destruction. A return to recent ecosystems is not always ecologically appropriate, however, because the pre-industrial ecological conditions can no longer tolerate current environmental pressures. For environmental security, urban structures and landscapes should support biodiversity enclaves for small, representative ecosystems that are protected from invasive species. The eDR should explain how the development increases ecological space beyond pre-industrial conditions and/or provides biodiversity incubators. (See PM analysis.)

14.1.2 How Will Net Habitats for Appropriate Indigenous Species Be Increased?

Current developments fail to support indigenous species and locally appropriate ecosystems sufficient to offset growing human populations, consumption rates and never-ending land-use conversion.

Stacking people in vertical towers or padded cells surrounded by ground-level gardens seldom increases net biodiversity. Ornamental, non-native plants involve high water use, deter native flora and fauna and invade the hinterland. Some RTs, and green design generally, encourage efficient outdoor landscaping for practical considerations like soil protection, low maintenance and low resource/water usage.[1] One RT assesses the ecological value of a site, and suggests retaining sites cleared for over five years, meaning the baseline is a degraded ecological condition.[2]

Creating biodiversity habitats has usually involved restorative landscaping, but this has seldom been informed by the historic evolution of ecosystems/species in the bioregion.

While some RTs mention biodiversity and habitat enhancement, what constitutes 'enhancement' is poorly defined and few RTs specify the level of ecological information needed.[3] One RT, for example, mandates the inclusion of native or naturalized species in brownfield development that emulates the damaged ecosystem's density and diversity, which need not be similar species.[4] The eDR would also consider the natural history of the bioregion since pre-historic times, such as changes in waterways, microclimates and species, which might suggest land reshaping.[5] (See ET analysis.)

14.1.3 How Will Biodiversity Incubators and Ecological Corridors Be Increased?

Green roofs/walls can be designed to preserve the bioregion's ecosystems and threatened species as well as to contribute to a building's passive efficiency/effectiveness.

Roofs can support many functions simultaneously. Many multi-residential buildings have flat roofs that can support intensive green roofs, social spaces and amenities while contributing to insulation, storm-water reduction,[6] cooling in hot climates and so on.[7] However, RTs often omit the other potential benefits, such as carbon sequestration, food production, fire protection and habitats for particular species.[8] The eDR would also consider ways to maximize the amount of eco-services in both separate or integrated spaces above or around buildings [Chapters 5–6].[9] (See HU analysis.)

Green Space Walls and nature corridors could provide far more environmental, social and building services, and other sustainability gains, than RTs yet contemplate.

Even an ordinary facade provides multiple functions.[10] Due to their reductionist orientation, however, one RT encourages vegetated roofs and walls only as 'dual function surfaces' in a credit concerning material reduction.[11] Green facades do far more: reduce heat loss due to wind effects, create habitats for selected birds and plants, channel breezes into buildings and so forth.[12] Native ecosystems in scaffolding can create habitats for endangered bugs, bats and birds, and link ecological corridors while providing water and energy efficiencies.

14.1.4 How Will Watercourses Be Protected, Runoff Reduced and Rainwater Stored?

Water storage ponds in urban parks can support urban and regional ecosystems while ensuring water availability during long rainless periods or dry seasons.

Some RTs reward storm-water management and/or water-efficient landscaping.[13] Another dry climate RT sets more stringent requirements for water usage.[14] While such strategies help, however, they do not proactively address the increasing global shortage of water. The withdrawing of water for urban and agricultural uses is affecting river flows which in turn affect their entire catchments and ecosystems, and beyond. The eDR should consider how proposals can increase/support urban water reserves through rain gardens, landscape ponds, inbuilt water tanks or other multifunctional systems.

Passive water treatment/reuse and urban flood prevention measures should consider the optimal scale and location in the urban landscape, not just building uses.

Since urban flooding sometimes allows sewage to overflow into streams, one RT requires water for occupants' use to come from storm-water reuse (closed-loop) systems, and all grey-water/storm-water to be treated onsite.[15] Other RTs reward strategies, such as intensive vegetated roofs that reduce runoff and pollution by capturing significant amounts of rain.[16] However, biological water diversion and treatment systems at the neighborhood scale can be more manageable, safe and efficient.[17] The eDR should explain the scale used to optimize nature-based systems.

14.2 Create Eco-positive Onsite and Offsite Impacts

14.2.1 How Will Ecological Space Be Leveraged?

Offsets granted for creating new offsite spaces for ecosystem/biodiversity habitats should ensure both projects combined are net-positive and avoid interference in offsite ecosystems.

Net-positive cities would reseed the regions, just as reefs replenish the oceans. Physical development can offer a unique variety of orientations, edges, minerals, microclimates and so on that different biodiversity habitats require. Sometimes developers are given additional (beyond code) floor area simply because they reduce other impacts beyond code requirements – the legal minimum. However, incentivizing architecture that creates more space for ecological gains and/or environmental amenity may warrant a floor area bonus. The eDR should justify any trading/offsetting arrangements.

Ecological compensation, which is generally only remedial, should require net-positive offsetting (onsite or offsite), and trading systems should include retrofitting for ecological space.

As discussed earlier, biodiversity offsetting schemes have usually been partial.[18] That is, they allow extra damage in exchange for remediating sites, yet do not deduct points for the ecosystems damaged during resource extraction. Sometimes greenfield development is compensated for by retrofitting other buildings.[19] The idea behind offsetting is to allow compensation where it is cheapest to make improvements, and some buildings are more easily retrofitted than others. Therefore, retrofitting incentives should prioritize the most harmful buildings or most threatened habitats.

14.2.2 How Will the Project Increase Future Options?

Design credits should not be offered for innovations (novelty) alone, especially where these neither change unsustainable construction norms nor contribute to systems transformation.

Some RTs give credits for innovations regardless of the value of the outcomes, and some even give credits for applying a known technology to a new situation.[20] Some RTs even require an extra application fee.[21] One tool simply sets high mandatory standards/targets to encourage innovation.[22] These provide little real incentive to improve whole-system efficiency.[23] Moreover, many new technologies can actually lock-in old directions (e.g. 'clean coal'). The eDR should therefore explain how the innovation will contribute to the PD Test.

Reversibility and/or keeping options open is fundamental to sustainability, yet assessments have ignored this basic principle, partly because public choice is not considered.

RTs have failed to reward many building features that have positive ecological impacts or to penalize many with negative impacts. Building products can be energy efficient yet create unnecessary adverse ecological impacts. For instance, a zero-energy residential building can cause excessive traffic in a congested area or other negative impacts, yet still receive a high RT score. The eDR would consider projects in terms of their potential irreversibility for future public choice, as well as describing their measurable environmental impacts. (See GO analysis.)

14.2.3 How Will the Building Footprint and Ecological Footprint Be Reduced?

Land coverage should be reduced and permeability increased where appropriate, but these should not suffice as indicators of adequate biodiversity and ecosystem services.

Both reducing a building's ground coverage and increasing building occupancy are generally considered virtues in green building design.[24] One RT gives one point for minimizing ground coverage to increase the landscaping area.[25] However, the benefits of vegetated open space will usually depend more on landscape design and plant selection than the dedicated horizontal area. For example, layers and edges can support more ecological functions than lawns. Off-ground, internal and/or vertical open spaces can add eco-services that benefit occupants and neighbors.

Residential areas should be largely self-sufficient in food, water and oxygen for public and environmental health, as well as to reduce transport impacts.

Social housing usually lacks many amenities other than basic shelter. The onsite production of nutritional food can save residents substantial funds.[26] A few square meters of garden in courtyards, balconies, green roofs and green walls can provide most of an individual's vegetable needs. A rule of thumb for the minimum (vertical) building-integrated food is 10 square meters per person. The eDR should describe how the functional green space is designed to provide each resident's fresh air, water and food needs.[27]

14.2.4 How Will Sensitive Natural Areas and Construction Sites Be Protected?

The use of brownfield sites is often encouraged over greenfield sites, but this is not enough to counteract losses of sensitive areas elsewhere.

Some RTs award credits for construction on brownfield sites or areas of low ecological value.[28] Remediating brownfield sites is, coincidentally, a good investment since contaminated land is cheap.[29] One RT simply withholds certification for projects on land near ecologically sensitive sites.[30] This, again, does little to preserve land of high ecological value, since harmful projects simply do not seek certification. Where applicable, the eDR would explore means to preserve any relatively natural areas that are under threat, through net-positive offsetting/trading schemes. (See CD analysis.)

Offsite waste/pollution should be prevented and remediated, not just managed within the boundaries of construction, as pollution flows in environmental media across borders.

Green construction management guidelines usually focus on reducing site damage from construction. This can include soil loss, sedimentation due to storm sewers, dust and particulate pollution or the preservation of onsite natural elements.[31] One RT includes the protection of vegetation and watercourses.[32] This approach reduces or repairs the immediate damage caused by construction site activity. It does not ensure 'ongoing' land/water management. The eDR should outline how the landscape will reduce maintenance, and state the provisions made for future maintenance.

14.3 Reduce Waste and Total Material Flows

14.3.1 How Will Total Lifecycle Waste Be Reduced?

Upstream material flows caused by manufacturing need consideration in design, as these are not adequately addressed by closed-loop production systems or recycling programs.

Recycling at the end of life has substantial economic benefits, but does not reduce material flows during production. There are significant impacts in recycling processes,[33] and the waste due to mining materials for buildings can far exceed building construction and operational waste, in volume, weight and/or toxins.[34] Design can reduce the need for environmentally damaging materials throughout the product life, unnecessary upstream use of fossil fuels and ecological waste, or products sourced from distant places (e.g. rainforest timber from tropical countries).

Waste management that is limited to onsite construction activity only diverts downstream waste from landfill, and seldom eliminates toxins embedded in construction materials.

While green buildings avoid toxic materials, much construction and demolition waste can still be hazardous. It is often dumped or mixed with other residues.[35] Recycling centers may divert some post-construction waste to other uses and even upcycle some. Although most construction waste occurs before materials reach the site (e.g. mining with cyanide), some RTs count onsite waste reductions as environmental gains. The eDR should therefore research and specify materials that are non-toxic, low-waste and designed for disassembly, reuse and recycling.

14.3.2 How Is Eco-retrofitting Prioritized over New Construction?

Retrofitting for energy efficiency has often been at the expense of opportunities to add ecological and social value, let alone increase eco-positive outcomes.

Research suggests that renovations cost, on average, 30% less than new construction,[36] while the energy, health and productivity savings from eco-retrofitting can pay for the renovations.[37] Specialist firms can be contracted to retrofit the other property. However, most retrofits only concern energy, because it is the low-hanging fruit.[38] To offset greenfield development, one RT suggests that the same amount of floor area should be retrofitted elsewhere. However, this may not actually offset the ecological costs of both construction projects. (See CC analysis.)

RTs, in general, do not favor eco-retrofitting, and credits are easier to obtain through new construction, even though their impacts are usually greater.

Some RTs apply almost the same criteria to both new construction and major renovations. This arguably discriminates against retrofitting. Although retrofitting saves money, it is complicated and can involve more management costs. Therefore, RTs should provide extra incentives. The eDR should examine the potential for eco-positive retrofitting in order to increase structural resistance and longevity of buildings, and to improve occupant health and life quality, provide surplus eco-services and public benefits, increase passive solar energy, and so on [Chapters 5–6].[39]

14.3.3 How are Ecological Waste and Designed Waste Reduced?

Embodied and ecological waste accumulating upstream during production can often best be reduced by substituting products and processes, rather than efficiency measures alone.

Some RTs address several site management practices, such as product stewardship, chain of custody or recycling processes such as waste separation, storage, handling and disposal.[40] However, waste accumulating throughout the construction process can be massive.[41] For example, many RTs treat timber products as if they sequester net carbon, but most of the forest is wasted, and most remnants are usually downcycled.[42] Although timber waste reduction and reuse is improving, much of the timber waste in forestry is, at best, downcycled.[43]

Durable design can cause waste because it seldom allows for adaptability, upgrading or disassembly – although social, climatic and technological change is likely.

Some RTs promote design for durability,[44] but this can mean more embodied energy and waste and a lack of flexibility. Durable buildings are costly to modify/repair, especially in case of earthquakes, demographic changes, building settlement and so forth. Although durable buildings may slow the demand for new buildings, they are often demolished simply because of the 'desire for the new'.[45] In contrast, design for future expansion, contraction and retrofitting can satisfy this appetite while reducing the number of buildings demolished. (See DW analysis.)

14.3.4 How Will the Design Create Beauty/Quality without Luxury (Waste)?

Luxury is usually defined by price, and is often proportional with embodied energy, whereas design can provide life quality without using high-cost materials.

Some have argued that prestige design lasts longer because it is highly prized, but it usually means excessive embodied energy/materials. Luxuries limit the resources available to others, and create consumer 'needs' with no social value. Design that evinces luxury and fosters conspicuous consumption also increases the experience of poverty and resentment by the have nots. (Again, far less than 1% now own 99% of the world's wealth.[46]) Design can create the appearance or feeling of luxury without the negative impacts.

Beauty and quality are goals of virtually all design, although perceptions of both vary, yet sustainable design has been stereotyped as lacking aesthetics.

Designers can transform ordinary building functions into works of art, using low-tech natural systems that increase environmental quality and aesthetic value (e.g. sculptural water features that double as downpipes). One RT encourages 'features intended solely for human delight and the celebration of culture, spirit and place appropriate to its function',[47] but does not suggest how to evaluate beauty or require a positive socio-ecological impact. The expression 'beauty is as beauty does' is a more relevant consideration for an eDR. (See DF analysis.)

14.4 Eliminate Fossil Fuels and Sequester Carbon

14.4.1 How are Highly Polluting Sources of Energy Avoided?

Pollution from fossil fuels, in addition to carbon dioxide emissions, is harmful to human health, yet wind power is readily available in many places.

Wind power, while not without costs, has far fewer negative environmental impacts overall than fossil fuels. Mining impacts are largely irreversible and it is expensive and complicated to restore the sites. The land beneath wind generators can be used and they can be moved when not needed. They do not use rare earths or increase cadmium and atmospheric mercury.[48] When coal mines are phased out due to automation, many areas can be converted to wind energy, to reduce social dislocation.

Hydroelectric power has huge environmental impacts, and energy from dams may be less reliable in the future due to impacts of climate change.

Dam power is 'renewable', but dams destroy ecosystems during construction. There are now growing efforts to unplug dams in order to restore environmental flows.[49] Some hydroelectric plants are becoming unreliable. They lack adequate storage capacity during peak demand periods, because droughts are more frequent with climate change.[50] Dam storage has already become a problem in some places (e.g. New Zealand, Tasmania). Furthermore, dam backup systems still often rely on fossil-fuel-based power, which cancels out some of the benefits of dams.

14.4.2 How Will Renewable/Passive Systems Be Maximized?

Site analysis to optimize building form and orientation and to consider optimal community-scale renewable energy systems should be conducted, especially in new construction.

Building orientation and configuration should always optimize site conditions for thermal factors such as shade, slope, wind and solar energy. One RT aims for energy autonomy, and allows embodied energy to be offset elsewhere.[51] However, as discussed above, community-based renewable energy sources may be more efficient.[52] For example, solar thermal disks occupy little ground area in neighborhood parks or shop carparks, yet can supply energy to 50 conventional homes. Renewable systems can also be used during construction to supplement energy.[53] (See PM analysis.)

Using fossil-fuel-based energy instead of passive design (due to a lack of full-cost accounting) has contributed to the disconnect between people and nature.

With the availability of cheap petrochemical sources of power and various forms of monopolies and indirect subsidies,[54] passive design has not been prioritized, even in new buildings. Even impoverished communities use petrochemical equipment for heating/cooling systems, which creates dependency on fossil fuels. This causes a lack of awareness about how the built and natural environments affect human psychological and sensory experiences.[55] Viewing the world through computer and TV screens, as well as car windscreens, further detaches people from biophysical reality. (See SE analysis.)

14.4.3 How Will Community Energy Generation/Conservation Be Encouraged?

Energy produced in buildings where it is efficient to do so can be exported to other buildings using exchange systems, such as 'blockchain'.

Some roof/wall solar arrays and/or windows with invisible solar cells can produce enough solar energy to export a surplus.[56] (Some call energy beyond that needed for heating, cooling and ventilating the building and its electronic office equipment 'positive energy'.[57]) There are now many examples of existing and proposed buildings that generate surplus energy for delivery to storage, adjacent properties or the grid. Means to sell/trade this energy are already being developed using internet exchange systems including blockchain, to avoid middlemen.[58]

Use of roof or vertical surfaces for greenery and/or renewable energy systems around public spaces can improve their comfort and ambient outdoor temperatures.

The many benefits of urban trees are now recognized, but they can sometimes conflict with solar access for passive design or solar cells on individual homes. Where buildings are overshadowed or future solar access may be restricted, the eDR should consider offsite, renewable energy sources. Buildings with permanent, large, blank sun-facing walls could be retrofitted with 'Trombe walls' which occupy almost no ground area. Roofs or exterior shade structures with inbuilt solar cells can also mitigate urban temperatures [Chapter 5].

14.4.4 How Will Insulation Be Used in Optimal, Multifunctional Ways?

Passive solar heating/cooling and renewable energy systems can be combined with building-integrated thermal storage for rainy or wintery days to avoid/reduce auxiliary heating.

In hot and cold climates, insulation is essential to prevent the loss of passive or active solar energy generated by the building, and prevent occupants from using electric space heaters.[59] Electric heating/cooling equipment can have negative externalities, even if powered by renewable wind or solar cells. For example, many air conditioners pump hot air outside, wasting heat energy and even contributing to the urban heat island effect. Building-integrated (passive) thermal storage 'heat banks' can at least reduce diurnal temperature swings.[60]

Thermal mass for storing solar heat/coolness can have high embodied energy, so these building elements need to serve multiple functions (beyond just insulation).

Passive design systems in cool climates typically use thermal mass such as stone and/or earth wall construction for heat storage and insulation. These materials generally have significant embodied energy, especially if transported – as do industrially manufactured materials. However, these structures can serve multiple purposes while providing opportunities for unique environments and aesthetic qualities. For example, glass-covered gabion walls, attached greenhouses or variations on Green Scaffolding can frame atriums, semi-outdoor social areas or indoor gardens, while collecting, storing and distributing heat.[61] (See MS analysis.)

14.5 Increase Ecological and Human Health

14.5.1 How Will Urban Environmental Health Be Improved?

Since the industrial age, conventional construction practices, building materials and heating fuels have created many health risks to humans and the natural environment.

Many health risks are caused by built environments, such as asbestos, volatile organic compounds, radon and other toxins, and CO_2 is produced in the transport of construction materials. Indoor activities also produce pollution. In economically deprived regions, where natural gas or timber are used for cooking and water heating, CO_2 and particulate concentrations are a particular problem. Further, outdoor

318 *Decision Making and Assessment*

contaminants seep inside to combine with indoor pollution, multiplying the toxins.[62] Many developing world cities/buildings fall below achievable World Health Organization standards.[63]

Built environments expose the poor to health risks disproportionately and make them more aware of their poverty, which can also affect their health/wellbeing.

Built environments in developed nations insulate the wealthy from the realities faced by the socio-economically deprived on a daily basis. Poverty prevents the treatment of even the most common illnesses, but the buildings inhabited by the poor are an indirect cause of many serious illnesses. While the urban environment cannot cure poverty or reform the economic system, it can make everyday life less expensive and more salubrious. It also reduces obvious wealth differentials which are known to contribute to illnesses.[64]

14.5.2 How Will the Ecological Impacts of Poverty Be Mitigated?

Poverty and the diversion of building investment to rich areas affects the capacity of citizens in disadvantaged areas to improve their environmental conditions.

Urban planning has played a role in limiting economic opportunities through segregation. Rewarding green buildings in wealthy areas does little for intra-generational equity. There is a lot of research about the unfair distribution of negative impacts but, again, little in planning fields on how urban development transfers wealth away from poor districts or developing regions. There have been many initiatives in disadvantaged regions to tackle issues like poverty through community initiatives, but these self-help activities have had little external support.[65] (See HI analysis.)

Low-cost, low-impact buildings are compatible with high living standards, whereas industrial technologies are often more expensive and can have more negative life-cycle impacts.

Residential buildings, especially in temperate climates, can create the environmental qualities of eco-resorts with relatively little embodied waste, materials or energy. The investments in green projects also deliver benefits to local communities in the form of health, education, jobs, etc. Such exemplars can be more effective than indirect kinds of foreign aid,[66] by helping to ensure that poorer nations do not emulate the western model of development which, some argue, has created a karmic circle of waste, inequity and conflict.

14.5.3 How Will Healthy Indoor/Outdoor Air Quality Be Increased?

Design that encourages and accommodates outdoor exercise is important, yet is undermined by landscapes that fail to provide quality food, air and water.

The lack of walking and biking paths or swimming pools correlates with cardiovascular problems, diabetes, depression and stress.[67] Exercising in middle age reportedly prolongs life and delays dementia significantly.[68] Some RTs credit provision for exercise such as pedestrian and cyclist pathways,[69] bicycle storage and changing facilities,[70] or recreation areas, playgrounds or sport fields.[71] In many developing cities, however, outdoor exercise can increase exposure to toxins, due to car and building emissions, which can be reduced by vegetation and/or Living Machines.

Natural ventilation and good indoor air quality are essential to health and can be provided very inexpensively using passive solar design and vegetation.

Most RTs address air quality and some RTs have a healthy outdoor category.[72] Another includes VOC-emitting materials for indoor air quality.[73] In disadvantaged areas, natural ventilation can expel smoke, cooking pollution and condensation on cold mornings, but this does not treat it. Buildings are seldom designed for growing plants. In polluted inner-city residential areas, building-integrated planting, or even window boxes or planters, can increase oxygen, absorb some toxins and particulates, and contribute to air circulation, environmental amenity and healthy food.

14.5.4 How Will Biodegradable, Adaptable and Renewable Materials Be Selected?

Embodied energy in materials can be reduced by design, whether the development requires durable and permanent, or adaptable and flexible, forms of construction.

Fired-brick structures are environmentally destructive, but there are durable substitutes that look similar and can blend in with an existing brick architecture. Brick-like materials, such as stabilized earth blocks, can be demountable and repairable if suitable mortar is used, and therefore can have a useful second life. Likewise, biodegradable materials (e.g. strawboard) and/or modular components like ICF (insulating, integrated, Styrofoam concrete formwork), assuming low-impact forms of concrete,[74] can also blend into local historic architecture while causing far fewer negative impacts.

Recyclable materials are important but, in some developing nations, such products should not excuse the use of unregulated materials, such as rainforest timbers.

Most RTs give points for using recyclable materials, such as credits for product stewardship and use of reused or rapid growing renewable materials.[75] In some developing nations, however, there is still little information on product origins, or distinctions between pre- and post-consumer recycled content.[76] Timber is generally deemed recyclable and 'sustainable' per se. Yet forestry is more damaging in some places than others (depending on its biodiversity, etc.). Voluntary RTs may forestall the adoption of appropriate codes and recycling regulations.

14.6 Recognize Complex and Interdependent Open Systems

14.6.1 How Will Exogenous or Unexpected Consequences Be Designed For?

Due to ecological uncertainty and complexity, system boundaries in assessment should be avoided as they cause impacts to be overlooked or compound errors.

Due to the complexity of social-ecological interactions, environmental assessment tools involve assumptions and predictions based on available data, or what has traditionally been measured. Although building science is improving, most negative impacts cannot be measured with certainty, because bio-accumulative phenomena interact differently with various immune systems. An increase of the natural life-support system is a hedge against uncertainty. System boundaries conceal cumulative, distant impacts. Since there is no upper limit to positive impacts, however, there cannot be 'too much' good.

Although urban design and architecture are considered spatial arts, the whole spatial dimension has been neglected in RTs and other economics-based, closed-system tools.

Biodiversity assessments purport to measure species richness, biomass, pond density, bio-acoustics and so forth. These measurements do not guarantee resilience to offsite land conversion in the surrounding area or urbanization more generally. Creating suitable multifunctional, adaptable spaces for ecological space requires design. Ecological space, if properly conceived, would not take anything away from people, and could greatly improve the urban experience. The eDR should consult urban ecologists to create suitable spaces for appropriate species and for seeding the new/reclaimed spaces.

14.6.2 How Will the Ecological Base Be Increased?

Investment in urban biodiversity enclaves is necessary to create the ability to restock the bioregions, as ecological corridors across cities are not adequate.

Most concerns in RTs end at the property line and do not attempt a symbiosis between the built and natural environments. One RT awards points for collaborative strategies to create nature corridors and link nearby habitats or ecological stepping stones across urban areas.[77] However, escape routes seldom stop invasive predators from following native species. Until urban ecology gains political support, biodiversity enclaves or niche spaces for small ecosystems can be accommodated in empty lots, unused walls, roofs or abandoned buildings. (See ES analysis.)

Efforts to reduce negative inputs-outputs may be nullified by the unintended consequences of development, such as increasing consumption, whether populations rise or fall.

Preserving what is now left of nature cannot achieve a plausible balance, given past/ongoing pollution, GMOs, invasive species and other bio-cumulative impacts. If the living standards of the poor improve, then resource production, consumption and depletion will likely increase to satisfy new consumer demands. In the alternative scenario, economic collapse, consumption of land and natural resources could also increase consumption through desperation, disorder and/or mobocracy. Design should recognize that 'making nature more resilient' to the impacts of development cannot suffice.[78]

14.6.3 How Will Wildlife and Nearby Ecosystems Benefit?

Light and noise pollution have ecological impacts and require physical solutions, not simply reliance upon people to turn off lights and/or stay quiet.

Common nuisances like dust, noise, vibration, nightglow and glare from buildings and construction affect wildlife. For instance, light affects the bio-rhythms of bats and threatens their very existence. One RT rewards activities like switching off unnecessary outdoor lights at night, and using more efficient fittings for safety/security lighting.[79] Behavior controls are unreliable, however, as one person can cancel out the efforts of many others. The eDR should discuss how the design is either fool-proof or makes good behavior much easier.

The heat island effect kills many people and animals each year, and heat reflected off walls, windows and roofs contributes to urban overheating.

Urban temperatures are often several degrees warmer than the hinterland due to the heat island effect. Collectively, buildings that contribute to the heat island effect result in far more deaths than structural design failures.[80] Some RTs reward vegetated surfaces, open-grid pavements in exterior hardscaping and high-reflectance materials.[81] Some heat energy from reflective materials bounces downward off shiny surfaces and contributes to ambient heat and glare. The eDR should therefore examine the effectiveness of alternative design measures for mitigating urban overheating.

14.6.4 How Will Site Planning Contribute to the Bioregion?

Planning analyses should consider developments in their regional context to identify priority regional ecological and social problems that they could help to counteract.

Since buildings are part of a complex ecological and socio-economic environment,[82] they shape human-human and human-nature relationships. Land use decisions have often alienated land from potentially positive uses, yet RTs largely ignore issues such as irreversible land-use change. There are RTs for communities or neighborhood-scale developments, but they tend to formalize green design concepts from decades ago, rather than encourage site-specific analyses. While some aim to mitigate the impacts of sprawl, they tend to perpetuate the suburban model – sprawl.

Long-term recovery of resource extraction sites in nature must be considered, as opposed to just ranking the general sustainability characteristics of building materials.

RTs encourage responsible materials selection based on generic criteria, not actual ecological impacts at the site of extraction (having side-lined EIAs). Durable materials arguably 'amortize' some impacts, but the ecological damage can be permanent and irreparable. One RT encourages regeneration, but not an increase in total land area.[83] Even where ecological damage is remediated, ecosystems seldom recover to their earlier state.[84] The eDR should consider the relative vulnerability of the ecosystems and recovery times at alternative sites of resource extraction. (See EW analysis.)

14.7 Conclusion

These two chapters have proposed a collaborative, cross-disciplinary eDR process that focuses on wider socio-ecological sustainability issues, as compared to conventional project approval processes.

The eDR process is a low-cost approach for raising the standard of ordinary buildings, the forgotten majority – not just rewarding the high achievers who benefit financially from efficiencies and prestige anyway. It minimizes transaction costs and frontloads design. Therefore, it can be adopted voluntarily by communities, clients or design teams. It can also be adopted by states, town or countries with limited financial resources, or implemented as an interim measure, while they develop more rigorous kinds of regulations that would raise the minimum level of all developments. In particular, the eDR questions are aimed to encourage design teams to:

- Emphasize or frontload the preliminary design stage;
- Address regional sustainability and transboundary socio-ecological issues;
- Engage with lay and expert communities on problematic or contentious matters;
- Keep updated on advances in potentially applicable eco-innovations;
- Find ways to increase positive public benefits and design synergies.

The eDR explains the way the design team has solved problems in a transparent manner to enable meaningful input and learning by others.

Generic rules can lead to arbitrary on-ground applications. Also, developers and their design teams end up competing with each other instead of competing against a sustainability standard. The underlying principles of PD sustainability standards are reviewed in Box 6. The eDR process is meant to enable people to learn from both project successes and failures, rather than from marketing claims for business purposes. Since the demand for quantitative approaches to assessment is entrenched among the management community, however, quantitative approaches are also needed. Therefore, a more technical tool has also been developed to incentivize and verify net-positive design [Chapters 15–16].

14.8 Exercises

1. Examine an RT in detail to see how it addresses each of the questions above.
2. Find examples of designs that address each of the above eDR questions.
3. In coordination with an urban design or architecture class, apply the questions in Chapters 12 and 13 to a set of design projects that concern residential development. Pair up students with the design students and work on brief answers together. Review what changes appear in the final design. Alternatively, apply the questions to an actual major residential development that has been drawn or actually built, whether a green project or not. Recommend changes.
4. Identify significant missing issues that are not covered in Chapters 12 and 13.

Box 6 Sample biases to be reversed (Source: Birkeland 2014)

The following list is meant to suggest how everything in the area of sustainable development, due to its legacy issues, is negative, and suggests a positive and whole-system alternative.

Code: **PD** = positive development, **DP** = the dominant paradigm

Design (project level)

Beyond reducing negative externalities to increasing positive externalities

DP ideally makes things better than before, relative to conventional practices or conditions, or what 'might have been' if mitigation measures had not been added. **PD** means not only eliminating negative impacts but making improvements that benefit the whole community and/or nature: increasing positive impacts, not merely internalizing negative impacts. (See HI analysis.)

Beyond zero waste in manufacturing to avoiding 'designed' waste

DP seldom considers waste by design (e.g. planned obsolescence, disposability, fashion changes) and emphasizes reduction and recycling over the redesign of products or production systems.

PD aims to reduce total/global material flows and to avoid waste due to the 'rebound effect' (where savings from efficiency are spent on more products). (See DW analysis.)

Beyond rationalizing supply chains to changing demand by design

DP aims to reduce waste in industrial supply chains (e.g. fossil-fueled factories, forestry, farms and fisheries), but seldom substitutes healthier products that use fewer materials altogether.
PD recognizes that only design can reduce overall consumer demand and material/energy flows which originate from poorly designed products with wasteful extraction and/or manufacturing processes. (See EW analysis.)

Beyond first-past-the-post approvals to assessing public values/purposes

DP means (legal) developments or land uses are approved unless very harmful, because, historically, 'freedom to pursue happiness' has been privileged over 'freedom from harm'.
PD considers whether the project's purposes will have net-positive public outcomes and, if a project is approved anyway, seeks means to increase positive public impacts. (See DF analysis.)

Beyond accountancy/awarding points to creating positive incentives

DP 'design tools' are retrospective decision aids to make choices that require a complete design to assess, and treat design as optimizing separate elements to satisfy occupant needs.
PD tools encourage integrative, whole-system, transdisciplinary or fluid design actions by incentivizing net public benefits that contribute to community and nature. (See HI analysis.)

Beyond streamlining review processes to frontloading design thinking

DP design review processes occur after basic decisions are made about siting, massing, infrastructure and energy sources, which are seldom altered during the post-review stage.
PD encourages cross-disciplinary engagement from expert and local communities early in the design stage – where the greatest positive impacts at least cost are possible. (See DF analysis.)

Beyond energy efficiency to integrating passive systems

DP usually optimizes costs, rather than considering lifecycle impacts, including repair/replacement of energy systems, so even when passive solar design is used it is often under-designed.
PD puts passive solar energy first, while minimizing embodied energy and ecological disturbance, to ensure thermal security is provided regardless of future energy supply. (See PM analysis.)

Beyond a focus on human comfort/health to increasing ecological health

DP tools primarily concern impacts on the human health and environment, such as air and water quality in the building, but virtually never increase nature.
PD aims to increase the positive ecological footprint of nature beyond the ecological footprint of development, in part by integrating eco-productive multifunctional systems in cities. (See MS analysis.)

Planning (city level)

Beyond eco-efficient production to design for life-support systems

DP emphasizes efficiency (optimizing inputs and outputs) which often leads to reducing public amenities, rather than using space to increase ecological and social life-support systems.
PD increases multi-functional and mixed uses of structures to reduce material flows and create public spaces and environments that increase life quality and reduce consumerism. (See NS analysis.)

Beyond resource/space minimization to amplifying spatial resources

DP planning minimizes public spaces to reduce energy and maintenance, which limits the potential for future multifunctional uses to increase benefits for the wider public.
PD recognizes that ecological space, framed by low-impact materials, creates opportunities for public spaces to support solar energy, social interaction and eco-services in mutually beneficial ways. (See ES analysis.)

Beyond densification to increasing natural security and biodiversity

DP often supports urban densification in ways that reduce adaptability, natural security and urban ecological/diversity, without reducing resource flows or pressures on distant wilderness areas.
PD begins by determining the highest ecological use of the site and links urban biodiversity habitats through vertical and horizontal nature corridors and stepping stones. (See HU analysis.)

Beyond predetermining future choices to expanding future options

DP development approval processes allow incremental but often irreversible ecological losses, which can lock in excessive consumption patterns, or the lifestyle choices of future generations.
PD recognizes that democracy requires meaningful, diverse choices and built-in resource security through social/natural life-support systems: future citizens cannot vote for things that have disappeared. (See DI analysis.)

Beyond planning for narrow indicators to planning for ecological spaces

DP tools, in assessing biodiversity, focus on numbers (e.g. species richness, water density) that are unreliable indicators of appropriate biodiversity, ecosystem resilience or ecosystem needs.

PD suggests that cities could serve as 'arks' by functionally integrating ecosystems with urban spaces/structures that support ecosystem nurseries and biodiversity incubators for the bioregions. (See ET analysis.)

Beyond weighting impact factors to finding leverage points for change

DP decision tools emphasize resource efficiency and marginalize social and ecological factors, although they can have serious cumulative impacts because they are hard to quantify.
PD aims to fill gaps in ethical, social and ecological information to assist in finding multiple ways to generate positive ripple effects throughout urban systems. (See MS analysis.)

Beyond closed-system frameworks that deny complexity to celebrating it

DP conceptual frameworks use systems boundaries in ways that limit planning to impact mitigation, which side-lines the potential of urban design to support natural systems.
PD sees buildings and cities as integral parts of complex open urban systems and assesses design proposals by their public benefits, not just resource efficiency. (See NS analysis.)

Beyond resilience within nature's limits to increasing nature's capacity

DP concepts like 'limits to nature' imply that nature can be made more resilient to absorb more damage – up to the point of collapse.
PD suggests that 'resilience' is about repair or recovery, not prevention, and nature's resistance to damage must be increased well beyond the rates of depletion/degradation. (See ES analysis.)

Policy making level

Beyond specialization to integrating eco-logical sciences in design

DP has focused on 'easy to measure' factors (energy, waste, etc.) and amounts of pollution in environmental media, with less attention to the ecological base.
PD would include urban ecologists in collaborative design processes and adapt new digital technologies to socio-ecological issues, rather than defining problems to fit existing tools. (See EW analysis.)

Beyond 'relative' baselines/benchmarks to whole-system measures

DP treats current ecologically negative urban conditions or buildings as a neutral baseline, and only counts impacts after the start of either property ownership or construction.
DP avoids counting past investments in a (failed) system as positive, and instead compares alternative design concepts as if no system or project yet existed. (See SC analysis.)

Beyond protecting property rights to ensuring human rights and life quality

DP allocates land on a first-come-first-served basis, believing that property rights are sacrosanct and that industrial growth/wealth can solve any environmental problems that it creates.

PD recognizes that disasters do not respect property lines and impact those without or without property, and aims to avoid/reduce natural disasters with bioregional-scale planning. (See RS analysis.)

Beyond predicting performance to creating adaptable cities and buildings

DP assessment tools focus on prediction instead of learning from past mistakes, and largely ignore design for adaptability to meet changing conditions and occupant needs.

PD emphasizes design for adaptability as there will be a need to retrofit most new 'green' buildings for climate change, as well as older buildings. (See CC analysis.)

Beyond interest-balancing to achieving a whole-earth balance

DP suggests that economic, social and environmental issues should be 'balanced' but, in reality, the environment or future is balanced-off incrementally with each major development.

PD looks at whole systems, so balance would mean achieving pre-industrial conditions such as pre-urban forest cover, reef systems and oxygen to carbon dioxide balance. (See ET analysis.)

Beyond calculating process inputs-outputs to assessing whole-system gains

DP analyses identify pockets of waste that can be recycled in sequential, segmented industrial processes, but seldom advocate changes in the design of underlying systems.

PD analyses aim to consider upstream and downstream impacts on nature, such as impacts caused by energy 'sources', not just the amount of energy used. (See SE analysis.)

Beyond deferred maintenance to valuing benefits of immediate action

DP spreads costs over space, time and populations to reduce the intensity of impacts (e.g. pollution mitigation), but often discounts cumulative damage and deferred maintenance.

PD counts compounding benefits of actions to benefit public/environmental health/welfare through improvements to built/natural environments, rather than just improving the per capita or average impacts. (See BA analysis.)

Governance level

Beyond interest balancing to resolving the causes of conflicts

DP often accepts 'developer contributions' as offsetting project externalities, such as paying to extend the sewerage system to a new suburb or planting replacement trees.

PD would not sanction unjust enrichment, or offsets that allow excessive damage to the ecological base and public estate, as these cumulatively increase social conflict. (See DI analysis.)

Beyond resource substitution to counting ecological recovery time

DP does not count the time and space that ecosystems need to regenerate after resource extraction, often assuming economic benefits compensate for the environmental damage.

PD considers the 'ecological waste', or the time and space required for ecological restoration, and not just the embodied waste or materials lost during manufacturing. (See EW analysis.)

Beyond compensation to reducing cumulative disparities of wealth

DP does not consider how development transfers rights which enable further wealth creation and reinforces power relationships that, in turn, influence future land development decisions.

PD makes social/environmental justice issues in development visible in order to explore how development concentrates wealth and control of resources and limits future sustainable options. (See RT analysis.)

Beyond Pareto Optimum to increasing the net public good

DP implicitly suggests that a development should be allowed if it does not unduly harm others, and places the burden of proof on opponents to prove harm.

PD reverses the Pareto Optimum decision rule and contends that developments could and should result in socio-ecological gains, while compensating developers where appropriate. (See GO analysis.)

Beyond assessing agencies by activities to tracking overall stocks/flows

DP charts trends in measurable factors that depend more on fluctuating exogenous conditions such as economic forces, rather than identifying action that could benefit society.

PD assesses agency action, not by activities, but by overall improvements in the condition of built and natural environments: the ecological base and public estate. (See ID analysis.)

Beyond political policy declarations to making judicious decisions

DP often allows agencies to follow the partisan ideologies of ruling parties rather than to uphold organizational charters which are based on the public interest.

PD examines agency policy and decision rationales for consistency with the agency's purpose (enabling legislation and/or preambles) and examines why outcomes differ from stated intent. (See CD analysis.)

Beyond balancing risks against costs to maximizing the prevention of risks

DP often predicts risks and balances costs of repair against likelihood of occurrence, which relies on insurance or gambling, rather than prevention through physical design.

PD calculates the worst-case scenario as the upper limit on expenditures for preventing risks, and also adds other savings or income-generating features to physical solutions. (See RA analysis.)

Beyond counting economic costs to counting costs to the economy

DP has sometimes treated resource scarcity as the mother of invention, or driver of innovation and efficiency, ignoring the long-term costs to the economy itself.

PD treats natural resource scarcity, losses of ecological space or unequal environmental space as indicators of system failure as these risk peace, justice and environment. (See EI analysis.)

Notes

1 PEARL: Abu Dhabi Urban Planning Council (2010) *The PEARL Building Rating System for Estidama: Design and Construction* (NS-R3). http://estidama.org/PEARL-rating-system-v10/PEARL-building-rating-system.aspx.
2 BREEAM: BRI (2010) *Code for Sustainable Homes: Technical Guide*, Dept for Communities and Local Government, Building Research Establishment, London, p. 296. www.breeam.com.
3 LEED: Leadership in Energy and Environmental Design, Section WE:1. https://new.usgbc.org/leed.
4 LBC: Living Building Challenge http://living-future.org/lbc/.
5 See Natural Sequence Farming. www.nsfarming.com/.
6 E.g. BREEAM Sustainable Homes and LEED include green roofs for environmental functions.
7 In LEED and PEARL (above) green roofs also count as a cooling strategy.
8 Velazquez, L. (2008) Advantages of Eco-roofs, in Birkeland, J., *Positive Development: From Vicious Circles to Virtuous Cycles through Built Environment Design*, Earthscan, London, pp. 292–3; Grant, E. J., and Jones, J. R. (2008) A Decision-Making Framework for Vegetated Roofing System Selection, *Journal of Green Building* 3(4), pp. 138–53.
9 Birkeland, J. (2014) Sustainable Resilient Buildings, in Pearson, L., Newton, P., and Roberts, P. (eds) *Resilient Sustainable Cities*, Routledge, London, UK.
10 Ken Yeang designs large buildings that use facades to exploit sun, wind, rain and other environmental factors. E.g. Yeang, K. (1999) *The Green Skyscraper: The Basis for*

Designing Sustainable Intensive Buildings, Prestel Verlag, Munich; Yeang, K. (2006) *Ecodesign: A Manual of Ecological Design*, Wiley, London.
11 PEARL (section SM-2).
12 See list of facade functions in Birkeland, *Positive Development*, p. 281.
13 BREEAM.
14 PEARL.
15 LBC.
16 BREEAM (section Pol: 03). See Freeborn, J. R., Sample, D. J., and Fox, L. J. (2012) Residential Stormwater: Methods for Decreasing Runoff and Increasing Stormwater Infiltration, *Journal of Green Building* 7(2), pp. 15–30.
17 Living machines were introduced by J. and N. Todd by the 1990s. Todd, N. J., and Todd, J. (1994) *From Eco-Cities to Living Machines*, North Atlantic Books, Berkeley, CA.
18 Birkeland, J., and Knight Lenihan, S. (2016) Biodiversity Offsetting and Net Positive Design, *Journal of Urban Design* 21(1), pp. 50–66.
19 The LBC encourages an equal or greater amount of land than that used by the project to be set aside in perpetuity and greenfield development to be compensated for by retrofitting another building. http://living-future.org/lbc/.
20 McDonald, A. (2011) personal communication, architect, Brisbane.
21 BREEAM adds 10% for exemplary performance, determined by a committee, while exacting an application fee.
22 LBC.
23 PEARL awards 2% and LEED awards 5% of total points for 'innovations'.
24 Boake, T. M. (2008) The Leap to Zero Carbon and Zero Emissions: Understanding How to Go beyond Existing Sustainable Design Protocols, *Journal of Green Building* 3(4), pp. 64–77.
25 See LEED (section 5.2). The appropriate design of private yards or internal courtyards may depend on local cultures, however.
26 Public housing residents were ordered to stop gardening (2016). www.treehugger.com/culture/public-housing-residents-told-tear-their-gardens.html.
27 Birkeland, J., Systems and Social Change for Sustainable and Resilient Cities.
28 E.g. see PEARL (section NS-1). LEED, BREEAM, LBC have similar provisions.
29 The profitability of brownfield remediation depends on economic circumstances. See www.lincolninst.edu/es/publications/articles/promoting-more-equitable-brownfield-redevelopment.
30 LBC.
31 LEED.
32 BREEAM.
33 Recycling has been subject to excessive corruption, but usually has fewer impacts than manufacturing that includes mining or forestry.
34 Apparently, the research indicating that 97% of waste is from manufacturing and mining is not well documented. See https://discardstudies.com/2016/03/02/municipal-versus-industrial-waste-a-3-97-ratio-or-something-else-entirely/.
35 In the case of Bogota, for instance, construction causes nearly 950,000 m³ of waste each month. 20,000 m³ of this waste is usually dumped or mixed with other residues, without separation or treatment. Bogota produces about 11 million tons of waste per year, and 73,000 tons are hazardous. See Secretaría Distrital de Planeación, 2011.
36 Thornton, B. J. (2011) The Greenest Building (is the One that you Don't Build!): Effective Techniques for Sustainable Adaptive Reuse/Renovation, *Journal of Green Building* 6(1), pp. 1–7.
37 Romm, J. (1999) *Cool Companies: How the Best Businesses Boost Profits and Productivity by Cutting Greenhouse-Gas Emissions*, Island Press, Washington, DC, p. 55.
38 LEED awards up to four points for building reuse.
39 Birkeland, Sustainable Resilient Buildings.
40 BREEAM and LEED.
41 Santana, M. E. (2002) Timber Waste Minimization by Design, in J. Birkeland (ed.) *Design for Sustainability: A Sourcebook of Eco-logical Solutions*, Earthscan, London, pp. 188–91.

42 Downcycling means reduced to a lower economic value such as sawdust instead of timber. The term was apparently coined by McDonough, W., and Braungart, M. (2002) *Cradle to Cradle: Remaking the Way we Make Things*, North Point Press, New York.
43 Jehne, W. (2002) personal communication (forest microbiologist, formerly of CSIRO).
44 PEARL.
45 Hill, G. (2002) Designing Waste, in Birkeland, *Design for Sustainability*, pp. 43–5; Mithraratne, N., Vale, B., and Vale, R. (2007) *Sustainable Living: The Role of the Whole Life Costs and Values*, Butterworth-Heinemann, London.
46 World's 26 Richest People Own as Much as Poorest 50%. www.theguardian.com/business/2019/jan/21/world-26-richest-people-own-as-much-as-poorest-50-per-cent-oxfam-report.
47 LBC.
48 Rare earths are often bound up in mineral deposits with thorium which causes cancer. See www.nature.com/articles/s41598-017-10256-7.
49 Sneddon, C. S., Barraud, R., and Germaine, M. A. (2017) Dam Removals and River Restoration in International Perspective, *Water Alternatives* 10(3), pp. 648–54.
50 El Niños are becoming more frequent due to global warming which intensifies droughts. See Watts, J. (2017) Global Atmospheric CO2 Levels Hit Record High, *Guardian*, Oct. 31.
51 LBC.
52 Lovegrove, K., and W. Stein. (2012) *Concentrating Solar Power Technology: Principles, Developments and Applications*, Woodhead Publishing, Elsevier, Cambridge.
53 E.g. cranes could theoretically double as wind generators at night that feed into the grid, and portable solar cells could be used on construction storage sheds.
54 While government subsidies for renewable energy began to surpass those for coal, gas and oil in 2010, there was 12% jump in fossil fuel subsidies in 2017. www.iea.org/weo/energysubsidies/.
55 Appleton, J. (1975) *The Experience of Landscape*, Wiley & Sons, New York.
56 Cole, L. (2017) New Tech Could Turn Windows into Solar Panels, *Sydney Morning Herald*, www.smh.com.au/business/energy/new-tech-could-turn-windows-into-solar-panels-20171027-gz9goq.html. Oct. 30.
57 'Net positive' energy is impossible, but some still assume sustainability is only about energy.
58 www.energymatters.com.au/misc/peer-to-peer-solar-energy-trading-guide/.
59 A recent tour of a green office building revealed that most offices had private little space heaters.
60 A ceiling can be shaped to capture the heat given off by ceiling lighting fixtures.
61 Birkeland, J. (2009) Eco-Retrofitting with Building Integrated Living Systems, in *Smart and Sustainable Built Environment Conference Proceedings*, Delft, Netherlands, www.sasbe2009.com/.
62 Indoor air pollution can often be four to ten times greater than the outdoor air.
63 Barton, H., Grant, M., and Guise, R. (2010) *Shaping Neighbourhoods: For Local Health and Global Sustainability*, Routledge, London and New York.
64 Sapolsky, R. (2005) Sick of Poverty, *Scientific American* 293(6), pp. 92–9.
65 See Mendoza, S. S. (2018) Box 16: Making Positive Impacts, in Birkeland, *Positive Development*, p. 295.
66 The argument is often made that giving survivors or socio-economically deprived people money instead of indirect levers and pulleys is more effective but, arguably, retrofitting the built environment would be more direct and cost effective, once emergency conditions were addressed.
67 Schmitz, A., and Scully, J. (2006) *Creating Walkable Places: Compact Mixed-Use Solutions*, ULI, Washington, DC.
68 See e.g. www.health.harvard.edu/blog/regular-exercise-changes-brain-improve-memory-thinking-skills-201404097110.
69 BREEAM.
70 LEED.
71 PEARL.
72 PEARL.
73 BREEAM.

74 Hempcrete can substitute for concrete for most purposes.
75 PEARL.
76 Castro-Lacouture, D., Sefair, J. A., et al. (2009) Optimization Model for the Selection of Materials Using a LEED-Based Green Building Rating System in Colombia, *Building and Environment* 44(6), pp. 1162–70.
77 PEARL. A new Green Star tool in Australia promises to increase ecological considerations.
78 This is like giving the target of a firing squad a cardboard shield.
79 PEARL.
80 The Center for Disease Control and Prevention estimates that excessive urban heat contributed to more than 8,000 premature deaths in the United States from 1979 to 2003 (1,600 per year). www.cdc.gov/disasters/extremeheat/index.html.
81 LEED.
82 Kaatz, E., Root, D. S., Bowen, P. A., and Hill, R. C. (2006) Advancing Key Outcomes of Sustainability Building Assessment, *Building Research and Information* 34(4), pp. 308–20.
83 LBC.
84 Birkeland and Knight Lenihan, Biodiversity Offsetting.

Section H
STARfish (A Quantitative Tool)

15 The STARfish Tool Described

15.1 Review and Preview

Since built environments are complex systems, design tools will emphasize some issues and omit others, and will therefore reflect or reinforce certain values.

In ecological design, everything is interconnected. Hence, decisions/designs regarding one impact category affect other categories, as illustrated below. In assessment, however, reality is separated into discrete units for enumeration. This reinforces technocratic values from the outset – as opposed to ethics or ecology. For example, measurable conditions affecting the human environment (e.g. daylight, indoor air quality, thermal comfort), were counted as improvements to the natural environment. Not only can the wrong things often be measured in the wrong ways, measurements are often fudged for expediency.[1] Assessment tools need to be relevant to design, rather than making design conform to assessment.

The main purpose of design tools should be to reveal opportunities for planning/design alternatives that avoid harm entirely and make everyone better off.

The ability to calculate interconnected, complex problems is rapidly improving. Many generic impacts of industrial materials are already linked to computer-aided drawing programs for rapid calculation of lifecycle impacts (e.g. LCADesign).[2] Nevertheless, decision tools tend to oversimplify or disregard multi-dimensional sustainability issues. Logically, design tools should assist in avoiding negative impacts entirely and create opportunities for positive impacts – instead of treating abatement as positive or not even recognizing and rewarding net-positive ones. Since there are no bounds to positive impacts except limited imaginations, design tools should stimulate structural/spatial solutions that over-compensate for unavoidable impacts and create net public benefits.

The STARfish tool aims to address criteria developed from the preceding critique of RTs and build design capacity for achieving PD sustainability standards.

While the eDR process [Chapters 13–14] should aid in developing the basic plan and brief, the STARfish supports the design process itself by stimulating design synergies. Both processes support collaborative, creative thinking, but the STARfish provides scores to rate or rank alternative buildings or design concepts. Assessment is increasingly deemed necessary to accommodate managers and approval authorities and give investors confidence. Therefore, the STARfish is

336 *Decision Making and Assessment*

linked to a spreadsheet tool. This means it can be combined with LCA data for quantitative assessment. The free STARfish tool is described and illustrated in Box 7.[3] Some objectives of the STARfish are to:

- Reframe design as opportunity creation, rather than reductionist problem mitigation;
- Emphasize the preliminary design stage, creativity, goal-oriented collaboration and fun;
- Include both positive and negative sustainability issues that are currently omitted by RTs;
- Foster a whole-system view of the environment, not buildings 'as objects' out of context;
- Integrate regional sustainability issues with site-specific planning considerations;
- Avoid latent anti-sustainable biases by making assumptions, values and reasoning transparent;
- Prioritize the use of multifunctional, eco-positive natural systems over industrial equipment;
- Reduce the gap between so-called sustainable design and objectively sustainable environments;
- Suggest eco-positive design concepts that could, in combination, meet the PD Test;
- Foster engagement of designers in different locations by providing an interactive game.

Because crucial ecological issues have been marginalized in building assessments, the STARfish starts from the ecological base and nature (the basis of sustainability).

The first version of the STARfish (2010) centered on design for eco-services, because ecology had only been nominally included in RTs.[4] RTs largely omitted ecology and environmental ethics and only counted negative impacts. Several RTs credit outdoor landscaping around the building, such as providing native plants or permeable paving, and label that 'ecological'. This might offset a small portion of impacts caused by buildings and paving but it fails to increase ecosystems or ecological space beyond the 'no building' case. Landscaping could increase the 'effective land area', by creating vertical surfaces/spaces for eco-services and habitats, but this is seldom encouraged.[5]

The STARfish can work like a game where the protagonists (design team) represent the public interest and the adversaries are malignant past practices.

RTs appeal to some who like competition but competition should target whole-system issues. RTs also exclude non-numerical issues that are not easily quantified (e.g. ethics, happiness).[6] The design-based PD approach to assessment can encourage integrated, collaborative, interactive design by putting everyone on the same team – against ignorance, apathy and prejudice. Here, the design team competes with itself. The PD STARfish aims to help find positive design opportunities across the supply chain before and after construction [Box 7]. The STARfish could be a physical board game,[7] but computer apps enable designers in different locations to collaborate in the design process.

Post-occupancy evaluations (POEs) should be used after commencing building occupancy to uncover/correct problems and amend the tool where predicted performance proves inaccurate.

POEs assess actual, not expected, performance. Some RTs check performance after a year of occupancy. Most have no penalty for failing to meet commitments, other than being deprived of another award. However, when predictions do not match performance, the tool should be re-examined. POEs would be more useful if buildings were designed to be adaptable and reversible, as shortfalls in occupant satisfaction and/or resource efficiency could be corrected after construction. Someday, regulations could require retrofits of any buildings that fall below a certain sustainability standard.[8] Retrofitting could be (and sometimes is) subsidized to the extent that it saves taxpayers money.

15.2 How Impact Categories Overlap

Before studying the design tool, it should be remembered that any separation of impact categories is conceptually problematic as all environmental issues interact.

RTs often fail to identify design opportunities because, being decision tools, they focus on separate parts. A compilation of efficient building components may focus on the trees and miss the forest. For instance, it is sometimes claimed that there is no timber waste in forestry today because (most) timber waste is recycled, even when the whole forest has been laid to waste. Of course, both reductionist analyses or decision making and design syntheses are necessary ingredients in sustainable development. One impact category, 'materials/waste', is used here to illustrate how impacts are interrelated. This indicates that positive reciprocal relationships are possible.

- *Materials – efficiency/energy*: The material flows associated with the manufacturing of building products are huge contributors to global energy usage. Some materials have relatively little embodied energy in production (e.g. bio-based materials), but might nonetheless be transported long distances. New efficient (cheaper, stronger, lighter) materials are becoming available which can reduce the total energy/resources used. They can create more space using less heating-cooling energy and/or more functions using fewer resources. Nevertheless, many price-efficient modern building products are high in embodied energy. Hence, materials designed for deconstruction, eco-cycling and/or multiple functions can often do more to reduce energy consumption over the project's whole lifecycle.
- *Materials – health/life quality*: Many materials affect health due to pollution throughout the product supply chain and some building products even off-gas toxins in situ. When sick building syndrome has caused new buildings to be demolished, their materials were totally wasted.[9] The toxins from building implosions affect a wide area,[10] and the debris that is taken to landfill eventually leaches into the environment. At the city scale, urban forests can remediate brownfield sites and clean the air while producing timber. At the building scale, indoor air quality can be improved by using innovative building materials/products that absorb toxins,[11] or simply by adding building-integrated vegetation.

- *Materials – greenhouse/carbon emissions*: The emissions from building construction and operation depend primarily on whether fossil fuels are used, not just energy usage.[12] Materials that use coal-fired power generation have serious climate impacts, along with other negative impacts such as cumulative atmospheric mercury.[13] Therefore, materials selection is critical in reducing carbon emissions in both production and transport. Timber is considered to cause relatively modest emissions, but soil disruption through forestry can be a significant cause of carbon release.[14] Some materials sequester carbon in buildings (e.g. timber, bamboo, olivine, hemp, mycelium-based bricks), although the amounts absorbed can be small compared to emissions caused during production.
- *Materials – ecology/biodiversity*: The selection and sourcing of materials is a primary cause of ecosystem damage. Avoiding mined materials/products reduces pollution and habitat destruction. Selective harvesting of timber reduces ecological waste, soil erosion and habitat losses (although this is subject to debate).[15] Building products can be 'grown' using agri-waste. If and when such buildings are eventually retrofitted or demolished, building materials from agri-waste (e.g. strawboard, hempcrete) and bio-based crops (e.g. bamboo, timber) can become soil additives, habitats and or nutrients depending on the local circumstances. Other new technologies (e.g. nanotechnology, printed buildings) are efficient, but do not yet seem to address ecological issues.
- *Materials – planning/spatial relationships*: It is now recognized that concrete megaliths designed to hold back nature can not only have large production impacts, but can magnify the consequence of floods, storm surges and earthquakes. With sea level rise and flooding, many homes will need to be moved, elevated onto structural tables or retrofitted for being quickly 'plastic wrapped' – or else abandoned. If abandoned, toxins will be released into waterways (while saltwater seeps into aquifers). Cities cannot easily be dismantled and moved, so the waste and toxins will be huge. Over time, cities must be decontaminated and ground levels retrofitted for flood proofing.

15.3 Description of the STARfish

The General STARfish can be used as a preliminary design tool in workshops and expanded during design stages for detailed analysis and assessment.

The General STARfish, a variation on radar diagram (described below), has six impact categories which were selected mainly because they overlap common impact categories used in several RTs.[16] This may facilitate cross-referencing or the transfer of information between other RTs and the STARfish. The STARfish can expand, like a fractal pattern, into many sub-categories. Generally speaking, the more parameters that must be met, the easier good design is. Blank canvases encourage reliance on design precedents, while more criteria create a challenge to find synergies through multifunctional design. The major categories and criteria in the General STARfish (discussed below) are:

- *Ecology/biodiversity* (e.g. carrying capacity, biodiversity, ecosystem functions/services)
- *Materials/waste* (e.g. resource depletion, waste, toxins)

- *Efficiency/energy* (e.g. energy and resource minimization)
- *Greenhouse/carbon* (e.g. fossil fuel avoidance, oxygen, carbon sequestration)
- *Health/life quality* (e.g. physical and mental wellbeing, environmental quality/amenity)
- *Planning/spatial relationships* (e.g. ethics, equity and environmental space).

The STARfish diagram combines the configurations used in radar and spider diagrams and impact wheels to facilitate the exploration of positive design opportunities.

The radar diagram can have any number of impact factors. In the preliminary stage or in community design workshops, a single radar diagram may suffice to define the issues and compare basic ideas. Although there are only six impact categories here, the radar diagram is combined with a spider diagram configuration, which can expand into many sub-categories. Thus, issues can be examined in more detail as the brief, context and/or special issues demands [Figure 15.1]. Radar diagrams allow different impacts with different metrics or units to be displayed together and summed, because the scales on each 'leg' can be different.

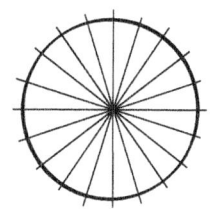

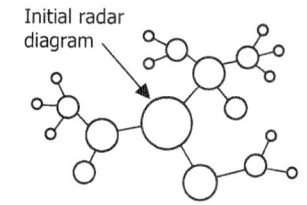

The radar diagram which has different factors on each radius, can be combined mathematically with radar diagrams that are subcomponents of each factor

Figure 15.1 The constituent diagrams

15.3.1 The Diagrams Combined

***Radar diagrams** register negative and/or positive impacts, but they do not register net-positive impacts because zero is at one end of the scale.*

Although biophysical sustainability cannot be achieved without net-positive development, ordinary radar diagrams cannot show net-positive gains. Where the scale ends in 0, positive impacts are really reductions in negative ones. Omitting the possibility of net-positive impacts may have resulted from the engrained supposition that public benefits cost more.[17] Ironically, cost is not an issue when the objective is to display conspicuous consumption or engineering prowess.[18] Further, design with public benefits would not cost more if full-cost accounting were used. After all, cleaning up irreversible problems in natural and urban environments, long after the fact, would cost far more than prevention.[19]

340 *Decision Making and Assessment*

Spider diagrams *can allow an expansion of issues and/or prioritization (weighting) of particular issues and helps to see relationships in time and space.*

The spider diagram can expand like a fractal pattern to help visualize relationships between issues/impacts. They can also help to make connections between separate issues, as in impact wheels (below). Such 'mind-mapping' diagrams are often used in workshops to identify problems or visualize complex issues that have many impact factors with subcomponents, any of which could have subcomponents. Tracing tributary impacts back in time and space can help to find opportunities for early design interventions that avoid compound damage downstream (as in industrial metabolism). Thus, a Satellite STARfish can highlight places where waste during production and construction could be reduced.

Impact wheels *usually trace negative impacts but, in PD, this is reversed to find opportunities for creating positive synergies between the various issues/impacts.*

This STARfish draws upon a PD version of an impact wheel, which maps how positive impacts affect other impacts.[20] An example used in *Positive Development* (2008) showed how many actions that caused a lack of soil quality were linked to soil structure.[21] Soil structure is how soil granules aggregate to create soil pores which improve water movement, biological activity and root growth. Reversing the wheels shows that improvements to soil structure (e.g. programs delivering urban compost to farms) could reduce other environmental problems related to soil quality that are often addressed separately, such as erosion or excess fertilizer usage [Figure 15.2].

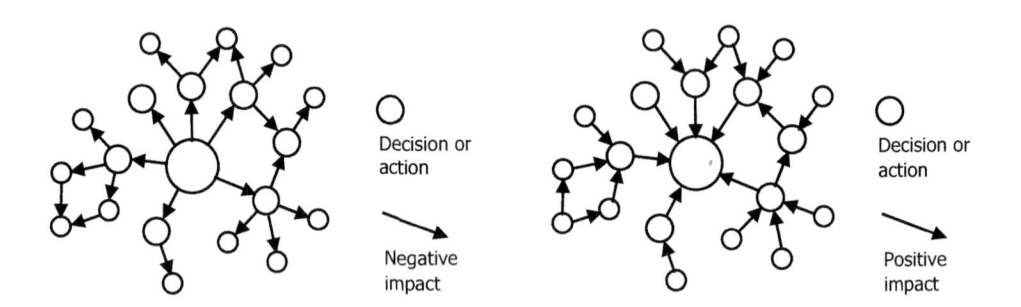

In the PD version of the impact wheel, the focus is on reversing negative impacts at each stage, as a means to affect the original cause of the problems

Figure 15.2 Reverse impact wheel (Source: Birkeland 2008)

The STARfish *combines the radar, spider and impact wheel diagrams, but also makes some fundamental changes to be more relevant to net-positive design.*

The General STARfish has six Satellite STARfish listed above. Each Satellite STARfish has several impact factors and more can be added [Chapter 16]. These define the radiuses or legs [Figure 15.3]. Each of these impact categories (e.g. waste, carbon, health or biodiversity) can be extended out further, as in

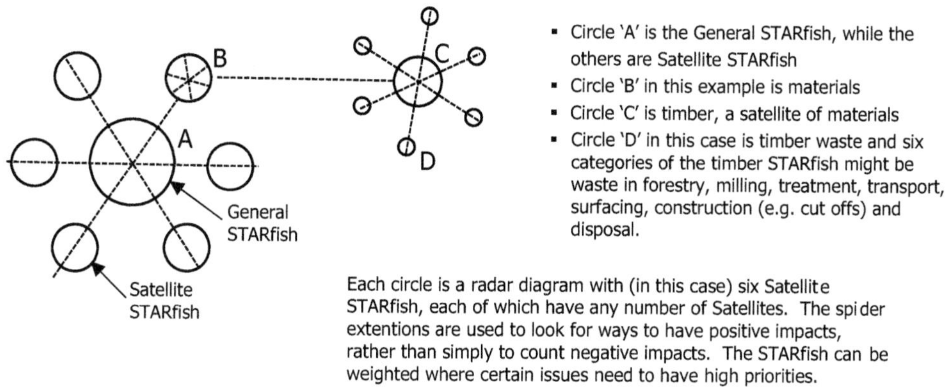

- Circle 'A' is the General STARfish, while the others are Satellite STARfish
- Circle 'B' in this example is materials
- Circle 'C' is timber, a satellite of materials
- Circle 'D' in this case is timber waste and six categories of the timber STARfish might be waste in forestry, milling, treatment, transport, surfacing, construction (e.g. cut offs) and disposal.

Each circle is a radar diagram with (in this case) six Satellite STARfish, each of which have any number of Satellites. The spider extentions are used to look for ways to have positive impacts, rather than simply to count negative impacts. The STARfish can be weighted where certain issues need to have high priorities.

Figure 15.3 The STARfish diagram

a spider diagram, to compose Satellite STARfish. These in turn can be extended out into more sub-categories. For example, in a desert, water might have another Satellite STARfish, whereas in a developing city air pollution might have a separate STARfish. The STARfish can be weighted where some issues are more important.

The STARfish diagrams distinguish worst case, neutral/zero and net-positive impacts, which allows for analyzing and crediting genuine progress, as opposed to unsustainable development.

As discussed below, radar diagrams need only two measurements to create a scale which facilitates estimates, based on a percentage of damage [Box 7]. The usual scale goes from '0' at the centre of the circle to '-1' at the outer circle. In this case, a smaller polygon means more sustainable. This is sometimes reversed so the outside circle is '+1'. Hence, most radar diagrams only show negative or positive impacts. The STARfish, in contrast, goes from '-10' to 0 to '+10' to record improvements beyond the 'no development' condition. This allows negative, restorative and net-positive impacts to be summed.

15.3.2 The Circles on the Diagram

The circles on the diagram establish the benchmarks (worst-case, net-zero impact and net positive) for each impact category or leg of the STARfish.

Different sustainability standards are provided for each basic impact category [Chapter 16]. The definitions of criteria/benchmarks appear as pop-ups on the tool where the estimated impact meets the center (worst-case scenario), the inner circle (neutral-net impact) or the outer circle (net-positive impact) of the diagram [Figure 15.4]. By using benchmarks linked to sustainable outcomes, progress toward sustainability could eventually be tracked (in a perfect world). Users would ideally state the basis for positioning an impact in writing, so others can learn. Links to inspirational solutions on the internet for the particular criteria can be added continuously.

342 *Decision Making and Assessment*

A: Centre (-10) = Total destruction caused by the project without any redeeming actions or mitigation measures being deducted

B: Inner circle (0) = The condition that would exist if there has been no development or negative impacts at all (ever)

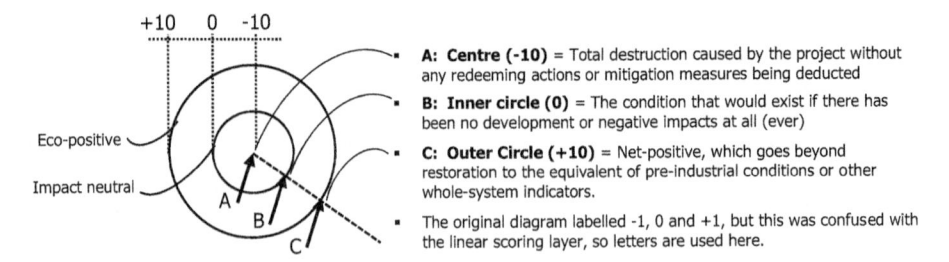

C: Outer Circle (+10) = Net-positive, which goes beyond restoration to the equivalent of pre-industrial conditions or other whole-system indicators.

The original diagram labelled -1, 0 and +1, but this was confused with the linear scoring layer, so letters are used here.

Figure 15.4 The circles on the STARfish diagram

The 'Sliders' in the app allow impacts to be estimated (and automatically displayed on the diagram) to be later refined as information improves.

Criteria that pop up on the app [Box 7] remind the user of the criteria/benchmarks for negative, neutral and net-positive impacts. Negative impacts appear on the diagram from the zero impact position inwards. Net-zero or neutral impacts effectively shrink those negative impacts. That is, they are connected to the negative impacts on the diagram. Remediation/regeneration actions can mitigate or even reverse the negative impacts caused by the development. For example, where more sustainable timber is regrown than used, these could exceed the '0' circle. Net-positive actions are separate actions, not remedial ones, and are generally actions that have public benefits.

15.3.3 The STARs on the Diagram

When the points for different (negative, regenerative and net-positive) actions/impacts are plotted using the Sliders on the app, three corresponding star/polygon shapes appear.

On each STARfish, the separate layers for negative impacts, and restorative and net-positive gains have transparent colors or patterns for 2D representation [Box 7] [Figure 15.5]. In this example, since only six legs are used, the shapes are polygons. The negative BlackSTAR, restorative GreenSTAR and net-positive BlueSTAR remain separate to preserve a record of the actual impacts and may aid in achieving a sustainability standard in the future. RTs generally record the remaining negative impact after it is mitigated, and only a single number is presented. Similarly, typical radar diagrams usually only show the net impact, even if the negative impacts remain.[22]

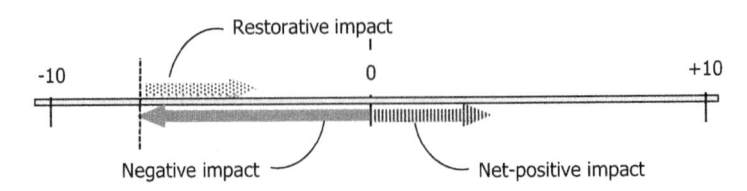

Figure 15.5 A typical leg (radius) on the radar diagram

The BlackSTAR *(negative impacts) goes from the central circle 'B' on the diagram toward the center point 'A' (-10) – the worst-case scenario.*

In the STARfish, negative impacts are measured from zero, as defined in each impact category (other display options are available). They are not hidden by remediation. If a building has sick building syndrome or asbestos and it is later remodeled, the past damage is not undone, and additional health risks may be created in the demolition-construction process. A retrofit encasing the asbestos might be better than removing the asbestos in a whole-system framework. New green buildings do not usually compensate for past harm to human/environmental health. Hence, negative impacts remain visible as a reminder that past impacts should be offset.

The GreenSTAR *represents remedial, restorative and regenerative actions that reduce the development's negative impacts and could conceivably outweigh those impacts in some cases.*

A restorative action is a reversal of the project's negative impact. If the arrow/bar reaches the inner circle '0', it means mitigation/restoration activity achieves the equivalent of impact neutrality – on a lifecycle basis. Restorative impacts go from the end of the above negative impact to '0' or even beyond. For example, air filtration is mitigative. If a filtering system, such as green walls, cleans more air than used by building occupants, it may remediate some urban air. Similarly, if substantial green roofs/walls clean urban air and add oxygen to support the wider urban area, it may go beyond zero.

The BlueSTAR *represents additional designs/actions that create public benefits and would usually involve multifunctional, reversible and/or adaptable design, or at least net-positive offsetting.*

Again, zero impact is not sustainable in the context of escalating problems. In a whole-system framework, improvements over current deteriorated environmental/social conditions are not net positive. Design outcomes depend on interactions with socio-economic and ecological circumstances. Improvements over average performance (code compliance) usually increases global depletion and pollution. Often, depending on how things are counted in assessment tools, a large project can be more efficient than most buildings with similar functions, yet have larger actual negative impacts.[23] Such contextual issues can be explored using the SMARTmode analyses [Chapters 7–8], which suggest ways to create extra positive, multiple and/or synergistic impacts.

Net-positive offsetting *can be offsite or offshore as long as the project improves whole-system (global) sustainability and does not excuse avoidable negative impacts.*

Net-positive actions/designs benefit the public and/or planet wherever located, so they can take place in disadvantaged countries. Therefore, if the subject project avoids harm and regenerates the affected environments, actions in disadvantaged regions or nations could provide additional offsetting. Collectively, this could reduce the 'circle of poison' that has often characterized DP development.[24] Eco-positive offsetting should compensate for unavoidable damage but also for possible future eventualities. For example, there are risks inherent in intervening in natural ecosystems, even when the aim is to increase

344 *Decision Making and Assessment*

biodiversity. Nonetheless, there is no upper limit to positive impacts, as they can pay for themselves.

The SummarySTAR displays total scores for comparing designs visually, for awarding credits or for other management purposes where single scores may be useful.

After the locations are determined for each impact category on the STARfish legs (using the Sliders), the tool automatically produces a summary of the end result of all negative, remedial and positive actions. This SummarySTAR can be displayed as just negative or just net-positive impacts. It can also be shown on the same diagram as the other three STARs although, for clarity, Box 7 shows it separately. The app also provides a numerical score when needed for various pragmatic reasons, such as to compare a proposed design to other competing products, design elements or other buildings assessed using this tool.

The basic STARfish app is illustrated in Box 7, which is available on a website and can be modified to suit particular projects.

Box 7 shows the basic elements of STARfish app for those not wishing to access it online. In the illustrations, a sample (simplified) radar diagram is shown, along with a bar diagram, in case one version seems easier to understand by users or their clients. These are interconnected, so moving any Slider changes all of the diagrams and their calculations. Any number of positive impacts can be added to the diagram. The website app may occasionally be updated or modified, so criticisms, questions or suggestions are welcome and may be incorporated into the app (which can be found at www.sustainability.org.au).

15.4 Summary of STARfish Benefits

Aids visualization: Whereas lists and numbers align with reductionist thinking, radar diagrams may assist in seeing people-building-nature relationships and thus help to stimulate synergistic design.

It can be hard to comprehend real-world interactions using lists, tables or even 'mandalas' (lists in artistic circles). The STARfish can help people visualize the relative scale of impacts and spot weaknesses in the design's potential contributions. A visual 'gap analysis' can facilitate group design by focusing on these problems/opportunities. It can reduce complexity without excluding information. Since the diagram changes automatically as data are added, participants can be stationed in different locations. As the design gels, the estimates can be refined when data on products and impacts are added into the spreadsheet program (this can occur at any stage).

Avoids normalization: These diagrams enable different impacts to be summed, even though they have different scales, if any two conditions can be defined and measured.

Normalization is where different kinds of impact factors are converted into the same units to enable them to be added or subtracted (e.g. weight, energy, volume or carbon equivalents). However, when everything is converted to the same unit of measure to produce a single score, errors are introduced. For example, waste to landfill is usually assessed by weight or volume, and toxins have little of either, yet toxins are often omitted from scorecards on waste management. The STARfish, like radar diagrams, avoid this because they record different impact factors on different legs, or radiuses, while keeping their own measurement scale.

Avoids unitization: Because each leg or impact category can have different kinds of measurements, it is not necessary to convert ecological phenomena into abstract units.

Unitization (here) means that inert units are used as surrogates for living systems or biodiversity. It bears repeating that when the life-support system is, in part or in whole, measured as a material resource, life is reduced to a number. For instance, ecosystem services and biodiversity are often converted to monetary units, such as the monetary 'costs of replacing natural services with mechanical systems'.[25] This legitimizes trade-offs between incommensurables such as biodiversity and energy. Further, monetary values are subject to fluctuation, speculation and exogenous political-economic forces. Instead of using prices/costs, therefore, the STARfish uses fixed biophysical benchmarks that represent sustainability.

Avoids thresholds: The scale from -10 to +10 allows for points for additional actions even though they exceed zero impact, to encourage more public benefits.

Minimum and maximum thresholds are common in RTs (e.g. 'four points for more than 10% recycled materials'). Once a threshold is reached, design teams have no reason to seek further improvements, as they would not count. Similarly: 'ensure that the coefficient of performance of cooling and heating source units for the HVAC system is greater than relevant federal or local standards, whichever is more stringent'.[26] Such thresholds encourage the simple addition of equipment with performance warranties, instead of passive solar design that minimizes the heating-cooling load.[27] In contrast, the STARfish can properly reward lateral thinking that leads to game-changing innovations.

Exposes negative impacts: The STARfish records negative impacts permanently, by showing reductions and gains separately, since irreversible/ongoing negative impacts are not actually eliminated in real life.

Again, not all negative impacts go away just because they are reduced by efficiencies and mitigation measures. For example, pollution can biomagnify in species and ecosystems. If a project gets credits for using recycled materials, it may use extra, and not compensate for the damage caused by the remanufacturing and transport impacts. Further, the chain of custody may be inaccurate, as there is still corruption in recycling industries.[28] Since negative impacts remain transparent in the STARfish, the scores/impacts can be audited in the future. Over time, more past damage may be compensated for as design standards, capacity and/or solutions advance.

Rewards impact avoidance: In the STARfish, unlike some assessment schemes, projects that mitigate negative impacts do not appear better than projects that have avoided them altogether.

RTs reward specific actions, so more points can be awarded for reducing a portion of negative impacts than avoiding them entirely. For instance, a maximum number of points is sometimes given for using at least '20% sustainably harvested timber'. Hence, projects may simply not use more sustainably managed timber than 20% of the total timber needed. Similarly, a project that uses '30% less natural gas' may receive more points than one using no gas at all. Large fancy projects can be very efficient and recycle more materials, yet do more harm than more modest buildings that provide the same functions.

Considers whole systems: *Instead of rewarding reductions relative to typical buildings, the STARfish aims for reductions that are proportional to growing rates of regional/global human impacts.*

Tools that record only the percentage of damage remediated can be misleading. Using more timber waste previously left on the forest floor as mulch is not a 20% reduction in timber waste. Further, the forest ecosystems may need that 'waste'. In a context of uncertainty and complexity, reductions do not increase resilience to change. A building should not just clean the environmental media that it damages, it should improve offsite media. Although still a stretch goal, net-positive impacts would ideally be in proportion to rates of increasing regional, even global, environmental degradation and resource depletion (not reductions compared to the norm).

Identifies opportunities: *The spider diagram configuration can help to identify new opportunities and inspire design elements that combine to create multiple restorative and/or net-positive impacts.*

Ecological design concepts can add value in several impact categories. For example, a roof/wall with Green Scaffolding can provide two dozen additional benefits, spanning most of the basic impact categories [Chapter 6]. Typical assessments only count impact reductions in one category by specifying points for easily measured actions (e.g. provide a certain amount of outdoor shading). When the same or similar design elements make distinct improvements in several impact categories and add to the positive public impact, they should also count. Many benefits can be explored and credited by adding Satellite STARfish in priority areas and weighting certain important factors.[29]

Prioritize problems: *Spider diagrams can prioritize critical issues or impacts, and they can also be used to focus on unique opportunities created by particular projects.*

Although all buildings should improve urban air quality, a building in a noisy, congested, polluted central city location should prioritize producing oxygen and filtering/purifying pollution. The health leg can be extended out into Satellite Air Quality STARfish to assist in identifying and exposing opportunities for air improvement strategies. Similarly, a building in a tropical setting has different design priorities than one in an isolated desert location, so Satellite Water Quality STARfish might be useful. However, since some LCAs have weighted certain categories more heavily to make projects/products look better, any changes in weightings in the STARfish should have written/public rationales.

Provides examples: *The STARfish tool can have links to relevant internet examples, case studies and websites to help inspire designers in developing their project-specific ideas.*

Designers' skill sets vary. Therefore, just as each leg has pop-up descriptions of the benchmarks, the STARfish can have pop-ups that show a range of potential solutions that are drawn from the web. For example, callouts on the 'water' leg might refer to various natural water treatment systems that purify water as it enters or leaves the site or building. Many websites (e.g. Inhabitat and Treehugger) now feature new design concepts. While not always suitable in themselves, they can seed ideas for innovations in other contexts.[30] Users could gradually contribute links to good ideas to cover more situations.

Supports public benefits: Radar diagrams show relationships among impacts, and highlight areas that need more attention, but the STARfish also highlights opportunities for positive public impacts.

Because RTs divide up impacts, specify particular actions and limit the points awarded to impact mitigation measures, they can encourage conventional solutions.[31] Most tools assign points for specific single-function mitigation measures – not for multiple public gains. Hence, green building elements often just serve one function, partly because actions only get credit in one assessment category. For instance, one RT credits green roofs for reducing runoff and providing insulation, but not for incorporating biodiversity habitats or providing substantial nature air-filtering systems on roofs. Multifunctional design can achieve more socio-ecological gains in relation to space, energy and resources than technical fixes.

Allows systems analyses: The STARfish could amalgamate other sustainability dimensions, such as governance or management performance, in one giant urban system assessment app for comparing cities.

Although built environments could improve most biophysical issues, STARfish diagrams could also integrate other sustainability issues that are concerned with management or organizational performance. Currently, cities are developing uniform criteria for comparing cities to each other. These often focus on one priority such as carbon emissions. An urban rating system using the STARfish could add dimensions such as environmental justice or socio-economic equity. For example, some of Bhutan's Gross National Happiness indicators include time expenditure, education and cultural or institutional factors. The STARfish diagram concept allows for very different issues to be calculated and summed (hopefully retaining the PD Test).

15.5 Exercises

1 Scan some RTs for a list of variables that are often used in assessments. Do they set specific measurements that are found in typical buildings and then expect the design teams to achieve that number or better? Of the list of sustainability issues covered by SMT analyses [Chapters 7–8], how many of these are covered by the RT provisions?

Box 7 The STARfish net-positive design app

The website (sustainability.org.au) has instructions on how to operate the app. Terminology note: Significant restorative actions would usually be required to compensate for negative impacts recorded in the BlackSTAR. The GreenSTAR represents remedial or regenerative actions that ameliorate a particular negative impact. These might restore the particular negative impact to the equivalent impact of 'no development', but these might not be enough to cause the impact factor to pass the zero-impact point to create net gains. The BlueSTAR is net-positive, meaning actions or design elements that create positive public gains.

Main diagram: The General STARfish (main diagram) is a radar diagram with (currently) six 'Legs', or impact categories, for measuring basic impacts caused by a project. These are: ecology/biodiversity, materials/waste, health/life quality, planning/spatial relationships, greenhouse/carbon, efficiency/energy. While these topics correspond generally with categories in conventional green building rating tools, they are not checklists of specific design measures. They can be examined in more detail in sub-diagrams, Satellite STARfish, which are also radar diagrams. The STARfish tool automatically calculates the results and displays them visually.

Radar diagram: In the preliminary design stage, or in community workshops, the General STARfish (with or without the six Satellites) might suffice on its own. There is a 'Slider' for locating negative, restorative/regenerative and eco-positive impacts. The impacts are estimated against stationary biophysical benchmarks in each case. These benchmarks for negative/black, restorative/green and eco-positive/blue STARfish pop up below the Slider when it moves near '-10', '0' or '+10'. Note that offsets do not erase negative impacts, even when they are offset.

Satellite sub-diagrams: Any number of Legs and Satellites can be added to the Constellation. That is, impact factors can be sub-divided further if a set of related impacts would have a particular bearing on the project performance. For example, if the project will be located in a highly polluted area, an 'air quality' Satellite STARfish could have another Satellite with several impact factors. The results of all sub-diagrams feed back into the General STARfish to provide an overall visual and numerical result.

Weighting: When the impacts of the Constellation of impacts are calculated by the program, they create the shape of the main General Starfish (that has six or more Legs). The STARfish app 'weights' the six main impact categories, which can be altered. For example, although many consider greenhouse emissions to be the most important factor, a project with few emissions (e.g. a plant nursery) should not emphasize that factor.

Graphic Options: The data can be displayed in different kinds of diagrams by using the sub-diagram options panel. Many options are available for different graphic presentations. For example, you can: change the relative size of diagrams; add, delete or rename Legs, diagrams and sub-diagrams; change the distance between them; change the colors or their transparency; rotate the diagrams or; swap the position of the Legs. Basic diagram types can be selected. For example, one option summarizes the total net-negative or net-positive impacts for a quick comparison of design concepts. Another is the classical bar chart view of the diagram.

ZeroCircle Graph: In the preferred diagram, the aim is to get out of the inner circle. The negative impacts begin from '0' in the middle of the scale. This can be presented as either a pie or star diagram configuration.

The STARfish Tool Described 349

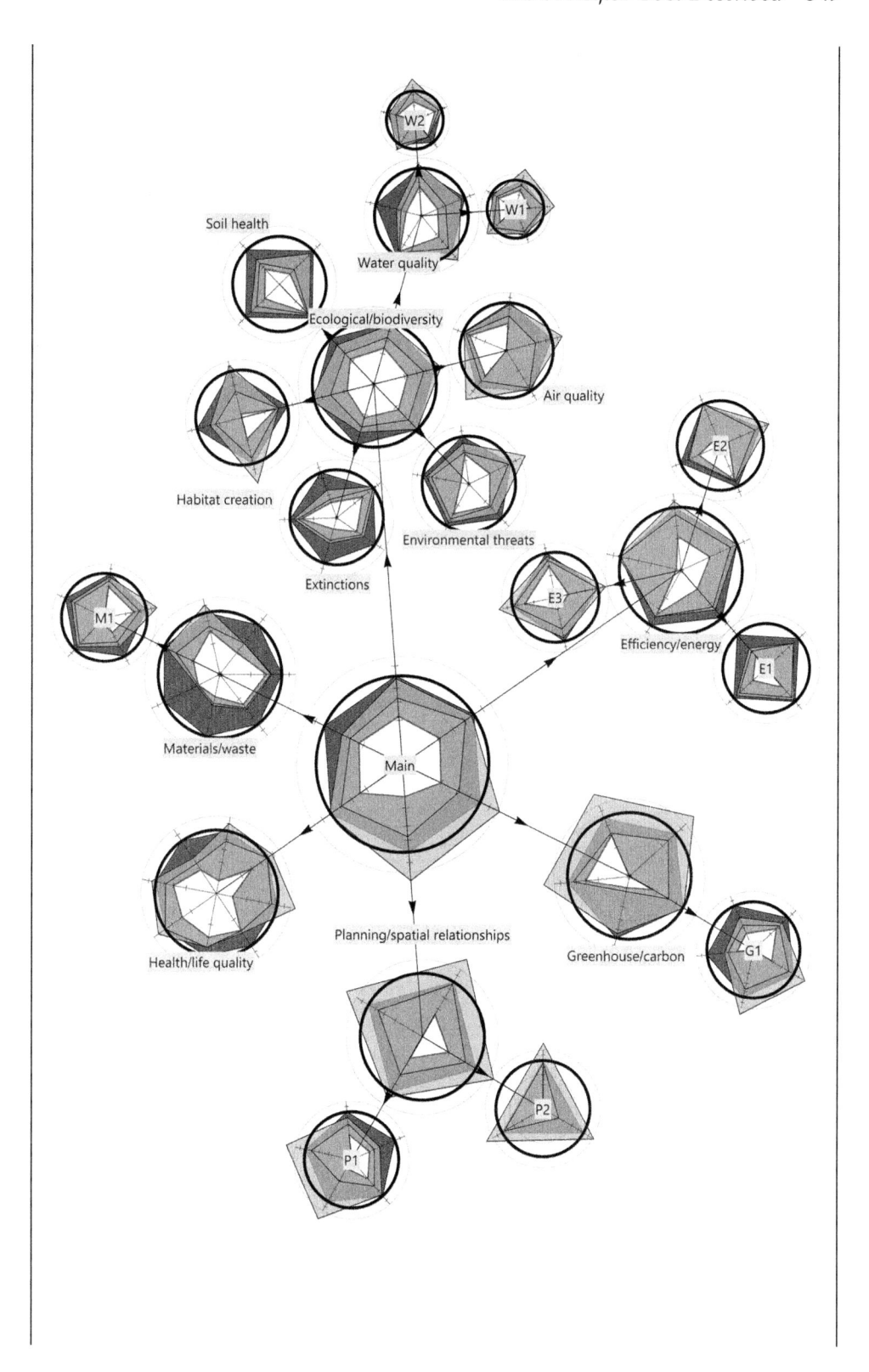

350 *Decision Making and Assessment*

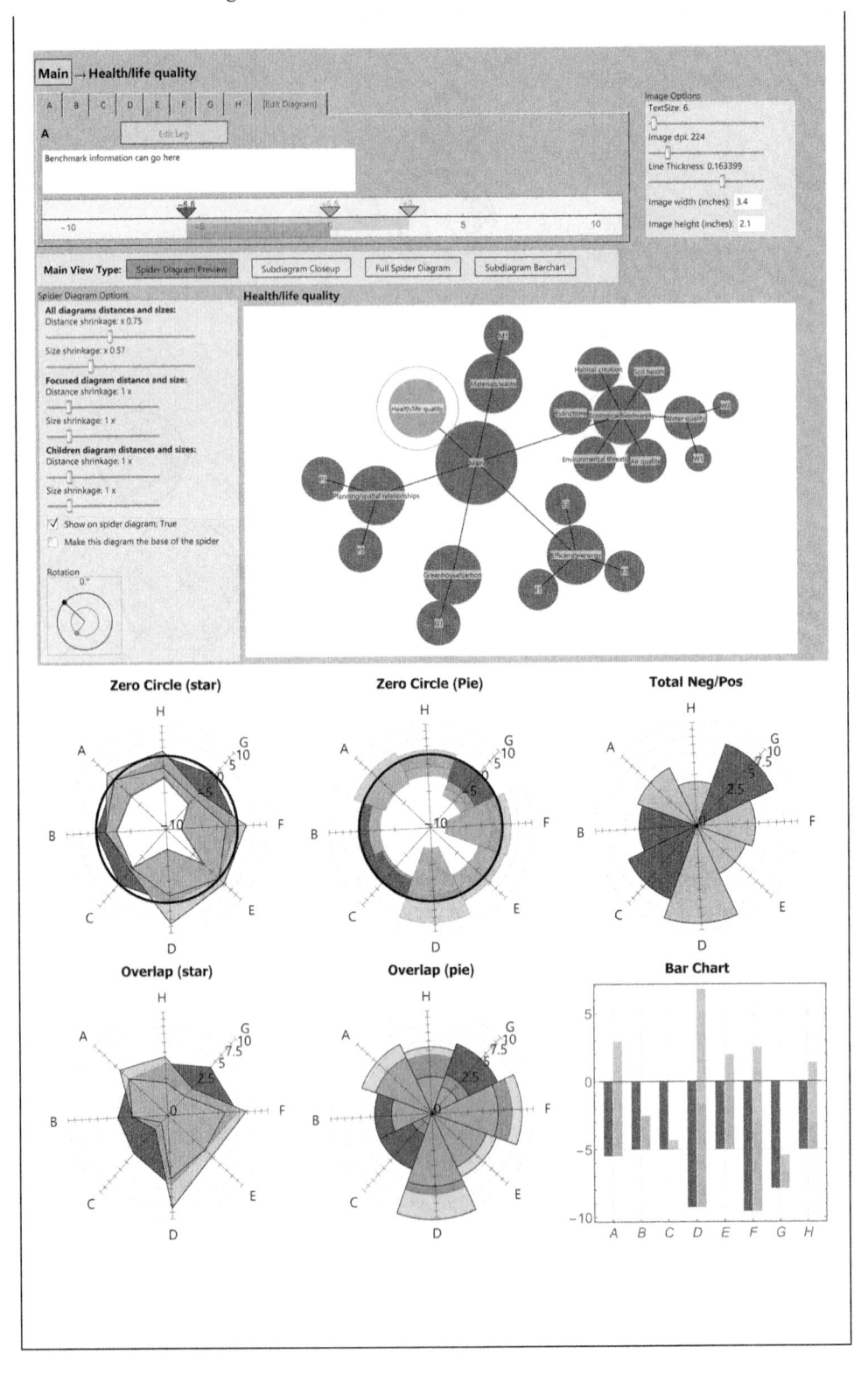

Notes

1 Several lifecycle assessors have admitted to me that the numbers are often fudged as even tangible variables cannot always be accurately measured.
2 https://sbenrc.com.au/app/uploads/2013/10/22-lcadesignbrochure.pdf. See also www.evah.com.au/.
3 The APP can be downloaded (free) from www.sustainability.org.au or contact janis.birkeland@unimelb.edu.au (or contact the author via the Linkedin website).
4 Birkeland, J. (2010) Starfish Tool for Net Positive Design, Presentation at Positive Communities, DEEDI (Queensland Government), Brisbane. Birkeland, J. (2012) Design Blindness in Sustainable Development: From Closed to Open Systems Design Thinking, *Journal of Urban Design* 17(2), pp. 163–87. Jackson, D and R. Simpson (2012) *D_City: Digital Earth/Virtual Nations/Data Cities – Connecting Global Futures for Environmental Planning.* http://dcitynetwork.net/manifesto/.
5 No examples of actual design for eco-services were found in any RTs.
6 The concept of 'gross national happiness' was apparently coined by the King of Bhutan in 1972. https://ophi.org.uk/policy/national-policy/gross-national-happiness-index/.
7 A physical game could be made of cork and use colored tacks along the legs where impacts are estimated. The star shape would be created by elastic string. The pin board would have paper overlays with rulers that define the benchmarks and criteria.
8 In most cases this means simply organizing for an eco-retrofit company to do it at virtually no cost to the owner (see Chapter 5).
9 Rostron, J. (2008) Sick Building Syndrome: A Review of Causes, Consequences and Remedies, *Journal of Retail and Leisure Property* 7(291), pp. 291–303.
10 An implosion in Canberra was promoted as a public spectacle and caused the death of a child by shrapnel. www.abc.net.au/news/2017-07-13/canberra-hospital-implosion-20th-anniversary/8702712.
11 E.g. hemp-lime and hemp fiber purportedly sequester carbon. www.greenoptimistic.com/bio-material-made-hemp-absorbs-pollutants-improves-insulation-20141007/#.XKfwSZgzayI. Other materials can absorb pollutants. See also Europa.eu/rapid/press-release_IP-04-301_en.pdf.
12 The energy intensity of a building is not the same as the total energy used by a building, which depends on the source of energy.
13 Scheer, H. (2002) *The Solar Economy: Renewable Energy for a Sustainable Global Future*, Routledge, London.
14 Adger, W. N., and Brown, K. (1994) *Land Use and the Causes of Global Warming*, John Wiley & Sons, New York.
15 E.g. see www.debate.org/debates/Selective-logging-is-not-sustainable./1/.
16 E.g. LEED divided impacts into (1) Sustainable Sites (2) Water Efficiency (3) Energy and Atmosphere (4) Materials and Resources (5) Indoor Environmental Quality (6) Innovation and Design Process.
17 Hedonic pricing supports green building and retrofits, but often only concerns things that affect property values. See Kok, N., Miller, N., and Morris, P. (2012) The Economics of Green Retrofits, *Journal of Sustainable Real Estate* 4(1), pp. 4–22.
18 Many websites boast about how expensive or tall a building is, although this usually has no public benefit.
19 As suggested in Chapter 5, cross-subsidies and trading schemes can be used to enable improvements in the environment where least expensive to do so.
20 For an example of an impact wheel, see Bell, N. (2002) Box 7: Waste Reduction Checklist, in Birkeland, J. (ed.) *Design for Sustainability: A Sourcebook of Integrated, Ecological Solutions*, Earthscan, London.
21 Birkeland, J. (2008) *Positive Development: From Vicious Circles to Virtuous Cycles through Built Environment Design*, Earthscan, London, pp. 174–5.
22 E.g. when a greenfield site is destroyed, the loss of land is often deemed compensated for by landscaping.
23 More efficient use of water is not necessarily more sustainable if the design uses more water overall.

24 The circle of poison refers to how recycled materials, e-waste or other toxic materials dumped in third world countries often are used in products that are sold back to richer nations containing toxins.
25 This was presumably intended to make nature 'count'. See Heal, G. M. (2002) *Nature and the Marketplace: Capturing the Value of Ecosystem Services*, Island Press, Washington, DC.
26 Section 5.2.4 of China's green building code, referring to the standard for energy efficiency in public buildings, GB 50189.
27 Several architects have stated that clients sometimes instruct them not to exceed the requirements for the rating or use passive solar design (presumably because they believe sustainable design must cost more).
28 Wheeler, K. (2019) Is There Any Point in Recycling? The Conversation, Jan 22. https://theconversation.com/is-there-any-point-in-recycling-109550.
29 Weighting is very common practice in RTs and multicriteria analyses. For example, if climate change is considered the most serious issue, carbon emissions will be weighted more highly than other categories.
30 These would be referenced to reduce plagiarism and to respect the originators.
31 For instance, a display home had an interior freestanding thermal mass wall with no other function and without direct sunlight, just to get points.

16 The STARfish Tool Benchmarks

16.1 Review and Preview

This chapter provides benchmarks and examples for the main six negative/black, restorative/green and net-positive/blue stars while others are provided in the tool itself.

Previous chapters argued that traditional assessments have been misleading by defining less-damaging buildings as sustainable, ignoring many negative impacts, only encouraging reductions in new impacts, and lacking flexibility for unusual project-specific conditions. Since there is still resistance to net-positive design, RTs do not provide incentives to create ways to use spaces, structures and surfaces to maximize socio-ecological gains. Further, they do not require design for changing climatic and ecological conditions, or to facilitate future retrofitting. Few buildings over-compensate for unavoidable impacts, and offsetting is still used to allow extra negative impacts, not to counteract the cumulative impacts of urban development.

Although each kind of impact has different biophysical benchmarks, general principles can be used to distinguish restorative or regenerative actions from net-positive ones.

Restorative gains are usually a result of decisions that mitigate or repair problems or regenerate conditions degraded by the project itself. Traditional design involves making choices among alternatives to select the most favorable location, project form, pollution controls, energy systems, remediation methods, technologies and so on. These choices often depend tacitly on price efficiency. Net-positive design requires 'thinking outside the box' to invent new strategies, spaces, structures and surfaces that generate whole-system benefits. Assuming the project is optimal/efficient, sustainability gains can be achieved by onsite/offsite mitigation and regeneration measures, but eco-restoration alone is no longer enough. Again, the differences are:

- **Restorative** (remedial-regenerative) actions directly address the specific impacts caused by the project's negative impacts. They tend to result more from a decision-making approach (choosing) than redesigning systems. Regeneration is seldom net positive. For instance, when surplus energy or water is transferred offsite, the amount delivered seldom offsets the embodied energy/water. When a greater area of forest than that used by the project is reserved in its natural state, there is no actual gain. Restoration does not increase overall regional/global sustainability.

- **Net-positive** design over-compensates for the damage caused over the project's lifecycle, for pre-existing onsite damage or offsite pollution entering the site. For instance, a project that replaces a natural wetland with a larger engineered wetland seldom offsets the ecological impacts. However, using natural systems to clean water from a river upstream could improve the health of downstream wetlands. The standard may seem utopian, but once a project minimizes its impacts, offsite gains provide low-hanging fruit, which could even be cross-subsidized.

The restorative and net-positive benchmarks set high standards, but a demanding scoring system does not change the sense of achievement, which is relative.

The benchmarks are based on stationary, real-world conditions and focus on matters that design teams can affect. The six STARfish benchmarks are fixed, but subcategories (Satellite STARfish) can be added to suit different contexts, functions and issues, and weighted if appropriate. While the benchmarks set high standards, a 'less negative' score rates/ranks better and shows relative improvements. Moreover, since multifunctional design is encouraged, some actions can count in more than one category and net-positive actions count more. If a building has no public benefits, it simply has a negative score. Something should not pass for 'sustainable' if it is not.

While this tool can be used to compare or assess projects, it is primarily for uncovering means to maximize positive impacts by design.

The overarching aim in PD is that the positive ecological footprint of nature should exceed the negative ecological footprint of the development. Partly because sustainability was not of concern to private development interests, PD sustainability standards were not considered or measured. Until sustainability standards are institutionalized, proxies or rules of thumb may be necessary. Today, however, technological advances are making 'genuine sustainability' assessment more feasible. These include digital tools such as building information modeling (BIM), the ability to measure physiological stresses and responses in real time, and increasing capacity to map, model and analyze complex multi-dimensional ecological and urban systems.

There are many things that make net-positive design standards more feasible than usually assumed, despite the entrenched cultural biases against creating public benefits.

Altruism has traditionally been associated with irrationality. Although deeply embedded in the culture, this is only a social construct. Planning systems can enable private development that provides public benefits to be rewarded or remunerated. For example, offsetting can work both ways. First, instead of offsetting being used to allow 'extra' negative impacts, it can be used to incentivize net benefits. Second, existing mechanisms can be used to offset costs incurred by developers when/where they can provide public goods more effectively than government (e.g. tax breaks, code variances, easements, transferable development rights, extensions of the allowable floor area or building envelope).

16.1.1 *The Benchmarks*

The following only discusses the benchmarks for the six main STARfish, but benchmarks for Satellite STARfish (second tier) are provided in the tool.

The benchmarks for the first tier, or six main STARfish, are provided below. '-10' is the worst case but, usually, the result would be between '-10 to 0'. '0' is a neutral impact but takes into account the whole lifecycle of the development. Net-positive concerns the whole-system context, including social impacts, diminishing resources and biodiversity losses. Pointers or 'hints' for net zero ('0') and net positive (+10) design for the six main STARfish are also offered below. When more detail is possible, the second tier or Satellite STARfish are used, but these are defined in the tool, not here.

16.2 Ecology/Biodiversity STARfish

16.2.1 *Key Issues Reviewed*

RTs tend to label buildings as green even when they cause ecological damage. Mitigating some manufacturing and construction impacts or using sites of 'low ecological value' are very narrow and short-term aspirations in an economy system that relies on perpetual growth. Many tools and guidelines call for 'enhancing' biodiversity on the site that remains after construction – which ignores the reduced ecological carrying capacity. Some biodiversity offset schemes encourage land rehabilitation at the sites of resource extraction, but even developments that remediate some of the air, water, soil and vegetation after construction usually have net and often irreversible ecological impacts.

Ecosystems are complex, uncertain and contextual, and therefore difficult to measure. This does not excuse conflating or confusing the quality of the human environment (psychological health, energy, thermal comfort, etc.) with ecological value. Ecological points should not be granted for things that are not really relevant to biodiversity. Some tools treat a reduction in 'relative' material flows as a surrogate for ecological gains but, because ecosystems vary, ecological damage is not always proportional to material flows. Furthermore, material flows are actually increased. Still other tools assume that building longevity will somehow amortize the ecological losses incurred over the building's lifecycle.

Paradoxically, only development can support more overall ecological space, carrying capacity, eco-services and/or (appropriate) biodiversity incubators than existed before development occurred in the region.[1] Likewise, ecological waste (replacement/recovery time) is most easily minimized in the early design stages. Hence, in PD, negative impacts are measured from pre-industrial or pre-urban conditions (again, whichever is more appropriate) and ecological space is calculated on a gross floor area basis. The rule of thumb is that ecological space in cubic meters should exceed the square meters of gross floor area, supplemented by net-positive offsetting where necessary. This requires a different kind of urban design/architecture.

16.2.2 Benchmarks

'-10' (worst-case ecology/biodiversity outcomes) represents the total destruction of ecological conditions and environmental quality at sites of resource extraction and construction. Most projects have negative ecological impacts in several locations. They may be constructed on an ecologically sensitive or greenfield site, destroy ecosystems during resource extraction (e.g. native forests, streams, wetlands) or involve the demolition of otherwise viable buildings. Eco-positive retrofitting usually has fewer negative impacts.

'0' (ecological restoration/regeneration) is where the resulting ecological conditions/space leave the sites ecologically equivalent to 'no development'. Although definitions of ecological regeneration are evolving, it typically only envisages the restoration of the left-over land. This would not compensate for the ecological waste, let alone future remodeling impacts. Compensatory onsite/offsite actions could reverse the residual ecological impacts of a development, although probably no verified examples exist.

Examples:

- *Eco-restoration*: Onsite multilayered landscaping can make biodiversity more resilient, and even compensate for some of the ecological impacts of the development itself. Restoring the remainder of the development sites to pre-construction conditions cannot be impact neutral. However, the eco-restoration of landscapes or eco-positive retrofitting on other sites can offset many of the (otherwise unavoidable) ecological losses.
- *Eco-services*: Environmental amenities and most eco-services primarily benefit people (e.g. indoor air quality). Things like outdoor recreation areas, green walls/atriums or gardens can support native ecosystems – but may also introduce invasive plants or otherwise conflict with the needs of local biodiversity. These should not count as an ecological benefit unless they also tangibly benefit nature.
- *Environmental media*: Reducing pollution and improving environmental media, such as restoring water and soil biota, is essential. Simply replacing natural resources will seldom neutralize the damage (e.g. biodiversity may not recover when forests are regrown after development, fires, floods or droughts). A project should aim to rehabilitate/restore more environmental media than it damages over the project lifecycle.

'+10' (ecologically-positive) means the project increases total eco-services and carrying capacity beyond pre-industrial/pre-urban conditions on a floor area basis – not just beyond pre-purchase or pre-construction conditions. Ideally, ecological space for biodiversity habitats should be sufficient to reverse the project's portion of the harm caused by development in the city.[2] The lifecycle impacts of the multifunctional structures used to support ecological space should be minimized.

Examples:

- *Eco-positive retrofitting*: By definition, eco-positive retrofitting combines building-integrated eco-services and ecological space with building services and functions.[3] Usually, conventional energy retrofitting only pays back its financial costs through energy savings. Where a site lacks adequate space, there is often space in peri-urban areas for creating urban ecosystems, parks or gardens (e.g. Green Scaffolding structure over low-scale warehouses).

- *Eco-positive biodiversity offsetting*: Urban planning can provide incentives to make biodiversity trading schemes more effective and eco-positive. Traditionally, they make it easier to meet statutory requirements, and can result in using more resources overall. However, net-positive offsetting/trading schemes would make it possible to support the bioregion's ecology as well as reduce the region's overall ecological deficit [Chapter 5].
- *Eco-positive functions*: Eco-positive project functions are where the development itself provides public benefits such as environmental education, ecological research facilities, or long-term eco-restoration programs. Again, reserving an existing wilderness area, creating an eco-education facility or converting a rural landscape back to wilderness conditions would count, but would seldom be enough to offset the project's added ecological damage.

SMT analyses relevant to determining ecological/biodiversity impacts: ecological transformation (ET) analysis; highest ecological use (HU) analysis.

16.3 Materials/Waste STARfish

16.3.1 Key Issues Reviewed

Disposable parts and planned obsolescence are often used for economic advantage despite wasting countless resources. Building products should use recycled materials and be recyclable. However, most building products end up as waste eventually, even if upcycled to a higher value in the interim. Thus, most materials/waste criteria only delay the eventual disposal, demolition or decay of materials. Reducing waste through long-life, durable buildings, recycling building products, or efficiency by using fewer materials or reducing space can lead to false economies. For instance, durable materials/products can cause 'extra' waste if the building has a short lifespan due to various other reasons.

The use and function of the materials matter. For instance, public buildings should last centuries as they preserve cultural heritage/identity for future generations. Generally, materials or products within structures should last as long as practicable, but this can be less critical to total lifecycle waste than design for disassembly and/or retrofitting. Materials/waste factors that should be considered but are often neglected include: the public benefit of the resources used over the project lifecycle; resource replacement actions; eco-cycling; modularity or adaptability; and the total amount of materials used and not recycled – not just the percentage of materials that are recycled.

More materials should be replaced, restored or regrown than used, so organic materials are generally preferable. Unavoidable waste from materials over the project or product lifecycle should be eco-cycled. (While upcycling reuses materials in ways that add value, it is not necessarily net positive.) Project/product functions should be considered, as an end use that is socio-ecologically harmful is a waste. A valuable rainforest felled for a private mansion on a beach, for example, wastes materials but also deprives others. Similarly, imported marble in a building for prestige is pure waste.[4] Further, redistributive outcomes can be as important as resources used.

16.3.2 Benchmarks

'−10' (worst-case materials/waste outcomes) represents the degradation, disposal or demolition of the building or building products over a short lifespan (which in the case of buildings is about 30–50 years), the materials are not replaced/regrown, or it has demonstrably negative social or environmental end uses. Mined materials involve significant waste but are usually necessary, long-lasting and potentially recyclable, whereas luxury items have little use value.

'0' (zero waste) is where building materials/products have a socially acceptable use, appropriate lifespans, minimal designed waste and the materials are reused, regrown and/or eco-cycled. This usually requires a building and its components to be adaptable, demountable, biodegradable or recyclable, and/or designed for retrofitting. The early design stage generally determines the type and amount of materials and waste, and space where positive gains can be added.

Examples:

- *Recycling systems*: Recycling of materials/products reduces waste, pollution and resource consumption, and thus the time required for natural resource regrowth and recovery. However, recycling is seldom net positive as it involves substantial reprocessing, energy, packaging and transport. Sometimes, toxic waste materials have been shipped to other countries and new products containing toxins have subsequently been sold back.
- *Biodegradable materials*: Building demolition usually causes more waste and pollution than retrofitting. However, biodegradable or compostable materials enable more low-impact retrofits and/or future demolition. Skeletal structures allow for replaceable parts using healthy materials. In contrast, concrete buildings can be high in embodied carbon and energy and have greater maintenance costs over time (e.g. cracking from earth movement).
- *Modular components*: While durable structures can sometimes be costly to adapt, repair, remodel or rearrange, durable modular building components can be designed for deconstruction, moving and so on. This could reduce demolition rates by enabling building expansion or contraction over time to meet changing needs. Similarly, modular roof or wall planters could reduce building maintenance and repairs.[5]

'+10' (restoring/increasing resources) means the equivalent of all materials used in the construction are recycled/recyclable or regrown. Designed waste should be avoided and unavoidable waste should be eco-cycled. Many tools count waste that is recycled but ignore the total materials that are not replaced or eco-cycled.[6] The total materials used, recycled and/or replaced are the main consideration here, since other impacts count in other STARfish.[7]

Examples:

- *Eco-cycling*: Since eco-cycling is recycling that creates public value, the end uses of eco-cycling would be sustainable and certainly not anti-social (e.g. recycling plowshares into weapons). The end products/projects resulting from upcycling or eco-cycling processes should also not be located in harmful locations, increase overall material consumption, encourage disposability or downstream waste or do socio-ecological harm.

- *Multifunctional*: Multifunctional, adaptable design can reduce more waste over time than the use of recycled or recyclable materials. Single-function products often have a poor ratio of materials to functional benefits. For example, free-standing water tanks have fewer benefits per unit of material than water storage walls that multi-task as thermal mass, noise/heat insulation and fire-fighting supplies.
- *Organic materials*: Organic materials are low-impact, often sequester some carbon, are recyclable or compostable and are regrown quickly (e.g. strawbale, bamboo, timber, mycelium).[8] Ideally, more materials should be regrown than used. However, in the process, sensitive ecosystems should not be damaged and nutrients/biota removed from the soil should replenished. Identifying appropriate locations for regrowing materials requires bioregional-scale analysis/planning.[9]

SMT analyses relevant to determining materials/waste impacts: ecological waste (EW) analysis; reverse sunk cost (SC) analysis; designed waste (DW) analysis.

16.4 Efficiency/Energy STARfish

16.4.1 Key Issues Reviewed

The efficiency/energy category is separated from greenhouse/carbon in the STARfish diagram, despite their close interconnection. The greenhouse/carbon STARfish (below) concerns ways to sequester carbon that has already been emitted. Typically, efficiency refers to the amount of work performed by a process/mechanism relative to the energy used (not to sustainability). This definition of efficiency is often conceived within a narrow input-output framework which leads to fine-tuning existing systems. Further, efficiency is often confused with the economic price instead of environmental cost. Conflating price and efficiency sometimes results in producing/selling more products even though at less cost, waste or energy per unit.

The efficiency/energy STARfish focuses more on 'design efficiency' than 'engineering efficiencies' which tend to improve upon existing systems.[10] In PD, design efficiencies change the system or environment and increase public benefits relative to resources and energy. In RTs, energy efficiency often just considers the amount of energy used compared to typical buildings per floor area. This ignores the source of energy, whether fossil fuel or renewable. Further, even if efficient in themselves, projects can nonetheless perpetuate fossil-fuel-based energy systems or equipment. Some tools treat energy as net positive when surplus energy is sent across property lines (ignoring whole-systems entropy).

Although solar energy is defused and cannot yet satisfy the needs of a military-industrial-corporate order,[11] it would be sufficient to support high-quality sustainable living environments.[12] Some buildings purchase 'green' energy from the grid yet continue to waste energy due to insufficient insulation or draft-proofing. Most RTs ignore a project purpose or even an energy source that is harmful. There is now a clear price incentive to use renewable energy, despite the long history of subsidies to fossil fuels.[13] However, since the public costs of fossil fuels are largely irreversible, incentives are necessary to speed up the transformation to renewable energy.

16.4.2 Benchmarks

'-10' (worst-case efficiency/energy outcomes) is where fossil fuels are used, the energy is used for harmful purposes or the design increases overall consumption through, for example, designed waste. Single functions, redundancy, rebound effects, excess embodied energy and anti-social functions all waste energy.[14] Postponing the transition to renewable energy systems has a great opportunity cost due to the damage caused by fossil fuels throughout the lifecycle.

'0' (energy autonomy) means energy produced equals energy used in project construction and post-construction operation – at an efficient domestic-district scale. While rebound effects should be minimized and multifunctional benefits should be maximized, the source of energy is critical. Fossil fuels are 'inefficient' as they take thousands of years to produce and have irreversible long-term costs. Multifunctional spaces are an important means of increasing efficiency.

Examples:

- *Renewable energy*: A building can produce renewable energy and maximize passive energy. It can be considered energy neutral 'for practical purposes' when it provides as much clean, renewable energy as is used over the project lifecycle, including embodied and operating energy and future interior fit-outs.[15] During construction, onsite portable solar arrays could help offset some energy usage.[16]
- *Scale*: Scale is always an important consideration. Generating electricity at a neighborhood scale (e.g. a community thermal disk or wind generator), is often more efficient than individual rooftop solar systems. Similarly, a community-scale Living Machine may be more efficient in maintenance and management than individual domestic systems or a central industrial-scale water treatment or energy plant.
- *Energy sources*: Low-impact and healthy sources of energy can be more significant than the amount of energy used. For example, new dams are ecologically irreversible.[17] Fossil fuels should not be used, even if offset, since a building's energy demand can be met by renewable energy. Retrofitting buildings can reduce existing urban energy usage while adding eco-positive gains.

'+10' (net-positive efficiency/energy) refers to whole-system design efficiencies. A design can add public benefits relative to the resources and energy used without reducing the value to occupants. Using less energy but for anti-social purposes is negative. Even though energy cannot be 'increased', using adaptable, multifunctional design (combined with engineering efficiency or reduction) and avoiding designed waste and/or rebound effects, can multiply the benefits of energy.

Examples:

- *Design for change*: Design for retrofitting can be more effective than setting higher standards for new buildings that will not be easily modified or upgraded, since social needs and climates will change. Adaptability for changing occupants, uses and conditions is essential, as an energy-autonomous

building designed for the current climate or context will need retrofitting in the future.
- *Positive functions*: In whole-system efficiency, long-term consequences should always be considered. For example, where 'surplus' energy may upset the grid, it should perhaps be stored. Stylistic changes that do not improve environmental safety/security or reduce material flows are wasteful even if technically efficient. If energy-efficient buildings with harmful functions are approved they should add significant public benefits.[18]
- *Spatial optimization*: Interior space is often reduced to save heating/cooling costs, and exterior space is often reduced to save land costs and reduce transportation. However, since the reduction of space reduces adaptability, urban retrofitting costs may be increased. Multiple uses of space and material resources are usually necessary to increase public gains relative to total energy consumption.

SMT analyses relevant to determining efficiency/energy impacts: **d**evelopment/design **f**unctions (DF) analysis; **d**esigned **w**aste (DW) analysis; **s**ource of **e**nergy (SE) analysis.

16.5 Greenhouse/Carbon (Sequestration) STARfish

16.5.1 Key Issues Reviewed

In addition to CO_2 emissions, fossil fuels cause air pollution, heavy metals like mercury and cadmium, and oil spills in waterways. Such public health impacts are recorded in the health/life quality STARfish, while the energy source is recorded in the efficiency/energy STARfish. Although efficiencies are a factor in every impact category, the greenhouse/carbon STARfish focuses on carbon sequestration, climate mitigation measures, and urban oxygen production (the converse of carbon emissions). Spaces, surfaces and structures in urban development can sequester significant carbon through multifunctional design using, for example, substantial permanent building-integrated vegetation, bio-based materials, or additives such as biochar or olivine.

Since net-carbon sequestration in the built environment is now possible,[19] carbon trading and offsetting should not allow credits for reducing a project's 'additional' carbon emissions. Likewise, buying and conserving a forest should not be a license to deplete other public goods. Such schemes align with the outdated 'polluter pays principle', or the right to do harm in exchange for financial offsets. Since every development can and should give back, there should be no right to continue carbon emissions through exemptions or grandfathering. Therefore, carbon sequestration is necessary, even if the project is energy efficient and somehow uses no fossil fuels.

Urban development should produce oxygen to offset the urban oxygen deficit in dense urban areas, as well as during construction, operation and demolition. In addition to producing more oxygen and sequestering more carbon than it emits over the lifecycle, development should also mitigate urban climate change and withstand the impacts of climate change, such as storms, droughts and urban overheating. This can be done in ways that provide additional benefits. Again, where a hardship to the developer or owner would be created, the public sector can offset costs to developers and owners, to the extent it saves long-term public costs.

16.5.2 Benchmarks

'-10' (worst-case greenhouse/carbon outcomes) represents the case where no carbon is sequestered by the development, no oxygen is produced, the project increases the urban heat island effect and there is no provision for future proofing against extreme weather. Although not the norm, each development should be expected to contribute to urban carbon sequestration, oxygen production and urban climate mitigation (or at least sponsor urban/rural reforestation).[20]

'0' (greenhouse/carbon autonomy) is where the carbon emissions caused over a development's lifecycle are compensated for. This does not include the portion of total urban emissions reduction to which buildings should ideally contribute. (Renewable energy usually only reduces the future demand for more fossil-fuel-based building equipment.) Greenery has been considered too inconsequential, but substantial permanent building-integrated vegetation can sequester its own emissions and produce oxygen.

Examples:

- *Carbon trading/offsetting*: Carbon trading could be net positive but most schemes just slow the rate of increased emissions, which means the building actually adds atmospheric carbon. Moreover, carbon offsetting/trading schemes often only count carbon emitted in building operation, not manufacturing. Since doing less than average harm is not net zero, carbon trading should reduce overall carbon emissions.
- *Building-integrated sequestration*: In high-density developments, permanent building-integrated vegetation/landscaping has multiple benefits in addition to carbon sequestration. For example, biochar sequesters carbon but also benefits plants and soil productivity. Developments can also use organic building components that sequester carbon. When concrete or brick and mortar are necessary, there are now versions of such products that can sequester carbon.[21]
- *Industrial solutions*: If geo-sequestration or in-ground carbon storage is used, it should be certain that collateral damage from geological changes (as happens in fracking) is not possible.[22] There are also various novel mega-industrial sequestration machines under development. However, they are generally single function,[23] and their construction and operation impacts would usually cancel out many of their gains.

'+10' (climate mitigation and carbon sequestration) means the development sequesters its embodied and operating carbon emissions. Ideally, projects would sequester their share of urban carbon, produce oxygen and mitigate the climate. Reducing urban climate impacts/risks and overheating can mitigate the immediate impacts of excess atmospheric carbon. In regions with fewer emissions, new projects should still sequester their portion of the excess carbon in the area.

Examples:

- *Urban vegetation*: Using little extra energy, urban vegetation can reduce the urban oxygen deficit while diluting/treating air pollution in inner city areas. There is still disagreement on how many trees are needed per person, but a figure can be agreed upon. The carbon emissions embodied in the materials for supporting and watering plants should also be minimized.
- *Vertical composters*: Rural sequestration offsets for using vertical composters for food waste in cities can have multiple benefits, such as increasing agricultural productivity.[24] Investments in rural carbon sequestration programs should be socio-economically redistributive and revitalize rural communities/economies. Farms should not displace more ecologically or socially sustainable land uses and should return a portion of land to wilderness.
- *Micro-climate mitigation*: Design for urban climate mitigation should protect buildings against extreme weather events. For example, wind-proofing shading structures using carbon sequestrating materials can support integrated solar cells or vegetation while cooling the area. Building-integrated water sprinkling systems can combat urban overheating. Development that is allowed near coastal areas should be designed for likely sea level rise.

SMT analyses relevant to determining greenhouse/carbon impacts: passive maximization (PM) analysis; resource security (RS) analysis; risk avoidance (RA) analysis.

16.6 The Health/Life Quality STARfish

16.6.1 Key Issues Reviewed

Typical green buildings provide shelter, reduce health risks and avoid pollutants or 'sick building syndrome' (e.g. mold, toxins). However, few increase lifespans. Having fewer illnesses among fewer people does not 'increase' health. Urban overheating causes many deaths each year, and people have even frozen to death in brownouts. Crucial factors in public health include stress,[25] social inequity, disparities of wealth and lack of opportunity.[26] For example, life expectancy is going down in the USA, partly due to growing inequality.[27] Urban environments affect all these factors.[28] Buildings that advertise inequality can reinforce a sense of injustice, fear, stress or hopelessness.

Like cigarettes, average buildings should be labeled 'harmful to human health', especially since urban environments can have a positive effect on private and public health. Recreation/relaxation spaces and gardens have been shown to improve health and life quality.[29] Many health-giving functions cost little (e.g. clean air, noise dampening, white noise and ironically named negative ions). Since recovery time in hospitals is increased by views of the outdoors or access to gardens, these can be presumed to be good for regular people. Amenities should not be restricted to visitor areas. For instance, working in hospitals should also improve the health of staff.

Urban office or residential building occupants should be able to become more physically and mentally fit by virtue of built-in health opportunities and conditions. That means the building user's biological age is potentially reduced relative to their chronological age, or their life expectancy increases. Designs must also be sensitive to the needs of disabled, deaf, blind, elderly and so on. Further, occupants change over time through real estate turnover and permanent residents change their lifestyles when aging. While developments should not be undertaken on unsafe sites (e.g. swamps, earthquake fault lines), credit should not be given for avoiding harmful sites.

16.6.2 Benchmarks

'-10' (worst-case health/life quality outcomes) is where the development has negative health impacts during construction, operation and/or occupancy. Priority health issues vary geographically and demographically. In disadvantaged regions, for example, air quality often suffers from poor sanitation or air pollution (e.g. indoor wood cooking/heating).[30] In wealthy regions, many 'modern' buildings still off-gas harmful chemicals (e.g. formaldehyde, volatile organic compounds, radon) and/or cause nature deprivation disorder.

'0' (health/life quality) means things that shorten average lifespans in development are virtually eliminated, such as untreated air or water, soil pollution or anything that increases rates of cancer disease, accidents or stress. In brownfield sites, treating existing toxins is a precondition. It counts, but does not, in itself, achieve a healthy condition for occupants, or compensate for the health impacts during construction and operation.
  Examples:

- *Offsite health improvements*: Buildings should not be given extra credits for not doing harm, such as not locating in a swamp or ecologically sensitive site. Projects should not rely on proximity to healthy environment, since building users benefit from sites near existing parks, lakes or health-giving surroundings, regardless of the design. However, developments could contribute improvements to those environments.
- *Public health impacts*: Public health should not be reduced when improving the health and comfort of building users/occupants. For example, air-conditioning units exhaust can harm neighbors,[31] and reflective wall/window surfaces in hot cities can increase urban overheating.[32] If a project receives credit for enhancing the surrounding environment, the community must not have to pay for those benefits.
- *Exercise/lifestyle options*: Unhealthy lifestyle choices and obesity cannot be controlled by built environment design. However, buildings can make healthy food and exercise choices available and provide stress-reducing garden environments. In office buildings, built-in exercise facilities are increasingly common. Multifunctional design can make these and other health options and opportunities affordable in office buildings or residential structures.

'+10' (health/life expectancy and wellbeing) is where the occupants (and, ideally, visitors and neighbors) can improve their biological age (versus chronological age) or increase their life expectancy within a reasonable period (e.g. a year). Individual health improvements can now be assessed in real time. Design can make exercise fun (e.g. a thermal power plant exploited its height to create a ski run around the building).

Examples:

- *Environmental justice*: Urban design could counteract many negative physical consequences of poorly designed economic systems. Environmental justice can be increased by developments or retrofits that create healthy living conditions, environmental amenities, access to nature and so on. Offsetting that provides quality, low-cost built environments or housing in poorer districts can have beneficial trickle-up effects while reducing health costs.[33]
- *Health offsetting*: Health offsetting schemes could provide health improvements in villages in developing nations, once the health benefits to development users/neighbors are optimized (assuming building products do not export toxic wastes and so on). Benefits to recipient communities should be equitably distributed and sustainable. For example, pumping clean water for villagers should not deplete their local aquifers.[34]
- *Eco-tourism*: Environmental remediation and eco-tourist programs/projects can often deliver personal health benefits to participants as well as to recipient communities.[35] For example, eco-restoration activities in priority regions can include remediating damaged environments, restoring local water quality, monitoring biodiversity or providing environmental education. Eco-tourist programs should have a lower ecological footprint than if the participants stayed home.[36]

SMT analyses relevant to determining health/life quality impacts: negative space (NS) analysis; ecological space (ES) analysis.

16.7 Planning/Spatial Relationships STARfish

16.7.1 Key Issues Reviewed

Conventional urban design guidelines, among other things, aim to respect the surrounding built environment aesthetically, make spatial relationships effective and efficient, work with nature and provide public infrastructure and amenities. However, site planning criteria/credits in RTs do not call for tangible offsite gains to address the negative sustainability impacts of urban development. Future proofing is now a common phrase, but it generally refers to defensive actions that mitigate the risks created by built environments themselves or the environmental risks created by new developments. Instead, PD aims to improve the impacts of buildings on cities, and of cities on the planet.

Many developers try to fill the allowable height and setback envelope to maximize profit, while planning codes and development controls often only prescribe what not to do. Hence, collaborative processes between developers and planning agencies are essential, as planning controls, like building codes, sometimes perpetuate outdated premises. Planning rules are often flexible or negotiable. For example, planning agencies can allow extensions of building envelopes, setbacks, floor area ratios or allow variances, easements, transferable development rights – where they demonstrably improve the surrounding urban/natural environment. Urban planning agencies should also allow experimental developments when they are likely to increase urban sustainability.

Site planning should provide direct access to basic needs (e.g. food, water, shelter, safety), wellbeing (sense of community, security, equity, opportunity), provision for civil or environmental emergencies (e.g. safe havens for refugees/evacuees) and expand future choice. Spatial proximity provides efficiencies and supports social interaction, but space for adaptability should not be sacrificed.[37] Planners and developers should ensure public urban facilities and environmental amenities are equitably distributed and contribute to environmental justice/equity or reduce disparities of consumption. Ideally, the fair resource share would be calculated, legislated and then gradually reduced. Finally, both private/public planning should aim to meet the PD Test.

16.7.2 Benchmarks

'-10' (worst-case planning/spatial outcomes) is where the development does not contribute to urban planning objectives, exceeds the average environmental space, fails to provide for basic needs and socio-ecological diversity or creates risks (e.g. building on flood plains). Since development usually reduces future land-use options and space, a lack of eco-positive planning outcomes is negative. Thus, affirmative action is necessary to increase equity and sustainability.

'0' (planning/spatial security and equity) means the project or development provides for onsite security and basic needs (e.g. food, shelter, water), has no negative impacts on the wider area, supports urban planning objectives and is within the development's environmental space allocation. To be impact neutral (given the opportunity costs of unsustainable development), site planning should improve the amount and distribution of social and environmental benefits.

Examples:

- *Address local deficits*: Collaboration with local planners can help identify socio-ecological needs/deficits in the area, as traditionally done for economic growth. While points should be given for the use of brownfield sites or retrofitting old buildings, they should not be awarded for (coincidental) benefits only to building users/owners, such as being located near transport hubs or shopping areas.[38]
- *Urban infill*: Infill urban renewal projects often make cities more compact and efficient and stimulate the local economy. However, densification can also cause gentrification, social dislocation, congestion, pollution and urban overheating.[39] Hence, infill development should preserve public open space, views, sunlight, access to environmental amenities (e.g. nearby parks, riverfronts) and increase natural security and future public options.
- *Mixed uses*: Most siting decisions are still based on private economic/energy analyses, not community needs analyses. In collaboration with planning agencies, appropriate mixed uses can be determined, such as public open space, multifunctional social facilities and public amenities, in combination with additional private benefits. Mixed uses can increase spatial efficiency, improve socio-economic impacts and revitalize the community.

'+10' (planning/spatial gains) means site planning that provides diverse, reversible land uses where possible, ensures local resource security, addresses regional deficiencies and ameliorates disparities in environmental justice. Site planning, building forms and landscaping can increase the public estate and ecological base in real terms. There are already many indirect subsidies to developers, such as public investments in infrastructure, but contributions from developers could be reimbursed.

Examples:

- *Developer contributions*: Developer contributions/exactions seldom cover the full public impacts of a development or pay back its resource consumption, let alone compensate for withdrawing land/resources from public use.[40] However, where onsite space is limited, offsets/credits can be granted for public benefits created on other sites if they are shown to meet public needs and save public money.
- *Emergency facilities*: The disabled, elderly, poor and otherwise less-mobile people need accessible emergency facilities, such as flood-proof structures with secure roof spaces, storm shelters for cyclones, or fire-proof bush/forest structures. Integrated multifunctional mini-shelters could create safe places for inner city residents or evacuees in cases of civil strife, water shortages, food system breakdowns or extreme weather events.
- *Environmental space*: Development should reduce the average environmental space in the region. This means limiting consumption to the region's per capita resource allocation, or the current average material/energy flows per unit of floor area. This should be determined by planning authorities. Improving resource efficiency means little if more resources are continually consumed per capita and/or per building.

SMT analyses relevant to determining planning/spatial impacts: costs of inaction (CI) analysis; resource transfer (RT) analysis.

16.8 Conclusion

Decision versus design: The distinctions between reduced, neutral, regenerative and net-positive impacts align with the extent to which actions result from a design or decision-making standpoint.

A central theme in this book has been the importance of design to sustainability. Decision making was regarded as an intellectual activity while design was seen as intuitive, yet both have intellectual and intuitive dimensions. Unfortunately, both have been dominated by binary thinking: choosing from among planning or design options, methods and processes, or merely selecting among existing products and technologies. Being a process of comparing and eliminating options, decision making usually results in fine-tuning for efficiency, not creating new kinds of cityscapes. PD is about changing the underlying dysfunctional systems to generate positive ripple effects throughout the urban environment.

Sustainability safety factor: '*Net-positive*' *is parallel to engineering safety factors, but considers ecological/climatic uncertainty, not just foreseeable and quantifiable risks from natural forces and human negligence.*

Engineering safety factors mean structures are designed to withstand several times the predictable forces/loads on buildings. The idea of mandatory engineering safety factors is generally accepted, despite the increased upfront costs. Not so for investments in sustainability. Yet far more people are killed by unsustainable buildings/cities than by buildings that collapse due to structural failure.[41] While working to reverse climate change, biodiversity breakdowns, escalating over-consumption and other consequences of socially constructed systems, net-positive design standards also provide a 'sustainability safety factor'. Eco-positive cities must go beyond restoration, regeneration and resilience to increase the ecological base, public estate and future social options.

16.9 Exercises

1. Provide benchmarks for new layers or tiers of Satellite STARfish that follow the above pattern of negative, restorative and net-positive outcomes.
2. Send a reasoned critique of the book or STARfish app to the author for direct feedback at Janis.Birkeland@unimelb.edu.au (or use LinkedIn).

Notes

1 Over-compensation is necessary because, during recovery time at resource extraction sites (e.g. forests, open pit mines, crop lands), restoration may be affected by fires, floods, disease and other forms of ecological uncertainty.
2 E.g., 'progressive forms' of zoo design – not conventional zoo design – for small animals in peri-urban areas might achieve this. www.washingtonpost.com/news/animalia/wp/2016/07/06/we-are-at-a-precipice-of-a-major-evolution-in-zoos/?utm_term=.29b1372f9f86.
3 Birkeland, J. (2009) Eco-Retrofitting with Building Integrated Living Systems, in *Smart and Sustainable Built Environment Conference Proceedings*, Delft, Netherlands, www.sasbe2009.com/. Birkeland, J. (2008) Space Frame Walls: Facilitating Positive Development, in *Proceedings of the 2008 World Sustainable Building Conference*, Melbourne, Sept. http://trove.nla.gov.au/.
4 Imitation gold or marble is almost indistinguishable to average citizens.
5 In about 2011, a sustainability committee recommended a living wall and green roof be included in a new university building. A higher-up committee, not understanding the concept of modular design, rejected the idea on the grounds that green roofs and walls could not possibly work.
6 That is, using 'percentage recycled' can allow for excessive materials and pointless luxuries.
7 Large buildings generally do more harm than small ones, but this is not well-reflected in RTs.
8 Mushrooms can be used to grow bricks using various waste products. See https://theconversation.com/scientists-create-new-building-material-out-of-fungus-rice-and-glass-98153.
9 Nanotechnology could change architecture dramatically but, arguably, the points made in this book still apply. There are few papers that even purport to link nanotechnology, architecture and sustainability. Abdelrahman, M. (2010) Towards Sustainable Architecture with Nanotechnology, in Al-azhar Engineering 11th International Conference 154, Cairo, Dec. Armstrong, R. (2010) Systems Architecture: A New Model for Sustainability and the Built Environment Using Nanotechnology, Biotechnology, Information Technology, and Cognitive Science with Living Technology, *Artificial Life* 16(1), pp. 73–87.

10 Again, engineering can involve design and vice versa, and designers can be talented engineers and vice versa, but they use different ways of thinking (reduction versus synthesis) as discussed in Chapter 1.
11 Parkinson, G. (2019) Australia has Enough Solar, Wind Storage in Pipelines to Go 100% Renewables, in Renew Economy. https:reneweconomy.com.au, Mar. 21.
12 More power from the sun hits the earth in a single hour than humanity uses in an entire year (without any fossil fuels). Renewable energy is infinite until the sun dies.
13 Government subsidies for coal, gas and oil were reduced from 2012 to 2016, but according to the International Energy Agency, support for fossil fuels increased by 12% in 2017 to more than $300 billion. https://reneweconomy.com.au/fossil-fuel-subsidies-increased-in-2017-says-iea-78934/.
14 Things that people desire and are willing to pay for are often more 'valuable' than things people actually need.
15 Again, some call a building energy positive if it generates more energy than it uses per year, ignoring embodied energy which would far exceed the operating energy over green building's lifecycle.
16 A wind generator or solar array on a construction site would be no more annoying to neighbors than a crane.
17 There is a movement to unplug dams and restore rivers on economic as well as ecological grounds. https://news.nationalgeographic.com/2016/06/largest-dam-removal-elwha-river-restoration-environment/.
18 Lead in bullets is allowed in some countries, including the USA, although it serves no good purpose.
19 Renger, C., Birkeland, J., and Midmore, D. (2015) Net Positive Building Carbon Sequestration: A Case Study in Brisbane, *Building Research and Information* 43(1), pp. 1–24.
20 www.theguardian.com/environment/2019/jul/04/planting-billions-trees-best-tackle-climate-crisis-scientists-canopy-emissions.
21 Carbon dioxide is emitted when limestone is converted to lime (calcification), but as the cement ages it reportedly absorbs nearly half the carbon dioxide (carbonation). www.abc.net.au/news/science/2016-11-22/concrete-is-a-carbon-sink/8043174.
22 Carbon dioxide has leaked out of underground reservoirs, polluted water supplies and caused tremors due to the build-up of pressure.
23 Some 'Doctor Strangelove' proposals were reviewed in *Positive Development* (2008), pp. 18–19, such as pumping sulfur dioxide into the atmosphere. Some solutions could develop (unusual if not ugly) aesthetic potential, such as 'mechanical trees' made with electromechanical materials that can convert winds into structural vibrations to generate electricity. https://phys.org/news/2016-02-mechanical-trees-power-sway-breeze.html.
24 Mycelium can transfer carbon from air to soil. See https://cleantechnica.com/files/2019/04/HiveMind_Tech_OnePager.pdf.
25 Neumayer, E., and Plümper, T. (2016) Inequalities of Income and Inequalities of Longevity: A Cross-Country Study, *American Journal of Public Health* 106(1), pp. 160–5.
26 Research is increasingly linking chronic stress to illness. www.bbc.com/future/story/20120619-how-stress-could-cause-illness.
27 Inequality contributes drug use, depression, hopelessness and other problems affecting health and the immune system. www.vox.com/science-and-health/2018/1/9/16860994/life-expectancy-us-income-inequality.
28 Things like equality are not really rewarded in RTs because they are not easily associated with particular actions that apply to all buildings.
29 Cooper Marcus, C., and Sachs, N. (2013) *Therapeutic Landscapes: An Evidence-Based Approach to Designing Healing Gardens and Restorative Outdoor Spaces*, John Wiley & Sons, New York.
30 The World Health Organization found that biomass or coal cooking stoves led to 4.3 million deaths in 2012 (more than from outdoor air pollution), and wealthy homes or buildings have significant air pollution from 'modern' chemicals.

370 *Decision Making and Assessment*

31 Air cleaning/cooling systems can leak HFCs (which trap heat in the atmosphere) and transfer polluted or hot air to the outside. Builders relying on air conditioners often do not build efficient or passive solar homes.
32 Some have proposed that solar-powered air-conditioning systems could capture carbon dioxide and water from the air and convert it into hydrogen and then into hydrocarbon fuel. Dittmeyer, R., Klumpp, M., Kant, P., and Ozin, G. (2019) Crowd Oil Not Crude Oil, *Nature Communications* 10(1818). A more biological solution is to use mycelium in green roofs.
33 Jacobs, D. E., Wilson, J., Dixon, S. L., et al. (2008) The Relationship of Housing and Population Health: A 30-Year Retrospective Analysis, *Environmental Health Perspectives* 117(4), pp. 597–604.
34 For collecting water from the air, see www.watercone.com/product.html.
35 For a summary of costs and benefits see www.worldtrips.com/blog/pros-and-cons-of-ecotourism.
36 Hunter, C., and Shaw, J. (2007) The Ecological Footprint as a Key Indicator of Sustainable Tourism, *Tourism Management* 8(1), pp. 46–57.
37 A book that challenges the association between sustainability and high-density living is Du, P., Wood, A., et al. (2015) Life-Cycle Energy Implications of Downtown High-Rise vs. Suburban Low-Rise Living: An Overview and Quantitative Case Study for Chicago, *Buildings* 5(3), pp. 1003–24.
38 LEED rewards siting buildings in close proximity to commuter rail or bus lines to reduce pollution and other impacts associated with increased automobile usage.
39 A key LEED provision is: 'Develop a site with a minimum density of 60,000 square feet per acre'.
40 Capital gains is a tax on unearned profit from increases in land value due to activities and investments of society as a whole, and land tax pays for government services to property owners. However, having people pay for services is not the same as expecting land owners to contribute to the public estate.
41 In 1995, a five-story department store in Seoul, South Korea collapsed causing the deaths of 502 people because of an air-conditioning unit placed on a weak roof.

Index

Abu Dhabi 280, 282n11
abundance/plenitude 76
acoustics 143; *see also* noise levels
acquaponic systems 44
adaptability: adaptable design 290–91; and the built environment 39; Costs of Change (CC) Analysis 183; Designed Waste (DW) Analysis 164; eco-positive retrofitting 113, 131; eDR 292–93, 298–300; flexible planning 230–31; Green Scaffolding 137; Multifunctional Space (MS) Analysis 169; Negative Space (NS) Analysis 172; positive development theory 103; rating tools (RTs) 263; reversible buildings 211; of spaces generally 156; STARfish 360–61; in sustainability 50; and waste management 314–15
advocacy planning 233
aesthetics 74, 113, 117, 138, 242, 279, 297, 315
affirmative action 39
affordable housing 94, 95, 298, 300–301, 303
Agenda 21 94–95
Agenda 2030 94
agri-waste building materials 42, 338
air quality: and the built environment 44, 49; design for nature 139, 140, 145; eco-positive retrofitting 123; eDR 294, 312–13, 318–19; and health 363; public health 49; rating tools (RTs) 276; Resource Security (RS) Analysis 170; STARfish 343, 346
air transport 114, 116, 118
algaetecture 25, 118, 142, 145
algorithms 50
altruism 354
American Association for the Advancement of Science (AAAS) 305n19
animal rearing 19
anthropocentrism 5, 15–16, 25, 65

anti-ecological bias in decision-processes 158, 206
anti-human conspiracy 94
anti-social functions 15, 69, 105, 162, 166, 260
'appeal to nature' arguments 67
appeals boards 207
approval processes 95, 148, 166, 183, 186, 190, 228, 233, 262, 271, 288; *see also* planning regulations
aquaculture 144–45
aquariums 125, 140, 144–45
architecture 74, 223, 296–97
Architecture without Architects (1964) 75
Arctic 90
artificial microcosm experiments 91
asbestos 49, 117, 129, 317, 342
as-of-right approvals 262
assessment tools 6–7, 125, 136, 146–47, 158, 159–60, 164–69, 343; *see also* certification schemes; performance assessment; rating tools (RTs)
assimilation policies 16
atriums 125, 131, 140, 145, 175, 282n10, 317
Australia: Australian GBC 248n46; Environmental Protection Act 1994 (EP Act) 283n31; Green Star 237; Smart Cities Plan 94; Sydney green bans 233
autonomous architecture 77–78
Autonomous House (1972/1975) 77–78
autonomy 63, 64, 293
aviaries 125
awareness raising 65, 120, 206, 294

back-casting 221–22
Bacon, Francis 63
bacteria 43, 50, 145
Balance Diagrams 8
balance/harmony, ideal states as 64, 68, 72
balconies 24, 131, 139, 148, 279
bamboo 42, 140–41, 178n43, 304, 338

baselines 9, 17, 160, 162, 181–82, 185–86, 255, 271, 325
basic needs, meeting 19, 48, 81n27, 114, 137, 156, 187, 213, 292
bats 128, 320
Bauhaus Architecture 74
bay windows 148
bears, falling 144, 151n37
BEES 267n31
benchmarking 125, 162, 280, 325, 341–42, 353–70
Benefits of Action (BA) Analysis 184, 194–95, 326
Benyus, J. 83n50
BESS (Built Environment Sustainability Scorecard) 267n31
best practice standards 131, 233, 253, 256
'better than the norm' 160, 211, 260
Bhutan 347
big data analytics 158, 223
bioaccumulation 260, 274, 319
bio-based building materials 42, 338, 359, 361
biochar 40, 361
biodegradable materials 42, 164, 183, 211, 263, 319, 358
biodiversity: aiming to return landscapes to earlier ecological conditions 120; banking schemes 18, 149; biodiversity credits 147; district/landscape scales 77; eco-positive retrofitting 123; enclaves 18, 148, 278, 309, 320; Green Scaffolding 139–40, 147, 148; incubators 18, 37, 105, 138, 139, 147, 162, 174, 310–11, 355; loss of 6, 13, 38, 47, 91, 136, 188; nature as the ultimate source of supply 209; oceans 37, 43; offsetting 119, 149; rating tools (RTs) 244, 256, 278; STARfish 338, 355–57; and transport 143
biofuels/biogas 142, 143, 144
biological sciences 256
biomagnification 50, 116, 260, 345
biomimicry 12, 29, 68, 76
biophilia 12, 29, 49–50, 76, 115, 120, 122, 256
biophysical tolerances 49
bioregional planning 28–29, 67, 91, 98, 116–17, 159, 160, 162, 170, 270, 274, 310
bioremediaton 50, 143
biosphere 72
Biosphere II 91
biotechnic society 76
birds 15, 25, 44, 128, 138, 145, 152n44, 178n41, 310–11
black box mindsets 67
black coal 182

blackouts 46, 187
blockchain 316
Blueprint for Survival (1972) 66
Bogota 289, 329n35
borderless nature of environmental media/pollution 90–92, 105, 277
borderless thinking 12
boundary management 90–92
bounded systems 73, 159
brain structures 13, 72
Brazil 171, 284n50
BREEAM tool 234, 248n52, 266n2, 266n10, 280, 305n30, 308n94
bricks 319
brittle systems 75
brownfield 50, 119, 143, 290, 310, 313, 364, 366
brownouts 43
Brundtland Report (1987) 7, 91, 92–94
buffer zones 148
building codes: blunt instruments 229; design for nature 146–47, 148; development control and assessment 228, 235, 238, 240; eco-governance 212; eco-positive retrofitting 132; eDR 303; grandfathering 183; and rating tools 262; STARfish 365; Systems Mapping Themes (SMT) Analyses 164, 173
building envelopes 74, 148, 277, 365
building information modeling tools (BIM) 54n30, 244, 256, 281, 302
bush fires 45, 171
butterflies 123
butterfly effect 80n5

camel roofs 146
campaign financing 96
capacity building 258, 280, 291, 303
car parking 75, 113, 116, 117, 118, 183
carbon autonomy 362
carbon emissions 38, 40, 48, 178n45, 237–38, 274, 315, 338
carbon sequestration 9, 40, 118, 145, 278, 306n50, 310, 315–16, 359, 361–63
carbon trading 198n28, 243, 362
carrying capacity, ecological 9, 18, 39, 73, 91, 98, 119, 123, 160, 174, 175, 209
cars 75, 117–19, 169, 238, 281, 297
Center for Disease Control and Prevention 331n80
centralized urban systems, risks of 46, 187
certification schemes 28, 147, 148, 164, 168, 234, 236, 237, 255, 260, 274, 281, 291; see also rating tools (RTs)
chain of custody 345
change, design as driver of 205–11

change management 71
charrettes 158, 232, 259, 294
child labour 160
children, design for 299
China 352n26
Churchman, C. W. 84n74
circadian rhythms 50
circle of poison 352n24
circular systems: city-region balances 76; closed compared to open systems 73–74; and the historical context of sustainable design 67–68; three streams of 69–72
citizen juries 230, 259, 271
city-region balances 76
climate adaptation 278
climate change 40, 43, 46, 114, 144, 216, 263, 278, 280, 305n19, 361; *see also* extreme weather events
Climate Council 179n61
closed systems: compared to open systems 73–74; Dominant Paradigm (DP) 40; energy and water are 14; ethics of 214; and the historical context of sustainable design 65, 68, 76; mainstream green design paradigms 11; metaphors for 11–12; outdatedness of 7; shifting to open-systems 100; sustainable design paradigms 61, 87
closed-loops: and the built environment 38; domestic properties 78; eDR 313; historical context 61–62; and the historical context of sustainable design 67–68; innovations 196; as mitigation measures 160
Closing Circle (1971) 68
coal 182, 315
coastal areas 90
co-evolution by integration 116
co-evolution in partnership with nature 16, 76
cognitive science 13, 72
co-housing projects 78
collaborative processes 106, 158, 211, 233, 256, 259, 294–95, 335; *see also* eDR (eco-positive Design Review)
colonization 281
commercialism 66
commissioning processes 295
Commons, The (1968) 73
community benefits *see* public benefits
community building 19, 29, 116
community consensus methods 157, 207
community engagement 208, 211, 259, 287, 290–91, 294
community facilities 169
community food gardens 293
community gardens 296

community participation 20, 228, 233, 239
community refuges 137, 142
community safety 137
community-based action 72, 94, 106
community-expert panels 106, 259
compact cities 85n101, 115
compact factory farming 123
compensation 91, 95, 117, 146–47, 165, 311–12
competition 207–8, 235, 237, 238
complex systems 319–20, 321, 335, 355
compliance costs 188
composting 144, 363
compound benefits 162, 184
comprehensive/master planning 219
computer-aided design 50, 335
concrete 319
confidentiality 261
conflict resolution by design 7, 12, 158, 207, 272
congestion 47, 75, 183
'conquering' nature 63
consolidation 114; *see also* infill development
conspicuous consumption 41, 189, 205–6, 315
constitutional change 212–14
construction industry 124, 131, 164, 303
construction site protection 313
consultants, use of 238, 256, 257
consultations, public 20, 207, 209, 232, 259, 287–88
consumer sovereignty 65
consumerism 38, 91, 115, 164, 189, 206, 208, 210
contamination 15, 25, 45, 49, 145, 165, 182, 188, 317; *see also* pollution
contingency plans 231; *see also* emergency escape routes
cooking fuels 294, 317, 319
cooperative neighborhood improvement programs 294–96
coral reefs 37
corporate sustainability reporting 177n24
corruption 213, 345
cosmic forces, balancing of 64
cost-benefit frameworks 17–22, 49, 100, 126, 160, 171, 209, 239–40, 265, 268
Costs of Change (CC) Analysis 183, 194, 326
Costs of Inaction analysis 184, 367
courts and the judiciary 212, 291
Cradle to Cradle (2002) 78
cradle to grave concepts 78, 273
crime prevention by design 293, 297
cross-border impacts 90–92, 105
cross-disciplinary decision making 89, 258

Crystal Waters 86n121
Cuba 82n32
culture and heritage, respecting 121, 138, 184, 186, 233, 242, 280, 281, 295, 296
Cumulative Decision (CD) Analysis 186, 195, 313, 328
cumulative impacts 41, 51, 62, 90, 96, 105, 255, 265, 274, 277
Curitiba, Brazil 171, 302
Currumbin Eco-villages 86n121
curtain glass walls 127, 139
cybernetics 51
cycle lanes 118, 318

dams 266n16, 316
data analytics 158, 223
daylighting 143–44
Death of Nature (1980) 64
decentralized living 67
decision tools, defined 12
decision-making, defined 12
decks 139, 141
de-constructability 211
deconstruction 129, 139, 263, 337, 358
decontamination 50, 115, 338
deep ecology 81n12
deforestation 55n58
degeneration 113
degrowth 38, 39, 96
deliberative processes 271
democracy 20, 65, 67, 71, 163, 210, 212
Democratic Impact (DI) Analysis 187, 195, 324, 327
demographic changes 169, 185, 290–91
demolition 50, 117, 129, 236, 255, 276, 277, 290
demountable design 183, 263, 319
Denmark 68
densification, urban 77, 96, 111, 112, 114, 115, 118, 172, 279, 292
depreciation 124
depression 318
deregulation 214
desalination 151n25
Descartes, René 63
desert cities 141, 145–46
desertification 144
design, definition of in Positive Design paradigm 11–12
design briefs 158
design for nature 136–52, 210, 241
design profession 6
design review boards 242
'design tools,' as misnomer 160
Design with Nature (1969) 75, 77
design-based change 210–11

design-based versus decision-based frameworks 11, 12–13, 100, 114, 162, 367
designed waste 314–15
Designed Waste (DW) Analysis 164, 191, 315, 359, 361
Designers Without Borders 226n14
devaluing future options 184, 265
developer contributions/exactions 148, 301, 367
developing nations 121, 140–41, 189, 254, 280–81, 294
development bonuses 301
development control and assessment 146, 228–49, 258, 291; *see also* building codes; planning regulations
development credits 125, 132, 136, 147, 149, 172, 175, 279, 301
Development Functions (DF) Analysis 166–67, 191, 315, 323, 361
digital cities 223
digital engagement platforms 233
direct action principle 216–17
disabled citizens 299, 363, 367
disadvantaged areas 137, 187, 189, 280–81, 287–308, 318; *see also* developing nations; poverty
discounting 184, 265
dislocation 48
dispersed settlements 116
displacement of local populations 117, 121, 129
disposal costs 164
distributed energy 187, 293
distributed systems 46, 142, 293
distributive justice 163, 187
district/landscape scales 77
Do No Harm 100, 160, 214, 275
Doing Net Good 100
Dominant Paradigm (DP) 5, 39–40, 61, 63–65, 74, 164, 322–28
donut model, mainstream 97–98
double counting 276
double-skin walls 175
downcycling 196
driverless cars 75, 114, 118, 183
drones 172
drought 316
due process 159, 214, 271
durability 263, 314–15

Earth Overshoot Day 53n27
earthquakes 41, 43, 47, 75, 121, 137, 139, 142, 146, 292
Earthwatch 188
easements 148, 175, 365
eco-cities, retrofitting for 111–35

eco-cycling 68, 197, 358
eco-efficiency 138, 217
ecofeminism 63
eco-governance 211–17, 291
eco-industrial parks 117
eco-innovations 167
ecological base 9, 320, 366
ecological baselines 17, 160, 336
Ecological Basis for Architectural Design (1972/1995) 77
ecological envelopes 137
ecological footprints 41, 48, 119, 274, 309, 312
Ecological Space (ES) Analysis 157, 175, 193–94, 324, 325, 365
ecological spaces 9, 25, 125, 157, 169, 172, 175, 178n57, 311–12, 319–20
ecological standard, defined 9
ecological stepping stones 320
Ecological Transformation (ET) Analysis 156–57, 173, 174, 193, 324, 326, 357
Ecological Waste (EW) analysis 165, 191, 321, 323, 325, 327, 359
Ecologist, The 66
economic dimension in PD 21–23
economic growth 38, 65, 88, 89, 93, 155, 158, 173, 214, 279
Economic Impact (EI) Analysis 187, 195, 328
eco-philosophies 71–72
eco-positive principles 7, 17
eco-positive retrofitting 23–24, 111–35, 164, 262, 263, 290, 314, 356–57
eco-productive technologies 25, 264
eco-resorts 318
eco-restoration 18
eco-sensitive landscaping 45–46
eco-services: basic design strategies 25; defined 9–10, 122–23; design for eco-services 136; Ecological Space (ES) Analysis 157; eco-positive retrofitting 122–23, 125; eDR 310; Green Scaffolding 142–46; offsetting ecological impacts 119; positive development theory 105; rating tools (RTs) 274; STARfish 336, 356; and sustainable design 17; trading and banking schemes 149
Eco-solutions (TV program) 206
EcoSpecifier 34n71
ecosystem nurseries 18
ecosystem services: basic design strategies 25; Economic Impact (EI) Analysis 188; eco-positive retrofitting 122; Green Scaffolding 137; and Positive Design (PD) 9; rating tools (RTs) 244
eco-tourism 365
eco-villages 78

Ecuador 213
edges/spaces, cities create 114
eDR (eco-positive Design Review) 101, 157, 159, 160, 236, 258, 287–308, 309–31
education 138, 239, 241, 256, 294–96
efficiency: basic design strategies 23; business-led approaches focus on 210; eco-efficiency 138, 217; and ethics 41; formulaic approaches to urban form 116; green building councils (GBCs) 235; Green Scaffolding 138; mainstream green design paradigms 11; rating tools (RTs) 160, 239, 270, 275; and retrofitting 112; Source of Energy (SE) Analysis 182; STARfish 337, 345–46, 359–61; and sustainable design 6
EFTE 143
El Niños 330n50
elderly people 43, 46, 120, 292, 298, 299, 363, 367
elevated pathways 47
embodied energy 40, 41, 74, 119, 164, 168, 189, 273, 274, 295, 315, 317, 319
embodied waste 165, 197, 314–15
embodied wealth 189
emergency escape routes 47, 137, 139, 171, 231, 367
emergency situations 137, 146, 368
emotional needs 113, 164, 171
empathy 307n71
'empty' spaces 137, 174, 274, 298, 320
endangered species 38, 123, 136, 138, 145, 157, 188, 278
end-of-pipe mechanisms 73, 241
energy: autonomy 142, 316, 360; closed system 14; distributed energy 187, 293; eco-positive retrofitting 112, 121, 122, 124, 132, 314; embodied energy 40, 41, 75, 119, 164, 168, 189, 273, 274, 295, 315, 317, 319; energy flows 70, 167, 168, 182, 277; energy security 142; exchange networks 316–17; metering 295; Passive Maximization (PM) Analysis 168; rating tools (RTs) 270, 274; Source of Energy (SE) Analysis 182; STARfish 337, 359–61; surplus 15; zero-energy buildings 6, 28, 117, 119, 260, 274, 312
energy ratings 236; *see also* rating tools (RTs)
engineering 114, 207, 272, 368
Engineers without Borders 47
enlightenment 63, 226n21
entropy 197
Environment, Power and Society (1971) 70
environmental education/action 47–48, 138
environmental governance 157

Index

environmental impact assessment (EIA) 51, 88–90, 156, 161, 165, 166, 184, 229, 245, 253–65, 268–84
environmental justice 10, 98, 117, 280, 289, 297, 365
environmental regulations 241
environmental reporting 242
environmental risks 171
environmental security 19
environmental space calculations 170, 367
equitable living environments 19–20
equity: eco-cycling 197; eDR 296, 318; mapping 170; and misconceptions about sustainability 63; and the PD social standard 10; positive development theory 89, 93, 103–4; rating tools (RTs) 275; Resource Transfer (RT) Analysis 189; and sustainable design 7; Systems Mapping Themes (SMT) Analyses 159, 163
essentialism 64
ethical design 41–42, 106, 158, 229, 233, 257, 271
ethics-based frameworks 167, 212, 276, 288
Eurocentricity 64, 281
evidence-based decision making 89, 258, 271
evolution 49–50, 71–72
exchange networks 68, 149, 316–17
exclusionary practices, avoiding 296
exercise 318, 364
expert design panels 167
expertariat 207, 233, 259
externalities 12, 87, 105, 186, 188, 190, 322–28
externalization of environmental impacts 73, 217
externalization of positive impacts 160
extraction industries *see* mining/extraction
extreme weather events 46, 187, 280, 330n50, 361
extremism 48–49

facade preservation 140, 143
factory farming 123
failure to act 216
fairness 63, 93, 159, 187
fallacy of the middle 5
fashion 41, 117, 164, 238
fertility 104
fertilizers 144–45
filling stations 117, 142
filtration systems 145
finite planet 66
fire protection 45–46, 137, 142, 146, 171, 310
first principles, designing from 74
fish 144–45
fixed baselines 162
flexible planning 230–31, 292, 312
flood barriers 75
flooding 43, 46–47, 75, 137, 146, 171, 227n33, 292, 338
flow analyses 155–80
flyscreens 151n26, 179n65
flytraps 144
flywire 179n65
fog water collectors 151n25, 152n48
food chains 120, 123, 209
food gardens 77, 293
food security: and the built environment 44, 46; city-region balances 76; eco-positive retrofitting 123; eDR 293; Green Scaffolding 137, 141, 144; and the historical context of sustainable design 66; Resource Security (RS) Analysis 170; self-sufficiency 312–13; urban farming 141; *see also* permaculture
foreign aid 48–49, 121, 292, 318
forensic flows analyses 20–21, 155, 159
forest fires 171
form follows function 74, 114
formaldehyde 49, 129
fossil fuels 70, 93, 121, 167, 181, 182, 216, 313, 315–16, 359, 361
France 213
free rider concept 215
freeways 47, 113, 143
Friends of the Earth 178n57
frontier ethics 275
frontloading towards design stage 122, 288
fuel cells 182
full-cost accounting 105, 123, 136, 182, 260, 301–2
functional fences 141–42
funding 124, 129, 139, 183, 217, 266n17
fungal building materials 42, 43
futures planning 205–27, 265

gabion walls 128, 138, 317
Gaia (1979) 72
gambling 171
gamification 258, 336, 347–48
García Patino, María Alejandra 289
Garden Cities 75
gardening boxes 118
gardens 44, 75, 77, 144, 293, 363
gated communities 275, 298
GDP (gross domestic product) 243, 265, 276
gendered dimensions of domination 64
gene pools 91, 120, 144
genetic change 213
gentrification 163, 233
Genuine Progress Indicators (GPI) 243, 301–2

geodesic domes 91
Gilded Cage Syndrome 49
glass walls 127, 139
Global Footprint Network 53n27
Global Reporting Initiative 242
globalization 29, 67
gold mining 54n29
governance 185–90, 205–27, 228–49
grandfathering 183, 361
gray infrastructure 218, 232
grazing, land for 18, 123
Great Pacific Garbage Patch 54n43
green agriculture revolution 281
green architecture 74
green bans 233
green bombs 54n36
green bridges 47
green building councils (GBCs) 234, 235, 237, 238, 239
green building rating tools 234–35
Green Building Voice 247n27
green buildings 28, 38, 210–11
green chandeliers 140
green consumerism 239
green design criteria 6
green design paradigms, mainstream (defined) 11
green facades 77
green 'mansions' 164, 275
Green Optimum (GO) Analysis 190, 196, 214–15, 275, 327
green roofs 43, 44, 49, 123, 145, 175, 248n45, 279, 310–11, 347, 368n5
Green Scaffolding 17–18, 19, 25, 44, 118, 122, 123, 128, 136–52, 172, 310–11, 317
Green Space Walls 25, 139–40, 310–11
Green Star (Australia) 237
green tape 148
green technologies 295–96
green walls 25, 40, 44–45, 123, 239, 310–11, 343
greenfield land exchange schemes 15
greenfield loss 119, 120
green-growth, alternatives to 112–13
greenhouse windows 128
greenhouses 141, 144
grey water 311
gross national happiness 347
guidelines, design 231

habitat creation 15, 138, 139, 140, 144, 145, 148, 278, 310
Habitat for Humanity 47
habitat loss 165, 188, 338
hacking 119
hard/technocratic orientations 69, 74–76
harm reduction 6, 260

healing environments 210
health, human: and the built environment 49, 50; development control and assessment 241; Economic Impact (EI) Analysis 188; eco-positive retrofitting 120, 123; eDR 317–18, 324; effects of artificial environments 50; governance 216; Green Scaffolding 143–44; positive development theory 88; rating tools (RTs) 270, 276; STARfish 337, 342, 363–65; Systems Mapping Themes (SMT) Analyses 165, 170, 182, 187
health and safety 213, 276, 292–93, 302–4
health offsetting 365
heat banks 317
heat deaths 55n51
heat inversions 43–44
heat island effect 43–44, 144, 320–21
heavy metal contamination 50, 177n34, 315
hedonic pricing schemes 121, 351n17
hempcrete 42, 51, 338
heritage values 121, 138, 184, 186, 233, 242, 280, 281, 295, 296
Hierarchy of Eco-innovation (HI) 160, 167, 192, 196–97, 272, 318, 323
High Line Park, New York 47
highest ecological use 279, 309
Highest Ecological Use (HU) Analysis 173, 193, 324
historic buildings 140, 142, 295, 296, 319
hoarding 76, 97, 122, 206
Hobbes, Thomas 63
home/land ownership 120
homelessness 169, 292
housing: affordable housing 94, 95, 298, 300–301, 303; co-housing projects 78; cooperative neighborhood improvement programs 294; demand for resources 209; eco-positive retrofitting 120; eDR 298–99; exclusionary practices 297–98; Green Scaffolding 140–41; rented accommodation 132, 294, 301; risk mitigation 171; self-help homes 151n22, 304; Smart Cities Plan (Australia, 2016) 94; spatial inequity 280; Suburban Bootstrapping 129; and sustainable design 77–78
human rights 44, 170, 187, 213, 214, 325
human-nature separation 47, 206
hurricanes 146, 171, 280
husbandry 69
hybrid rating tools (RTs) 280
hydroelectric power 316
hydrogen peroxide 69
hyperaccumulator plants and worms 151n35

ICF (insulating, integrated, Styrofoam concrete formwork) 319

ideologies 206, 207, 211, 271
immigration *see* migration
impact avoidance versus mitigation 345–46
impact category overlaps 337
impact wheels 339–40
imported labor 189, 270, 280, 302
inaction, costs of 184, 260
incentives 96, 97, 124, 131, 136, 137, 146–47, 231, 243, 272, 301, 323
inclusive design 299
incremental-adaptive planning theory 219–20
India 302
indigenous landscapes, mapping 174
indigenous plants 144
indigenous species 310
indigenous states, return to 18
indoor air quality 45, 49, 144, 145, 319
indoor plants 144, 234, 241
industrial infrastructure 46
industrial metabolism 38, 208
industrial revolution 63
industrialism 11
industrialization 66
inequality 37, 96, 120, 163, 206, 210, 363; *see also* equity
infill development 96, 111, 114, 115, 279, 298, 366
informatics 223
infrastructure: eco-positive retrofitting 122; eDR 292; and the expertariat 207; gray infrastructure 218, 232; public benefits 190; transport 118
innate need for contact with nature 49–50
institutional design 181–200
Institutional Design (ID) Analysis 185, 195, 327
institutional reform 26, 158, 205–27
instrumentalism 65
insulation 69, 140, 317
integrated planning 95–96
intentions, assessing 186
interdependent open systems 319–20
interdisciplinary decision making 105–6
interest balancing 106
interest groups 96
inter-generational equity 63, 88, 89, 102–3, 159, 212
interior space-saving 301, 361
international cooperation 90
International Energy Agency 199n48
International Federation of Red Cross and Red Crescent Societies 55n50
International Living Future Institute 30n10
International Red Cross 305n19
International Style (Bauhaus) architecture 74

internet 162, 205, 207
invasive species 145, 147, 157, 165, 320
isolation 114, 298–99
iterative processes 257, 272

jet packs 118
job creation 121, 126, 138, 164, 238, 264, 276, 294, 298, 302–4
Journal of Cleaner Production 52n9
judicious approaches 271

Kennedy, Robert F. 243
kinetic energy 118
knowledge, privatization of 167, 217, 258
knowledge transfer processes 258

Lake Pedder, Tasmania 198n25
land, ownership of 120
land clearances 117, 185
land degradation 18–19, 119, 147
land reclamation 56n75, 143
land use planning 161, 166, 173, 183, 213, 218–20, 272, 288
Landcare 47, 188
landscaping 17–18, 46, 244, 263, 279, 300, 310, 312, 336
Lanzarote 174
large species 120
latent values 242
LCADesign 307n85, 335
Le Corbusier 36n114
least change options 183, 217
LEDs 49
LEED 246n12, 247n35, 248n51, 280, 307n76, 307n89, 370n38
legal systems 211, 212, 291
legume production 18
life quality 48, 66–67, 91, 131, 163, 230, 254, 296, 337, 363–65
lifecycle assessment (LCA) 51, 181, 190, 191, 236, 244, 256, 273, 277, 281, 302, 336
lifecycle impacts 119, 122, 146, 164, 237, 270
light levels 49, 139, 140, 143–44, 320
lighting 124
Limits to Growth (1972) 66
'limits to nature' position 91
linear causality 65
linear progress 64, 87
lives saved calculations 188
Living Building Challenge (LBC) 32n41, 33n63, 34n71, 238, 248n55, 266n4, 305n25, 308n96, 329n19
Living Building Council (LBC) 178n47, 246n1, 281
living buildings 72
living environments, improving 48–49

living in place 29, 67
Living Machines 25, 45, 49, 72, 145, 148, 197, 290, 318, 360
living systems 69–72
living wallpaper 138
living walls 294, 368n5; *see also* green walls
lobbying 66, 213, 238
local culture and heritage, respecting 138
local governments 112, 160, 213, 236, 288
local sustainable practices 303–4
Lovins, Amory 83n65, 197n1
low-cost loans 49
low-impact concrete 319
low-impact energy sources 360
low-impact lifestyles 39, 116, 120, 164
low-impact materials 41, 51
low-impact rural development 114
luxury goods 38, 159, 161, 164, 197, 315, 357

maintenance 15, 23, 40, 101, 105, 121, 127, 164, 217, 295
Manila 294
mapping 174, 223, 243
Marina City, Chicago 178n53
marketing research 208
marketing tools 160, 234–35, 258
markets 10, 19, 65, 88, 96, 97, 185, 207–8, 209, 211
masculinity, historic systemic imbalances towards 64
Masdar 117
master/comprehensive planning 219
material flows: and the built environment 41; and green-growth strategies 114, 117; historical context 68; positive development theory 91; rating tools (RTs) 265, 270, 277; STARfish 337, 357–59; Systems Mapping Themes (SMT) Analyses 156, 167, 189
materialism 65, 66, 254
materials substitution 142–43
mechanisms of nature 63, 65
media facades 49
mediation 212
medicinal plants 144, 293
mega-structures 74–75
mental flows analysis 277
mental health 50, 318, 363
mercury 40, 165, 177n34, 182, 198n9, 315
metabolic systems 67–68, 76–77, 78
Metabolism of Cities (1965) 68
metering 295
methane gas 50
metrics for assessment 101
microbial fuel cells 105
micro-climates 137, 363

micro-ecosystems 18
micro-gardens 144
micro-habitats 140
microorganisms 120; *see also* bacteria
microplastics 42
migration 48, 292, 302
mind-mapping 340
mini Trombe walls 41
mining/extraction 155–56, 165, 212, 213, 216, 264, 274, 276, 315, 321
mini-parks 172, 297
mini-shelters 367
mirrors 138, 140, 143
misanthropy 63
miscommunication 294–95
mixed-use spaces *see* multifunctional design
mobocracy 320
modernist architecture 297
modular design 183, 319, 358
mosquito-borne illnesses 144
multifaceted problems 71
multifunctional design: design for nature 122, 137, 139, 140; eDR 296, 297, 320; meeting competing needs 158; overview of net-positive development 23, 24–25; rating tools (RTs) 257; STARfish 338, 347, 359, 361, 366; Systems Mapping Themes (SMT) Analyses 156, 164
Multifunctional Space (MS) Analysis 156, 169, 174, 192, 324, 325
multinational corporations 67, 212
multi-scalar planning analyses 49
multistory apartment buildings 129
municipal/regional planning scale 162–63, 170–75
Murray Darling River, Australia 199n31
mushrooms (mycelium) 42, 50, 51, 368n8, 369n24
mutual learning 232
mycology 25

NABERS 246n15, 248n42
nanotechnology 18, 41, 51, 338, 368n9
national/regional planning scales 162–63, 185–90, 212
natural disasters 37, 46, 137, 146, 171, 305n19
natural security 170
Natural Sequence Farming 27
nature: defined in PD 15–17; demise seen as inevitable 13; human dominance over 16; mainstream green design paradigms 11; offsetting past human consumption of nature 15
nature corridors 47, 123, 145, 162, 175, 320
nature deprivation disorder 50

nature interpretation displays 138
nature reserves 119
need for nature, human 115, 120
negative ions 145
negative space 162
Negative Space (NS) Analysis 156, 162, 169, 172, 193, 324, 325, 365
neighborhood solar thermal disks 182, 316
neo-classical economics 67
neoliberalism 215
NEPA (US National Environmental Protection Act, 1969) 88–90, 91, 102, 245, 266n6
nested systems 270
net, defined in PD 14–15
net positive, defined 14–15
net public benefits 100
net-positive offsetting 9, 290, 297, 311–12, 343
neural networks 13
New Orleans 46, 137, 179n59
New Urban Agenda (NUA) 95–96, 113
Newton, Isaac 63
NGOs 226n14, 243
no development options 184, 260, 275, 278, 336
no loop systems 197
noise levels 49, 139, 143, 292, 320
normalization techniques 244, 344
nuclear power 115, 182, 188, 226n30
null alternative 260
nuts and berries architecture 75
nuts and bolts architecture 74

Obama, Barack 307n83
obesity 55n56
objectification of nature 63, 113
oceanic gyres 42
oceans 90, 311
OECD 248n49, 301
off-gassing 284n39
offsetting past human consumption of nature 15, 105
offsetting schemes: design for nature 136; developer contributions/exactions 148; development control and assessment 243; eDR 311–12, 313; Green Optimum (GO) Analysis 190; Green Scaffolding 146–47, 149; net ecosystem/biodiversity losses 6; net-positive offsetting 290, 292
olivine 361
Omega 3 production 144–45
open houses 294
open spaces 169, 173, 297, 299, 312
open systems 6–7, 12, 62, 73–74, 98–101, 100, 270
open-plan spaces 140

operating costs 164
operational performance 295
operations research 71
opportunity costs 5, 162, 166, 183, 192, 217, 240, 264
opportunity gains 184, 217, 346
organic materials 359
over-compensation 7, 9, 14, 15, 24, 105, 288, 290, 354
overcrowding 114
over-development 174
over-exploitation of resources 73
overheating 43
oxygen 44, 145, 241, 312–13, 343, 361

parabolic concentrators 151n27
Pareto Optimum 190, 214, 215
parking lots 75, 113, 116, 117, 118, 183
part-earth model 98
partial extensions 148
participatory decision making 89, 105–6, 209, 211, 233, 259, 290–91, 294
passive energy systems: building codes 148; and the built environment 40; design talent for 132; eco-positive retrofitting 116, 123, 126–27; eDR 316, 317; environmental regulations 241; Green Scaffolding 137, 138, 143; historical context 75; overview of net-positive development 25; paradigms 27; Passive Maximization (PM) Analysis 168; positive development theory 105; Solar Core 126; Source of Energy (SE) Analysis 182
Passive Haus movement 78
Passive Maximization (PM) Analysis 157, 168, 192, 316, 323, 363
passive water treatment 311
payback 132
PEARL 235, 248n51, 266n5, 282n11, 305n24, 306n53, 307n88, 308n93
pedestrian paths 118, 178n54, 307n68, 318
performance assessment 146, 161, 185, 229–31, 240–41, 291, 337
performance bonds 239
performance contracting 124
permaculture 12, 27, 76, 77, 116, 120
permanent greenery 44
permeable surfaces 256, 312
personal air transport 114, 119
personal resource security 120
pest control 44, 144
pesticides 65–66
phase change materials 40
philosophy 71–72
photovoltaic cells 127, 138
pigeons 145
Piggyback Roofs 25, 126–27

Pinchot, Gifford 226n22
place-sensitive design 296–97
planning regulations: anti-social functions 166; Cumulative Decision (CD) Analysis 186; design for nature 137, 146–47, 148; eco-governance 212; eco-positive retrofitting 131, 132; eDR 288; as governance 218–20; grandfathering 183; Green Scaffolding 139; Highest Ecological Use (HU) Analysis 173; positive development theory 95, 106; STARfish 365–67; Systems Mapping Themes (SMT) Analyses 155–80; whole-system accounting 183
planning tools 155
planting walls 15
plastic 42, 141
Playgardens 25, 128–29, 148
plazas 172, 175
point systems 234, 256, 271
policy development 87–108
policy planning 220, 231
politics: and the built environment 20, 26; and collaborative approaches to reform 206–7; Democratic Impact (DI) Analysis 187; and eco-positive retrofitting 124; and the historical context of sustainable design 66; policy planning 220; and public interest assessments 186; resource security 170; and systemic bias against nature 206
pollution: and the built environment 38, 45; construction site protection 313; Costs of Change (CC) Analysis 183; cross-border impacts 90–92; in developing nations 294; development control and assessment 243; Economic Impact (EI) Analysis 188; eDR 315–17; environmental impact assessment (EIA) 270, 274, 275; Green Scaffolding 139, 145; and the historical context of sustainable design 65, 67, 88; polluter pays principles 361; rating tools (RTs) 274, 276, 278; Reverse Sunk Cost (SC) Analysis 181; STARfish 345, 356; Systems Mapping Themes (SMT) Analyses 156; toxic contamination 50
polyvinylchloride 129
Population Bomb (1968) 66
population growth 48, 66, 114
positive, defined in PD 13
positive butterfly effects 62
Positive Development (PD): basic concepts 9–17; defined 6–7; outline of theory 97–101
positive public purposes 166–67
post-modernism 107n7, 121, 159
post-occupancy evaluation (POE) 161, 291, 337
post-traumatic stress 171

poverty 91, 117, 137, 280, 294, 301, 317–18
power outages 46, 187
precautionary principle 215–16
predator species 145
pre-emptive action 184
pre-European occupation, defined 14, 152n62
prefabrication 139
pre-human states, return to 18
pre-industrial states 14, 152n62
prescriptive rules 132, 148, 228, 229, 241, 256, 259, 271
preventative actions 162, 170–71
'printed' buildings 41, 51, 183, 338
private-public-community partnerships 243
privatization of infrastructure 187
privatization of knowledge 167, 217, 258
proactive PD principle 216
product specification tools 256
property lines 73, 74, 264, 277, 320
property rights 147, 258, 325
property values 121, 123, 132, 137, 161, 166, 189, 279, 300
protectionism 238
psychological dimensions 70–71, 113, 115
public benefits: eco-positive retrofitting 123; eDR 288; mapping 162; positive development theory 89, 97; STARfish 343, 347, 354; Systems Mapping Themes (SMT) Analyses 166–67, 169, 190
public consultations 20, 207, 209, 232, 259, 287–88
public estate 10, 169, 214–15, 268, 275
public good 15, 23, 74, 147, 171, 275
public health 49, 67, 172, 364
public interest 95, 186, 213, 234, 272, 275
public social spaces/'the commons' 6, 10
public space 156, 169, 274, 275, 279, 293, 297, 298, 299–300
public transport 118, 183, 279, 281, 292, 297
public-private dichotomy 64
pyrolysis 53n15

quality control 228, 240

radar diagrams 339–40, 348
radon gas 49, 117, 129, 317
railways 143
rainforests 55n58
rainwater collection 145–46, 292, 311
rating tools (RTs): benefits of 235–37; compared to STARfish 336; critiqued 253–67; and design guidelines 231; development control and assessment 229; eco-positive retrofitting 125, 131, 132; Green

Scaffolding 146; and innovation 167; overview of 234–40; and retrofitting 314; social waste 166; Systems Mapping Themes (SMT) Analyses 157, 167, 168; Triple Bottom Line (TBL) 17, 22
rational actors 69, 89, 225n12, 241, 271
reasoning and relational thinking 289
rebound effect 164, 197
reckless disregard for life 216
recycled plastic 141
recycling: basic design strategies 23; closed-system mindsets 87; eDR 314; mainstream green design paradigms 11; and Positive Design (PD) 15; recyclable materials 319; STARfish 345, 358; and sustainable design 6; water 45
reduce, reuse, recycle (3Rs) 205
reductionist decision-making: development control and assessment 238; eco-positive retrofitting 131, 132; green walls 310; and green-growth strategies 114; over-emphasis on numbers 159, 289; overview of net-positive development 8; rating tools (RTs) 253, 270, 271, 277; seen as higher-order thinking 261; sustainable development 40, 63, 65, 100
reforestation 165
refugees 48
Regen Village project 86n121
regeneration 63, 119, 147, 165, 278, 321, 343, 353; *see also* remediation
regenerative design 12, 16, 29, 47, 76
regional governance 162–63, 185–90, 213, 281
regional issues 116–17
regional planning scales 162–63, 170–75
regionalism 242, 281, 296–97
regulation: action-forcing legislation 89; Cumulative Decision (CD) Analysis 186; development control and assessment 228–49; eco-governance 212; environmental regulations 241; Green Scaffolding 146–47; health and safety 303; New Urban Agenda (NUA) 95; retrofitting 337; Reverse Sunk Cost (SC) Analysis 181; 'revolving door' 185; waste 164; *see also* building codes; governance; planning regulations
reification, nature as a 17
remediation 13, 122, 185, 311, 313, 321, 342, 343, 353, 365; *see also* regeneration
renewable energy: eco-positive retrofitting 115, 123; eDR 316; expectations of a fast payback 181; Green Scaffolding 137; as investment, not cost 184; Passive Maximization (PM) Analysis 168; Source of Energy (SE) Analysis 182; STARfish 360; *see also specific types*
renovation 129, 132, 183, 314
rented accommodation 132, 294, 301
repairability 319, 353
reseeding bioregions 162, 311
resilience 16, 39, 46, 63, 120, 124, 278, 319–20
resort-like living environments 164
Resource Autonomous design 28
resource autonomy 293
resource efficiency 6
resource exploitation 158, 213
resource industries 212
resource loop closing 6, 9, 39
resource management agencies 209, 212
resource security 137, 265, 278, 292, 297
Resource Security (RS) Analysis 170, 187, 192, 326, 363
Resource Transfer (RT) Analysis 189, 196, 327, 367
resource yields 66, 88
restoration 119, 165, 290, 310, 343, 353
retrofitting, eco-positive 23–24, 40, 46–47, 49, 111–35, 136–52, 263, 311–12, 314
Reverse Curtain Wall Units 127
reverse engineering 221–22
reverse impact wheels 340
Reverse Sunk Cost (SC) Analysis 181, 194, 325, 359
Reverse Trombe Walls 128
reversibility 104, 211, 263, 312
revitalization 163, 172
right brain/left brain 13
right-left dualisms in politics 206–7
rights of nature 213
rights-based ethics 100, 206–7, 212, 213; *see also* human rights
Rio Declaration 94, 226n29
risk, and the precautionary principle 215–16
risk aversion 132
Risk Avoidance (RA) Analysis 171, 193, 328, 363
risk mitigation 171
risk-benefit analysis 171, 209
river basins 90
river catchments 47
roads 75, 116, 117, 118, 183
robotic cars 75, 114, 118, 183
rock walls 53n22
roof gardens 25, 144, 175, 178n43
runoff 45, 145, 311
rural farming 18–19, 141
rural settlements 117

Sacred Balance (1997) 72
San Francisco Embarcadero Highway 47

Save Beeliar Wetlands (Inc.) v Commissioner of Main Roads (2017) FCA 4 199n33
scenario planning 220–21, 222
science, cross-fertilization of design principles into 256
scientific revolution 64
sea level rises 43, 280, 338
seating (outdoor) 118, 144, 299, 300
security/safety 170, 187, 292–93, 299, 368
seed banks 144, 147, 293
segregation of populations 19, 50, 96, 233, 275, 296, 300
self-assessment 157, 159, 160, 236
self-funding 125
self-help homes 151n22, 304
self-regulation of industry 235, 253
self-sufficiency 12, 77, 117, 120, 145, 292, 312
semi-outdoor spaces 131; *see also* atriums
semi-passive retrofitting 40
semi-rural settlements 120
semi-wilderness experiences 169
Senegal 308n97
sense of community 299
sense of place 19
'sensitive' growth 112
sensory overload 49–50
shared land 73
sick building syndrome 49, 276, 342, 363
Silent Spring (Carson, 1962) 65–66
sink holes 47
site planning principles 162, 321, 365–66
skybridges 139
skylights 140
skyscrapers 75, 77, 178n53
slavery 159, 160, 303
slums 113, 179n66
Small is Beautiful (1973) 66–67
Smart Cities Plan (Australia, 2016) 94
smart meters 295
smart-city technology 223
SMARTmode 101, 106, 155, 157, 158–61, 218, 233, 295, 343; *see also* Systems Mapping Themes (SMT) Analyses
social baselines 17, 160
social change 205–27
social cohesion 297
social construction, nature as a 17
social contract 94, 213
social equity 291
social housing 312–13
social impact assessments 187, 242, 276
social interaction 114, 187, 298–99
social justice 11, 63, 98, 115, 117, 122, 189, 297
social media 205
social needs 296

social reform following from design 7
social safety nets 44
social spaces 299
social standard, defined 10
social sustainability 19–20
social transformation, design as driver of 205–27
social waste 166–67
socialization 298–300
socially detrimental products 41
socio-economic independence 187–90
socio-political systems 19–20, 26
Soft Energy Path (1976) 70
soft-system approaches 69, 70–71, 74–76
soil quality 144, 340
Solar Core 25, 126
solar energy: eco-positive retrofitting 115; energy exchange 316; Green Scaffolding 142; overview of net-positive development 15, 24, 25; Piggyback Roofs 126–27; solar design 116; solar ponds 43; solar thermal disks 182, 316; solar windows 198n13, 316; solarization 129, 137; Source of Energy (SE) Analysis 182; STARfish 359; *see also* passive energy systems
soundproofing 143
Source of Energy (SE) Analysis 168, 182, 194, 316, 326, 361
space: Ecological Space (ES) Analysis 157, 175; rating tools (RTs) 273; and synergistic relationships 69; Systems Mapping Themes (SMT) Analyses 156
space exploration 70
space tourism 48
spaceframe structures 137–38
spaceship earth 70
spatial inequity 280, 297
spatial optimization 361
spatial reduction 23
spatial relationships 156, 274, 319–20, 338, 365–67
special interests 210
specialist retrofitting companies 125
species islands 143
species richness 120, 256
spider diagrams 339–40, 348
spiritual dimension 29, 72, 113
sports hardtops 118
sprawl 120
sprinkling systems 44, 146
stakeholders: collaborative planning processes 106; financial benefits 276; mainstream green design paradigms 210; nature seen as 185; as problematic term 31n32; versus public interest 275
STARfish 101, 157, 160, 236, 257, 258, 291, 335–52, 353–70

State of Environment Report (Australia, 2000) 177n23
Stegall, N. 54n36
Stern Review (UK Government) 52n12, 184
stewardship 69, 229
Stockholm Conference (1972) 95
storm waters 45, 145, 171, 311
stowaway concept 215
straw 42
strawbale construction 306n50
strawboard 319, 338
street easements 148
street trees 144, 241, 316
stress 49, 114, 171, 318, 363
strip malls 113
students 299
stylistic variation 164
subsidiary principle 67
subsidies 199n48, 215, 330n53, 337
substitutability of nature 93
Suburban Bootstrapping 129
sunk costs 181
superfund sites 181
superinsulation 78
supply and demand 38, 209
supply chains 41, 159, 323, 336
surveillance 49
sustainability: definitions of 92–94; reframing as positive design challenges 102–6; as a right 159
sustainability reports 242
sustainability safety factors 368
sustainable (futures) planning 220–23
sustainable design: design paradigms outlined 11; difference scales of 76–77; and the ecological base 9; paradigms 27–29
sustainable development: can pay for itself 6; current situation 5, 6; historical context 61–86; misconceptions about 62–63; and nature 14; Positive Development (PD) 6; and positive development theory 87–108
sustainable yield 88, 93
symbiotic relationships 71, 174
synergistic relationships 69, 277, 338
synthesis versus reduction 12
system boundaries 277, 319
systems change, design as driver of 205–11
Systems Mapping Themes (SMT) Analyses 272, 289–90, 291, 347, 357; for institutional design 181–200; for physical design 155–80

tall buildings 115, 121, 123, 128, 171, 175; see also skyscrapers
tax 124, 160, 370n40
technocratic processes 11, 69, 74, 79–80, 218–20, 256, 271, 335

technology: blockchain 316; building information modeling tools (BIM) 244; eco-positive retrofitting 131; green technologies 295–96; and green-growth strategies 114; and the historical context of sustainable design 66; and job creation 302; and maximization of natural systems 162; smart-city technology 223; and urban cultures 115
terrariums 125, 140
terrorism 45, 46, 115, 137, 187, 225n11
thermal audits 132
thermal comfort 143
thermal mass 126, 128, 146, 168, 317
thermal storage 317
thorium 330n48
three pillars of sustainability 8
3D mapping 172, 302
timber 38, 40, 140–41, 164, 184, 306n50, 314, 319, 337, 338
time and space 273, 277
tipping point 92
total quality analyses 270
toxic waste 129, 314
toxin accumulation 41, 49, 50, 68, 116, 129, 144, 284n39, 338; see also contamination; pollution
toxin removal 144, 197
trade-offs: encouraged by built-environment assessment methods 160; mainstream planning tools 209; positive development theory 87, 89; rating tools (RTs) 244; seen as inevitable 5, 8; Triple Bottom Line (TBL) 21–22; zero-sum 157
trading and banking schemes 243, 311, 313
training 239, 295, 302, 303
trains 117
transactional relationships 65, 100, 162, 185, 215, 276
transboundary assessment methods 101
transboundary issues 90–92, 105
transdisciplinary workings 233, 256
transferable development rights (TDRs) 148, 172, 226n28, 243
transformational tools 162
transformative potential of design 37
transparency 158, 163, 258, 261, 271, 295–96, 345
transport: cars 75, 117–19, 169, 238, 281, 297; Costs of Change (CC) Analysis 183; eco-positive retrofitting 116; eDR 288, 291; Green Scaffolding 143; and green-growth strategies 117–19; Multifunctional Space (MS) Analysis 169; public transport 118, 183, 279, 281, 292, 297; risks of relying on 187; zoning 218
transport-oriented development (TOD) 118

trees 144, 165, 168, 306n36, 317
trickle-down economic theory 95, 97, 117, 186, 275, 279
Triple Bottom Line (TBL) 8, 17–22
triple-glazing 143
triple-skin buildings 137, 139
Trombe walls 126, 128, 316

unexpected consequences, designing for 319–20
United Nations (UN): Earth Summit (1992) 94; full cost assessments 301; Habitat-III 95–96; Millennium Development Goals 94; Millennium Summit (2000) 94; NEPA (US National Environmental Protection Act, 1969) 266n6; Stockholm Conference (1972) 88; Sustainable Development Goals 52n7, 53n18, 94; UNEP (United Nations Environment Program) 37, 53n26, 54n31, 88; UN-Habitat 53n18
United States: Acid Rain program 243; advocacy planning 233; Clean Air Act (1977) 243; constitution 214; design review boards 248n53; dust bowl 200n61; EPA 197n4; EPA Green Lights program 125, 267n37; inequality gaps 225n5; NEPA (US National Environmental Protection Act, 1969) 88–90, 91, 102, 245, 266n6; rating tools (RTs) 255
unitization techniques 244, 345
unjust enrichment 104
upcycling 6, 15, 23, 68, 197, 357
upstream-downstream impacts 41, 119, 156, 161, 164, 206, 270, 271, 273, 277, 313–15
urban acupuncture 10, 163, 293, 302
urban ecology 76–77
urban farming 141, 292
urban forests 143
urban infill 96, 111, 114, 115, 279, 298, 366
urban renewal 219, 233
urbanization 63
UV radiation 143–44

vacant buildings 166
value-adding paradigms 11, 166
values-centred levers of change 205–11
van der Rohe, Mies 85n100, 227n36
vegetarianism 19
vernacular architecture 296–97
vertical composting 144, 363
vertical farming 19, 91, 104, 123, 141
vertical gardens 142, 299
vertical planting walls 145
vertical structures: and biodiversity 120; eco-positive vertical spaces 278; green spaces 263; multifunctional design 24; offsetting ecological impacts 119; open spaces 312; and Positive Design (PD) 9; vertical planting 44; vertical vegetable food production 19
vertical wetlands 145
vested interests 147
visibility of nature systems 47–48
volatile organic compounds (VOCs) 49, 317, 319
voluntary nature of assessment tools 146, 236, 238, 240, 255, 268, 319

walls, city 119
waste: and the built environment 38; and carbon emissions 40; caused by poor design 164; certification schemes 237; construction process 41; Designed Waste (DW) Analysis 164; eco-cycling 15; Ecological Waste (EW) analysis 165, 191, 321, 323, 325, 327, 359; and eco-positive retrofitting 124; eDR 313–15; embodied waste 165, 197, 314–15; exchange networks 68; forensic flows analyses 159; and material flows 41; mining/extraction 41; plastic 42–43; rainwater collection 45; rating tools (RTs) 264; social waste 166–67; STARfish 357–59; Systems Mapping Themes (SMT) Analyses 156, 161; timber 40; toxic contamination 50; and wealth 48; zero waste 119, 197, 260, 322, 358
water: and the built environment 38, 44; closed system 14; contaminated 15; desert cities 141; eco-positive retrofitting 121; eDR 311, 313; embodied water 45; externalization of environmental impacts 73; fire protection 171; flooding 43, 46–47, 75, 137, 146, 171, 227n33, 292, 338; Green Scaffolding 145–46; grey water 311; industrial approaches to controlling 75; pollution 49; and public health 49; rainwater collection 145–46, 292, 311; rating tools (RTs) 274; resource autonomy 293; Resource Security (RS) Analysis 170; storm waters 46, 145, 171, 311
water cones 145, 370n34
water transport 116
watercourse protection 311
waterpipe degradation 45
watersheds 45, 244
Waterwatch 47, 188
weak sustainability 81n10, 93, 107n24
wealth 48, 212
wealth inequalities 206
wealth stratification 19
wealth transfer 163, 189, 297
wealthy individuals 48, 120, 315

wellbeing, human 91, 122, 170, 216, 243, 317–18, 364
wetlands 15, 25, 49, 145, 200n65, 354
wheelchair users 299
white roofs 43, 178n43
whole-earth model 98–99
whole-system accounting 162
whole-system analyses: development control and assessment 238; eDR (eco-positive Design Review) 288; going beyond business-centered change 207–8; historical context 70; overview of net-positive development 7; and Positive Design (PD) 14; rating tools (RTs) 270, 277; setting whole-system baselines 181–82; STARfish 346; Systems Mapping Themes (SMT) Analyses 162, 163; whole-system accounting 183–84; whole-system biophysical baselines 17
wicked problems 71
Wicked Problems (1967) 71
wilderness, return to 104, 123, 141, 278
willingness to pay 265, 278
wind energy 115, 142, 178n41, 182, 315
win-win design options 207, 209, 212
'wise use' of resources 88
women 48, 64

worker productivity 44–45, 49, 121, 234
workshops 158–59, 232, 287–88
World Bank 249n65
World Business Council for Sustainable Development (WBCSD) 225n6
World Commission on Environment and Development' (WCED/Brundtland Report) 91, 92–94
World Conservation Strategy (1980) 90–92, 93, 98
World GBC global network 237
World Health Organization 318
World Je 369n30
worms 50

yard easements 148
Yoff, Senegal 308n97

zero 'additional' impact 238
zero carbon 28, 117, 274
zero impact buildings 260
zero waste 119, 197, 260, 322, 358
zero-energy buildings 6, 28, 117, 119, 260, 274, 312
zero-operating energy targets 124
zero-sum 161, 272
zoning 95, 113, 162, 173, 218, 219, 241, 262, 296